A Bond of Love

Srila Prabhupada and His Daughters

Compilation copyright © 2020 by Bookwrights Press

All rights reserved. In accordance with the U.S. Copyright Act of 1976, the scanning, uploading, and electronic sharing of any part of this book without the permission of the publisher constitutes unlawful piracy and theft of intellectual property. Authors of individual memories may share their own memory. However, if anyone would like to use material from this book (other than for review purposes), prior written permission must be obtained by contacting the publisher at bookwrightspress@gmail.com.

Cover photographs © Bhaktivedanta Book Trust International. Used with permission.

Dedication page painting © Anuradha devi dasi. Used with permission.

Bookwrights Press
1060 Old Ridge Road
Woods Mill, VA 22949
www.bookwrightspress.com
Bookwrights Press is an imprint of The Bhaktivedanta Center, Inc.

ISBN 978-1-880404-29-4 print book
ISBN 978-1-880404-30-0 ebook

Cover and text design by Mayapriya devi dasi, Bookwrights.
Printed in the United Satets of America

For bulk order discount, contact publisher@bookwrightspress.com

Profits from sales of this book go to ISKCON's Vaishnavi Ministry.

We dedicate this book to our spiritual master,
His Divine Grace A.C. Bhaktivedanta Swami Prabhupada,
who created a bond of love with his disciples that is eternal.

This book is also dedicated to all his female followers who worked hard to help him establish his mission, and are still working to advance it.

Preface

God sisters, initiated disciples of A.C. Bhaktivedanta Swami Prabhupada between 1966 through Nov 1977 were asked the following question: "After so many years, your life is still reposed around Srila Prabhupada's lotus feet. Why?" What are your memories and how has it changed your life? The answer to these questions begot fragrant flowers for a garland of memories that we have offered to Srila Prabhupada together with gratitude: *A Bond of Love: Srila Prabhupada and His Daughters.*

The intention of this book is to document Srila Prabhupada's exchanges with his female disciples for the benefit of existing and future members of ISKCON as well as for anyone interested in knowing more about our beloved spiritual master and how he deeply and personally affected the lives of his beloved women disciples (spiritual daughters). Most of the available books are from the men's perspective and there's not so much out there by or about his female disciples. We want to amend that perception. Our intentions for this book include:

1. To insure that Srila Prabhupada's women disciples' voices are on record for posterity.
2. To show how his women disciples strongly felt Srila Prabhupada's signature love and care.
3. To reveal the instructions and lessons Srila Prabhupada imparted to his women disciples.
4. To show that Srila Prabhupada had equal love and affection for both his male and female disciples, giving both due credit for their lovingly performed services.
5. To show how Srila Prabhupada transcended the constraints of physical age, time, place, and mundane social customs as he implemented standards of ancient teachings and included the participation of women in his successful effort to establish a world wide mission.

This book is an important, collaborative effort with Srila Prabhupada's female disciples. Through its pages we will be united with god sisters throughout the world and will grow even closer to our dearly beloved Spiritual Father, Srila Prabhupada. Every effort was made to locate as many of our god sisters as we could, through Facebook, by asking god sisters to tell others, by having god sisters in larger communities connect us to them. Still, some may not have known about the book, and to those we are sorry. Also due to the size of the project and volume of work being done by just a few, most entries were edited but then not shown to the devotee who wrote them. Most, we had no way to contact, and if we had gone through a review process the book would have taken many more years to complete. So, again, please understand, we did the best we could.

Riding in the back of a taxi with a close god sister in Mumbai one fall evening around 2008, discussing the seemingly eternal topic of friction between genders, even in a god centered institution, where this topic is certainly no stranger, I paused for a moment to reflect on a particularly sweet remembrance where Srila Prabhupada put this topic nicely into perspective, as reiterated by my god sister.

"The men need to hear this!" I exclaimed. Then countered myself by adding, "We all need to hear this, men and women! But, still, how do the women's voices get heard?" And thus hatched the idea for a book of interviews with Srila Prabhupada's initiated spiritual daughters. I am an "idea" person. My third grade teacher once wrote on the top of an assignment where we each had to write a story. Mine was quite existential for a third grader and she wrote: "Where do you get your ideas?" While most of us are filled with "ideas," many of us, including myself, do not have the ability or capacity to manifest our "great ideas."

Those who can and do are rare wonderfully empowered persons. I'd like to mention a few of those who came to the rescue and profusely thank and appreciate them since they were the ones who made this "great idea' happen, bringing it to the finish line. Their Graces Visakha devi dasi (ACBSP), Kaisori devi dasi (N BBT), and Mayapriya devi dasi (ACBSP), with help from Arundhati devi dasi (ACBSP), Dinadyadri devi dasi, (ACBSP) Gokula Priya (RNS), Pranada devi dasi (ACBSP), Gandharvika Keli devi dasi (IDS) and others. Whoever has been inadvertently omitted, I beg forgiveness.

In addition, there were some kind-hearted devotees who gave donations here and there to keep the wheels turning and to those souls, we are very grateful.

Malati devi dasi
February 29, 2020
New Vrindavan, WV, USA

Srila Prabhupada's Daughters

These women are not ordinary women.

They are preachers.

They are preachers.

They are Vaishnava.

By their association,

one becomes a Vaishnava.

– Srila Prabhupada, morning walk,
Bombay, March 27, 1974

Abhaya devi dasi

Abhaya was twenty when she received initiation in Portland on Lord Nityananda's appearance day in 1975.

I was amazed and deeply affected that Srila Prabhupada gave me the name Abhaya, the feminine of his own name. When I saw him in Los Angeles (L.A.), California, his effulgence flabbergasted me. He almost floated and was regal and graceful.

Prabhupada shaped my life at a time when I was impressionable and needed guidance, and in that way he's like my father. He instilled values in me I'll never forget, like vegetarianism, simple living and high thinking.

I live on some acreage and grow food; I'm not what I'd consider a good devotee, yet I've tried to instill Prabhupada's values in my children and they seem to get them. They're not practicing devotees, but they consider the material world a temporary place and aren't too attached to it.

Aditi devi dasi

In the mid 1970s, Kamalakrishna dasa, a disciple of Srila Prabhupada who was living in Mayapur, went to Bangladesh to preach and as a result seven or eight families from Bangladesh moved to Mayapur–Aditi and her family among them.

My in-laws were so poor they were not able to take care of their family, so when my husband and I heard from Kamalakrishna Prabhu that in Mayapur, in exchange for our work, we could receive *prasadam* and our three children could go to the *gurukula*, my husband and I thought, "OK, maybe we can maintain our family if we go to Mayapur."

When we got to Mayapur, initially I was sweeping the roads and cleaning the bathrooms in the ISKCON complex. After that every morning I began husking paddy from the crops the devotees were growing and sometimes, as he was going on his morning walk, Prabhupada would stop by and observe me and the situation in the kitchen. I also cleaned the kitchen and it was really clean, *pukka*. Prabhupada asked the in-charge, Tapomaya Prabhu, "Who is doing this wonderful service? It's so clean. This must be a good Bengali girl. Who is that?" Tapomaya Prabhu told Prabhupada, "This is done by Arati." My legal name was Arati. After that, at Gaura Purnima in 1977, Prabhupada initiated my husband, our eleven year-old son, Sudhir (who now serves in the ISKCON temple in Dallas), me, and some others.

Prabhupada wanted to see his new initiates. He said, "You all must come to my room." I didn't go because my third child was a baby. Tapomaya Prabhu said, "No, you can't go there, you can't go there." He wouldn't allow me to go close to Prabhupada so I offered obeisances to Prabhupada from a distance. Sometime later Prabhupada was sick and leaving Mayapur for the last time. I made a beautiful, thick rose garland for him that he was happy to accept. After that he never came back to Mayapur.

How was I so fortunate as to have Srila Prabhupada as my spiritual master? I was only husking grains and keeping the oven and a few pots clean, but Srila Prabhupada was pleased by my service. Even though he's absent now we can go on pleasing him by surrendering to him, thinking of him, and by serving him. I am uneducated and don't know how to speak well, but I can serve by cooking and by making garlands for Prabhupada. I can go to the temple and take darshan. I'm shy and when I see other women devotees I just give them a hug and say a few words, "Are you okay?" I can try to have my heart in the right place; I can wish them well and try to see to their needs.

When I was new here, we served with a simple heart, a very simple heart. That simplicity has to be there. Simplicity in Krishna consciousness is a blessing.

Aditya devi dasi

In 1972 Aditya went with the Boston sankirtana devotees to meet Srila Prabhupada in Pittsburgh. Once there she made a huge garland of gardenias and American Beauty roses–a beautifully fragrant, dark red rose, with petals that felt like velvet. When she saw that garland on Srila Prabhupada, swaying by his feet as he walked, Aditya was ecstatic.

Before Prabhupada gave the Pittsburgh arrival address he emphatically said, "No one should take notes unless you can write down every single word. Just hear me." I thought, "Wow, I can take shorthand; Prabhupada is giving me permission to take notes." I was in the back and couldn't hear properly but I saw an open spot right next to the *vyasasana*. Somehow I walked through all the devotees, sat down in that spot, looked at Prabhupada and smiled. He was looking at me, didn't smile, but turned and started speaking. In shorthand I got every English word he said and felt happy: "Prabhupada mercifully let me sit here in the middle of a sea of saffron." But after he left devotees chastised me: "What do you think you're doing sitting here? You're proud!"

Shortly after that I went to Dallas to be an assistant teacher and secretary in the *gurukula*. When Prabhupada came he went to the temple room and Nandarani opened the curtains for him to have darshan of Radha-Kalachandji. Prabhupada said, "*Ah*, Nandarani, how are you?" Hearing Prabhupada address her first, Nandarani burst into tears and I did also.

Shortly after that, in 1973, I went to Bombay. Once, while Prabhupada was on his walk, in front of Prabhupada's doorway, Mahati made a big, beautiful *rangoli* with a lotus flower design and the name Krishna in the middle. When Prabhupada saw it, he said sternly, "Who has made this?" Somebody said "Mahati," and he said, "Bring her here." Mahati came, sweet, humble, and delicate. Kindly, Prabhupada said, "You have made this beautiful *rangoli* so nicely. But you've put Krishna's name in the middle. If someone walks on Krishna's name, it will not be good."

Prabhupada didn't like these "Prabhupada said" quotes. Once he got heavy, "Prabhupada said! Prabhupada said! What I have said is in my books! Read my books!"

In 1977, twenty-four hours a day, workers were carving marble to finish the Bombay temple. One old Muslim worker carved by himself and never stopped chanting, "Allah, Allah, Allah, Allah," even during lunch. Surabhi Maharaja told Prabhupada how the name of Allah was this worker's meditation all the time. Prabhupada said, "I want to go and meet him!" Surabhi Maharaja said, "Prabhupada, I can bring him to you." Prabhupada said, "I don't want to disturb his work. I want to go there and meet him."

I feel closer to Prabhupada now than when he was physically present because he's powerfully present in his *murtis*. Prabhupada wants to talk with us and is waiting for us to want to talk to him. If we have faith in him, we can talk to him.

Akuti devi dasi

In the summer of 1970, Akuti was in Boulder, Colorado looking for a beady-eyed, long-haired, bones-sticking-out, sitting-on-a-deer-skin type guru, but when she heard the philosophy of Krishna consciousness she forgot all those preconceptions. Three weeks later she went to Los Angeles to attend Ratha-yatra and to have Srila Prabhupada's darshan.

I didn't know anything about Krishna consciousness, so for me to see the most divine person, Srila Prabhupada, and to be with all the devotees attending the most ecstatic festival on the planet, Ratha-yatra, was a powerful experience. After that I didn't have any doubts; I was convinced that Krishna consciousness wasn't just ideas but real, active spiritual life. At first I was concerned about myself – how I was going to become self-realized – but Prabhupada ecstatically swept me and all of us into his mood of saving others.

Srila Prabhupada visited Los Angeles quite a few times when I lived there and it was fun being in the "Prabhupada is coming" mood, organizing, cleaning, and raining flowers on him. Prabhupada knew how to throw a party – we had many Krishna conscious festivals that attracted me. I was also attracted by how serious Prabhupada was about Krishna consciousness – and how powerful he was – and by how he was a sweet person and could be light and make us roll over laughing. Prabhupada had different moods and kindly shared them with us. Each morning after his walk he and all the devotees would have a sweet exchange of flowers. Once, after he put a flower in my hand, I bowed down and saw his tan canvas shoes in front of me. I thought, "Oh, my gosh, should I touch his feet?" I touched his shoes softly, so that he couldn't feel it, and then I put those fingers to my head. That was a big lift-off.

Once in his Los Angeles garden he was sitting on a bench swaying back and forth as he read from the *Krsna* book. He loved it; it was nectar to his ears. When he heard the pastime of Krishna and Balarama stealing butter and yogurt and Mother Yashoda chastising Them, Prabhupada leaned back and laughed in enjoyment. That pastime is dear to me because I saw Prabhupada experience and relish it. It was a Friday night and from the garden we heard devotees getting into vans and closing the doors. Prabhupada said, "Where's everybody going?" Someone said, "They're going on *sankirtana*, Prabhupada." Prabhupada said, "Ah, yes, this is Lord Nityananda's movement. Going door to door getting everyone to chant Hare Krishna." We all felt ecstatic to be part of Lord Nityananda's flow of mercy.

I got first and second initiation at the same ceremony. At that time Prabhupada looked at me and gave me a personal instruction. He said, "Just chant Hare Krishna and be happy." So I'm still trying to be happy in chanting Hare Krishna and serving him.

Prabhupada wants to build a house that the whole world can live in. Whatever devotion I have in my life is like part of the foundation for his big construction project; I'm dedicated to him and want to help him, and I've always liked to build things. Now, after he's gone, beyond all the good and bad, uglies and mishaps and rough waters, to maintain and increase his ISKCON house, knowing that it's his heart, is the most absorbing thing anyone could do. We're all not *brahmana*s or pure devotees, so we need to engage people in Krishna's service according to their means and interests, and by developing *varnashrama* we can gather people to fill his house.

We're daughters of the most wonderful father who's bringing all his children back to his hometown. Prabhupada didn't want us to hang around; he wanted us to always be engaged in Krishna's service, otherwise *maya* will get us one way or another. So I beg, borrow, or steal to get some service for Srila Prabhupada. He's done so much for me and for all of us. He's engaged us, and if we can learn from him how to engage others, that will keep all of us happy. We have a lot to do.

Every day I think of Srila Prabhupada and his instructions – to come to *mangala-arati*, to read and chant and go on *sankirtana* – the basics. And I think of his missionary work of spreading Krishna consciousness to every single person. For the twenty-six years of my *gurukula* service, trying to fulfill Prabhupada's wish to have a *gurukula* ashram, I thought of him. Those years were a big sacrifice and struggle, but Prabhupada wanted us to stretch and I learned that unless we do what Prabhupada says, we're going to fail. For example, Prabhupada said men and women shouldn't associate with each other. But the teenager girls in our school wanted to do service with the teenage boys and when they did, within days the boy and girls started pairing up, thinking they had to have a mate, sneaking out at night. It was a disaster. Prabhupada has the perfect formula, and our challenge is "Okay, Prabhupada said this *but* he also said to use our intelligence, and it's a different time and circumstance…"

Now that Prabhupada's gone this is what makes it hard. Prabhupada wanted us to be innovative, but he also didn't want us to change things. Our challenge is to have a Prabhupada dictionary to understand what is "innovation" and what is "change." We need to pray to Prabhupada and not think we can figure this out by trial and error. Our sincere dedication to Prabhupada through thick and thin is what's going to keep this Movement pure and keep it going.

We pray to Srila Prabhupada to get Krishna, but my lifetime goal is to serve Srila Prabhupada, so I pray to Krishna to help me please him. Krishna can help me understand how I can satisfy Srila Prabhupada. We're fortunate to be under Prabhupada's guidance, and if we pray to please him ISKCON will go on strongly. It's our duty to keep it going strongly and to inspire the younger generation to follow Prabhupada – to support the BBT, for instance. The BBT is Prabhupada's heart; how can we expand unless we keep book printing and distribution alive?

We have many opportunities to surrender and we shouldn't let them pass by because if we do we'll regret it later.

Alarka devi dasi

When she was in high school in New York in 1970, Alarka started coming to the temple and chanting thirty-two rounds because she thought a round was both ways on the japa beads. In April of 1971, Prabhupada came to New York for a week.

I moved into the temple a month before Prabhupada came. When I first saw him, he was coming out of the airport elevator and looked effulgent, as if he wasn't from this planet. It was purifying to be in his presence. I felt fortunate and sensed he knew me from beyond time and loved me, a soul.

Srila Prabhupada came every year and to be in his presence made all our austerities worth it. Whatever we did, our whole meditation was, "We're going to see Prabhupada soon, we're going to get his mercy." In my initiation letter, Prabhupada wrote that we should distribute the little booklet, *The Reservoir of Pleasure*. We distributed millions of those. Once at the airport he told us to distribute the *Perfection of Yoga*, so we immediately started selling them. That was the biggest book distribution day I ever had.

Later, four of us from the New York *sankirtana* party went to Vrindavan and Mayapur. Once we were waiting to get on a plane in India when Prabhupada wanted us to have a kirtan. I was playing *mridanga* and Prabhupada was looking at me, nodding his head and smiling. He was happy I was playing. He knew what was on my mind and looked at the good things there, not the bad things. He cared about all of us.

When we were on 55th Street in New York, Prabhupada handed cookies out to all the kids. Then all the *brahmachari*s wanted cookies but Prabhupada said, "Women first," and at that time I got a cookie from Prabhupada.

The day Prabhupada passed away I was looking out over Manhattan at sunset feeling so much sorrow for the Earth and all the living entities on it, because this pure devotee had left and was no longer blessing us with his presence.

Prabhupada saved me not just spiritually but materially also because I was not moving in a positive direction. Through him I feel strongly connected to Krishna and His protection. The underlying feeling that Krishna is present has kept me going on all these years. I chant sixteen rounds and feel my spiritual life is a personal, inward relationship between Krishna and me.

I'm fortunate I got Prabhupada's association and was able to imbibe a small amount of the Krishna consciousness he emanated. No matter who you were, it was hard not to get affected by Prabhupada. Everyone could feel his love and beauty.

Ambika devi dasi

The devotees in Australia had so much enthusiasm for Srila Prabhupada and told so many lovely stories about him that even before she moved into the temple at the end of 1971, Ambika was attached to him.

When Srila Prabhupada came to Sydney at the end of March in 1972, I was over-awed by him and a bit scared of him. But I was impressed by how personal he was with Chitralekha.

In February of 1973, when I was a *pujari* for Radha-Gopinatha, Prabhupada came to Sydney again. One evening I cooked, made the offering, and then Srutakirti said, "Why don't you give the *maha-prasadam* to Srila Prabhupada?" I put the plate of *maha-prasadam* on Prabhupada's desk, backed out in great fear, and offered obeisances. Srila Prabhupada said, "Oh, what is this?" and pointed to various preparations. Madhudvisa said, "Srila Prabhupada, this is pineapple chutney, this is *pakoras*, this is *halava*." With his fingers Srila Prabhupada deftly took a little *halava*, put his head back, threw it in his mouth, and said, "Very good. Who has made?" Madhudvisa said, "She has made, Srila Prabhupada." Prabhupada inclined his head toward me and Madhudvisa said, "Now she has pleased her spiritual master. She'll go to heaven." Prabhupada smiled and I left in ecstasy.

At Hare Krishna Land in Juhu I'd regularly clean Prabhupada's room while he was on his morning walk. One morning when it was still dark, Srila Prabhupada was walking toward the gate and passed some of us streaming along with buckets, mops, and brooms. We offered obeisances. He smiled and said, "All glories to the *gopi* devotees!" We were so encouraged. Every day we'd change his sheets, but Prabhupada said, "Only change them when they're dirty." We thought, "But they're never dirty after Prabhupada slept in them." So we changed them every three days.

In Juhu, Srila Prabhupada was lecturing about Devahuti from the Third Canto of *Srimad-Bhagavatam* and he mentioned being attached to fine, opulent clothing. He seemed to know that I was attached to the opulent silk *saris* some Life Members had been buying for us *pujaris* and he didn't approve. He seemed to be personally instructing and correcting me.

Srila Prabhupada had compassion for the poor children around Hare Krishna Land and had Moksa Laxmi start a school. The kids got baths, their lice removed, *prasadam,* and decent clothes. Every night when we all lined up to get the *prasadam* Srila Prabhupada gave from the *maha* plate, sometimes these kids would try to get seconds. The devotee men said, "*Shoo*, go away, you've already had *prasadam!*" Prabhupada said, "No, let them come."

We had Srila Prabhupada's darshan every night on the Juhu rooftop. Although we devotees didn't always get along with each other during the day, at darshan I used to feel, "Here I am in the spiritual world, and I love all these devotees." We ladies didn't have positions in ISKCON, but we didn't feel our service was unimportant. When we saw Prabhupada reciprocating with the Deities we'd dressed we felt, "Oh, my gosh, to be able to serve Prabhupada like this is important."

In Juhu in 1977, I went with a Life Member to see Srila Prabhupada, who was unwell and weak. He was sitting cross-legged on his bed with a pillow across his lap and I was aghast at his thinness. The Life Member said, "Oh, Swamiji, they have built the temple facing the wrong direction." Prabhupada said, "Why don't you come and help these boys and girls?" and for twenty minutes preached like a lion. He was so strong no one would have dreamed his frame was so emaciated. It was a lesson that we're not these bodies and can preach in any condition.

There comes a time in Krishna consciousness when our internal life begins to grow: our understanding deepens, our hearts soften, and we have a taste for Krishna. The process works; we simply need to keep going with patience and determination and cultivate love for Krishna in our heart by chanting with as much focus and sincere prayer as possible. Although his physical form isn't here, we can still talk and pray to Srila Prabhupada and he can instruct us through his books and *murti*. Srila Prabhupada can place his blessing upon the head of anyone who takes up devotional service and comes to his Movement, Krishna's movement.

Srila Prabhupada transformed my life and I feel blessed by and eternally indebted to him. He always signed his letters, "Your ever well-wisher." He's everyone's well-wisher and he's particularly so for the fortunate souls who follow him.

Amekhala devi dasi

In Manchester in 1971, Ranchor dasa gave Amekhala a Back to Godhead magazine. Impressed by Ranchor, Amekhala began visiting the Manchester temple. Then in 1973, not long after the devotees acquired Bhaktivedanta Manor, she moved into one of the cottages on the Manor property, and in 1974 Srila Prabhupada initiated her by letter.

I had the wonderful service of helping to clean Srila Prabhupada's rooms at the Manor. As we cleaned, the devotees talked about Srila Prabhupada, and then one day they told me Prabhupada was coming to the Manor along with hundreds of devotees from throughout England and Europe who wanted to be with Srila Prabhupada. The day Prabhupada came, I stayed back from the airport to help ready his room and the temple room. When I heard the huge kirtan that meant Prabhupada was nearby, my heart pounded. I shook with nervousness. Finally the temple door opened and I saw Srila Prabhupada face to face. He offered his *pranams* to me and as he walked by I threw rose petals on his path. Afterwards my hairs stood on end and tears streamed from my eyes. Externally I was a mess on the floor but inside I felt like I was home. It was amazing.

Then one day a few months later a group of ladies ran to my cottage and banged on the door, screaming. I thought, "My God what's going on? Is somebody dead?" They yelled, "You have a letter from Srila Prabhupada!" I thought ,"What? Prabhupada doesn't even know who I am." I opened the letter and read, "My dear daughter, thank you for cleaning my room. If you continue in devotional service and follow the regulative principles, you will go back to Godhead in this lifetime." I was honored to clean Prabhupada's room and couldn't believe that he took the time to thank me for doing that small service.

Later I was in charge of the kitchen in New Mayapur in France, and when Srila Prabhupada came I was assigned to buy groceries. I couldn't find *chapati* flour, but I was painfully shy and didn't want to ask the devotees for help. The French merchants thought I was insane: "What the hell is *chapati* flour?" I thought, "If I don't get *chapati* flour Prabhupada will never write to me again." I didn't tell anyone my problem but instead bought some flour that looked like *chapati* flour. Later when I took Prabhupada's lunch plate to him, he looked at the plate, looked at me and said, "So you could not find *chapati* flour." That was mystical; how did he know it was me who couldn't find the *chapati* flour?

Later I was involved with the restaurant in New York City. Rsi Kumara, who's an absolutely amazing cook, was teaching me cooking. But Rsi Kumara become confused to the point that he was blaspheming and blaming Prabhupada. The devotees told me, "Don't talk to him, don't look at him." But something in my heart told me that no matter what a devotee does, we have to somehow or other let that person know that he or she is still a friend. I thought, "If nobody talks to him, how will there be a chance of his coming back or feeling welcome in any way?" So I was friendly with Rsi Kumara. When Prabhupada came to visit the New York City temple, he got out of the car, walked to Rsi Kumara and rubbed his head. Prabhupada said, "How are you? Are you going to cook for me?" The big leaders all around said, "Prabhupada, he eats meat, he blasphemes you." Prabhupada said, "That's okay." So Rsi Kumara cooked for Prabhupada and asked me to help him, which I did. Srila Prabhupada loved his cooking.

This incident let me see Prabhupada's compassion and love for the devotees. Prabhupada saw that Rsi Kumara never completely cut himself off, that there was still an opening. I think it's important that we all learn to keep the door open, because you never know when the devotee's heart is going to change again. After all, we are all devotees and at the same time, we are all fallen. So, the experience with Rsi Kumar and Srila Prabhupada was also amazing.

Amrita Keli devi dasi

When Prabhupada came to Toronto in 1975 he told the devotees, "I'd like you to buy the church on Avenue Road." Later the devotees asked Amrita Keli and her husband, Manhar Patel, for a donation to help buy it. Her husband gave them a blank check and said, "Write whatever you want," and the devotees wrote $5,000.

Amrita Keli and Manhar didn't have that much money, but they were both working and happy to serve Prabhupada by donating for the new temple.

Prabhupada came to Toronto in 1976 and when I first saw him I felt, "He has so many temples and disciples, but he's humble. I've never seen such a humble person." I'd made a garland for him from fragrant yellow and pink roses from my garden and in the airport, Prabhupada stopped walking so my husband could put that garland on him. Prabhupada had many garlands on and I thought, "I hope Prabhupada doesn't take off my garland." When he sat down on the *vyasasana* in the temple, Prabhupada took off all the garlands but mine. That touched me.

In his talk Prabhupada said, "How much you are doing for your body and how much you are doing for the soul?" My husband thought, "I just serve my body, I don't do much for the soul." And in a darshan Prabhupada asked my husband, "What do you do for a living?" My husband said, "I'm an engineer." Prabhupada said, "There are so many engineers but I want preachers. There are fifty thousand Indians in Toronto; you and Subhavilasa make them devotees. Become a preacher." Since Prabhupada told him, "Become a preacher," without asking me, the next day my husband left his job. He came home and said, "If we do what Prabhupada says, everything will be okay." He started making Life Members and helping the devotees at the temple.

I was happy Prabhupada picked us up from the material world, happy that my husband was distributing books, and happy to do *seva* at home and work part time to support our family so my husband could serve Krishna. Ever since Prabhupada told us to preach we've been preaching. We don't want to live in Vrindavan; we want to preach for Prabhupada and I think he's pleased. By his mercy our three daughters are all married in Vaishnava families.

Every time I have a problem, I open Prabhupada's book or play his tape and he solves my problem. Once, some criticism upset me and on Prabhupada's tape I heard, "The elephant walks and dogs bark behind him but he keeps on walking." I thought Prabhupada was telling me, "Don't worry who says what. Just serve me and everything will be okay." By reading Srila Prabhupada's books and hearing his lectures I always have a relationship with him. Sometimes I feel I wasted the twenty-seven years I lived before I met him.

Anandamurti devi dasi

When she fell very ill as a young woman, Anandamurti prayed to be allowed to live so that she could get to know God. She met the devotees in Argentina and was initiated in 1975 in Brazil.

I never met Srila Prabhupada, but I always felt very connected to him. Before I came to the Movement, I almost left my body. I was maybe twenty years old. In that moment, I prayed to God, "Please, God, don't let me die. I want to live to know You. I don't want to live just to have a house and kids, all these things that everybody has. I only ask You to let me live to know You." At one point, I thought, "What did I ask? What did I pray for?" I was questioning myself, "What is this prayer? Why did I do that?" I didn't know that I had that sentiment or those feelings about God.

The same day early in the morning I went to walk alone by myself to think about God, and at that moment I saw the devotees. It was incredible. I said, "What is this?" I went running to the feet of the devotees just to see who they were, what kind of people these were. They gave me a card. I said, "Yes, I will go to the temple." So I started to visit the temple for one year. I didn't move to the temple right away.

My impression from the devotees I met was that these devotees had a lot of love for this person they called Prabhupada. I always saw Srila Prabhupada through the devotees. Everything the devotees did was for Prabhupada, it was very clear.

The day of my first initiation, Hridayananda Maharaja brought to me the *japa mala* in the name of Prabhupada. So I went to the *asana* to get my *japa mala* that Srila Prabhupada would have chanted on from Hridayananda Maharaja, and he told me my spiritual name, Anandamurti dasi. He said, "Your name is Anandamurti, and this means you are the servant of the eternal form of the spiritual blissful."

I said, "Prabhupada really knows me." I felt that Prabhupada knows me because this name to me was a very special name. *Anandamurti* means spiritual blissful. I thought if I serve what my name means, servant of the blissful form of Krishna, if I serve this form, I myself will become blissful too. Because I was a very unhappy person as a child. So this contact with Prabhupada was the beginning of my new life. It was everything for me. Even if I do many very wrong things in my spiritual life, I always feel Prabhupada's sentiment for me and union. I felt very blessed and even if I did some wrong things and my spiritual life was not perfect, I felt that Srila Prabhupada knows me and there is a big connection. I always felt it. Every day I have new sentiments for Srila Prabhupada that I experience in my daily life. Maybe they are not pure, but I try to be under the lotus feet of Srila Prabhupada and serve him to my best ability.

I feel like I have not taken Krishna consciousness very seriously, and right now I am suffering because I am regretting that. By seeing so many other devotees serving, I regret that I have not stayed on the path constantly serving Srila Prabhupada. Now I regret that so much, that I have wasted so much time.

Another sentiment I have is that now Krishna is giving me back the opportunity to be around devotees and come back and to steal from *maya* to give to Krishna, to give to Prabhupada. This is very important for me now. I don't only cry because I don't do anything for Krishna, for Prabhupada. Crying is okay, but this other sentiment is very important because it gives me inspiration and strength and courage to get closer to the devotees again.

Ananga Manjari devi dasi

At sixteen Ananga Manjari was attracted to chanting the Hare Krishna maha-mantra and first felt connected with Prabhupada in Boston in the early spring of 1970.

Chanting always did something to me so I knew it was spiritual and intense, but I wasn't sure what it was. One day I was chanting with the devotees on the Boston Common near Park Street Station when I saw a booklet, *The Reservoir of Pleasure*. My question was, "What is this Hare Krishna mantra?" I opened this booklet up and read, "We can get our actual spiritual form again and be blissful, full of knowledge, and eternal life. That is the purpose of evolution. We should not miss this. The entire process of liberation begins just as we have now begun this chanting and hearing. I wish to point out that this chanting of the holy name of God and hearing the truths of the *Gita* is as good as bodily association with Krishna. That is stated in the *Gita*. This process is called kirtan. Even if one does not understand the language, still, just by hearing, he acquires some piety. His assets lead him to a pious life, even if he does not understand – it has such power." I thought, "So *that's* what it is! That's why I'm so caught up in this – because the mantra is waking up my soul to love of God." This was exactly what I wanted.

In the booklet I saw a picture of Prabhupada and I thought, "He has the knowledge that I'm looking for and I can learn it from him." That same day I went to the Sunday Feast in the Boston temple and was totally in ecstasy the whole time, chanting and dancing and hearing the philosophy from Saradiya. The next morning I told my mother, "I'm never eating your food again," and ran to the temple thinking, "Anyone who hears this is going to become a devotee, it makes so much sense." That was the potency of Prabhupada's knowledge and love.

In 1971 Hrdayananda and I were managing the Krishna House, a little preaching center in Gainesville, and Hrdayananda and Amarendra invited Prabhupada to come there. They made all the arrangements for his visit. It was exciting – lots of devotees from Miami came too.

Prabhupada had initiated me by letter and a month later, when he was in Gainesville, I was supposed to get my *brahmana* initiation. So I walked into Prabhupada's room. Prabhupada was sitting informally on a chair and wasn't wearing a *kurta*. Gravely he said, "Sit down." I sat at his feet and he said, "Repeat after me." He was formal at first, serious. *"Om bhur bhuvah,"* I tried to repeat. I knew how to move my fingers but I had no idea of Sanskrit pronunciation. When we got to *"svah tat savitur,"* I lost it. I couldn't repeat properly. I didn't know what Prabhupada was saying and whatever I said must have come out like Greek. Srila Prabhupada said, "Repeat, I said repeat." He tried again and I tried again. We got to the middle of the first line and I was messing up. He looked at me and said, "They did not give you a paper with it written down?" I said, "No, Prabhupada, no one gave me a paper." He said, "That's all right, Hrdayananda will give it to you tomorrow." I got up and I started walking out. I didn't want to turn my back to him, so I walked backwards with my hands folded, thinking, "I blew it." I said, "Thank you, Prabhupada, thank you."

He took a garland off his desk, looked at me, tilted his head back, smiled and said, "Here," and threw the garland. I caught it and held it near my heart. I walked out the door and into about twenty devotees who were listening to Prabhupada talk to me. They said, "He gave you a garland! He's been so merciful to you," and started grabbing the garland. It was ecstatic.

I feel that my spiritual life is a perfect mercy case. There's nothing proper about me. I never got anything right. Mercy was bestowed on me and I'm glad, I'm happy for that.

In one of the classes he gave in Gainesville, Prabhupada made his famous statement, "We are very much obliged to you that in this remote place, which is thousands and thousands miles away from Lord Chaitanya's birthplace, Navadvipa, you are carrying His desire, chanting the Hare Krishna mantra." The thing that struck me most about that class was when Prabhupada said, "Because one of my students, this boy Kartikeya, is Krishna conscious, many times he was talking of Krishna to his mother. So at the time of her death the mother asked the son, 'Where is your Krishna? He is here?' And immediately she died. That means at the time of death she remembered Krishna, and immediately she was delivered." Hrdayananda and I were sitting at Prabhupada's feet and Prabhupada moved forward, looked right at us, and continued, "That is stated in the *Bhagavad-gita*. At the time of death if one remembers Krishna, then life is successful. So this mother, on account of her Krishna consciousness son, got liberated without actually coming to Krishna consciousness. This is the benefit."

I was in Vrindavan for the opening of the Krishna-Balaram temple when Lokamangala and Rasajna and some other devotees performed "The Age of Kali" drama. Prabhupada was sitting in the rocking chair under the *tamala* tree in the courtyard. The devotees were sitting on the steps watching, and the actors and actresses were in the middle of the courtyard. I was watching the drama and watching Prabhupada. Prabhupada was glistening. The whole time his smile was ear-to-ear and his eyes were wide. I thought, "They're making him smile. They're entertaining him and making him laugh. I wish I could make Prabhupada smile and laugh like that." That desire came from deep inside my heart.

Hrdayananda wrote to Prabhupada, "I have an important proposition to talk to you about when you come to Los Angeles." He wanted to take *sannyasa*. I had joined when I was sixteen, was married when I was seventeen, and was eighteen by then. I got all excited, "Wow, we're going to do this for Prabhupada, how cool." I was thinking it's the best thing to do. Hrdayananda and I got along well, like brother and sister friends, because in those days we weren't like householders. We never had a house, we never had our own place. We lived in the temple and we did service. When we walked into Prabhupada's room in Los Angeles he had just finished eating some fruit. He was in a happy, light mood. He handed us some fruit and we sat down in front of his desk.

Suddenly he looked at us gravely. The mood changed. He said, "So, what do you want?" Hrdayananda started a little speech that he had practiced, "Srila Prabhupada, Vedic literature says first you get trained under the spiritual master as *brahmachari*, then you have *grihastha* life, then you take *vanaprastha,* then *sannyasa*. So now I'm asking if I could take *sannyasa*." Gravely Prabhupada said, "Does your wife agree?" I sat with my hands folded, nodding my head. Hrdayananda said, "Yes, Prabhupada, she agrees." Prabhupada looked at us for a while and said nothing. Then he leaned forward. He said, "Sometimes it's difficult." He looked grave and serious. I thought, "Yes, it's difficult, but we take on these difficulties for the spiritual master, for preaching, for Krishna, so Krishna will help." I minimized that "difficult."

A second time and then a third time Prabhupada looked at both of us and asked, "So does your wife agree?" Each time I folded my hands and said, "Yes, Prabhupada." Hrdayananda said, "Yes, Prabhupada, she agrees." Prabhupada gave Hrdayananda a whack on the back and said, "You have a good wife because she agrees," and he was happy. "So, all right," he said and told Srutakirti to get a *danda* and cloth.

Then he turned to me and got totally compassionate like I've never seen anyone so compassionate. He looked right in my eyes and said, "So, what do you want to do?" I thought, "This is it. I can have anything in the whole universe because whatever he says I'm going to get because Krishna will make it happen." I had to step back because his presence, his aura, his universal love, was taking up space.

I took time because all these thoughts were running through my head.

In a split second desires were shooting through my head like a roll of film just like your whole life goes by at the time of death. I thought, "Where's this all coming from?" and I said, "Oh, Srila Prabhupada, I just want to be Krishna conscious." It was like Srila Prabhupada reached deep inside my heart and pulled those words out from somewhere, maybe from a speck of my desire, and I almost saw those words drift out of my head. I looked at Prabhupada. Prabhupada stepped back and looked at me almost like an artist looks at his own painting, "Did I get the right angle here?" Because of the way he looked at me I realized my words had come from him. It was mystical. Then he waved me off saying, "You're already Krishna conscious." I could feel he gave me something. Again that was mercy because I didn't work for it. I didn't do anything. I was in the right place at the right time. Somehow or other he pulled those right words out of my heart. And that's how I'm still around, that's how I'm still here. Then he came close again and he brushed his hands together and said, "These bodily relations, they are superficial. Our real relationship is with Krishna."

One evening in Delhi I was sitting in darshan and Prabhupada was talking about karma with about fifteen people – a mix of Life Members, Indians, and devotees. Prabhupada said, "Everyone is trying for happiness, and everyone's trying to avoid distress. But no matter how much you try for happiness you are only going to get this much happiness and this much distress." He made a little measurement with his hands. He said, "So the idea is to become a devotee of Krishna, then there is no more happiness, no more distress." He repeated that a couple of times and looked around the room. There was a long moment of silence. I thought, "What do you mean? I'm trying to be a devotee and I'm happy, I'm distressed." I waved my hand meekly, Prabhupada looked at me and I said, "Srila Prabhupada, we're trying to be devotees, but sometimes we feel happiness and sometimes we feel distress. Is that Krishna or is that karma?" Prabhupada said, "It's all Krishna." He looked compassionate and said, "Any time you're feeling happiness, that is coming from Krishna." I thought, "Yeah, I get that. But what about distress?" In an emotional way I blurted, "And the distress too, Srila Prabhupada?" He said, "Yes, it's just like the *cataka* bird." He put his hand up like a bird's beak, "The *cataka* bird prays to the clouds, 'Where is rain, where is rain?' but sometimes he gets thunderbolts." Prabhupada threw his hand out at my eyes like he was throwing a thunderbolt. He said, "Yes, sometimes he get thunderbolts," and with his eyes big, he threw a thunderbolt at me again. "Still he goes on only praying to the clouds for rain. Similarly a devotee only depends on Krishna. Whether he gets happiness or distress, it's coming from Krishna."

That was ecstatic because it keeps me happy all the time. Even distress comes from Krishna, it's not karma. I call it Krishna karma. It's what we need, what we deserve, what we have to go through. But it's not coming from the material energy.

At that same darshan, one young Western *brahmachari* said, "Srila Prabhupada, at the end of a Rama-*lila* drama, I saw people offering money to Rama's feet and touching the actors' feet. I thought, 'No this is not right, they're not Rama and Sita, they're just actors and people shouldn't do that.'" Prabhupada said, "No! For the time someone is acting, they are the personalities they portray. It is Rama and Sita. It's okay that the people are worshiping Rama and Sita through the actor."

Ananta devi dasi

In 1972, Ananta devi dasi began seeing devotees on harinama in downtown Chicago. Their kartalas and drums sparked her curiosity and one day she asked one of them what they were about.

One friendly devotee lady had a bag full of magazines and was trying to stop people. I asked her my question and she was pleased to answer. She looked at me with intense, bright eyes and, with an accent, told me how we're not these bodies and how Krishna consciousness was a way to love and serve God. I had never experienced a person looking at me and speaking to me like that before. Her name was Labangalatika. Before I knew it she had a BTG in my hand and I was giving her donations until I had to stop myself. I gave due to her friendliness and the way she looked past my body to me, the spirit soul. When she invited me to a Love Feast the next day I agreed to go.

I went to the temple in Evanston with my two children. The smell of pleasant incense hit me, the devotees welcomed us, sat us down, and served us *prasadam*. Afterwards, on the L train all the way back to the south side of Chicago, my children and I chanted Hare Krishna. After that, we came to the temple as many Sundays as we possibly could. But my husband at the time was unfavorable. He didn't like me going to a strange place, hanging out with strange people, and chanting a strange mantra. My home situation was becoming more and more intense.

One Sunday in 1973, when my son Shyamasundar was three months old, I had left the temple feeling distressed because I wanted to move in, but I didn't know if it was proper to leave my husband. I prayed to Krishna to send me a sign. I was tearfully holding Shyamasundar when out of nowhere I heard "Krishna!" My infant Shyamasundar said "Krishna" clearly, and that decided it. A week or two later I made the difficult decision to leave my husband and move in the temple.

I really wanted to see Prabhupada, the great soul who was answering all the questions I ever had in my life, questions that my mother or even the Christian pastors or the Bible could not answer. When Prabhupada came, in July 1974, I was initiated during a huge initiation. Prabhupada asked me if I knew the four regulative principles. I was nervous thinking that Prabhupada could see my lowly qualities, and the apprehension must have showed on my face because Prabhupada said, "It's okay," and chuckled. He reassured me. I told Prabhupada the four regulative principles and he asked if I knew the requirement of chanting sixteen rounds. After I said yes, Prabhupada handed me my beads, and as I reached for them I touched his hand. I was frightened that I'd done something wrong but Prabhupada was tickled at me and again laughed and said, "It's okay." I'll never forget his deep, resounding voice when he said, "Your name will be Ananta devi dasi," and all the devotees said, "*Jaya* Ananta Prabhu!" That was wonderful.

The second time Prabhupada came he looked more somber. When he was leaving he was waving at everybody and I wanted Prabhupada to look at me. I thought, "Prabhupada, just look at me. Just look at me, Prabhupada." He seemed to be looking at everyone else but me. Then I thought, "With all these great *sankirtana* devotees and *pujaris* here, why would Prabhupada look at you? You're just cleaning the bathrooms." As if Prabhupada could hear me, the instant I thought that, our eyes locked. And then I, the spirit soul, shimmered. It was the most brilliantly lit situation. Tears burst out of my eyes and I experienced a love of such intensity that I could hardly bear it, a love I had never felt from anyone, not even my own mother. I felt Prabhupada loved me so much that I could not even hold his glance; I had to look away. As I did so I was crying, saying, "Prabhupada loves me, he loves me. He doesn't even know me, but he loves me."

After some time I wanted to tell Labangalatika how much I appreciated the gift of Krishna consciousness that she'd given me. When I saw her years later in L.A. I said to her, "Prabhu, I know you don't remember me, but you saved my life. You gave me my first BTG. I want to thank you so much." And we both ended up sobbing.

Andha-rupa devi dasi

Andha-rupa was initiated in 1975 in Miami by letter. Srila Prabhupada originally gave her the name Vishnu-kanta, but the initiation letter got lost. When Prabhupada wrote back he gave her a different name: Andha-rupa devi dasi.

For years, I never knew what my name meant. No one else seemed to know either. I always thought it would be in the next book that came out. Since I was a book distributor, I would read all the new books and then distribute them. It usually took me about seven hours to read the book, and then I would go out on *sankirtana* and tell everyone what I had read. But I was also looking for my name.

Twenty-seven years later, someone in India finally told me what my name meant – it is a name for Radharani when She was a baby. She was born blind; *andha* means "blind" and *rupa* means "form." It appears in the *Brahma-vaivarta Purana*. I was thrilled to hear that Prabhupada had given me a name meaning I was a servant of baby Radharani when Her eyes were closed. She opened them when She saw Krishna.

I met Srila Prabhupada in 1974 in the *tulasi* garden in Miami. I wasn't initiated yet when I first saw him. Of course, I was reading his books. I thought he was very big, grand, because his books were big and grand in knowledge. So I was in the *tulasi* house and standing next to Srila Prabhupada. He had this golden hue. Standing next to him I said, "He's the same size as me!" But he was really big – he was just so saintly.

About four hundred devotees were in India, and twenty-five were chosen to travel with Srila Prabhupada: Nartaka and Sukhada were among them. Because we were all from the same temple, we got to travel with Srila Prabhupada. He would go speak in Hindi at different *pandals*. We would sit onstage while Prabhupada gave his lecture. The men were to one side and the women on the other. The Indians would be taking pictures of us – they just couldn't believe these white, Western devotees were following Vedic culture.

There's one picture of me with Srila Prabhupada. I saw it printed in Hari Sauri Prabhu's *The Transcendental Diary*. The story goes that Prabhupada was in a (I think) Lakshmi-Nrsimha temple. He was on the *vyasasana* in the back and all the devotees jammed into this small room. I was in the doorway and couldn't get in. All the men got in, but the women were outside. I was thinking, "I'm never going to get in to see Srila Prabhupada." Then all of a sudden, there was a gush of wind and I was just blown up front. I was so close to Srila Prabhupada that my legs were under his *vyasasana*. I was looking up at Srila Prabhupada, and someone took a picture.

Then we traveled to Vrindavan and four other cities. We traveled by school bus, and Prabhupada wasn't with us in the bus. In Vrindavan I was taking care of his quarters. While cleaning his bathroom I would pick up his razor and look at it, look at his tongue scraper – I would examine all of Prabhupada's paraphernalia. I would shine his spittoon.

Then when Prabhupada came back from his walk, we would all run out. Prabhupada was walking by himself along the side of the Krishna-Balaram temple. I ran up ahead in front of everybody – I wanted to get up close to Srila Prabhupada. As he was walking I said, "*Jaya* Srila Prabhupada." He looked at me with a sidelong glance, and in that glance I saw a ray. It was just the mercy. It was a ray of light. I offered my obeisances.

I felt like that ray of light was giving me the ability to distribute books. He gave me that ability to distribute books for thirty-four years on *sankirtana*.

Then one time there was a *pandal* he was going to attend. Before he came, we were all under the tent and the tent collapsed. Hari-sthanu and I were trying to get out from under the tent and had to crawl out. Luckily Srila Prabhupada didn't arrive until later with the Gaura-Nitai Deities. They put the *pandal* back up. Everyone was just so happy that Prabhupada wasn't there yet.

I knew Srila Prabhupada from his books. I have a relationship with Srila Prabhupada through his books. When we were distributing books at the Miami airport, someone said that Prabhupada left his body. We all went back to the temple. Nartaka, Sukhada, and I were crying in the van. I was sitting in the back, and I had a book in my hand. I said, "Prabhupada's not really gone, he's in his books. I really feel that he's right here." And to me he has never left the world. To me, he is always in his books. As I read the purports, they are like his emotions. I always feel his presence when I am reading. This is my association with Srila Prabhupada – through his books.

The day I saw that sidelong glance, I got so excited. Now I'm not distributing books on the front lines anymore – I'm sixty – I have other services taking care of Prabhupada's books. I order them from the BBT and put them in our BBT warehouse, which is only a small closet where the books are stacked. Whoever wants books comes to me. I also take care of the scores by putting them into the BBT newsletter every month. I run around and get everybody's scores. It's exceptionally ecstatic. We had seventy devotees go out on *sankirtana* for the Christmas marathon. Everybody was just in ecstasy. We had a lot of spots and even had a few Spanish devotees. We had to order more Spanish books for them. *Sankirtana* book distribution is real life. That's what it really is.

Annada devi dasi

Annada was born in Ceylon from Indian parents. In 1972, two weeks after she joined the devotees, 18-year-old Annada hitchhiked to the Paris temple at Fontenay-aux-Roses to meet Srila Prabhupada. Although the temple room was small, she noted that Prabhupada brought an oceanic feeling with him so there was plenty of space for everyone.

Meeting Srila Prabhupada face-to-face was transcendental, something I'd never experienced before. I knew there was no one in the world like Srila

Prabhupada and meeting him was a point of no return – it completely changed my life.

I'd barely joined the Movement when Bhagavan asked me to marry a *sankirtana* devotee. I wrote my father that I was going to be married, and my father got upset because he didn't know the boy. My father asked Srila Prabhupada for me to return to India and Prabhupada wrote to Bhagavan saying there shouldn't be a marriage unless the parents agree.

In December 1973, I was in India when Prabhupada came. Prabhupada asked me how the Paris temple was and I said, "It's dynamic, Srila Prabhupada. There's a lot of preaching going on." Prabhupada was pleased and said the temple should always be dynamic, that there should always be a lot of preaching, chanting, and *prasadam* distribution. One night in his room, Prabhupada was having an informal talk with a few devotees when he started to play the harmonium and beautifully chant different tunes of the Hare Krishna *maha-mantra*. Then he stopped and said, "You can learn how to please Krishna like this, it's very simple – different melodies of chanting the holy names."

In Delhi I found it difficult to fit in the temple so I was living at my parents' house. One day Srila Prabhupada asked me, "Where are you living?" I said, "At my parents' house, Srila Prabhupada." He said, "What would you do there? Sit on your mother's lap?" He didn't want me to hide away at home but to be a bit courageous by living and serving in the temple. Later my father wrote to Prabhupada saying that he wanted me to go to college. Prabhupada wrote back saying certainly I could go to college if that's what my father wanted, but as far as he was concerned, by studying his books – the Vedic literature – my education would definitely be complete. Prabhupada was merciful to put that in writing and it worked. I didn't go.

Once in New Mayapur, Prabhupada said, "If Krishna has recognized you and sent you a nice spiritual master, what else do you want?" Another time Prabhupada asked me, "How old is your father?" I replied, "He's about 60." Prabhupada was about 80. Prabhupada said, "Oh, that's old enough to be my son." Prabhupada was a father for everyone; his compassion was not limited and it was without bodily attachment. After Prabhupada saw Ganga and me in London, then in India, then in London again, and then finally in New Mayapur, he said, "Oh, you are here, now stay here."

When Prabhupada was at Bhaktivedanta Manor in August of 1977, he'd sit and look at the devotees during *guru-puja* every morning. No words were said but there was an amazing, beautiful exchange. We were all in love with Srila Prabhupada and he was in love with his disciples. The whole temple room was filled with a gentle loving mood. The devotees would forget all animosity towards each other because Srila Prabhupada had made such an endeavor to come to London to visit the devotees. There was no way we could stand in front of him and hold anything bad within our hearts. The kirtans were so moving, so filling. Often tears were rolling down Prabhupada's cheeks. Later, at the airport when Prabhupada was leaving England, devotees took him into an elevator and as the door closed we were all chanting, "*Jaya* Prabhupada!" The elevator went up one flight, so we all ran upstairs and as the doors opened, Prabhupada saw us all standing there. He smiled. He wasn't well but he hadn't lost his sense of humor. He was enlivened that the devotees were so enlivened.

When Srila Prabhupada left the planet my first thought was, "Who's going to answer our questions now?" And it dawned on me that, "Yes, we have to get out of here. We have to go back home, back to Godhead." That was the first time that I thought of going back to Godhead. When Prabhupada was on the planet, where would anyone want to go? My second thought was, "Prabhupada hasn't left, he'll never leave. We just have to keep chanting." Prabhupada is here through his books, his tapes, his devotees, and granddisciples. Prabhupada is spiritually accessible to anyone, any time, always, so there's no barrier. Love is spiritual.

Prabhupada appreciated everyone whether they were in men's or women's or children's bodies and he was sweet and kind to everyone. He wasn't the least bit prejudiced or unfair; he was always perfect in all his dealings and satisfied everyone. As followers of Srila Prabhupada, we should follow this example. We should learn to appreciate each other and see each other with love and devotion as servants of Prabhupada. We have to learn how to deal as gently, efficiently, and perfectly as Prabhupada. If we can follow him in that way, we'll be a lot happier.

Srila Prabhupada said that if we can learn how to please Krishna by chanting the holy name, then our lives will be successful. Prabhupada changed my life by giving me the holy name. And he gave me an example in himself that was so attractive that nothing can take its place. I'm praying to him that somehow the impossible becomes possible and I'll develop some sincerity so he'll will be pleased and will empower and guide me to do what he wants.

Annapurna devi dasi

Annapurna, divorced and with a 7½-year-old son, started coming to the Detroit temple in April 1976.

I was getting a basic understanding of what it means to be a devotee – no meat, eggs, or fish – okay, got it. Stop smoking and drinking – okay, did that. What, no garlic and onions too? Okay. Govardhan first talked to me and answered my questions brilliantly.

Then in June that year Srila Prabhupada came – it was the first time he'd seen the Fisher Mansion since they'd bought it – and the temple room and balcony were packed shoulder-to-shoulder with devotees jumping up and down and playing *karatalas* and drums in a tumultuous kirtan. After Srila Prabhupada offered his obeisances to the Deities everybody separated just enough for him to walk to his *vyasasana*. As he walked past the women, Sukti and Yasogami pushed me in front like an offering to Srila Prabhupada: "Look, we're making devotees here!" Prabhupada stopped and smiled at me. I thought, "Please accept me as a devotee. I want to give up all my nonsense." Prabhupada looked at me like he could see my soul. It seemed he knew exactly what I was thinking, and nodded as if to say, "Yes, I will accept you." It happened in slow motion and everything else was blocked out, as if just Srila Prabhupada and I were in the temple room. It was wonderful.

Maya has challenged me many times and I've had many hard and rough times, but Prabhupada's smile has gotten me through. My encounter with him was brief, but it meant the world to me.

Arcana-siddhi devi dasi

Arcana-siddhi always felt cared for and protected under Srila Prabhupada's shelter. Even though she didn't personally meet him she feels she knows him through service. She moved into the Potomac, Maryland temple and was initiated in 1976.

When I first joined, the temple president, a married man with children, was having an affair with one of the *brahmacharinis*. When the affair became public knowledge he asked Prabhupada if he could take the *brahmacharini* as a second wife. Prabhupada told him that if he wanted to take a second wife he would have to move outside of the temple. He didn't send the girl away. I thought it was really wonderful that Prabhupada continued to give her shelter.

This gave me a sense of Prabhupada and his mood. I felt very, very safe by the way he looked at the situation and I admired his solution. Prabhupada was just an amazing person, and he gave a perfect solution.

I had a very deep connection with Srila Prabhupada right from the beginning. I felt he had lifted me out of my material situation and given me shelter in his Movement. I really felt this. In September, right after Prabhupada had visited Washington, D. C., I moved into the temple. When the devotees were driving me to the temple, they had a tape of Srila Prabhupada singing and it was so otherworldly. I had never heard anything like that. I was transported into a whole other realm of consciousness. I felt, "Yes, this is what I need to do, I need to be here." Everything at the temple was so foreign, but I had a feeling of connection with Srila Prabhupada. He wasn't foreign.

I also felt a connection with him because I distributed his books. It was such a difficult service for me. It was really against my nature to go up to people and ask them for things. I don't even like to go up and ask people what time it is, what to speak of try to sell somebody a book. I really had to take shelter of Prabhupada to do that service. About five times a day I would be up in the balcony crying and looking at a picture of Srila Prabhupada in the BTG. There would be tears every day, "Prabhupada, I can't do this service. You have to help me. Please give me strength." And then suddenly from within I would feel, "Okay, you can do this." I would get up and go out and be able to approach people for another hour or so before another wave hit.

That was my early relationship with Prabhupada, and I always felt strength as soon as I prayed to him. He never let me down. I never felt that he wasn't there for me in every way. And really, my relationship was through serving him.

The other way I really felt his presence was through serving the devotees. I felt reciprocation with him by serving the servant of the servant of the servant. So I loved to serve the older devotees, and also, I loved serving the new people who came. I knew he would be pleased if I took care of the new girls. Whenever anyone came to the temple, I would make it a point that they got *prasadam* and I would sit and talk to them. I felt so much mercy from him by offering these services.

I don't feel any lack from not seeing him personally because he's so much a part of my life. I never felt like I didn't know him. I don't feel that I didn't have or don't have his personal association. I definitely have.

I guess I've been really fortunate, too, even being in a woman's body, because in Potomac, Rupanuga treated the women in a way that Prabhupada wanted the women to be treated. One time he had me give class. That was scary. It was probably one of the few temples where women were giving classes after Prabhupada left. That was my fortune, to have a leader who had had so much association of Srila Prabhupada and who understood his mood.

Archya devi dasi

When Prabhupada came to Stockholm, Archya was only fourteen years old. The devotees rented a large house that was just one block from her home–the same home she and her husband live in today. Neighbors were talking about the strange people that had turned up. One morning Archya looked out her bedroom window and saw an assembly of gentlemen dressed in orange clothing walking down the street. She didn't realize until afterwards that Prabhupada was among those men, who were going on a japa walk past her house.

A year or so later, just two days after I finished school, I joined the Stockholm temple. That same month – June 1974 – I took off with all the other devotees for Germany to meet Prabhupada at Schloss Rettershof. People ask me, "What was it like the first time you saw Prabhupada?" I'm an extremely analytical person, but I can't describe what it was like because spiritual feelings can't be described with material words. Prabhupada came around the corner of the Frankfort airport and the kirtan exploded a million times louder than it had been. There were hundreds of devotees and hundreds of *karmis* around, but for me no one was there except Prabhupada. It was a strange feeling and whichever way I try to put it in words, it's not right.

The first time I saw Deities was at Schloss Rettershof because in Stockholm we worshiped pictures of Gaura-Nitai. When the curtains opened for *mangala-arati* I saw the small brass Deities and thought, "Wow, that's so wonderful. I wish I could worship Them." The next day I was initiated and got the name Archya, which means "the worshiper of the Deity." That was fantastic. I was fifteen.

Toward the end of 1976 I was a *pujari* at Bury Place when Prabhupada came to see Radha-Londonishvara. We *pujaris* had worked hard and we thought everything was perfect. Lila Shakti was doing the *arati* and I was sitting on the floor by Prabhupada, who was sitting on his *vyasasana*. As Lila Shakti offered the *chamara,* Prabhupada looked at it and said, "They didn't clean it." Every day we used to wash the *chamara* with Johnson's Baby Shampoo and hot water to make it clean and white. But now, although we'd done everything else, we'd forgotten to clean the *chamara*. Prabhupada wasn't saying, "Oh, it's not good enough," but, "Oh, I have noticed everything you have done, but you forgot this." He spoke in a loving manner.

Later I was in charge of the kitchen at the Manor and my husband used to help cook the *mangala-arati* sweets. When Srila Prabhupada came he took a bite of *burfi* that my husband had made and said, "This is dry," and put it down. Then he ate a piece of Bombay *halava* that I had made. Later that week I made more Bombay *halava* for Prabhupada and one of Prabhupada's servants came and said, "Is there any more of that Bombay *halava*?" I gave him more and it never came back, so I believe Prabhupada ate seconds of my Bombay *halava*. My husband and I still tease each other about it. I say to him, "Well, he ate my Bombay *halava*."

Something spiritual can't be measured materially. We can count how many temples and disciples there are, but Prabhupada's impact on society, on literature, on Western philosophy, can't be measured. People are still writing Ph.D. theses about Prabhupada's use of Eastern philosophy in the Western world. And even for those who have no spiritual interests, Prabhupada has done a great thing – he's made the spiritual dimension respected, which it wasn't before. His impact can't be described.

On a couple of occasions Prabhupada said, "If someone says, 'Prabhupada says,' then we should immediately ask, 'Where does Prabhupada write that?'" The most important thing is to read his books because what Prabhupada said is there. How many times have we read the same verses and purports over the years? But when we read them again we find new nectar and depth that we didn't appreciate before. The circumstances and our growth help us understand different things. Prabhupada's books are the treasure which we absolutely mustn't lose. New books are being written, which is good for a new era of people, but just as the Bible is never out of date so neither are Prabhupada's purports. If we want to know *Bhagavad-gita* as it is, we simply need to read his purports. His instructions are straightforward and, like a cookbook, if we follow the recipe then we'll get the dish. But if we start to put other things in we won't get the same thing. It's quite simple.

We can't underestimate the power of following Prabhupada's instructions. We have to read but if we also practice and ask Krishna to clear our mind and help us understand what those instructions mean in our circumstance, that's more complete. People will always reinterpret things for their own good or for others' good, but we're never really going to know what Prabhupada meant unless Krishna tells us. There's no formula to stop misinterpretations, but it's very important to be humble, to appreciate other devotees' endeavors, and to have open discussions so we can learn from each other. Together devotees have an enormous power of spiritual understanding. We underestimate this.

As a *sannyasi* Prabhupada had to show the correct standard of behavior, so on the outside he treated women disciples different from the way he treated men disciples, but he didn't ignore the women or think that women were less valuable than men. Prabhupada showed his appreciation of women in other ways, and he was very appreciative. His vision was that we are spirit souls; he didn't look at us as women and men.

Ardra devi dasi

Although she didn't like to read, Ardra immediately became attracted to Krishna consciousness when she read Sri Ishopanishad. She thought, "Yes, this is all correct!" and seriously tried to follow Prabhupada's instructions. She moved into the Amsterdam temple, chanted Hare Krishna, served Krishna, and went on sankirtana.

I'd been terrified to think that the absolute truth was impersonal, like a light, and when I heard that God, Krishna, is a person with a form, name, pastimes, and that His place, Vaikuntha, is without fear, I was happy. Of course, still I fear because I'm not a pure devotee, but I know that Krishna is taking care of me and helping me, and one day, by His mercy, I'll go back home.

The taste I got from my temple experience made me completely convinced about Srila Prabhupada and Krishna. I can't forget that taste. All the time I think, "When am I going to feel close to Krishna again?" I can relate to the pastime when Krishna appeared before Narada Muni as Lord Vishnu and said, "You will not see Me again in this lifetime."

From the day Prabhupada gave me initiation I've felt comfortably situated because I know Prabhupada's always there for me. Prabhupada gave us Krishna, the biggest treasure. Once we're in contact with Him and the devotees, then there are no anxieties of "Who am I?" "What am I doing here?" "Is the absolute truth a person or not?" All these worries drop away.

I keep my link with Prabhupada by worshiping his *murti* and following his instructions. When I listen to Srila Prabhupada's lectures or read his books, there's always something that hits me, "Oh, yes, that's what I have to do."

Krishna consciousness is beautiful. Whatever we see as not beautiful is due to our forgetfulness of Krishna. If we can be satisfied with little things like *prasadam* or an offered flower, and can see the mercy in those things, that's sufficient.

Arundhati devi dasi

In 1966, seventeen-year-old Arundhati was walking through Tompkins Square Park when a friend of hers said, "I want to show you something," and brought her to Srila Prabhupada. Arundhati chanted the Hare Krishna maha-mantra along with Prabhupada.

I wasn't drawn to Prabhupada and after I walked away, I didn't think about him or the chanting. Later I moved to the East Village and when I passed Matchless Gifts storefront I'd think, "This is weird." Then in the spring of 1968, on the invitation of Kirtanananda, my boyfriend Randy, who became Ranadhir, and I visited New Vrindavan. One morning we all took acid and I went on a bad trip. Kirtanananda was playing the harmonium and chanting and I asked if I could play. He said, "Okay." As soon as I said, "Hare Krishna," my severe craziness dispersed. I was hooked on the holy name and chanted nonstop all day. But I didn't know the philosophy; I was still taking acid.

I moved to Berkeley and had the best food I'd ever eaten at the Sunday Feast at the San Francisco temple. Then I went on another bad trip and was sinking into total despair. Without even knowing what I was doing, I sang and danced for hours crying out to Krishna in the Sanctuary at Berkeley University. My whole life changed. I understood that Krishna, not LSD, was the answer.

Around September 1968 I moved into the Boston temple and started transcribing Prabhupada's tapes. Boston was austere but we were blissful, chanting and serving Prabhupada. Sometimes I cried when I chanted and I wrote to Prabhupada asking about that. He wrote back, "Your tears in kirtan are very good, it means that Krishna is pleased upon you."

In April 1969 I went with all the Boston devotees to New York to meet Prabhupada at the airport. When I offered obeisances I stayed down a while and, when I peeked up, Prabhupada was by me and he patted my head. I was blissful. I had a fairly loving family when I was growing up but at that moment I thought, "I haven't known love until now." After that, all the women – Lila-shuka, Kanchanbala, Indira, Rukmini, and me – walked alongside Prabhupada and stood in front of him chanting when he sat down.

Later Prabhupada asked, "Would somebody like to take care of my Deities each morning?" I immediately said, "I'll do it, Srila Prabhupada." He said, "Come to my room tomorrow morning." He showed me how to bathe and dress the little Radha-Krishna Deities he traveled with and I did that every day while he was in New York and Boston.

In Boston Satsvarupa said to Prabhupada, "The women are always fighting with each other." Prabhupada said, "That's because they need to be married. Immediately arrange, I will perform the wedding." Prabhupada said I should marry a devotee from Montreal, but I had no attraction to him and didn't want to marry him. I was crying. Prabhupada said, "That's all right. Nothing is by force in Krishna consciousness. If you don't want to get married now, you can get married later."

The next day Prabhupada performed the wedding for the others and then left. I started praying, "Prabhupada, I didn't get married when you asked me to, but I'm praying to you now to send me a husband." Prabhupada thought Pradyumna and I would be a good match because we were both working on his books, and he asked me if I'd like to marry him. I immediately said yes, and Prabhupada married us in Columbus. When ISKCON Press moved to the new Boston temple, Pradyumna and I moved there. I gave birth to Aniruddha in 1970 and once I'd recovered, continued my service on the composing machine.

I once wrote Prabhupada asking if it was all right for me to do Deity worship while others took care of Aniruddha. He wrote back, "I am simply surprised that you want to give up your child to some other persons, even they are also devotees. For you, child-worship is more important than Deity-worship. If you cannot spend time with him, then stop the duties of *pujari*. At least you must take good care of your son until he is four years old, and if after that time you are unable any more to take care of him then I shall take care. These children are given to us by Krishna, they are

Vaishnavas and we must be very careful to protect them. These are not ordinary children, they are Vaikuntha children, and we are very fortunate we can give them chance to advance further in Krishna consciousness. That is very great responsibility, do not neglect it or be confused. Your duty is very clear." I immediately started taking care of Aniruddha again.

I moved to Los Angeles and when Prabhupada came I'd transcribe his tapes. Once he said, "You are very speedy. Your husband is not as speedy as you." A few minutes later he called me to his room, took out a bangle and said, "An Indian lady gave me this. It's solid gold. I'd like you to have it, you're working so hard on my books." I was tongue-tied but said, "Thank you, Srila Prabhupada." I still have that bangle.

In Los Angeles, Aniruddha was imitating the devotees dancing Bengali-style. Later Prabhupada said, "He's imitating the others and in a child, imitation is a sign of intelligence." Srutakirti said, "He's intelligent like his father." Prabhupada said, "No, he's intelligent like his mother. His mother is more intelligent."

Aniruddha had been in the *gurukula* for two years and didn't know how to read. I was upset and Prabhupada said I could teach him myself. Then in the summer of 1976 Prabhupada invited me to travel with him to transcribe his tapes and bring Aniruddha also. We went to London, Paris, Tehran. In Tehran, Nandarani told Prabhupada that she was giving her two daughters a good education. Prabhupada said, "Teach them to be like Aniruddha. He's always chanting Hare Krishna."

Eventually we got to Bombay where Palika cooked for Prabhupada. I thought, "I wish I could cook for Srila Prabhupada." A week later Palika got eczema on her hands and Prabhupada said, "Teach Arundhati to cook for me." When an Indian woman cooked something delicious for Prabhupada, he said to me, "Learn how to cook like this. Radharani was able to please Krishna because She was such a good cook. You should also learn to be a good cook."

Prabhupada said to Aniruddha, "So Aniruddha, you are going to be a Sanskrit scholar when you grow up?" Aniruddha said, "No, Prabhupada, I'm going to be a cowherd boy." Prabhupada said, "You do not want to be Sanskrit scholar? Your father is very good Sanskrit scholar." Aniruddha adamantly said, "No, Prabhupada. I'm going to be a cowherd boy." Prabhupada laughed.

Aniruddha usually stayed with me, but one night he stayed with Pradyumna and the next morning Prabhupada asked Aniruddha if he'd brushed his teeth. Aniruddha said yes, but Prabhupada knew he hadn't. When I saw Prabhupada later he said, "Take very good care of your son. The husband cannot do. You must do." I said, "Okay, Srila Prabhupada."

Prabhupada was even-keeled and Krishna conscious wherever he was. Whether living in a hut or a mansion he was unbothered and focused on preaching and translating his books.

I was cooking all of Prabhupada's meals, typing his books and letters, and taking care of Pradyumna and Aniruddha. Aniruddha used to play with the calves and I'd let him come into the kitchen, but Hari Sauri didn't like that. One day Hari Sauri yelled at me so loudly that Prabhupada came to the kitchen. Hari Sauri said, "I've told Arundhati many times not to let Aniruddha in the kitchen. His hands are dirty and she lets him serve you food." Prabhupada called Hari Sauri to his room and spoke to him for a few minutes. Then he called me into his room and said, "I told Hari Sauri that if he has any complaints about you he should either speak to the father or the husband – me or Pradyumna – not directly to you. From now on if Aniruddha wants something to eat, ask him to stand by the door and bring him something. But don't let him come into the kitchen. Is that all right?" I said, "Yes, Srila Prabhupada." Prabhupada satisfied everybody, including Aniruddha.

In 1977 we returned to Bombay and Palika was supposed to cook again, but I was attached to that service and continued cooking. One day I didn't cook well and Prabhupada yelled at me, "The *subji* is burnt! I've been teaching you for so many years and still you do not know." I said, "I'm sorry, Srila Prabhupada," but he seemed disgusted with me. He said, "Tomorrow Palika will cook." I was crushed. Later Prabhupada cooked *bati-chachari*, a vegetable dish that's burnt on the bottom, for himself and he called both Palika and me into the kitchen to help him.

Theoretically I know the spiritual master lives on, but I was attached to being with Srila Prabhupada's *vapuh* and really miss that relationship I had with him. I'm not doing service like I was during those years, but I still feel strongly connected with Srila Prabhupada. When I talk about him I can feel his energy.

Arya devi dasi

During the most auspicious Deity installation and opening of the Sri Sri Krishna-Balaram Mandir in Sri Vrindavan dhama, on the Rama Navami celebration in April 1975, Arya and her husband Vijeta dasa received harinama initiation. Bhargava snapped a close-up photo just as His Divine Grace Srila Prabhupada handed Arya her japa beads.

In the photo we see Srila Prabhupada sitting calmly while surrounded by his devotees who are engaged in different types of activities. Hamsadutta looks strained while dutifully fanning Prabhupada, and Akshayananda looks on with a concerned expression. An Indian mataji and a young devotee boy stand behind Prabhupada looking on attentively. Paramahamsa sits in front to the right of Prabhupada, while gazing away in the distance with his hand looming in the foreground. Subdued tones of saffron and ivory white seem to enhance the transcendental composition, creating an overall mood of serenity.

Prior to the ceremony, I learned that it was proper etiquette to wear new cloth while receiving initiation, so in an effort to honor tradition we spent time searching through *sari* displays for just the right one. But as you can imagine, that task quickly became a tedious distraction compared to the up-coming transcendental event I was anticipating. So in a mood of exasperation I settled on a soft, natural fiber *sari* with modest trim of gold *jari*, in ivory white! Back then we didn't know that pure white was reserved for widows. Just four months earlier my husband and I had discovered Prabhupada's Movement while passing through Bombay on our way to the hippie mecca of Goa. As spiritual seekers, we came upon Hare Krishna Land and discovered, much to our delight, that the author of the spiritual books we had been reading was personally present at the time, and would be attending the temple worship that very evening. On the advice of Daivi-sakti devi we ventured to Juhu Beach to collect flowers to offer Srila Prabhupada upon our return. Losing track of the time we finally returned at 7:25 pm that evening, just in time to see the devotees bowing down while Srila Prabhupada, sitting on a raised seat, recited the *prema-dhvani* prayers with his deep resonating voice. That was a life-altering moment for both of us.

Within three days the temple administration interviewed us and welcomed us to ashram life. Our first service was cleaning Srila Prabhupada's quarters. Returning from his morning walk he noticed that I was donning a full-length Tibetan dress, and he instructed Palika devi to "give that girl a *sari*." I have since read Prabhupada refer to the *sari* as the "pure Vaishnava dress," with no mention of it originating from any civilization other than the Vaikuntha culture. I appreciated that on the recommendation of his disciples, he so readily and willingly included us in his ranks. We recognized what a rare gift he was offering us, and we very seriously took to Krishna consciousness. Although the initiation picture was taken a mere four months later, I did not see it until fifteen years later, when Lola devi recognized me in the picture at a New York temple reunion and very kindly had Puru dasa print a copy for me. I wish to take this opportunity to express my gratitude to all those kind Vaishnava devotees of Lord Krishna for their role in preserving such a timeless gift of the most precious memory of my spiritual life.

By Lord Krishna's mercy, I live a very simple lifestyle revolving around my *sadhana, japa,* and transcendental reading in the pristine West Kootenay Region of British Columbia, Canada. "He reasons ill who tells, Vaisnavas die, When thou art living still in sound! The Vaisnavas die to live, and living try to spread the holy name around."

Ashalata devi dasi

When Ashalata, who's from Uttar Pradesh, started going to the Toronto temple in 1968, she thought, "Prabhupada must be a great personality for he has changed the Western people." Seeing Prabhupada's photograph, she had a strong desire to touch his lotus feet.

In 1975, my husband, Subhavilasa, and I went to Chicago to see Prabhupada. One day after Prabhupada's lecture, Subhavilasa said, "Prabhupada, we came here to fulfill my wife's desire to touch your lotus feet." Prabhupada mercifully said to me, "Come and touch my lotus feet." I did. Krishna fulfilled my mission. Touching Prabhupada's feet was so wonderful I cannot tell you what I felt.

In Chicago, every morning my husband and I would attend *Srimad-Bhagavatam* class and every evening, darshan. Once I didn't go and Prabhupada asked Subhavilasa, "Where is your wife? Why didn't she come?" One day we bought a pair of shoes identical to a pair he was using. When Prabhupada was going out of the temple room that Upendra put our new shoes on him and gave us his old ones. We still worship those shoes in our home.

When he came to Toronto in August 1975, Prabhupada visited our home. We had a big kirtan and a feast. I wanted to cut a chiku fruit for Prabhupada but he said, "I'll cut it myself." He and I had a sweet, natural relationship; it wasn't like Prabhupada was "guru"!

Somebody asked Prabhupada, "When are you going to come to Toronto again?" Prabhupada said, "When you buy the building on Avenue Road. You have to get that building." It was hard to buy that building, but by Prabhupada's blessings Krishna gave it to us.

In the beginning of 1976 Prabhupada initiated my husband and me by letter; my name means "creeper of hope." That June we went to see Prabhupada in Detroit, but his secretary wouldn't let us into Prabhupada's room. Subhavilasa sent a note, "Prabhupada, this is Subhavilasa and Ashalata, we want to see you." As soon as Prabhupada read that he said, "Call them right now!" Then, as Prabhupada's disciple, I asked, "Prabhupada, will you keep us at your lotus feet?" He said, "You are already at my lotus feet." I felt my husband and I truly had a close relationship with Srila Prabhupada; he knew us forever.

In Vrindavan in 1976, once we were sitting in Prabhupada's room and my son Indresh, who was two, fell asleep on Prabhupada's lap. Subhavilasa said, "What should we do?" Prabhupada said, "You go, I will bring Indresh." Indresh slept in Prabhupada's lap for a few hours and when he woke up he held Prabhupada's finger as Prabhupada walked him to our room. Prabhupada was thinking, "He's my grandson."

Minakshi, my daughter, wrote a letter to Prabhupada and Prabhupada wrote back, "From your letter I can understand that you and your brother Indresh are both great devotees. You are very fortunate to have devotee parents and to take to Krishna consciousness from your very childhood. I also had the good fortune to have a devotee father and mother and when I was young they gave me Radha-Krishna to worship and I was also performing Ratha-yatra festival with my young friends. I am always thinking of you and your brother, what nice devotees you are. Please continue with your service to Srimati Tulasi devi and to Radha and Krishna and your life will be sublime."

After Prabhupada passed away, ISKCON faced many obstacles. I felt the problems – I was crying at home – but my family and I did not give up Prabhupada's service and we still went to the temple to see Prabhupada and Sri Sri Radha-Gopinatha. Whatever strength I have is from Prabhupada's association. Everyone can see Prabhupada is an extraordinary person; everyone can see what he has done all over the world and everyone can have his association and be touched by his mercy.

Krishna is sweet, yet Prabhupada was put into such difficulty and had so many tests. Sometimes we go through hard times but we can still stay on track spiritually. My husband and I tell our children and grandchildren about our sweet memories of Prabhupada and about his glories. By hearing about him, the new generation can also naturally love and follow him. Seeing us worshiping Prabhupada and Radha-Krishna also keeps them in Prabhupada consciousness, in Krishna consciousness.

Asta-sakhi devi dasi

After devotees visited her Denver high school in 1974, Asta-sakhi became inquisitive about Krishna consciousness and began attending programs at the Denver temple. A year later–the day after she graduated high school and shortly before her eighteenth birthday–she moved in. Like the other fifteen women in the one-room brahmacharini ashram, she got a spot on the floor for her sleeping bag and an army locker to keep her belongings. One week later, in June 1975, Srila Prabhupada visited Denver for six days.

This was at the height of the tension between the men and women devotees. The Radha-Damodara party was visiting Denver, and just before Prabhupada arrived almost every temple class was about how bad women were. I thought I'd taken the wrong birth and prayed to leave my body and take birth as a man.

When Srila Prabhupada came, his mood was loving and kind to everyone – man, woman, child, it didn't matter – and I felt better knowing that Srila Prabhupada loved us all equally. During *guru-puja* Prabhupada would look around at everyone and when his eyes fell on me I felt he saw beyond my material body. He really saw me, a spiritual being. It was humbling, for I knew he could see my faults.

After Denver, we attended the San Francisco Ratha-yatra where Prabhupada gave *sannyasa* to Gurudas and jokingly said, "Yamuna, Gurudas's wife, is doing very nicely; therefore I advised her husband that 'You also take *sannyasa*.'" Everybody laughed.

The day after Ratha-yatra we went to a big hall where Prabhupada was to speak in Hindi, but the Hindi-speaking people there were talking and socializing during Srila Prabhupada's talk. Their disrespect disturbed me and I felt like standing up and saying, "Shut up!" But Prabhupada was calm and undisturbed and kept speaking, although he did speak in English for the benefit of his disciples. Seeing Srila Prabhupada so tolerant and undisturbed touched me.

The year 1977, during which Prabhupada was sick, was like a rollercoaster. We'd get word that he was really bad and we'd all pray and have twenty-four-hour kirtan. I had two hours in the evening. Then we'd hear he was a bit better and we'd feel some relief. It was a constant back-and-forth. I'm fortunate that I was in the Denver temple during this time, for it was Prabhupada conscious and Krishna conscious. We each had personal exchanges with the Deities, read the book distribution results to Them, and we used to think that Lord Jagannatha could come walking down the temple stairs and through the temple at any moment so everything had to be clean. Those were my boot camp years – austere and surrendered – and I'm incredibly grateful for that training. I don't know if I'd want to live that way now, but I feel blessed that I had that opportunity.

Even though I had many doubts, I also had the sweet feeling that despite them Prabhupada loved and accepted me. And his love and acceptance further inspired my love for him. But I also feel sad that I wasn't mature and wise enough to appreciate Srila Prabhupada when he was with us. I was too young and inexperienced to fully grasp what Srila Prabhupada had brought us.

Asta-sakhi devi dasi

In the fall of 1971 in Bury Place, Srila Prabhupada initiated twenty-year-old Asta-sakhi saying, "Asta means 'eight' and sakhi 'friend.' Asta-sakhi is the special intimate friend of the eight principal gopis. I want you now to become the special friend of all the devotees."

Once we rented Camden Town Hall for Prabhupada's discourses and I felt embarrassed for Prabhupada because few people attended. But Srila Prabhupada gave an electrifying lecture as if the hall was completely full of people we couldn't see. A Christian in the audience said, "What about Christ?" Srila Prabhupada looked at him intensely and explained that the love Christ had for God is the same as our love for Krishna. The Christian was shocked.

Srila Prabhupada's publisher, Macmillan, arranged a book promotion event with *The Times* and other London newspapers, publishing houses, and famous bookstores. I was cooking for the event and was horrified when Srila Prabhupada told me to make *gulabs*. I thought they wouldn't go down well with the dignitaries and said, "Maybe we can serve cakes or biscuits." Srila Prabhupada said, "No, I want *gulabs*." So for two nights I cooked *gulabs*. Many professional people attended and Srila Prabhupada lectured about how we're not the body. Then he had *prasadam* on a plastic plate and ate seven *gulabs*. The next day *The Times* had a wonderful article glorifying Srila Prabhupada, the lecture, the kirtan, and even the *gulabs* – they were a hit.

Once Srila Prabhupada said, "Just from the smell, a good cook can know even down to the last spice what's in a preparation."

One devotee acted strangely and had an extremely wild face. Srila Prabhupada told us, "When they're in this condition don't preach to them. Just be kind and serve them *prasadam*."

Another time tears were flowing from Srila Prabhupada's eyes while he was driving down Oxford Street. He said, "The people are suffering so much and they don't even know it."

I was Lord Jagannatha's *pujari* on the Ratha-yatra cart when Srila Prabhupada danced and walked and twirled the whole way to Marble Arch. I had to look after Lord Jagannatha but my heart was pulling and pulling because I wanted to dance with Prabhupada. Every so often Srila Prabhupada would stop and look at Lord Jagannatha with such intense love it made me cry. I'd never seen and felt anything so incredible.

Atitaguna devi dasi

Atitaguna joined in New Zealand in 1975, and the first time she was aware of having a spiritual desire was when she wanted to be personally initiated by Srila Prabhupada.

In April of 1976, when Srila Prabhupada arrived in Australia, the airport kirtan was going and everybody was completely joyful. All of a sudden there was a big cry, "Srila Prabhupada!" When I first saw him I couldn't believe it because he was effulgent. It seemed he was walking about twelve inches off the ground. I knew right there and then that he was my spiritual master. When I saw him I realized that he was the person I'd been searching for.

The day after I was initiated I went on the morning walk. Srila Prabhupada stopped at a tree, picked up a leaf, crushed it, smelled it, and asked what kind of tree it was. A devotee said it was a Japanese camphor tree. Prabhupada said that camphor was Radharani's favorite aroma. A devotee asked, "Srila Prabhupada, I thought we were supposed to be in Vaikuntha when we're doing devotional service, but I find that we're always in anxiety." Prabhupada said, "Yes, we should always be in anxiety. If we're not in spiritual anxiety, then we'll be in material anxiety, and if we are not in anxiety, then we're a zombie." From that I understood that this Movement is alive, that we don't just do our service, but we do it with the spiritual anxiety to please Krishna.

Atmavana devi dasi

Atmavana was eighteen when, in May of 1971, she visited the San Diego temple.

A very nice devotee suggested that I borrow *The Nectar of Devotion* and the *Krsna* book from the library. After I read *The Nectar of Devotion* I started going to the temple, and a week or so later – June 1971 – Bhakta dasa, the temple president, encouraged me to go to the San Francisco Ratha-yatra. He said, "Srila Prabhupada, our spiritual master, is going to be there." I thought, "Sure, why not, I'll go."

In San Francisco, a series of people helped me get to the parade, and before it began I set a mango for Prabhupada down before him as he sat on Lady Subhadra's cart. Prabhupada was grave and nodded his head in appreciation. There were many people around, but Prabhupada, detached, was looking around happily. I paid my obeisances, and the Ratha-yatra parade began.

Later, after my husband, Aja, and I were initiated, we moved to the Los Angeles temple with our children. Srila Prabhupada frequently visited there and I used to cook the afternoon offerings – the cookies and delicacies. Sometimes, Srila Prabhupada honored my sugar cookies and, I heard, enjoyed them very much.

When we'd walk through the alleyway next to the temple to attend *mangala-arati,* we'd see the back of Prabhupada's head from the window as he worked through the night. We were encouraged that he was there working and couldn't believe he'd been up all night. But if he did it, we'd do it. We'd go to *mangala-arati* dragging our babies.

Once when we were greeting the Deities, the temple room was so packed I got pushed against the corner wall near Gaura-Nitai, where Srila Prabhupada would offer his *dandavats* to the Deities. When he came in, Srila Prabhupada looked at me sternly and waved me off. Get out of the way! He didn't want to offer *dandavats* with his feet facing me, being such a kind and honorable man. I felt humiliated that I'd disappointed him, but later thought that I was blessed by the wave of his hand. All things from the spiritual master are good.

At the Los Angeles airport, I wanted to take a photograph of Prabhupada, so I got ahead of the crowd and looked back to see Srila Prabhupada walking abreast of the pathway, completely filling it. The Hare Krishna mantra was reverberating most gloriously. Prabhupada was so proud, walking with his cane – very slowly! Prabhupada usually walked quickly, but he was taking his time, tapping his cane as he went.

Then Srila Prabhupada sat down, quietly chanting his *japa* with the devotees around him as he waited for his plane. He looked at each of the devotees and also looked at me. Our eyes caught. I felt so dirty. I felt all of my sins and karma. Then telepathically I heard him say, "And this girl, she should be protected." He cared about his female devotees and wanted them to be protected and cared for.

Atri devi dasi

In Melbourne in 1972, Atri saw Srila Prabhupada for the first time, a tiny figure getting out of a blue van on Burnett Street.

My first impressions were overwhelming. Here was a personality who scared me due to his unknown power. I'd never experienced anything like it and knew he wasn't from this world. I could almost sense that if I followed him, he was going to tie me up for the rest of my life and my whole life would change. I was just seventeen and knew nothing, but I could feel this was a total clash of worlds. I had to either run away or forever try to figure it out.

I didn't have a one-on-one personal relationship with Srila Prabhupada but by observing him I formed a loving spiritual bond with him. That relationship isn't explainable in a mundane sense because it's not of this world. It's based on service. We only love Krishna if we do some service for Him and as soon as we engage in that giving, that service exchange, our relationship develops. Similarly, when we're engaged in Prabhupada's service our love for him develops. That was the strongest love I ever felt; it overwhelmed me.

Srila Prabhupada was impressed by devotion, like Krishnapremi's and Kamarupa's singing. He enjoyed the emotions in their voices and wanted to hear them.

When I went to Bombay and saw Prabhupada relaxed in his natural element, my love for him increased. In one darshan Prabhupada saw my discomfort when the setting sun was coming straight in my eyes. He said, "Come and sit here," next to him. I was insignificant yet my spiritual master said, "Come and sit with me."

Once after class in Mayapur, Prabhupada was walking from his *vyasasana* to Radha-Madhava while Visakha was taking photographs. Prabhupada picked flowers off his garland and threw them at her. These weren't ordinary flowers; she was being hit by waves of pure transcendental energy. She could barely contain herself. If you look at this from a mundane perspective, it's nothing. But if you look at what was actually happening it was complete ecstasy.

Because Prabhupada loved everyone, everyone loved him. His love was spiritual and the soul responded to it. To come into the presence of such a personality is a rare and mind-boggling experience.

If a person has a strong desire, she will be led to real Vaishnavas. The higher the quality of Vaishnava, the more the creeper of devotion is nurtured.

Bala Gopala devi dasi

A follower of Siddhasvarupa, Bala Gopala's sister sent her a photo of Krishna. Bala Gopala was already dissatisfied with material life. After high school she visited her sister in Hawaii. Her sister's car died right where a group of Prabhupada's devotees were performing harinama. She chanted with them and went with them to stay for the night. She thought she would only stay a few days.

Around August or September 1970 Prabhupada passed through Hawaii on his way back to India. There was some bad feeling between ISKCON and our group, but we all went to see Prabhupada – sixty or seventy of us. Prabhupada was very excited to see us and he gave a lecture. Siddhasvarupa decided there and then to surrender the whole yoga group to Prabhupada. I recently learned that Prabhupada encouraged him not to do that but he did it anyway.

So early in December 1970 half of us went to New York and half to San Francisco, and a very small group went to England – Tulasi (who was Tusta Krishna's wife), Sananda Kumara, Bhakti, Sudama, and me. We stopped off in New York where we met Kirtanananda, then we flew on to London. It was a big adventure. It was winter and dark when we arrived, and on the very first night we were invited down to the Apple studios to record. It took me years to adjust to the cold. Bury Place was austere, but in the beginning it was so exciting that I don't remember the difficulties.

I was determined to become Prabhupada's disciple and within weeks I wrote to him asking for initiation. In January 1971 he wrote back accepting me as his disciple. He changed my name from Gopala to Bala Gopala. I was the first of our group to ask for initiation.

It was a well-rounded time. We did *harinama* every day. In the mornings we studied *Ishopanishad,* after lunch *Nectar of Devotion* and in the evenings *Krsna* book. Everybody participated in everything. There was no man-woman divide. No segregation. Other-worldly Mondakini was the *pujari*.

Dhananjaya had come over from Amsterdam and asked Mukunda if he could marry me. We had an arranged marriage that was carried out on Lord Nrsimha's appearance day. I called up my parents and my mother said, "Do you love him?" and I said, "We love everybody, Mum." We went up to Scotland to visit Dhananjaya's parents then traveled around Europe a little and on to Amsterdam.

When Prabhupada came I was still very involved in London. My first brief personal encounter was when I got second initiation. I sat really close to him alone with him in his room. He tried to put me at ease but I was so nervous that when he asked my husband's name I couldn't remember it for the life of me.

I learned how to make one complete meal, which I cooked for Prabhupada every day for the remaining week of his stay. I cooked in his three-tier cooker: *lauki subji, dal, chapatis,* rice. For a sweet he might have had powdered milk *burfi*. He was very particular about his rice – it had to be cooked at the last minute to be fresh. I used to sit on the staircase and wait to hear that he had come out of his room to bathe after his massage. That meant I had exactly twenty minutes while he bathed and chanted his noon Gayatri until he was ready to eat. So I dashed down to put the rice on and make *chapatis*. I would carry the meal up to him and then bring up more *chapatis*–one at a time as each one was cooked. He asked me to try to dry-roast a popper but apart from that he just accepted whatever I cooked.

Dhananjaya became president and I became joint head *pujari* with Lilasakti. As the president's wife, I pretty much had free access to Prabhupada's room. When we moved into the Manor it seemed so big you almost got lost in it. I helped to fix up Prabhupada's quarters. We didn't have much money so it was simple. We spread a white Indian bedspread over his cushions. He had the simple chrome glass-topped table. He sat by the window to take *prasadam* alone. The weather was beautiful and he would sit out every afternoon. I would sit on the lawn in the afternoon – I could do that because I had hand sewing to do. He sat on the grass and just talked.

Life was really tough, but in the midst of difficult times–such as the men-women thing–whatever austerities, however cold, however lousy the *prasadam* was, all that you went through was tolerable because Prabhupada used to come every six months or so. The austerities were washed away like a drop of water in the bucket. It seemed that any difficulties were nothing. It was all worth it, he made it all better.

Prabhupada was very mothering. I never felt less valued by him as a woman. He never once, ever, chastised the women. He chastised the men, but never the women. Sometimes he would chastise the servant instead. I was always in awe.

Prabhupada told Dhananjaya not to worry too much about the Indians, but to concentrate on preaching to the Westerners. He made Dhananjaya the president, but Syamasundara had his own ideas as to who he wanted as the president. So Prabhupada deferred to Syamasundara. It wasn't meant to be, so we chose somewhere else to go. At the time I had no bitter feelings, but I realize now I did feel slighted. Because we had Prabhupada to encourage us it didn't affect us at the time. So we went to Rome and we got such mercy. He told us to go to Rome and find a house and he would come immediately. That was the hardest service I ever did. We had no money, we didn't know anyone, we didn't speak the language, and there were reduced options for *bhoga*. But the rewards were unbelievable. Srila Prabhupada visited us for ten days there.

Throughout our devotional life he always encouraged Dhananjaya and I to be together. He said he never expected his householders to live in temples. He told us he wanted us to live in nice homes. He wanted us to live nicely and eat nicely. He encouraged us to start the *mukut* business and live in the *goshala* house. Very different from that heavy *sannyasa* mood.

Ballavhi devi dasi

During her search for life's meaning and for God, Ballavhi met devotees and was immediately attracted. She moved into the Atlanta temple and, in 1971, when she was twenty-two, went to Boston to receive initiation from Srila Prabhupada.

I first saw Prabhupada at the Boston airport and knew immediately that he was a majestic, exalted personality. He emanated spiritual energy and it seemed he'd descended from the spiritual world to be with us in this material one.

During the lecture Prabhupada gave when I was initiated, he asked us what the ten offenses were. Jadurani said, "The first offense is to blaspheme the pure devotee of the Lord." Prabhupada said, "No. It is an offense to blaspheme *any* Vaishnava who is sincerely spreading Krishna consciousness, propagating the holy names." That point – that every devotee is to be honored – stuck in my mind and heart.

After the initiation I was standing outside the temple door when someone handed me a garland for Prabhupada. I garlanded him and then Prabhupada humbly offered me respect by bowing his head and folding his hands. It was remarkable.

During the Janmashtami celebration in 1972 in New Vrindavan, I was honored to once again see Prabhupada and spend time in his association. After one of his talks someone asked, "Prabhupada, why is *maya* so strong if our purpose in life is to be with God?" Prabhupada said, "Your purpose is not strong." That struck me. *Maya* has a big bag of tricks to pull us away from Krishna, but if we're determined to be Krishna conscious, if our purpose is strong and we're resolute, then we're protected. *Maya's* bag of tricks no longer has power over us and vanishes.

When he came to Atlanta in 1975, Prabhupada was pleased with the temple. One of the *sankirtana* devotees there asked him, "Prabhupada, what pleases you the most?" Everyone thought, *Prabhupada will say, Book distribution.* But Prabhupada said, "If you love Krishna." We were happy to hear that. While he was in Atlanta I felt ecstatic nectar from cleaning his quarters; I didn't feel that I was being left out, but that cleaning was a special opportunity. I did my best and, although I wasn't with the other devotees while Prabhupada lectured or went on his walk, I felt the satisfaction and joy of service.

Those few words of instruction I directly heard from Prabhupada – to honor all Vaishnavas who are helping to spread Lord Chaitanya's *sankirtana* movement in whatever way they are able, and to remain strongly resolute in purpose – have stayed with me all these years. We may distribute books or be a Krishna conscious mother – what service we do doesn't matter – but if we do it sincerely, without letting ourselves be distracted by *maya*, we'll please Srila Prabhupada.

Even though I didn't have much of Prabhupada's physical association – his *vapuh* – I felt close and connected to him through prayer and through reading his books. And I still feel that today.

Bhadra Priya devi dasi

Bhadra Priya was a traveling hippie when she first met devotees chanting on harinama sankirtana near the American Express office in Amsterdam. A day or two later she became vegetarian, and later returned to her native Canada.

I began studying different yoga practices and studied under a guru, Swami Satchitananda of Integral Yoga. I needed a *Bhagavad-gita* and went to the Montreal temple to get one because the Integral Yoga people told me the Hare Krishnas had the best *Gita*. I stayed for the Sunday Feast and met Urvasi, who spoke with me. She was very convincing. A few days later the devotees invited me to go with them to New Vrindavan to see Srila Prabhupada. Since I was gainfully unemployed at the time, being a good hippie, I said, "Sure." We piled into a 1957 Chevy and went first to Toronto, where I was mesmerized by the volume and purity of the sound vibration in the temple. It was simple, but I had never heard anything like it. I broke down. Instantly I was attached to the beauty of getting up early, being with spiritual people, and hearing the Hare Krishna mantra.

In New Vrindavan Prabhupada spoke under a canopy on a hill. I was impressed and knew my life would never be the same from that time on. I took in what I could understand, but somehow I found that I absorbed more from what his disciples said – and they had a lot to say compared to my yoga and silent meditation groups. A couple of days after we got back to Montreal I joined the Movement and eventually served in New Vrindavan.

In my life I hadn't had much contact with death. Srila Prabhupada was the first person who I really cared about who died. In November 1977, I stood in Prabhupada's unheated Palace of Gold, absorbing the news that Prabhupada had left this world and thinking that nothing would ever be the same again. It wasn't. After Srila Prabhupada left I couldn't find any joy in my service. I went to Toronto, got a job, and went through my own personal growth.

Then my spouse died. Then I almost died. What I learned from Prabhupada's and my spouse's deaths and from my near-death is that I didn't appreciate what I had when I had it. It took three horrendous events, but now I appreciate Srila Prabhupada more than I did when he was present. I also appreciate Srila Prabhupada's followers and believe that Srila Prabhupada lives on in them. Even though they would never admit it, they're a lot like him, and in them I see him. I try to appreciate every moment with them and make up for my offenses. My lessons came hard, but I get it now. Srila Prabhupada taught me to appreciate my life with him and his followers.

Everything has been for my spiritual evolvement. Had all these things not happened, I wouldn't be in a good place spiritually – I'd continue to be "out there." I really disconnected from spiritual life.

I came back because the devotees felt like my family and I wanted to go home. It's wonderful coming back. When I was in the world, I barely thought of ISKCON and didn't give the devotees credit for growing and evolving. But it wasn't only me who grew. Now that I'm back I see there's a new wave of Krishna consciousness in ISKCON. I like that.

Even though I continue to struggle with disease and possible death, within my heart of hearts I'm deeply happy. I can't expound on it; it just is. I have sad moments, I cry a lot, but I'm happy I'm here, happy I made a good choice coming here.

Bhagavati devi dasi

At nineteen, Bhagavati dasi received first initiation. She describes that the Detroit temple room was full of devotees chanting like the hum of bees going for the nectar. It was overwhelming. The building seemed like a transcendental spaceship. There was an effulgent-like light around Srila Prabhupada. "It was the safest–it was the best feeling in the whole world that I had ever felt."

I was standing in a long line to go into Srila Prabhupada's quarters in New Dwarka to receive Gayatri mantra. I was happy and excited. I was afraid to go in by myself. I wasn't afraid of Srila Prabhupada, but that I might say or do the wrong thing. Prabhupada showed me how to count. He said, "Now show me." I did it all wrong. So then he said, "Just follow your husband." When my husband was in the room I felt more relaxed, and then I was able to count after he did. I felt that Prabhupada knew everyone's heart. He knew their fears, he knew their inadequacies. He was endearing like a father. I felt that from the very beginning. From the first time I heard his voice, the first time in his room, just the three of us.

In New Dwarka, as Prabhupada would approach the temple, he would talk to the children and pat them on their heads. We would have to run to keep up with him when he was just walking. When he would arrive at the airport he would walk so fast. He walked down the center and we rode on the moving walkway. At the time, you were supposed to just stand, but we would have to run on the belt to keep up with his walking.

It was very exciting to see Srila Prabhupada. Everywhere he went he transformed matter into a spiritual place. It was unanticipated. Just like hearing his voice. When we first joined, Indira and Vamanadeva gave us the Hare Krishna album. We could hear the sound vibration over and over and never become bored. It was never repetitive; it just got increasingly better.

Like the song says, "The spiritual master is the ocean of mercy and he bestows transcendental knowledge." This is something that can't be understood from study but from his mercy.

Once I made *kurtas* for all the boys in the *gurukula*. I was so excited to see all the boys in their new *kurtas* and I also gave each boy a gardenia to give to Srila Prabhupada. I wanted to see Prabhupada's reaction. I wondered if Srila Prabhupada would acknowledge my son Baladeva. Maybe he would know that I made all those *kurtas* and gave all the boys the gardenias. I thought in an egoic way. I didn't want him to know these things exactly, but I wanted him to acknowledge my son. The temple was so full I didn't see what transpired when Prabhupada came in. But some days later someone said, "Did you see what happened to your son in the temple room? Srila Prabhupada touched his head, and it lit up like a light bulb." I thought, "Well, that's very nice that they said that, but this is a new temple room so the lighting is different." But the picture of that moment is in a Vyasa-puja book. Prabhupada is touching my son on the head, and my son is looking up at him smiling. Prabhupada is looking down at him smiling and there is an effulgence. It's just an amazing picture. Once again Prabhupada fulfilled my desire. I felt very blessed.

I wanted to learn anything I could about becoming a *brahmana*. In an initiation ceremony Srila Prabhupada had said, "So now you have been given the Gayatri mantra, and so now you must become *brahmana*." It made me understand the humility and the position. It's not that we have been given *brahmana* but we must become that. I was very happy to hear that, and I felt like my understanding was much better.

The mothers used to pace on the sidewalk with their children, back and forth and back and forth, until someone would come around to the front of the temple from the alleyway and say, "Srila Prabhupada's car is coming!" Prabhupada got out of the car and someone handed him a plate of cookies. I think he might have taken a cookie. Then someone took the plate and started to hand cookies to the leading men there. And Srila Prabhupada said, "The children first." So they lowered the plate and all the little children were offered cookies. My heart felt relieved. I had wondered how children fit into spiritual life and how they're to be acknowledged. After all, if they made noise they would always leave the class. I felt that Prabhupada was like my father and he was sticking up for the children. So Prabhupada answered me. It was a special moment. Being with Srila Prabhupada was always a special moment like that.

I felt safe as a mother. After my second son was born, I was in the L.A. temple room, and all the mothers were up in front with their children to get the cookies. A tray of cookies was brought in for *guru-puja*, and then Prabhupada would hand the cookies to the children. It was always so crowded but it was very exciting. The devotee women were pushing me up front, "Bhagavati, you have to go up. Take your baby up to get a cookie from Srila Prabhupada."

Prabhupada liked it when the mothers held their baby forward to get the cookie. I was just so afraid to be that close. I was always feeling inadequate in some way and that I wasn't a good disciple or I didn't do things right or understand everything. So I passed my son forward and another woman held my second son, Sridhar, up to get the cookie. Then they handed him back to me. I always thought, "Gosh, that was so silly. I should have gone up there with him, and I could have experienced the happiness of seeing Srila Prabhupada look at Sridhar while I held him to get the cookie." Then I thought, "Oh, no." I had mixed feelings about it and thought maybe it was just my bodily consciousness and attachment and pride.

Then sometime later Nitya-trpta came to me with a great big huge picture. A colored, glossy, bigger than an 8 x 10 and she handed it to me. It was a picture of Srila Prabhupada handing Sridhar the cookie. It was a perfect profile of the two of them, and they were both smiling and touching the cookie at the same time. It was just a perfect picture of their heads and their hands and the cookie. I felt that Srila Prabhupada had reciprocated with me since I had regretted that I didn't go up there. He personally came in the photograph. The photograph didn't feel like simply a piece of paper. It seemed like a gift from Srila Prabhupada. He was present in the picture and the picture was completely a transcendental experience. I am always very grateful to Prabhupada that no matter what blunders I make, he always reassures me that he's still present.

Over the years, every once in a while something like that will happen again. A few years ago my mother passed away and I went back to St. Louis for her funeral. My family was very unhappy that I became a devotee. They didn't understand anything at all about Krishna consciousness. When I left them to go to the airport to return to California to my children, I felt very alone and afraid. It was right before 6:00 a.m. in the morning. I had been up since 3:30. I reflected on why I went to California and left my family. The St. Louis temple had closed and we had moved to Detroit. But it was very cold so we went to California, where my last two children were born. I remembered the reasons for the moves, but I still felt empty that I was again leaving my family in Missouri. At the airport, all of a sudden, I felt Srila Prabhupada's overwhelming presence. It felt as though he was walking with me to the plane. I didn't feel alone anymore. My mother was gone and even though Srila Prabhupada left physically, he was still mystically with me and knew my every feeling. I was so comforted by his presence. When I arrived in California a couple of devotees–neither one knew the other or had heard what I thought had happened–said to me, "It was Srila

Prabhupada that was walking with you." It was such comfort at that great sad time of losing my mother.

Once I made a hat, *kartala* straps, a bead bag, and a *kurta* for Srila Prabhupada. Srutakirti kept saying, "Maybe it would be good if you went into Srila Prabhupada's room so you can fit the hat on him. It seems like you need to know where to put the button." I would say, "No, I might stick the pin and hurt him, so you go up. Plus I wouldn't want to go up, being a woman. I might make an offense or something." I told Srutakirti, "Now, make sure that Prabhupada wears the hat with the silk on the outside, and the wool on the inside." Anyway, many years later I went to Badger to visit a devotee, Yashoda. I was looking through her photo album and found a picture of Srila Prabhupada wearing my hat. There were no buttons on it and he wore it inside out. Later when I saw Srutakirti, I asked him why Srila Prabhupada wore the hat inside out. He said, "Because Prabhupada never wore wool right next to his skin. It would always be lined by cotton or silk because the wool drains the energy from the body."

In separation his presence is strong and I feel his association is available. The association of the devotees keeps his presence alive.

Bhagavati devi dasi

In 1971, Bhagavati and her husband, Vasudeva Prabhu, saw Western devotees in Sydney. Vasudeva thought, "Who changed these Western people? I want to meet that person." He asked the devotees, "Who is your guru?" "Srila Prabhupada," he was told. Then, on July 3, 1974, when Prabhupada was en route from Melbourne to Hawaii and had a thirty-minute stopover in Fiji's Nadi airport, Bhagavati and Vasudeva met him.

In the airport lounge we offered Prabhupada a garland and some *prasadam* – sweet *puris* and tomato chutney. Prabhupada asked Vasudeva, "Is there a Radha-Krishna temple in Fiji?" Vasudeva said, "No, there's no Radha-Krishna temple here." Prabhupada said, "You make a nice Radha-Krishna temple." And he told Vasudeva, "From now chant sixteen rounds." Since that day Vasudeva has chanted sixteen rounds. When Prabhupada was leaving, Vasudeva said, "Come to Fiji." Prabhupada said, "Next year when I go from Australia to Hawaii, I'll stop in Fiji," and in May 1975 he came.

We advertised a program for him in Natabua Hall, Lautoka and two or three thousand people attended. There was kirtan and then Prabhupada explained that Krishna is the Supreme Personality of Godhead and the importance of chanting Hare Krishna. In my family we had worshiped Shiva and Durga as well as Radha and Krishna. But after we met Prabhupada we understood that as watering the root of a tree nourishes the whole tree, so worshiping Krishna includes worship of demigods, so we stopped demigod worship. Vasudeva and I had hosted many Indian *sadhus* but only Prabhupada taught us how to engage in Krishna's service daily by chanting and reading the *Bhagavatam* and *Bhagavad-gita*. Prabhupada said, "You don't have to stop anything, just add Krishna to your life. Whatever you cook, offer it to Krishna, and then take *prasadam*. And chant Krishna's names."

In 1976 Prabhupada came again for the foundation-laying ceremony of the Krishna-Kaliya temple. At that time he said, "Fiji is a beautiful place and now the temple is here, I'll come again and again." The day before the ceremony Vasudeva said, "Prabhupada, I want to take initiation." Prabhupada said, "Okay, shave your head and get ready." I said, "I want to take also." So Vasudeva Prabhu, his elder brother, Bhuvan Mohan, and I were initiated on the same day as the ceremony. The next morning Prabhupada gave Vasudeva and me second initiation and taught us how to say Gayatri.

My sister, Nandarani, and my mother were cooking for Prabhupada and he told them, "Cook whatever you like but daily make these two things – stuffed karela and stuffed bhindi." When I brought him a little pot of rice he said, "Is it hot?" He opened it, steam came out, and he said, "Okay, close it." He liked hot rice.

Prabhupada was a great personality, but he was humble and simple. That attracted me. I wasn't qualified, but by Prabhupada's mercy he accepted me as his disciple.

Just as Vasudeva and I were attracted to Prabhupada, so Prabhupada's books and lectures attract people coming today. And everything he established – Deity worship, kirtan, *tulasi-puja,* temple service – is also attractive. Just seeing devotees engage in Krishna's service is attractive.

Bhaja Govinda devi dasi

After reading Srila Prabhupada's purports for a month, Bhaja Govinda moved into the Gainesville temple. That was the effect his words had on her.

In 1976, we drove from Gainesville to attend the first Ratha-yatra down New York's Fifth Avenue and I finally saw Srila Prabhupada, the wonderful personality I'd heard so much about, along with many bright-faced devotees. Prabhupada was so regal it was like he was from another planet. He was a big golden merciful person with a glowing gold effulgence. Before class he motioned for the women and children to come first to get cookies from him. My twelve year-old daughter and I went first and got a cookie.

From day one Amarendra, our temple president, had drilled us, "Your relationship with Prabhupada is through book distribution. The way to please him is by distributing his books." I was a book distributor and since my association with Srila Prabhupada was through his books, when he left the planet, my reaction was different from my godbrothers and godsisters. For me, Prabhupada's books were still here, so he was still here. The physical separation wasn't traumatic. Prabhupada is also in the heart of the wonderful daughters he left to help take care of me and raise me; by their mercy I'm still here.

Bhakti devi dasi

From India, Bhakti's husband, Brahmatirtha, was writing stream of consciousness letters to her. When he started writing about A. C. Bhaktivedanta Swami Prabhupada, a name Bhakti couldn't pronounce, she thought they were more stream of consciousness letters and didn't give them much credibility.

As I was growing up there was a lot of death in my family and no one could answer my questions: Why were people dying so young? Where were they going? Why was there pain in the world? After my husband came back from India and we started going to the temple I realized the depth of Krishna consciousness, but I was a "don't tell me what to do" person and couldn't relate with the devotees or the philosophy. I only went to the temple because of my husband and when devotees said "Hare Krishna" to me, I'd say, "Hi." I'd never say "Hare Krishna." I felt I'd say it when I was ready.

After several years my husband was clearly ready for initiation and I was clearly not. I still hadn't said, "Hare Krishna." A dear friend, Atreya Rsi Prabhu, suggested that my husband and I meet with Srila Prabhupada in New York City on July 4th, 1974. I was intimidated to meet Prabhupada and didn't know what I would say or even why I should go, but together my husband and I walked into Srila Prabhupada's beautiful, long narrow room. Prabhupada was sitting at a table at the head of the room, my husband sat in the middle, and I sat at the opposite end, terrified. I wanted to blend into the wall. Srila Prabhupada was golden. He looked right at me and in perfect English said, "So you are interested in Krishna consciousness?" But I couldn't understand a word he said. I was embarrassed. Prabhupada, knowing precisely what was going on, said to my husband, "Translate." It didn't matter to Prabhupada that I didn't understand and right away I felt embraced by Prabhupada. I didn't have to stand on ceremonies or to pretend. I could just be me and it was okay.

Prabhupada asked me if I had questions and then a young lady came in with a large bowl of white round sweets that looked like golf balls. Prabhupada thanked her, she left, and he called me over. I went to his desk and he said, "Hold out your hand." I held out my left hand and he said, "No, no, other hand." He wasn't condescending, he was loving. I held out my other hand and he put a wet drippy golf ball-looking thing into it. I had no idea what to do with it. He saw my bewilderment and motioned to me with a very open mouth as if to say, "Pop it in your mouth." I thought, "How am I going to get this in my mouth?" Somehow I squished it in. My eyes must have bugged because Prabhupada burst out laughing. I washed my hand, sat down, and thought, "This is a magical experience. This person has made Krishna consciousness real and available to me." I couldn't concentrate on what Prabhupada was saying because all I was thinking was, "How am I going to thank this person?" Somebody said, "Srila Prabhupada, it's time to go to the airport." My husband was the driver so he ran out. I was standing in the threshold of the door about to walk out when I stopped, turned around, folded my hands, and said to Srila Prabhupada, "Thank you very much." Without a moment's hesitation Srila Prabhupada said, "Hare Krishna," and for the first time I said, "Hare Krishna." It was a magical, life-changing experience.

I had felt like a square peg in a round hole – I was misunderstood and didn't fit anywhere. But when I met Prabhupada, everything changed. He was loving and welcoming and fatherly and everything I was looking for. And I became good friends with phenomenal, like-minded devotees who understood me, Yadubara Prabhu being foremost of them. He acknowledged me and said, "Yes, there is a place for you here," and showed me where. And by Srila Prabhupada's and Krishna's grace, I'm still here.

Bhavatarini devi dasi

Bhavatarini first saw Srila Prabhupada at the airport in Atlanta, Georgia, in June 1971. She had been living in the Atlanta temple for a few months and searching for the truth.

I had not only found the truth in Krishna consciousness but I was also being taught a practical way to attain it – by chanting the Hare Krishna mantra. Through reading Srila Prabhupada's books and hearing from his followers, I developed some attraction for Krishna and the philosophy, but I had no real understanding of the importance or potency of the spiritual master.

The day I met him, Srila Prabhupada was flying back to New York City from Gainesville, Florida, where he had done a television interview. During his two-hour layover in Atlanta, the devotees arranged a conference room at the airport so we could have a brief visit with him. Preparations for his visit actually began weeks in advance, and devotees from other centers in other cities gathered to help. The atmosphere was surcharged with anticipation and excitement. A handful of devotees had built a small *vyasasana* for him to use at the airport, others prepared a play, and others a feast. We decorated the conference room with fabric, flowers, and paintings.

Devotees, friends, and relatives gathered at the airport to greet him, chanting Hare Krishna, dancing, and playing *karatalas* and drums. The small plane landed and a metal staircase moved up to the plane's door. Then we saw Prabhupada in the doorway. The entire doorway filled with light, suddenly. He had a glowing golden complexion, and his silk saffron robes rippled slightly, although there was no breeze. With his head held high, a cane held gracefully in one hand, he descended the steps to the tarmac.

I was astounded. I had not expected him to be so extraordinary. I thought, "He appears so regal – like a lion."

When he reached the tarmac he lifted a bright orange and yellow marigold garland from around his neck and garlanded the disciple standing next to him. Then, the garland I had made of red roses, carnations, and miniature magnolias was draped over his neck. It fell all the way to his feet, framing his entire form. As he started toward us, it seemed as if his feet weren't touching the ground, like he was gliding across the pavement. I thought, "He appears so elegant, like a swan gliding across a lake."

We followed him into the conference room. He climbed onto the *vyasasana*, which had been placed on top of a table, and sat down on the beautiful, round blue-velvet seat. The wall behind him was a light blue, but it paled in comparison to the bluish effulgence that he seemed to emanate. Like a lotus flower sprouting from mud, Prabhupada bloomed in our midst. The entire room was transformed into the spiritual world and in his presence we were completely free from anxiety. He stole our hearts and planted the seed of bhakti in them. I began to have a slight realization of the glories of the guru.

This occasion has been described in detail in *Srila Prabhupada-lilamrita* by Satsvarupa dasa Goswami, so I will leave my personal memories of it for another time. Needless to say, the two hours were over much too soon. Prabhupada boarded his plane to New York and flew away, taking our hearts with him.

Bhismaka devi dasi

On Radhastami, September 23, 1977, in front of Radha-Gopinatha in the Toronto temple, Bhismaka and her husband, Visnutattva Prabhu, were initiated. Feeling their life was useless if they didn't see their spiritual master, two weeks later they decided to go to India.

My husband said to his business partner, "Why don't you buy the business?" His partner said, "Your share is worth $250,000 but I can give you only $8,000." My husband said, "OK, I'll do it." We sold our three-story home for no profit and bought tickets to Vrindavan.

I was a neophyte with no service attitude and a big ego. In Vrindavan I started serving Pishima and she'd talk only about Nityananda Prabhu, Lord Chaitanya, and the devotees. She treated me like a daughter and gave me so much love that my ego was smashed and I got purified.

While we all danced in ecstasy, Prabhupada, on his palanquin, would circumambulate the temple three times, take *charanamrita*, and then pay his obeisances to his Guru Maharaja, to Krishna-Balarama, and to Radha-Syamasundara. Prabhupada hadn't eaten for a long time and after *mangala-arati* on the 7th of November, everybody was excited because he requested Gujarati *chapatis* and *dal*. I was asked to cook. I showered, ran to Prabhupada's kitchen and cooked while constantly praying to Radharani, "I don't know how to make these dishes well but they are for Your pure devotee. Please help me."

Everybody wanted Prabhupada to eat and be healthy, but every day he'd been sending his plate back untouched. When the plate with Gujarati *chapatis* and *dal* came in front of Prabhupada, the whole room was quiet: would he eat or not? Prabhupada looked at the food for a couple of minutes then picked up the *chapati,* dipped it in the *dal* and ate it. The devotees started jumping, "*Jaya* Prabhupada!" Of the five *chapatis* I made, Prabhupada ate three, all the *dal,* and half the chutney and *shak*. Upendra gave me Prabhupada's plate, "This mercy belongs to you," and I gave everybody a little bit.

Prabhupada asked my husband, "Does Bhismaka know how to make *malpura* and *srikhand*?" Excited, my husband said, "Yes, Prabhupada! You can request anything any time of the day or night, and she'll cook it for you." Prabhupada was calm. He said, "You devotees are so nice, you're all serving me so well," and became quiet.

On the evening of the 14th of November, all of us were around Prabhupada's bed chanting and crying loudly when Prabhupada sipped Yamuna *jal* and left this planet. That consciousness, that environment, that cry of love from all devotees cannot be expressed. It was beyond this material world. I thought, "Why does Prabhupada have to leave us? We don't want to be separated from him." The garland I'd made for Radharani that morning was on Prabhupada's neck when he left.

If an ordinary person dies, his body becomes stiff but Prabhupada's body was like a flower. It wasn't material but completely spiritual. The Gaudiya Math devotees came and we chanted the whole night while Prabhupada was on his palanquin on the *vyasasana* in the temple room. One after the other all the devotees fanned him. Nobody slept. In the morning, we went with Prabhupada's body on *parikrama* of Vrindavan and the Brijbasis paid their final respects to him. And by Prabhupada's previous request, we distributed *prasadam* to all the Brijbasis. I thought, "Prabhupada asked about *malpura* and *srikhand*," so I made those for him and by his mercy they were offered to him.

Prabhupada is my life and soul and I cannot leave him. Every day I ask him for mercy. His books are full of nectar and when I read them I hear him giving instructions – what to do, what not to do, how to preach. If I miss hearing him lecture even one day I feel, "I'm missing out." This material world is full of misery; we can't always trust others, but if we follow Srila Prabhupada, then Radha-Krishna and Gaura-Nitai are pleased and we're fine.

Bhogini devi dasi

In August of 1973, when Srila Prabhupada installed Sri Sri Radha-Parisisvara in the temple on Rue le Sueur in Paris, he also held an initiation. At that time, Bhogini received initiation from him.

We had never seen large marble Deities before, and for the installation They were being bathed in huge aluminum cooking pots in the center of the temple room. Prabhupada was sitting on the *vyasasana*, observing. I was going back and forth to the kitchen and I just happened to be looking into the room when Srila Prabhupada got off the *vyasasana*, walked up to Radharani, and stood stroking Her cheek with his forefinger. I felt that Srila Prabhupada was seeing Radharani in a personal way, which reinforced my understanding that once the Deities were installed, then Radha and Krishna are personally present. That tender moment touched me and contributed to my attraction to *pujari* service.

Once, when Srila Prabhupada offered his obeisances to Radha-Parisisvara, I was directly behind him. My head was inches from his lotus feet as he bowed down. We'd been instructed not to touch Srila Prabhupada's lotus feet, but I could feel the very soft and delicate warmth from them. I was blessed to be that close to Srila Prabhupada's lotus feet.

The second time Prabhupada came to Paris I received *brahmana* initiation. One of Prabhupada's disciples performed the ceremony while Prabhupada sat on the *vyasasana*, completely relaxed, almost as if he'd fallen asleep. Later, I was suddenly catapulted into Prabhupada's room to receive the Gayatri mantra. I didn't know what was going on, but Prabhupada patted the carpet on his right side and said, "Come, sit down here." It was the only time I was alone with Prabhupada. I sat next to him and it was beautiful. I felt that I wasn't just one of a crowd, I wasn't just a woman in the back, but I mattered enough to be requested to sit beside him. I loved watching as he used his own long fingers to show me how to count the mantras from one digit to the next. He said, "Can you do that?" And I did the same thing. He had me repeat the Gayatri mantra after him word by word, and I couldn't say one word in the last line, so he had me repeat it three or four times until he was satisfied that I said it correctly.

When I think of Srila Prabhupada, those beautiful long lotus fingers and the softness of his lotus feet still appear in my mind's eye.

One morning Prabhupada took darshan of the Deities and then gave a talk in which he spoke extensively about Krishna's lotus feet. At the end of the class he said, "And, therefore, we are asking why Krishna is not wearing ankle bells." He also made a comment about Radharani being a cowherd girl who wears a skirt and a veil, not a *sari*. After that we learned to make skirts and veils for Radharani.

My grandparents died around the time I was born, so I grew up without grandparents, but Srila Prabhupada was everything a grandfather would be insomuch as I could respect him unconditionally and he was incredibly wise and loving. He entirely fulfilled my needs and I knew I could really trust him. My association with Srila Prabhupada inspired me. It's not that I'm the most faithful disciple, I've got very lax standards, but those don't remove the bond of love I have with him.

Bhranti devi dasi

Bhranti, Shranti, and Akincana Krishna were living in Largo, Florida in 1974 when a mutual friend, Garuda Pandit, introduced them to Prabhupada's books and chanting. When Bhranti read Easy Journey to Other Planets she felt, "Oh, my gosh, this book makes total sense." Immediately all her confusion cleared.

During Christmas time in 1974, Garuda Pandit and I went to the Seattle temple, where a devotee told us about book distribution. I thought, "That's the coolest thing I ever heard. You remember this person, Srila Prabhupada, and you become full of some kind of power. It's far out." Garuda Pandit and I went back to Florida and rejoined our friends, Shranti and Akincana Krishna, made an altar in our house, cooked from the *Hare Krishna Cookbook*, and went to the Gainesville temple for Sunday Feasts.

We heard Prabhupada didn't like hippie-looking people and both the men had long hair. We cut their hair, got better clothes, and went to see Srila Prabhupada in Atlanta in February of 1975. The temple room was packed. When Prabhupada came in wearing a beautiful saffron coat with peacock feathers, I couldn't decide if he looked more like a king or a saint. Right away I fell on the floor and said to myself, "I don't know who you are, but I want to surrender to you and serve you. My life is never going to be the same again."

It was Srila Bhaktisiddhanta's appearance day and seeing Prabhupada offer *arati* to his spiritual master impressed me. Then we saw a well-done play of the Chand Kazi, and I noticed that the devotees were watching Prabhupada to see how he liked it. Prabhupada was the devotees' life and soul.

The next day at *guru-puja* the temple room was totally packed again with women on one side, men on the other and an aisle down the middle so Prabhupada could see the Deities. When it was my turn to offer flowers to Srila Prabhupada, I walked toward him down that long aisle feeling, "This is scary because Prabhupada just sees me," and knowing I didn't understand the significance of what I was doing.

The times I was with Prabhupada were important, but from the beginning I was attracted to his books. In the Gainesville temple I'd get up an hour before *mangala-arati* to read *Chaitanya-charitamrita* and I'd read the *Bhagavatam* while I ate lunch. Starting with *Easy Journey to Other Planets* until now – 35 years later – I've stayed connected to Prabhupada by reading his books. Reading clarifies everything. Bam! Everything's put in the right place.

Bhumata devi dasi

In 1975, Bhumata devi dasi, received a letter from Srila Prabhupada that was a source of encouragement for her for the rest of her life. In it he said, "You are a good lady and a good devotee."

Bhumata joined the Hare Krishna movement in 1970 in Cleveland, Ohio at thirty-eight years old. When she read a *Back to Godhead* magazine that she received from her eldest son, Jasper, Bhumata realized that she had finally found the spiritual science she had been looking for most of her life. A spiritual seeker since a young age and the daughter of a strong southern Baptist minister and a faithful evangelist mother, Bhumata had immersed herself in a few religious practices including Pentacostal, Nation of Islam, Mormon, Unity and Moorish Science, and Seventh Day Adventists. As a long-time, dedicated follower of Lord Jesus Christ, she saw Srila Prabhupada as an extension of the Christ spirit and always claimed both as her beloved gurus. In her estimation, Srila Prabhupada fulfilled the Biblical prophecy that a messenger of God would come from the East in the last days. Later, when she read that a precocious child had called Srila Prabhupada "Swami Jesus," Bhumata wasn't at all surprised.

Bhumata immediately gave up her materialistic trappings, sold her furniture, and gave the proceeds to the fledging Hare Krishna storefront temple that was under the jurisdiction of Sri Govinda and Srilekha. She had her male children and students cut their hair with *shikhas* and right away she started wearing *sari* and *tilaka*. She brought several of her eight children and some of her students (she was a metaphysics teacher) with her to the temple. Coming from a strong Christian background, many of Bhumata's relatives were aghast that she chose to participate in a strange cult. Though her early days in Krishna consciousness were fraught with many challenges, she received initiation, along with her husband, Rupchand Das, and three of her children in Dallas, Texas on Radhastami, 1972. The same day, Srila Prabhupada installed the gorgeous Radha-Kalachandji Deities. Along with her daughter, Krishnanandini, Bhumata opened the Radha-Syamasundaraloka Temple of ISKCON in Cleveland, Ohio in 1974, after being authorized by Srila Prabhupada to open a center in the inner city. "Birds of a feather will flock together," he wrote them in a letter.

Bhumata always claimed Lord Jesus Christ as her first guru who guided her to her beloved Srila Prabhupada. And, because of her love and commitment to Srila Prabhupada, many of her children, grandchildren, and spiritual children took to Krishna consciousness also.

Bhumata passed away in a hospital in 2014 chanting Hare Krishna during the *brahma-muhurta* hour, on the auspicious day of Bhismadeva's passing. The nurses in the hospital felt impelled to inform us of the time. One of her sons, Krsnadasa (Otis Lee Christ) asked the nurse, "What was my mother doing when she passed?" "Your mother was speaking a foreign language," she replied. "What language? I don't think she knew any foreign languages." "Yes," the nurse said emphatically, "she was saying, 'Ha ray Krishna. Ha ray Krishna.'"

Bhumi devi dasi

For years, Bhumi saw devotees chanting on the streets of New York, but she was not at all attracted. She thought the devotees were weird and, like anybody who took up anything religious, had nothing else going for them.

What changed my mind about the Hare Krishnas was hearing them on The David Susskind Show. They explained Krishna consciousness in such a way that I thought, "Wow, that's cool." The thought of having inner peace and a oneness with the universe attracted me. My sister was watching the show too and I said to her, "You should check out the Brooklyn temple." She did, and moved in right away.

I visited the temple a few times. I was happy that my sister had found something that inspired her, but there was no way that I was going to do it. Then, just before Prabhupada was going to come in July 1972, the devotees asked me if I wanted to stay during his visit. I said, "Sure." Every morning they gave me *mangala-arati* sweets. For me, it was all about *prasadam*. At the temple I tasted *puris* and caramel made from condensed milk for the first time.

I don't remember much from Prabhupada's visit, but when he left, I went home, played the "Govindam" song on the Radha Krishna Temple album and, looking at the picture of Prabhupada on the back of the album, thought, "That's my spiritual master." I was startled by that realization and cried, because I knew that there was no turning back – they'd gotten me. I moved into the temple in July 1972, just after Prabhupada's visit.

A few weeks later it was my very first Janmastami and I went to New Vrindavan with other New York devotees to hear Prabhupada give the Bhagavata Dharma discourses there.

Janmastami was the first time I'd ever fasted. At the Nrisimha prayers after the midnight *arati,* we all sat down and I was thinking "When can we take *prasadam*? I can't wait until I can eat!" Then Srila Prabhupada indicated that we should read from the *Krsna* book. So we read the first chapter and I heard the name Bhumi for the first time.

After we'd finished that chapter, I thought, "Finally, I can take *prasadam*. I'm so hungry and tired." It was one am. Prabhupada indicated that we should keep reading.

We read the second chapter of the *Krsna* book. It's a long chapter. And that night it seemed even longer. Prabhupada was in ecstasy hearing Krishna's pastimes. I was thinking, "When will this be over? I want to sleep. I want to take *prasadam*." Then Prabhupada indicated that we should read another chapter. We read three chapters of *Krsna* book to Srila Prabhupada and took *prasadam* around two-thirty in the morning. My purport to the New Vrindavan Srila Prabhupada *Krsna* book reading marathon was that I was very happy to take *prasadam*.

In April of 1973, Prabhupada came to Brooklyn again and I got initiated. My name means Mother Earth. Bhumi took the shape of a cow, prayed to Lord Brahma and because of her prayers, Krishna appeared and performed His pastimes on earth. When Krishna left this planet, Bhumi's feelings of separation were the most intense because she was accustomed to having Krishna's lotus feet always on her body.

I didn't enjoy distributing books, but every day I distributed books in Port Authority because I heard it made Srila Prabhupada happy. At night while we drank hot milk, we'd have *Krsna* book readings, and we also had *Nectar of Devotion* and *Bhagavatam* classes, so I knew what was in Prabhupada's books. I grew up in Krishna consciousness listening to classes by Jayadvaita, Jadurani, and visiting *sannyasis*. I felt connected with Srila Prabhupada and his Movement by hearing from his books, by hearing classes by his followers, and by associating with his disciples.

To me, Prabhupada wasn't a father figure. He was larger than life and I almost couldn't relate to him as a person. I was reverent toward him. After he left this physical world, my relationship with him deepened.

Brahmi devi dasi

Brahmi's first memory of meeting Srila Prabhupada was in a book she found in a secondhand bookshop. The book was called Krishna Consciousness: The Topmost Yoga System. *She also found* Easy Journey to Other Planets. *She was so intrigued by these titles that she bought them both.*

One paragraph made a deep impression on me—as I remember it, it said, "Why are we sending all these young men to the war in Vietnam when there is a fighting class of men?" That is when I recognized my spiritual master, and I told myself, "This man is beautiful." I looked at the back of one of the books and saw the number for the Toronto temple. I called and asked the person who answered the phone whether I could visit, and of course I was welcome to. I have loved Srila Prabhupada from the moment I read his books. He has been my life and soul from then on, and I am, by Krishna's mercy, in a seventy-seven-year-old body—in the "dwindling" stage, to be precise. I shudder to think about what my life would have been without his loving guidance and teachings.

I saw Srila Prabhupada for the first time at my initiation in West Virginia. We were like excited children, and I felt completely inadequate and unworthy to be initiated by him. When I approached his dear lotus feet he looked at me with his beautiful, noble, dark eyes, and said, "Your name is Brahmi devi." I felt ashamed to dare to stand before him. He was sitting on a *vyasasana* outside in the open, and all the devotees were looking on that glorious, pure figure with adoring eyes. We were his children, lost in the material world and coming to his lotus feet for security. There was a dog under the *vyasasana*, but he didn't let us remove him. "Leave him there," he said. Fortunate dog!

The devotees felt jubilant to have Srila Prabhupada with us. The joy of it! I remember dancing in the temple with maybe fifty devotees, and there was a devotee who had been a ballet dancer. He was jumping high in the air, and we danced with him, as if we were in a ballet. I swear I felt time stand still. I felt such joy in my heart that I couldn't feel my feet touch the ground. The bell was ringing, and it felt like being suspended in time.

It was either in Los Angeles or Dallas when I was asked to help prepare Srila Prabhupada's room and make his bed. I had a fourteen-year-old to help me. We cleaned everything and put new sheets on his bed—we had washed them and they had dried just in time. We set his slippers and Deities near his sitting place. I put some blue stuff in the toilet to remind him of Krishna (how silly of me—but that's what I was thinking!). We had just finished and were coming out of the kitchen when Srila Prabhupada and some of his disciples passed by. Srila Prabhupada looked at me with such a gaze of nobility—his eyes like black gems. I pushed my assistant back and we both crawled back into the kitchen and paid our obeisances very loudly.

What a wonderful blessing to have been seen by my beloved spiritual master. I'm not being puffed up, but to have had his lotus eyes look on me makes me feel blessed beyond description. The thought of it makes me weep even now.

When our beloved Srila Prabhupada left this planet I felt adrift. My only friend and guide had left; the world seemed empty. Our father and best friend was gone. Then I realized he hasn't gone at all—he will always be with me if I follow his words. I have his books, which he translated for us. He is there. So now his books have become my life and soul. When I read them I know Srila Prabhupada is with me. I also have wonderful association with all the devotees of the Lord. They are my family and friends.

Since I was accepted by Srila Prabhupada I have never stopped looking to him for guidance and strength of purpose. He is always with me. There has never been a time when I thought otherwise. If I need an answer to anything, I consult him through his books. All answers are there, quite clear and explicit. Srila Prabhupada is always with us. We may leave him, but he does not leave us. I could not bear to live without him. I prostrate myself at his beautiful lotus feet again and again.

I always think, "What would my spiritual master want me to do in everyday life?" And then I remember his words and deal with whatever disturbances arise. I must think from a Krishna conscious point of view—this viewpoint is learned through Srila Prabhupada's purports in *Srimad-Bhagavatam* and *Bhagavad-gita*. Everything we need to know is there. I may be the greatest fool, but if I repeat his words, people will listen. Actually, I've seen that whenever I preach to someone in his words, they are amazed at those words. I myself feel amazed. I have firm faith that simply using his words with conviction will transfer those words into people's hearts. People evolve at different rates, and we can't force anyone to become a devotee. So it is essential that we be kind, friendly, and understanding—empathic instead of judgmental. People are suffering. Srila Prabhupada accepted us and took it on himself to train and guide us although we had no idea how to behave. We should emulate how he treated us when we speak to others.

I am a humble servant and a godsister in our beloved Srila Prabhupada's family. All glories to His Divine Grace, our dearest father and eternal spiritual master, and to all the devotees of Lord Krishna. May we continue to have his blessings and service to his beautiful lotus feet.

Caitanya devi dasi

Once, in 1970, during a rip-roaring kirtan in the Los Angeles temple, Caitanya dasi, along with all the other devotees, went wild when Prabhupada suddenly walked in, put his arms in the air, and started dancing like he was floating.

Sometime later I married Kanupriya, went with him to Trinidad to preach, and then returned with him to Los Angeles where I was to receive *brahmana* initiation. Prabhupada did the ceremony and I was told to go to Prabhupada's room. I was pregnant and huge, so I offered my obeisances on my knees. Prabhupada said, "How did the preaching go in Trinidad?" I said it went nicely but because I was going to have a child, I wanted to come back to America. Then, extremely nervous, I sat down on a cushion next to him to receive Gayatri. I knew how to chant on my fingers but suddenly I couldn't do it. Prabhupada said the words of the mantra and told me to repeat. I felt like he saw all my horrible sins and faults and I went into a state of shock. I froze and was sitting there like a complete foolish idiot. He took my hand and said, "Do like this." I thought, "Oh, my God, I have to do this." With my heart pounding, I moved my fingers and said the mantra.

When Prabhupada was to leave L.A. and had just gotten into his car, Srimati and I quickly picked roses and went to the car. Prabhupada rolled down the window, I handed him my rose and blurted out, "Please hurry and come back, Srila Prabhupada!" He said, "Yes, I shall return soon," and smiled. Srimati gave him her rose and he said, "Are you coming to India?" Srimati said, "I'm making money to buy my ticket." Prabhupada said, "OK, I'll see you in India."

In 1972, I went with my fourteen-month-old twins, Draupadi and Gandhari, to Vrindavan. When we arrived, we went into Prabhupada's quarters in the Radha-Damodara temple. He was wearing his simple *sannyasa* top and was leaning back, relaxed, with his hands behind his head. He said, "Oh, Krishna has brought you here." I thought, "Wow, Krishna brought us here!" Then he said, "So you are following Ekadasi?" I thought, "My God, I forgot it's Ekadasi." I put my head down and said, "I'm sorry, Srila Prabhupada, I didn't know it was Ekadasi. I broke it." Prabhupada said, "Go ahead, take sweets." It was a brief, sweet exchange and I felt blessed to be in his presence in the holy *dhama*, and to experience his mood of being at home.

Back to Los Angeles, I used to play the *mridanga* and sing for the devotee dance troupe, the Vaikuntha Players. Once I sat on the temple room floor next to Prabhupada's *vyasasana* when we did a private performance for Prabhupada, "The Killing of Pralambasura." When Balarama punched and killed Pralambasura, Prabhupada's expression was incredible; his eyes got wide and he smiled broadly. He very much enjoyed that show. Another time I sat in Prabhupada's garden and read to him, "Lord Brahma Steals the Cows and Cowherd Boys." Sometimes Prabhupada listened with closed eyes and other times he commented. It was personal and transcendental.

When Prabhupada distributed cookies in the temple room it touched my heart how he always took the time to make sure each child received that special mercy from his hand. It showed his patience, tolerance, love, compassion, and how he saw everyone as equally important.

When Prabhupada toured the devotee apartments in Los Angeles it was like Krishna entering Dwarka. Incense was billowing, the ladies were on the balconies, and everybody was waiting in anticipation. It was a transcendental game – which apartment would he visit, where would he go next? Prabhupada had fun and relished these exchanges with the devotees.

Cakrini devi dasi

Prabhupada initiated Cakrini, twenty-three, under a big tree in the New Mayapur garden. It was the first time Cakrini saw him.

Prabhupada's eyes were shiny. With his eyes he conversed with and understood me. And from his eyes I realized how fallen I was. My heart told me, "This man is going to give you something special. How can you thank him for what he'll give you?" Prabhupada closed his eyes for a moment and said, "Cakrini." I touched my head to the grass to offer obeisances. He said, "Everything will be all right if you follow my instructions." My mind had been unsettled but he gave me lifelong direction.

I've never experienced a lot of love in this world. When I was fourteen I lost my father; my mother was left alone and poor with five children. It was difficult. But, although I wasn't with Prabhupada for a long time, when I lost him I cried all the time – he was the father who created me when he initiated me and I didn't want to accept that he was gone.

I'm not intellectual but I wanted to read *Srimad-Bhagavatam* and *Bhagavad-gita*, listen to Prabhupada every day, and keep him prominent in my heart. His words are deep. They never fail me, and they help me feel his sweetness and love. He is my irreplaceable refuge. Love is love and everybody should understand another's heart. No one could ever replace Srila Prabhupada in my heart.

Prabhupada is always speaking to Krishna, and for us to be happy, he's the only person we need to know in this world. Thank you for coming Srila Prabhupada.

Camari devi dasi

In 1973, Camari went from the Sydney to the Melbourne temple to help prepare for Prabhupada's arrival.

We had assembled in the temple room to greet Srila Prabhupada. He was sitting on the *vyasasana*, and I was about two meters away from him. Being a young devotee, I was finding it difficult to follow the many regulative principles of Krishna consciousness, and my mind was giving me trouble. I remember looking at Srila Prabhupada's foot and thinking, "If I can completely meditate on that foot, my mind will never give me trouble again! This meditation will conquer all." Then I looked up at Srila Prabhupada's face. He was looking directly at me, quite serious and stern. It was not a sentimental glance. In that moment I realized I had to get real about my Krishna consciousness and embrace it. It was a genuine lifestyle choice, and if I was to become serious, I had to get off the mental platform and immerse myself in my spirituality. That realization took a weight off my shoulders and helped my Krishna consciousness.

On another occasion when Srila Prabhupada was visiting the Melbourne temple, the carpet in the house where he was staying was not clean. I sewed several white sheets together to cover the carpet in the large lounge room, but the center joins were all a bit off. When Srila Prabhupada walked into that room, he immediately noticed the white sheeting on the floor and said, "This is not centered. This is not correct." That was actually a sweet moment for me. In doing something to serve Prabhupada or Krishna, I needed to get it right. Near enough is not good enough.

On this same visit, we heard that the back cushion on Srila Prabhupada's lounge-room *asana* was uncomfortable, so we pulled the *asana* cushion apart and redid it to ensure that Prabhupada had no discomfort while he translated. We wanted to help Srila Prabhupada in his writing–that was the most important thing for us, because we were a distribution center for his books. During the day we were all out distributing with our hearts and souls.

I've stayed enlivened in Prabhupada's service over the years because of my memories of Srila Prabhupada and the association of his devotees. As I and my godsisters were enlivened by Srila Prabhupada, there's a new generation that have that same love, that same passion, for their Gurudevas and for Krishna consciousness. Srila Prabhupada is present in his books, in the temple, and in his disciples who love him and who are passing on that love to new people who come to Krishna consciousness.

I came to Krishna consciousness because I wanted to follow a true spiritual path. I found great happiness in chanting the Hare Krishna mantra; there was no turning back from that. And that's just as true today as when

I came. The process has not changed. And the result is still available to anyone who follows the process.

Candravali devi dasi

Candravali was searching for some reason to be alive when she saw Srila Prabhupada. She thought, "Here's someone who looks like a very good person." Srila Prabhupada was in kirtan and to Candravali it seemed that Srila Prabhupada had chanted "Hare Krishna" his whole life. Although Prabhupada was old, she thought he looked wonderful. In fact, Candravali didn't believe anybody could be that old and look that good. "Maybe Prabhupada's wearing makeup," she thought. She got close to him and saw that Prabhjupada wasn't wearing makeup. It was mysterious. Not much later, Srila Prabhupada initiated Candravali devi dasi in San Francisco in 1967.

The first time I saw Srila Prabhupada I was twenty-two. He was sitting chanting Hare Krishna with his eyes closed and I was captivated. It was hard to believe that he was really so beautiful. I never saw anyone like him before. I started responsively chanting to the kirtan that was going on. It was great. When Prabhupada opened his eyes, what I saw there was beyond the goodness of heaven. I saw an active life in the spiritual sky. Now finally I had a life, I had a direction. When I saw Srila Prabhupada a blessing came into my life.

Later, when I was initiated, I tried to figure out what my name meant. Prabhupada told me that Candravali was one of Krishna's *gopi* lovers. He said that Candravali liked to pretend she was Radha and that she and her friends used to entice Krishna. I didn't understand much about *gopis,* but I was happy with my name because it took me into another level, another insight. Krishna consciousness continually expanded me, it was like nothing I had ever experienced before.

Once in Los Angeles I paid my obeisances to Srila Prabhupada and while I was doing that, my little son, who had a snotty nose, crawled to Srila Prabhupada. Srila Prabhupada picked him up and, with his index finger, wiped my son's nose. Then he looked at me and said, "Do you not use mustard oil?" I didn't know what mustard oil was. He said, "You should use mustard oil." I'd never done that before. That's how I learned of using mustard oil.

When I had my first child, I wrote to Prabhupada, who was in Bombay. Prabhupada read the letter, turned to Malati and said, "Your friend Candravali has had a son and I have named him Candrasekhar." Prabhupada laughed and said, "The mother's name is Candravali, and I have named the son Candrasekhar." Sometime later, when our second child was born, we wrote to Prabhupada and this time he turned to Malati and said, "Your friend has had a baby girl. You name this one." Malati named our daughter Nalinaya, which means "eyes like a spreading lotus."

The last time I saw Srila Prabhupada, everybody was lined up to say goodbye and pay obeisances to him, and I noticed they all had flowers. I didn't have flowers so I ran nearby, got some common flowers, went to him and handed him those flowers. He took them as if they were something precious, smiled, and looked at me with gratitude. I didn't give him anything of value, but he knew I wanted special attention from him, and he gave it to me.

Before I met Srila Prabhupada I didn't have a life. I was asking, "Why was I born? Why am I here?" Srila Prabhupada is my good fortune. If I hadn't seen him I would have died. I had to see someone who was happy with their life, who was doing something meaningful.

Catura devi dasi

Catura first saw Srila Prabhupada walking toward the New Dwarka temple. He looked noble, beautiful, humble, and loving all at once. She fell to her knees and with tears, paid obeisances to her beloved guru.

Later, while walking from the Press, where I was fortunate to be rendering a little service, I saw Prabhupada on a rooftop looking out over the city. I thought that this was my golden opportunity. After offering my obeisances I looked up and said, "Hare Krishna, Srila Prabhupada." His eyes met mine as he said in a most powerful voice, "Hare Krishna!" This memory is the favorite moment of my life.

Another time I heard that Prabhupada was giving an informal talk in his garden. I was late and knew the garden would be filled to its limits, but still, I approached Ramesvara Swami and begged to be allowed to squeeze in somewhere. He looked at me with his intent look, and then finally said, "Okay, Catura." I ran to the garden with relief. On entering the area, I was motioned to sit somewhere and found myself close to Prabhupada. He glimmered; his transcendental vibration extended to all, and I'm sure that each devotee felt his personal loving concern. Each of us had placed an offering into a pile that had become like a haystack, and after His Divine Grace spoke, he reached into the middle of this huge stack and pulled out one offering. It was mine! He opened the box and tossed out the figs, dates, nuts, and cherries it contained to our waiting hands. This memory is magical to me, as I saw my guru accept and appreciate my humble gift. *Jaya* Prabhupada.

I was so fortunate to have the service of cleaning Srila Prabhupada's bathroom at New Dwarka. I got to ever so carefully move his little golden tooth, which he left on the sink counter in the mornings. Later, I got to distribute his used eucalyptus twigs to devotees, which made me quite popular. Also, it seemed that Srila Prabhupada was satisfied with my efforts, as I didn't hear otherwise.

These are a few of the important memories that help me remain enlivened, because "a moment in the presence of the pure devotee . . . " The devotees who helped Prabhupada lay the foundation of his Movement needed him in this way. However, my most cherished, deepest realizations and reciprocations from and with Prabhupada come as I read his transcendental books.

With a concerted effort to share with one another our Prabhupada experiences, our feelings and thoughts of him, we all can remind each other to find time each day to meditate on his transcendental qualities, on how he loves each of us, on how he saved us. And we can assist one another in developing more devotee qualities by associating with respect, kindness, and patience, by inspiring each other to each day spend time reading Srila Prabhupada's books, by lovingly reminding ourselves and others to chant Hare Krishna very attentively, to chant all of our rounds every day, and to do that which so pleases Prabhupada and Lord Chaitanya: tell folks about Lord Krishna, give *prasadam,* and distribute Prabhupada's glorious books.

Realizing that his *vani* is more important, *shiksha* is more important and that he's everyone's topmost *shiksha-guru,* we all have an equal opportunity to receive Srila Prabhupada's mercy according to our own desire and set of devotional circumstances.

As Pankajanghri Prabhu of Mayapur *dhama* once optimistically said, "Just do your best and see what happens when you leave your body." So we have no worries because we're in Srila Prabhupada's loving hands.

Jaya Srila Prabhupada! *Jaya* daughters of Srila Prabhupada! *Jaya* granddaughters of Srila Prabhupada! Jaya followers of Srila Prabhupada!

Chayadevi devi dasi

In 1969 in San Francisco, Chayadevi saw Srila Prabhupada at the second Rathayatra festival.

The Ratha-yatra procession went down San Francisco's main street where hippies hung out. My friends and I were there waiting for the procession to start when Srila Prabhupada came out of a fancy car and everybody around us immediately offered *dandavats* in the street. We were the only ones standing and I was thinking, "This is crazy, what's happening?" Srila Prabhupada was standing a couple of feet away from me. I looked at him and was overwhelmed, thinking, "Who is this person?" Immediately I was attracted to him, as if there was some communication between us. He walked slowly to the cart and got onto it. There was a lot of excitement and chanting and the parade began. I pulled the ropes and felt ecstatic. My hands became blistered and rough and I thought, "Oh, I should stop," but it was too much fun.

At one point the whole festival stopped before a bridge and Srila Prabhupada got up, put his arms up and danced. All the devotees were so excited and thrilled that I got excited too. I was chanting and dancing. Then we were rolling again and I pulled all the way to the beach where we all ate a big feast. Then, at the Family Dog Auditorium, Prabhupada spoke on how we are not God. I was shocked to hear I wasn't God. The whole mood of the Haight-Ashbury drug culture was merging with the void and the white light and being one with God. All around me people in the audience didn't like what Prabhupada was saying. There was a strong feeling against him. I thought, "What an amazing person to fearlessly say the truth although he knows it's unpopular."

Later I was in a tumultuous greeting at the New York airport when Prabhupada arrived. The whole airport was overtaken with devotees. When I saw Prabhupada I immediately felt, "He is my spiritual master for eternity. I definitely want to take initiation from him." It was wonderful to know that this person was always going to be with me, that our relationship was endless.

In Hawaii, Govinda dasi and I had a personal darshan with Prabhupada. I had my son Baladeva, who was four months old, with me, and with a tremendous grin, Prabhupada looked at Baladeva and said, "Who are you?" Govinda dasi said, "This is Balabhadra's son, Baladeva." Prabhupada looked right at Baladeva and said seriously, "You are very nice." Govinda dasi said, "And this is Balabhadra's wife, Chayadevi." Prabhupada looked at me and after a little time said, "And you are very nice, too." Then Baladeva, sitting in my lap, became animated. He was gurgling and babbling while looking at Prabhupada. Prabhupada laughed and said, "He's talking to us!" Prabhupada was kind and obviously enjoyed seeing Baladeva. It was a sweet exchange.

Another time in Hawaii Prabhupada was lecturing when Baladeva was sitting in my lap staring intensely at Prabhupada. Prabhupada was speaking about how we are limited and he turned to Baladeva and said, "Just like this boy here, he's limited because he's in a baby body, but he will grow. When he grows up, he will do great things." At that time I thought, "Oh, yes, Baladeva's a ray of Vishnu!"

In college I'd studied to be a teacher and as a devotee I started working with Satsvarupa Maharaja to develop the *gurukula*. I wrote a letter to Prabhupada and he wrote back answering my questions: "How am I supposed to educate the girls?" "What about the intermixing of the boys and girls?" Prabhupada said, "My instructions to you will be what you will build the *gurukula* on." I also told Prabhupada, "I have a desire to marry but I'm doing this *gurukula* service, so what should I do?"

In reference to the boys and girls together, Prabhupada said that there's no problem up until the age of ten or twelve. He said there was one girl, Saraswati, who asked her father, "Were you a boy or a girl when you were young?" Prabhupada said, "They don't know anything about boys and girls before ten or twelve so you shouldn't worry about that." He said the boys and girls should always sleep in different ashrams, but in the classroom we can separate them at ten or twelve. And at twelve they can be initiated.

Prabhupada also wrote, "I want every woman in the Movement to be married." And about educating the women, he said, "They should be learning how to cook and sew, and if there's plenty of milk, they should make ghee, yogurt, curd." He said, "What is this training to be wives and mothers? You don't have to train them. They will learn by your association. If you are doing, they will follow by associating with you."

And Prabhupada wrote, "What is this question of higher education? There is no higher education. They will learn everything they need to know from my books. You just teach them some English so they can read nicely and some mathematics so the nondevotees will not think we are fools."

The children of our Movement don't have a future in the Movement unless we establish *varnashrama* in rural communities. Picture a little community centered on Krishna that grows all its own *bhoga*, gets all its milk from protected cows that pasture there, and all the agriculture is done with oxen. Within that environment, a whole lifestyle develops – farmers, people to sell the produce, blacksmiths, carpenters – all these occupations are necessary. It widens the horizon of how children with so many capabilities can fit in within the devotee realm, not that they have to get a *karmi* job to support themselves and in the process become influenced by nondevotee association. Prabhupada said by developing cow protection properly, we'll have the economic base for a rural community and from that, life can develop. That's what the International Society for Cow Protection, ISCOWP, that my husband and I started, is all about. I feel very close to Prabhupada with this service; I'm happy. Anyone is happy when they're fully engaged because devotional service wipes away all envy, the tendency to criticize, and the tendency to doubt.

Chitralekha devi dasi

Just days after the temple in Laguna Beach, California opened–in September 1969– Chitralekha moved in. A few weeks later she moved to the Los Angeles temple where Vishnujana was temple commander and sankirtana leader. Then a few months later, in December, Prabhupada came to Los Angeles.

It was the first time I was going to see Srila Prabhupada. We were all very excited to greet him at the airport. All arrangements were being made to receive our guru in the most regal style. Tamal Krishna, Gargamuni, and Vishnujana devised the plan: One person would sprinkle rose water on the ground in front of Prabhupada, and another person would throw flower petals for his lotus feet to step on and another would carry an umbrella over his head. We were all anxiously waiting to hear who the chosen ones were. Sahadevi would throw the flower petals, Nanda Kumar would carry the umbrella, and I was chosen to throw the rose water! What mercy for a first encounter with my spiritual master.

It was an unexpected blessing to be chosen to walk beside Prabhupada as he strolled through the airport to his car. I was carrying a bright orange, plastic mixing bowl of rose water, which stood out against my blue flowered *sari*. Walking next to Srila Prabhupada carrying a bowl of rose water wasn't easy. Prabhupada walked very fast, almost floating across the floor. I had to keep up with him and, at the same time, be careful not to spill the water, or throw too much on the ground in front of him. At one point he looked at me, almost eye-to-eye. I nervously said, "Hare Krishna, Prabhupada."

During January 1970, initiation was going to take place and I was on the list. I had been told that your Sanskrit name usually starts with the first letter of your name. Wondering what my name would be, I thought, "*Hmm*, I wonder if Prabhupada will know that my middle name is Cheryl, which is pronounced like the 'ch' in 'cherry.' " No one knew my middle name, I had never used it and I didn't tell anyone what I was thinking. I was amazed when I realized that Prabhupada had responded to my thoughts from the very beginning. He named me Chitralekha – pronounced like the "ch" in "cherry"! He knew from the beginning what was on my mind.

After I received first initiation, Gargmuni asked me if I would marry Upendra. I was caught off guard. Quickly considering the option, I thought, "Upendra is Prabhupada's servant – being Prabhupada's servant is a pretty good qualification." So, I said, "*Umm*. I guess so, I will marry Upendra." We were married the next weekend and I was given second initiation the following day. So after being in the temple for four months I had a major purification program going on – initiation one weekend, marriage and second initiation the following weekend – and I didn't have a clue what I was getting into!

The intensity of having three fire sacrifices in two weekends was beyond expression, and the culmination was when Silavati, an older lady who was the head *pujari*, said to me, "Prabhupada is coming to the temple and you are going to do *arati*." I was very new to Deity worship and felt so unqualified, but wasn't going to give up the opportunity to offer *arati* to Prabhupada. During *arati*, the *pujari* would walk from altar to altar to offer the different articles, first to Radha-Krishna, then to pictures of the Pancha-tattva and Lord Jagannatha and finally to Prabhupada while he was sitting on his *vyasasana*.

I walked up to each altar and then to Prabhupada sitting on his *vyasasana*, offered the articles to him, then held them out for him to honor the fire or smell the flower. It was such an intimate, intimate experience. I was nervous and my emotions were running wild, while I was trying to keep my mind together enough so I could do everything without mistake.

As was customary, after *arati* I knelt with folded hands on the corner of the stage by Radha-Krishna's altar. As Prabhupada was leaving the temple, he turned to Radha-Krishna, folded his hands and said, "*Govindam adi purusam tamaham bhajami.*" I was right there, two feet from Prabhupada, caught in the electrical charge of Prabhupada directly communicating with Radha-Krishna. I could feel the energy surging through my body. I couldn't talk, let alone believe what I was experiencing. It was the most intense, purifying, and eye-opening experience in my life – feeling the energy of Prabhupada communicating with the Deities.

In October of 1970 Upendra and I went to Fiji by ourselves to start preaching there. Upendra had a wonderful relationship with Prabhupada. Prabhupada was like his protective and sometimes chastising father. Upendra wrote Prabhupada letters two or three times a month about what he was feeling or thinking and what was going on in Fiji. Prabhupada answered promptly and gave us direction, nurturing and cultivating his young children who were spreading this Movement.

Our visas for Fiji expired and the government wouldn't renew them, so in April 1971, with Prabhupada's permission, we went to India. Every afternoon while Prabhupada was in Calcutta, before his afternoon nap Prabhupada's servant would put *chandan* on his head. One afternoon the servant kindly asked me if I wanted to do this service. I had never done any personal service for Prabhupada before, so I agreed. I cautiously went into Prabhupada's room. He was sitting on the edge of his bed and just sat there waiting as I used a flower to dot the *chandan* across his forehead. He nodded his head and said, "Thank you." I offered obeisances and left. It was personal and sweet and a special moment.

While in Calcutta we used to go with Prabhupada to life members' homes for kirtan, a talk, and *prasadam*. One such program we were going to attend, but there wasn't a car left for the ladies to go; the men had taken them all. So, we ladies stood by the door to say goodbye to Prabhupada. As Prabhupada was leaving he stopped, looked at us, and said, "Aren't you coming?" We explained that there wasn't a car for us, and Prabhupada said, "Oh, you come with me." So Prabhupada sat in the front seat and we all crammed in the back seat. Prabhupada took care of his daughters. We felt protected because we knew that Prabhupada was watching out for us.

Once in Calcutta we were in Prabhupada's room for a darshan when he started telling us a story of Krishna and Jatila. All of a sudden he burst in to his big smile with his eyes as wide as they could get and was clapping his hands just like Jatila did in the story. Everybody laughed; his playful side was special and endearing.

Every moment with Prabhupada was special and endearing and sweet. I didn't say a lot to him, nor did he say a lot to me, but it was his presence and knowing that his well-wishes and blessings were always there.

In Melbourne, Australia, 1973, Srila Prabhupada was arriving at the temple soon. My son, Saumya, was only three months old, but I wanted him to have Prabhupada's special mercy. I was waiting in the hall near the front door of the temple with Saumya in my arms, thinking, *How am I going to get his head on Prabhupada's feet?* The door swung open and there was Prabhupada surrounded by devotees. I offered obeisances and as I lifted my eyes I saw Prabhupada standing right in front of me. I quickly put Saumya's head on his lotus feet as he patiently waited. Prabhupada was the supreme mystic, always knowing what was on my mind and perfectly responding.

He knew what was going on with you and he would say something instructive or something that would hit right on. While we were in Melbourne in 1973, Upendra was cooking for Prabhupada. Once, Upendra was outside Prabhupada's room talking to some devotees when Prabhupada called him in and said, "What are you doing?" Upendra said, "I'm just talking to some of the devotees in the hall, Prabhupada." Prabhupada said, "Gossip. It will ruin this Movement." Regularly Prabhupada would chastise Upendra. Upendra would shrink away and then come back.

Upendra was Prabhupada's servant off and on throughout the years. So my children and I usually had a back door in to have personal darshan with Srila Prabhupada. When my son was two years old, he started wearing glasses. When Upendra took him for darshan, Prabhupada joked, "His glasses are larger than his head." When I took Saumya for darshan, Prabhupada patiently allowed him to touch things on his desk, saying, "Naughty means intelligent." Saumya proceeded to wander into Prabhupada's bedroom, picked up his slippers, and put them on his head. Prabhupada was the most patient, loving grandfather, always encouraging, instructing us how to help our children become Krishna conscious.

When we lived in Los Angeles in 1974, I was always running late to see Prabhupada, with two children in tow. This time he was leaving to go on to another temple. Prabhupada was already in his car in the alley along the side of the temple. Saumya always had a flower to give Prabhupada whenever he saw him, so I had to get him there. I pushed the stroller as fast as I could up the street, right in front of all the devotees standing near the car, and pulled Saumya out of the stroller with his flower. Prabhupada looked at Saumya, told Tamal Krishna to stop the car and roll down the window, so Saumya could give him the flower. Such sweet nectarine moments always made my day.

Once in Los Angeles, June 1975, when Upendra was Prabhupada's servant, Prabhupada gave him $20. Upendra said, "Oh, Prabhupada, I can't take this, you are my spiritual master." Prabhupada said, "This is not for you, this is for your children. I'm not their spiritual master, they will have to find their own spiritual master." Upendra brought that $20 home. At that time my son was two-and-a-half and my oldest daughter was six months and I thought, "What am I supposed to do with this money?" I bought some gifts for the children and then wrote to Prabhupada, thanking him for the money and explaining that I used it to purchase some fabric to make a dress for my daughter and I also bought some *Krsna* book tapes with it. Prabhupada was like a grandfather to my kids, reciprocating with them, giving them gifts and special attention.

In November 1975, my children and I had just arrived in Vrindavan. Upendra was Prabhupada's servant at the time. Prabhupada was having darshan, so right away I went to take my children in to see him. The *brahmachari* at the door was reluctant to allow me in because my daughter, Shantaya, was just a year old. Prabhupada saw me at the door and motioned for me to come in. I went in and sat toward the back of the room with the children. Shantaya squirmed away from me and started walking toward Prabhupada. I immediately got up to get her, but Prabhupada put his hand up, motioning to stop me. She continued walking up to his desk and climbed on to his lap. Prabhupada talked to her and teased her with a flower. Then he gave her the flower and nodded, signaling me to come get her.

It was *guru-puja* in Vrindavan, Saumya was three years old, and a rather serious child. Prabhupada was on his *vyasasana* while a loud, energetic kirtan was going on. Saumya walked right in front of Prabhupada and stood there looking at him. One of the *brahmachari*s in the kirtan picked him up and tried to remove him but Saumya kicked and screamed until the *brahmachari* put him down. Saumya continued looking at Prabhupada and the *brahmachari* tried to remove him. Again he kicked and screamed until the *brahmachari* put him down. After looking at Prabhupada a few more minutes, Saumya went outside to play in the dirt. When Prabhupada walked out of the temple to return to his quarters, he saw me, stopped and asked, "Where is your son?" I responded, "Playing in the dirt, Prabhupada." Prabhupada gently tilted his head saying, "That's okay."

Prabhupada was leaving Vrindavan. As Prabhupada walked out of his quarters, devotees gathered around him near the side gate to see him off. Running a little late, I got there with Saumya and his flower to give to Prabhupada. I gently pushed Saumya through the devotees in to the open space in front of Prabhupada. Prabhupada stopped to wait for Saumya to hand him the flower but Saumya didn't see Prabhupada. Prabhupada waited saying, "Here I am, over here. Over here." Then Prabhupada raised his cane and tapped Saumya on the shoulder again saying, "Here I am. Here I am." This loving exchange between Prabhupada and Saumya went on for several minutes while all the devotees watched in amusement. Finally I reached in the circle, turned Saumya toward Prabhupada, and said, "There he is, Saumya."

Prabhupada knew our deepest intentions and secrets and mental excursions. He received so many gifts and passed them on to his disciples. but I wanted to give him something that he wouldn't give away. Then I had my chance, in Melbourne, 1972. Any devotee who had something to give Prabhupada could have personal darshan. My mother had given me an oval locket with a flower etched on the front of it. I had a small piece of cloth and cotton from the quilt in Rupa Goswami's *samadhi* in Vrindavan that the *samadhi pujari* had given me. So I put a small piece of the cloth and cotton on one side of the locket and on the other side. I put a picture of Prabhupada's Guru Maharaja, Srila Bhaktisiddhanta Sarasvati Thakura. My turn for darshan came, I entered Prabhupada's room and offered obeisances. He was sitting at his desk, so I leaned over the desk, gave the locket to Prabhupada and showed him how it opened. He said, "Oh! What is this?" I said, "This is from Rupa Goswami's cloth from his *samadhi* in Vrindavan at Radha-Damodara temple." Prabhupada's eyes got big and he said, "Oh!"

After Prabhupada left his body in 1977, Tamal Krishna Goswami gave some of Prabhupada's personal things away, and I heard he gave Pishima a necklace of Prabhupada's. Later, in early 1978, when I was living in Mayapur I went for darshan to see Pishima, who was also living at the Mayapur temple. I couldn't believe what I saw – she was wearing a chain with that oval locket on it. *Ah!* All of a sudden everything came together. She was wearing the very locket I had given Prabhupada. Prabhupada knew my intentions – I wanted to give him something that he wouldn't give away – and that locket stayed with him all those years. I was shy, so in my relationship with Prabhupada I would think something and he would answer my thoughts by his actions more than by his words.

Prabhupada had so much faith in us, much more than we had in ourselves. He would send Upendra and me to spread Krishna consciousness where there were absolutely no devotees for association. Prabhupada told us, "You only need two devotees." We were on our own, away from the community of devotees and depending totally on Prabhupada to direct us. So from early on all I knew was to depend wholeheartedly on Prabhupada and Krishna because that's all I had. My only shelter was Prabhupada. Every day I would pray to Prabhupada to help me through the situation at hand. No matter where Upendra and I were, it was always trying for me, but the endearing moments I had had with Prabhupada kept me together. Prabhupada was my shelter. He was right there saying, "Oh! Chitralekha, is she all right?" He fully accepted whatever token of love and devotion we could offer him.

Prabhupada knew that if he said anything harsh to me I would shrivel up, so he captured me by reciprocating with whatever I was thinking. He was my father, my guru, and my well-wisher all rolled into one. And Prabhupada knew what was going on. Even today if something's on your mind or you have a question, you can open *Bhagavad-gita* and there will be a *shloka* that answers your question. It was like that. Whatever little thing was going on in my mind, no matter how silly it was, Prabhupada responded.

Cintamani devi dasi

Cintamani was a freshman at Ohio State when she attended Prabhupada's visit to the University with Allen Ginsberg. When she saw him and heard him speak, she knew he was a God-realized soul. Just being in his presence was so reassuring and blissful. She joined and was initiated four days later.

A year and a half later I was sent to open the first temple in Japan with Sudama, my new husband, and Bali Mardan. By Prabhupada's grace so many things were happening quickly. He visited Japan twice when I was there and blessed many souls. He commented that "these Japanese people are very nice." We had the first *Krsna* book printed in Japan.

I ended up with the Jagannatha Deities from Japan after Sudama took *sannyasa* in 1972. I had been Their only caregiver, and from Tokyo I went to Hong Kong and then Manila. Coming back to America I was one of the few people who had Deities.

In Los Angeles devotees did not think I should have my own Deities because Srila Prabhupada wanted us to focus on worshiping the Deities in the temple. Even though I had always been too shy to talk to Srila Prabhupada, I got the courage to speak to him about Lord Jagannatha since this was so important to me. I scheduled a darshan to see Srila Prabhupada and brought the Deities with me in a nice box.

I had gone up to his room and no one else was there. He smiled and handed me a sweet ball and said, "Cintamani Prabhu." I was shocked that he called me "Prabhu." After giving him a report on the temple in the Philippine Islands, which I also helped open, I said, "Srila Prabhupada, I have Lord Jagannatha in this box and I want Them to see you."

I opened the box and stood the Deities up so Srila Prabhupada could see Them. He was really smiling and said, "Oh, very nice. They are gorgeous. *Jagannatha swami nayana patha gami bhava tume.*"

I said, "Everyone is telling me I can't worship Them." He immediately said, "Who's telling?" I said, "But Srila Prabhupada, you said . . ."

He interrupted me and said, "Never mind! You just make Lord Jagannatha your life and soul, and you will be happy your whole life." He then said, "So your husband has taken *sannyasa*?" I said, "Yes." Then he slowly said two times, "You just make Balarama your son, Subhadra your daughter, and Lord Jagannatha your husband, because every woman needs a son, daughter, and husband."

He also told me not to divert my mind, to treat Lord Jagannatha as God, and to bring the Deities wherever I went "inside or outside the temple."

Then I also asked, "Srila Prabhupada, is there any chance of me going back to Godhead?" He said, "Take care of Lord Jagannatha as I have told you and you will be fully liberated, Krishna conscious, and you will go back to home in this very lifetime."

I was feeling greatly encouraged. I left the room with all my doubts removed and so happy with his merciful instructions!

From then on, wherever I went someplace with Lord Jagannatha, all I had to say was that Prabhupada said for me to worship these Deities, and it was like, "*Jaya.* You can put Them on the altar," and everything was okay. This is an example of different instructions to different people.

It is almost fifty years later and I still have these merciful Deities by the grace of Srila Prabhupada. We should all follow his instructions to the best of our ability for a fantastic future.

Citraratha devi dasi

In the summer of 1976 in New Mayapur (south of Paris), it hadn't rained for months. It was scorching hot. There, late one morning, Srila Prabhupada sat in the shade of tree and presided over a fire sacrifice in which he initiated devotees from all over Europe. Citraratha, sitting in the full sun near Prabhupada, was waiting to receive initiation and sweating profusely.

When I was called–Bhaktin Catherine–I went to Prabhupada and offered my obeisances deeply. My whole body and my face were floating with water. As I lifted up my eyes I couldn't see anything because my glasses had steamed up. I thought, "Anyway, you shouldn't look directly at your spiritual master's face." I put my head down and said the four regulative principles. Then, when I said I would chant at least sixteen rounds every day, I looked up at Prabhupada. At that moment I thought, "Will I really be able to chant sixteen rounds every day for the rest of my life? I knew I wouldn't be able to–that sometimes I probably wouldn't do it. Prabhupada looked at me with a half smile that seemed to say, "I know you will have difficulty, but I also know you will try to chant for your whole life." This is how I understood him and also what happened.

While Prabhupada was present on the planet I was easily bewildered in spiritual life, and when he left I was in full *maya*. In fact, I was on my way to do a very sinful activity, when, in the street, I met a friend of the devotees who told me that Prabhupada had left the planet. I was devastated. My mother died when I was a little girl, and when I heard that Prabhupada had left, I felt like an orphan. I renounced my abominable activity and three months later was back in the temple in Rome.

Now I realize that Prabhupada initiated revolutions on different levels: in Western countries people think that the caste system in India (and other aspects of Indian culture) are horrific, but by following Chaitanya Mahaprabhu's instruction to make Krishna consciousness available to all classes of people, Srila Prabhupada taught us how the traditional Indian spiritual culture is glorious even if Indians themselves wrongly apply the *varna* and *ashram* system. Even though as a Westerner I sometimes have difficulty following all the instructions Srila Prabhupada gave, I understand that by the grace of Srila Prabhupada and the whole *parampara*, everyone gets the same chance to become Krishna conscious, whatever his or her class, caste, abilities, or gender.

These days I am trying to cultivate the desire to have a personal relationship with Srila Prabhupada, not only by offering him my obeisances but also by always speaking to him, by praying to him, by asking him questions, by begging for his shelter, and by thanking him. I mix awe and reverence with considering myself Prabhupada's eternal daughter who is struggling against her rebellious nature.

One of the difficulties I'm slowly solving is "the women's issue." Seven years ago, when I came back to Krishna consciousness, I wanted to test my determination by reading the two or three "heavy" sentences on that topic in the *Bhagavad-gita*–where for instance it says that in general, women are considered less intelligent. First, "in general" doesn't mean all women, but some women sometimes. Then I thought about my own life. "Yes, I've been stupid. I've let myself be abused. I believed flattery and imagined things were wonderful that weren't." I had acted less intelligently.

Prabhupada said that intelligence is humility. Humility doesn't mean to act like a doormat, but to be a servant of Krishna and guru. I decided not to validate the *shastra's* general statement about women by acting stupidly again, but to be intelligent, to be a devotee, to serve Krishna and guru.

In the beginning some of our godbrothers who were leaders didn't know how to properly respect devotees–men or women–how to understand and to apply Srila Prabhupada's teachings, or how to manage in Krishna consciousness. Above all, they didn't know what it meant to protect women. By his example Srila Prabhupada demonstrated how much he cared for the material as well as the spiritual comfort and happiness of women, and he set the standard of protection, affection, and esteem they deserve. He always cared for us and he wanted us to remain in his ISKCON family. As Gopalasyapriya devi dasi of New Vrindavan remembers, Srila Prabhupada asked her if she was warm enough, if she had sufficiently warm clothes. Then Prabhupada told the temple commander, "Women need to be protected. They will not ask. So you have to ask once a month and make sure they have everything they need."

Prabhupada also recognized the intellectual capacities of his female disciples and engaged them in Krishna's service. Nrihari dasa recalls his sister Bhakti dasi's position as Art Director of the BBT. And Jyotirmayi did wonderful service in the *gurukula*.

Srila Prabhupada wanted men to be responsible, to look after and protect women, not to deprecate them; this attitude is the basis of a stable and balanced society. When he came to America, Srila Prabhupada studied and reflected on the situation, saw that men and women were treated more or less equally, and figured out how to advance Krishna consciousness in that milieu. If we want to continue to move forward we need to continue to do as he did, analyzing, observing, and adapting with care according to time and circumstances.

When I was living away from ISKCON I never found any other philosophy or philosopher–no other spiritual leader, living or not living–who satisfied my questions. Seven years ago when I came back to Krishna consciousness I started to offer my food again, and from one day to the next it was not the same food any more, even though the ingredients were the same. I also started chanting rounds. At first the rounds were painful, like when sobs are stuck deep in your throat. Then, by Krishna's mercy, chanting became tasty again.

Each time I came back to Krishna consciousness after falling down, I was not rejected. Of course, the more a devotee is known and did wonderful things, the more difficult it is for that person to come back. But since I've never done wonderful things, it was not difficult for me.

It's important that we don't reject people when they come back. Prabhupada was disturbed if devotees didn't properly welcome back those who had left–and it's rare to find devotees who never leave. Vaiyasaki Prabhu quotes Srila Prabhupada while answering a question about how to recognize a devotee who fell accidentally from one who fell purposefully. Srila Prabhupada said, "If the person comes back, it was an accident."

Daivi-sakti devi dasi

Daivi-sakti was initiated in August 1970 in Philadelphia. She was eighteen. Srila Prabhupada told her to learn the art of loving Krishna from her senior godbrothers and sisters.

My sweetest memories with Prabhupada were here in Vrindavan. Prabhupada had me go through a three-month training program living with his sister Pishima, learning to cook for him. She trained me Bengali style, and then he called me in one day and said he was satisfied that I had learned from her, and now he wanted me to modify what she'd taught according to his health so that she could rest. I then began cooking independently for Prabhupada here. That was from 1974 to 1975.

Prabhupada had a beloved friend and neighbor here named Bhagatji Visvambar Dayal. Bhagatji had donated the land and construction of our *gurukula* here, and he adored Prabhupada. He respected Prabhupada's preaching and Prabhupada as a person so deeply that he was very protective of Srila Prabhupada. He also loved to cook for Srila Prabhupada. He cooked Brijbasi style, being from U.P., Kanpur side. He was a retired college principal who came to live here. He would bring things for Prabhupada, and Prabhupada would also go to his house. With Bhagatji's style of cooking everything had to be exactly perfect. The fire had to be perfect, the rice had to be ten years old, the spices had to be perfectly cleaned, the wheat had to be hand-cleaned and then ground perfectly. The ghee had to be perfect. He was so conscientious of Prabhupada's health.

One day Bhagatji expressed to Prabhupada that because of his rheumatism and old age, he wanted to teach one of Prabhupada's disciples how to cook. The first person who was assigned was a dear godsister who had been cooking for Prabhupada, and Bhagatji began to train her. But coming from the West, she had her own concepts of what Prabhupada needed. Once while Bhagatji was teaching her how to cook eggplant *subji*, he showed her how to cut it up, but she insisted on peeling the eggplant because according to her standard everything had to be peeled for Prabhupada. An argument ensued, tempers flared, and Bhagatji went to Prabhupada and asked for someone else to train. Then Prabhupada assigned one of his *brahmachari* servants.

At that time, Prabhupada's kitchen was just a small room, hardly big enough for one person to fit. But every day Bhagatji, the *brahmachari* and I would cook for Prabhupada together in that small kitchen. I would make the staples from his cooker according to Prabhupada's health requirements, and Bhagatji would make extra Brijbasi dishes to train the *brahmachari*. To make the *capatis*, the Brijbasi *rotis*, Bhagatji insisted on having a coal stove prepared every day. The coal stove had to be made in the temple restaurant kitchen and then carried by two men into our little kitchen for Bhagatji to make the *rotis*. It took about one hour to get the coals right for making the *rotis*. One day the workers forgot to make the stove. When Bhagatji was about to make his *rotis* and found out there was no stove he nearly had a nervous breakdown because he couldn't get the *capatis* made in time for Prabhupada.

Prabhupada was strict about timing. Bhagatji could not compensate that there was no stove, and he knew no other way to make a *capati*. Seeing the dilemma I said, "Bhagatji, no problem. I'll make *capatis* on the gas stove." He couldn't believe *capatis* could be made on a gas stove. I took his *capati* dough and made the *capatis,* and they puffed up like balloons as he watched in amazement. He had never seen anything like that. He took the *capatis* in to Prabhupada and when he came back he said, "Prabhupada says I should train you to cook."

Then I had a new assignment. I had to learn how to cook Brijbasi style from Bhagatji. He was the best teacher I ever had in my life. He was father, mother, uncle, big brother, teacher, cooking guru, everything combined. Every day he would hobble to the kitchen and teach me how to make different preparations exactly right. Prabhupada knew how to draw out the love in everybody, and Bhagatji was able to express his love for Prabhupada by this cooking.

Bhagatji was so dear to Prabhupada that he was the only person who would go up to Prabhupada's upstairs room at night to be with him. Otherwise Prabhupada would be alone, just his servant would go up. The cook, myself at the time, would bring his evening meal. Bhagatji would come up and massage Prabhupada's legs at night until about eleven o'clock at night, and they would talk privately. Nobody would be there. One night I brought up Prabhupada's hot milk and *prasadam.* Usually Prabhupada was sitting at his desk and Bhagatji would be there by his side, but that night Prabhupada was sitting at his back veranda with Bhagatji. I would never speak to Prabhupada when I served him. But that night he said to me, "Come and sit down." I sat down at Prabhupada's feet, and it was such a beautiful drama that Prabhupada carried out there for Bhagatji. He said, "You have been learning how to cook from Bhagatji, and he has taught you nicely. Now Bhagatji can rest and you cook the things he taught you for me." It was like a rerun of what Prabhupada had done with Pishima. I could understand that Prabhupada had allowed Bhagatji to express all of his love and do what he wanted to do, which was to train somebody, and then Bhagatji could rest because he was old. After that, from that day, Bhagatji would come and watch to make sure I did everything right and he would bring the plate in for Prabhupada, and in that way he felt very accomplished in passing down his knowledge to somebody.

Daksinavari devi dasi

Daksinavari was initiated in 1973 in St. Louis. The following year she received second initiation from Srila Prabhupada in Chicago.

It was quite a crowded scene there in Chicago. The Radha-Damodara buses were there, getting their Deities installed. Lots of *brahmana* initiations. There was a very long line in the hallway. Even though there were so many of us, maybe twelve or more in the hallway, Prabhupada initiated each one of us individually. He didn't do any group Gayatri. Each person individually heard the mantra from his mouth.

We were all in line, very nervously waiting. Every time someone came out after receiving Gayatri, we would ask them what it was like, to tell us something. Each one would say, "Don't do this, because Srila Prabhupada was irritated with me." Different things. For instance, one devotee had just offered obeisances and then stayed by the door. He was far away from Srila Prabhupada. Prabhupada told him to come over, come close to me. We were all trying to memorize the mantra while we were in line and thinking, "Don't do this, don't do that."

When I went in the door I was trying to remember all the don't dos, don't dos, but I was thinking, "Let me not waste Srila Prabhupada's time. Let me do what he wants me to do and get out, because there are so many other devotees. I'm not the only one." I sat close to him and he said the mantra. I repeated it. He showed me how to move my fingers and I did it. He showed me on his hand–he lowered his hand and showed me where to put the thumb. Then when I began to move my fingers around I looked out of the corner of my eye and saw that he was leaning over and scratching his arm. This is embarrassing, but I was just totally surprised that he was a person and he had an itch and was scratching it. Previously, he was the author of books, the picture on the *vyasasana*–I had never seen him before. I had this two-dimensional kind of understanding of him.

So I did that quickly and successfully without any blatant offending or wasting of his time. I was happy with that.

I was feeling so grateful and I wanted to give a gift, but I had nothing. But I was one of those *brahmacharinis* who had two slips and three *saris*, and I didn't even own my own *Bhagavad-gita*. I owned nothing. So I went outside and just walked around chanting. The Chicago temple was in the inner city and there were many vacant lots with overgrowth. I saw some wildflowers. I thought, "I can give some flowers." I tried to get different colors and made this bouquet.

The next morning I went into the lobby and was just waiting there with my pathetic little bouquet because I wanted to give my gift to Srila Prabhupada. He came in from his morning walk and there was no one with him. At the time I didn't think anything of it. I just ran up to him and said, "Srila Prabhupada, I really wanted to give you this gift, and thank you so much for giving me initiation." I'm not sure what I was expecting, but he was genuinely surprised. He nodded his head and was smiling and said, "Thank you very much." He was appreciative. I didn't know what else to say, so I just dropped to the floor, offered my obeisances, and ran away. He went through a set of doors, I suppose to his own quarters.

Just a few minutes later I was thinking, "Oh, no, he's about to greet the Deities. He's going to get a solid gardenia garland and roses and those Hawaiian flowers. I gave him a bunch of weeds that are going to wilt in a few minutes." I thought, "He just accepted my love and appreciation for him." He wasn't thinking he was the big shot of the Hare Krishna movement. He was genuinely appreciative that someone wanted to give him a gift. I was just enthralled with the small realization that I had a genuine spiritual master who was totally humble and just wanted to serve Krishna and encourage me to serve Krishna. That he would have that genuine reaction. I felt loved.

We went to O'Hare airport to greet Srila Prabhupada. When he first arrived, he seemed very short, and my idea was that he was very big. However, because he was walking down the airport hallway, I was looking from the side view, he was walking and everyone else was running. They couldn't keep up with him to keep the umbrella over his head. He was walking and they were running. It just didn't make any sense at all. I thought, "Something's wrong with this picture!"

I feel like he has enough love for every single person who comes to this Movement. There's no question that he is so much representing Lord Chaitanya's magnanimity. He has love for every person who reads his books and tries to understand what he's written. I have faith that he will take care of everyone despite the apparent discord. He has the qualities that are described in the *Bhagavatam,* and we met a person who is actually like that all the time. He's the walking *Bhagavatam.* There's something written about just a moment's association with such a person. One can travel for millions and billions of births and never meet such a person. I hope that new people will join and hear these stories and feel that they can come to know and love Srila Prabhupada. I think that they will because these stories are not about an ordinary person. They're not just sentimental stories, reminiscences. They're actual descriptions of the person *bhagavata,* and just hearing about these exchanges will bring a person to the point of developing love of God. I'm glad to be part of the magic.

Damayanti devi dasi

Although she saw him in London, New York, New Vrindavan, Chicago, and Detroit, the only personal exchange Damayanti had with Srila Prabhupada was in London in September 1971, when he gave her brahmana initiation.

I had a desire to know "Who am I?" and "What is life's purpose?" I was attracted to temple life and to transcendental knowledge and I quickly experienced some purification from eating *prasadam,* chanting the holy names, the ashram program, and going to *mangala-arati.* There was a lot about Krishna consciousness that was wonderful and since I liked to sing, I thought, "Wow, singing in the street – *harinama-sankirtana* – was especially designed for me."

The devotees helped me understand Srila Prabhupada's significance and his teachings and from that point, I felt inspired to serve Prabhupada. I decided I wanted to be a devotee, a disciple of Srila Prabhupada. That became my identity. Krishna attracts His servants by giving them a spiritual taste. The devotee takes a little step and gets some mercy from Krishna, and that encourages the devotee to do more. Just continuing to do some service and to follow Prabhupada's instructions, the simple process he gave us – chanting, offering our food to Krishna – we become purified, our spiritual eyes open, and Krishna gradually reveals Himself and gives us enough bliss to inspire us to keep going even if our service is difficult.

Although I was attracted to temple life, many aspects of it were difficult and I would then think, "I don't like living in the ashram. How can I stay in the temple?" Krishna consciousness wasn't easy. However, by hearing Prabhupada's instructions in his books, associating with devotees, engaging in devotional service under the direction of the guru, and by being determined for spiritual life rather than material life, I was inspired to go on despite difficulties. To achieve something great we must endure difficulties. Prabhupada wants us to keep connected to Krishna, the greatest person, for this connection gives us real life. If we stay away from Krishna we'll dry up, we'll be dead.

I look back and think that before Prabhupada came into my life I was confused, lacking direction, ignorant of what was truly beneficial. After meeting him I gained access to divine knowledge and to the mercy of Lord Chaitanya and Lord Nityananda. I always try to appreciate that Prabhupada made my life auspicious; that he brought all blessings. It's crucial that we don't lose this chance we have.

The life of Prabhupada is a source of inspiration for our spiritual life so it is beneficial to hear his biography and anecdotes that his disciples tell. We learn how to be a pure devotee from both the instructions and personal example of the pure devotee. Yet Krishna's pure devotees are often difficult to understand for a conditioned soul or beginner in Krishna consciousness, so it is probably better to rely more on his instructions.

It was only after living a few weeks in the ashram that I was able to sit down and read the *Bhagavad-gita* through and appreciate it. If someone never had personal contact with Prabhupada, it's not an impediment. I connected to Prabhupada through his disciples. Because Prabhupada is empowered, our connection is not to only one person, it's to the *guru-tattva*. Through our connection with our guru we're connected with Lord Nityananda, Lord Chaitanya, Krishna. No one should feel, "Oh, I don't have the founder-*acharya* as my guru," because you do if you're connected in that line. He is your *shiksha-guru* which can sometimes be more important than the *diksha-guru*. You do have that connection, just as we're connected to Srila Bhaktisiddhanta, Srila Bhaktivinoda, and all the way to Rupa Goswami. Somebody doubting their connection is on the mental platform but the connection is through the soul, not just the mind. To feel unconnected is some trick the mind is playing. Through the soul we can experience our connection with *guru-tattva*, with the whole *parampara*.

We have to be determined to make this connection by hearing from the guru and by serving him; that's the process. In this way we will make spiritual progress and become fully Krishna conscious.

How do I know if Prabhupada approves of my activities or is pleased with me if I never have his personal association? He has instructed us what pleases him, what we should be doing with our lives, and how to engage in devotional service. If we are doing that we can know we are on the right track. Sometimes a disciple falls away, stops or neglects her *sadhana*, becomes full of doubts and material desires. Perhaps her attachment to Srila Prabhupada was only sentimental which is very dangerous. One has to have a firm resolve: I'm going to do my devotional service whether or not Prabhupada notices me. I'm convinced that to become a pure devotee is the supreme goal of life and is the goal I should attain. I think, "This is what I have to do; I have to chant my *japa,* hear the *Bhagavatam,* the *Gita* classes, read, do my service." Our part is to do the activity of the disciple and to know Krishna is always paying attention, that He knows everything in our heart, He sees everything we do, He knows our every thought. Also, Prabhupada knows how we are doing. Many devotees had the experience where he let them know he knew their heart, their level of consciousness.

In the early days, many of us felt rather shy about writing to Prabhupada or having his darshan in his rooms if that was available. I also felt that all my questions were answered in his books so why should I bother him with letters. Even now, for those who want and need Prabhupada's personal help or approval, he will give it. Prabhupada doesn't want anyone to feel distant if that person wants to be close. Anyone can talk to Prabhupada, can tell him their thoughts and problems or offer prayers. Prabhupada is fully present at his *samadhis* in Vrindavan and Mayapur. We can get his mercy there, or in his rooms at the temples where he lived, or at any temple or place where he is remembered and loved. Prabhupada is always available to everyone; we should know that he cares about every single disciple, every granddisciple, every child.

Daru Brahma devi dasi

Daru Brahma, twenty, was shopping at East Ridge Mall in San Jose when a book distributor inspired her to give a donation and get the Srimad-Bhagavatam Second Canto, Part 2, "Lord of the Heart."

I was raised Catholic but was questioning my faith and how everyone fit in God's world. I took this book home, read a little, and put it on the shelf. But it kept calling me. So one evening I sat by the fire and read it through without stopping. For a couple of years I read this book over and over and it became my connection to Srila Prabhupada. Although I hadn't met him yet, in my heart I secured a position of love for Srila Prabhupada, who had come to me in this book and answered my questions. He was my guru.

I started serving in the Berkeley and L.A. temples and everything I did, I did for love of Srila Prabhupada. He's why I'm a devotee. When he blessed me with the name Daru Brahma, I thought, "Wow, Srila Prabhupada, you know my heart." Because I worshiped Lord Jagannatha and Daru Brahma devi dasi means servant of Lord Jagannatha.

I was in charge of the *pujari* room in L.A. and when Srila Prabhupada came, I'd work all night so I could hear him dictate – that had the same potency as being in his presence. Once when Prabhupada was walking through the *pujari* room he asked my godsister and me, "Are you happy?" I was choking to speak but we both said, "Oh, yes, Srila Prabhupada!" He said, "That is very good." He smiled and walked on. My heart filled with love. I will forever have this interaction of his glance, his love, his question. I thought, "He didn't ask if I was chanting sixteen rounds. He asked if I was happy." If we follow Prabhupada's instructions, we will be happy.

Later, Pushta Krishna, who had been a *sannyasi* and Srila Prabhupada's secretary, and I married. Pushta wrote Srila Prabhupada and sent pictures of our Deities and a donation. Srila Prabhupada wrote back encouraging and honoring us. That again showed me Srila Prabhupada's heart: It's all about helping us serve and come to Krishna. In his letter, Prabhupada praised our Deities but nicely corrected me, saying I shouldn't put Nityananda and Chaitanya on each side of Radha-Krishna by explaining that Gaura-Nitai always stand together.

My pastimes with Srila Prabhupada play all the time in my mind. I feel he's with me every moment. He's blessed me by protecting me, giving me good association, coming to me in dreams, and keeping me on track. He owns my heart. For some reason Krishna gives me the mercy of serving Srila Prabhupada, who's forever present and ever-fresh.

Devadidhiti devi dasi

Devadidhiti's first connection with Krishna consciousness was seeing the back of the "Happening" album. The picture of Srila Prabhupada convinced her that he was her spiritual master. He chanted the maha-mantra and spoke on its meaning.

Most of us were protesting material life and searching for the truth and Srila Prabhupada was the magical genie who appeared. My good fortune came shortly after, in 1971, at the San Francisco Ratha-yatra when his glance captured my heart. From then on my only ambition was to be part of his Movement.

I was living in the Henry Street temple in Brooklyn, where he formed an army to help all the conditioned souls. When Srila Prabhupada visited, he showed his young followers so much loving kindness and mercy.

Later I went to New Dwarka in Los Angeles. Srila Prabhupada had his headquarters there and sometimes stayed for three months translating his books and strengthening our faith.

The women with children had extra mercy since we weren't allowed to be in the temple room during his lectures. He was very loving and generous with the children. Cookie time was after his lectures. We all lined up with our children as he gave each child a cookie. My daughter still remembers his loving exchange through the cookie connection.

Prabhupada's daughters received his love in abundance. His love was unlimited and still exists. Srila Prabhupada's instructions are deep rooted and are a constant reminder of the truth. Srila Prabhupada saw the soul within the body, our true selves. That is the soul-to-soul connection. He tried to help us realize our true nature and encouraged any service that could help him serve his spiritual master.

Srila Prabhupada is the true master *acharya* and only he can transform our low births. Srila Prabhupada will always reside in my heart. His love and his instructions play a tape in my brain. By his mercy I take shelter of his lotus feet. My prayer is not to forget him and that the next generation will take serious his instructions through his books.

Devaki devi dasi

1974 was a trying year in Devaki's life. Emotionally suffering to the point she couldn't even eat, she understood there was no happiness in this world and was looking for spiritual truth. One day she became so miserable she couldn't take it anymore. She left her six-month old baby with his grandmother while she and her husband drove from Augusta to Atlanta, Georgia.

It sounds crazy, but we were going to be gone for a day or two to visit all the spiritual groups in Atlanta: 3HO, Kundalini, Hare Krishna, until I found the truth. On the way we talked about these different groups and I decided, "Hey, we've got to go to the Krishna temple first."

When we got to the Atlanta temple I couldn't leave. I had no idea why, but as soon as I walked in I felt that we didn't have to go anywhere else. I couldn't even go back to Augusta to get my baby. So while I stayed at the temple, the temple commander, Gokularanjana, and my husband went and brought my baby back.

Srila Prabhupada was coming in a week. I said, "Wow, who's Srila Prabhupada?" The devotees were telling me and we stayed up three nights straight preparing Srila Prabhupada's *vyasasana* and sewing, and I was learning everything. They said, "You need to offer your obeisances to Srila Prabhupada when he comes." I said, "Yeah, but there's no time for me to learn the prayers. Somebody has to teach me." They said, "Well, it's okay. Just put your head down and say 'Hare Krishna.' We'll teach you later." We had so much to do to get ready.

At the airport, I wanted to say the prayers everybody else was saying but I didn't know them. When Srila Prabhupada came I put my head to the floor and – this has never happened before – a big force came through my brain, my mouth opened and closed and I said, "*nama om visnu-padaya krsna-presthaya bhutale* …" I had no idea what I was saying, but I felt beautiful and wonderful and had chills all over my body. I looked up and Prabhupada was looking in my direction. I thought, "What!" That was my first connection. Later I had to learn the prayers word-for-word because I didn't know them.

A few days later I really wanted to hear Srila Prabhupada's class but I had a high fever and could not get up. I was looking at the Lord Sheshanaga picture on the wall and suddenly I had no fever. I had so much energy that I ran to the temple, heard class while my baby slept, and afterwards headed back to my room. There, within a few minutes, my fever raged and again I couldn't move. I can't explain this from a material viewpoint. I knew Prabhupada is not from here but is from someplace where I want to go. Within the year Srila Prabhupada initiated me.

I realized Krishna talks to Srila Prabhupada and Srila Prabhupada does absolutely nothing without Lord Krishna's sanction. All of Srila Prabhupada's books come directly from Krishna. They contain Krishna's words. When Srila Prabhupada read his own books, he would become ecstatic because he was reading Krishna's words. He never thought the books were his.

Since 1975, in my heart all I wanted is to know what Srila Prabhupada wanted me to do. I wanted to do that and to try to remember Krishna. But throughout the years I was falling down in different ways and feeling very bad. Then, during one of Prabhupada's disappearance day celebrations, I was feeling that I had abandoned Srila Prabhupada and was so fallen that I couldn't get his mercy again. But when I looked up, someone had thrown one of Srila Prabhupada's garlands at me and it hit me in the face like a bullet. I cried and cried and cried. I still have that garland. I realized Srila Prabhupada's mercy will always be there, and all I have to do is pick myself up and keep going.

My conclusion is, we should simply chant Hare Krishna, follow the principles, do some service, and delve deeper into Srila Prabhupada's books. If we can do that, Srila Prabhupada will be there for us. As long as we're trying Srila Prabhupada is there.

Devamaya devi dasi

Around fourteen years old, Devamaya dasi started exploring Buddhism, Zen, and Taoism and shortly later became a vegetarian.

I did secretarial work at the BBC at Radio 1 and got to know DJs. I liked music and went to rock concerts. Then I was attracted to devotees chanting on the street. I saw them on TV once and was impressed. I began chanting with devotees at different places like the stage at Quintessence concerts, and sometimes along the street, spontaneously, burning incense and blowing bubbles. I noticed how chanting uplifted people. I wanted to do it all the time. I went first for Sunday Feasts, then gradually went more often. My parents didn't like that. They didn't want to lose me. I was allowed to go to the temple twice a week. Then I began going to the temple every day and staying there for most of the day. The philosophy was better than Zen. It was more colorful and devotional.

I left my job and ran away from home. I took my potted plant and a little Indian table that it stood on, to put in Prabhupada's room. The sacrifice of joining the temple was a lot more than I expected. I remember being hungry and tired a lot. But we thought if we felt that way we were in *maya*.

When Prabhupada visited in 1971 the temple was packed and so warm it made it really difficult to stay awake in his classes.

When I went up to get my initiation beads, Prabhupada said, "Your name is Devamaya. When the mind is thinking of Krishna it is in Devamaya. *Deva* is 'God' and *maya* is 'energy.' When the mind is with Krishna it is Devamaya."

The men tended to force themselves to dislike women because they had to give them up. In the beginning, women were on right side and men on the left. Then at some point the men were complaining and we had to go to the back.

I made Prabhupada a cake in the shape of a temple. Prabhupada said, "I don't want to eat a temple I want to build a temple."

Dhanistha devi dasi

When Srila Prabhupada came, everything was washed clean by his presence. Thank God for his pure devotee, who indiscriminately blesses us both from near and far. As the guru of us all, we are his spiritual children eternally. Realization of this special privilege takes place deep within, but it was very helpful to have his physical presence, even just for brief times.

Because I was distributing his books, I felt close to Prabhupada. During his visit I was given the extra service of cleaning his quarters. In the early morning hours, just before class Prabhupada would take a morning walk. That's when we would clean and freshen his rooms. The particular quarters I'm speaking of were a few blocks from the apartment where Jayananda and his wife, Trayi devi, lived–appropriate rooms were cleared and arranged to accommodate Srila Prabhupada's needs.

Srila Prabhupada liked bare floors kept very clean by spreading white sheets over them and taping down the edges. The sheets were changed and washed every day. Everything was always kept sparkling clean.

One day, just as we were finishing the cleaning, Srila Prabhupada returned earlier than usual with several of the men who had accompanied him on his walk. The stairs leading up to the second-floor flat entered the apartment in the middle of a long hall. If you turned left at the top of the stairs, you ended up in the kitchen; turning right led to Prabhupada's room. Since Srila Prabhupada had arrived early, Keli-lalita and I were caught in the narrow hallway that opened into his room. There was nowhere else for us to exit from. There were several devotees with Srila Prabhupada, and in such a small space, there was also no room for us to pass and go down the stairs. Srila Prabhupada, however, turned left and headed toward the kitchen with his men. Keli and I offered our obeisances, and when we rose to our feet, we saw the crowd heading in the opposite direction from us. We edged toward the kitchen to try to see what was going on.

Everybody was standing closely around Prabhupada, and he, being smaller in physical stature, was hidden momentarily. Then one devotee bent down to sprinkle *kunkum* powder over his lotus feet. The scene was jubilant and sweet to watch. The devotees were laughing with such gentleness. Srila Prabhupada was smiling and reciprocating the love of his devotees. I could see him quite well, because when the devotee offering the *kunkum* bent down in front of Prabhupada, the rest of the men crowded to the sides and we were suddenly directly in front of him, with a clear view from the hallway. We felt we were onlookers and might not be welcome if the men noticed us there, so we carefully exited. But the last thing I saw was Srila Prabhupada smiling in our direction.

The next morning when we went to clean his rooms, we saw Srila Prabhupada's *kunkum* footprints here and there throughout the room, distinctly visible on the white sheets and pillows behind his desk. To this day I curse myself because I washed those sheets. Before I removed them, however, I sought out every lotus footprint and offered it my obeisances, placing my head on each one.

We cleaners salvaged various items Prabhupada had used during his visits, like the eucalyptus twigs he used for brushing his teeth, bits of flowers and paper he'd touched. We took these back to the temple for distribution to the other devotees, who didn't have the same opportunity to get close to Prabhupada. I gave everything away. What I wouldn't give for just one eucalyptus twig now.

During an informal darshan Prabhupada asked if there were any questions. I raised my hand. I had just received initiation and my beads from him during a fire sacrifice at the temple. He also gave me my name, Dhanistha devi dasi. Now, a few days later, I was concerned. Srila Prabhupada would be leaving soon to continue his travels to other temples. I knew that the cleaning I had been doing might be my last opportunity to serve his form directly, so I asked, "Srila Prabhupada, how can we get more personal association with you?" Before the words were even out of my mouth he raised a hand and said softly, "Just distribute my books." Then he smiled. The temple president said, "That's what she does, Srila Prabhupada. She goes to the airport every day and distributes your books."

"Then that is very nice," Prabhupada said. I was in the very back of the room, sitting next to Jayananda. All mental obstacles between myself and my guru were in that moment removed. I understood what real association with the guru meant, at least for me.

One day during the same visit, Prabhupada was standing in the temple foyer. One devotee asked out of the crowd, "Prabhupada, how do we get more of your association?" Prabhupada said, "Just read *Krsna* book. Even I read *Krsna* book." And he smiled a broad, effulgent smile. We all laughed. I felt so close to him then. If we remember what he said, we can feel close to him now, too.

Dhrti devi dasi

Devotee students at Dhrti's New York art high school told her about the Hare Krishnas. Dhrti found the Hare Krishnas irritating.

The irritation was that I liked to talk to them and when I did, I'd think too much. I'd ponder, "What is life?" and I didn't want to deal with that—it was too complicated. So I avoided the devotees, who looked too strange. If I saw them at the end of the street, I'd go out of my way to not have contact.

Then, with leftovers from the Sunday Feast, some of the students at my school who were becoming interested in Krishna consciousness held a Monday feast in the cafeteria. *Prasadam* was very wonderful. One of them told me, "You have to check out the temple." So I went with a friend to the Brooklyn temple for a Sunday Feast. The temple was tiny, and full of incense and flowers. Everyone seemed beautiful and happy. My friend was grim and hated the experience, but somehow I decided I wanted to be with these people. For a year I went to the temple without ever telling my parents. I went before and after school and gradually became more and more serious.

One morning at the temple, one of the *brahmacharinis* told me Prabhupada was coming. "Come with us to the airport!" I'd never skipped school before, but that day I did. The airport hoopla was amazing. My first impression of Prabhupada was surprise at how small he was. I had imagined him to be grand, a lion. But he was beautiful. At first sight I was in awe of his spiritual manner, which was somehow not of this world.

The morning Prabhupada was to leave, again a *brahmacharini* said, "You have to come to the airport to see Prabhupada off," and she gave me a large bag of flower petals to throw before him as he walked through the airport. I'd never been close to Prabhupada before, and all of a sudden I was within a foot of him and mesmerized as I walked through the entire airport–a long way–throwing flower petals. My heart pounding, I was staring at Prabhupada. I couldn't believe my good fortune. When Prabhupada sat down to wait for his plane, an airport employee complained to him that we'd littered the corridors with flower petals. Prabhupada laughed and said, "See how they think that beautiful flowers are litter."

In June of 1975, when I was seventeen, I graduated high school, and in July I went with the *brahmacharinis* to the Philadelphia Ratha-yatra. Srila Prabhupada was seated on the center cart, and we watched him from the side. A *brahmacharini* said, "There's no one between the ropes, dancing for Prabhupada. Let's go!" For the whole procession we danced for Prabhupada and had his full attention. It felt wonderful. We blocked out everything else: it seemed like it was us and Prabhupada, so sweet. Days later, I flew to L.A. where the BBT production department had moved. Devotees were in the midst of the mad *Chaitanya-charitamrita* marathon, and I was immediately put to work painting. My first painting is signed Bhaktin Miriam. Later, when I received the name Dhrti and heard that it meant "determination and steadfastness," I thought it was a perfect name for me. I decided to embrace the meaning of my name as Prabhupada's instruction to me.

Prabhupada's quarters in L.A. were upstairs, and one morning I was standing with a few others under the stairs. Prabhupada started up them, glanced over at us, came down, and walked over to us. We had our hands folded and were looking at him. He said something, but my heart was pounding so fast I couldn't hear. Prabhupada pointed. I turned around to see who he was pointing at, but he was pointing at me. It was like a dream. Devotees were laughing and Prabhupada was smiling. One of the *sannyasis* standing with Prabhupada told me what he had said: "I saw your photograph in a newspaper article about the Ratha-yatra, and it was very nice."

That was wonderful on many levels. One is that Prabhupada remembered such a tiny detail. Another, that he made that effort–to me it was a huge effort–to acknowledge what he saw and to say it pleased him. Third, I felt he knew that that particular kind of attention was perfect for me, a young girl. I didn't do anything fabulous. I danced nicely, he saw it, and it made him happy. His tenderness has kept me going for many years. When I hear other devotees speak of their tender exchanges with Prabhupada and of how he treated them as his daughters, I feel, "Yes, he also acknowledged me as his little daughter."

As one of the artists, I went with the others to bring our paintings to

Prabhupada in his quarters. Calm and casual, he looked at the paintings as he was receiving his massage. It was wonderful that he viewed the paintings at his leisure. I think he enjoyed seeing them. What I understood and hold on tightly to is that we artists were part of Prabhupada's team. His books were dear to him and we were embellishing his jewels. I always and definitely felt that connection with him and didn't require Prabhupada's physical presence for acknowledgment. The books were his, he felt some personal pride in them, and I knew that he would be looking to see how they were decorated.

In the art department we played Prabhupada's lectures at all times. They were my lifeline to Prabhupada. His voice was nondifferent from him, and he spoke to me directly through those recordings. To see him speak in person was overwhelming, but I loved how he'd end his lectures with the summum bonum: "Chant Hare Krishna and be happy." Hearing that, I'd think, "Yes, I can try to do that." I'd try to bring that joyful consciousness into whatever service I did. And if I couldn't do that, then maybe I wasn't meant for that service.

My time in the L.A. art department while Prabhupada was with us was brief–from 1975 through 1977–just two years. It was very challenging, but there was a fabulous intensity to it. I felt some energy and enthusiasm and got caught up in its whirlwind, went with it, and stuck it out. It was solidifying. I tried to do my painting service with good intent and happiness and bhakti so that it would please Prabhupada and Krishna. I had no doubt that Krishna consciousness was perfect and that Prabhupada was perfect. I feel very fortunate that I could give art, which was already my direction in life, to Prabhupada. I got to do something for him that meant a lot to me. Devotional service that was ideal for me cemented me to Prabhupada.

Dinadayadri devi dasi

Dinadayadri dasi prays to Queen Kunti Devi, the most intelligent woman: "I beg that my story will not invoke lamentation in the heart of the reader. I truly believe that in order to receive the great boon of meeting such an exalted transcendental personality as His Divine Grace Srila A. C. Bhaktivedanta Swami Prabhupada in this life, some sacrifice would naturally be required."

I was initiated, and entered a consensual marriage with a devotee I didn't know, two months after joining the temple in late 1969. Srila Prabhupada certainly desired an auspicious outcome for all his householder disciples when they served in his mission with doubled strength as spiritual helpmates. He sent a letter to our temple president containing a sprig of dried narcissus flowers along with the message: "I am enclosing the beads with flowers of my blessings for N. and Dinadayadri dasi on the occasion of their marriage."

Unfortunately, my spouse quickly became abusive. I was born and raised as a middle-class "daddy's girl" in mid-20th century America and was in no way prepared to cope with the situation in my marriage. In fact, I was literally falling apart, and the other devotees could see it. How could they not notice when the abuse sometimes took place right out in public and my screams could often be heard from behind closed doors? My husband and I traveled a lot from temple to temple, and we ended up in India for a year from 1971 to 1972.

Some devotees had alerted my parents, who liked Krishna consciousness, that I was in trouble and needed help. So they went to meet Srila Prabhupada in New Vrindavan in 1972. Prabhupada received them graciously and gave them *prasadam* from his hand. He told them, "I am also concerned about my children." They thanked him for saving their daughter from a degraded hippie life and Srila Prabhupada replied, "Yes, many parents thank me." He also assured them that I would be returning from India soon and that everything would be all right. Looking back on it, I recall that he sometimes arranged for me to stay at the Detroit temple for a while and would send my husband elsewhere. I believe he did this to give me some relief and allow my parents to see that I was all right.

The kirtan, *japa,* and classes in the temple were my only shelter, and I threw myself into these activities with all the abandon I could muster – especially the kirtans, which in those days were performed using the beautiful, accessible melodies that Srila Prabhupada himself sang. The chanting would start out slowly and meditatively until everybody was fully absorbed in the transcendental sound vibration of the holy names of Krishna, gradually building to a crescendo of natural heart-felt ecstasy at the end. Sometimes it seemed as if thousands of demigods were singing with us and showering flowers on the transcendental proceedings. Indeed there were several occasions when Srila Prabhupada informed the devotees that Narada Muni had been present at one of our kirtans.

By the time we were sent to India, I had become so demoralized that I was seriously contemplating suicide much of the time. In Calcutta, a godsister urged me to talk with Srila Prabhupada, and a private meeting was arranged. I was certain that my predicament was an aberration that had nothing to do with real Krishna consciousness. I had read about the qualities of a Vaishnava and seen in Srila Prabhupada that a devotee is kind, benevolent, peaceful, self-controlled, sane and compassionate – a far cry from the animalistic fury and violence that I was subjected to. All my life I had been sheltered and protected by a gentle, loving father and could not comprehend what I was doing to elicit such rage from my husband, who was said to be my protector and guide in spiritual life.

Upon entering Srila Prabhupada's room, I wasn't quite prepared for the force of being in his personal presence as he looked at me with full attention, waiting for me to speak. In the few seconds it took to gather my thoughts, Srila Prabhupada transmitted a vision into my heart. All of a sudden, as if from outside of my body, I could see both myself and Srila Prabhupada sitting there as shining spiritual sparks – the vast and significant difference between us being that my spark was covered under a mountain of debris whereas Srila Prabhupada's blazed clean and clear in all its glory. I realized that his intention was to elevate me from my grossly polluted condition to his level of pristine purity, and I became infused with the certainty that this was indeed possible if I followed his instructions conscientiously. So the relationship between Srila Prabhupada and me as master and disciple was established, and I realized it in a most tangible way in the flash of that vision.

Then the most astonishing thing occurred: what I had thought was an insurmountable problem suddenly shrank down to the size of the hoof print of a calf (the exact analogy that came to mind). All this happened before either of us spoke a word. I thus began to feel very foolish that I had come to waste Srila Prabhupada's time with what now seemed to be a small problem. But there I was, having already disrupted him. So I gathered my courage and blurted out that I was being physically and psychologically tormented by my husband and my mind was so disturbed that I was thinking of committing suicide and I was not able to be Krishna conscious in this situation and could I please live in the temple separately from my husband.

Srila Prabhupada's facial expression was attentive and thoughtful, but he did not reply right away. I explained that the devotees had said that the marriage vow was so sacrosanct that only he could make the decision to separate a husband and wife, and that's why I had come to him. I also told him that my husband insisted that my only relationship with Srila Prabhupada was through him and that if I left him I would lose my connection to my spiritual master.

The first thing Srila Prabhupada said was, "No, it is not like that. These material relationships are not so important. The important thing is to be Krishna conscious." As he said this, an incredible feeling of warmth and empathy enveloped me like a father's comforting embrace. I weep to remember his sweetness and humility as he posed his instructions as requests: "You will stay in our temple?" "Oh, yes, Srila Prabhupada!" "There will not be other men?" "Oh, no, Srila Prabhupada!" "All right, you can stay here and assist Palika." And that was it.

I was, of course, elated that Srila Prabhupada had mercifully relieved me of this burden but now was faced with the fearful task of informing my husband. It was a mistake for me to do this myself because of the dynamic of intimidation in such relationships, but there was no one else available. All the devotees were frantically preparing for the Mayapur cornerstone laying ceremony on Gaura Purnima in just a couple of days.

My husband returned from a preaching engagement in Kenya shortly before the festival, and it wasn't until we were walking down Bhaktisiddhanta Road in Mayapur that I was able to gather the courage to tell him what I had done. The next thing I knew, I was sitting on the ground seeing stars. He had knocked me down right in front of scores of shocked Bengali pilgrims who were in Mayapur for the most holy day of the year for Gaudiya Vaishnavas. Then he dragged me to a secluded place and battered my mind for hours with rhetoric, finally persuading me that I had committed the greatest *guru aparadha* by asking Srila Prabhupada to sanction my desires and that I should stick to my duty like Arjuna in the *Bhagavad-gita* and remain living as his wife.

Later that day, my husband entered a darshan in Prabhupada's straw hut that was attended by several leading ISKCON men. Prabhupada greeted him with a smile, "So, now you will take *sannyasa*?" Sheepishly, my husband had to tell him no, that he had persuaded me to stay with him as husband and wife. Srila Prabhupada was very expert at disarming a person's false ego defenses and then imparting an important truth into the person's newly opened heart and mind. Prabhupada brought up the saying by the sage Tulasi das that "you can beat a dog, a drum, or a woman until you get a nice sound." In a teasing tone, he turned to my husband and said, "N. understands this principle very well." Then Prabhupada became very grave, looked right into my husband's eyes and exclaimed, "But don't do it! These are not ordinary women, these are devotees!" Srila Prabhupada then apparently praised me at some length and advised my husband, "Do not tease her or she will close the door."

After being corrected by Srila Prabhupada, N.'s behavior improved for a while but then again deteriorated and the situation became worse than ever. I finally made my escape from the marriage a year later in 1973. Returning to live with my parents for a while to try to recover from the trauma, I then discovered that I was with child. Not knowing that N. had taken another wife as soon as I had left, I wrote to Srila Prabhupada right before my son was born to ask if I should return to my husband to raise the child, even though this was the last thing in the world I wanted to do. I explained that I was living with my parents but was chanting sixteen rounds a day, offering all my food to Krishna, and reading his books and listening to his recordings regularly. Srila Prabhupada replied:

"You are a very good girl and a sincere devotee, therefore, even though you have experienced difficulty you are remaining pure in Krishna

Consciousness and keeping faith in Krishna and the spiritual master. This faithfulness has pleased me very much. So many great devotees have had to undergo difficulties, and the great example among women was Queen Kunti whose family life was perpetual danger, but because she always thought of Krishna she was saved. There is no question of your returning to N. He has remarried. . . . You have got one child, so now make Krishna your husband and take shelter of our temple. . . So take spiritual instructions from your elder Godbrothers and sisters, forget the past, and make all progress in Krishna Consciousness without any material lamentation or hankering."

Upon receiving this letter, I felt unbridled joy and once again the warmth of Srila Prabhupada's fatherly affection flooded over me. It's not that he was rejecting me because I had left my husband, but rather he was drawing me closer under his own protection and offering me the shelter of his ISKCON temple, where I could find spiritual support and fellowship with my godbrothers and godsisters. He also reinforced that he was very serious about his disciples following the basic regulative principles of *bhakti-yoga* and that this was what pleased him the most.

As representatives of Srila Prabhupada and Lord Krishna, it would seem that the husbands and managers of ISKCON are duty-bound to be on the side of Srila Prabhupada and Lord Krishna as protectors of the devotees under their charge rather than in the camp of the predators and abusers. Of course, mistakes are endemic to life in the material world, so the question then becomes how one will react in the event that such a tragedy does occur.

When a woman's natural nurturing and emotional tendencies are dovetailed in service to Lord Krishna, they become transformed into purifying devotional sentiments that give women the advantage of being "blessed by the Lord because they believe at once in the superiority and almightiness of the Lord, and thus they offer obeisances without reservation. . . . This simplicity of acceptance of the Lord's authority is more effective than showy insincere religious fervor." [from *The Teachings of Queen Kunti*]

It appears that these blessings of the Lord upon women can sometimes literally be the envy of men. In fact, such envy was later admitted by my former husband to be the main cause of his harsh treatment of me during our marriage. I have noticed that the women who take up Krishna consciousness are some of the most extraordinarily intelligent people I have ever met. The mistreatment of devotee women that has unfortunately occurred within ISKCON, which is irrational and destructive to everyone, needs to be rooted out and eradicated. Srila Prabhupada worked so hard to make Krishna consciousness available to everyone ("even a dog can take part in it"), and we as his followers have no right to restrict or deny shelter at Srila Prabhupada's lotus feet to anyone. And we certainly have no right to harass such persons, especially based on something so superficial as their external "shirt and coat."

Dina-sarana devi dasi

In 1974, along with thirty, perhaps fifty, other devotees, Dina-sarana dasi was initiated by letter in Germany at the Schloss Rettershof castle in front of Radha-Madana-mohana, who reside in Abentheur, Germany, Goloka-dhama.

I was wondering what kind of name I was going to get. I thought, "What is my real name? It would be nice to have a name that expresses being the servant of the servant of the servant." What we receive at initiation is the real name that we carry for our soul for the rest of our lives. I thought along these lines. I was meditating on being the servant of the servant of the servant. My name was "Dina-sarana." In German, the word *servant* is "dina." I was completely happy. I was in tune with my name before I received it. That was important to me because it had this notion of servant, *dina*.

Cakravarti, the temple president at the castle, wrote Srila Prabhupada asking permission to marry me. Prabhupada agreed. A friend said, "The temple president wants to talk to you." I was surprised as I'd never spoken to him before. I thought, "What does he want? Did I do something wrong?" The temple president was sitting on a chair like a teacher who is going to chastise you. He handed me his letter and I began reading. I still couldn't understand why I was there. The letter was addressed to Srila Prabhupada explaining what kind of preaching he had been doing. At the end of the letter, he wrote, "I'm thinking of getting married." I thought, "Oh, maybe he wants to ask my advice about his choice of a wife." So I kept reading. "The person I have been thinking about is Dina-sarana." I read this name like it was the name of my neighbor. I thought, "Oh, he wants to marry Dina-sarana," without thinking it was me!

Before I became a devotee, I had many opportunities to marry, but I always avoided it. I felt my life was for more than a marriage. But then I considered, "If I want to remain in this Movement my whole life, then I should marry. Otherwise, later, I might get an idea to leave and do something else." I thought, "Krishna knows better than me what kind of person I need for my life." Very quickly, I figured that this was Krishna's arrangement and I would agree, even though I had no idea of what I was getting myself into it.

Then in the middle of a class Cakravarti was giving to the *brahmacharis*, an announcement came through on the speakers, "Cakravarti, Srila Prabhupada is on the phone. Come immediately." So he left class to take the call. But somehow, the speaker remained on so we all heard Srila

Prabhupada say, "You wrote saying you want to marry to Dina-sarana and I give you my blessings." The *brahmacharis* completely broke apart because their temple president was marrying a woman!

After six months Cakravarti decided he preferred being a *brahmachari*. He told me he changed his mind and he was sending me to Radha-kunda (India) as a widow. He sent me with one pair of shoes and one *sari*. A *babaji* named Krishnadasa received me there. I was about twenty-four years old, a young girl. He asked me, "What do you want here?" I said, "My husband sent me as a widow to be here for the rest of my life."

He said, "You can't stay here. It's only a matter of time before someone is going to rape you." So I said, "But I'm supposed to be here. I have nowhere to go." So he hid me in a place, that as far as I can remember, was the ruins of a temple associated with the Six Goswamis. I lived there for three months, hiding under a roof that was falling down. I could only crawl in there. I had to stay in there during the day, and at night Krishnadasa would bring me a plate of *prasadam*. I would go to the lake to take a bath while everyone was sleeping. So nobody knew that I was there.

But after some time, Krishnadasa said I had to leave because rumors had started that there was a young girl at his place. So I went to the Krishna-Balaram Mandir and Prabhupada was there. It was 1975 or 1976. I was scheduled to have darshan with Prabhupada. But every time I had an appointment, there was no one to go with me into Srila Prabhupada's room.

One day his door was open and I dared to stick my head through. Prabhupada was sitting at his desk and saw me. He said, "Who are you?" I said, "I'm Dina-sarana." Prabhupada repeated, "Who are you?" I said, "I'm Cakravarti's wife." He said, "Come in." He asked me to come all the way to his desk. He sat on one side of the desk and I sat directly on the other side so I could see him perfectly. We were speaking face-to-face.

He was talking about this so-called wonderful husband that I had who had just sent me into a desert. He said Cakravarti was doing good service in Germany. My conversation with Prabhupada gave me another perspective and the strength to remain in the relationship despite all the ups and downs. Prabhupada had such a high regard for this person. I thought, "If Prabhupada thinks so highly of him, who am I to reject him?" He told me that if I happened to have a son I should take care of him as if he was Krishna. I should make him the all-in-all in my life.

I stayed for three months at Krishna-Balaram Mandir and Srila Prabhupada was there the whole time. At one point, someone asked me to clean his bathroom. Germans are trained to clean, so I took a particular effort to clean Srila Prabhupada's bathroom. On the shelf were his glasses and his watch, which I also cleaned.

In the afternoon Srila Prabhupada gave class in the courtyard, sitting under a tree. There were so many *sannyasis* and *brahmacharis* that there was a wall of saffron in front of him. Behind them were the *grhastha* men, and behind them the *matajis*. I could only found a place to sit at the top of the stairs. The whole time I lamented, "What an offense I'm committing sitting here higher than Srila Prabhupada." In the middle of his class, Srila Prabhupada said, "Who cleaned my bathroom?"

I was embarrassed. He asked again, so very shyly I raised my finger. He looked at me and said, "Cleanliness is next to godliness. If someone strives for perfection, success is guaranteed." He sent an arrow that pierced my heart. I had the impression that Prabhupada had given me a personal education – for me, for my life, for me to set my intention. From that moment on, my whole life went in a particular direction. It seemed that success in my life was guaranteed.

During the class, at one of the doors, an Indian woman appeared in a red *sari* with flowing black hair and a big red flower in her hand. I took her to be a prostitute because of her dress and unbound hair. She crossed the whole crowd – stepped over the *brahmacharis* and *sannyasis* – and went to Prabhupada to offer him her flower. Prabhupada took the flower, she bowed down, turned around, stepped over everyone again, and walked out the door. Prabhupada followed her with his eyes.

This was significant for me because although she was in a woman's body, Prabhupada accepted her service. That was another indication that I was okay even though I happen to be in a woman's body. I felt very awkward and silly because of having this woman's body.

If it wasn't for my husband sending me away, I would never have had the opportunity to be in Radha-kunda and meet Prabhupada. I'm grateful for it.

Eventually my husband came and picked me up and shortly later we had a son.

Some years later, I had an important dream. I was in the temple at the castle and Prabhupada was due to arrive. At a road crossing, he said that he was too tired to travel the rest of the way. So he got out of the car and sat down under a tree. I had to go to him. When I arrived Prabhupada was sleeping under the tree. So I sat at his feet and waited for him to wake up. While Prabhupada was sleeping, rows and rows and rows of Sanskrit writings transmitted to me from Prabhupada while he slept. This kept going and on and on and on. While this was happening, I understood that all the knowledge Prabhupada knew was being transferred to me. When this finished, Prabhupada woke up and said, "Now you know everything you have to know. I told you everything you need to know." In my dream

Prabhupada left his body. One or two weeks later, Srila Prabhupada actually left his body.

Thirty years later, I was scraping a pot in my kitchen. Srila Prabhupada "appeared" to me complaining that his Movement was falling apart and there was nobody there to take care of it. I felt that he was directly speaking to me, and I felt obliged to do something. At that time I wasn't much involved in temple activities. Most devotees didn't even know me. I was wondering how I would even be able to do anything for him.

On Vyasa-puja, I was asked to garland Srila Prabhupada even though there were other devotees there who should have done it. I was reluctant but I did it. As I offered obeisances at the base of his *vyasasana* I was "hit" on my shoulder. It was so hard I had to keep myself from screaming out. I got up and hid myself in the crowd, thinking, "What's going on? What is this all about?" And then a kind of order came to me again, "I've told you everything you need to know." My dream came back to and I knew I had to go and do something. But what I should go and do? Then I realized that Prabhupada told me that he had told me everything I needed to know. But my objection was, "Who am I? I'm in this woman's body." The answer came, "You know you're not the body." In other words, don't make a fuss of it.

It occurred to me that what I was supposed to do is in my mind and being – whatever I understood. This is how I was to serve his Movement. From this experience I gathered the courage to stand for an election of the National Council. So six months later I was elected as one of the National Council members. I hadn't been a member of anything! A year after that I became a deputy. The following year I became the Euro GBC.

Prabhupada infused in me that understanding that if someone strives for perfection he'll be successful. And later he told me that I knew everything I needed to know. I feel that though I had very little association with Srila Prabhupada, I am always in contact with him. That carries me.

Dinatarine devi dasi

Dinatarine joined the temple in New York in the summer of 1970 and after a few days went to the temple in Columbus and then to one in Denver. Strangely, every time she joined a temple, something catastrophic was happening in it. She was chanting and following the principles, and from Florida wrote a letter to Srila Prabhupada saying, "What is the condition of someone like me who likes Krishna consciousness but finds she can't live in the temples with the devotees?"

I sent the letter and one month went by, two months went by, and at three months, I decided 'Never mind, I'm going to join again.' In the fall of 1971, on my way to hitchhike to Tallahassee, my friend said, "Let's stop by the house where we used to check for mail." She opened the big mailbox and there was a tiny blue air envelop from Srila Prabhupada. In a one page handwritten letter Prabhupada wrote, "In order to become successful in Krishna consciousness three things are necessary: You must have enthusiasm, you must be determined, and you must be patient. If any one of these is missing, you'll find the process difficult. So please learn to be patient." Prabhupada knew my problem and his letter was my saving grace. From then on, every time I had trouble I'd look at that letter and see where I was lacking. I went to the Tallahassee temple, then to Dallas for almost two years.

My big mistake was I became dogmatic and was unable to see the person behind the Supreme Lord's fervent, strong instructions. I thought that Prabhupada wasn't a person but a visual incarnation of those instructions. In 1973, I came to a point that I had to see who Prabhupada was, otherwise my faith in and commitment to the process of Krishna consciousness couldn't continue. Unauthorized, I went to India and as soon as I sat in front of Srila Prabhupada my life changed. I saw an incredibly compassionate, loving, humorous, knowledgeable, regulated, convincing, and faithful person. In one second his personal qualities finished all of the disruption dogmatism had caused my life.

My relationship with Srila Prabhupada was unique. Before him I acted like a fool, intimidated and not knowing what to say, and he ignored me. But every time I sat with him, I felt incredibly blessed and in the spiritual world. It didn't matter whether he exchanged with me or not; just to be in his presence was a wonderful gift I never took for granted.

From Prabhupada's instructions to Yamuna and me when we went to Oregon, we understood that he was going to pass away soon and he wanted to protect and encourage us. He said, "You are like widows now so live simply and keep a mood of renunciation." He engaged us in Deity worship, in chanting, and in trying to help others in a wonderful way.

Seeing how Srila Prabhupada acted with and treated women showed me clearly that Srila Prabhupada didn't make distinctions based on the body but rather based on the sincerity of the soul who was coming forward. He engaged and encouraged and loved his women disciples in a powerful and real way. With us Westerners Srila Prabhupada dealt with every configuration of strangeness, yet did it with aplomb, compassion, and care. He wanted us to adopt the culture of Vaishnavism, so that by living with morals within *varna* and *ashram*, we'd be relieved of the difficulties of this chaotic world and learn what it means to be a devotee.

Today's world doesn't encourage us to go within, to become introspective and thoughtful; rather, today's world necessitates a loss of true intelligence, namely the ability to discriminate, to reason, to put things in their proper perspective, to properly see our place within things. True intelligence includes character and integrity and moral compass. Srila Prabhupada wanted us to develop our spiritual intelligence so we could go within and advance in Krishna consciousness.

One of the wonderful things about Srila Prabhupada was that he could hear just a sentence or two from someone not in line with Vaishnava *dharma* and with one or two sharp swords of his words, he'd cut down the whole thing, "Nonsense rascals." In Srila Prabhupada's absence no one can do that and so a continuing stream of detrimental ideas has come forward. In order to remain positive, focused, and enthusiastic in Krishna consciousness, we have to see those ideas as an opportunity to grow as Vaishnavas. If we consult with our senior godbrothers and godsisters and Srila Prabhupada's books and see them in that light, then we can remain strong. I was helped and encouraged when I read that the same problems we face were also there after the departures of previous *acharyas*. Such challenges are Krishna's grace so we can develop firm faith, become introspective and understand Krishna consciousness on a heart level that's independent of outside circumstances, and draw strength from any circumstance.

Aspiring devotees can connect with Srila Prabhupada every day, develop their relationship with him, be encouraged by him, and stay strong by watching his DVDs and reading about how he lived, acted, and instructed his devotees. It's one thing to read his Bhaktivedanta Purports, but if we see him in a video take *prasadam,* go on a morning walk, speak to people in a loving and humorous and convincing way, we get an understanding of his remarkable, extraordinary, unparalleled, insuperable nature and that increases our faith and enthusiasm. Then when we read his Bhaktivedanta Purports we can put his words in perspective.

There'll be many challenges to our faith and commitment to the Krishna consciousness process. These challenges, whether from without or within, should be seen not as impediments but as a firm affirmation of our devotional life. In that way we'll have the strength to go through the invariable trials and tribulations in addition to all the joy that comes from re-establishing our relationship with Krishna. This process is so full of life and happiness and wonder that we should never become discouraged by challenges. If we continue forward with faith, enthusiasm, and determination, then wonderful spiritual rewards will come.

Dirgha devi dasi

One day when she was in Canada, Dirgha saw a film about Jesus Christ, a preacher who spread God's message worldwide. Dirgha was attracted to having a spiritual master who traveled and preached and, deciding to show God her desire, she sat in an armchair without eating or sleeping. After three days a man came and gave her a BTG, and two months later she joined the movement.

I had been living in the Paris temple for three months when Prabhupada came in June 1973. I offered Prabhupada some small portraits I'd painted of the disciplic succession. Prabhupada said, "Oh, very nice." Then he turned to Yogesvara, who was translating into French, and said, "Oh, she can do big posters for the Movement." I thought, "Wow!" It was a blessing. I was very shy; I didn't ask any questions. I paid my obeisances and ran out.

The next day Prabhupada was giving initiations but Bhagavan told me, "You've been here only three months, you're not ready. There's no way you can understand what initiation means!" I was very disappointed. But Prabhupada told me I could be initiated so I was.

The next year when Prabhupada came to New Mayapur I went on all his morning walks. Being next to him I felt happy, totally fulfilled. I didn't need anything else. Later I was in Los Angeles when Prabhupada came in 1976. We were at the airport saying goodbye and when Prabhupada stepped through the door to go to the airplane, I started to cry. I don't cry for anything, but I knew I would never see him again and I felt abandoned.

In my life I've gone from one desire to another and I see my desires have become more and more purified. When I was outside I wanted to become an artist and I did. I wanted to join the Movement and I did. I wanted to work with the devotee artists and I did. I wanted to marry a devotee and I did. I wanted to have nice land and a house and I did. Now I have to desire to become a pure devotee I don't need anything else! More or less I've finally exhausted my nonsense desires.

Now I try to follow Prabhupada's instructions and read his books. And I built a temple in my mind where I go see him and talk to him. But since I'm not advanced it's hard for me to be by myself. I realize I need to take shelter of one of Srila Prabhupada's advanced disciples. Prabhupada said we can become pure devotees within a second if we do whatever Vasudeva or Vasudeva's representative say. I'd like to be totally engaged again in serving Prabhupada, in making paintings for him or whatever. That's my goal now.

Divyadristi devi dasi

In San Diego in 1975, Srila Prabhupada initiated Divyadristi by letter. He wrote, "Your name is Divyadristi, which means the servant of transcendental taste, and by reading my books and distributing them profusely you will develop this transcendental taste."

In 1974 I went with a friend of mine to the San Francisco Ratha-yatra. It was a dark, gloomy, cold, rainy, overcast, freezing, and miserable day.

Everyone was bundled up. But when Prabhupada got on the stage, put his arms up in the air and started to dance, the clouds separated and it became sunny. In my heart, Krishna made me realize that Prabhupada was a special personality.

In 1975 I was late in getting to the airport when Prabhupada arrived in Los Angeles. Prabhupada was coming down the escalator and he lovingly acknowledged my friend and me, standing at the bottom. I was one of the bigger book distributors and later on, when Prabhupada was sick, my constant meditation was to try and distribute as many books as possible to try and help him get better.

Today here in Los Angeles, I can see that due to Prabhupada's Movement and his energy, many people are becoming vegetarian and in that way taking the first step in becoming God conscious. The devotees have distributed so many books, have had a temple here for so many years, and have conducted Ratha-yatras in such a glorious way, that many people are taking that first step. It's growing bigger and bigger and I feel blessed that I'm able to be part of it, that Prabhupada is still allowing me to do some small service for him.

Draupadi devi dasi

Many years ago, Draupadi, a native of England, was looking for a life other than what her parents, who had lived through two world wars, had experienced. Krishna sent her Prabhupada and Prabhupada offered her Krishna consciousness, the topmost consciousness achievable.

In 1968, after I'd been chanting Hare Krishna for three months and had attended a Ratha-yatra festival, Srila Prabhupada came to England and lectured in Conway Hall. Although I couldn't understand much due to his accent, I sat in front of him absorbing his transcendental vibration. I knew, "This is my guru." After Srila Prabhupada's lecture I asked the devotees, "When can I move in?" They said, "Immediately."

One week later I arrived at John Lennon's Tittenhurst estate with my thirteen-month-old boy and all my paraphernalia. Malati introduced us to Srila Prabhupada, "These people are just coming to Krishna consciousness." I was on my knees looking up at Prabhupada who was looking down at me. It was a moment in eternity; it was the moment I'd waited so long for! Prabhupada said, "Hare Krishna!" and with a big smile welcomed me to Krishna consciousness.

The next day Prabhupada invited my son to walk with him but my son was shy. Prabhupada laughed and took Malati's daughter Saraswati, who was beside him, by the hand and the two of them walked together. A week later Prabhupada initiated me and named my son Dhruvananda. I was young, not intellectual or philosophically inclined, but sincerely looking for the truth. Prabhupada quickly captured my heart by asking me about my son, my big attachment. Prabhupada was always personal like a loving father.

Prabhupada's Radha-Krishna Deities were in a little room in the Tittenhurst estate. As we'd pass by this room we'd hear Prabhupada playing his tamboura and singing "*Govindam adi purusam*" to Them. One day it was pouring rain when I came out of the kitchen and I met Prabhupada coming through a little gate. I was preparing to offer *dandavats* into a big puddle but, smiling, Prabhupada looked at me compassionately and said, "That's all right." Once I asked Prabhupada, "*Prasadam* is a new taste for my son and he's not eating much, so what should I give him?" Prabhupada said, "Take a little milk, a little rice, a little sugar, and a little bit of ghee and give him this." He explained in detail how to feed him nicely. He was always very concerned about and very kind to the children.

We all went in a big truck to Prabhupada's Conway Hall lectures. Prabhupada would be in the front with the driver, and thirteen-month-old Dhruvananda, fifteen-month-old Saraswati, Malati, and me would climb in the back. When the kirtan started, the two children used to chant, "*Hari Yiya, Hari Yiya!*" and at the end of his class Prabhupada would say, "This Krishna consciousness is so simple that even a child can take to it." He liked the children coming.

Many university students attended a morning engagement in Oxford Town Hall. Prabhupada gave a wonderful class. The kirtan started and Prabhupada jumped off his *vyasasana* and danced with his arms in the air. At the same time the students jumped up and put their arms up. Prabhupada picked everybody up and had them dancing.

For seven years my husband and I lived in the Alps. One beautiful day I was sitting in those mountains chanting Hare Krishna when I clearly heard Srila Prabhupada saying, "I want you to live peacefully with your husband, to take care of your children and to paint." It was an incredible experience! As an artist I feel I must develop my service for Srila Prabhupada. My husband and I consider our paintings Prabhupada's. Painting in that way is a meditation. We try to be as Krishna conscious as possible and to be instruments for what Prabhupada wants to express. I pray that Srila Prabhupada will allow us to be good instruments and we keep our link with him strong.

When my daughter passed away for an unknown reason one night, that same night I had a dream about Srila Prabhupada. Looking at Prabhupada I said, "Srila Prabhupada, I love you. Is the relationship with the spiritual master eternal?" He said, "Yes, always." After that I felt pacified because Srila Prabhupada was there to guide my daughter on. Prabhupada's always there to guide us through life and through death.

Although Prabhupada had the external form of an elderly person, he had internal beauty, grace, wisdom, and freshness that he manifested externally at every moment. All of us can develop ourselves so Prabhupada can give us indications. That depends on us. We can have Srila Prabhupada as much as we want. Prabhupada's compassionate; he guides anybody who follows him. If there's uncertainty in my life, I turn to Srila Prabhupada and my doubts are dispelled.

Prabhupada said in ancient times people used to look for the guru but in Kali-yuga the guru comes to you. Out of his mercy, Prabhupada came, picked us up, and guides us. I can't conceive where pure devotees are situated – how they are seeing, hearing, smelling, and thinking. They're in an ocean of transcendental intoxication. In the material world the people are supposed to be sane but are actually crazy, and in the spiritual world people are in a crazy state but actually they're sane. Radharani is embracing trees. But we're so resistant, we're so afraid of nectar, we so much like to suffer. If we could just be done with this material world we'd have a life so wonderful we can't imagine. We are as free and as high as we want to be.

Once Prabhupada wrote to me, "I'm so pleased to hear that Krishna has blessed you with a new child. So you can call her Devaki and raise her to be a staunch devotee right from birth. And by increasing the number of children, in that way we can increase the number Lord Chaitanya's devotees at large."

Krishna is working for the good of all. Even if we don't make it for millions of lifetimes, our future is assured because we've met Srila Prabhupada. Now it's up to us. By the grace of Krishna, everything is possible. We have to keep beating out Srila Prabhupada's message and keep faith in our Movement even though we see it's bumpy sometimes. What's the meaning of faith if the path is easy? If it's easy, there's no meaning. It's up to us to give our life to Srila Prabhupada and to Krishna.

Duhkhahantri devi dasi

Duhkhahantri saw devotees at a "Yes" concert at the Spectrum in Philadelphia and thought, "They're so happy. I want to be that happy without having to get high every day." She bought a Sri Ishopanishad.

I was interested in Eastern philosophy so this book immediately made sense to me. I thought, "This author knows what he's talking about. I like this." At the time I was a typesetter at Princeton University Press, working on a thousand-page book called *The Arab-Israeli Conflict*. One day I bought the *Bhagavad-gita As It Is* at a bookstore and then bought ten more as Christmas gifts for my friends. When I saw the Bhaktivedanta Book Trust published this book, I became wistful for service there. I thought, "If I could work for these people, I wouldn't need pay. I could type this stuff all day."

Before I went to the Brooklyn temple I was totally dedicated to Srila Prabhupada and as soon as I walked into the temple I felt, "Oh, yes, I'm home." In February of 1973 I moved in – I was nineteen – typeset all day and helped the *pujaris*; I loved it. Within weeks Prabhupada came.

I moved to Los Angeles with the BBT and was part of the *Chaitanya-charitamrita* marathon. It was heaven. One day I heard that Srila Prabhupada was going to tour the press. Frantic, I thought, "I have to do something!" I ran around the corner to a little bush with little white flowers that I thought smelled wonderful. I whipped off a branch and when Srila Prabhupada came to the typesetting room Radhavallabha introduced me, "This is Duhkhahantri. She has much experience in typesetting." Prabhupada said, "She is married?" Radhavallabha said, "No." "And she's still working?" "Yes, she is still working." I was star-struck. I handed Prabhupada my flowers, he smelled them and said, "They have no flavor." I was crestfallen. He smiled at me and said, "Flower with no flavor is like a woman with no intelligence. She might be very pretty, but what is the use?" He left, I offered my obeisances and was happy as could be, forever mortified.

Dwijapriya devi dasi

Dwijapriya dasi met the devotees in 1972 in Denver, Colorado. Her boyfriend had a paper route and they'd go to arati and then return home. Her future brother-in-law and sister-in-law joined the temple in New Vrindavan.

One day I sat down with my mother and said, "Gerald and I are going to join the Hare Krishnas. They don't eat meat, they don't have illicit sex, and they don't take intoxication." I was pretty wild at that time, so she said, "Wow, I think that would be a great idea. It sounds perfect! I think you should do it." I was one of the few people whose mother thought she should actually join the Hare Krishnas.

So at sixteen, I joined the temple with my boyfriend. We were going to get married but they wanted everyone in Denver to be *brahmachari* and *brahmacharini*. It was a heavy ashram temple. They said, "Okay, if you're going to get married, you have to move to L.A., because that's where all the nonsense householders live." That's exactly how they put it. "We don't want any householders here." They shipped us off to Los Angeles. In 1973, after we moved there, I had a baby.

I had been hearing Prabhupada's lectures and seeing pictures of him in Denver. Because Prabhupada is larger than life you thinks he's so big.

When I saw him I thought, "He's a lot smaller than I thought." It's funny I would think that. But I imagined him towering over everyone.

But he was so effulgent. He was glowing. He would be walking in a group of devotees, and you could tell he was there, because there was kind of like a glow.

Prabhupada came to Los Angeles regularly and would spend at least two weeks so we got a lot of his association. Since I was pregnant, devotees said I should go and sit close to Prabhupada so the child could hear Prabhupada. I'd try to squeeze in the temple room two hours before he even came in because it would be packed. You'd never see anybody missing. Then maybe after three days or four days, the temple would be half full even though Prabhupada was still there giving lectures. After a week, he would ask, "Where are all the devotees?" He noticed that after a while people wouldn't show up for *mangala-arati* or wouldn't show up for the *guru-puja*. We didn't realize how fortunate we are to hear from a pure devotee. We were too lazy.

He would give amazing lectures. One time he spoke about Bhaktisiddhanta and it really was incredible. Everyone was there–Jayatirtha, Ramesvara, Hrdayananda – everybody would come and listen attentively. Prabhupada was talking and every single man, *brahmachari*, *sannyasi* in the temple was crying. There wasn't a dry eye in the house when he said at the end, "You are all like my guru, because you're helping me to spread my Guru Maharaja's mission, so I have to thank you very much." We just cried for the longest time. First there was dead silence, then everyone broke out crying.

In lectures he would say, "You should chant properly," or "You should get up early. Everyone should come to *arati*." "You should bring the kids." Maybe you'd leave the baby at home. He'd say, "These children should come." So those kinds of instructions he was giving to all the householders.

He also gave instructions in not so subtle ways. One devotee's daughter was always making noise. The child was about three years old, but she was always making noise, making a disturbance, moving around. One time the little girl sat cross-legged but she wasn't wearing underwear.

Prabhupada said, "She should not be allowed to be behaving like that and sitting like that in front of Krishna." The mother turned beet-red. She started crying, got really huffy mad, took her child, and left. She was so upset she actually left the temple because she couldn't take the heavy instruction. But who brings their kid to the temple not dressed properly?

My son Partha-sarathi was maybe six months or a year old. A woman brought in a tray of cookies and said, "I made these for you. Do you want to give them out to the devotees?" Prabhupada would eat one, and then give one to each of the little kids. There were dozens of little kids who would come and see Prabhupada.

It became a ritual. Every day a lady would make cookies, bring them in, and Prabhupada would eat one or two, then hand them out to all the little kids. There are videos of that. We'd all take our babies up. He would look at them and us. Every time Prabhupada would look at me I would feel terrified, like a lightning bolt would hit me, he was so intense and so powerful. I could never understand it, but I always felt terrified of it. I would come and sit in class, and if he would look my way I would just freeze.

Prabhupada was so kind to the kids. When he would give out cookies, he would say something and pat them on the head, or he would hold one of the kid's hands. He took the extra time and energy to relate personally to little children in a really nice way–always kind and loving. Sometimes he'd be out on the street and a little boy would be there with a *japa* bag and he would say something encouraging to him or start talking to him and smiling. I just thought he had so much kindness and so much love. It impressed me that he was such a perfect personality.

I could relate to him because of his kindness to children. I was just a lowly householder, which was considered pretty out there. I was motivated to be a devotee because of his relationship with the children. From that I've always thought we have Prabhupada no matter what happens in ISKCON, because there's been so much that's gone on. Somehow or other we have to follow or try to be a better devotee for him, because he's never disappointed us or shown any kind of weakness in spiritual life or any kind of characteristics that are less than pure.

I went to a Ratha-yatra in San Francisco–the one where Prabhupada stood up and everyone started dancing. All the big *sannyasis* were there. I'll never forget how amazing it was. All Prabhupada did was put his arms up, and it seemed like the huge crowd–you couldn't see the end of the people because Ratha-yatras in San Francisco were huge–the entire place rose up and down ecstatically dancing for the longest time. You can't even imagine what it was like unless you were there, how spiritually surcharged it was. That was a great experience.

My husband and I both got initiated at the end of 1973. We got first initiation, and then maybe six months later we got second. Both times by letter. At that time, initiations were happening really quick, because they needed *pujaris*. So you'd get initiated and then three months later you'd receive second initiation. It was happening so fast. But of course, a lot of those people didn't last for more than six months, unfortunately.

Kirtanananda came to visit. Ambarisa, our brother-in-law, was living in New Vrindavan then, so he said we should go to New Vrindavan and we moved. My little boy was maybe a year and a half. It sounded like a good idea to be on a big farm. It was very austere. There was no heat and no running water. You had to carry buckets of water. It was freezing. There was always ice or mud on the road. It was really hard. We had oat water–I'm sure you heard of the oat water. That's all we ate every day for breakfast and it was burnt half the time, sometimes too salty. Whatever they could scrounge up for vegetables in the wintertime we'd have for lunch. It was so hard to get any *prasadam* then. Everyone would steal *prasadam*. They used to lock the *maha* room. There was one cabinet that had twenty locks on it. That means however many locks they had, somebody would get in there and steal *maha*. The cabinet was locked in such a way that someone could reach underneath the door and take *maha*. Then they put nails below, so if you reached underneath, you cut your hands. Still people were desperate for nice *prasadam* so you'd do anything to get it.

I used to make *burfi* at New Vrindavan for Radha-Vrindavancandra. I didn't actually get to make it for Prabhupada, but I made it and they would give it to Prabhupada. He called me the *burfi* queen–the queen of *burfi*–one time. He didn't say it to me but I was so excited that he was pleased by it.

Prabhupada came in 1976. All the *sankirtana* mothers came back to the farm just for that. Prabhupada talked to the *sankirtana* mothers and we were asking questions. I was too afraid to say anything. But the others would ask, "Prabhupada, how should we do this? How should we do that?"

Maharha was the head *sankirtana* lady. She had many questions. Other ladies would ask, "What should we do if we're not chanting our rounds on *sankirtana*," and he would always say the most important thing was to chant. "Chant sixteen rounds. Take *prasadam*. Those are the basic things you have to do first." Already by that time, we weren't doing that and we were in anxiety. But we were trying to build the palace so Prabhupada would come and live there. At the same time, he didn't want us to give up our Krishna consciousness to do that. He made that really clear to us while we were there.

Bhadra Priya went through a lot of struggles. She was always so sweet and so humble. She asked Prabhupada, "What do we do if we're struggling?" He encouraged her and said, "Just continue to try to practice Krishna consciousness as best you can." Everyone was just so happy because he was there. We were out on a marathon and we got to come back, and Prabhupada would make us feel like we were fired up to go out for another few months.

And as soon as he left, we had to go right back out on *sankirtana*. And even when he was there, half the time we had to go out and do different picks. The whole thing was building Prabhupada's palace, so that's what we were really focused on for many years.

A couple of times mothers went and got to see Prabhupada in India, but I didn't get to go, because you had to have a certain amount of money you had collected to be able to go.

One day while we were on *sankirtana* we heard that Prabhupada was leaving his body. Our *sankirtana* party was living in Pittsburgh at the time. All the mothers came together and cried. No one could stop crying. We rushed to New Vrindavan to be there to pray, to go and see the Deities and to pray and hope Prabhupada would not leave his body. When Prabhupada left the planet we were so devastated. We kept building the palace in memory of Prabhupada being there in spirit.

I joined pretty young and Krishna saved me because I was going downhill quickly. I realize that if it wasn't for Prabhupada, I probably wouldn't even be in this body right now. I owe him my life.

Ekabuddhi devi dasi

When Ekabuddhi was a sixteen-year-old a high school student, she visited New York's Greenwich Village where "spiritual masters" were on every corner. Later, Ekabuddhi's boyfriend started getting involved in New York's ISKCON temple.

For a couple of years my boyfriend brought me magazines and books and when I read the *Bhagavatam* I got interested. I moved into the Henry Street temple but the men devotees were acting strangely with the women devotees, sometimes even spitting on them, and I felt unwanted. Prabhupada was unhappy about this mistreatment and sent a representative to try to straighten it out. Fortunately, everyone accepted Prabhupada's word as final. Prabhupada's mood was to warmly welcome everybody and not to judge people. Over the years I see the devotees who criticize others ended up falling down. Each of us can follow Prabhupada's example of humbly avoiding criticizing.

I got initiated in 1976 at New York City's 55th Street temple. It was wonderfully exciting. There were devotees from everywhere and every *sannyasi* you could think of was there. Everybody was in awe and nervous, worrying about having everything just right.

Once Prabhupada looked at me like he knew me from a past life, as if he was saying, "Oh, you're back again!" But because of my laziness and insincerity, while Prabhupada was with us I didn't take full advantage of his presence. Yet in another sense Prabhupada is still with us – he hasn't left us alone. We can feel his fire, his aliveness to gets things done, and his desire that we attract as many people as possible to Krishna's army. We need to analyze our motives, look into ourselves, and be sure that we don't act out of false ego. Prabhupada was a genius in moving with the time, in using people in the proper way to get spiritual things done and in letting people express themselves in their own way. Everybody can do some service. Prabhupada has compassion for everybody and his Movement is something everybody can be a part of because everybody wants to have a purpose, a meaning in life.

I was interested in spiritual life, and Prabhupada's books and mood made me understand all religions are good and the whole world is a temple with one God. Krishna consciousness has a lot more information than other religions, and Prabhupada's trying to give that information to everybody. Prabhupada thought universally and eternally. He was always saying, "Just think of Krishna." And, "Put Krishna in everything in your life. He's everywhere." That was Prabhupada's mood. Our only worry should be how we can somehow help him.

Gangamayi devi dasi

In a letter, Prabhupada wrote Gangamayi, "You are right that politics should be avoided. In my personal life I did not participate in the political diplomacy of my godbrothers. I was simply thinking how to fulfill the order of my Guru Maharaj. He gave me his blessings, and I was saved from any implication. Now I am trying to carry out his instructions strictly, and it has come out successful. I note that you are planning to come to India, and I have no objection. We will be needing experienced pujaris for our Vrindavan temple."

In England the temple's politics were bad and Prabhupada told me to stay out of politics, chant Hare Krishna, and go on with my service. He said he never got involved with politics at all in the Gaudiya Math.

After Prabhupada gave class at Bhaktivedanta Manor he'd say, "Thank you very much," and then, "Kirtan." The devotees would start a slow kirtan and as it gradually built up, they would stand up and soon the whole room would be bouncing as everybody leapt up and down while Prabhupada's *kartalas* were beating up and down. Our hearts burst open and we wanted to jump and shout Hare Krishna! It was an ecstatic, wonderful, joyous time.

Once in Vrindavan I was cleaning Srila Prabhupada's floor with a rag. Prabhupada said, "I will show you how to clean." He got down with his knees and calves suspended above the floor, dipped the rag into the bucket, and wiped over the floor. He put the rag in again, screwed it tightly, got all the water out of the rag, looked at me in the eyes and said, "You do like that." "Yes, Srila Prabhupada." The next day he said, "Did you do like that?" and I said, "Yes, Srila Prabhupada." I felt greatly honored to be in his presence, what to speak of saying anything to him.

Srila Prabhupada made me understand that breaking the four regulative principles wasn't good for me. He convinced me that I didn't want to do those things. I'm almost within reach of being with him, I just have to get out of this material world alive – by remembering him. I want to be as Krishna made me, totally sober. All our training is to remember Krishna at the time of death. I don't want to come back again. I don't want to disappoint Prabhupada. I owe Prabhupada something for what he's put into me, and the least I can do is try to be conscious and follow the principles. I don't want to leave Prabhupada. He didn't let me down, so why should I let him down? But I don't accept Prabhupada's words blindly. I accept what he says and never doubt the truths he spoke because everything he says works. If I don't understand something, if something doesn't work out, it's due to my stupidity.

My friend Annada and I want to somehow preach and to serve Srila Prabhupada, the devotees, and Krishna. The more we do to make our life centered on Prabhupada, the more Prabhupada comes around us. As much as we follow Prabhupada, that much Prabhupada reciprocates with us. She and I hear Prabhupada's lectures and *bhajanas* and we offer food to Prabhupada's Deity. By following this simple process we're happy.

Gauri devi dasi

In New Dwarka in 1985, Gauri, age forty-five, was diagnosed with terminal cancer. Before leaving to spend her final days in Vrindavan, she gave this talk to the devotees.

During a darshan in his room in New Dwarka, I was sitting next to Prabhupada and watching his expressions carefully. One by one, devotees were presenting their preaching services to him – on a college campus, with a newspaper, paintings for his books. Prabhupada looked exhausted as he leaned back on his pillows and nodded in approval. Then Ramesvara presented the book distribution report. Immediately, Prabhupada sat up, put his elbows on his desk, his chin in his hands and grinned broadly. He looked like a young boy. Book distribution was dear to Prabhupada.

I wasn't good at painting for Prabhupada's books, so I became a full time book distributor. But I was a complete introvert. When I was growing up, I was so shy nobody ever heard a word I said. My father would say, "Elizabeth, speak up!" I had a heavy, morose, grouchy, and intellectual personality – completely wrong for stopping and meeting people. I couldn't even carry on a light conversation or be nonthreatening. In the beginning, book distribution was hellish for me. But I kept at it because I saw that other devotees relished it. Prabhupada said everything comes with practice and I thought, "If Krishna helps the others distribute books, He'll help me, too."

Even though I had a huge false ego and was puffed up, one day Krishna blessed me and I suddenly found it easy to approach people, smile, and be free from the clouded personality that I'd had all my life – and I was free from it forever after. I started liking approaching people, giving them books, talking about Krishna and getting donations from them. I found that if I gave my heart and soul to book distribution, more love came from me and Krishna used me more by making me more clever and quick-witted. Krishna can make the dullest stone-like person into the most brilliant poet and philosopher and joker. Anything can happen on book distribution. It's amazing.

To immediately understand where a particular conditioned soul was coming from and how to deal with each one, I had to be clear-headed and in an urgent mood. Everybody's different and to engage them is an incredible challenge that requires total concentration and commitment. It can't be done mechanically. My mind couldn't be anywhere else but absorbed in wanting that soul to be engaged. I had to really give myself to each soul and in the process of doing that, I was also praying to Krishna on behalf of that soul and giving myself to Krishna. Just stopping each person was absorbing and fascinating. When a person saw that I was focused on them, they felt it. I got through to that soul and they couldn't help but reciprocate.

Book distribution requires extreme enthusiasm, because the people we're speaking with are extremely enthusiastic for their fruitive activity. It also requires surrender, dedication, and energy to engage a soul who's bewildered by the modes of ignorance and passion. When I distributed books, I didn't present Krishna consciousness as a religion but as a great science that has been handed down for thousands and thousands of years and which, in this materialistic Western culture, is totally unknown. People were interested – fascinated even – by Prabhupada's books. And they were appreciative; they were getting Krishna's mercy and progressing. I relished the sweet experience. I always tried to see how I was engaging the soul and how much they needed it and I needed it, how we were both getting purified and how Lord Chaitanya's mercy was somehow present.

Book distribution, engaging the conditioned souls, is a sportive activity with Krishna; it's the highest Vaishnava sport. Through its intensity we unavoidably experience the presence of Lord Chaitanya and Krishna and Prabhupada. We pray to them for empowerment, and we feel their reciprocation. The more I prayed to be steady on book distribution, the more Krishna allowed me to concentrate and experience rapport with the conditioned souls.

Maya tries to make us doubt that we're doing the right thing. She tries to make us feel that we're cheating the conditioned souls because that's the way materialists think. Actually, we're doing the greatest service. A devotee has to have so much knowledge that she'll never be shaken. She has to understand the position of the conditioned souls and her service to them. The goal of our devotional service is to be purified from all material identification and desire, to be Krishna's pure instrument – His puppet – and eventually to participate in loving pastimes with Him. We want Him to use us as He likes, we want to become His touchstone. By distributing Prabhupada's books, we get purified and we purify others. We act as guru. It's incredible, for we have no qualifications, yet here we are to some degree or other acting as a guru for the conditioned souls that we meet.

In my present situation, I've realized Krishna is kinder than I can imagine. Krishna loves me. Because I've been goofing off for so long, He wants to free me from illusion and to purify me, so He's given me an ultimatum.

There comes a point in every devotee's career when she gradually begins to sever herself from superficial motivation and transfer her energy to a much deeper motivation. Since I'll be passing away in a short time, I have a special opportunity to purify myself and to realize the goal of my service. At the fag end, Krishna's forcing me to get it together quickly. It's great mercy, but I lament that I didn't do more service, that I wasn't more serious and attached to Prabhupada. Although I'm trying to surrender, in the last few weeks I've been seeing duplicity, cheating, and foolishness in my thoughts. I know that if I continue trying, if I give my best, then when the time comes for Krishna to take me from my body, He'll also release me from those unwanted things. Krishna will help me come to my senses and realize I'm His humble, menial servant.

The process of leaving the body definitely changes one's consciousness a great deal. It increases commitment and seriousness and surrender. Before I was hanging onto sense gratification, to the hope of material happiness, to so many illusions. Please all of you, please don't be like me and wait until you're in the position that I'm in.

When Krishna makes some arrangement beyond our control and it becomes obvious that this body is definitely finished, immediately a devotee thinks, "What mercy Krishna has given me!" Death is a blessing. We want to do all we can to purify ourself while we're in this body, but as King Kulashekara prayed, "Now that my mind is in good condition and I can chant Your holy name, please allow me to leave this body so that I can find a shelter at the network of Your lotus feet. If You let me live to a ripe old age, I may be so choked up with mucus and my mind may be deranged, that I may not be able to chant Your holy name or remember You."

Krishna has made this arrangement for me. If He had wanted me to be cured, He would have given me something that was easy to diagnose in the early stages and I would have been cured. To me, it's clear that I had so much difficulty increasing my surrender and service, that Krishna decided this is the best program for me. Krishna's wants His devotee to have every opportunity to become Krishna conscious. Every one of us will be leaving our body, and it's an intense experience. If we're not prepared for it, it's going to be unlimitedly frightening and painful. I'm not old and I was as strong as an ox, but Krishna took my health away. He could do it to anyone.

Death is nothing to be afraid of. It's another step in purification, another step in coming closer to Krishna. My prayer is, "I don't care whether I go back to the spiritual world. I want to be free from all material sex desire. I want to be free from all sense gratification. I want to be pure so that I can actually serve You. I want to become Your instrument. I want to chant Your holy name twenty-four hours a day. I want to love You." This should be our constant concern. It isn't something that we wait to think about until we find out we've got terminal cancer.

Don't think that you're getting rid of me; you're not. I'm not going anywhere. Book distribution is an eternal party that we're going on together. But in the very near future, something needs to be done with the particular material body I have. When I got this disease, I got a closer view of how the body is a messy, disgusting business. I had no intention of stopping book distribution or even of cutting down to six days a week; I was getting energy from book distribution and was planning to continue to the very last ounce of energy I had, until Krishna stopped me.

In Vrindavan, I'll be hearing and chanting, visiting Krishna's places of pastime, meditating on Krishna's and Prabhupada's pastimes. I'm fully convinced it's going to be thoroughly enlivening right up until the end. Krishna wants to purify me, to free me from my false ego, from the desire for honor, fame, and distinction, so ultimately I can say, "*Jaya*, Krishna, I'm ready. I'm Yours, whatever You want, I'm into it and completely excited about it. I'm going to give my heart and soul to try and do it." I'm expecting and hoping that I'm going to see Krishna face-to-face. It doesn't matter a bit to me where I go, as long as I'm with Him and Srila Prabhupada.

Gayatri devi dasi

In July 1971, Gayatri's husband, Amarendra, along with Hridayananda, his wife Ananga Manjari, a few brahmacharis, and Gayatri invited Srila Prabhupada to come to their small temple in Gainesville, Florida for an engagement at the Gainesville university campus.

We didn't know how to do anything, but we tried the best we could. In three days we painted the temple psychedelic pastel colors – yellow, pink and blue – and Ananga Manjari somehow upholstered the *vyas-*

asana. It was amazing to watch her. I loved her. It was because of her and Hridayananda's incredible devotion I became a devotee. Srila Prabhupada sat on the *vyasasana* and spoke about Lord Chaitanya to the two hundred devotees from Tampa, Tallahassee, Jacksonville, Miami, Gainesville, and Atlanta who'd all squeezed into our little, freshly painted temple room, along with another two hundred people from the campus.

I wasn't a very good artist, but I'd done a painting of Lord Chaitanya that Srila Prabhupada liked. He was so touched by it he cried and said, "We are here in this Gainesville, very far from the birthplace of Lord Chaitanya, yet Lord Chaitanya is here." He talked about how the chanting of Hare Krishna along with feasting and dancing would make everyone in every town and village happy. In Gainesville we had no money. We'd used my parents $3,000 wedding gift to pay our rent. We went on *sankirtana* and Prabhupada was grateful we were helping Lord Chaitanya and him spread this Movement. His presence was so powerful, I have chills thinking about it. I didn't stop crying the whole time he was there. His love for the conditioned souls and for Krishna was beyond anything I'd ever experienced. He acknowledged Lord Chaitanya was with us because we were trying so hard.

At the university, Srila Prabhupada talked about the *ashtanga-yoga* process, the Sixth Chapter of the *Bhagavad-gita*. I thought, "Who can understand this?" But a thousand college students and professors filled up the Plaza of the Americas to hear him and were amazed. Later lots of people came from the campus to hear Prabhupada speak at the temple. After that he was on a university radio show. I was worn out but Prabhupada kept going.

When Prabhupada spoke strongly, he did it with valor and gentleness. I was convinced he was a pure devotee of the Lord. I wanted to take initiation from him, to be his devotee, and to follow him. Until then, I wasn't convinced, but after I saw what he was doing and heard him speak I wanted to emulate him. That night I got initiated along with ten or fifteen others. We didn't have *tulasi japa* beads, we just had wooden beads that we had strung together. Prabhupada told me my name, Gayatri, and later said, " '*Gaya*' means 'to sing' and '*tri*' means 'to deliver.'" From then on I thought, "We're supposed to help people, tell them about Krishna, sing, and they'll be delivered." I'm supposed to deliver the song, just like Srila Prabhupada.

The next morning we took Prabhupada to the Jacksonville airport. When we got there, devotees sat at his feet singing beautiful hymns while looking at him in total love. But Prabhupada's eyes were on Ananga Manjari and Hridayananda, who were distributing his magazines and books. Prabhupada recognized they were the ones really in love. I started to distribute books too so he would look at me. I felt rightly situated. I was with the highest people in the world, exactly who I was supposed to be with, and I was being trained in Krishna consciousness by devotees whom I loved. Meeting Srila Prabhupada was the most powerful experience of my nineteen-year-old life.

Prabhupada's love was outstanding, like a father. He was kind, not chastising, not angry, just loving and forgiving. I was grateful and wanted to be with him all the time. At that time there was no discrimination. I was treated just as a mother, and if I wasn't, I'd let the men know and they'd shape up or they wouldn't get any *prasadam*.

In 1976 I had the most painful experience of my life. I was chanting and following the principles but intensely depressed. I prayed for an answer. Amarendra wrote to Prabhupada, "My wife is suffering immeasurably. She's crying all the time, she's depressed, she can't think straight." Prabhupada wrote back, "For Gayatri, your wife, she should continue the program of chanting sixteen rounds on beads a day, she should follow the four regulative principles, and every day she should read *Bhagavad-gita*, and this will help her." This was my instruction for my ultimate help. I took the reading of *Bhagavad-gita* seriously. I'd read to the girls in the sewing room, listen to tapes, and write down verses, but eventually I left the temple. Since then I've gotten a lot of help. I know all the answers are in the *Gita* and still take that instruction seriously. Pain and suffering only concern the body, and we have to rise above it by serving the spiritual master, the pure devotee, and Lord Chaitanya's mission. Now I think I can do some service for Srila Prabhupada.

Girija devi dasi

Girija, a devout Christian, became interested in Krishna consciousness when she learned of Srila Prabhupada's respect for and openness to all bona fide, sincerely practiced religions.

As I got older I saw my religion declining and felt sorry. I tried Sri Aurobindo's ashram for a year, then I tried Maharishi, then went to a convent to be a nun, but these weren't what I was looking for. Then in 1976, when I was twenty-four, I went to the Govardhana-puja festival at the Montreal ISKCON temple. A week later I renounced everything and joined the Movement. What first impacted me was the *Bhagavad-gita*. I found all the answers in that book–answers to who I was, where I would go in my next life, who God is, and how to dedicate myself to Him. It was perfect.

My husband and I wanted to raise our five children in Krishna consciousness, so we moved from farm to farm so they could grow up in a natural environment, in the mode of goodness, and in the association of devotees in a spiritual community. By the mercy of Krishna and Prabhupada it was possible, and our children are beautiful and wonderful devotees. Now I have five devotee grandchildren. It's rewarding.

I love being a devotee. I stay enthusiastic and inspired by strongly focusing on my goal: to go back home, back to Godhead. I do whatever's needed to achieve that end. In old age I see myself being blissfully focused on Krishna, and this is all because of Prabhupada and the association of devotees. Anybody who wants God and wants to go back home, back to Godhead, can be inspired and happy by the mercy of Srila Prabhupada and his teachings.

Girindra Mohini devi dasi

In the spring of 1972, Girindra Mohini and her husband were living as hippies in Colorado when she got a Back to Godhead from the Denver devotees. She and her husband started going to the Denver temple but since there were no grihasthas in the temple, she, her husband, and their baby moved to New Vrindavan.

In 1972, when I was seventeen or eighteen years old, Srila Prabhupada initiated my husband and me at the New Vrindavan Janmashtami festival. Devotees from the entire East Coast were there. When I went to get my *japa* beads Srila Prabhupada said, "What are the four regulative principles?" I answered like everybody else and he said, "Your name is Girindra Mohini," but I couldn't understand him. I was blank so he repeated, "Girindra Mohini devi dasi." I still didn't understand a word. He laughed and said, "I will write it down." I kept that paper he wrote my name on until it crumbled into shreds.

In New Vrindavan I would watch my son along with Syama dasi's son, so she could transcribe Prabhupada's translations of the *Bhagavatam*. Hladini and I used to read those transcripts – the Third Canto – and that's how I became connected to Prabhupada and learned about Krishna consciousness. Whenever I sat down and nursed, I read Prabhupada's books. And since I always had a baby, I was always nursing. So I read a lot. For that reason alone I credit my kids with making me Krishna conscious.

Later we moved to the Los Angeles temple where my husband and Naranarayan were making the temple room. Prabhupada would give me his input on the milk sweets I made and my son, Kiba Jaya, and husband would go with Prabhupada on his morning walks.

Once Prabhupada said to me, "Are you taking special care of Kiba Jaya?" I said, "Of course, I am because he's so special." Prabhupada said, "Because he is special." I said, "Yes, all these children are special." Prabhupada said, "No, Kiba Jaya is special among devotees." That's when I knew that my life was about raising my children very carefully.

I was very close with my dad, who was a Presbyterian minister. He read Prabhupada's abridged *Bhagavad-gita*, and on my first visit home with the nose ring, pierced ears, and *sari*, my father wrote to Prabhupada and expressed his joy. Prabhupada wrote back saying how he appreciated all the young people who were joining the Krishna consciousness movement. My father said to me, "I don't understand your culture or it's importance. But any man that brings about a change in two people like I've seen in you and Steve [my husband, Syama Kunda] has nothing but my admiration." My father fully supported everything I did in Krishna consciousness and encouraged me. He said, "My only concern is that you keep the vows that you have made to God." I said, "Yes, I will."

I didn't get much personal association with Prabhupada, but I think every aspect of my Krishna consciousness experience is special. I see the beauty in my experience, and I know that anybody who is truly seeking spiritual life will find that beauty regardless of what happens.

Every morning of my life I recite the *Guruvastaka* prayers because to me they are the most beautiful prayers and the most sublime method of positive affirmation that there ever was. Srila Prabhupada connected with the Supreme on a level that can only be described as *ananda*, as blissful. Every morning I give thanks that Srila Prabhupada is my spiritual master, and every day I chant the holy names. In my world, to chant the holy names is all there is.

With various degrees of intensity, I've been practicing this process of self-realization for forty years, and I'm grateful to be a devotee.

Gokularani devi dasi

Gokularani was working as a nurse in Melbourne. Her life seemed useless. She saw Srila Prabhupada at the Melbourne Town Hall where he said, "Take up Krishna consciousness, everything else is useless."

Those words had an amazing affect on me. I couldn't stop thinking of them and how they really applied to what I was experiencing at the time. I went traveling to avoid joining. I stayed on a farm in Yugoslavia. On the radio I heard *My Sweet Lord*. Wherever I went I would meet devotees and receive BTGs. By the time I reached London it was winter and the only bright place in the city was the temple. In London I worked in a hospital in the East End.

I started visiting Bury Place. Vichi was giving classes. England can be a hard place when you first live there. I didn't know many people but I was made very welcome and made friends. The *prasadam* was nice. I met Malati, Jayalastita. The Saturday night *harinama* attracted me to overcome my shyness. I gave up my job and in December 1974 I joined at the manor where Himavati took me under her wing.

In 1975 I went with Himavati to meet Prabhupada at Heathrow. She told me to put my arms up and start yelling, "Prabhupada!" I felt embarrassed, but he looked at us and grinned. I was relieved to see him smiling, because she was being outrageous.

I felt he was my real father, whom I had been searching for all my life, and in previous lives. I saw him before in Melbourne but this was different. I went on a couple of morning walks. It was hard to get close because of all the men.

Gopa Patni devi dasi

One day in 1975, a friend of Gopa Patni's, who liked caring for plants as much as she did, came to Gopa Patni's house and told her about Tulasi devi–how the devotees worshiped this plant with incense and water and flowers, how they danced around it, and how they made skirts for it.

The devotee who visited me, Sranti Prabhu, had just come from the Bhaktisiddhanta disappearance day festival in Atlanta, and she also talked to me for hours about how Srila Prabhupada loves everybody, how he knew everything, how the absolute truth is Krishna, how Krishna is God, and how I'm not my body. I thought, "Wow, these are coolest things I ever heard!"

Then Sranti left, and I was still in the material world. But every once in a while she came back, and once she invited me to a rock and roll concert at the Tampa Stadium with the Radha-Damodara Party. I thought, "No, I've got to work." I was an assistant manager at a Pizza Hut. Sranti said, "You've got to come because Radha-Damodara is out of this world." So I went. I realized that the devotees chanting and dancing were beautiful, but on the way home, when the devotees said, "You should come to the temple," I said, "No, I have to go to work." But they kept preaching to me and finally I decided to go to the temple. There I met Amarendra and Gayatri who fed me and enveloped me with love. I decided, "Okay, I'll stay the weekend." And not much later I said, "What happens if I don't want to go home?" Sranti said, "Yay!" The next week was my twenty-first birthday.

The next year, in May of 1976, I got initiated in Gainesville, Florida, on Lord Nrsimhadeva's appearance day, and in July I went to New York to attend Ratha-yatra. I was standing next to Kaulini's son, three-year-old Ramachandra, in the New York temple when Prabhupada walked in carrying his cane. Ramachandra was shaved up and had big beautiful eyes. As he immediately focused on Ramachandra, Prabhupada's eyes glistened and in a deep voice said, "Hare Krishna!"

For three days in New York we heard Srila Prabhupada's classes on the *Chaitanya-charitamrita* and made garlands for the carts. Then, while Prabhupada was on Subhadra's cart during Ratha-yatra, I helped pull that cart all the way to the park.

My husband and I left Krishna consciousness in the 1980s. We had two kids to feed, we went back to school, we were floundering, and, of course, *maya* poured many coats of lead on top of us. For eight or nine years we gave up chanting, hearing, and associating with devotees. Then my husband got multiple sclerosis. When his kidneys were failing he was supposed to go on a dialysis machine, but he decided he wasn't going to do that. He said to me, "Gopa, bring me my bead bag and my *Nectar of Devotion*." I thought, "What? Wow!" Finally he said, "Take me home. They're *rakshasas* in this hospital, they're taking my blood." I had to sign many papers to get him out, and five doctors were talking to me at one time telling me I was a murderer. I told them, "This is what he wants."

A week later he sat up in bed and said, "Hare . . . Hare . . . Hare . . . " I said, "He's leaving his body, he's leaving his body!" and immediately turned on a kirtan. I was running around, "My God, he's leaving his body! What should I do? What should I do?" But Srila Prabhupada was so kind and so merciful that although we hardly had done anything for him, he came through his instruction to tell my husband to chant Hare Krishna.

I was absorbed in the bodily concept of losing my husband so it wasn't until about a year-and-a-half later that I realized, "Srila Prabhupada came here just to help us. He is so kind and merciful that he gave us Krishna consciousness so we would know how to quit this material world. Krishna consciousness is where it's at. That's what it's all about."

Prabhupada pulled me back, and ever since then I wish I could do something for him. Every time I look at him, Prabhupada says, "Distribute my books." All the time I beg Srila Prabhupada to please let me be a dust particle at his lotus feet, to let me hang on somehow, and, "Please let me help you do something, even if it's in my next lifetime."

Gopalasapriya devi dasi

Gopalasapriya spent a month in the Ann Arbor temple before moving to New Vrindavan in 1975. In the fall of 1975 she was initiated. She saw Srila Prabhupada, and when he stayed for a while in New Vrindavan, she was able to experience his compassion.

When I first became a devotee, I hadn't met Prabhupada. I didn't know anything about Prabhupada though I had seen pictures of him all the time. I had seen *BTG*s and then I visited the temple in Ann Arbor and

Badrinarayana was in charge of that temple. I had no idea what it was all about, but somehow or other the vegetarian food and the chanting was attractive, and you know, the Indian clothing and the incense. I was drawn in by different things. I was wondering who Prabhupada was and why everyone was excited by him, why his picture was everywhere. I just didn't understand. But after I started staying in the temple there would be a tape of Prabhupada singing while we took *prasadam*. Badrinarayana would tell us stories of the different things that happened to him with Prabhupada and stories about Prabhupada. Just during that one month I started to think, "Yes, I see why everyone is so excited by Prabhupada."

Just hearing his voice and the way he spoke–you could hear the purity and the sincerity and the concern. It seemed he was so concerned about the conditioned souls and all the suffering that goes on in the world. Myself, I felt like I had been suffering. I was only twenty, twenty-one–I wasn't even twenty-one at that time. When I took initiation I was twenty-one. But I felt like I had been through the ringer in my twenty years of existence in the material world and just felt like I had no attraction to get involved in things anymore after the things I'd been through. The devotees seemed to have such a nice thing to offer. It felt so safe at the temple. I felt like I didn't have to worry anymore about a lot of things that I used to have to deal with that were very distasteful. The four regulative principles just made so much sense.

When he was here at New Vrindavan that summer of 1976, there were darshans up at the house where he was staying. The *vyasasana* was out on the grass.

It wasn't like everyone could go see him all at once. They kind of broke it down into smaller groups so that it wouldn't be too overwhelming. So maybe thirty or forty people would go one night, and another thirty or forty would go another night. The night that I was there with all the *sankirtana* women was the one time that he actually spoke to me.

We were all sitting outside and it was evening. The sun was starting to go down. It wasn't really warm out. Most of the devotees were wearing *chadars* or sweaters or something. I was sitting without any other kind of extra cloth. I just had on my *sari*. So he was just looking at me. He was saying, "Are you all right?" I didn't think he was talking to me. He had just paused. It was quiet for a few minutes and he was just looking at me and he said, "Are you all right?" Finally I just put my hand to my chest like, "Are you speaking to me?" He said, "Such a thin cloth, haven't you got a cloth?" I was sitting a little toward the back. I told him that I actually had one, I just didn't have it with me. But he didn't really hear that. He turned to Kuladri, who was standing near him–Kuladri was one of the main managers at the time–and he said, "You have to ask the women if they have everything they need and find out once a month if they do. Women really need to be protected." He said once a month you should go to them and find out if they need anything.

I remember when we were walking away, one of the devotees I was with was crying and just feeling so fortunate to be a disciple of Prabhupada and to see how much he just cared about everybody. Unfortunately, it doesn't seem like too many people took that instruction very seriously, but somehow that really struck me. I don't know, I've always kind of taken that on for a personal thing for me to do. I somehow have this really good feeling when I can give someone something they need. I started the thrift store because I would always have things. If someone needed a sweatshirt or anything special, I like to provide a basic material necessity. It seems for some reason that it's not too hard for me–I always have everything I need, so I like to help other people when they need things.

Govardhan devi dasi

Govardhan dasi first met the devotees in 1972, when they invited her to the temple in Manchester. She went and found that Krishna consciousness was what she'd been looking for; she loved it. And two weeks later–the day before her seventeenth birthday–she joined.

I was extremely pleased and gratified and felt good about myself to belong to something so unusual and spiritually strong and potent as the Hare Krishna movement. This was even before I met Srila Prabhupada. Once Kishore said, "How many of you haven't seen Prabhupada yet?" Many of us put our hands up and he said, "Just see, you've given your lives to Prabhupada and you haven't even seen him!" Later, in May of 1973, Prabhupada was going to the Bury Place temple in London, and all of us – the men and women together – went there, to that small, narrow temple room, and we all huddled in without distinction between the genders and had a long kirtan as we waited for Prabhupada to arrive.

A lot of what Prabhupada said in his classes went over my head. The Krishna conscious philosophy had inspired me to join, but it was who Prabhupada was and his causeless and complete acceptance of me that overwhelmed me. There was no reason for Prabhupada to accept me, but he did. The crown jewel of my life is that Srila Prabhupada accepted me as his disciple.

Later, Prabhupada was going to the airport to leave and all the devotees crowded into the temple vans like baggage to go to the airport to see him off. One Scottish devotee, Brahmajanani, was hanging onto the outside of a van shouting, "He's my spiritual master as well! I'm going to go as well!"

Somehow, after Prabhupada flew off, we couldn't fit into those same vans that had taken us to the airport. Prabhupada brought transcendental, spiritual potency with him that took us out of our bodily concept of life, that swept us off the mental platform, and that made us remember that we're eternal servants of Krishna.

In his darshan room at Bhaktivedanta Manor in the summer of 1973, Prabhupada personally gave me the Gayatri mantra. I was still seventeen. I paid my obeisances by the door and said, "*Nama om visnu-padaya ...*" I knew what every word of Prabhupada's *pranam mantra* meant – it gives me great pleasure to understand what I'm saying in different languages. And because Prabhupada was personally hearing me, I was smiling as I said it. When I looked up I saw that from across his large room Prabhupada was smiling at me. He patted the floor in a fatherly way as if to say, "Come and sit down here." I went over and he took the strip of paper I had with the Gayatri mantra faintly printed on it. He looked at it and said, "It requires transcendental eyes." I thought, "Wow!" Then he became grave. He told me the mantra and showed me how to count on my fingers.

I'm no one special but you don't have to be anyone special, you don't have to have seen Prabhupada or to have been initiated by him. If you love Prabhupada he loves you. I felt his love and I feel it's ongoing. He makes me feel protected and comforted like a girl with her father. When a person appreciates Prabhupada even momentarily, that stands in eternity and forges a link of love that won't go away. Why should Krishna and Prabhupada forget a soul who is able to put *maya* aside, even for a short time – time enough to join their Movement, to chant Hare Krishna, to see the Deity properly. These fleeting experiences forge a link that will never go away and when we're conscious of that link we feel close to Krishna and to Prabhupada. It's wonderful to feel that you belong, that you're protected, and it's got nothing to do with being a woman. It has to do with that yearning of the soul to be back home again; it's got to do with the pure soul seeking the pure devotee and the shelter of Krishna's lotus feet.

In a *Bhagavad-gita* purport Prabhupada writes, "One may not fully discharge the injunctions of the Lord, but because one is not resentful of this principle and works sincerely without consideration of defeat and hopelessness, he will surely be promoted to the stage of pure Krishna consciousness." We just keep doing what we can to serve and whatever spiritual advancement and ecstasy we feel is coming from Prabhupada's kindness because he's delivering Krishna to us and delivering us to Krishna.

My experience of Prabhupada's love and acceptance didn't come from those few times I was in his personal presence, because in those days I was an extremely shy, spaced-out girl. Those feelings that I've got now have come since then; they've come in Prabhupada's absence. It's a wonderful thing to have known that I was there at the right time and was able to come forward. But the bliss in Krishna consciousness is always available. It can be a small thing like reading in the *Krsna* book that Krishna takes His father's slippers on His head and brings them to His father. Whatever it is that devotees love about Krishna, whatever enlivens them, whether it's a kirtan or a class or a bit of *Krsna* book or their devotional service or association with each other, all of that ecstasy is coming to us because Prabhupada did what he did. We'd have no access to Krishna and the bliss of Krishna consciousness if it wasn't for Prabhupada. He's giving Krishna to every single one of us. That's Prabhupada's kindness and it's the same for everyone. Without Prabhupada there wouldn't be a Krishna consciousness movement, there wouldn't be any of this spiritual ocean that we bathe in. What he did was a wonderful, marvelous thing, and anyone who learns about it will find their heart overflowing with gratitude.

If we simply do some service, whether at the temple or in our home, remaining aloof from distractions, we'll get the nectar Prabhupada has to give. By sharing things that make us blissful we'll go back to Godhead together. Prabhupada will reciprocate with our prayers to him and will allow us to rejoin our eternal family. We're an eternal part and parcel of Krishna and we're taking steps, however "baby" they may be, to revive our consciousness of that.

And we all have a special relationship with Prabhupada; he knows us whether we had a lot of association with him or not (and I'm one who didn't). He knows our hearts and our service because he's in close touch with Krishna. So how could we abandon him, or he us?

Just thinking about Prabhupada is distressing, but it's blissful and sweet as well. I feel close to him and as time goes on he means more and more to me. Prabhupada displayed and mirrored Krishna's attractiveness; in this world there was nothing like Prabhupada's attractiveness. And he acknowledges our desire to serve him, even though our service is insignificant. Srila Prabhupada is irresistible. I just adore him. His love is causeless and all of us are dear to him. What could we be or have done to "deserve" that love of his?

Govinda dasi

Govinda dasi met Srila Prabhupada in January of 1967, just after his arrival in San Francisco for the Mantra Rock Dance. She was a senior art student at the University of Texas, so he engaged her in artwork for his temples, books, and Back to Godhead *magazine. She served as his secretary, servant, and cook for over a year until January of 1969, when she was sent to spread Krishna consciousness in the Hawaiian Islands.*

In San Francisco, my husband Goursundar and I daily relished Srila Prabhupada's kirtans and classes. He also gave me many personal instructions for depicting art of the spiritual world. Once I asked about the color of Krishna's eyes, and with a faraway look of love he replied, "Blackish!" I felt he was actually seeing Krishna in the room!

For two years, from January of 1967 until January of 1969, I was with Prabhupada almost continuously. After his heart attack in May 1967, my husband and I served him at the New Jersey seashore for weeks. That was the most wonderful time of my life. There, I heard wonderful Krishna pastimes from him and also experienced his love and concern for me as his spiritual daughter. Daily I would pick roses for his room while softly singing Hare Krishna. He told my husband, "Govinda dasi is simple-hearted. This is good for bhakti."

Early on, Prabhupada studied our lives. He asked questions like "Can you drive? Can you swim?" He understood that both boys and girls are educated similarly in the West. So he patterned his ISKCON like this; he encouraged both his sons and his daughters to study scripture, give classes, lead kirtans, create temples, and preach to the world about Krishna. He engaged everyone according to his or her abilities and psychophysical nature of each disciple. He encouraged us to dovetail our existing talents for service to Krishna as the perfection of life.

In early 1967, Prabhupada held classes in Sanskrit for my husband and me. Each day he would recite the Sanskrit alphabets and we would imitate. One morning he taught me the beautiful *shloka: vande sri-krishna-chaitanya, nityanandau sahoditau, gaudodaye pushpavantau, chitrau sandau tamonudau.* This verse describes Lord Chaitanya and Lord Nityananda as the simultaneous rising of the sun and the moon. Every morning he then asked, "Govinda dasi, you have remembered that verse?" And I would chant it for him as he had taught, and he would beam and chuckle with delight. It seemed to give him great joy to hear a young American girl chanting *shlokas* glorifying Lord Chaitanya and Lord Nityananda. He wanted all of his disciples to learn *shlokas* and preach Their glories all over the world.

Prabhupada once said to my husband, "Govinda dasi is a very beautiful young girl. Don't try to enjoy her, send her to Krishna. Krishna likes all beautiful young girls!" Girls coming to his Movement should know that their soft hearts are very attractive to Krishna, and their loving attempts to serve Him are much appreciated by Srila Prabhupada.

When Jagannatha Deities arrived in New York, Prabhupada explained, "Just see how They are riding on the chariot with Balarama on one side and Krishna on the other, and Their sister Subhadra is sitting between Them. Krishna and Balarama are protecting Her from all harm. I would like that the boys in our Movement should protect our girls, just like Krishna and Balarama are protecting Their Sister Subhadra." So Prabhupada's definition of protection was like this. It was loving protection, as if we were sisters, not oppression or abuse.

Often he said, "I want that you all should work together to spread this Hare Krishna movement all over the world. This will save everyone from all calamities. It will change the face of this earth planet!" Prabhupada wanted that his boy and girl disciples work cooperatively and spread Krishna consciousness everywhere, and that did indeed happen in the beginning. Yamuna, Malati, Jadurani, Palika, Rukmini, and others are great stalwart examples of this. But due to the ambitious nature of some of the men, this original concept got perverted and often became one of misogyny and abuse. Prabhupada tried to correct this, but after he left everything changed–from instructions on how to deal with one another, to kirtans, even to his books! So now we must try to recapture the original mood given us by Srila Prabhupada.

In 1968, for a whole wonderful year I served as Prabhupada's secretary, taking dictation as well as typing his letters, transcribing his books, as well as cooking his *prasadam*. Prabhupada would sometimes say, "We have become just like a family."

In May of 1968, I was sitting in Prabhupada's room taking dictation when my husband came in and asked, "Swamiji, can I call Govinda dasi 'Govindaji'?" Prabhupada replied, "No, 'ji' is a very third class form of address." So I asked, "Then why are we calling you 'Swami-ji'?" He was very humble, saying it was not so important. But I insisted that it was indeed important to us, and that we wanted to address him in the most respectful manner. He then said, "Srila Prabhupada is nice."

He explained, "Srila Prabhupada means the great master at whose lotus feet all masters take shelter. Prabhu means 'master.' You are all masters who have taken shelter of me, the Prabhupada. So you should all call one another as Prabhu, all of you who have taken shelter of me, the Prabhupada." He told all of us, boys and girls alike, to always address one another in this way. Nowadays the word "prabhu" has taken on a gender connotation, but Prabhupada, who knew Sanskrit, didn't relate it to gender. Rather, it was related to our personal relationship to him as "the Prabhupada." He called me "Govinda dasi Prabhu," and my husband "Goursundar Prabhu," and others, such as "Malati Prabhu," even in letters. This had the effect of instilling in us respect for one another, regardless of gender.

Years later, Prabhupada ordered me to sculpt Gaura-Nitai Deities and send Them to all temples. It was an important project, one very dear to his heart. But I was blocked at every angle by the *sannyasi* in charge of Honolulu.

When Prabhupada heard about this, he began exclaiming, "Why?! Why?! Why?!" each time louder than the last. He was practically roaring, "WHY?!" Then he shook his head in disgust and said, "What can I do?" He knew that he could not always control the independent mentality of his strong-willed leaders. I never did get to make those Deities and became heartbroken that for the first time I was unable to fulfill Srila Prabhupada's request of me.

When departing Kumbha Mela in 1977, one *sannyasi* wanted to leave me and one godsister and her young child behind at the Mela. Some twenty million people were there, so this would have spelled disaster for us. Prabhupada became adamant and exclaimed, "The women and children will come with us!" He protected us from harm, and we traveled in the train compartment next to his.

Because of our austere lifestyle of traveling from place to place and preaching all over, especially in India, Prabhupada once told me, "You are not a woman, you are something else!" Often women are materialistic, attached to clothes and jewelry and family. But Prabhupada's daughters were not like this. They were like soldiers, willing to undergo any type of austerity to serve Lord Chaitanya's mission, and they still are. He often said, "You have all been sent by my Guru Maharaja to help me."

In 1969 Prabhupada sent me to Hawaii. He said, "Preach to the people, they are suffering, although they do not know it," and a tear of compassion trickled down his cheek. He also said, "You are a good cook, an excellent secretary, and you are serving me very nicely. Only problem, you are a woman and I am *sannyasi*." Since my husband had already left for Hawaii, his concern was that a *sannyasi* may be criticized for having a girl disciple serving in close proximity, even though he was the age of my grandfather. Srila Prabhupada was above all criticism, but the people of the world are not.

I prayed to Krishna that I would always be allowed to visit Prabhupada wherever he was. He was like my beloved father. I prayed like this because later on there were many wonderful godbrothers but some were agitated and even cruel, and the weird attitudes toward women had begun. Once in 1974, Prabhupada was in Honolulu and I was halfway up the stairs to his room when a *sannyasi* blocked me, saying, "You can't come. He's resting!" At that very moment, Prabhupada opened his door and called out, "*Ah*, Govinda dasi, come on!" Prabhupada foresaw everything. He saw the problems with his men and often tried to correct them. He even said they should to go to the forest if they were so agitated by the presence of ladies.

In my own life, I have been greatly blessed by having Srila Prabhupada as my beloved father, spiritual master, and "well-wisher" since my youth. I was also blessed to have a brilliant husband, who was an accomplished devotee as well as a Sanskrit and Bengali scholar, and one whom I loved very much. Indeed, my husband did the transliteration for Srila Prabhupada's *Chaitanya-charitamrita,* while I transcribed the taped chapters. His articles and lectures were appreciated by many. However, even such brilliance can be hazardous, for scholars often become enamored with their own scholarship. Such superior intelligence can easily become an ego trap. As in the case of my husband, after he left the temple, Srila Prabhupada made the famous comment, "He is suffering from the disease of too much intelligence. He now thinks he knows more than his spiritual master!" Soon after my husband left, I received a letter in April of 1974, wherein Srila Prabhupada wrote, "Forget this nonsense [husband]. These are all material relationships and have nothing to do with spiritual advancement."

Srila Prabhupada's favorite part of *Srimad-Bhagavatam* was the chapter "Prayers of Queen Kunti." He explained that her simple-hearted love for Krishna, her dedication and devotion are exemplary for everyone–regardless of gender. He would sometimes point out that women by nature are gentle because they are meant for motherhood, which is the most selfless love in this material world. He would say that their hearts are not crooked with ambition and false ego, so they can more easily surrender to the Supreme Lord. He would point out that in every church, temple, or mosque there are mostly women and few men because, he would explain, women generally lack the hardened false ego of men. It is men who exploit them, create wars, and suffering, and women become misguided by such men. But, Srila Prabhupada would also say, "If women have a good guru, or a good husband or guide, they can very quickly make spiritual advancement."

In January of 1977 in Bhubaneswar, Srila Prabhupada stayed in a cow dung hut that he loved. He was sitting outside with the sunlight shimmering on his golden face, softly chanting *japa.* I was sitting on the ground nearby. Meditatively, he looked out over the freshly plowed fields and prophesied, "So the fields have been plowed, and now some plants are starting to grow and they will become small bushes. And in due course of time they will grow into big trees, and then they will bear fruit." Then, spreading his arms wide he exclaimed, "*Ah,* then you shall see what is this movement of Lord Chaitanya!"

For those devotees who had no personal association with Srila Prabhupada, he said, "I am present in my books." Srila Prabhupada is not limited by time and space as we are. He is available to everyone even now in his books, pictures, and *murtis.*

In spite of all difficulties, we need to maintain faith that Srila Prabhupada is ever watching over us, cheering us on, and encouraging us to use our lives fully in the service of Krishna, whether it is by preaching, serving as *pujaris,* creating temples, raising our children to be devotees, whatever service is given to us by Krishna. Let us do this with the feeling of being loved and protected beneath the shelter of his lotus feet–as "the Prabhus who have taken shelter of the Prabhupada."

Gunamai (Gunamayi) devi dasi

Gunamayi was born and raised in Laguna Beach, California and always was a sort of seeker. During the 1960s everyone experienced a period of change, with a curious gaze towards the East looking at all that it offered in the form of philosophy, yoga, mysticism, self exploration, gurus, and incense. It was in the ether and everyone could feel it.

After graduating in 1968, I thought deeply about what I was going to do with the rest of my life. I wondered how I fit in, because I couldn't imagine the normal agenda. Apart from the music, I wasn't much into the "get high" life of the 1960s. I was a vegetarian and fasted, which brought me a higher sense of awareness and more questions.

There was a bookstore along Coast Highway called "Mystic Arts." They stocked spiritual books and paraphernalia related to India. In one room were photos of gurus and saints lined up on a wall. There were photos of bearded, stereotypical gurus, some lof whom looked a bit sleazy, and I wasn't impressed. Then my eyes landed on a picture of A. C. Bhaktivedanta. Instantly I thought, *This man is completely honest, and he knows God.* His eyes had a compassionate gaze into the soul. I was sold.

Later, I heard devotees chanting on the streets and received a BTG, which had an article explaining how to offer your food. I thought, *Oh, that's what's missing. Food isn't just for eating.* I read *Bhagavad-gita*, *The Nectar of Devotion*, and *Krsna* book in a very short time. The first thing that attracted me was how the names sounded: Balarama, Krishna, Radha, Sri Chaitanya, the cowherd boys, the *gopis*. Everything made perfect sense. My first Sunday Feast at the temple in Laguna Canyon was after I had fasted. The taste was otherworldly, but I couldn't understand why these "yogis" would eat so much!

When I heard that Srila Prabhupada was going to lecture in Los Angeles I had to go! It was raining hard and I had never been there by myself, but I headed out in my old 1950's bread truck. When I first saw Prabhupada I felt like I was seeing a god. He was effulgent and seemed all knowing.

I was at the temple when they first played "Govindam." The heavens opened up to an indescribable, transcendental transportation.

As a devotee living in the temple, we would wear polyester *saris* which we took from a communal stock everyone shared. We packed into vans to go for *harinama* on the streets of Hollywood and Vishnujana often led.

Soon we moved to Watseka Avenue and Srila Prabhupada was with us. There I was initiated along with four others in April 1971.

I used to stay up late painting. One night I was working on a painting of Krishna and Arjuna to give to Prabhupada. I had a premonition and suddenly I was called up to his room. Prabhupada's kindness is hardly anything that can be put into words. I was wondering how I could be in the presence of such a great personality. He wanted me to help illustrate the *Bhagavad-gita*, but I felt unqualified and never completed that service. Rather he had me paint the disciplic succession. He asked if I liked my name and said I could come up and see him any time.

His presence with us was like living in a transcendental bubble. Meeting Srila Prabhupada felt as if it was fated, as if I was handpicked to be in this *sankirtana* pastime led by Srila Prabhupada. It was above all, his loving kindness that softened my heart so that I could receive the transcendental message of Godhead and chant Hare Krishna. *Jaya* Nimai, *Jaya* Nitai!

Gunavati devi dasi

After reading a friend's BTGs, Gunavati started going to the Melbourne temple. In February of 1973, she saw Srila Prabhupada there and his compassion and wisdom overwhelmed her. She knew he was from the spiritual world and was capable of taking her there.

When I first saw Srila Prabhupada I immediately accepted him as my spiritual master and for the first time in my life cried cold tears. I was amazed that such a swan-like person could exist, floating through this horrible Kali-yuga. All my questions were answered in his books and lectures and the only question left was, "How can I serve you?" When I got initiated, Prabhupada said, "Gunavati is a very nice name. It means 'one who possesses all good qualities.' " As guru *dakshina*, I gave him a pair of handmade pink slippers with laces on them.

I have a strong attachment to and absolute faith in Srila Prabhupada as Krishna's pure representative. He was exemplary in the way he executed loving service to Krishna; he was the highest example of selfless pure devotional service. When I open a book or listen to a lecture I feel connected to him; he's there. When I read his Conversations books I'm at all the darshans I missed. Srila Prabhupada's completely transcendental personality and his incredible example inspires and enlivens me, as does the association of devotees who are dedicated to him.

I was a suffering lost soul who didn't know which direction to turn. Srila Prabhupada changed my life completely. It was hard in the beginning because the temple was small and crowded; nobody knew anything, and the men were mean to the women. But my attachment to Prabhupada and my faith in him kept me going through all those tough tests. As long as I stay under the shelter of his lotus feet I know I'm connected to the *parampara*.

Guru Charana Padma devi dasi

Originally from a Jewish background, Guru Charana Padma was on a spiritual search. She practiced Transcendental Meditation, read all sorts of spiritual literature, and then left university to go to Israel. In Amsterdam she got a Bhagavad-gita and a Back to Godhead, and throughout Europe she kept meeting devotees. She thought, "God is trying to tell me something."

During the two days I was in Israel I developed a strong desire to go to Vrindavan and explore Krishna consciousness. I journeyed overland on a bus, which took three or four weeks, and visited Vrindavan in July 1975, when it was 140 degrees. During my return trip, also overland, I was chanting the holy names. When I arrived at my home in Winnipeg, my parents didn't know what had happened because I was talking about Krishna. I was supposed to return to my university, but I was increasingly frustrated with material life and only wanted to immerse myself in spiritual life. I dreamt about devotees and developed a longing to be with them.

Eventually I read the whole set of *Chaitanya-charitamritas* that were in the university library, and in November 1976 finally joined the Chicago temple. At Chicago's O'Hare Airport I got a taste for book distribution, became one of the top distributors, and, immersed in and focused on serving Srila Prabhupada, I pushed myself to the limits. Through this service and through the people I met, I felt connected to Srila Prabhupada and felt his reciprocation. Tripurari, Praghosa, and Vaisesika were also there and all of us were unified in trying to please Srila Prabhupada by distributing his books. In April 1977, when I was twenty-one, I was initiated.

I never saw Srila Prabhupada and have lived a life of service in separation from him. But by his mercy and the company of my godsisters and godbrothers, whose great love for him gives me strength and increases my faith, I'm still here. I prayed for my children and it gives me extra faith that they've also developed a taste for the holy name and a love for Srila Prabhupada. I'm fortunate. With the young children I teach at the Manor *gurukula*, I try to share Srila Prabhupada's life and mission and help them develop some commitment and taste.

My life is an example of how we can have a relationship with Srila Prabhupada and feel connected to him by following his instructions. Now I intensely want to strengthen my relationship and connection by studying his books and properly reflecting what he said.

Harakanta devi dasi

Ever since she was a little girl, Harakanta felt that her real life wasn't the one she was living. She was always searching for that real life, that place where she belonged.

In the winter of 1974, some friends that I had gone to school with stopped over to visit me and my boyfriend. They had been to the Boston temple and were eager to tell us about Krishna consciousness. We talked for hours; I was amazed at how the philosophy they were presenting was giving satisfying answers for all my questions. That following Sunday we went to the temple for the first time. We attended the program and met devotees. We bought lecture tapes and a *Bhagavad-gita*, and after that started regularly reading and hearing from Srila Prabhupada. We lived over an hour away from the temple and were busy with our garden and orchard, so our visits to the temple were infrequent.

What stands out in my memory is that the devotees I met there were filled with such happiness. Their love for Srila Prabhupada was palatable and contagious. They were totally absorbed in devotional service, and by being with them I met Srila Prabhupada, felt his love, and found the home I had been searching for.

The devotees kindly manifest Srila Prabhupada's magnanimity and took the time to guide us in our new quest for Krishna consciousness. They visited us on the farm, engaged us in growing vegetables for the temple, taught us how to cook and offer our food, and encouraged us to chant sixteen rounds. We started to serve at the temple, too—the new building needed to have its temple room floor structurally upgraded to support all the ecstatic dancing! So my boyfriend worked until that was accomplished. I got to sew for the devotees and eventually for the Deities.

In the summer of 1976 Srila Prabhupada was scheduled to be in New York for the Ratha-yatra. Yola and Gus, our new devotee friends, had a prosperous flower business in Boston, and they were going to bring a vanload of flowers to NY, so we hitched a ride with them. We went to the morning program at the Radha-Govinda Mandir, a large room filled with a sea of excited devotees, all looking forward to the Ratha-yatra and, of course, seeing Srila Prabhupada!

I was in the front foyer when Srila Prabhupada returned from his morning walk. The doors opened to the sidewalk, where there was an ocean of saffron-clad *sannyasis* moving devotees aside to create a path. Srila Prabhupada entered with an elegance and grace I had never seen. His feet did not appear to touch the ground as one would expect. It was surreal. The devotees took up every inch of space in the foyer, and they all offered obeisances the moment he walked in. I could find no space to bow down in, so I folded my hands and watched Prabhupada pass, effulgent and carrying a depth of love unknown to me. I couldn't take my eyes off him, but yet I felt I wanted to hide from him. (I offered my obeisances after he had walked by.)

Srila Prabhupada gave class, and there was *guru-puja*, after which he distributed cookies to the children and then to the women. I was too shy to go up, but Vijaya devi dasi pushed me from behind until I stood in front of Srila Prabhupada. He looked at me–he really looked at me, all the way through, all the details of my many lives exposed, everything revealed. What an incredible feeling of being so small, honestly humbled, yet not judged. He extended his hand with the gift of a cookie, and I extended mine to accept it. He pushed it into my hand with a firmness I didn't expect. A moment's association, a moment of eye contact, a moment of physical contact in a room filled with hundreds of people–that was my only meeting with Srila Prabhupada, yet it was a very personal reconnection.

That winter we moved into the Boston temple, and when spring came my boyfriend returned to the farm and I stayed at the temple. In the fall of 1977, a few of us received formal initiation by letter from Srila Prabhupada. Shortly thereafter, while in my infancy as an initiate, Srila Prabhupada left this world. I felt lost.

I followed the flow of temple life and accepted the changing conditions. Satsvarupa Maharaja gave me second initiation on behalf of Srila Prabhupada in the spring of 1978 (he said Srila Prabhupada would have given it to me anyway). I was then sent to the New York temple to serve.

Srila Prabhupada has continued to guide this aspiring disciple through his books and lectures. It's truly amazing how if I need a question answered he gives the perfect purport at the perfect time. His lectures have corrected my misunderstandings. He comes to me in dreams, instructing me to do a certain service or patting me on the head when I offer my obeisances to him. I see his hand in the lessons that life presents on my path, and feel his love when I cry out to him from the pain of those lessons. The more I keep him in my thoughts, the more I feel him reciprocating. Srila Prabhupada is still preaching and pushing on his Movement. Just look and listen for him. He is available for all who seek him out.

Harilila devi dasi

When Harilila was a child, her father used to tell her, "When you grow older, you'll discover God for yourself." When she was older, she found herself searching for more out of life than simple materialism, so she left her native England for Africa, where she lived in a mud hut, taught high school students, and learned how to do without newspapers, radio, and TV.

Everyone has a long journey before they become interested in spiritual life and begin to seek out a spiritual master. I'd been searching for something since I was eight. At eighteen, I went to a Greek island, and while there I felt God's presence in the sheer beauty of His creation. I couldn't believe I'd spent my life not knowing much about His existence. Yet I wasn't satisfied with what I found out about Him.

When I was a young woman, I was good at giving speeches and getting crowds of people to agree with me. Once somebody told me, "You were overwhelming. I don't remember a word you said, but it was great." At that point I vowed to myself that I wouldn't speak before crowds until I had something worthwhile to say.

I loved the African people and appreciated the simple life I had in Africa, but after two years of living there I went to India in search of spiritual knowledge. I wanted to fill up inside, to become internally strong. When I was on a beach in South India a *sadhu* told me, "If you really want to know spiritual life, you should go to Mayapur and Sri Caitanya Mahaprabhu." I never made it to Mayapur–I spent my time in Nepal, which is where I met my first Hare Krishna devotees. I helped them paint and set up the small altar in the first temple there. Krishna was guiding me along my path even though I didn't make it to Mayapur at that time.

After Nepal, I traveled through Pakistan, Afghanistan, and Iran. Then, back in England, I taught in the slums for some time, then went to Canada, where I met my first husband, Nitai-pada, who introduced me to ISKCON and Krishna consciousness. He used to read me stories about Krishna and we'd chant together.

In the different books I'd read before Prabhupada's, the authors were waffling or guessing: "God may be this or may be that." But Srila Prabhupada said, "Krishna is God." My first connection with Srila Prabhupada was realizing that he knew God. I read *Teachings of Lord Chaitanya* and found it so profound and exact that when I finished it I found myself crying. I felt an intense personal connection with Srila Prabhupada and knew he was my guru.

When people ask me if I had a personal connection with Prabhupada, I never know what to say, because I did have one: Srila Prabhupada was right there with me and we made a connection that's never left me. I'd found the person I was looking for, the person who could bring me to God. Srila Prabhupada was the culmination of my spiritual journey.

Nitai-pada and I hitchhiked throughout the States, stopping at different temples along the way. In 1975 we went to the Vancouver temple and never left. I have spent most of my devotional life serving Srila Prabhupada in Vancouver and at Sharanagati, and I feel blessed to have found such a wonderful and inspiring spiritual family.

I brought up my children with Srila Prabhupada, and they love him. Srila Prabhupada is a disperser of spiritual knowledge; he epitomizes all the wealth of Krishna consciousness. If we understand how great he is, that understanding will invoke our love for him and for Krishna. Srila Prabhupada embodied the compassionate understanding that comes from knowing Krishna. He's our lodestone; the root of our Krishna consciousness, and he links us to the *parampara* and to Krishna. If we feel that link, we will always have stability in Krishna consciousness.

Many times Srila Prabhupada helped me. My husband died. I had a car accident. I was lonely, deeply distressed, and crying inside. It was a very difficult time for me. I prayed to Srila Prabhupada, "I'm yours. You have to help me. I can't do this on my own," and then everything changed.

Srila Prabhupada looks after us. If we can get bedrock faith in him and Krishna, we can deal with anything. That faith comes by reading, practicing, experiencing, thinking, wanting, searching, chanting, association. Our link with Srila Prabhupada, with the *parampara*, with the Lord in our heart, brings us everything.

Harinama devi dasi

Harinama made a decision in high school that because the world was so harsh, she would not show her emotions to anyone. She decided she would have a face in public that never cried or showed weakness. She described herself as a "tough cookie." But when she was one of the girls dropping flower petals onto Srila Prabhupada from above a walkway, she was amazed to find tears gushing from her eyes.

I didn't think anybody could make me cry that fast. Srila Prabhupada didn't have false ego so there was no difference between his pictures, his lectures, and seeing him. There was no disappointment, there was no, "Oh, I thought that . . ." It was as if the person that I'd heard and seen in the pictures just came to life and was standing and walking into the temple room where we all were.

I went to Philadelphia with Ananga Manjari for a Ratha-yatra there. I kept her in my sight because I knew she was determined to see Prabhupada. When I didn't see her for five minutes, I knew something was up. So I found out she had gone across the street. Sure enough Balavanta was standing guard. She was just about to go upstairs, so I grabbed hold of her, and she grabbed me, and we went upstairs. A press conference was to be held and there was a low table that Srila Prabhupada would sit at. Ananga Manjari made sure we were in the front so that if the room filled up it would be very uncomfortable to try to get us out. Ananga was very bold.

I think what surprised me the most is Srila Prabhupada's gracefulness because I was close enough to be able to watch his movements. There was one reporter who was very intelligent and she asked good questions, but she was challenging. Prabhupada answered her in a curt way, in a very short way. Another lady reporter had put on a *sari*. It seemed she wanted to please Srila Prabhupada. She appreciated him and had more of a mood of submission. Even though her questions were not particularly clever, Srila Prabhupada would elaborate at great length. But when the other woman would ask questions, then Prabhupada would be a little short.

At one point he was putting some sugar in his tea and I thought, "How amazing. . . . He's going to drop the spoon." It didn't seem he was using any effort, the spoon just sort of lifted. And then when he held the cup I thought, "That cup's going to fall to the ground." Because the cup lifted effortlessly. It was very beautiful to watch him do even simple things because of his grace. I thought, "Now I understand what it means to observe somebody who is swan-like."

When I look back on my years of *sankirtana*, Krishna was very clever because I was very competitive. In those days, the boys and the girls were pitted against each other for *sankirtana* scores. I wanted to be the best and the most austere – there was a lot of ego there. And, of course, I wanted to please Srila Prabhupada and I believed what Prabhupada said, that these books would save people. I wanted to help in the world because there was so much suffering.

There was a large window just a few feet from where Srila Prabhupada stood doing *arati* for Srila Bhaktisiddhanta Sarasvati Thakura. A few of us had the same idea at the same time. We all ran out to the window and clamored to see Prabhupada. I thought, "This is amazing. We're all piled on top of each other, boys and girls, and nobody could care less." We were just focused on Srila Prabhupada, and whatever enmity had been there because of our neophyte condition completely dissolved. We were just concentrating on Srila Prabhupada. It was wonderful.

I was very proud of my intelligence, which now I'm completely embarrassed about. I used to ask questions, but they were abstruse questions. They weren't questions that made any difference on the path of bhakti. They were the kinds of questions that a *jnani* would ask like, "There is the *virata-rupa*, the Karana Ocean, and the material world. Exactly where is this and where is that?" Like who really cares, right?

Anyway, Srila Prabhupada had said something in his lecture that had sparked one of those questions and I was very close to the *vyasasana*. So I was on fire to get that question answered. I thought that the question was the most important question in the whole wide world and I had my hand waving all over the place. Prabhupada never called on me. I was in complete shock, "How can he not see me? I'm right in front of him with my hand waving, he must see me." He didn't call on me, and I couldn't believe it. I wondered, "How could I not get my question answered?" So, as is always with the pure devotee of the Lord, they are great teachers, and if one day we finally get the lesson, then we can consider ourselves very blessed because it was something very particular for your journey. So it's something that I've often reflected on.

In Atlanta, Srila Prabhupada played *mridanga* for the first time in many years and he taught us how to sing "Parama Karuna." That was also the shortest arrival lecture that he ever gave because wherever he began to speak he would say, "Oh, these are the most beautiful Deities." But he was crying and he couldn't go on. That was really something to see how moved he was in speaking of the mercy of Sri Sri Gaura-Nitai.

Because Srila Prabhupada said that he was in his books, they have really been a shelter for me. Prabhupada's books have been an incredible shelter and guide and a very powerful process of purification. I have full faith that *Bhagavatam* is nondifferent from Krishna and that any good which has developed in my life is directly from Prabhupada's mercy through his books and through his wonderful disciples who have taken his mood and mission to heart. I'm so grateful for all of them.

I also want to encourage everyone to listen to Srila Prabhupada directly and to hear from those who have really absorbed his mood, because that direct connection is so powerful. Srila Prabhupada is without envy. He only came to this world to deliver us out of such deep compassion that we don't even have an ability to understand it.

As I've traveled I've met many people who don't listen to Srila Prabhupada's tapes; they only listen to the lectures of their guru. I think it's very important to listen to the lectures of your guru, but it's so important to listen to the words of Srila Prabhupada because those words are very powerful. They will give deeper insight into the relationship that anyone has with their guru because that's where the knowledge and the inspiration is coming from.

Haripuja devi dasi

At nineteen, Haripuja joined the Pittsburgh temple in Pennsylvania in 1971. She was initiated there by a letter from Srila Prabhupada in 1972 after writing him a letter requesting initiation.

I was a simple devotee in the Pittsburgh temple going out on daily *sankirtana*, selling incense, taking care of the altar, and Tulasi Devi.

One day the roadshow came with Vishnujana Swami. I was offered the opportunity to use some of my artistic talents in the roadshow and I accepted. So I was "traded" for a cook who stayed behind. The roadshow took me to Brooklyn where I soon got married to Kirtiraja dasa in 1973.

We soon went to Calcutta, India where we saw Srila Prabhupada. One day he expressed his happiness to see the Polish Consulate's wife attending *arati*. Someone told Srila Prabhupada that Kirtiraja was of Polish ancestry and Srila Prabhupada said, "You should go there and preach."

Later Kirtiraja and I were living in Los Angeles and I had given birth to our daughter Raga. On Prabhupada's visit to Los Angeles in 1975 he told Kirtiraja, "Go to Poland immediately. I want that our preaching be pushed in the Eastern European countries. You are an intelligent boy and I know that you will be successful in preaching there."

We left the comforts of Los Angeles and went to Poland in the middle of the winter with our one-year-old daughter, Raga.

At that time, Poland was very bleak and gray. The sky, the buildings, and people's clothing were all gray. Finding food that would suit a one-year-old child was very difficult. Carrots, potatoes, and cabbage was about all that was available.

When we first arrived, we rented all ten beds in a hostel so that we could have some privacy. But it was cold and damp and the cement floors seemed to increase the cold and damp. It was seriously austere.

We decided we'd make sweets and go to hotel lobbies to distribute them and meet people. Whoever we met, all week long, we invited to come to a Sunday Feast at a professor's home. I would cook the best I could with the limited ingredients available.

Srila Prabhupada wrote to us encouraging words. "I am very happy that you are taking a chance for Krishna, do everything very carefully and sincerely. Krishna will help you."

I wanted to participate in this exciting preaching mission, but I was a twenty-three-year-old new mother in a foreign communistic country in the middle of a gray winter who didn't know the language or have one friend outside of my husband. I was very concerned with my inability to adapt.

Srila Prabhupada wrote again, "I am very pleased to note your activities in Poland. If you can arrange for the translation of my books into Polish that would please me very much. I am pleased that you have taken so much courage and I pray that Krishna will bless you with more and more success."

We lost our place of residence and decided to temporarily leave Poland and try to figure out a solution. I was not very happy performing the austerities of living in a frigid hostel.

My husband wrote to Srila Prabhupada of our dilemma and he wrote back, "What can I advise if your wife doesn't want to take inconvenience. Preaching means some inconvenience. There is no reason you need to be settled in one place. My advice is that you preach together."

I was devastated. I had displeased my spiritual master. I was not strong enough to live in those conditions in Poland and preach. I worried day and night.

One night Srila Prabhupada came to me in my dream. He was ascending a staircase, much like the one at Schloss Reterschoff in Germany. Srila Prabhupada looked at me and I said, "I will preach in Poland and the communist countries!"

Srila Prabhupada said, "Thank you very much."

Prabhupada went up a few stairs and then turned and looked at me again. I looked at him and said," I will preach in the communist countries, Srila Prabhupada!"

Srila Prabhupada again said with complete acceptance of me, "Thank you very much."

When I woke from the dream, it was confirmed within my heart that Srila Prabhupada would give me the will, confidence, strength, and ability to preach his mission with my husband and family in the communist countries.

We moved to England and then onward to Sweden. We spent twelve years getting books translated, printed, and distributed in many languages of Eastern Europe, Poland, and the Soviet Union, as it was called then.

We always felt that we were just puppets in the hands of Srila Prabhupada in his mission to spread the glories of the Lord through the *sankirtana* mission.

It was such a spiritual pleasure to be involved in such a mission in the communist countries. As Srila Prabhupada said, "Preaching in the snows of Russia is sweeter than any mango."

Hrimati devi dasi

Hrimati, an animal lover, decided to become a vegetarian when she was eleven. Later, her twin brother gave her an old "Govindam" single record, sung by Yamuna devi and others. The album cover had on it a picture of Krishna worshiping a cow. As Hrimati was already a vegetarian, it was significant to her that God was worshiping a cow. Sometime after that, on hearing Srila Prabhupada's voice she was drawn to him. She learned English by listening to Prabhupada's lecture tapes. When she was fifteen, disappointed with her family and religion, she came to Krishna consciousness.

I felt Srila Prabhupada was my father and I longed to see him. I was in Germany when he visited Sweden, so I boarded a Sweden-bound train and, while traveling, crocheted a hat of soft white angora wool for him. I wanted to do something for Prabhupada, not just to take from him. The next morning, Prabhupada wore the hat I'd made. He buttoned it under his chin.

Srila Prabhupada went to Uppsala University to lecture, and when he entered the hall, I fell flat on the floor in full *dandavats* (as all the women and men did), not realizing my stretched out arms were blocking his *vyasasana*. Srila Prabhupada stepped on both my hands as he walked to the *vyasasana*. It was a wonderful feeling–he was light and his lotus feet were soft. Prabhupada was not of this world.

In 1976, I was pregnant with my second baby when I went to India with my son, Raghunatha, who was almost two. I delivered the baby in Vrindavan on Prabhupada's Vyasa-puja day. When my baby was fourteen days old, Prabhupada was sitting behind his desk in his room in Vrindavan when Himavati put my daughter onto Prabhupada's lap and rubbed her head into Prabhupada's feet. He raised his arms and smiled, "Oh, so small!" and then talked about his childhood and children while my daughter lay on his lap. I told him she was born on his appearance day, and Prabhupada smiled and named her Nandini. I asked what it meant, and he said, "Oh, there was so much excitement around that day for Nanda Maharaja with his daughter and son." Srila Prabhupada put everything in relation to Krishna, not himself.

Once at the Hyderabad farm, where there was no running water or much to eat, at one o'clock in the morning I heard Prabhupada translating his books. He was selflessly serving Krishna with dedication and determination that were beyond my comprehension.

At that farm, my son used to cry so much that Prabhupada became angry. He said, "Why is your son crying twenty-four hours a day? Can't you take care of him?" I hadn't seen that side of Prabhupada and wanted to disappear in the ground. I was speechless and felt bad. Sometime later, after his massage, Prabhupada was sitting in a chair in the sun with one leg down and one leg on his knee, wearing a *dhoti* but no *kurta*. My son showed him a homemade book of paintings of Krishna from the German *Krsna* Book. Prabhupada rubbed my son's head, hugged him, and together they looked at the paintings. My son said, "Oh, here is Krishna." Prabhupada looked at me, smiled, and said, "Now your son wants to make friends with me." Prabhupada had kindness in his eyes as he gave this innocent child love. He took away all the fear that I might have developed from his harshness.

Sometimes emphasis is put in designations and ranks, but I don't think Prabhupada emphasized that. He emphasized a service attitude. Prabhupada worked hard to create a Movement where we had an opportunity to serve and remember Krishna. Just as the love that mothers instill in their children will stick with the children when they grow up, so Prabhupada raised us with love and made us part of an eternal family. We can love others as Prabhupada loved us. He instilled in me that my life's duty is to give Krishna consciousness to others. I owe it to him. Out of love he went to every corner of the world and picked us up. He went to Germany to find me, and he loved me in a way that a father or grandfather would.

Jadurani (Syamarani) devi dasi

Syamarani had been trying to ignore the vague but penetrating questions drifting in and out of her mind: "Where are we really all going?" "Where are we really from? What does it all mean? What is the point of it all?" In 1966, at nineteen, attracted by the transcendental sound vibrations she heard while walking through Tompkins Square Park, she had her first meeting with Srila Prabhupada.

Prabhupada was dressed in pale peach-colored robes, playing a small bongo drum. He sat cross-legged on an oriental rug under a huge oak tree, his were eyes closed, his demeanor peaceful yet intense. He seemed completely absorbed in his chanting, as if experiencing a different reality. He appeared ageless, timeless, and yet right there in our midst.

Here was the person who knew the answers to my deepest questions. With kindness emanating from his eyes, he explained that because the chanting of the Hare Krishna mantra was coming from the depths of the soul there was no need to understand its language. It was universal; all nationalities could benefit equally. I couldn't imagine the whereabouts of the soul's depths, but his voice was so sonorous and commanding that it sounded as if it had surely come from there. When he finally turned his attention to me, it was electric.

His radiant eyes pierced through me, as if in an attempt to cut my speculative misconceptions. I felt he could see my very soul and that he already knew me thoroughly, but I fought the feeling and looked away. I told myself, "You're making all this up! This person is your own creation!" I had taken LSD earlier that day, which would account for my exaggerated sense of self.

He looked squarely into my eyes and spoke calmly: "This is not a concocted process – or something that we have made up. This process is very old, simple, and sublime."

He sat back comfortably and slowly looked around the room. "We are eternal and everything around us is temporary." Though he spoke softly, his words penetrated my being. I found myself anxiously wanting to hear what he would say next. Rather than expound on other philosophical truths, however, he politely asked me, "Do you live near here?"

I was nervous, not knowing exactly how to reply in a way that would demonstrate how "enlightened" I was. I deliberately drew out my words in a strange affected way. Trying to imply that I, as the ultimate divine being, lived everywhere, I answered, "Yeeeees. . . . I live veeeery near." Again, it was more the LSD talking than me.

"Good," he said, smiling. "Then you will be able to attend the morning program at 7:00 a.m."

I immediately realized my blunder. I lived in the Bronx, an hour and a half subway ride away! Still, the conviction in the Swami's voice made me want to try. How could I say no?

At that point, I asked him a totally unrelated question, "Do I have to come down from LSD?" He looked at me quizzically. Remembering the trance-like state of the dancers in the park and in the temple, I said, "Is there a way I can stay high on it forever?"

"No. It is material, and therefore temporary. Only Krishna consciousness can give lasting pleasure; it is spiritual and therefore eternal."

Later, when he first asked me to paint, it took several minutes for the gravity of the exchange to sink in. He was actually requesting me to paint for him – to paint that same Supreme Entity I had previously envisioned as unlimited but formless.

"You can paint one copy?" he asked, gesturing towards the dancing figures on an Indian print. "This is Chaitanya Mahaprabhu's *sankirtana* party," he explained. "They are Mahaprabhu's associates and pure devotees. They are all singing in ecstatic love of God."

I was thrilled to think of how, by guru's mercy, I might become a conduit, elucidating his message to the children of the world – through *art* of all things. I covered a corner of the temple room floor with newspaper. Surrounded by my paints, palette, brushes, and a bottle of turpentine, I sat on an Indian rug and began a routine of painting for several hours a day.

In 1967, he gave me a position as his first art director. While waving his hand and arm in the air as if painting the air, he told a newer artist, "I have taught her how to paint. Hare Krishna Hare Krishna Krishna Krishna Hare Hare, Hare Rama Hare Rama Rama Rama Hare Hare." Nine years later, he said, "In the beginning she could not paint, but by following the process of *shravanam, kirtanam, vishnu-smaranam* the talent has come out."

I was painting his spiritual master, Srila Bhaktisiddhanta Sarasvati Thakura Prabhupada. When I finished for the evening, I left the painting and reference photograph on the newspaper covering the floor. When I returned the next morning, I was surprised to find soft pillows under both the canvas and the small print. I smiled, recognizing this simple gesture of respect given by our Prabhupada to his superior. I became determined to always do the same.

A year later, I painted "the eternal spaceman," Sri Narada Muni, who travels through universes without the aid of a spaceship, chanting Krishna's name and glories. When I touched my paintbrush to the canvas to paint the topknot in Narada's hair, I felt like I was connecting with a real person. That small beginning gave me a joy I had not known before meeting Srila Prabhupada.

As my paintbrush touched the canvas, it was a thrill to be even minutely aware that the divine personalities on the canvases were really present. Although I knew that Chaitanya Mahaprabhu's mission was being spread by the mercy of Sri Guru and Mahaprabhu Himself, at the same time, working on the paintings made me feel vital to their mission. Having pictures in Prabhupada's books would help the devotees to distribute them, and this would help everyone to visualize the philosophy and histories within them. Srila Prabhupada wrote to us artists more than once that the pictures help make the message in the books more clear.

Srila Prabhupada would often describe his work of translating and explaining the ancient Vedic texts as the life and soul of his mission. Regarding the role of his art department, he said during a visit to his Brooklyn temple in 1971. "The paintings are the 'life department' of ISKCON, and the publication of books is the 'soul department.' "

There were times when the urgency of Srila Prabhupada's mission to spread the bhakti movement seemed overwhelming to his BBT artists. For example, he wrote in a letter (October 21, 1968, to Muralidhara, the second artist to join him): "I wish that some of my disciples, either individually or collectively, may produce at least half a dozen pictures daily. Anyway, I think Krishna will give you strength more and more."

In an attempt to fulfill his desire, the artists sometimes worked on a single canvas – a form of efficient collaborative art they called "the assembly line process." At other times the team worked individually and, at the beginning of each set of paintings, met for what they called "idea-meetings." They would sit in a circle on the floor to discuss themes for an upcoming set. They would read together Srila Prabhupada's unpublished transcripts and select specific pastimes or philosophical concepts.

Sitting in a small circle, we worked on our individual 2" by 3" idea-sketches as fast as we could, with strong concentration – we had one minute to do this. These sketches were our instinctive feelings put onto paper as a response to the given pastime. After that, we all placed our idea-sketches in the middle of the circle. Then, after one sketch, or after a combination of a few elements from more than one sketch, was chosen, this would become the basis for a painting.

When the artists had questions regarding aspects of the paintings, they submitted them to Srila Prabhupada. While waiting for his replies, they continued their service. They never had to just wait, because they usually worked on several paintings at the same time – there were lots of books to illustrate.

Besides giving detailed replies, Prabhupada showered the artists with his encouraging words. In a letter to me dated May 26, 1970, he wrote: "You are all being inspired just how to portray the Lord and His associates for the devotees' eyes, so everyone who sees these transcendental pictures will turn to become devotees – that is our aim."

When I was too strong in my criticism of the others' work, they let me know, and when I was too over-sensitive to others' critique of my work, they also let me know. This was an asset in the ultimate outcome of my art, and a great help in my personal spiritual development. (Extract from Syamarani's memoir *The Art of Spiritual Life*.)

Jagaddhatri devi dasi

Jagaddhatri was always interested in "spiritual things." Her first husband's sister, Joanie, had met Srila Prabhupada in New York and told them about Krishna. A few years later she saw the devotees on harinama in Seattle and she walked up to them. She bought some books and they invited her to the Sunday Feast. She attended and never left.

The first time I met Srila Prabhupada I believe was in December of 1973 in L.A. In those days the women and men stood opposite each other in the temple room. Later on with the influence of Tamal Krishna, I guess, and Radha-Damodara, the women had to stay in the back. But in those days we were side-by-side with the men. So I would get up early, like three in the morning, and sit down to claim a spot so I could be right next to Prabhupada's *vyasasana*. You had to get dibs on spaces, so you could be close to him. So I got to sit next to Srila Prabhupada and to see him as he gave classes. There are so many wonderful things about Srila Prabhupada. The way he played *karatalas* struck me. He was so graceful with his hands and his thumbs would go up to let the *karatalas* ring a little bit more. I was just fascinated by that. But I had no real personal interaction with him because I was just one little *brahmacharini* amongst a forest of *sannyasis*.

I received my *brahmana* initiation in L.A.. That was my first opportunity to meet Srila Prabhupada in person. I had heard he liked gardenias. I scraped some money together to buy a box of beautiful gardenias that were beautifully wrapped in cellophane. I went up the stairs and paid my obeisances to receive my *brahmana* initiation. Prabhupada was lounging on the floor on his pillows in front of his desk, and he patted the space with his right hand to the right of him. He had his knee up. I offered him the flowers, but they were all wrapped up so he couldn't smell them. He tried to open them up for a few seconds, got disgusted, and put them down.

He repeated the Gayatri mantra and then he showed me on the fingers how to count the Gayatri mantras. Of course I couldn't get it. He had to go over and over. And by then, of course he knows my heart anyway, but it just kind of verified what he intuitively knew, that I'm just a real dunce. However because he wants to serve his spiritual master he proceeded to allow me to be a *brahmana* by initiation from him. I always hid in corners and when Srila Prabhupada would pass with all the men, I would say, "*Jaya* Prabhupada!" He would look at me kind of dryly and say, "*Jaya.*" But he was so patient. He tolerated me. That happened several times throughout the years. I remember one time Hamsaduta got really mad at me for doing that, and glared at me in a manner that looked like, *What are you doing here as a woman?* I just said to him, "He's my guru too!"

In 1973, I wrote Prabhupada a letter. When everybody was flat-out prone on the floor offering humble obeisances, I ran over to Prabhupada – because nobody could stop me because they were all down on the floor – and handed him a letter. I only gave him three or four letters, and every time I delivered my letter like this. He knew – it was like a conspiracy between him and me. He would grab the letter and stick it in his pocket and pretend he never got it. And then I'd run down to my spot and get down on the floor and nobody even knew till his secretary had to answer the letter.

I had a platinum, sapphire, and diamond ring. I gave it to my son Raghunatha with a little note rolled inside of it, so that Raghunatha could go up to meet Srila Prabhupada. So I presented the ring via my son. I was not present. He gave the ring to Srila Prabhupada and then he wrote a letter, "I received your gift of one," he spelled it "one" and then in parenthesis "(1) ring. Just now I am wearing it on behalf of my Srila Gurudeva, although I am not worthy." And he said, "I have met your son. His lovely features are very appealing, and he appears to be a very nice *brahmachari*. Always go on being an example in Krishna consciousness and your motherhood will be perfected." There are some pictures of Srila Prabhupada wearing that ring. He wore it on the pinky of his left hand. And I have one of those pictures. So he did wear it for some days.

In Mayapur, during the spring of 1977, I utilized my son once again, and I gave him a note to give to Srila Prabhupada. They wanted to give me away. Dallas had closed. Devotees were traded like baseball cards in those days. And I was supposed to be traded to Tamal and Adi Kesava to serve in New York. I really didn't want to go there. I told Prabhupada I did not want to go to New York, I wanted to collect for the Vrindavan *gurukula*, which would mean Vrindavan would be my home temple. Prabhupada was ill, and it was the one letter he didn't answer in written form, but he told Tamal Krishna to tell me that I could go to Vrindavan.

I was in Vrindavan in October of 1977 when Srila Prabhupada was very ill but I did not get any association with him. My son, Raghu, was in the room when Prabhupada left this world.

Jagaddhatri devi dasi

Jagaddhatri attended an all-girls Catholic school in Edinburgh, Scotland. When she was thirteen a friend suggested that they go see some people who had opened up a "center" which was a five-minute walk from their school. Her friend had wanted to go to the newly opened Guru Maharaj ji center on one side of the street, but by mistake they went to the Hare Krishna temple which was directly opposite!

Between the ages of thirteen and sixteen I visited the temple regularly and was very attracted by the purity of the philosophy and the dedication of the devotees. Unfortunately the temple would sometimes close down due to lack of devotees. But I took it as Krishna's plan that maybe I should try to "enjoy" life for a while. Krishna was always kind and another group of devotees from London would arrive to Sweden and encourage me in my devotional life.

When I turned sixteen and was allowed to leave school, the temple decided again to close down. I decided to leave home and move to the Bhaktivedanta Manor to be able to continue in my spiritual life. I left Edinburgh with a couple of devotees who had volunteered to give me a lift.

Under the care of Sri Sri Radha-Gokulananda at Bhaktivedanta Manor I felt happy and eager to serve in whatever way the authorities felt fit! Attending the morning program, hearing, chanting, cleaning, serving *prasadam,* going out on *sankirtana,* and associating with like-minded devotees convinced me that by following Srila Prabhupada's instructions I could also be a devotee of the Lord.

In 1975 Srila Prabhupada came to visit and a few of us ladies were asked if we wanted to take initiation – which of course we did! We were *so* excited and happy that Srila Prabhupada was going to be here at Bhaktivedanta Manor and give us initiation in person. The day before our initiation Srila Prabhupada's servant asked us to give him our *japa* beads for Srila Prabhupada to chant on. *Japa* beads were difficult to get in those days. We had been given, what we thought, were wonderful colorful wooden beads from the Bead Shop in London. Mine were purple which I thought was great! Taking my beads out of my bead bag to give to Srila Prabhupada's servant, I could see a look of disapproval on his face and immediately felt scared. He wouldn't take my beads and said, "I can't give these to Srila Prabhupada." And then he walked away. We didn't know what to do and wondered if we would be initiated the next day. Had we committed some offense chanting on these beads? We had a sleepless night and in the morning, we still weren't sure if we would be receiving initiation. We decided to get ready for the ceremony and hope that Srila Prabhupada would be merciful to us.

Cushions were placed on the floor around Srila Prabhupada's *vyasasana*. Some men sat down, but we were still waiting in great anxiety. Eventually Srila Prabhupada's servant looked over and pointed to the cushions and we eagerly sat down. Srila Prabhupada arrived shortly after and sat down on his *vyasasana*. After a short talk we were called up to receive our names. Srila Prabhupada's kindness and mercy on a sixteen-year-old unqualified girl has never been forgotten and the great fortune to have been handed my "new" initiation beads from the hands of Srila Prabhupada is, I am sure, why I am still here trying to be a devotee.

Jagajanani devi dasi

The day after she graduated from high school, Jagajanani's boyfriend took her to the northern California mountains where they lived for three years. Immediately she and her boyfriend, Larry, stopped taking intoxicants and eating meat, fish, and eggs. Seeking purity, they lived a simple lifestyle of gardening and trying to find themselves.

Larry's mother sent us a *Back to Godhead* magazine that she got at Kmart in Berkeley. We were amazed that there were people who believed the same things we believed. Larry sent for the *Bhagavad-gita* and I sent for the cookbook and *Easy Journey to Other Planets*, which I loved. From that book I felt a connection with and trust in Srila Prabhupada. We left the mountains the day of my twenty-first birthday, May 26th 1976, and went to Denver, Colorado. A week later we moved into the Denver temple.

We both became airport *sankirtana* devotees and Larry decided that we shouldn't have any connection for six months because we had no training. I was a young girl in a new city, a new state, with a new lifestyle, a new group of people, and for the first two weeks I was struggling.

Once Kurusrestha, the temple president in Denver, said to Larry, "You should spend time with your girlfriend – read with her or eat a meal with her. I joined the temple with my girlfriend and since I wouldn't associate with her she left Krishna consciousness." Out of nowhere I said, "Oh, I'm not going anywhere." Then I thought, "Oh, my gosh, where did that statement come from?"

After that, one evening I got emotional with Larry (who later became Lalitananda), "Why are you doing this to me? Why can't you help me? I'm struggling!" Then I went to the *arati*, chanted, and prayed to the Deities, and in that half-hour my anxiety, fear, and distress left. I felt peaceful, protected, and comfortable. I told Larry, "I understand what you're doing and why you're doing it, and I'm going to be okay." That was my first tangible experience of Krishna and Prabhupada.

During *sankirtana* at the airport I'd constantly daydream about Srila Prabhupada arriving and coming to the temple. I'd imagine seeing my spiritual master. But when Srila Prabhupada physically left the planet in 1977, I still hadn't seen him. Sometime later though, Prabhupada allowed me to dream about him so vividly that I fell to the floor and wept. The dream was so real I knew Srila Prabhupada was fulfilling my deep desire.

When I look back on my life before and after becoming a devotee, I feel that Srila Prabhupada was always taking care of me and bringing me to him. As a young girl I didn't have a firm faith or religion, yet I knew God existed and I always felt protected in amazing situations, although I didn't know by whom or how.

Srila Prabhupada has helped me in so many areas of my life. He gave me my husband, Naikatma Prabhu, who has guided me, kept me on track, and given me a wonderful daughter, Remuna, who's my best friend. I'm grateful for all of the other devotees Srila Prabhupada gave us to associate with and help us, and I hope I can be helpful to them. I'm happy to be involved in the family business of preaching and giving Krishna everywhere we go.

I can't imagine life without feeling Srila Prabhupada's presence at every moment. So I'm grateful to him and pray every day that I will eternally be in his service.

Jaganmurti devi dasi

Jaganmurti felt too insecure and shy to go to the Saint Louis, Missouri, temple. Finally, in 1975, Jaganmurti's mother brought her to the temple. The devotees were kind to Jaganmurti who had been reading Prabhupada's books, so on the day of her first visit she moved in. Three months later she saw Srila Prabhupada when he arrived in New York City.

At the airport, Srila Prabhupada chanted the *samsara* prayers clearly, beautifully, and spiritually. He transcended his age and nationality and his chanting brought tears to the devotees' eyes.

Srila Prabhupada automatically knew I was attracted to the universe and stars since I was four. He gave me a name that means "the servant of the universal form." On a morning walk in Chicago in 1975, Prabhupada looked right at me, into my heart, and saw past all my contaminations and weaknesses, to the spiritual soul, the part of me I don't see myself. It was intense, almost as if a lightning bolt jolted me, but it was blissful.

Srila Prabhupada never tried to impress. He gave pure Krishna consciousness philosophy straight – as it is – without deviation or compromise, and he did it in a way no one can duplicate. It's hard to feel inspired without him. I didn't have much of his association but I can never forget the effect he had on my life. He could see Krishna and was with Krishna all the time. He was a first-class devotee acting on a second-class platform for our benefit, for preaching. He didn't need to come to this austere, cold, strange country, America, but he went through so much trouble to come. Our mission is to show the world what a great personality Srila Prabhupada is.

My hope is to somehow or other serve devotees, and I pray that Srila Prabhupada's lotus feet, his instructions, his words, his beauty, and his intelligence will be imprinted in my heart forever. Whatever condition I'm in, Srila Prabhupada's and Krishna's lotus feet are all that matter, because there's no material situation that satisfies. I've tried to enjoy many times, and without Krishna it's just suffering. But if you suffer remembering Krishna, that's not suffering. Srila Prabhupada gave us jewels, unlimited, eternal wealth – Krishna consciousness – because no one can be satisfied with material riches or beauty. I'm very imperfect in Krishna consciousness but if I try to be Krishna conscious and pray to Krishna and Srila Prabhupada, one of these days I'll wake up in the spiritual world.

Jagannathesvari devi dasi

At twenty-two, Jagannathesvari dasi was initiated by Srila Prabhupada. While not speaking directly to him, she basked in his association in classes and darshans in Vrindavan, Mayapur, and London during the final two years of his time with us.

I arrived back in Vrindavan just two days before Srila Prabhupada left this world, so I got to be there for that momentous occasion, which was also very difficult. There was an announcement at lunchtime that the *kaviraja* had given just a few hours to Srila Prabhupada – five hours or something – that he had left. That news didn't really sink in. It was hard to accept or even believe that it would be possible to carry on without Srila Prabhupada, so it took a long time to deal with that. When that announcement came, I just thought, "These Ayurvedic doctors are all bogus. They don't know what they're talking about."

But the doors to Srila Prabhupada's room were opened to everyone and we all went and spent the whole afternoon there. Many devotees were in the room doing *bhajanas*. I was engaged to grind sandalwood paste for Srila Prabhupada. In my naiveté I thought the paste was going to make Srila Prabhupada better. I didn't realize that the sandalwood paste would be to go onto Srila Prabhupada's body after he had departed.

I was grinding and grinding. At some point I left the room to take a break and take some *prasadam* because I was feeling very weak. The time that Srila Prabhupada was supposed to leave had already passed. So I thought, "It's not going to happen, don't worry. Take a break, come back." Just on my way back to his room, I heard someone say Srila Prabhupada had stopped breathing. I thought, "Well, he stopped breathing, but he's going to start breathing again, just in a moment. It can't be true." Then, eventually, after a few moments, it sank in that the time had come and it was very, very devastating.

We stayed up all night making garlands in the temple room. After Srila Prabhupada was bathed and dressed, his body was brought onto his *vyasa-sana* in the temple room with the sandalwood paste. All the garlands were placed on his transcendental body and we stayed all night like that.

In the morning there was the procession to take Srila Prabhupada's body to visit all the seven temples of Vrindavan with the *harinama* party. We all followed in procession. Then we came back to place his body in *samadhi*. Then after that there was a feast for the devotees.

I wasn't feeling well so I didn't take the feast. I just went to the ashram and decided to fast. Actually, at that point I just thought, *I'll fast until I leave my body. What's the point of living?* But then Parvati came and persuaded me to eat something, and in that way we gave strength to each other. We had to give strength to each other to carry on.

It took time to deal with separation from Srila Prabhupada and learn how to actually associate with Srila Prabhupada in separation.

For many years I've been worshiping my deity of Srila Prabhupada. I receive a lot of mercy to be able to personally serve Srila Prabhupada by bathing him, dressing him, offering him food, and *arati*. And, of course, I have Srila Prabhupada's *vani*. Srila Prabhupada told us that *vani* is more important than *vapuh*. By the mercy of the devotees, we have all his recorded lectures, and, of course, by Srila Prabhupada's mercy we have his books. So we have so much. We have so much.

I think that the physical association of the spiritual master is just the beginning of our relationship, actually, because it's an eternal relationship. We just have to keep on trying to serve Srila Prabhupada. I feel some burden of responsibility as Srila Prabhupada's disciple, which I'm not qualified to carry. Hopefully by the mercy of the devotees I can carry on his teachings.

I've had a few dreams that are important to me. Srila Prabhupada has given me a lot of encouragement. I guess because I need to feel his shelter. Just one little dream is so special that it can stay with you for the rest of your life. A little exchange can mean everything, like Srila Prabhupada allowing me to take shelter of his lotus feet or him touching me in the dream – touching my hand, patting me on the shoulder, things like that.

I feel I got a lot of Srila Prabhupada's mercy through his disciples who were close to him and who have been empowered by him to lead this Movement. Any of his disciples, or any devotees, actually, can act as his instruments to inspire us or to encourage us. So that's been very important as well, and it still is for me. For example, I'm married to a disciple of Tamal Krishna Maharaja and in that way I got a lot of shelter from him. He's helped me a lot in my spiritual life. And many others as well – Giriraja Swami, Indradyumna Swami, Radhanatha Swami, and so many other devotees have helped me and engaged me to serve Srila Prabhupada.

When I was a new devotee in Vrindavan, the twenty-four-hour kirtan was going on, which was established by Srila Prabhupada when the Vrindavan temple was opened. We all had our slots. Himavati, Rasajna, and myself used to chant together from 11:00am to 12:00 p.m. during the *raja-bhoga* offering. We used to chant the *bhaja-bhakata-vatsala* – the noon offering song. It was very beautiful. Srila Prabhupada was present in Vrindavan during some of this time. Himavati used to take me sometimes for the morning walk. Most of the ladies wouldn't go, but she would go, and sometimes take me with her to tag onto the back of Prabhupada's morning walk. Himavati was very kind to me.

Jagarini devi dasi

In Los Angeles in May of 1973, Srila Prabhupada initiated Jagarini, who was twenty at the time. Prabhupada said "Jaga" means sleep and "Jagarini" means "one who has conquered sleep, and sleep is ignorance. Jagarini is one who has conquered ignorance."

In 1971, Nirakula, Tirtharthi, Brahmarupa, and I were hippie friends in Brooklyn, New York. Once we were in Tirtharthi's house watching a baseball game on TV when there was a special news broadcast of the Swami arriving in the New York airport. We were all raised Catholic, knew nothing about Krishna consciousness, and had never seen anything like this before. That was the first time we'd seen Srila Prabhupada and all four of us were glued to the screen. "Wow, look at him!" His countenance was regal yet humble and he was powerful and gentle at the same time.

When I joined the temple in Los Angeles, the men and women stayed on different sides of the temple room and didn't associate closely, but there was a brother-sisterly mood between us. Srila Prabhupada spent lots of time there and his desk was next to an upstairs window. Whenever I walked through the alleyway I'd see Srila Prabhupada's head in the window. Once, unexpectedly, Srila Prabhupada visited our apartment, which was next to the Los Angeles temple. He looked in every room, closet, and cabinet. At the end, Prabhupada looked at me, smiled, and said, "Very nice, very clean." All my cleaning worked in my favor – it pleased Srila Prabhupada and I was happy. And my home had been blessed with his lotus feet.

Recently I started the hospice project in the Mumbai hospital. I prayed intensely to Prabhupada's *murti* in the hospital and meditated on doing it the way he would want it. I felt his hand in it; I felt guided by him. We can have Prabhupada's association; he's here now in his books and instructions. It's strong and prominent, comforting, and wonderful. How fortunate we are.

My parents were not supportive of my Krishna consciousness, my husband was an alcoholic, and I raised three sons. I was determined to stay, and during my many hard times I'd pray to Prabhupada and feel his guidance, comfort, and strength. And I was happy! My mother would say, "Aren't you having a nervous breakdown?" But this wonderful consciousness that Prabhupada blessed us with, this perspective that we could actually feel happy in any situation, was his gift to all of us. And he is still giving that gift to all of us.

Jagatam devi dasi

In 1975, Jagatam had been living in the Pittsburgh temple for a month when she and other devotees drove to meet Srila Prabhupada at the New York airport.

There were two hundred devotees from different parts of the East Coast engaging in an amazing, ecstatic kirtan at the airport. When Prabhupada came it felt like tears started from my toes and rushed right up my whole body to squirt out my eyes. I didn't know what a pure devotee was, but on a deep level I understood that Prabhupada was a pure devotee. I was crying and everyone else was crying. It felt like we were in an ocean.

In Vrindavan I got a chance to help make Srila Prabhupada's fruit offering. We had to peel everything thoroughly – all the white segments had to be pulled out of each orange and every grape was peeled and seeded. So much thought and devotion went into the offering I realized serving the spiritual master is the same as serving God.

I was so contaminated by impersonalism that, because Prabhupada never looked at me, I was convinced he didn't like me. It was a kind of egotism based on a material conception, not on the spiritual relationship between the guru and disciple. But for years I fretted about this in my heart. Then, in a dream, I saw Srila Prabhupada sitting cross-legged on a cushion and looking at me with an incredibly beautiful, oceanic smile that dripped with softness and love. It seemed Prabhupada was personally there. He put his head to the side and said, "You should train my devotees." That instruction and his personal loving look were the most special things to me.

Once at the Manor I said to Yamuna, "You're so lucky to have had so much personal association with Prabhupada. I'm so unlucky I didn't have that." Soft-spoken Yamuna slammed her hand down on the desk with so much force I jumped. She said, "That is a misconception. If you read Srila Prabhupada's books and follow his instructions, you are in association with Srila Prabhupada. So many devotees were with Srila Prabhupada personally and now they've gone away." It was important for me to hear that.

Prabhupada wants me to act according to my nature, which is to preach and give Krishna consciousness. There's nothing else I can do, and by Prabhupada's mercy that's the only thing I could ever do. When I'm not doing that, I'm unhappy. I pray that Srila Prabhupada helps me to stay on the path and continue to share Krishna consciousness with others, because there's nothing else really. As Prabhupada says, "Without preaching, there's no life."

Jagatpriya devi dasi

At a Town Hall program in Sydney in 1973, Jagatpriya saw Srila Prabhupada, got some prasadam, liked the devotees, and later visited the temple.

At the end of 1975, after my husband and I had read Srila Prabhupada's books, we moved into the Sydney temple where everything was revolving around Srila Prabhupada. Everybody spoke about him and was conscious of him. By serving, following the regulative principles, chanting sixteen rounds a day, and going to the program, I became more and more attached to Srila Prabhupada.

When Srila Prabhupada visited Melbourne in 1976 we heard his morning *Bhagavatam* classes and attended his evening darshans. But what cemented my relationship with Prabhupada was after he left in 1977. I was in New Govardhan wondering, "What's going to happen now?" when Prabhupada came to me and said, "Don't think that I have gone." That was the turning point of my relationship. I thought, "Of course he's not gone. He's with us," and I felt much closer to him. Just those six words coming from Srila Prabhupada's mouth cemented my relationship with him and I've never ever thought of doing anything else with my life but serve him.

From my experience, *vani* is more important than *vapuh* – hearing is more important than personal presence. Prabhupada isn't gone at all. Devotees who didn't see him are not any less fortunate than those who did. In fact, many devotees who never saw him are much better than I am and much better than devotees who had a lot of personal association with him.

Today, devotee friends keep me inspired by their services, their attitude, and their *sadhana*. If we're genuine devotees, Prabhupada and Krishna will help us go back to Godhead. It's quite straightforward: we need to follow the four regulative principles and chant sixteen good rounds a day.

Jagattarini devi dasi

In the early 1970s, Jagattarini, a movie actress, started coming to the Sydney temple.

When I met Srila Prabhupada in Los Angeles, he was gracious and grandfatherly and on hearing I was an actress said, "I was an actor once. I played the part of Advaitachandra." He said, "We've been attracting hippies but if we present the culture of Krishna consciousness, we can attract a higher class. You should put on plays for Krishna." We had an enthusiastic conversation about dramas and toward the end he said, "Are you married?" I said, "No." He looked at me with soft, penetrating eyes and said, "You are alone?" I said, "Yes." He nodded with a grave look and said, "I will find you a nice husband." It was an amazing moment, because on one side I was almost disgusted at the thought of somebody finding me a husband. Culturally, it was unbelievable. And on the other side, because he was so attractive and endearing, I felt touched and honored. I came out of the room confused and thinking, "I don't think I'll tell anyone about this."

Some months went and Srila Prabhupada gave his blessing for me to marry Bhurijan Prabhu. Bhurijan and I met and got married in Hong Kong, where we opened a center. Hong Kong was crowded, dirty, and permeated by the smell of dog stool. We had a rat nest in our kitchen roof and were isolated from devotees. My husband wanted to stay but I didn't. I thought of Prabhupada all the time and when I saw him next, in 1972 after one-and-a-half years of struggling, I burst into tears and cried and cried. Prabhupada asked, "You haven't been fighting with your husband, have you?" Nervous and flustered I said, "Oh, no, no, no, Prabhupada," and thought, "My gosh, I just told him a lie." He said, "Good. Husband and wife shouldn't fight. When a husband and wife fight, it shouldn't be taken seriously. It's just like sometimes there's lightning and thunder but no rain." He made a serious point first and then became humorous and sweet.

Later my mother and father met Prabhupada in Melbourne. My father was respectful, my mother nervous. Prabhupada told my father, "Your daughter will deliver you." My father said, "Yes, yes. We always thought she'd do something like that." Prabhupada said, "Don't think that she's given up your service. Because of her, so many generations of your family will be delivered." My father said, "Yes, that's very nice." Srila Prabhupada said, "Wherever I go throughout the world, parents come to see me and thank me for what I've done for their children." Then turning to my mother, he slowly, gently, and gracefully took off his garland and gave it to her. My mother liked flowers and was excited and grateful to receive the garland. After that my parents were more reasonable about Krishna consciousness.

In Hong Kong, I felt Srila Prabhupada asked me to do something impossible. And when I did it, he added to it, and added to that. Bitterness and anger towards Srila Prabhupada arose in my mind, and subtly I started becoming rebellious and pushing him away. This planted the seed of offenses in my heart that later fructified into weeds. I got back into my career, started mixing with wealthy Indians, became fashionable, wore silk chiffon saris, lots of makeup, and put my hair up. So by the time Srila Prabhupada came to Hong Kong to save Bhurijana and Jagattarini at the end of 1973, I was a different person. I felt uncomfortable and nervous that Prabhupada was going to be critical of me. At the airport, Srila Prabhupada, looking stern and grave, gazed right through my husband and me (my husband had hair) and kept looking. Where are the devotees? My husband started to faint. I was terrified and somewhat defiant.

Srila Prabhupada asked, "What is your morning program? I heard you closed the temple. Why?" I had no *sadhana*; I wasn't chanting *japa*. My husband and I thought that Siddhaswarupa was special and we had some malice toward ISKCON devotees and didn't find them likable. Srila Prabhupada said Siddhaswarupa was a nonsense and gravely asked, "Jagattarini, what do you think of our lifestyle?" He had caught me. I said, "I don't know." He said, "You are following a cheater, you have become cheated, and now you are cheating others." I was flabbergasted and wanted to get out of the room, but tried to be composed. Later I cried, and whenever I could that's what I did during Prabhupada's visit. I felt lost, desperate, rebellious, turbulent, and heavy-hearted. I was crawling along with the motions without any eagerness or feeling for Prabhupada.

Then the day before Prabhupada was to leave Hong Kong, I was sitting outside his room and heard Prabhupada with his dictaphone translating the *Chaitanya-charitamrita*, Madhya 19, on Rupa Goswami's teachings. He said, "It is just like . . . *click* . . . the mad elephant offense . . . *click*. When an elephant enters a garden . . . *click* . . . it destroys everything . . . *click*. It uproots everything . . . *click*. Similarly, offense against the spiritual master . . . *click* . . . uproots everything . . . *click*." My whole body went limp as I heard him explain my situation. My husband said to me, "Please come in and see Prabhupada." I went in, paid my obeisances, and didn't come up because I was crying. Prabhupada gently took the ring off his finger, gracefully turned around, and said, "Jagattarini, this is for you." I put the ring on my finger, paid my obeisances, and cried.

In two intense days, Srila Prabhupada realigned my husband and me, and before he left he asked us to come to the Mayapur festival in February. We arranged for a Chinese devotee to come with us to Mayapur and when this devotee got initiated, Prabhupada was emotional and said, "From a dog-eater. Just like in a forest, if there is one sandalwood tree, the whole forest becomes fragrant. Because of this one devotee, the whole Chinese race is glorious." And in Mayapur, in front of all his *sannyasis*, Srila Prabhupada said to me, "Thank you so much for coming."

When we returned to Hong Kong, however, we had trouble and my husband decided to leave. I said to him, "Prabhu, I suffered so much when Prabhupada was angry with me. I don't want Prabhupada to be angry with me again." My husband said, "When we see Prabhupada again, he won't be angry with you, he'll be angry with me."

Prabhupada learned we'd left Hong Kong and wrote, "What are they doing? What is this restlessness?" He wasn't angry but concerned, and in Melbourne Srila Prabhupada tried to maneuver us back into service. He was an expert psychologist. He said, "So you did not want to stay in Hong Kong. Maybe you should go to China instead." My husband made some excuse why we couldn't go to China. Prabhupada said, "Maybe you can go to Africa." And, "You can become my servant and travel with me." At a certain point my husband said he liked Singapore and Srila Prabhupada said, "You could go to Singapore, open a bookshop, and sell all kinds of books along with our books. You don't have to wear a *dhoti* and you can put *tilaka* on with water." He didn't stress any externals. But by this time I was five months pregnant, so instead of going to Singapore we stayed in Australia and started a business making tapestry bags. Every month we sent Prabhupada some money and every time he wrote back, "Thank you so much."

In 1976, my husband decided that he wanted to be active in ISKCON again. We started traveling with Srila Prabhupada but, when we were in Fiji and Hari Sauri spoke critically of Siddhaswarupa, I said, "I don't want to live in a temple." Srila Prabhupada called for us. He said, "What is the difficulty? It's been going on so long. You are here and I am here. Let us solve this difficulty for good." Srila Prabhupada brought up many things expertly and artfully, and we had an amazingly illuminating discussion. I explained that I had the impression of the spiritual master as someone that burdens you with tasks beyond your capacity. Prabhupada told me, "Your duty is to listen to your husband," and he leaned over his desk and in a fatherly way said, "And if you think your husband is incompetent, then you write to me and I will direct you. But nobody else." That was sweet. He was staying in Vasudeva's brother's house. He said, "Just see this couple. She has her Deities and she is perfectly happy and never restless." I said, "But Prabhupada, I wasn't brought up in this culture." He didn't dismiss that. He said, "I know. But if something is good, why not try for it?" It was such a reasonable, sensible answer. Then Prabhupada said to my husband, "Why doesn't she follow you?" My husband said, "Because I change my mind a lot." Prabhupada said, "You change your mind, then she becomes disturbed. Of course she cannot follow. First, you fix your mind on the spiritual master and follow his instructions." That was the last time we saw Prabhupada.

I was incredibly fortunate because Prabhupada taught me what to do if you get into difficulty with your spiritual master: Srila Prabhupada insisted on obedience. I saw that he would save us if we remained dutiful and kept going. It took years for me to heal and re-establish my commitment. Now my relationship with Srila Prabhupada is flourishing. I pray to him and respect everyone who's serving him because I know Srila Prabhupada respects them.

Jahnava devi dasi

In a letter dated 14th February 1969, Srila Prabhupada accepted Jahnava as his disciple and wrote to her, "This process of Krishna consciousness is offered to everyone, but only one out of many thousands of people will accept it. Therefore you should be very serious about perfecting your life in Krishna consciousness, and thereby becoming qualified to enter into the Kingdom of God, Goloka Vrndavana. So please receive these beads, duly chanted upon by me, and chant at least 16 rounds daily and follow all of the regulative principles. Take assistance from your godbrothers and godsisters there, and engage yourself purely in the business of Krishna consciousness. This will bring all success to you. You can be certain of this."

One of my first impressions of Srila Prabhupada was that he was inconceivably humble. And his humility was multifaceted, like a multifaceted jewel. With only a moment's association with him we were able to get a glimpse of the relationship of the spirit soul to Krishna, we were able to see that Krishna is wonderful, generous, and giving, and that the soul is in the position of receiving the mercy of being protected. Srila Prabhupada showed us all that. And then we became confident of him and of Krishna.

At every moment Srila Prabhupada was remembering his spiritual master, Srila Bhaktisiddhanta Sarasvati Thakura. Srila Prabhupada was proud of how great Lord Krishna is, he was proud of how merciful Lord Chaitanya is, and he considered himself the menial servant of his spiritual master. He is our ever well-wisher because he is the representative of Paramatma and a representative of Srila Bhaktisiddhanta Sarasvati Thakura. And we aspire to become representatives of Srila Prabhupada.

Together we can approach his lotus feet through devotional service. We're all suffering in this material world and Srila Prabhupada has kindly created this Society by which we can take one another's association and compassionately assist one another in Krishna consciousness. This is real friendship. And this is a gift which Srila Prabhupada gave. New devotees can develop their devotion to Srila Prabhupada by hearing about how he talked, how he walked, what he did, how he communicated. We can mediate on something that Srila Prabhupada did and then consider how that instruction relates to us here and now. And how we can take it into our future. Each and every word of Srila Prabhupada's contains volumes of meaning; each action that he did, each exchange that he had, has volumes of meaning which we can discuss and digest. We have plenty of time to do it. Devotees viewed Srila Prabhupada's actions from different perspectives. Sometimes our impressions were the same, but sometimes we naturally saw the same activity from many different angles of vision. This is wonderful.

When Srila Prabhupada arrived in the Boston airport in 1969, it was lightly raining and Rukmini and I ran out to the airplane to greet him as he came down the latter holding an umbrella. We were young and with childlike eagerness to receive him, we bowed down in the sprinkling rain and Srila Prabhupada was pleased. It was as if he had come from the spiritual sky. We hadn't seen Srila Prabhupada for a long time and when we got back to the temple from the airport, Brahmananda sent me into Prabhupada's room with a silver glass of water. I just fell into full *dandavats* – full, prostrated obeisances – in front of Srila Prabhupada. Once I was down I began to think, "Oh, I don't know if women are allowed to do this!" so I got scared and, as I sheepishly and slowly got up, I looked intently at him to see if I'd made some offense. Srila Prabhupada was really pleased. After that everybody started making *dandavats* – the men and the women – and Srila Prabhupada was pleased.

Srila Prabhupada explained that as we advance in Krishna consciousness we may become expert in different arts and sciences and so forth, but Krishna is pleased by our devotion. Srila Prabhupada was pleased with even a child's drawing of Krishna, which was no more than a scribble, but on seeing some technically accurate and well-executed artwork, Srila Prabhupada could chastise, "You have not presented Krishna well."

Another point about Srila Prabhupada is that he's already given us everything. The whole road is laid out before us. In one sense the only relevant question to ask is, "Within our own hearts how can we accept the mercy that he is giving?" Real humility means to have faith that Prabhupada can make a devotee out of us. It's up to us to simply submit to him, to accept his mercy. If we love Srila Prabhupada then we will try to at least endeavor constantly to accept his mercy, and we won't break our promises to him. And it will be possible for us to go back to Godhead in this very lifetime.

When I'd been in the temple for less than two weeks, I had the opportunity to be in Srila Prabhupada's room with him for two hours, but I was having a difficult time. I was unable to hear Srila Prabhupada properly because of his accent, and I was unable to listen very well or retain what he said. Srila Prabhupada was compassionate. He saw that I was trying to hear him, trying to take advantage of his association, and he looked over my shoulder intently and said, "Just see how beautiful Krishna is." I thought, "Well if I turn around I might see air, or I might see a painting, or I might see brass. I don't know what form of Krishna is there, but I have such mundane vision." For the first time I began to get a glimpse of my dependency on Srila Prabhupada and I thought, "My position is that I don't know Krishna and Prabhupada is describing Him to me, so let me hear his description rather than trying to see with my mundane vision. Let me see Krishna through hearing Srila Prabhupada." That was important. I'm a testimony of Srila Prabhupada's mercy, because I was practically unable to cope with this material world and Srila Prabhupada was able to give my life meaning and hope.

Srila Prabhupada took careful care of his newly initiated neophyte devotees who were pioneering this ISKCON movement. My husband and I and two other couples were married at the same time and Srila Prabhupada performed the ceremony. Here he is, a Vaishnava *paramahamsa* and a *sannyasi*, yet he kindly took the role of a dutiful father and a priest. He's so merciful.

Another quality of Srila Prabhupada was that when he wanted to notice you, he would notice you and give you confidence that you've just done something right in Krishna consciousness. And if he didn't want to notice you, to cut down your pride, he wouldn't notice you for anything. It has taken me twenty years to digest the idea of not trying to enjoy the spiritual master but trying to understand the confidential aspects of serving his mission.

I gave my life to Srila Prabhupada. I want to be honest about how I'm progressing or backsliding in Krishna consciousness and I constantly endeavor to correct myself. One major point is *japa* – that's one of the main ways that I see myself staying linked with Srila Prabhupada. Also to be enthusiastic about assimilating his books in a personal way, for they contain the answers to all of the dilemmas of life.

Jalatala devi dasi

Jalatala had a family relation to Srila Prabhupada: Prabhupada's mother was the younger sister of Jalatala's great grandmother. Prabhupada's brother, Krishna Charan De, lived at Jalatala's house and raised her. Jalatala used to go everywhere with him and he'd often buy her little saris. Krishna Charan would tell her how much he loved his brother, Srila Prabhupada.

When Srila Prabhupada had a pharmacy business in Allahabad, on business trips he'd sometimes visit my grandfather's house. Prabhupada loved my grandfather's large orchard with jackfruit and many other fruit trees, and he'd give my father and my father's nine brothers neem toothpaste from his pharmacy.

Many years later, Prabhupada's European and American disciples arranged a big, successful *maidan pandal* program in the Esplanade in Calcutta where Prabhupada spoke daily. I was eight then, and my father, sister, and I attended those programs.

A few years later, at the *pandal* program in Calcutta's Deshapriya Park, Prabhupada was lecturing when some Naxalites threw bombs. I was afraid but Prabhupada wasn't. In Bengali he told the Naxalites, "We have a bigger bomb than yours." The Naxalites were surprised, "Prabhupada has a big bomb?" Prabhupada said, "Krishna can do anything. He can finish you." Those Naxalites never threw bombs again. Prabhupada was fearless – and surprising.

Once I was pounding the *mridanga* and trying to sing in front of Radha-Govinda in the Calcutta ISKCON temple when Prabhupada came in. I thought he would be angry but in Bengali he said, "Play, play, no problem." Prabhupada mercifully accepted my poor playing and chanting. I was living at home and going to school, but whenever Prabhupada came to Calcutta I'd stay with the lady devotees in the temple. I'd help clean Prabhupada's room and I'd help Pishima and Yamuna cook for him. When Prabhupada ate lunch, he'd savor and take a little of everything we cooked, but he'd always finish his big bowl of *shukta*. The *sannyasis* – Bhavananda Maharaja, Tamal Krishna Maharaja, Gargamuni Maharaja – would wait outside Prabhupada's room, and when his plate came out they'd grab the remnants. This surprised me; I'd never seen disciples honor their guru before. I slowly learned how to worship and love the guru and started celebrating whenever Prabhupada came to Calcutta, "Prabhupada's coming! Prabhupada's coming!"

I'm from a Vaishnava family and all my life I've been doing *puja* and going to temples. I'd seen lots of gurus and I knew that how Srila Prabhupada preached, wrote books, and made disciples all over the world was extraordinary. When it came time for me to choose a guru, how could I choose anyone besides Srila Prabhupada?

Prabhupada was perfectly regulated. When he took bath, when he napped, when he ate, and what he ate – I can't imagine how he was so regulated. Every day at four o'clock I used to give him a cut guava, the juice of a coconut, sandalwood paste with saffron, a little camphor for his forehead, and a garland that I'd made.

These days sometimes I'm sick and alone in the house, but I put a lecture on and hear Prabhupada telling me, "You're not this body. Why do you think this body is yours?" Prabhupada said, "I will never die. I live in my books and you shall utilize." He is always with us, watching.

Srila Prabhupada is from the spiritual world. When people feel his love for them, they become magnetically attracted and attached to him just as I did.

Jambuvati devi dasi

Jambuvati had been chanting at home for about a year-and-a-half before she moved into the New York temple in 1969. She was seventeen.

From New York I was sent to become *brahmacharini* in Boston, and when Prabhupada came I went to greet him at the airport with all the other East Coast devotees. On seeing him I felt him deep in my heart and knew Krishna consciousness was for me. I was crying.

Whenever Srila Prabhupada spoke all the suffering and fears I ever felt dissipated. I decided to follow him, so I hopped on a bus and went to Philadelphia and it was there that, by letter, Prabhupada initiated me and married me to Lalit Kumar, my childhood friend who had first told me about Krishna consciousness. Then by phone Prabhupada told us to start a temple in Wilmington, Delaware. He said, "Just go and funding will be there for you."

Wilmington was in the Bible Belt and Lalit and I explained to Prabhupada that we weren't accepted there. Prabhupada said, "Just keep pushing forward because somebody there is going to be a devotee, even if you're pushed out eventually," which is exactly what happened.

Henry Street in New York was like Vaikuntha and when Prabhupada came, Lalit and I were to get brahminical initiation. I made some Simplies the size of golf balls and put them in a big basket. Lalit and I went into Prabhupada's room and Prabhupada touched my head and directed me to sit behind Lalit. His touch went through my whole body. Then Prabhupada put his hand on Lalit's head and said, "Ah, Lalit Kumar, very nice boy." He gave Lalit the Gayatri mantra and said to me, "Follow your husband, do Gayatri together, and become the ideal Krishna conscious couple." Then he said, "Oh, what's that?" I said, "These are Simply Wonderfuls." He said, "Oh, Simply Wonderfuls are simply wonderful," took one, bit it, and said, "Now distribute the rest to the devotees." I said, "Right now?" He said, "No, not right now." He told Lalit how to take care of me nicely and told me to be a good wife by following Lalit's instructions. I was in ecstasy. When I came out the devotees said, "What did he say? What did he do?" I said, "He wants everyone to have one of these," and distributed the Simplies.

I used to write to Prabhupada, "What do I do about this? What can I do about that?" and to my shock he responded every time. In his first letter he wrote, "Give your baby one pound of milk every day." He also wrote, "Sometimes we have to accept help from regular doctors. But give your child Krishna consciousness and for things that are out of your hands see a regular doctor. Because that doctor is working on your child, who's a devotee, the doctor will benefit."

In New York I started ISKCON's first *gurukula*, and Prabhupada instructed me to take care of the students, give them Krishna, and add what academics I could. Prabhupada wrote to my husband, "Tell Jambuvati to keep pushing forward with the school," and gave me his blessings. For me, Srila Prabhupada's every word was encouraging. And his instructions now are the same as they were in 1969.

Janaki devi dasi

In the late summer of 1966, when she was twenty-one, Janaki was initiated at 26 Second Avenue in New York City. She was Srila Prabhupada's first female disciple.

Mukunda and I were planning on going to India. We had gotten passports, visas, and shots. Then one day Mukunda came home and said, "I met a guru just down the street." I was skeptical, "A guru on the Bowery?" We went to hear Prabhupada and it was difficult to understand his thick dialect. On a piece of paper he had written words for us to sing, "Hare Krishna, Hare Krishna, Krishna Krishna, Hare Hare, Hare Rama, Hare Rama, Rama Rama, Hare Hare," but it was hard for me because I had no idea what I was singing. The third time I went, we told him we were going to India. He said, "I can give you what you want to find in India." After that I saw him walking alone down the street, a blaze of saffron walking at me in the middle of the Bowery stench. I went up to him, he smiled, and I said, "Do you remember me?" He said, "Yes, of course I do." I said, "It's nice to see you. We live one block up the street." He started coming to our house once a week or more.

He'd instruct me, "When I visit its proper for you to offer me food." I didn't have food in the house because Mukunda and ate once a day in a macrobiotic restaurant. I offered Prabhupada orange juice. Prabhupada asked questions about the United States and the practice of boys and girls and why Mukunda and I lived together without getting married. He wanted to understand how America worked in a societal way. A couple of times we took walks together, which was lovely. He'd carry his umbrella, his robes would flow in the breeze, and he had an intoxicatingly delicious patchouli-sandalwood smell. Being next to him was always fabulous. Sometimes his robes touched me from the breeze and they felt soft and luscious, like Prabhupada.

Prabhupada shared a huge, empty loft with a crazy young man and in his part of that loft he held regular classes and kirtans. After going through the dark, dank hallway, we'd open his door, look across this room, and there would be Prabhupada sitting on a funny little platform and playing *kartalas* with a light bulb hanging from the ceiling over his head. He hung his robes from a clothesline to define his living quarters, which were 6 by 12 feet. He had a bed on the floor, a small sit-down desk, and a school-room-type chalkboard. He gave us Sanskrit lessons, which were extremely interesting, once a week. He taught us how to play the *kartalas,* and the cadence and sound vibration of singing Hare Krishna. He liked us to come and Mukunda and I came regularly. Mukunda took to it like a leaf floating in water, but I was more distrustful and nervous about religion, so I went more slowly.

When his crazy roommate got crazier, Prabhupada asked if he could live with us. I said, "No, that's not a good idea. We can't do that," which escalated him getting an apartment at 26 Second Avenue. Then he said that the Society needed to be incorporated; Mukunda was the secretary and I was the treasurer.

When Prabhupada initiated me it blew me out of the tub. I had recently gone to New York City from Portland, and saw very odd behavior there – 1966 was the apex of intense change in America. Prabhupada's 26 Second Avenue apartment was the size of a large closet and he made a good-sized fire in the middle of that room. Six initiates, including Mukunda, were around me – I was the only female – and there were bananas going in the fire, charcoal being put on our bodies, all kinds of incantations that were foreign to me, and it was extremely hot. Afterwards I left there by myself. I needed to walk the streets and get my feet back under me.

Prabhupada finally told Mukunda and me that we should not be living together, that it would be proper for us to get married, which was fine with me. I was a product of the 1950s, and being married was the right thing to do. Prabhupada told me, "You will become the goddess of the home, and that's important. That will be your domain, and you will rule it. You will cook *prasadam* and take care of your husband." He was explaining that women are not powerless in their environment, that we have a lot of responsibility and a lot of freedom to invent how we want to initiate that domain ruling. He told me that my wedding *sari* needed to be red silk. I picked it out and Mukunda and I bought it together. It wasn't inexpensive and it was beautiful: wonderfully soft silk with gold threads. Prabhupada wrapped me up in that *sari* so it stayed on.

That was the only *sari* in ISKCON for a while and other brides wore it – Yamuna, Malati. It became an instrument of sisterhood. I had my mother's wedding ring and I also gave that to Yamuna and Malati when they got married.

The cooking for our wedding was important. Fortunately I asked my sister in Oregon if she wanted to come – it was a big thing to go to New York – but she flew out for the wedding and Prabhupada immediately put her to work in the kitchen.

Meanwhile I was buying big Indian earrings, making garlands for Prabhupada, Mukunda, and me, and decorating the room from corner to corner with boughs of evergreens. In some ways the wedding was like the initiation: a large fire in the middle of the room and fruits being put into the fire. There were probably twenty, or thirty, people in that small room. People were standing in the hallway looking through the doorway because there wasn't enough room. Prabhupada tied the end of my *sari* to Mukunda's *chadar* and said it should stay tied for seven days. The *prasadam* was wonderful and the atmosphere festive.

For our honeymoon, Mukunda and I planned to go to my aunt's house at Lake of the Woods near Crater Lake. Prabhupada said, "As long as you're going there, see about a temple in San Francisco." My sister Joan, her friend Maurice, Mukunda, me, and my black cat, Sketzelbrenzer piled into a driveaway car and on the way decided to visit our friends Melanie and Sam [later Malati and Shyamasundar] who were working in a lookout tower at the top of a 10,500 foot mountain at Three Sisters. I cooked *prasadam* for them and Melanie was transfixed by the *chapatis* blowing up. Prabhupada had given me a pair of *kartalas* and we taught them to sing Hare Krishna. Pots, pans, and spoons were the accompanying instruments and we had a nice kirtan. Sam offered us some LSD and I said no. Malati said, "Wow, something's really changed here. They're married, they're not eating meat, and no acid."

Mukunda said, "We're going to start a temple in San Francisco," and asked them to help. Malati said, "What's a temple?" Very seriously Mukunda said, "It's a storefront painted white." Malati said, "Okay."

Getting that temple together was wonderful. We found a hippie storefront on Frederick Street, put pictures of Jesus and Buddha in it and invited Prabhupada. Prabhupada said, "It would be a good idea if we took down the pictures of Jesus and Buddha. Why would you want to have those when you can have the Supreme Personality of Godhead? And by the way, maybe Ralph, Sam's dog, should wait outside." He was uncritical; he instructed us how to focus and absorb ourselves in Krishna, refine our consciousness and go in a more specific direction. He offered positive alternatives, "Perhaps this would be a good idea," and left it up to the individual to decide.

His personality was always wonderful. Those were happy days for me because I had a lot of personal, informal contact with him. If I wanted him to taste something – mashed potatoes with butter or whipping cream – he would come down the hallway barefoot and be delighted to experience these things. Likewise he taught me things in the kitchen that were fabulously wonderful – like how to make *puris* puff up. Once I offered him an artichoke and said, "Here, I'll show you Swamiji." I plucked off a leaf, dipped it in melted butter, pulled it through my teeth and said, "Now you try it." He tried a few leaves and said, "So much trouble?"

When Prabhupada took a bit of whipping cream that was sweetened with sugar and delightfully fluffy and wonderful, his eyes blew up like *puris*. He was so excited by the uncommon taste that he took another bite in the kitchen. I said, "You're eating in the kitchen?" He smiled.

To make Krishna's Surprise I mixed together whipped cream, pineapple, mandarin oranges, maraschino cherry, and some rice and brought it to him, "Try this, Swamiji." He liked it and said, "What is it?" I hesitated, thought a moment, and said, "Krishna's Surprise." Prabhupada said, "Yes," and that became one of our staples. Another time I put two or three little cocktail parasols made in Japan on his plate. Srila Prabhupada looked up, smiled, and said, "Yes, Radharani also knew the art of serving Krishna so He was pleased. He was so pleased He would taste everything simply by His glance." Prabhupada encouraged us in so many ways.

Once the mailman came with an aerogram from India for Swamiji. This was exotic and exciting. Malati and I ran upstairs with it and knocked on his door. He came to the door and I said, "Swamiji, you have a letter from India!" He took it and said, "Yes." I said, "Swamiji, aren't you going to read it?" He opened the letter, read it, and folded it up. I said, "Swamiji, good news?" He said, "Yes, my sister has died." Malati and I looked at each other, "That's good news?" He said, "She was a devotee of Krishna. She has gone back to Godhead." We got a glimpse into the new world we were entering. He started reminiscing about his sister with tears in his eyes. There was a great deal of love between those two Vaishnavas. Prabhupada offered us a wealth of learning and taught us in overt and covert ways. We learned that death was not a bad thing or to be feared. And we learned that he could reminisce and have great emotion about his sister, yet be happy that she'd gone back to Godhead.

We had been immersed in impersonal nonexistent philosophy, but here was a philosophy that enveloped everything, including emotion, and yet there was detachment and transcendence.

Prabhupada never quit teaching us. I was at the window when the *mridanga* first arrived from India and he got so excited he was twirling around the room waiting for it to come upstairs. Then he ran into the hallway. He couldn't wait to get his hands on that drum. He sat down and started playing happily and afterwards he ripped the end of his *dhoti* to wrap the *mridanga* up.

Once somebody brought him powdered milk. He mixed it with butter and sugar, rolled out balls and asked me to try one. "What do you think?" I said, "Why, Swamiji, it's simply wonderful!" Prabhupada said, "Yes," and that became Simply Wonderfuls. Those were delicious days with Prabhupada. When he was leaving it was horrible. There's a picture of me at the airport leaning over a railing and he's sitting on the other side. I snatched his airline ticket out of his hand and said, "Now, Swamiji, you cannot go. I have your ticket." He looked at Mukunda like, "Do something." After he left I dreamt everybody was chanting and the whole planet was reverberating with this wonderful Hare Krishna vibration. My dream was so real that I wrote to Prabhupada. He responded, "Yes, this is the way it should be."

Some time went by and we heard that Prabhupada had a heart attack, was extremely sick, and may not live, so we started chanting and didn't stop for almost twenty-four hours. We chanted so hard and intensely while looking at the Jagannatha Deities and thinking about Prabhupada that the Deities started dancing. It was phenomenal. I turned to Malati with tears in my eyes and said, "They are real." I was one with Them in that there was no physical, material interruption between the chanting, the Deities, and me. We all chanted and chanted and Prabhupada survived. We got some royal accommodations for him at Stinson Beach and he got lots of rest and good *prasadam* and recuperated there. San Francisco was the time of new beginnings, where our innocence was coupled with great enthusiasm and unbridled decorations of our spirit.

My cat Sketzelbrenzer's favorite place was Prabhupada's bathtub, where he'd sleep. I'd hear, "Janaki, come and get the cat," and go down and scoop Sketzelbrenzer out of the bathtub. Prabhupada was patient about Sketzelbrenzer in his bathtub but at some point suggested that we should free ourselves from cats. He said, "For now, you don't want to have animal consciousness. You want to focus all your energy on Krishna consciousness." He wanted us to have more discipline in our lives.

I had a miscarriage and then got pregnant again, and Prabhupada initially told me, "You must do what the doctors say. Stay off your feet and mind them," because he knew I wasn't good at minding people. He also said, "But if you don't have this baby, that's all right." I was really sad and sick. He said, "Don't hold onto that sadness. Let it go because maybe you're not supposed to be pregnant." After three miscarriages I decided he was right; it was a clear sign and I was finished having children. Prabhupada said, "Maybe you should go to your Aunt Edna and let her take care of you," and I did that. I went to Lake of the Woods, wrote to Prabhupada from there, and he counseled me like a father. He told me Krishna didn't want me to be pregnant at that point, and, "There's nothing you can do about that. You're powerless to do anything about it. Ultimately it's up to Krishna." When I first went to him I was crying, but he wasn't patting me on the head saying, "Oh, I'm so sorry for you." He wasn't foolishly sentimental. He was instructive and kept me moving forward.

Later he said, "Go to London." So we did, stopping on the way to celebrate Janmashtami and Vyasa-puja at the Montreal temple cum bowling alley. In Bury Place I taught new devotees how to cook. That temple was crowded and we had to make lots of *prasadam*. I was disciplined in the kitchen, strictly following Prabhupada's rules – no snacking or tasting *prasadam* in the kitchen, keeping everything clean, not enjoying the *prasadam* before it was offered to Radha and Krishna.

After some time I got tired of the temple politics and the need to bow to men all the time. It seemed like the men were taking over, that they were injecting into Krishna consciousness something that really wasn't Krishna conscious. It got to the point where I had to leave the Movement. I went into Prabhupada's room and said I was leaving and he said, "Are you sure you have to leave? Is there nothing that I can do?" I said, "No, there is nothing you can do, I have to leave." He asked me to take care of myself and said that no matter where I was he would pray for me and that there was a place for me; I could come back anytime I wanted. And he cried.

Jarati devi dasi

In 1972 when Jarati was fourteen and had been in England less than a year, a harinama party at the Mander Centre shopping area in London attracted her. She had seen sankirtana in India but the London devotees looked different. They seemed to have dropped from heaven.

In my mind the devotees had come from the spiritual world and I wanted to watch them going back to the spiritual world. My sister was nagging me, "Let's leave," but I said, "No, you go." She said, "Here's your bus fare. You make it home." The devotees saw I was interested and said, "Do you want to come with us?" I said, "Yes, sure." I went with them to the Bury Place temple, where everyone was rushing to make everything beautiful for Srila Prabhupada who was coming the next day.

The devotees gave me delicious *prasadam* and I forgot about going home. I spent the night at the temple and the next day Srila Prabhupada arrived. Someone said, "Oh, Srila Prabhupada, this is an Indian girl who wants to join." Srila Prabhupada said, "Oh, very nice." I said to Srila Prabhupada, "I'm not sure who is God. Are you God?" He said, "No, I am a servant of God. Lord Chaitanya is God." I felt that Srila Prabhupada was my way to know God.

I also said to Srila Prabhupada, "I haven't told my parents that I joined the temple." He said, "That's not very nice. Go back with your parents." I was crying. Srila Prabhupada said, "Your name is Jarati, and you chant sixteen rounds daily." He gave me my beads and I left. My father was furious.

When I was fifteen-and-a-half, my father arranged my marriage. I didn't tell my husband or his family anything about Krishna, but my mother-in-law liked me and was happy with whatever I did. She asked me to get initiated by her guru and I said, "Oh, no, I can't." She said, "Why?" I said, "I have a guru in the Krishna mandir." She said, "Oh? Why didn't you tell me?" I said, "I'm new here and wasn't sure if I should." She said, "Invite them." So we invited all the Krishna devotees and cooked a feast for them. My husband and his brothers and everybody else in the house became Life Members. My husband was habituated to smoking and drinking but after the devotees left, the whole night and day he read the First Canto of the *Bhagavatam*. Right away he stopped drinking tea, smoking, and taking alcohol. He said, "I'm going to check them out at the temple." We went to the temple, he purchased all the books and then went door-to-door distributing them. He didn't know he was doing *sankirtana* but he brought the money to the temple. At Christmas the devotees wanted him to give up his work and do *sankirtana* full time. Eventually he did give up his work, we sold our house, and moved into Bhaktivedanta Manor.

Now my husband and I aren't engaged in direct service like we used to be, but we're still trying to fulfill Srila Prabhupada's desire. Srila Prabhupada is gone but not gone. He said, "If you think of me, then I'll be with you." My husband and I feel Srila Prabhupada's presence is in his books, and that keeps us going. I saw Srila Prabhupada four times and spoke to him once. But I'm part of his huge family and he's always present in my life.

Jatila devi dasi

In 1969, when the San Francisco devotees were still wearing white sheets, Jatila used to chant with them and go to festivals. At the Family Dog (a rock 'n roll ballroom), with her hair down her back and wearing patent leather Mary Janes, white lace tights, a pink and white checked baby doll dress with white lace, and a Victorian headband, she saw all the devotees offer their obeisances. She didn't know what they were doing and thought, "I wonder if I could do that?"

Then I saw a small figure enter the room and move like the wind to the foot of an enormous chair. He climbed the steps to the chair, sat down, and began to speak. I couldn't understand what he was saying. I thought he was speaking a foreign language and was waiting for a translation. Everybody was listening intently, although I don't know if they understood any more than I did. But somehow we understood the significance. Finally I thought, "I give up. I'm going to go get some more Krishna food." Later I read a transcript of the talk Prabhupada gave and at one point he said, "They are leaving now to get *prasadam*. That is all right. Let them sing and dance and take *prasadam* and one day they will understand."

Segue to the mid 1970s. My husband and I were running a vegetarian macrobiotic collective restaurant when we abandoned ship, moved into the Atlanta temple, and helped get everything ready for Prabhupada's visit. It was all fresh and momentous and exciting and I got to sew Prabhupada's white umbrella. When Prabhupada came into the temple, he said, "*Hmm*, fresh paint. Amazing. Everywhere I go I'm greeted by the smell of fresh paint." He had us learn the "Parama Karuna" song and we sang it with him.

Jaya Gauri devi dasi

At fourteen, Jaya Gauri was certain that her intense desire to meet an old wise man who would be her guru would be fulfilled. When she saw Srila Prabhupada's picture on the vyasasana in the Sao Paolo temple she immediately said, "That's him."

Srila Prabhupada was really present in his photograph. When I was getting initiated in New Mayapur in 1976 and was face-to-face with him, he had the same look that I'd seen in his photograph. I felt, "Yes, I know him. He's mine, he's my guru," because he was so close to my heart, so much a part of me. Srila Prabhupada had my *japa* beads in his hand and looked at me, seeing the soul. He asked, "What are the principles?" Firm and sure of myself, I looked straight at him and told him the four regulative principles in Portuguese because I didn't speak English. He looked at me deeply in a way that transcended material communication. He needed to see, "Who is this person? I don't understand what she's saying, so I need to give her a better look," and then gave me my name.

Later that year, my husband, Mahavira, and I arrived in Vrindavan at sunset, walked to the side of the Krishna-Balaram temple, and there was Srila Prabhupada sitting under the *tamal* tree. I received second initiation and, walking into Prabhupada's room to get the mantra, felt awkward and inept, but Srila Prabhupada was totally relaxed. I sat beside him like he was my dear father, held the Gayatri mantra paper, and he pointed to the words. Every time I have doubts about where I'm going, I remember Srila Prabhupada there and he carries me through my life.

One afternoon Srila Prabhupada was observing Mahavira and me talking and he told Mahavira, "You have a good wife." I was happy to hear that. I saw my marriage as my service to Srila Prabhupada, and wanted to live up to his comment. But raising kids and trying to be a good wife took its toll because I lost spontaneity; I was in a near torpor. Now I've paid my dues – I don't have to think about family and can focus on serving Srila Prabhupada with my life and soul. I want to improve myself so I can present something he'll be pleased with. I'd like to write a book for my grandchildren and, in my own words as a woman, a mother, and a grandmother, express who I am, what a devotee is, and what Krishna consciousness is, so they're inspired to try devotional service. My kids say, "Mom, all you talk is about Krishna." I say, "Yes, this is who I am. When I'm long gone you'll remember me talking about Krishna."

I always feel loved by Srila Prabhupada and that inspires me every day. I know in this lifetime or the next he's going to engage me in his service and I look forward to that. At seventy Srila Prabhupada traveled across the ocean to a country where nobody knew him; he was constantly on the spiritual platform and that's where I want to be. I'm working towards it and if there's an obstacle, I deal with it and keep moving forward. Determination is important for pursuing spiritual life. Now I'm working on chanting *japa* attentively because I want to be able to serve Srila Prabhupada eternally. Prabhupada's legacy has infused us with passion for spiritual life. We're passionate *bhaktas* running towards Krishna's lotus feet.

Jayabhadra devi dasi

The first time Jayabhadra saw Prabhupada she felt she had never seen such a humble person. She realized that she'd never seen humility before. His humility touched her heart.

In the L.A. airport, Prabhupada was walking with his hands folded and his eyes lowered and the devotees were going wild, "*Jaya* Prabhupada!" He was giving the glorification to Krishna. When he received a garland, to me it looked like he disappeared into an ocean of humility. I felt I only wanted to please him. It was an intense desire that came from deep within my heart and an unusual feeling for a conditioned soul, but the pure devotee arouses spiritual feelings.

At my initiation, on December 6th, 1973 in Los Angeles, my mind was uncontrolled and wandering. I couldn't focus on Prabhupada's lecture. I was upset and frustrated. It seemed that everyone else could hear Prabhupada except me. In the middle of the lecture I lost control and started calling, "Prabhupada! Prabhupada!" Prabhupada stopped speaking for a second and looked up. He wasn't angry that he was being disturbed, he was wondering who was calling him. Immediately I felt that he was concerned, compassionate. His look completely pacified me. Then he continued the lecture and I could hear better.

Prabhupada told me that my name was Jayabhadra. He said that *Bhadra* was a name for Krishna meaning "the most gentle" and that I was the maidservant of Krishna. Then all I could see was those golden hands coming towards me with the beads.

Once Prabhupada was saying that material enjoyment is like trying to enjoy a *rasagulla* with a Band-Aid on your tongue. Then he rolled his eyes and tongue at the same time, very expressively; he looked beautiful. His face looked like a lotus and his tongue like a petal of the lotus. It was funny – the devotees were laughing.

In his lectures, he'd say, "You are not this body," almost indignantly. As if, "How can you think you are this body?" I was impressed because we were trying to understand that we were not this body and we accepted it theoretically, but for him it was a fact. I didn't get direct personal instruction from Prabhupada to cherish deep in my heart. What happened was he gave knowledge that I'm not this body, that there is a Supreme Person who can give full shelter, that can free me from any kind of fear or unhappiness, and all I have to do is learn how to surrender to Him. When I heard how strong Prabhupada was on the point that you're not this body, it made me realize that for me to identify deeply with the body was outrageous. And that gave me strength when I was going through various kinds of difficulties. I remembered that I'm not this body, I'm an eternal spirit soul. Whatever difficulty I go through has nothing to do with me. It will pass. The knowledge, even though it wasn't fully realized, has a very deep effect on me.

Another time he said that if we preach and follow the four regulative principles we'd go back to Godhead in this lifetime. This is guaranteed. He said that with complete conviction; there was no doubt about it.

If we want to have a relationship with Prabhupada, we have to enter deeply into his books, and some devotees did that. I used to write Prabhupada letters after he'd passed away, and that was always very potent. I got immediate reciprocation from him. Especially when I was feeling some personal difficulties, I would write him a letter and I felt he'd reciprocate. I feel that whatever difficulty I'm in, Prabhupada will always be there.

After Prabhupada left, many of his representatives were not able to maintain their spiritual lives. I understood that if I was more self-controlled, regulated, dedicated and pure, then it wouldn't matter who came and went. The real problem was that I wasn't fixed enough in Krishna consciousness. If his representatives couldn't maintain their spiritual life, that was no reason for me to stop surrendering. Later we understood that someone doesn't have to be superhuman to represent Srila Prabhupada, that person just has to be sincere and sincerely cooperating with Prabhupada's servants. Now my connection with Prabhupada is strengthened by devotees who are taking shelter of Prabhupada. Those devotees, who stayed through everything and who cooperated together, were sincere. Seeing their sincerity, my faith became stronger. Over time, Krishna revealed different persons I can take shelter of who inspire me to overcome my weaknesses and lack of steadiness, to deeply study Prabhupada's books, to improve my *sadhana*. Now I feel Prabhupada's presence more in my life.

I also feel connected to Prabhupada through the deity of him I worship. By having him in my room, it's forced me to develop better regulation and cleanliness and more Krishna-orientation. I can't be sloppy or lazy.

It's also important for me to discuss Prabhupada's pastimes, and to keep his example fresh. The videos of Prabhupada are also important, because otherwise Prabhupada can become a theoretical person. Book distribution is also an important way to feel connected with Prabhupada because book distribution is very dear to Prabhupada.

Once a girl asked me, "What is it that keeps you Hare Krishna people together?" I told her, "It's Krishna. Somehow or other Prabhupada has planted Krishna in our heart. Even though we don't have a lot of realizations about our relationship with Him or who He is, He's so powerful and attractive we can put aside the nonsense of material life."

Any time things got difficult, what kept me going was the personal love that Prabhupada gave me. The most distressing thought of leaving would be separation from Prabhupada. I'm fully dependent on his mercy. I have no qualification but the goal of my life is to become his real disciple. I should surrender to him the way that he deserves.

Before I met Prabhupada I was in the hell of distress. I had no understanding of any purpose in life, and I didn't have the enthusiasm to pursue material goals and successes. There was no way for me but down. Before I even saw him, Prabhupada reversed the whole tide of my life through his disciples. They gave me his books and took me to the temple for the Sunday Feast, and I've never left. Prabhupada is acting through his disciples, the *sankirtana* devotees.

If we can develop a loving relationship with Prabhupada, then it's the same as loving Krishna in the sense that Prabhupada's only desire is to fulfill Krishna's desire. If we can surrender heart and soul to Srila Prabhupada, we get the same result as surrender to Krishna. We get surcharged with spiritual energy, we come off the bodily platform. And our mind and senses come under our control.

Jayarama devi dasi

Jayarama's boyfriend took her to a Sunday Feast at the Caracas, Venezuela temple. Later, she moved into the temple alone and soon realized she was pregnant. She asked a devotee, "What does Srila Prabhupada say about abortion?" When she heard the answer, Jayarama decided to have her baby.

Three months later, Srila Prabhupada visited the Caracas temple for six days. I was eighteen, and although I respected Prabhupada as an important person, at that point I didn't love him. A nondevotee heard Srila Prabhupada's morning *Srimad-Bhagavatam* class and said, "The *brahmacharis*, the *brahmacharinis*, and the *grihasthas* in this temple are in *maya*! Why are you talking about *maya* outside? *Maya* is in the temple." Srila Prabhupada said, "Tell me where *maya* is not and I will go there."

I got initiated in New York in 1976 when Srila Prabhupada came for Ratha-yatra. Once I went close to Srila Prabhupada as he was taking darshan of Sri Sri Radha-Govinda and I saw he was crying. His tears looked like diamonds.

We're lucky. Srila Prabhupada gave us a beautiful gift! We got his mercy and God's mercy for no reason and now we have to do what he says. I wish we'd all understand Srila Prabhupada is our father and we're a close, tight, family without friction or envy. To forever please Srila Prabhupada, we're meant to love each other deeply, putting aside material motivations.

After Prabhupada's departure, when our Society had so many problems, I understood that Krishna is the controller, we're not the controllers. Krishna has a plan and we have to surrender to His will. In my heart I keep Srila Prabhupada's instructions to distribute his books. That's the essence. There's nothing more important than that because the conditioned souls are in a dark night, but Srila Prabhupada's books are the light that illuminates our vision.

I know I can change my life if I follow strictly because I have my master. I strive to be humble, to have a simple life, to be honest, and to love others. We can learn from each other, from our godbrothers and godsisters. Every day, every minute, Krishna teaches us. We have to continue to spread Prabhupada's message so all human beings can take advantage of and taste this precious nectar of love of Godhead! When I see the living entity suffering, I suffer too.

Before he left Caracas, Prabhupada told us, "If you follow the four regulative principles, chant sixteen rounds, and go on *sankirtana*, I promise you will go back to Krishna in this life." I want to make a tight circle between Srila Prabhupada, the four principles, sixteen rounds, book distribution, and me. If I do, he promised he'd take me back to Godhead. That's my real desire and if I endeavor hard and work for him until I die, I'll be happy.

Jayasri devi dasi

Jayasri was twenty when she met Srila Prabhupada in Hawaii in March 1969.

I was a hippie girl from a well-to-do family from Hawaii who, at eighteen, had left home on a spiritual quest. I meditated daily and tried to understand the meaning of life. In Hawaii, many of my friends after high school were on similar spiritual quests. One of my friends had a closet-sized temple, and I would sit in it and read the *maha-mantra* she had posted on the wall. This was before Srila Prabhupada's followers had arrived in Hawaii, but somehow or other, I was already following the four regulative principles and reading a *Bhagavad-gita* translated by an Indian Swami, the Bible, and various Buddhist teachings. I was trying to find God, but was becoming more and more confused. Each of these texts said something different, so I became bewildered.

One day, I lay down in my room and prayed, "Dear God, I don't know if You are here, but if You are, please send me to someone who knows You." The next week I saw a handwritten poster on a small bakery window at Sunset Beach that said, "Chant while you can: Hare Krishna, Hare Krishna, Krishna Krishna, Hare Hare, Hare Rama, Hare Rama, Rama Rama, Hare Hare, A. C. Bhaktivedanta Swami." And there was an address that would take me only a few miles up the coast. I asked a friend to take me there.

It was an old Hawaiian house on a hill with a big yard and cows and a windmill. We drove up the driveway, and when we parked, I turned to look up at the top of the outside staircase, and there was an older gentleman in orange robes who waved to invite us in. So we went up the stairs, through the enclosed porch, through the temple room with its Brijbasi prints thumb-tacked to the wall and a string across the room holding a simple curtain that hid the altar, and up the stairs. Srila Prabhupada was alone in the house–the devotees had gone out on *harinama*.

We entered his room, and Srila Prabhupada sat down on an old Hawaiian cushion behind a desk made of a piece of plywood supported by cinderblocks. He immediately started talking about God. It was very simple, what he said, but at the same time it was very deep, and in the course of the discussion, I could see him looking into my mind and heart and seeing what I needed to hear. He answered all my spiritual questions without me asking anything. It was a profound experience. He was dynamic, effulgent, sweet, and seemed so familiar to me. He was the person I was looking for. For me, God had answered my prayer and, through Srila Prabhupada, all of my questions. It was a miracle that I met Prabhupada.

Then devotees returned from their engagement and one of them came in and offered him a plate of fresh-cut sugarcane. He asked me if I would like some, but I said, "No, thank you, I don't eat sugar." He took a piece of sugarcane, tilted his head back and popped it into his mouth, and said, "Oh? In India, we eat sugar." When he said that, volumes of knowledge went racing through my mind–of course, sugar is natural. What's wrong with sugar? And when I left the room and saw the plate of sugarcane sitting on the floor in the next room I bent down and put some in my mouth. It had already been chewed–most likely by Srila Prabhupada.

I came back to that house almost daily for the next week, and Prabhupada asked me to bring the *Bhagavad-gita* I had been reading. He had me sit next to him as he opened my book to 6.33, where Arjuna says, "O Madhusudana, the system of yoga which you have summarized appears impractical and unendurable to me, for the mind is restless and unsteady."

In the purport this Swami wrote, "*Astanga-yoga* is for this age and everyone should do it." Prabhupada said, "Do you see what he's doing? He's taking Krishna's words and saying they mean exactly the opposite of what Krishna actually said. He's inserting his own philosophy."

He closed the book and pulled out the purple paperback *Bhagavad-gita* he had translated and said, "This is *Bhagavad-gita As It Is*. Would you like one?" I said, "Oh, yes!" I thought that he was going to give it to me because I thought all things connected with God were free. He gave it to me, sat back, and said, "That will be $2.95." I thought, "Yes, of course, $2.95. It costs money to print a book. It's God's work." I bought four books and gave three of them to my neighbors.

After he sold me the *Gitas*, Srila Prabhupada turned to me and said, "Do you like me?" I laughed and said, "Yes, I love you!" He smiled. He was so nice to deal with.

I tried to get back to see him every day until he left Hawaii, and on one occasion Govinda dasi told me her iron was broken and asked if I could launder Srila Prabhupada's clothes. I took them home and washed them in an outdoor cement sink. I found as I was washing them that the fragrance and spiritual energy of his clothes was simply intoxicating. I had the same experience again once they had dried and I began to iron them. Somehow in later years whenever Srila Prabhupada came to a temple where I was someone would ask me to wash his clothes. My good fortune.

Govinda dasi was instrumental in getting me to move into the temple shortly after Srila Prabhupada left Hawaii. It was Goursundar, Govinda dasi, Balabhadra, and me. Then Turiya dasa came a month later.

Sometime later, Govinda dasi had the idea that she wanted a saffron coat made for Srila Prabhupada and she asked me to make it. We were in Hawaii, so wool was hard to find, what to speak of saffron wool. I ventured to the fabric section in Sears and wouldn't you know it, but Krishna arranged that the first fabric I saw was this beautiful saffron wool. Govinda dasi had an old coat of Srila Prabhupada's, and I would try it on so I could measure the components for the coat that I would make. We added peacock feathers on the tassels and a fur-lined hood. Govinda also asked me to make a flannel saffron cape with a hood that Srila Prabhupada could wear early in the morning to translate. She said his *chadar* would always slip off of his head or knees, so she wanted a garment that would keep him covered and warm. After he received them he wrote back to her that they kept him so warm that it was like being on the lap of his mother.

One time I wrote to Srila Prabhupada and he wrote back, "You are such a sincere devotee that Krishna has helped you to understand the philosophy so quickly. And this sincerity of purpose is the only means to attain perfection in Krishna Consciousness. I am so glad to learn that you are thinking of sleep as a waste of time. This is not an ordinary thing. So I have become very much pleased to hear this statement from you. Be blessed by Krishna. Just as you have already understood the benefits of this Krishna Consciousness Movement, try to realize and assimilate it more and more and distribute it to the suffering humanity. Our Movement is the greatest gift to the human race. They may not immediately appreciate it, but time will come and history will give evidence that this Movement saved the human society from being fallen into barbarianism.

"Regarding the things that Krishna is giving you, everything belongs to Krishna and He is giving everything, even to the nondevotees, even to the animals who have no consciousness of Krishna; and what to speak of His devotees. Just like the father maintains all his children without any grudge, but the child who is very faithful to the orders of the father is given specific care by the father. Similarly, Krishna being the Father of all living entities, he is supplying the bare necessities of their life; but for His devotees He has got special attention. So depend on Krishna, chant regularly Hare Krishna and you will find that He is talking with you face to face, what to speak of supplying your necessities. This is a great science, and please try to understand it nicely."

Years later Srila Prabhupada returned to Hawaii to rectify a situation that had deviated from the standard and, in a lecture he gave on Ala Aloha Loop, he said, gravely, "If you cannot see that what I have given you is the highest, then there's nothing I can do." Prabhupada had a purpose in asking us to follow the rules and regulations, to wear certain clothes, and to follow certain standards. He wanted the standards to be maintained.

To this day, whenever I smell gardenias I remember Prabhupada, because when he left Hawaii he was wearing a gardenia garland. As he drove off to the airport, he turned around from the back seat of the car and smiled. I thought, "This is the last time I'll see him." It was. All glories to Srila Prabhupada.

Jijnasi devi dasi

After Americans at Jijnasi's boarding school in Oxford, England, introduced her to radical politics, drugs, poetry, and jazz, she rebelled against her parents' values, which seemed hypocritical. Her mother considered her "difficult."

I'd wonder, "What's the point of working all week? Work for what?" I was frustrated and tortured that no one could tell me. George's song, "All you need is love," summed it up for me. Society seemed destructive and the mainstream world was becoming intolerable for me. The hippie lifestyle and philosophy offered me a meaningful alternative and the Indian influence attracted me. Yet at the same time, I saw that hippie life was an idealistic dream of love and peace, but couldn't work because it was artificial. It was based on drugs and corrupted by greed.

In late 1970, I found a packet of incense with the Bury Place temple address on it and, although none of my friends would come with me, I went. Ranchor answered all my questions in the course of his Sunday Feast lecture. It felt so right; it was what I'd been looking for. Within a month I was living in the ashram.

Mondakini and Jyotirmayi were always talking about Prabhupada and in August of 1971, this mythical person was coming at last. We were at Heathrow, dressed in our *saris* and *dhotis,* holding flowers and chanting, waiting and waiting and excited. Most of us had never seen Srila Prabhupada.

Suddenly he appeared. I felt shivers go down me and I was weeping. I'd never experienced anything like it. We fell down to pay obeisances and then went crazy, throwing flowers, chanting, and crying. The effect Prabhupada had was overwhelming and surpassed everything I'd been told about him. This amazing little man with an effulgent golden aura was floating and seemed so big. As he came toward us in his saffron robes, he was peaceful, and had the biggest, most wonderful smile.

Seeing him confirmed everything I'd heard about him, and everything he wrote in his books. Seeing him dispelled all my doubts. I've met many extraordinary people, but I've never met another human being as special as him. I can imagine Jesus must have been like that – the living embodiment of what he said.

Prabhupada embodied the intellectual words he spoke and I could feel the power of the living embodiment. It was his personal association that maintained in me a core acceptance of his teachings for all these years. I never renounced what he said or the organization he created. Nothing swayed my conviction that he was that embodiment.

We were a close and blissful family at the Bury Place temple, and he was our beloved father who'd come home. Like children, we gathered around him in his room.

His presence changed the whole atmosphere. It enlivened me and made me blissful.

When he initiated me, he said, "Your name is Jijnasi, which means one who is always inquiring about the absolute truth." Everyone laughed, because I had a reputation of forever asking: "Why this? Why that?" But Prabhupada became serious. "No, this is not funny." I felt protected by him, my father. He said, "It is a serious business. One cannot even begin spiritual life until one starts to inquire." It was wonderful.

Jitamitra devi dasi

Jitamitra joined in 1970 at the Henry Street temple in Brooklyn, New York.

I'd been spending weekends at the temple and going to Sunday Feasts. Then in July, devotees told me that Prabhupada was coming. Everyone was excited and busy cleaning and redecorating. When Prabhupada came, he spoke the basic philosophy–how we're not these bodies and how we can't enjoy in this world without Krishna. His peacefulness and contentment and awareness of Krishna were unique–I had never seen anyone like him. Over the years, whatever temple I was in, Brooklyn, or Dallas, or Los Angeles, Prabhupada would bless us with his association in the summers. I was shy and worried how I'd feel when Prabhupada saw me, but when he did look at me I realized he wasn't looking at me as a body; he looked at me as a spirit soul, and so I didn't feel at all self-conscious or awkward.

Once, after Prabhupada arrived at one temple, he was going to speak in his quarters. His room was crowded with *sannyasis* and other men. Prabhupada noticed the women trying to squeeze in through the back door and said, "Let the ladies come forward." Some of the men moved out of the way so we could sit near Prabhupada. He was gentlemanly.

In November 1977, when I heard that Prabhupada had passed away, I sat down where I was and tried to absorb it. I wondered how everything would work without him. Now the tests would really begin. That frightened me.

As the years have passed, there are times I've felt that today's ISKCON is not the Movement I joined. But, as a Movement, we have worked through a lot of things.

I feel connected to Prabhupada by reading his books and especially by chanting my rounds. Chanting and following the four regulative principles is a promise I made to Prabhupada. I know some devotees struggle to keep their initiation vows, but they have found other ways to keep their connection with Srila Prabhupada. They might be rendering service and feeling much devotion through that service or have other ways to show that they love Prabhupada. I don't consider myself better than them, but for me, keeping my vows is my minimal way of staying connected with Srila Prabhupada. I am very fallen and have not been able to remain so enthusiastic about spreading Prabhupada's Movement. Still, I feel connected by keeping the vows I made to him.

I am always conscious of the things I do in my life, weighing them based on what would please Srila Prabhupada and what would not. By no means do the scales always tip on the favorable side. But at least by Srila Prabhupada's mercy I can remain aware and know the difference between what I should and should not be doing as his disciple and pray for the strength and determination to improve.

By keeping my basic promises to Prabhupada and by reading his books, I have access to Prabhupada and somehow that's enough. It's a wonderful feeling to have one person that you totally trust and have faith in–faith not easily placed elsewhere.

I feel a certain hankering or loneliness for Prabhupada, because when he was here I could turn to him absolutely and totally accept whatever he said on any question that came up. I miss the simplicity of the Movement that we had while he was with us. A certain innocence is gone–the innocent trust that a child has for his parents is what we had toward Prabhupada. It was satisfying. Innocent acceptance was a very nice feeling.

Jivan Mukta devi dasi

Jivan Mukta's husband, Barry, was involved in Brooklyn's Henry Street temple and in the winter of 1973, Jivan Mukta saw Srila Prabhupada there.

Prabhupada wanted a building in New York City and in 1976 when he looked at the West 55th building for the first time, he saw it as a preaching element and blessed it by folding his hands. To see Prabhupada was the perfection of eyesight, to hear him speak was the perfection of hearing, and to get the *prasadam* cookie he gave out after *Bhagavatam* class was the perfection of mercy. Preaching is the essence and Srila Prabhupada was the perfection of preaching.

In the summer of 1976 I was pulling Subhadra's cart when Prabhupada joined the Ratha-yatra in New York. I can't put into words how special that was. It was the first Ratha-yatra in New York and thousands of people joined the festival. Prabhupada gave a lecture in the park on West Fourth, devotees served *prasadam*, and as Prabhupada left, I was just a few yards away and clearly saw him as he blessed us.

Later I went to Bhaktivedanta Manor. I loved the *sankirtana* women and thought, "These girls are the best." I was serving them, washing their clothes, and one day someone said, "Go out and distribute." I said, "Okay, I'm going."

I distributed books in Amsterdam, on the *sankirtana* party led by Malati devi dasi in Denmark, and in Paris airports. One day I was told: "Bhaktin Julia, you will be initiated in the summer." I said, "Oh, no, that cannot be. I'm not ready yet." But it happened. I was initiated in New Mayapur in the summer of 1977. Srila Prabhupada was in Vrindavan at that time and it was the last initiation that took place while he was present on the planet.

One day in November I came back to the temple to hear Prabhupada had left his body. It was confusing. I didn't comprehend what was happening. Prabhupada's mercy pulled me in and then he was gone. Even till today I don't understand that.

Jnana Murti devi dasi

Jnana Murti had been a devotee for about a year and then blooped – when, in 1974, she received a telegram from the devotees saying Prabhupada was coming to Melbourne. She went to see him and ended up staying.

I'd make sandalwood paste with saffron and camphor for Srila Prabhupada's forehead, make his garland, clean his room, and cook breakfast for the devotees. One morning at Danks Street I'd missed class and was walking across the courtyard when Prabhupada came out of the temple room surrounded by an entourage of men. Spontaneously I fell down flat to offer him *dandavats* and touch his feet. Srila Prabhupada didn't say anything but a *brahmachari* dragged me off the ground and severely chastised me for touching Prabhupada's feet. I thought I'd committed some terrible offense and felt absolutely dreadful but later the ladies told me, "You're so fortunate! You're so fortunate!"

Remembering Srila Prabhupada is what keeps me going today. There are times when I'm so down I think, "Is Krishna really real?" Then I think of Prabhupada, his dedication, and devotion, and know that Krishna consciousness is real because Prabhupada was the living example of it. My conviction returns.

Prabhupada left all his books for us to read and he set everything up – devotee association, *prasadam*, Deity worship, and other service. It's all there. We just need to be dedicated to and serve Srila Prabhupada, or someone who is dedicated to him and serving him, and we'll feel deeply connected with Srila Prabhupada.

Jyestha devi dasi

In Amsterdam, Jyestha had heard about Prabhupada and had pictures of him on her wall, but she was attached to her so-called freedom and didn't want to commit to Krishna consciousness. Finally convinced by Visva devi, she moved into the temple but wasn't sure why she'd joined because the devotees weren't personal with each other. Jyestha was looking for answers to questions like, "If there is a God, why is He so mean that one person is born crippled and another wealthy?"

Nothing prepared me for that moment in June 1974 in Paris when I first saw Srila Prabhupada. He was majestic, grand, and the most beautiful person I'd ever seen. His beauty was completely beyond anything material. It was an instant love affair. I cried and cried from the satisfaction of being in his presence and knew I'd made the right choice. I'd been involved with anarchist groups and had seen it wasn't safe to give my heart to anybody. But with Srila Prabhupada I felt, "Here's somebody who will not betray me. Here's somebody I can give my heart and life to." Srila Prabhupada had perfect answers to every question one can have in life.

I lived from one of his visits to the next, and although I served in the temple all day and night, in front of Srila Prabhupada I felt I'd wasted the whole year between his visits. My service wasn't enough to repay his kindness. At my initiation Prabhupada chanted on my beads and asked, "What are the four regulative principles?" Crying, I told him and, with glowing and tearful eyes and a look of compassion, he gave me my beads.

Prabhupada saw through all my coverings and accepted me as his disciple, and that's the greatest love, the greatest gift. Before Srila Prabhupada I had nothing and he gave me everything – my children, my service, everything I am. He's the reason for my existence and his mercy is my anchor and mast.

Over the years, I've taken shelter of my godsisters, have philosophical discussions with them, and together we go deeper and find rich realizations from our years of Krishna consciousness. When we joined we thought we knew it all but now we realize we're aspiring.

Our eternal family connection is with Srila Prabhupada and with all the wonderful devotees. The love affair between Prabhupada and the devotees is all-consuming and the impact he made is like a roller coaster. Some of us may take a little longer and may have to come back a few times because we haven't finished our journey, but at some point we'll meet again when these bodies are finished. I say, "Krishna, if I have enough time, then maybe I'll catch up with the others."

Srila Prabhupada said that service to the devotees is most important. There are difficulties, but if we can be personal, intimate, and keep a community spirit, his mission will go on. Service to Srila Prabhupada is eternal. He's still with us, and through service we're connected to him.

Jyotirmayi devi dasi

In September 1969, five devotees arrived in France to open the first French temple at Prabhupada's request. Jyotirmayi was planning to go to Nepal to become a Buddhist monk with Mondakini, but before they left France they began visiting the new temple for weekly engagements of kirtans, bhajanas, and japa. Then the devotees in Paris told them to visit Prabhupada in London.

On the day of our arrival in London in December 1969 the Deities were installed. The next day Prabhupada invited us to see him. He had been told that we were the three first French devotees. I was expecting that I would be filled up with enlightenment, like some transcendental fluid filling up my being. To my disappointment, it didn't happen. Prabhupada was practical and that put me off at first. Yet, I was attracted when Prabhupada looked at me, because I felt he was seeing everything inside me. He was very kind to us, and advised us to learn from the older devotees: Yamuna, Malati, and Janaki. To my astonishment, he asked us if we knew how to type. Later I understood that he was already thinking of his books being translated into French.

Three things made me become a devotee instead of a Buddhist. One, I loved the Hare Krishna mantra and the most extraordinary thing I'd ever heard was Prabhupada chanting it. Prabhupada made the kirtan a meditation. He was completely absorbed in the mantra and he absorbed us in it. Second, although I didn't appreciate Srila Prabhupada's philosophy of personalism and, on hearing his lectures thought, "I don't agree with that; this is not correct," he countered my mental arguments with philosophical points. I was weighing impersonalism vs. personalism, Vaishnavism vs. Buddhism. In every class he gave in the five days he was in London he defeated my doubts. It was as if he knew my mind. I started to think, "This is really strange." Little by little I became convinced that this philosophy was higher than Buddhism. Third, was seeing Prabhupada's love for his disciples, and his disciples' love for him and for each other. Prabhupada was personal with the devotees and they were personal with him and with each other. I'd never seen anything like that and it attracted me so much. By these three things, I became convinced. In later years, as Prabhupada had thousands of disciples, I was astonished to see that he stayed personal. Whenever he would come to France, if he didn't see me he'd always ask my husband, Yogesvara, "How is Jyotirmayi?"

On the fifth day that December, Prabhupada held initiations and told Tamal Krishna that he wanted to initiate us. Tamal Krishna told him we had been in the temple in London only five days, that it was too early. So Prabhupada initiated us by letter one month later in January 1970. It was customary that each new initiate would give a gift to the guru at the time of initiation. As I loved painting, I did a small painting of Radha-Krishna as a gift. Srila Prabhupada hung it in his room. Later, at Yamuna's request, I painted two more pictures to decorate the temple. The one of Lord Chaitanya was hung on the wall of the stairs leading to the first floor where Prabhupada's room was. Prabhupada saw it and asked who painted it. I was just behind him and told him it was me. He said I should paint for his books. I never followed this instruction because I became too busy with translating his books and preaching.

Fortunately, Prabhupada behaved exactly the same with the women as with the men, for otherwise I would not have joined. Both men and women went on Prabhupada's morning walks and both got as close to Prabhupada as they could. When Prabhupada told Mondakini and me, "Learn from the older women of the temple" (Malati, Yamuna, and Janaki), I tried to do that. Those women were absolutely wonderful and were my heroes – intelligent, in love with Prabhupada, active, enterprising, capable in many different ways. All the devotees had as many women heroes as men heroes. At that time, men had no harshness or tension or disdain toward women, and neither were they condescending. There was separation, not segregation, between the sexes; and between us there was tenderness and kindness and sweetness.

We had little money, no heating, only cold water, and were ten people in a room. Temple life was austere. But we were happy because the atmosphere was transcendental and there was a strong loving relationship between us. Every evening when we were in bed, Gurudas, who was the temple president and like our father, would read *Krsna* book to us. Yamuna, who was like our mother, taught both the men and the women. The men had no ill feeling, "Oh, a *woman* is teaching me." Prabhupada had brought a loving spiritual atmosphere, and the devotees were almost transparent in giving it to us. We did everything the way Prabhupada did it, because that's the only way we knew how to do it, and we felt constant spiritual ecstasy. It was completely out of this world. At that time, a wonderful part of the Movement was that we would take responsibilities immediately, which made us strong and expert. We would learn and develop.

I'd been a student at the Sorbonne in Paris, where I was studying ethnology – the study of the cultures and religion of different ancient traditions. I'd stopped my studies to become a devotee, but later thought, "It would be good to finish my studies because then I could teach Krishna consciousness." I asked Prabhupada and he said that I was a very intelligent girl and I should do it. But I didn't because I started translating Prabhupada's books. When I was translating, I became engrossed in Prabhupada's writing and in trying to render it in the best possible way. I loved Prabhupada's intelligence, and would think, "My God, he's so intelligent!"

Since I was the main French translator, I usually translated Prabhupada's lectures when he came to France. Once, we had an engagement at the College of Architecture in Paris and I asked Prabhupada to make short sentences, and he was careful to do that. When I missed a word, he told me the word I'd missed. I thought, "He understands French?" As Prabhupada saw that I was progressing in translating, he made longer and longer sentences. He adapted to my ability.

When I translated his classes, it obliged me to concentrate on what he was saying and I saw that the classes were perfectly structured with an introduction and a conclusion. Even when he'd stray to a side point, he'd always return to his main point. The time I noticed it most was when the Vice Mayor of Paris officially received Prabhupada at the Paris City Hall and I translated Prabhupada's talk. Later, when devotees wanted to know what Prabhupada had said, I was able to retell the whole lecture because it was so perfectly structured.

Also, Prabhupada was able to adapt to different personalities. Some people he'd talk to in a soft, sweet and friendly way, some he'd teach, some he'd be stern with. When he was talking to Christians, he'd speak about animal killing and that the animal has a soul. Whenever he'd preach in his room, he'd always ask the devotees to come in. I appreciated how Prabhupada wanted devotees to learn from his preaching. And I loved the way Prabhupada made devotees learn by having them give lectures in front of him, as he did with Yamuna and others. Prabhupada appreciated that some devotees had less knowledge, but impressed people with their love.

Following the example of Jadurani, Yamuna, Rukmini, and Himavati, I started very quickly to give Sunday classes to the guests and *Bhagavatam* and *Gita* classes to the devotees. As I loved reading Prabhupada's books, I gave erudite classes which devotees, men and women, greatly appreciated. I learned the philosophy and practiced preaching. I tried to give class in a lively way, as Prabhupada did. Sometimes he would make us laugh, sometimes tell stories, sometimes he was strong and stern. The devotees loved my lectures and I loved giving them. Along with translating, speaking was my main service, my life. But little by little, around 1974, devotees came from America saying, "Women should not give classes," "Women should not lead kirtan," and I became so disgusted by the attitude that I stopped. I asked Prabhupada about it, and Prabhupada said yes, women can give classes. He said, "The *varnashrama* way is that your husband is a *brahmana,* you are a *brahmana.* So he is preaching, you are preaching." But it was a time when women were not supposed to have any responsibilities. I stopped giving classes and my translating services were taken away. I wrote to Prabhupada and explained the situation. At the end of a letter he wrote to Bhagavan, who was the GBC in France, Prabhupada replied to me. He wrote, "And as far as Jyotirmayi's letter, she can give lectures." Bhagavan never told me what Prabhupada had written. He put that letter in a wastepaper basket where I happened to find it.

In 1972 in the temple in the suburb of Paris, Prabhupada noticed when he gave class that I could pronounce the Sanskrit better than others (I had been taught in the New York temple by Nitai, his personal Sanskrit secretary). So he said that from then on, I should lead the recitation of the Sanskrit verses before class.

In June of 1974, as the head of Public Relations, I invited many important French people to meet Prabhupada, with the help of Yogesvara and Prithu Putra. One of us would translate their conversations with Srila Prabhupada. We invited diverse personalities such as a Christian Cardinal, a UNESCO member, Sanskrit, Vedanta, and Hindu philosophy teachers, a Christian priest and nun, an Orthodox priest, Rosicrucian leaders, a communist journalist, a member of the Senate, the Buddhist Society president, the Founder of the first French vegetarian store, etc.

We also invited Prabhupada to give a lecture in a hall that could fit 2,000 people at the Salle Pleyel. I organized publicity all over Paris and 1,800 people came. But, typically for those times, men got credit for organizing the program. Anyway, Prabhupada lectured and I translated. When Prabhupada said, "If we abide by the laws of the state, then we are a good citizen, peaceful citizen," members of the audience started to whistle and complain. The French people were anti authority and anti government. One of them challenged Prabhupada, "Did God give you the authority to be seated on this big seat and receive obeisances from your disciples?" I was embarrassed to translate what he said, so I minimized it. Prabhupada told me, "No. Tell me what he said exactly." I told him exactly what the boy had said, and Prabhupada said to him, "You can also get this position. If you know God and if you can speak about God, then you are also welcome to sit here and speak about God." After we left, Prabhupada told the devotees, "From now on when I preach in France, don't give me a *vyasasana*. Give me a regular chair." Prabhupada was perfectly able to adapt to different situations and knew how to handle difficult situations. From him I learned how to answer quickly and in a way that avoided conflict, but made my point.

Prabhupada allowed all the devotees to develop in Krishna consciousness through their own personality. All of us were different and all of us were extraordinary and strong personalities. We developed as the persons we were. That made each of us happy and, when we were developed as our own personalities, using whatever good or bad we had, we were able do a lot. Prabhupada used even the bad in people. As he said, "Those devotees are GBCs because they have big egos." He was able to take whatever good or bad there was in a person and dovetail it to Krishna; the good became better, and the bad became good.

In August 1973, we wrote a letter to the Mayor of Paris, Jacques Chirac (who later became President) to propose that he meet with Prabhupada. He received Srila Prabhupada at the magnificent Paris City Hall by the Vice President of the Paris Counsel, M. Assouad. I translated the Vice President greeting talk and Yogesvara translated Prabhupada's talk.

In 1975, I became headmistress of the French *gurukula* in New Mayapur, which had started a few months earlier. I found that the children in many *gurukulas* were unhappy and disturbed when chanting with the adults in the temple room during *japa* with the regular *japa* beads. Prabhupada had said that devotional activities should never be forced on the children but made pleasant for them. He had also said, "Use your common sense." So I changed the system and had them chant on special small *japa* beads, only a quarter length of regular beads for the youngest and half length for those a little older. And I had them chanting in unison in a special rhythm. They loved it and were enthused to chant many rounds in a very amusing way. But I was strongly criticized by devotees for this initiative, which they considered not bona fide. When Prabhupada came to visit New Mayapur, he asked to see the *gurukula* children. So all thirty students, their teachers, and myself went to Prabhupada's room. After a very nice talk, Prabhupada asked the children to chant *japa*. So they started chanting in unison in that rhythmic way. Prabhupada loved it, he made them chant and chant. Then he had them stand up and go on chanting. The children were ecstatic.

Prabhupada also gave me very good instructions when I asked him about history, geography, and biology classes in the *gurukula* curriculum.

While I was headmistress of various *gurukulas* in France, the USA, and Belgium, I compiled a Gurukula Manual. In the manual I cited a conversation I had with a *gurukula* teacher. Some devotees were wondering if girls should also go to *gurukula,* or if they should rather just be trained in womanly duties at home. Prabhupada said, "*Putra, putri*" ("son" and "daughter"), both boys and girls should go to *gurukula.*

Once in the castle of New Mayapur, Prabhupada was going through the hallway on the first floor, surrounded by many devotees. Busy with my *gurukula* duties, I was coming the opposite way. When we met in the middle of the hall, Prabhupada stopped everybody, calling my name to ask me how I was doing.

What I particularly loved about Prabhupada was his intelligence. He was simultaneously transcendental and practical. One cannot understand Krishna consciousness only from his books. We have to understand also through Prabhupada's personal example, and all the instructions he gave through conversations and letters.

Kalalapa devi dasi

On her nineteenth birthday, August 6, 1973, Kalalapa devi dasi was initiated in Chicago. She thought it a wonderful gift, the best actually, the opportunity for no more "birth" days.

The first time I ever saw Srila Prabhupada was at the Bhagavata Dharma discourses in August of 1972 in New Vrindavan. My brother invited me to come. He was practicing Transcendental Meditation at the time. He also became an initiated devotee by Prabhupada. There was an initiated devotee who had come to our hometown in Saginaw, Michigan and said, "Ah, you guys, you have to meet Prabhupada." It was just the most wonderful thing. So somehow or other this particular event was happening at New Vrindavan. I had just turned eighteen and finished high school. I was thinking, *What am I going to do with my life?* We hitchhiked from Saginaw, which is in the middle of Michigan. It took us all day to get to New Vrindavan. Bhagavata Dharma discourses was a three-day event. I was walking on one of the rolling roads at New Vrindavan, and out of the blue I heard this *beep-beep-beep-beep-beep*. What's that? Better get out of the road, you're going to get run over. Prabhupada was in, I think it was, a Lincoln Continental. But that was interesting–they beep when he drives. It was the countryside.

When I actually saw Srila Prabhupada, he had an aura around him that I was not trained to see, but he really glowed. It was about five feet around him. It was a beautiful creamy kind of yellow-orange, like a Jesus Christ kind of energy in a way. Very significant. I had not read the books, nothing. It was my first encounter with Krishna consciousness. I said, "Wow." And on all the trees were all the four regulative principles listed. The signs said, "If you want to stay on this property, you must follow these principles." I thought, "Oh, my goodness, these are my people." That was the first time I ever went and saw Prabhupada.

A few years later, I was living in Chicago, and at that time it was the *maha* Hare Krishna explosion to get the books out. Chicago was key in many, many ways. Prabhupada had written us a letter, and in this letter he said to leave one man back and everyone else should go out. So we would have this major feast in the morning and everyone would go out the whole day. Everyone was so enthusiastic.

But I developed a condition so that when I woke up in the morning I had a major sore throat. I had to go to a specialist. I had nodules growing on my vocal cords. The doctor told me I was not allowed to speak for about a year in order for it to heal. I thought, "I'm going to go mad! This is impossible. I can't chant Hare Krishna?" I thought, "I have to get smart about this." I had to get clever. I had Prabhupada's *japa* tape and I would chant my rounds in my mind, all sixteen of them. And I thought, "What a wonderful lesson," because at the time of death, when all the bodily functions are failing and we may not be able to utter anything except in the mind, Krishna will always be there. It was wonderful–learning how to chant Hare Krishna in the mind, but listening to Prabhupada chanting *japa*.

The interesting thing is that Prabhupada was in Chicago I think in 1975. The Radha-Damodara buses were in Chicago and Prabhupada was also there, but this is when the Gaura-Nitai Deities were being installed on the buses. At that time, there was darshan, and my husband at the time, Visalaksa, asked a question on my behalf. "Srila Prabhupada, if my wife's not able to chant, what then? What do you do?" What can one do? Prabhupada said there are nine-fold processes of devotional service, so pick one. Hearing, chanting, remembering–those of course are the most important. He focused on hearing in his answer. In a way it gave me that insight into paying attention to the hearing aspect. *Sravanam-kirtanam. Kirtanam, sravanam, smaranam.* Remembrance comes afterwards. But hearing and chanting are the most important.

Kamadhuk devi dasi

Kamadhuk joined in Edinburgh in 1972, moved to Bury Place the same year, and then moved to Bhaktivedanta Manor, where she was the first devotee to be in charge of the kitchen. It was at the Manor that Kamadhuk was in Srila Prabhupada's physical presence for the first time.

I was quite young and from a small town in Scotland with no concept whatsoever of Indian philosophy. When you're a new devotee and you're hearing about the spiritual master, the concept is very new. I thought, "Gosh will I understand Srila Prabhupada when he speaks? Will I connect with him? How will I view him? Will I feel that I have a relationship with him?"

When Prabhupada first arrived at the Manor, my connection was instantaneous; it was just there. Actually, it's always been there and I hope it will always stay there. In those days I was busy working in the kitchen, which was a hub of activity. I wasn't able to have a personal rapport with Srila Prabhupada, but whenever he came he would look at me and smile. One smile from him was like a thousand benedictions. One gesture of his hand was like a thousand actions. He didn't have to speak.

I was part of a group of devotees who cleaned Prabhupada's rooms when he would go on his morning walk. One morning we were cleaning and, since the fire was roaring in the fireplace, we were too warm so we opened the windows. Then one of the devotees came in and said, "Prabhupada is coming back early, quick get everything ready!" We scurried to finish up and forgot to shut the windows. Prabhupada walked in and said with a big smile on his face, "Oh, you are the daughters of very rich men." We had left the windows open while the fire was going so we were letting all the heat out. We felt pleasantly chastised by Srila Prabhupada and that was wonderful.

Prabhupada was wonderful with the children and took an instant liking to Svati's son, Sivadvara. When Prabhupada sat on the lawn we would all sit around him quietly chanting and Sivadvara would play. In a loving way Prabhupada would tease Sivadvara and Sivadvara was never sure how to take it. Prabhupada would tell him to come, come, and Sivadvara would walk toward Prabhupada while looking at his mother to make sure he was doing the right thing. Prabhupada's relationship with Sivadvara went on for years. To be able to see and be part of that was the most touching and wonderful thing you could ever experience.

In 1974 the temple president at the time didn't want women living at the Manor or Bury Place temples and a lot of devotees, including myself, went to India. Svati, Sivadvara, and I landed in Bombay and Prabhupada immediately sent for us. We were in his room along with a number of *sannyasis* and he said, "Why have you come to India?" We explained the problems we faced in England and Prabhupada said, "If these men are agitated by the women then the men should live in the forest." Prabhupada was genuinely concerned.

I went to Mayapur and took charge of the dispensary. Most mornings I got to take Prabhupada's breakfast to him. That was wonderful because Prabhupada was by himself. I would put his breakfast down and he would smile and acknowledge me. Once I asked Prabhupada if I was doing the right thing being in Mayapur and he said, "Yes, you should be here for the rest of your life." That meant an awful lot to me. These are the small things that you hold dear in your heart through all the bad stuff. I stayed in Mayapur until March 1977.

Later I took charge of the *sankirtana* party in England and was present when Prabhupada visited England for the last time. So I was present when Srila Prabhupada first visited the Manor and when he made his last visit. It was traumatic because Prabhupada's physical condition distressed us. But it was also ecstatic, as much as we could understand ecstasy at the time. The boys used to carry the palanquin gently so Prabhupada wouldn't be uncomfortable. The kirtans were wonderful, and even though his health was failing, Prabhupada had energy for his disciples. Everybody was caring to each other, also. At that time we had a strong English *yatra* and the godbrothers and godsisters were closer than any family could be. We all felt deeply indebted to our spiritual master and we all wanted to do the right thing.

Prabhupada's servant asked me to do some shopping for Srila Prabhupada in London, and that was how I served my spiritual master. He didn't need to acknowledge me or speak to me every time. In all honesty I didn't feel I needed that. I didn't say I didn't want it, but I didn't feel I needed it. My relationship with Prabhupada was through service. The fact that I was a *sankirtana* leader and the money we collected built Soho Street is my contribution to Srila Prabhupada. My service was direct but also indirect. I was able to enjoy seeing others in the intimacy they shared with Prabhupada, but I was on the periphery and that's where I've always been.

By the wonderful energy of those devotees who had personal experience with Srila Prabhupada and those devotees who serve him and those devotees who read his books, newcomers are starting to understand who Srila Prabhupada is and how great he is. As these newcomers go on hearing the devotees' realizations, then from within their hearts they will want to know more about Srila Prabhupada and will want to know how they can serve him. The result is that everyone becomes stronger and better.

We can all make a contribution in some way or the other in spreading the Movement and we can certainly all look after each other as a family. Krishna has a plan for us. There will be a lot more preaching going on. Everybody wants to be able to preach, everybody wants to share Krishna consciousness. We will do it in a natural organic way, a loving, caring way. You can only attract people who see how beautiful it is. It always goes back to the people – the devotees – who are beautiful inside. That is happening now and it will happen more and more. Srila Prabhupada's disciples are like World War I veterans – we're not going to be here a lot longer. It's important that the real message is left behind for everyone to carry on and share these experiences with the next generation. It's time to get more serious. The fond memories we share sustain us and keep us fresh and help us understand what we want to achieve in the future and at same time we realize what true love really is.

Kamagiri devi dasi

While she was growing up, Kamagiri's mother shared everything she knew with Kamagiri and Kamagiri loved her more than life itself. When her mother passed away, Kamagiri was eighteen and devastated. She started managing a Barasini's sweet shop at Severance Mall in Cleveland, Ohio, but she wasn't happy and didn't know what would make her happy.

In my heart I felt there had to be more to life than the useless cycle of working, going out with friends, and getting intoxicated. I thought, "Lord, there has to be more to life than this." Then one day a devotee, Bhakta Tony, came into my sweet shop and we became friends. Tony never told me anything about Krishna, but after I'd known him for about a month, although I had never expressed this to anybody in my life, I told him, "I feel like I'm supposed to be learning something, but I don't know what it is." He gave me a *Krsna* book that I took home.

When I opened the book and saw a picture of Srila Prabhupada I thought he was the most beautiful man I'd ever seen. I couldn't stop looking at him and for the first time in my life, I fell in love. When I read the book I was so attracted and fascinated I couldn't put it down. I read it everywhere I went.

One Sunday Tony invited me to the feast at the Cleveland temple on Euclid Avenue. When I opened the temple room door, a cloud of frankincense and myrrh, the most beautiful smell I've ever smelled, slapped me in the face. The devotees were chanting and dancing and I started dancing a little bit. I thought, "Wow, this is like another world!" I was amazed at how the devotees were smiling and happily serving because in the material world nobody wants to work. Plus the *prasadam* was so good that for the whole week I couldn't stop thinking about it.

I started going every Sunday and I was bringing *prasadam* home for my neighbors. Then I went to *mangala-arati* and afterwards, as the sun was rising while I was chanting *japa*, I felt that the sun was rising inside me. I said, "This is what I want to do for the rest of my life." I was attracted by the devotees' ecstatic mood of selfless service.

I read the *Bhagavad-gita*, started offering my food, and started telling all my friends about Krishna. I felt I'd received the most wonderful gift and I wanted everybody to have it, but my friends didn't want to be around me anymore – they wanted to have fun in ignorance.

In the temple in those days we did everything together and nobody wanted to miss *mangala-arati*, *Bhagavatam* class, *tulasi-puja*, *guru-puja*. All day, year after year, the devotees ecstatically preached and served the Deities. It was an amazing, wonderful time.

For the whole year of 1975 I prayed, "Oh, Krishna, please, I have to meet Srila Prabhupada just once. Please, Krishna, please, one time." And I did meet him once, in Bahulaban in New Vrindavan in 1976.

When I saw Srila Prabhupada I was stunned; I couldn't believe Krishna allowed me that opportunity. The devotees pushed me up front so I could get one of the cookies Srila Prabhupada was passing out. I was so happy Krishna had fulfilled my heart's desire.

Without the devotees I never would have met Srila Prabhupada and I never would have had an opportunity or even a desire to engage in service. Reading about Krishna was enlivening, but it was just a wonderful story that I appreciated. It wasn't real to me until I started associating with the devotees and engaging in service. I'm so grateful for the mercy of the devotees who got the mercy of Srila Prabhupada and who are sharing it with me even to this day.

Kamalini devi dasi

In October 1972, Kamalini first received a Back to Godhead magazine. The first paragraph she read, which was an article by Srila Prabhupada, made her think, "This is it. Here are the answers to my questions." She felt deeply connected to Prabhupada.

I was reading Prabhupada's books and visiting the Brooklyn temple, and that summer Prabhupada came. When I saw him, I thought, "Wow, this is that person! His picture is on my altar and I offer my food to him and because he said I should follow the regulative principles and chant sixteen rounds, I've altered my entire life to do that."

I moved into the Brooklyn temple and at first helped Rasajna with sewing. Then Romapada dasa brahmachari, the *sankirtana* leader, snatched me up to be a book distributor and I began distributing Back to Godhead magazines. After awhile Prabhupada appeared to me in a dream and said, "I want you to distribute my big books." I took that seriously and the next day began distributing big books, mostly Bhagavad-gitas, and I still do that today. It's when I'm distributing his books that I feel most connected with Prabhupada, and I'm grateful for the opportunity to give his words to others.

Along with many other devotees I received Gayatri initiation in Mayapur in 1976, and I had to wait and wait before I was allowed to go into Prabhupada's room to get the mantra from him. After two days of tension and hearing "No, you can't see him, he's too busy," when I finally went in, Prabhupada was alone and totally relaxed like he had all the time in the world. He was sitting at his low table on the floor, and he motioned with his right hand for me to sit next to him. I paid my obeisances, sat down, and he showed me how to count. Then he patiently went through every word of the Gayatri mantra and if I didn't pronounce a word perfectly, he said it again and again. He never had to say a word more than three times, but he made sure I got the pronunciation. Afterward I paid my obeisances and left but felt, "Oh, I wish I had talked more."

Prabhupada's books are so dynamic I'm amazed how anybody could write them. When I read Srimad-Bhagavatam I feel he's entered the pastimes and at the same time his words appeal to people of any level of spiritual advancement. Whether a person is just coming to Krishna or is a *paramahamsa*, Prabhupada's books speak to them.

I've been distributing Prabhupada's books since 1974, especially during Christmas marathons. My husband always was and still is a great support. We even planned our children's births so I would be able to continue participating in the Christmas marathons. These days I go out at least once a week but, of course, I would like to increase.

Kancanbala devi dasi

Kancanbala dasi was only sixteen when, on December 19, 1967, Prabhupada accepted her as his disciple. Kanchanbala had sent Prabhupada, who was in San Francisco, a letter and japa beads from 26 Second Ave.

Gargamuni called from San Francisco and said, "Srila Prabhupada asked are these girls' or boys' names?" Then, although many of the initiates were in New York, Srila Prabhupada performed a fire sacrifice and chanted on our beads as well, sanctifying them as well as our whole existence.

I was underage and living at home, which was about an hour away from the temple. Without asking anyone I had sent my beads and letter to Srila Prabhupada. It wasn't done out of rebellion, but when Brahmananda, who was president of the New York temple discovered I was suddenly initiated, he took me aside and sternly asked me if I knew the gravity of accepting initiation and if I followed all the regulative principles–which I did.

Because I was young and my mother wasn't favorable, I wasn't allowed to go to the temple. So I stayed home and did paintings of Krishna. I wrote Prabhupada telling everything I was doing. I explained that I had cattails, moss, acorns, and interesting pieces of bark on my altar. Srila Prabhupada wrote, "I am very glad you don't go out but are engaged in Krishna Conscious activity. My sincere blessings are for you, for your nice prosecution of Krishna Consciousness. Whatever you are doing at the present moment is approved by me, and I think on account of your becoming a sincere soul, Krishna is dictating from within, and you are doing things so nicely."

Srila Prabhupada was returning from India when I met him for the first time. We all piled in a van and drove to the airport. I assumed Prabhupada was very tall, towering above us. When he arrived I saw that he was only about five feet tall, but due to his dignity and greatness he appeared grand and larger than he was.

One time, I was cleaning his quarters. I was still sweeping the adjoining room when Srila Prabhupada came back from his morning walk. When he saw me, he smiled and asked, in a deep and gentle voice, while holding his *kanti mala* with his thumb, "Are you initiated?" I said, "Yes, Swamiji." He asked, "What is your name?" I said, "Kanchanbala dasi." Srila Prabhupada nodded with kind feeling and said, "*Ah, Kanchanbala dasi.*"

Another time, I was washing his *dhotis* in his bathroom. Srila Prabhupada walked past the open door to leave his quarters to go downstairs to give the lecture. As he was about to pass the bathroom he stopped and asked, "Are you coming down to hear, too?" I nodded and said, "Oh, yes Swamiji." He then left, and I finished and hurriedly followed behind to hear the lecture.

The second time Srila Prabhupada came to 2nd Avenue we dashed out to greet him. As I lifted my head from obeisance on the sidewalk, I saw Srila Prabhupada gently glide his hand across Balai's head. Then, coming by me, he gently brushed and patted my head also. We felt the greatest joy just being sanctified by his holy touch.

The *brahmacharis* started to refer to the girls as "cows." Out of the blue, Srila Prabhupada said, "These girls are not ordinary girls, they are like Lakshmis, goddesses of fortune." Such is Srila Prabhupada's fatherly kindness.

Myself and around four or five godsisters were living at home and going to high school. I wondered if the proper thing was to give up going to this "karmi school," and move into the temple to have full association with devotees and perform devotional service. Lilasuka wrote a letter regarding the matter to Srila Prabhupada. He said we should all finish school and receive our diplomas. "If we just left, what would society think of us?"

I did a watercolor painting of Krishna with a cow, giving the cow a plate of *prasadam* with His hand petting her. When it was finished I bought a wooden frame and painted it gold. I then gave it to Rayrama who was going to San Francisco to see Prabhupada. Rayrama said that when Srila Prabhupada received it he had it hung up on the wall over his bed. That made me very happy beyond measure!

I was very happy being a *brahmacharini*; I had no desire to get married. Right around that time, though, Srila Prabhupada emphasized that all the young girls should be married. Thereafter an arrangement was made for me to be married. My prospective husband and I, along with another future couple, went up to Prabhupada's quarters for a darshan. At one point Prabhupada spoke strongly, "Women should always be protected. In the beginning they are protected by the father, in the middle by the husband, and in old age by the grown up sons. So she is never left alone and so-called free." Since I was still thinking that I was happy without getting married, I was awestruck how Srila Prabhupada seemed to be reading my mind and addressing the issue.

When my mother heard that I was to be married she came to speak with Srila Prabhupada and spoke with him in his room upstairs. She said, "I couldn't understand much that he said, but I see that he is a very wise man, and he fulfills a fatherly image for you." My godbrothers relayed that my mother told Prabhupada that she wanted me to date and associate with other boys. Srila Prabhupada had explained about the *varnashrama* system and how women are protected in all stages of life. After she left, Prabhupada said, "Just see, she wants her daughter to be a prostitute."

In the year of 1968-69 Prabhupada was in Montreal and I visited him there. A devotee came up to me and said that Srila Prabhupada's servant, Himavati, needed someone to bring over some *bhoga*. I wholeheartedly agreed. When I got to the door I listened to hear any stir, not wanting to make any noise to disturb him. Then I knocked cautiously and Himavati opened the door a crack. I wasn't intending to see Srila Prabhupada, but through the crack of the door I saw his flowing saffron robes. He was sitting against the wall across the room from the door. I handed Himavati the *bhoga*. Prabhupada asked, "Who is at the door?" She answered, "Kancanbala has come to bring some *bhoga*." Prabhupada said, "Tell her to come in." She opened the door wide.

I was overjoyed at the unexpected and merciful gesture. I just exclaimed, "*Ah,* Swamiji," and offered obeisances. Srila Prabhupada said, "Very nice," and pointed for me to sit down several feet away. Himavati then went into the kitchen to prepare a meal for the flight later that day.

Srila Prabhupada and I just chanted *japa* together. I marveled at his beauty and serenity as I chanted. He melodiously chanted softly. All of a sudden, Prabhupada asked, "Is it cold outside?" I said, "Oh, yes, it's very cold Swamiji." And we resumed chanting. Soon, presidents from different temples arrived, offered obeisances, and sat down in the space in front of me, closer to Prabhupada. As more people came in, Prabhupada started giving a small talk. After a while Himavati brought in a huge plate with nicely arranged fruit, carefully cut, with cookies around the edges. He popped a piece or two of fruit into his mouth, then he started handing out his *maha-prasadam*. I was in the back and felt too presumptuous to lean over everyone to receive a piece for myself. When he was handing the *maha-prasadam* in my direction, Prabhupada looked directly at me and said, "Did you get any?" I immediately leaned out my hand to gladly receive a piece. He passed out *maha-prasadam* to everyone three times around and I, of course, leaned forward each time, unreservedly.

In 1975, the year of the opening of the Krishna-Balarama temple, a large group of devotees had traveled to Hyderabad for a *pandal* program. While there, we took a trip to the newly acquired Hyderabad farm, which was forty-five minutes away. Prabhupada gave a lecture. Later, in the hot part of the day, a group of about five or seven ladies headed by Palika went to a stream to bathe and cool off. Though we returned earlier than the departure time, the bus back to Hyderabad had left without us. To our relief, a few moments later, we learned that a open-backed truck carrying the *pandal* equipment was leaving shortly and we could go with it. We waited in front chanting *japa,* when all of a sudden Srila Prabhupada appeared with his servant and some *sannyasis*. We all offered obeisances and when we stood up, Prabhupada was smiling and nodding to us. He asked, "Do you like India?" We all nodded and said, "Oh, yes, Prabhupada!" Then he added, "Better than America?" We all nodded, beaming, even though many of us were struggling with the heat and our health. I was so grateful for obtaining Srila Prabhupada's unexpected darshan.

As he was about to step into his car, he turned to the devotee near him and asked, "Are they attending the *pandal* tonight? Will they be able to get there?"

In the summer of 1976, Srila Prabhupada came to Los Angeles. At that time in Los Angeles there were departments like *sankirtana* department, the BBT, head *pujaris*, book artists, etc. They would meet for darshan with Prabhupada in his garden. This was going on all week and I was getting more and more anxious since I wasn't part of any department, hankering to get into one of the darshans. Finally, on the last day I was able to get "authorization" to get into Prabhupada's garden for a darshan. Srila Prabhupada walked through the *pujari* room into his garden and we all followed behind. He sat down on his *vyasasana*. I was towards the front and offered my gift to him. Then I bowed down to him and when I got up, I saw Prabhupada nodding and smiling at me. I felt so happy. His nod was like him saying, "It's nice to see you are still engaged in Krishna consciousness." All anxieties were completely washed away. That was the last time I beheld his Divine Grace in his *vapuh* form.

What made me stay all these years with Srila Prabhupada is his genuine care and love to all living entities what to speak of his disciple daughters. Throughout the years, there were bumpy times with many growth pains in the Krishna consciousness movement, either due to immaturity or motivation of individuals or groups. But remembering Srila Prabhupada's compassion towards his disciples, and how he administered justice in our interpersonal relationships, I imbibed such a solace in me and it reminds me why I want to be here.

All glories to Srila Prabhupada, our loving father. Hare Krishna.

Kanka devi dasi

While in Berlin in April 1970, Kanka, nineteen, read Srila Prabhupada's Who Is Crazy and Krishna, the Reservoir of All Pleasure and found what she was looking for. She visited the temples in Hamburg, London, and finally Brooklyn.

I stayed in Brooklyn as a *brahmacharini* for a year. In May of 1971, we received a letter from Srila Prabhupada saying, "Yes, Svarupa Prabhu has my permission to get himself married to Suzy O'Neil [me]." In June he wrote to Svarupa, "So now you are married in Krishna Consciousness; that is very nice. But sometimes married life is risky business because being attracted by the wife, one forgets Krishna. But if both the husband and wife remember Krishna, then their householder life becomes Vaikuntha. Our acharya Bhaktivinode Thakura was the perfect householder and we should take his example. How nice a householder he was and how nice children he produced; one of them is my Guru Maharaja. That is the example. So follow it and become successful in Krishna Consciousness."

On July 21, 1971, Srila Prabhupada initiated me. He said Kanka was the daughter of a great king who was also a great devotee and asked, "Are you going to be a great devotee?" I was embarrassed and said I'd try to be a good devotee. He said he named his female disciples after great women devotees so they can follow in their footsteps. Then, after I said I'd chant sixteen rounds daily, his eyes got big and he said, "That's all?" I said, "More if I can." He said, "What's your new name?" I couldn't remember and he laughed and said, "You've forgotten already."

Once I told Prabhupada that whenever my two-year-old son, Krishna Kumar, saw Prabhupada or his picture, he'd say, "Prabhupada cookie! Prabhupada cookie!" Srila Prabhupada threw his head back, laughed, and said, "Yes, the way to make a friend is to give him a cookie." Another time I was told to take Krishna Kumar out of class. I started walking out but Srila Prabhupada stopped me and said, "Where are you going?" I said, "I was told to take the baby out." Srila Prabhupada said, "No. Go sit down." It seemed he knew I wanted to stay for class and afterwards he patted Krishna Kumar, who'd been quiet the whole time, on the head.

In Berkeley in 1975, a reporter asked Srila Prabhupada, "What will happen to the Movement in the United States when you die? Prabhupada said, "I will never die." All the devotees said *"Jaya! Hari bol!"* and Prabhupada said, "I shall live in my books, and you will utilize."

In the early days, the men weren't so aggressive and there was no discrimination between the men and women. We were a loving family of brothers and sisters, enthusiastic and happy. As women, we never felt less but just as able to do service. Sometimes women would lead kirtan and stand next to Prabhupada.

I got and am still getting a lot of mercy. I'm learning from Srila Prabhupada how to love and be compassionate. I'm one of Prabhupada's daughters and I'm trying to live my life by his words, "Chant and be happy!"

Kanta devi dasi

Kanta joined in June of 1970, and got initiated in Los Angeles in February, 1971.

About a month after I'd joined, Bhavananda said, "Get a tape measure, you're going to measure Srila Prabhupada." I'd taught myself how to sew and wasn't expert, but in those days even if you didn't know how to do something, the mood was you did it anyway. I offered *dandavats* to Srila Prabhupada, and when I got up he was grinning. He took off his garland and handed it to me. I didn't know what to do with it, so I put it on. Then Prabhupada stood up, unfolded the silk and asked me, "Is this enough to make two *kurtas*?" I said, "Yeah." He turned around and I measured his shoulders. I was trying not to touch him, but I did touch his silk *kurta*. Then I measured his arm length, the length of the *kurta* and his neck. When I measured his neck, I couldn't help but touch him. That was ecstatic.

I stitched both *kurtas* but they were too small. Bhavananda was furious. I added a little panel on the shoulder, which made them big enough, and Prabhupada wore one the next morning at Greeting the Deities. Srila Prabhupada's comment was, "If someone makes a mistake and doesn't bother to fix it, he's a rascal. But if someone makes a mistake and fixes it, then he's expert in his art."

Later, when Silavati was the head *pujari* in Los Angeles, I was the head *pujari* in San Francisco; I used to do all seven *aratis* every day.

Then in October of 1971, I went to the Akash Ganga building in Bombay where Tungavidya was worshiping Radha-Rasabihari. There, once, Rsi Kumar was cooking soup by boiling milk and then adding spinach so it cooked in the milk. After the spinach was cooked–just a minute later–you're supposed to squeeze lemon so the milk curdles and you have a nice curd and whey spinachy soup. But as he was boiling the milk, Rsi Kumar added salt to it. I don't know where Srila Prabhupada came from, but I was standing outside the kitchen door when I heard him roaring like a lion at Rsi Kumar, who was in the kitchen, "I told you not to put salt in milk!" Suddenly, Prabhupada was standing next to me in the kitchen doorway. I couldn't go forward or backward so I paid my obeisances by sliding down the side of the door. When I got down there, I was right by his feet. By the time I finished saying *nama om*, he was gone.

Kanti devi dasi

Kanti and her school friend, Srutirupa, had been traveling in Europe and were on their way back to America when, tired, distraught, and hungry they arrived in Paris. They decided, "Let's go to the Hare Krishna temple. We can get vegetarian food there."

We were young – eighteen and twenty – and spoke no French, so it was difficult for us to get to the temple. On our way, someone chased us, which added to our drama and anxiety. As it was getting dark we came rushing down Rue le Sueur and pounded on the temple door. Indradyumna dasa opened the door and invited us in. After we'd taken *prasadam* and the temple president, Bhagavan, had spoken with us, he said, "Tomorrow is Ratha-yatra. We need some help. Why don't you help us a little tonight?"

I'd been a seamstress, and I ended up spending the whole night sewing for Lord Jagannatha, whom I'd never seen. I didn't know what was going on, but Kripa, Indradyumna's wife, gave me some instruction, and when I was confused about putting things together, she said, "Don't worry, He has a beautiful smile. It will all work out."

The next day we attended Ratha-yatra and heard Bhagavan's class. Srutirupa and I were dumbfounded by what we heard. She mouthed to me, "I'm not leaving." In my youthful search I'd made a commitment that if I ever heard the truth I'd accept it. That day in the park I cried because I'd found the truth and now I had to give up sense gratification, which I wasn't ready to do. Bhagavan told us, "Our spiritual master is coming in a few weeks. Why don't you stay and help us get ready?" And we did. The temple was a beehive of activity. We sewed Deity outfits, made furnishings, curtains, a *vyasasana*. The devotees were outgoing and friendly and always explaining everything, and I began praying to God, "I'd like to know if Prabhupada is your servant."

When Prabhupada came it was exciting, but I was working hard and relatively oblivious. Then one day I listened to a conversation Srila Prabhupada had just had with a Catholic Cardinal, Cardinal Danielou. I'd been Catholic in my youth and had never found a satisfactory answer to my question, "What about the animals?" On this recording, like a lightning bolt to my heart, Prabhupada asked the same question, "What about the animals?" My hair stood on end. The Cardinal was confused. Prabhupada said, "Suppose a man has two sons, not equally meritorious. One may be a Supreme Court judge and the other may be a common laborer, but the father claims both as his sons. He does not make the distinction that the son who is a judge is very important and the worker-son is not important. And if the judge-son says, 'My dear father, your other son is useless; let me cut him up and eat him,' will the father allow this?"

I was dumbstruck. Prabhupada answered a question I'd had when I was twelve, a question that I hadn't thought of in eight years. It was as if he knew my heart. It was completely clear that he was intimately connected to God.

After Prabhupada passed away and I was living in America with my husband and children, my fifteen-year-old son left his body in a car accident. I was so distressed over losing him that my perspective totally changed. I regretted that I hadn't been a strong devotee and that my son didn't have closer association with devotees. I got more focused on my daily devotional activities, but I didn't feel connected to the devotees and Srila Prabhupada.

Then two experiences changed that. One was a dream where Prabhupada accepted my service. The other was when I saw the photographs decorating Prabhupada's *vyasasana* in the New Raman Reti temple room in Alachua on Vyasa-puja day. I was dumbstruck because my services were visible in almost every picture – Prabhupada sitting on an *asana* I'd made, on the rocking chair I'd decorated, in front of the curtains I'd made, on his turquoise *vyasasana*, laughing with a tremendous smile and his hand in the air. When I covered that *vyasasana*, I had meditated that Prabhupada was the jewel and the *vyasasana* his setting. In the photo, on his lap he had a pillow that I'd made that we'd put the *Bhagavad-gita* on to offer to him. In another photo I was standing nearby Prabhupada, fanning him. It was amazing. I felt Prabhupada was reaching out and letting me know that he accepted my service. Instead of feeling alone and abandoned, I felt connected. I felt, *I have a corner in the house Prabhupada's created to shelter the whole world. Even a corner makes your life successful.*

On a daily basis, I feel that Prabhupada's mercy is real. I try to listen to a class of his every day, and it's astounding how many times he speaks on the exact thing that's troubling me or answers a question I have. On a deep level, anyone can connect with Srila Prabhupada at any time. He responds if we reach out and endeavor to understand or search or question in a way that's not resentful. Or maybe it *is* resentful! Even though I was stuck in lamentation, he responded. That's a concrete thing.

I still don't always feel like I'm doing anything that's pleasing him. I still struggle with that issue, but I've embraced my spiderhood. Not everyone is a Hanuman. Some people can do huge services, can throw big rocks. I'm struggling with my grains of sand. But I've embraced my spiderhood and have confidence and faith that Srila Prabhupada accepts the grains I'm throwing to help him build his bridge. And I'm grateful to the Hanumans who are throwing giant boulders.

If we can learn to be as loving, gentle, and respectful as Srila Prabhupada was, if we revere each other because we've somehow managed to find the shelter of Srila Prabhupada's lotus feet, if we encourage each other to stay on the path and stay connected, we will maintain the structure that Srila Prabhupada established. That is service, and sometimes I feel that that's my service – to be positive.

I pray every day that devotees will make a successful foothold in the material world for Lord Chaitanya's movement. I'm grateful that Prabhupada trapped me in his net of serving Krishna. And I'm grateful that the devotees haven't abandoned me!

KantiMati devi dasi

KantiMati's father was killed in an accident before she was born. Her family on her maternal side were Catholics, her deceased father's family were Mormons, and her mother had a Jewish father. So she comes from a background of Catholics, Mormons, and Jews. Her mom was very liberal about God, and gave her freedom to find him.

I lived with my grandparents most of my life because my mom was very busy. I really wanted to know who God was, and when my grandmother took me to Catholic church I'd sit in the front pew, watch the priest, listen to everything, light the candles, and go to Catechism. When I was twelve I started asking questions about God and the priest kicked me out of Catechism class, saying that I asked too many questions, that I was a nonbeliever, and that I was polluting the kids in the class. I decided I had to find out why I wasn't allowed to ask questions about God.

I got married, had a child, and started thinking more about God. My father-in-law was a nonsense, but he was a big shot in the church. So I decided, "Maybe I need to go outside of the church and look elsewhere." I started investigating Eastern philosophy.

During the Summer of Love in 1967 I was a hippie in San Francisco. My friends and I started looking into Meher Baba, Kirpal Singh, Baba Ram Dass, and quite a few others, but nothing resonated. I didn't feel that they knew God any more than the people in the Christian church. One day we saw a poster on a telephone pole that said, "Stay high forever," and advertised a concert at the Avalon Ballroom with the Jefferson Airplane, Big Brother and the Holding Company, Moby Grape, and others. We went and everybody was stoned. At one point Allen Ginsberg got on stage along with all these "pink people." The devotees had a kirtan, which was strikingly different from the rock music. Then Prabhupada spoke. I didn't want anything to do with being a pink person, but I felt there was something to this.

When my daughter turned five, I was looking for a school for her as we were not satisfied with the local public school. I heard the devotees had a school, so I went to the Seattle temple on a Sunday, had the feast, and asked the president about the school. He said, "I don't know much about it, but our spiritual master will be coming to Salem, Oregon, in a little while. Maybe you could go and ask him personally." We went to Salem to see Srila Prabhupada.

The engagement was at a Baptist church, and I sat in the first pew just like I used to when I was a little kid in church. I couldn't understand Prabhupada's accent but his presence was something I'd never experienced with any other guru. At the end of the talk, Prabhupada asked if there were any questions, and a Christian stood up and said, "What do you think about Jesus Christ?" Srila Prabhupada answered, "Lord Jesus Christ is our guru because he is teaching pure love of God, the Father." I had always felt Jesus was my guru. Another Christian rudely said, "Jesus Christ said, 'I am the way, the truth, and the light, and only by me can one come to the Father.'" Srila Prabhupada said, "Yes, that is all right." A third one stood up and said, "Are you trying to say that you're right and Jesus is right too?" Prabhupada said, "Yes, why not?" The Christians were disturbed by this and Prabhupada said, "Please try to understand. If a man has a son, does that mean he can have no other son?"

This is a terrible thing, but as Srila Prabhupada started to explain, I started to cry. Inside myself I said, "Oh, shit. Here is the person who is not going to lie to me." But I didn't want to be a pink person! I didn't want to have to surrender and do what all these pink people were doing! Yet I knew that this was the man because no red flags went up in my heart or mind. I didn't want anybody to see my crying so I started to leave. A devotee came up to me with a plate full of Simply Wonderfuls. I ate organic food, no sugar, no white flour, or white rice. The devotee said, "Would you like a Simply Wonderful?" I said, "Sure, why not?" I took a Simply Wonderful, went outside and ate it. I thought, "Okay, that's it." That was the beginning.

I was apprehensive about sending my daughter all the way to Dallas for the school, but she wanted to go. Finally we drove her there, and she wound up staying for seven years. Meanwhile, we started going to the temple and doing service, and I realized when I started associating with the devotees and listening to lectures that this was the way to God. In fact, Srila Prabhupada actually knew who God was. Nobody I had ever contacted could say that they knew who God was. All the yogis, all the swamis, all of the philosophies that I'd looked into, none of them could tell you who God was. And here was this wonderful little man from India, telling us that Krishna is God. It was so simple. Everything in my being said, "This is the absolute truth. This man won't lie to me." Just as I thought the first time I saw him. It felt very comfortable being under Srila Prabhupada's protection.

Srila Prabhupada said that we were all his daughters, and I never had a father. So he took that role as my spiritual father, one whom I could trust with every part of my life. I was extremely blessed to have no father because Srila Prabhupada became every kind of a father, protector, and teacher that I could ever possibly want in my life to be a happy person.

So all throughout the years, through lots of trials and tribulations and tests, Srila Prabhupada remains the only person that I know I can always trust. I believe everything he's ever told us. If I have any issues or problems, I remember things that Srila Prabhupada has said. There's overwhelming satisfaction and comfort in knowing that Srila Prabhupada is there in his instructions, that we never lose him. Srila Prabhupada is leaving a lifelong path that leads to absolute perfection if we actually follow it.

There isn't anything else I want to do but to please my spiritual master somehow or other. The material world is pretty much a phantasmagoric crazy place and without the association of devotees and eating *prasadam* and having all the spiritual things to put our eyes on, we're lost souls. Srila Prabhupada found us and picked us out of the mire and told us, "Now you're washed like the elephant that goes in the river and gets clean. Don't come out and throw dirt all over yourself again."

If I think I'm going to do this or that and enjoy myself, there comes Srila Prabhupada's words going through my mind, taunting me. And I say, "Okay, this isn't going to work." The only thing that can work in our lives is to try to develop some pure love for God, which was Prabhupada's desire for us.

We are blessed to have had Prabhupada's association, no matter how briefly, and to see how Prabhupada took us all in – with all our different backgrounds and beliefs and habits and problems and talents – and brought us together. I never had a lot of personal association with Srila Prabhupada, but he told us that he was more present in his instructions than he was in his material form.

I'm a goner. Not much can attract me to the material world after being attracted to the best of all there is. Srila Prabhupada gave us the best of everything there is. When everybody else in the material world is suffering from things, whatever those things may be, they don't have an ultimate solution. The material world gives you temporary this and temporary that. None of those things work for ultimate satisfaction of the soul.

Everyone is looking to find out, "Who am I?" Vishnujana Swami once said, "Everybody's looking for Krishna. They're just looking in the wrong places."

Karana Karana devi dasi

Karana Karana and other devotees from the Ottawa temple went to see Prabhupada in Philadelphia. Once there, she was nominated to babysit the children so she missed all of Prabhupada's Bhagavatam classes and most of the kirtans. She was regretful and upset.

Six months later we went to Toronto when Prabhupada was there and this time I was determined to see him. As he walked along the sidewalk surrounded by *sannyasis* with their mood of, "Stay away from our Prabhupada!" I thought, "No, he's my Prabhupada." A loud kirtan with banging *mridangas* was going on, but as he came close I piped up and said, "*Jaya* Srila Prabhupada!" He stopped, turned his whole body around, looked me in the eyes and said, "*Jaya!*" The *sannyasis* were shocked. I appreciated him stopping for me – a nobody – and felt a deep connection with him.

Another time in Chicago I came back from *sankirtana*, put my book bag down, went to the temple, paid my obeisances, and suddenly the mantra opened up. Every word was a beautiful, spiritual, eternal, floating sensation. I felt timeless; I didn't even know where I was. I didn't want the mantra to end but when it did I thought, "Thank you, Prabhupada. That was so nice. Why did that happen?" A few minutes later I heard that Prabhupada had left his body. I felt I got his mercy. For a few minutes he'd taken the time to come to me and let me be with him.

Sometimes when I get off track and the Deities and the spiritual world seem far-fetched, I look at Prabhupada's picture and know he's a real person. He's caught me by a rope and holds me steady. When I read his books I know he's talking to me and I'm still with him.

In my family, in my school, and even in the temple I was an outsider. I was never in a leadership role and I was always a nobody. Now I'm still an outsider. I accept this as my karma, yet Prabhupada made me feel that I belonged. From Prabhupada I learned not to worry about who I am. Every one of us can be who we are – there's no need to change – and we can add Krishna and Prabhupada to our lives.

My experience with Srila Prabhupada was limited, but it feels unlimited.

Karlapati devi dasi

Karlapati dasi began chanting Hare Krsna in 1968 when she heard it in the Broadway rock musical "Hair." A year later she visited the Laguna Beach, California temple.

Sukadeva (a heavy preacher) and Rukmini (sweet and kind) engaged me in devotional service. I wasn't your typical impersonalist hippie yogi. I didn't want to be God. I wanted to serve Him and I prayed for a teacher.

From Laguna I went to the Los Angeles temple to meet Srila Prabhupada. I remember that as soon as I heard the *maha-mantra* and started chanting it was like I woke up and had a reason to get up in the morning and a reason to sing and dance. I learned that everything could be done for the pleasure of the "greatest person" – the Supreme Lord Krishna and His pure devotee – not for fame or money or my personal sense gratification. When I saw the Lord's form of Krishna it captivated my heart. When I heard Srila Prabhupada's voice it was like hearing outside of me the voice that had been guiding me from within all my life. I was "drafted" into Srila Prabhupada's service. To be true to myself, and not wanting to be a hypocrite or speculate about how I should be trained, I moved into the temple.

Dayananda and Karandhara told me my service was to finish university – not the usual instruction in those early days of the Movement. I did both, I lived in the temple and went to school.

During that time I got my first taste of Deity worship. Even though I was uninitiated, Rukmini-Dwarkanath, the presiding small brass Deities in Los Angeles, and Silavati, their *pujari*, allowed me to go on the altar and repair the Deities' metal throne because I had fine art training in metal work. I felt so fortunate.

In the summer of 1971 Rukmini-Dwarkadish were installed. Their crowns didn't arrive from India in time and because of that I got to spend a day and night with Them in Srila Prabhupada's quarters prior to Their installation, making wire armature crowns and then decorating Them with flowers. I was still uninitiated.

That fall I became really ill. Four hours of daily bus commutes, a full-time schedule in fine art, and three hours rest nightly were too demanding for my body to maintain. I moved back to my apartment by school to recuperate, delaying my initiation. Srila Prabhupada had decided his Western disciples couldn't be initiated if they didn't live in the temple.

I dovetailed everything I did in Krishna's service. I went to school in a *sari* and *tilak*, chanted rounds on the school track, started a bhakti-yoga club with Danavir's guidance, distributed Srila Prabhupada's books from my locker, and did my art projects by centering them on the form of the Lord.

In the fall of 1972, after graduation in English and Art and moving back into the temple full time again, I was finally initiated. I received first and second initiation and got married within months. Karandhara had forgotten me, which he admitted when I asked if I had done something wrong to be missing the fire sacrifices going on day after day. I wanted to directly serve the Deities, so second initiation was especially important to me.

On his suggestion, I had pestered Brahmananda Swami every couple hours asking when we should gather so Srila Prabhupada could give us the Gayatri mantras. There were ten or more devotees waiting to see Srila Prabhupada. When I went to his quarters Srila Prabhupada asked if there were any men, and Brahmananda Swami said there were. But I was so eager, he had to take me up first. I regret that when I had the opportunity to sit next to Srila Prabhupada and have him personally instruct me that I didn't know what to ask or how to really ask for his mercy and blessings. My awe and reverence was too great.

Srila Prabhupada has always been the center of my spiritual life. Shortly after getting brahminical initiation I was asked to head up taking care of his quarters in Los Angeles. He was there for months at a time. I felt like his daughter and his quarters were his training ground for me. Punctuality, cleanliness, attention to detail, following instructions to the letter, the opportunity to engage others in the Lord's service, a servant mentality with no desire for honor or recognition, and love for guru were some of the lessons I remember best. Even when Srila Prabhupada was traveling, I got to maintain his quarters daily so they were always ready for his return with no notice. I learned how Krishna reciprocates with one's desire to serve Him and His pure devotee.

Once Upendra asked me if I knew anyone who could make Srila Prabhupada's breakfast. He was supposed to attend class. I asked if it would be okay if I did. A variety of fresh fruits in season, hot spiced puffed rice and raisins and nuts (called puffies), salt, pepper, ginger, fresh orange juice, and *sandesa* were Prabhupada's typical breakfast at that time. I got to prepare it, deliver it to his room where he sat to honor *prasadam,* and pick it up and distribute his *prasadam* remnants daily. I was ordered by Upendra to have the first choice of Srila Prabhupada's remnants. The service continued to expand and engage me until 1975 when I left Los Angeles for Vancouver.

It is a lifetime realization to see how Srila Prabhupada is continuing to train and guide us all, and that by pleasing him we can still receive his mercy and loving affection – it is all we are made of. I am happiest when I am fulfilling Srila Prabhupada's instruction, "I have made you fortunate, now make others fortunate." My goal is to be like Srila Prabhupada when he asked Krishna to make him dance, "Make me dance."

Karunaksi devi dasi

First, I give unlimited obeisance from the depth of my heart to Om Vishnupada Ashtottara Shata Sri Srila A. C. Bhaktivedanta Swami Prabhupada, whom, by the mercy of Sri Nityananda Rama Prabhu, I and my two young daughters were mystically moved from Michigan to Laguna Beach, California in time to meet him on his last tour to Los Angeles. We received the supreme mercy of *harinama* initiation from him by mail at the Seattle temple on the Vyasa-puja day of Om Vishnupada Sri Srila Bhaktisiddhanta Saraswati Thakura Gosvami Maharaja Prabhupada in 1977. Thereafter, coming upon me in a dream as an actual presence and occurrence, I received his potent, transcendental glance, wherefrom he planted the ecstatic seed of bhakti in my heart. That look of the sweetest supreme love remains fixed in me forever. Our beloved Srila Prabhupada did not just change our life forever, he gave us eternal life.

Kaulini devi dasi

In the beginning, Kaulini didn't have an attraction or a desire for spiritual life but was following her husband, Kesava Bharati, who was very serious about spiritual life. Kaulini thought, "I'm stuck now because I'm pregnant. But as soon as the baby's born, I'm leaving." That was her plan in January of 1973.

We got an apartment a block from the temple on Valencia Street in San Francisco, and immediately Jayananda and Vaisesika took Kesava Bharati under their wings and he jumped right into *sankirtana*. The first time I went to the temple, I heard that buzz from everybody chanting *japa* in the temple room. I was overwhelmed. I sat in the lobby and Harivallabha talked to me, which helped a little, but I wasn't really interested.

Jayananda knew I needed service to feel connected to Prabhupada and Krishna. He had me write the *Bhagavatam* verse on the board every day and I also helped make vases. Later, when the temple president recommended Kesava Bharati for initiation, I went along for the ride. In May, when our son Rama was barely a month old, we were initiated by mail.

Soon after, all the ladies, including me and my two-month-old baby, packed in a car and drove to see Prabhupada in L.A. Hundreds of devotees were there. When we arrived, the other ladies jumped out of the car. I was sitting in the car in the parking lot wondering, "What do I do?" I felt alone.

Prabhupada gave class and because of my baby I sat in the car in the parking lot. I still hadn't even seen Prabhupada, but a devotee told me, "Tomorrow morning before Prabhupada goes on his walk, wait in the alley." Holding Rama, I did that. When Prabhupada came he had a big beautiful smile and I immediately felt he recognized me. He planted the initial seed in my heart that made me not want to leave Krishna consciousness.

For the San Francisco Ratha-yatra in 1974, Prabhupada was going to stay in the house my husband and I shared with a few other couples and I helped get the house ready. I realized the truth of what Jayananda had said, that service makes the connection. You end up loving whomever you serve. Prabhupada had darshan with devotees in our house but, sad to say, because of Rama, who was about a year old then, I couldn't attend.

Then Rama and I moved to Dallas and were there when Prabhupada visited. Prabhupada was giving out *rasagullas* and I wanted to give him something, so I gave him a pomander ball – an orange filled with cloves that makes a room smell good. When I handed this ball to Prabhupada he was puzzled, "What is this?" He looked at it and set it down with a sweet smile, "I don't know what this is, but I understand you're trying to offer me something."

At the Philadelphia Ratha-yatra, with Rama on my shoulders, I didn't budge from the wheel of Subhadra's cart for the entire parade, and when I'd look up at Prabhupada I'd see him looking at me.

Prabhupada gave all of his spiritual daughters special reciprocation. Each time I saw him the distance that I initially felt got smaller; he brought me closer to him and the reciprocation got deeper. I've never experienced that with any other personality in my life. Because of Prabhupada my whole experience of life in Krishna consciousness has been wonderful. He's the force behind it all, the person responsible for my good life. Nondevotees are in so much anxiety and, guaranteed, it wouldn't have been any different for me, but Krishna is not letting me go away.

Krishna gives us exactly what we need to turn to Him, and He designs everything to purify us and help us come close to Him. It's not always easy or without struggles and trials, and we don't always think everything that happened to us is right, but Prabhupada is protecting and looking after us. According to our mindset we can look at something in a negative or a positive way. We have free will so we make choices and sometimes we make a mistake – that's human nature, but can anything bad outweigh all the good that comes from living a Krishna conscious life?

Prabhupada is freeing us from material anxieties and the fear that comes with material life. Every day we're given an opportunity and being reminded to turn to Krishna. We're protected. That's Prabhupada's gift to each of us.

Kausalya devi dasi

Kausalya, age nineteen, was looking for spiritual realization. When she first met Srila Prabhupada, she immediately knew that he could answer all her questions.

The thing that struck me the most about Srila Prabhupada when I first met him was his kindness, warmth, wisdom, and love. At that time, I didn't know there was a Hare Krishna movement.

I was fortunate to go to India in 1970 with Malati, Yamuna, Himavati, Madri, and baby Saraswati. There were only six women in the initial party, and Prabhupada cared so much about us that wherever we went, he'd ask, "Where are the women?" In Amritsar, the Sikhs' holiest city, the devotees and Prabhupada were assigned two small ashram rooms. Prabhupada said, "Well, of course, the girls will take one room and I will take the other room, and the rest of you [all the men] can sleep on the grounds." He made sure that we were always taken care of and protected.

Prabhupada never made me feel like a second-class citizen because I was female. Quite the contrary. In those days I didn't know I was female. I didn't think of myself as a female or a male, I thought of myself as Prabhupada's servant. When we were around him, he empowered us to lose our bodily designations. He gave us enough vision and strength to realize we are spirit souls and that these bodies are merely the soul's temporary housing. When we were with Prabhupada, it was a can-do situation. It was not, "Oh, they're women, they can't do that." No. Prabhupada was a hundred percent behind our ability to succeed.

In December of 1971, we were in a *dharmashala* in Delhi during the war between Pakistan and India. Every night there were blackouts, and Prabhupada was getting frustrated because we were sitting in the dark and he wasn't lecturing. As a surprise, I put black paper on the windows and that night when I turned on the lights, Prabhupada beamed and said, "This is first-class intelligence. First-class intelligence is you see a need and you do it. Second-class intelligence is I tell you what to do and you do it nicely. Third-class intelligence is I tell you what to do, you say, 'Yes, Srila Prabhupada,' run out and then come back and say, 'What was I supposed to do?' "

In the Calcutta temple, when I brought Prabhupada his fruit plate, he was sitting alone on the floor of his room. I said, "Srila Prabhupada, why are you sitting on the floor?" He said, "Because the mosquitoes have taken my *asana*." I said, "Do you want me to get a fan?" He said, "No, that is all right, the floor is very comfortable." He said, "Kausalya, we should go to the bank of the Ganges, chant Hare Krishna, and someone will come along and bring us a *chapati*. Is that all right?" I laughed and left. Prabhupada had a tremendously heavenly sense of humor. He made us laugh. When he was lecturing or debating he was grave, but in personal relations he was warm and funny.

Once I was complaining to Prabhupada about some criticism going on. I said, "I don't want to have to deal with my godbrothers saying these things about me, I just want to be left alone." He said, "Kausalya, why are you complaining? One little criticism and you are complaining. Look what I have to tolerate. You are looking for a calm sea, and you will not find it here in this material world. You will only find it when you are with Krishna."

Another time, in front of a group of a hundred people, he said, "Kausalya, you sing the *Ishopanishad* for them." I sang the whole *Ishopanishad* as Prabhupada watched me, beaming. He had so much presence that when he smiled his face lit a room. When I finished, he said, "Come here," and patted his knee. I started to pay my obeisances, and he took my head, put it in his lap and pat my head and back. He said, "You did very, very well." It was sweet.

Prabhupada sent Srimati and me to Jaipur to purchase marble Deities for several temples in the United States. In Jaipur, we met the *pujaris* of Govindadevji's temple and other leading people who, on hearing about Srila Prabhupada from us, said, "We'd love to meet your guru." Wealthy persons in Jaipur contributed funds to pay for Prabhupada and a group of devotees to come to Jaipur for a *pandal* program, which is where Tamal Krishna took *sannyasa*. Prabhupada was pleased that two women in a city they'd never been to were able to manifest a *pandal* program. It was the only ISKCON *pandal* that ISKCON didn't pay for – it was entirely financed by local people – and Prabhupada said that this should be a standard for ISKCON. Prabhupada empowered us; he didn't say, "You're only women, you can't do it."

Time and again Prabhupada broke the rules. He was quite the rebel. In India, we did things that women didn't do: Yamuna led huge public kirtans, Malati and Himavati spoke before huge crowds, I did *aratis* in public. We were empowered because Prabhupada didn't place limitations on us.

Srila Prabhupada empowered his daughters in the same way that he empowered everyone. He didn't make a distinction. In all of the many times that I spent with Srila Prabhupada, at no point did I feel that he saw me as a woman. Prabhupada saw us all as spirit souls. The greatest form of respect and love for Srila Prabhupada is to emulate – not imitate – his qualities. We need to emulate his fearlessness. We should be fearless as we go forward in our spiritual and material life. We should be fearless with our efforts to teach people about Krishna.

If there are any bodily limitations placed on anyone, they should be removed. Until we are free to be spirit souls, until we are free to manifest ourselves to our fullest destiny, the Movement cannot grow as it should. Women are an important and integral part of this Movement, women have a balancing energy that has been neglected and ignored. Prabhupada's Movement will grow and mature beautifully with all of our wonderful Vaishnava energies combined.

Kelilalita devi dasi

Kelilalita came to the movement in 1974 in San Francisco after having been severely burned in a car accident. She had met devotees in Isla Vista, the student community at the University of California at Santa Barbara, where she was a student.

I received a *Bhagavad-gita As It Is* and *Krsna* book from devotees and bought a *Nectar of Devotion* at a bookstore. I was beginning to embrace Krishna consciousness. Then I was in the accident. I lost my husband, and everything else, and for the next year and a half, as I rehabilitated, I read, studied, and began chanting Hare Krishna on my own. I say with conviction that Prabhupada saved me through his books. My future looked very dismal, and he was offering me hope for a happy and meaningful life. Needless to say, when I was able, I was ready to move into a temple.

As a new devotee, I was fortunate to have the association of Jayananda Prabhu. He was very kind to me and it was his example and association that showed me how a disciple devotedly serves and loves Srila Prabhupada. I wanted very much to have Srila Prabhupada as my spiritual master and was impressed and felt accepted and loved by this devotee. My confidence in the truth of Krishna consciousness and the stature of Srila Prabhupada grew. I began to distribute *BTG*s when I discovered that telling others about Krishna consciousness and distributing books was the thing that pleased Srila Prabhupada the most. I was inspired.

After a year or so, the temple management decided to put me on a women's party where I spent many years. We distributed thousands of books, but mostly collected hundreds and thousands of dollars. These were ecstatic times as well as very challenging, fearful, and painful times. The austerities we performed, and the immaturity and fallen nature of our leaders, were a fertile field for sexual, physical, and psychological abuse – more or less all the women on these parties were abused, some horribly.

Reading Srila Prabhupada's books saved me during this testing time. I would come home after a long, difficult, and challenging day, and I would read *Krsna* book in bed, and fall asleep feeling the mercy and comfort of Srila Prabhupada's words. I felt I was going to be all right. There were many times when I was on the abyss of some disaster and Prabhupada always saved me. It's amazing how Srila Prabhupada was able to use such imperfect and fallen souls to help others.

I only had Srila Prabhupada's personal association a few times. I saw and heard him give a few classes, and, with a small group of women, personally received the Gayatri mantra from him in Vrindavan. Prabhupada reciprocated with my service by giving me the practical blissful realization of how myself and my godsisters were given spiritual potency and material strength to help others by distributing literature and asking for donations. We were convinced that they were getting the mercy of Lord Chaitanya and that their lives were now a success, for they were on their way back home to Godhead!

After Srila Prabhupada left, and there was chaos in our Movement and the devotees scattered, I knew the solution to all these problems was to read Srila Prabhupada's books together and chant. I began a monthly devotional to distribute to my godbrothers and godsisters with hopes that this would contribute to healing our broken hearts and lead us out of the wrong direction that seemed to be overwhelming the whole Movement. Again, Srila Prabhupada was saving me through his books, and I wanted to remind and convey this to others.

Now, so many years have passed, and Srila Prabhupada is still the only person I can really trust. He gives me the insight and strength to tolerate a lot of things that I don't understand, especially as the Krishna consciousness movement has grown and changed. I live in such a way to protect my faith and don't really want to hear or be around anything that I perceive is not what Prabhupada says in his original books, letters, or lectures.

I'm currently living out my life in the association of a few devotees. I see how Srila Prabhupada continues to, and is always ready to, save me, even in small ways. I know he hasn't forgotten me. I think I'm still grieving that he's is no longer physically here, and I miss the blissful times we experienced when he was here. One thing that I haven't lost is the hope and reassurance that no matter what happens, Prabhupada will never give up on me if I don't give up on him. There's always hope in my heart that there's a new place to go to or aim for when I'm at his feet. I wait patiently for his grace as he sees fit. Maybe one day I can be a light of Srila Prabhupada's mercy to those who are suffering.

I heard one devotee recall that Srila Prabhupada told him, "How you treat people shows them how much Krishna loves them." Srila Prabhupada's love for me, for his disciples, followers, and the unfortunate souls in Kali-yuga sets the standard which none of us can hope to achieve but only by which our relationships with others can be compared. In my own imperfect way, I realize, in faith, that by remaining close to his lotus feet, and serving those lotus feet, will allow me to witness and experience the standard of love and compassion that he exhibits to this day. This lifts me above the inconsistencies and offenses of the time, and can catch a glimpse of the spiritual world where loving exchanges are eternally taking place. Thank you Srila Prabhupada. Thank you. Please let me always remember and glorify your love, your compassion, and your ecstatic expressions and revelations which are ever-present in your books!

Kilimba devi dasi

At thirteen, by some causeless grace, Kilimba got to take part in greeting Srila Prabhupada at Los Angeles airport in June of 1976, along with her mother, twelve-year-old sister, and hundreds of devotees doing kirtan inside at the gate. Just ten months earlier they'd made a bold move from Grand Rapids, Michigan to Laguna Beach, with the hunch that their lives would blossom there.

"His Divine Grace will be arriving in three minutes," announced a voice over the loud-speaker. Finally, as the very last but most radiant person from this plane from Honolulu, His Divine Grace emerged like a floating golden mountain, grave and beautiful. It was a stunning sight. There was an unmistakably visible golden effulgence emanating from around his head. To this day I don't know if everyone saw that or if it was subjective and personal to individuals who were being allowed to see it, but this really made a deep impression on me. I managed to dig through the crowd to walk nearer the conveyor he was now gliding on. He held four pieces of sugarcane, two of which somehow ended up with us!

Next, we drove to the headquarters of the International Society for Krishna Consciousness on Watseka Avenue for a fuller round of first impressions. The temple floor was solid marble and covered in rose petals. This being a first impression of this grand center, I assumed this is how it's done here. Heavenly! Suddenly, the thick carved wooden altar doors slowly started opening, with nothing to see but billows of frankincense. The first sight for me through the incense was very large white round eyes with deep black pupils in the center, altogether stunning but somehow like a *déjà vu*, as if this had happened before. *Jaya* Jagannatha Deva!

Early the next morning we drove up again from Laguna Beach to hear His Divine Grace give the morning class and attend the ceremonies. Our school friends, sisters Piper and Portia, had spent the night after coming with us for the airport greeting the day before. At one point while all four of us were up on the balcony observing, we noticed kids lined up in front of Srila Prabhupada's divine seat. We looked at each other and mutually expressed in a mood of, "Hey, we're souls, but we happen to be kids right now. Let's get down there!"

Once in line, we couldn't help but notice that each kid had something in their hand to offer Srila Prabhupada. We immediately held each others' place in line and took turns scavenging for something to offer. Marigolds were everywhere! Three of us got some of those, and my sister's friend, Portia actually found a marigold *garland*. *Woah!* Luckily we didn't know anything about "offered" or "unoffered." We just felt Portia had "scored" the best offering. We watched as she approached his seat holding this garland with both hands as a precious offering. Srila Prabhupada put down the cookie he had in his hand and, after searching, picked up a bigger one and handed it to her with an oceanic smile. How heart-warming!

When it was my turn, I started across that large empty space in front of his seat and came forward, gazing at him gazing at me, as if seeing through everything, deep into my soul. I could feel in that moment that he knew everything about my soul's journey across *lifetimes*. I could feel that although his glance was grave, more grave perhaps than any glance I had ever met, it was reliable, like God's love. My heart flung open. I felt, "Whatever he's here to teach, I'm *into* it."

That glance and all that happened within that moment was pivotal for me. It is still the most significant moment of my entire life, guiding my choices from within. I now know this glance to be that singular "moment's association" with a pure devotee that can liberate one from the cycle of repeated birth and death. Through that glance of mercy, that *kripa-drshti*, a seed of transcendental faith in Sri Krishna came in my heart from His Divine Grace's heart. One of Krishna's names is Adhoksaja. He is unknown, and He is unknowable. Except by the grace of a pure devotee of Krishna. We cannot know Krishna through mental speculation or even through scholarship! Krishna has actually hidden Himself in the hearts of His pure devotees who love Him completely, and *they* have the power to give this transcendental faith or *sraddha* in Krishna to us.

Funny, I don't remember handing him the flower or receiving the cookie in his hand, though I know those two things happened. But I will never forget what happened during that moment of receiving His glance, and how just remembering this event awakened me two months later.

Sometime after all these days in L.A. in which we were able to see Srila Prabhupada daily, we started summer break from school and got back into our rhythms of life with our friends and the beaches of Laguna. A periodical from Srila Prabhupada's mission came out with a feature article about "Gurukula," his ashram schools for children that were a part of some of his temples. My sister who was by then twelve, read that article and powerfully announced to Mom and I that in the fall she would be going to "that school."

This forced me to think. My first thought was, "I could go back to Michigan and live with my Dad." But then, "Why would I wanna do that? That'd be like going backwards!" Sitting with those thoughts for a minute or two, a flood of the memory of being before Srila Prabhupada came pouring in as I remembered my personal experience of faith: the gift in his glance. My concluding thought was natural, "Me too! I want to do that also." Whew! I'm glad I had my personal reason backed by some grace that I could remember now at another pivotal life change. Following someone else into the surrender process of accepting Sri Guru can be dangerous. Krishna says so Himself in *Srimad Bhagavad-gita*, "To follow another's path is dangerous." One must find their own internal reason for surrender to work. It has to make sense to one's own heart. I think what I'm reliving in this telling is how grateful I feel that Srila Prabhupada gave me that reason in that glance of mercy.

Meanwhile, come September, after having called our friends over and given away most of what we owned, we took Mahatma Prabhu (the Laguna Beach temple president) up on his suggestion to go to Seattle. He had said he had a friend in charge there, Bala Krishna Prabhu, whom he greatly trusted. He even had a ride for us. Mahesvari dasi was heading up to Seattle in her large, mostly empty station wagon to visit her parents. That was perfect timing. We traveled to Seattle and were beautifully welcomed at the front door by Madhumati devi dasi holding two-month-old Krsna Devata. They were wife and daughter of Bala Krishna Prabhu, who turned out to be a great temple president, as Mahatma had promised.

Five months later, after having adopted the discipline and *sadhana*-practice for the path of bhakti-yoga as set up by Srila Prabhupada, a letter signed by Srila Prabhupada came in response to Bala Krishna Prabhu's request for all three of us to become Srila Prabhupada's initiated disciples. The letter had instructions and our new names, which were given at our initiation ceremony on the birth-appearance day of Srila Prabhupada's own spiritual master, Om Vishnupada Sri Srimad Bhaktisiddhanta Sarasvati Thakura Prabhupada. This was in February 1977.

Our names became: Karunaksi Dasi (my mom was 36); Tamra Dasi (my sister was twelve) and Kilimba Dasi (I was thirteen).

Nine months later, on November 14th, 1977, Srila Prabhupada departed our earthly vision. That was both a very sad day of separation and singing, and a very blissful night, when we'd realized while out distributing some of his *Bhagavad-gitas*, that he is always with one who tends to his divine instructions.

As of this writing in the year 2020, we still feel Srila Prabhupada's presence every day through the process of bhakti-yoga he clearly teaches in his books. My husband and I relish at least one verse and purport daily from *Srimad-Bhagavatam*. I personally also read from *Sri Chaitanya-charitamrita* daily, and when the entire work is finished start again, finding fresh gems of transcendental inspiration and guidance each time. At the beginning of 2019 we started a nightly one-hour *Bhagavad-gita* conference call, which three to ten devotees join and keep going even when one or both of us cannot. Again, no matter how many times we go through these transcendental literatures, they are fresh every time! Different points stand out as dynamic guidance, always. "He lives forever by his divine instructions, and the follower lives with Him." Hare Krishna.

Kishori devi dasi

Kishori's family had been taken to Auschwitz. Afterwards, she would hallucinate and see Nazis everywhere taking people by buses into camps. She had a poster of Vishnu, and would think, "What they are going to do to me now I don't know, but I am Your servant." She relays, "I was in such state when the devotees found me. It's a miracle they found me." Kishori was initiated in London the second time Prabhupada gave initiation there.

Doctors said I would die. Then I heard the Hare Krishna *maha-mantra* and saw Dhananjaya and Bala Gopala. They were glowing. Dhananjaya said, "Oh, we have the medicine for you. Popcorn *prasadam*!" They made me laugh and I went to the temple. There were three boys. I remember Aksayananda and Dhananjaya. They were jumping up and down, "Haribol! Haribol! Haribol!" I could not believe it. I thought, "Now I have come to spiritual life. I am going to rest." Spiritual life was for me like a rest.

Just before my initiation, I had put up a notice for somebody to help me make flags for Ratha-yatra. One girl, Vivian, came. I asked Vivian, "What do you want to be in Goloka Vrindavana? Prabhupada is going to give us our names. He is going to tell us who we are." She said, "I want to be a cow for Krishna." I said, "I want to be a *gopi* for Krishna." And we didn't speak of this with anyone.

Then we went to Bury Place to see Srila Prabhupada. I fell at his feet and touched them. I was the most fallen person. Forever a prisoner, forever. And incredibly, he had come and saved me. So I screamed, "Help, help! Please save me, save me! Please!"

Later Prabhupada was on the *vyasasana* and we were doing kirtan. It was unbelievable to see Srila Prabhupada. He was not of this world at all. I looked at Surabhi, my husband, and I saw tears in his eyes. He said, "I've never seen anyone in this world like this person. He's not a normal person."

Srila Prabhupada called Vivian up and gave her the name Surabhi devi dasi. I was amazed. When she came back towards me, she was jumping, "I'm a cow for Krishna!" Then Prabhupada called me. He said, "Your name is Kishori devi dasi, an eternal *gopi* in Goloka Vrindavan, eternal servant of Srimati Radharani." I could not move. I was just looking at Srila Prabhupada, and I could not believe it.

When I went to Vrindavan, I arrived at Radha-Damodara temple. Yamuna, Palika, Madira, and Maithili were serving there and suffering in the heat. Prabhupada was not there but he was coming. Yamuna was in charge of Prabhupada's quarters and taking care of him. The big men were giving Yamuna a hard time. They would not be nice to her.

So one day Yamuna was leaving Vrindavan. Satsvarupa Maharaja said, "Kishori, we're looking for somebody to take care of Prabhupada's quarters and cook for him. And Prabhupada said, 'Kishori can do it.' " I had cooked some *samosas* for Srila Prabhupada at the Manor and he liked it very much. He said, "She's a good cook." Prabhupada always remembered the service, always.

I started to cook and to bring him his plate. Sometimes at noon I would put *chandan* on his forehead. One time he gave me a strong reprimand. Prabhupada's good friend was Bhagatji. Bhagatji became very attached to my family. Every night we would be with Bhagatji and Srila Prabhupada. Prabhupada would take some milk and they would talk.

One time after I delivered Prabhupada's plate, two *sannyasis* told me, "*Ah*, Kishori is so lucky. Prabhupada just said, 'Just see this Kishori. She is so young, so beautiful, so intelligent, and she is so happy simply serving me.' " It was like Prabhupada was saying, you have taken *sannyasa* and everything but look at this girl.

One afternoon I was sitting with Srila Prabhupada in the little garden after serving his meal and cleaning. I would simply go and sit there. GBCs and *sannyasis* came. Tamal Krishna said, "All our problems in ISKCON come from the women who are not married. We want to take them out of the temple." Srila Prabhupada put his head up like this. Not looking at Tamal, putting his head on the side a bit, looking past him. He was not very satisfied. He said, "Tamal, in this world the biggest burden is to be a woman alone with children."

Prabhupada was so gentle, and he knew everything. Then he said, "So in the temple, you take all these women, you keep them, you protect them, and you let them simply play with their children. Of course, if they want to do some service, they can do." So then Tamal, he waited a little. He was not satisfied, Tamal. Then he said, "But Srila Prabhupada," and he repeated the same thing, exactly the same. So Srila Prabhupada let a silence pass. And he repeated the same thing in the same order. Then silence. And then Tamal, he started to speak. Prabhupada said, "It's enough now. You can go."

Srila Prabhupada, he didn't differentiate at all. I just felt love from him.

One time I was next to him and I had a sensation. This is not ordinary, because Prabhupada was not an ordinary person. So we get rays from him which are not from this world. I was pierced. As if something came inside. I thought nobody has loved me like Prabhupada loves me, not my father, not my mother. It came very fast that I was receiving love from him. Love, rays of love, like piercing me. Always with love. His treatment was love, rays of love. He was like that.

I was cooking for three sets of *murtis* in Vrindavan at the Krishna-Balaram Mandir after the temple opened. It was hard work, all day. No gas, no this, no that, the fire was difficult. I had to put cloth on my face to protect me from the smoke. But I was so happy to cook for the devotees. We didn't have a big stock of things but I cooked with whatever was there. Aksayananda and the other temple president came and told me I was cooking too much. "We have no money," they said.

I said, "Why do you disturb me like this?" I was very philosophically inclined from my birth, but very simple also. I said, "Prabhupada told me cook for Krishna. I see what you eat and what everybody eats. How can I give less? Prabhupada said Krishna is a person." The temple president said, "You're a stupid, sentimental woman. Krishna has no stomach. When you make spiritual advancement, you'll give Krishna dry *chapati* with no salt on it."

I said, "I'm not Sanatana Goswami. I am just Kishori and Prabhupada told me cook for Krishna." The *pujari* started to pick things off of the plate which was already made, "Take this out and this." I said, "You can't do that." I couldn't sleep. I'm an emotional person.

So Prabhupada was coming that day. Brahmananda said, "Kishori, Prabhupada wants to eat what you cooked for Krishna this morning." I had made *parathas, subjis,* sweets, everything. I gave him the plate. Brahmananda came back and said, "Kishori, you should not cook like this because I was telling Prabhupada, 'Stop eating your stomach is not well.'" And Prabhupada leaned back and said, "What can I do? It was too good. She cooks too good. I could not help it." I felt like I had little wings on my feet; I was so happy.

Somebody called into the kitchen–I never left the kitchen–"Aksayananda wants you to come, there is a meeting." Then he said something horrible. "I don't want devotees to do service in the temple. We will hire people from outside. It will be more simple." Sometimes devotees used to get sick or come and go from the temple. But Prabhupada was not paid and we were not paid. There was just love. He came with love and we loved him. A bond of love. I felt like I was dying. This idea felt like a knife in my heart.

One *brahmachari* came and said, "Srila Prabhupada is calling you." So I knew I had to manage myself, otherwise I would cry. It was dark inside, the curtains were drawn because it was so hot. Prabhupada was sitting on his little cushion, leaning back. I paid my obeisances. It was all cozy ambience, very sweet. In a strong voice Prabhupada said, "Kishori, I don't like the idea that we will hire some people from outside for doing the service here."

I looked at Prabhupada and said, "It's a miracle! It's a miracle!" At least four times, "It's a miracle, Srila Prabhupada!" "What miracle?" he asked. I explained everything. I said, "I just cook for Him whatever He supplies. I know it's all coming from Him." Prabhupada leaned forward, threw his arms in the air, and smiled up to his ears. "Yes, yes, Kishori! This is the way to cook for Krishna! This is the way to cook for Krishna!"

I said, "Srila Prabhupada, please tell me what should I give to Krishna to please Him so that He likes to eat." Prabhupada started to make a list. "You give one plate to each Deity." I was giving three plates. When I came out of his room, I had to give ten plates!

Before I left his room, Srila Prabhupada said, "Kishori, can you cook for the restaurant?" "Yes, Srila Prabhupada." I always said yes. I wanted so much to serve him. Then, "Can you cook for the devotees as well?" "Yes, Srila Prabhupada." "And for the Deities? And for Krishna?" "Yes, Srila Prabhupada."

One evening Srila Prabhupada asked, "Do you know how to make namkeens?" I didn't know at all. I said, "Yes, Srila Prabhupada."

Sometimes Prabhupada would say, "Go to Loi Bazaar and watch how they cook such-and-such so you can learn." So I thought I would go the next day to learn how to make namkeens. But Prabhupada said, "*Ah,* you have the machine?" I had no machine, but I said, "Yes, Srila Prabhupada." He said, "Show me the machine." I had no machine.

Oh, my God, it's a terrible situation. So I ran to the kitchen—not the little kitchen where I cooked for him, but where we cooked for the devotees. I saw a strainer and a *dal* cleaner. So I put this heavy steel cleaner on my shoulder and I came back in Srila Prabhupada's room. Prabhupada started to laugh and laugh. And Bhagatji said, "This is your machine?" "Yes, Srila Prabhupada." He said, "All right. Make some for me."

I still don't know what got into me. I didn't have a recipe for namkeens! So I said, "Srila Prabhupada, how you like it? Do you like it with wheat flour, maida, or besan?" Prabhupada said, "Besan." "Do you like it with cumin, with ajwain, with . . . ?" In this way, he gave me the recipe without me asking for the recipe.

I was in Prabhupada's room with Bhagatji and he asked Prabhupada, "Srila Prabhupada, what is going to happen when you leave? Who will be the leader? Prabhupada said, "At night there are so many stars in the sky. Everyone can see the stars. But when the moon rises then everyone will see it."

One day Satsvarupa said, "Come, Srila Prabhupada is calling you." It was about five minutes after I had given his *prasadam* plate. He was *magnifique*–wonderfully grave. He said, "You put so many preparations on the plate. I eat one, then the second, and third. At the end, everything else is cold. I can't eat everything. Don't do like this." It was a test for me. So I began to cook only in his cooker: rice and *dal*. Every day he had bitter melon, sometimes *tinda, samosa,* or *kachori*. So I would just do what he wanted and nothing else.

But one day I went to Jaipur with Surabhi and Gunarnava. They took me to a hotel. I had some kind of namkeens–a mixture of *poha*, peas, spices, neem, and butter. When I tasted it, I thought, "Oh, I have to make this for Srila Prabhupada."

So I made it and nervously put it on his plate. A few minutes later someone called for me. I thought, "I'm finished. Why did I do that?" But Prabhupada was eating and said, "This is so good. Where did you learn this, Kishori? I want this every day–everywhere I go in this world. Call Hari Sauri."

Hari Sauri came, but he wasn't really happy. He had to learn from a girl how to make that preparation. A few months later, when he returned to Vrindavan he said, "Kishori, call Hari Sauri because he cannot make this preparation as good as you make it. You can teach him again." After so many months Prabhupada had remembered everything.

When my son Kirtan came to visit me in Vrindavan from the Dallas *gurukula* I felt something was very wrong. At one point, I heard a teacher tell him, "You are in *maya*, wake up!" I thought, "Why don't you teach them Hari Bol, Hare Krishna?" I took Kirtan to my room and gave him some *maha-prasadam*. So he was eating as we both sat on my bed. The person in charge of the *gurukula* came and knocked on the door. He said, "What are you doing, Kirtan? Sitting on a bed with a woman!"

Prabhupada didn't see any difference between men and women. He saw if one was sincere or not. So I stood up and said, "Prabhu, this woman is his mother!" You know sometimes men get mixed up about strong statements in the scripture. They misapply. No common sense. Prabhupada was always talking about common sense.

Kirtan started to open up a bit to me. He told me so many things. They wanted to put him in a washing machine in the *gurukula*. They beat him. They made him and others sit while holding their hands on their hands in front of *prasadam* and they could not eat. Horrible things. So I'm a little passionate person. I picked up a bucket, put some of my things inside, and my beads, and grabbed Kirtan by the hand and my little girl. "Okay, come."

I passed my husband on the way out. He said, "Where are you going?" "We're going to Bombay immediately to tell Prabhupada." I told everything to Surabhi in two minutes. "I'm going to tell him exactly what's happening in the school."

I took the train to Bombay. We arrived at dusk and I left my children with a friend. I rushed to the roof of Bombay, which was under construction. I started yelling, "It's very important!"

Prabhupada was in a darshan with many important rich men from Bombay. Many GBC men were also there: Bhavananda, Jagadisa, Tamal Krishna Maharaja, Gopal Krishna Maharaja, Hari Sauri, so many important people. Prabhupada saw me and he stopped, "Kishori! What's happening? Is there some problem?" "Yes, Srila Prabhupada, a big problem." "Come." Then he did *pranams* with his hands and looked at everyone and said, "Everybody can go." He had them leave the room. All these important people were asked to leave so he could talk to a mother who was upset.

I offered my obeisances. First I just told him about how the *brahmachari* spoke to us while Kirtan was taking *maha-prasadam* on the bed with me. Prabhupada said, "Just see, just see." He said it twice. "A mother giving some *maha-prasadam* to her son. Just see what they do. What is this?" He was really disgusted.

Then I got courage. I spoke for a long time because I relayed the story from the day I sent Kirtan to the school. Prabhupada was looking me straight in the eyes. I continued and told him everything Kirtan had told me.

At one point, one of the men said, "Srila Prabhupada, Kishori is a woman. She's a mother, so she's sentimental. She's making more out of this than there is."

Prabhupada—I never saw him like this. He came forward like a lion. I never saw him like that. Like a lion. He came like a lion and he banged both fists on the *vyasasana,* like this. We were eye-to-eye. He never lost eye contact with me. Without looking at the man, Prabhupada said, "She is telling the truth!" He was so angry.

It was like thunder. "She is telling the truth! Just see what they do in my name! They are all Hiranyakasipu teachers! I never said to beat the children, never! I said to show the stick. And I said sometimes you may go a little like this—a tap on the cheek with two fingers, but not a slap. Expel these teachers! Before you expel them, hang them up!" Prabhupada was so angry. I never saw Prabhupada like this. There was no question of ambiguity. There was no question of ambiguity with him. Everything was clear. Everything was decent. You didn't have to have shame about anything with him.

He said, "Actually there should be ladies teaching because they have a softer heart. Of course, there is no one better than the parents to raise their children." There were no ladies teaching then. I am so thankful that Krishna didn't show Prabhupada the rest of the ugly things in the *gurukula*.

We were sitting on the lawn behind the Manor. They were reading *Chaitanya-charitamrita* and I was sitting a bit away. There were only men sitting there. Prabhupada called me, "Come, come, come sit here." Yogesvara said, "Devotees who come to ISKCON must have done some good activities in their past." Prabhupada said, "Never think you have one pious activity. It's all Lord Chaitanya's mercy." Yogesvara again said something and Prabhupada said, "All Lord Chaitanya's mercy, grace of Lord Chaitanya."

In Bombay, I was late for the walk because I had been preparing his breakfast. I began running with my daughter, Bhakti Kishori, toward the beach. I could see Srila Prabhupada coming back from the beach. When I reached him I was going to fall in line behind and walk with them. But Prabhupada stopped and said, "Kishori, be very careful." He pointed with his cane. "There is a dog always barking there. I think there is a hole in the fence. Be very careful because you never know if that dog can come out and bite you." He was caring.

Prithu Putra took *sannyasa* and his wife Visvadevi had some gold bangles. Omkara told her to give them to the Deities. So I went to Srila Prabhupada because she was alone, she had no money, nothing. I brought her with me. Prabhupada told us that Visvadevi should keep the bangles for any emergency.

Some people say Prabhupada told Surabhi to take *sannyasa*. That is not true. Every time somebody was taking *sannyasa*, Prabhupada had to speak with the wife. He would say, "What I am going to tell Madri if Tamal takes *sannyasa*?" He was responsible, he cared.

Surabhi came to see me and said, "I have to take *sannyasa* now." I said, "No, you cannot do that. I have three children. I helped you, please help me now." The whole night, . . . I was almost . . . Then in the morning very early, I rose early before the time for initiation. I grabbed Surabhi and I went on my knees, "Please, please!" But he took *sannyasa*.

Prabhupada called for me. He wasn't very well. I sat with my three children. Prabhupada was deciding on a plan to protect me. Bhagavan took me to France.

Kripa Mayi devi dasi

Bhakta Brian (Indradyumna Swami) and Bhaktin Eileen (Kripa Mayi) were seekers living in Ann Arbor, Michigan, where Eileen was finishing her undergrad degree. One day they were walking on campus and heard beautiful music, ching-ching-ching, ching-ching-ching. Enraptured, they followed the sound and found Vishnujana, Gargamuni, Subala, and Brahmananda. Vishnujana said to them, "I want to tell you about my spiritual master." Hearing Vishnujana speak, Kripa Mayi felt she had met Srila Prabhupada.

When I saw Srila Prabhupada in the Detroit airport it was as though the spiritual world had descended. The airport became Goloka. Prabhupada was beautifully golden and regal and every aspect of him emanated the spiritual world.

I was in the kitchen of Srila Prabhupada's house hiding, feeling intimidated, when someone yelled, "Bring water for Srila Prabhupada!" Nobody else was around, so I brought water and offered my obeisances. I ran back to the kitchen and heard, "Bring fruit for Srila Prabhupada!" I cut up some fruit, ran in, handed the fruit over, and was going to run out when Prabhupada said, "Sit down." I was nervous and overwhelmed by his presence but I sat down. Prabhupada was distributing the fruit and everyone was taking a little. Prabhupada said, "When doing business and taking *prasadam*, one must never be shy." I've faithfully followed that instruction.

When Prabhupada was on his way to New Vrindavan to give the Bhagavata Dharma talks, I made a garland of yellow roses for him and was praying, "I hope Prabhupada likes the garland!" He wore it that day and the next morning as well. Prabhupada reciprocated even when our desires were self-centered and foolish.

When Prabhupada spoke in New Vrindavan I felt nothing could be better than sitting in that beautiful place with Srila Prabhupada and seeing Radha and Krishna. A sense of peace and happiness that I'd never experienced before filled me. Life was perfect. Prabhupada said, "This material world is a hard struggle for existence. But when this is over and you are back to Godhead, then life will be sublime." I thought, "Prabhupada, I'm so happy right now!" Srila Prabhupada's presence fulfilled our every desire for safety and security and love. I had no clue about the struggles of material life.

Even though it was crazy preparing for his visits and trying to make it wonderful for him, every time Prabhupada came to Paris, I got a sense of the spiritual world. I felt deep joy and peace and safety and security and affection.

When Prabhupada installed Radha-Parisisvara, somebody had painted over a small dark spot in the marble on Radharani's cheek. The bathing oils removed some of the paint and Prabhupada rubbed Her cheek. My heart was beating fast and I thought, "Oh, my gosh, is Prabhupada upset?" He rubbed off all the paint and we dressed the Deities in all Their finery. They looked beautiful. Prabhupada sat on the *vyasasana* and said, "The women of Kashmir have the most beautiful bodies, and the women of Paris have the most beautiful faces. Krishna has come to Paris to collect His Parisian *gopi,* She's the most beautiful." I took that lesson deeply. I realized Prabhupada's eyes were anointed with love of God and he saw Krishna and Radha as They really were. We didn't have the eyes to see Them.

There's a picture of Prabhupada standing with folded hands looking at Radha-Parisisvara. When Prabhupada saw that photograph his eyes got big and he said, "Ah, the photographer has caught me at a very intimate moment. I am looking at Krishna, and Krishna is looking at me."

Krishna Katha devi dasi

Krishna Katha devi dasi met Srila Prabhupada at the Hyderabad temple and he acknowledged her with "Hare Krishna."

I was sitting in the corner making garlands for Gaura-Nitai at the Krishna-Balaram temple in Hyderabad. Prabhupada asked his secretary if I was initiated. Then he said, "I will initiate her next year." I didn't ask him anything, but he kept looking at me.

I cooked potatoes for Prabhupada on Ekadasi. He was fond of potatoes. I boiled some potatoes and sprinkled them with a little Ekadasi salt. He really liked them and asked who had made it.

I got permission to clean Prabhupada's room and he was there at the time. I was able to clean the room and wash his clothes and I was happy; I was able to perform nice *guru seva.*

The next day a big snake came, and Prabhupada ordered that no one was to disturb it, saying it would go away on its own.

I had seen many other pseudo gurus in South India, especially Amma and other women gurus. I wasn't attracted to them. They came across as material. When I met Srila Prabhupada I felt there was no one like him; he was genuinely spiritual. Prabhupada gave daily classes on the *Bhagavad-gita.* He said that we wouldn't have problems if we would daily read one verse of the *Bhagavad-gita.* I really liked him immediately. I felt that he was my father, mother, and my well-wisher. He was constantly on my mind and I felt very lucky about being able to meet him. I felt immense gratitude toward him. I thought, *What more do I need, I have a nice guru.*

Prabhupada gave me my *shakti.* I tell newcomers there is only one *jagat-guru,* Srila Prabhupada. Others are simply Mayavadis. You will not find someone like him anywhere. You can stay at home and engage in chanting the holy name and follow the process of bhakti.

Krishna Kirtan devi dasi

Krishna Kirtan, fifteen and an active Christian, met the devotees in her hometown of Paris. She was impressed although she didn't understand anything about them.

My life changed completely from seeing the devotees chanting in the street. I became vegetarian, started practicing yoga and meditation, and became interested in India. In 1976, when I was eighteen, I was climbing the stairs of the Rue le Sueur temple when I saw a big picture of Prabhupada. Prabhupada looked at me through the picture. I recognized, "Yes, this is him," and immediately offered obeisances. I felt he was my authority and could speak to my heart. I stayed overnight in the temple library and started reading "Questions by the Sages" from the First Canto of the *Bhagavatam*. I read and read and at 3:00 am took a shower and went to *mangala-arati*. Locanananda started singing and I started crying. I felt, "Now I'm secure; this environment is good for me." I was where I should be and felt sheltered.

I'd clean the bathrooms, toilets, stairs, and entry, and when I had a free moment I'd sit by Prabhupada's *vyasasana* and sing the *maha-mantra*. In 1977 Prabhupada gave me my name, Krishna Kirtan and I felt, "Oh, Prabhupada, you could hear me singing for you and that's why you've given me this name." Then I started distributing Prabhupada's books. His books were my life and, although book distribution was intense and austere, I was inspired by knowing that book distribution pleased Prabhupada. My whole devotional life was service in separation: studying Prabhupada's books, preaching from his books, and distributing his books.

After Prabhupada left I went on with my service and Prabhupada was still there. Each time I had a problem, I shared it with Prabhupada and he encouraged me. Each time it got too difficult, Prabhupada made arrangements so I could continue. Prabhupada took care of me and for this I am eternally grateful. In the Christian religion I was preparing to go to the heavenly planets but Prabhupada hijacked my trip and gave me the great treasure of transcendental knowledge through his books, his strong disciples, his *seva*, Deity *seva*, and *sankirtana*. He transcendentalized my life and now I'm safe. Whatever happens, if I just keep following his instructions, Prabhupada will be there for me. I don't have to worry about anything. I can concentrate on sharing Krishna consciousness with others and Prabhupada will take care of the rest.

Krishna Kumari devi dasi

While living a life of seclusion on a mountain, Krishna Kumari had several pen pals, one of whom was a devotee. In his letters to her, this devotee wrote the Hare Krishna mantra and invited Krishna Kumari to visit him in the temple–although by the time she got to that temple the devotee had already left. Krishna Kumari, however, didn't leave.

The first time I saw Srila Prabhupada was 1972, the year I was initiated, when it seemed that practically every devotee in the whole country was driving to New Vrindavan for Janmashtami to see Prabhupada. In those days the whole Movement rotated around Prabhupada. Everybody knew where he was, everybody was thinking about him and getting letters from him, reading things from him or about him.

I'd only been chanting for a year, and when I saw Prabhupada it seemed that there was a halo around him and his feet didn't touch the ground. On Prabhupada's appearance day the big Jagannatha Deities and Prabhupada were all in the *pandal* along with five hundred or six hundred devotees, including the Radha-Damodara bus party. Gayatri and I cooked Prabhupada's big birthday cake. It was an incredibly austere service because we had to bake it in a wood stove on big, bent, floppy trays, but somehow or other the cake came out. It smelled a little like wood but it was nice. After the *arati* Prabhupada spoke and then we cut a piece of cake and gave it to Prabhupada, who was sitting in front of everyone.

As soon as Prabhupada finished eating his piece of cake, three or four of us madly cut the rest of the cake into small pieces as what seemed like millions of devotees descended on us. Suddenly the whole cake was devoured, finished. Not long afterwards Prabhupada's servant came and said, "Prabhupada wants more cake." Since there was nothing left except little gobs of frosting and some crumbs, I started crying, "Oh, my God Prabhupada wants more cake and there's no cake!"

A little after that Prabhupada's servant came again and said, "Prabhupada is ready for lunch," but between all the festivities and excitement, the noon offering for the Deities – which was supposed to be Prabhupada's lunch – had been distributed to guests and some newspaper reporters, and suddenly Gayatri and I were crying again, "Oh, no, somebody ate Prabhupada's lunch!" The servant told Prabhupada and came back to us saying, "Prabhupada simply said, 'Cook again.' " Knowing there were hardly any ingredients left to cook, it was just heart-sinking. We were terribly upset, but Prabhupada was not the least bit disturbed.

From the lectures Srila Prabhupada gave at this time in New Vrindavan, I understood that when you become a devotee you're becoming part of

Krishna's family. All the miserable things that we're going through in our life are temporary and when we become devotees – part of Krishna's family – these miseries slowly disappear. It gave me a lot of comfort during these days because I felt that now I have a real family, an eternal link with Krishna. Prabhupada's presence was so strong, his feeling for everyone was so strong, that it really came across and even the children were sitting quietly and listening intently to everything Prabhupada said.

I went to Dallas to help at the *gurukula* for some years. It seemed like I had hundreds of small children in my care, but I think it was only about thirty. For play sometimes we would dress the children up like cows with paper ears and a little tail. Once the children were mooing and walking like cows when Prabhupada saw them. Prabhupada went after the last little cow, pulled on his tail and laughed. Then all the children turned around, saw Prabhupada, and offered obeisances mooing. They started running towards Prabhupada like cows going "*moo, moo*," and Prabhupada was laughing. He enjoyed seeing them play like cows.

When Prabhupada came to the *gurukula* he always gave *rasagullas* or *sandesh* or cookies to the children, then to the ladies, and finally to the men, in that order. At one point all the children were in the temple room and one little girl wouldn't stop crying. I didn't know what to do so I took her into a classroom and I put her in the corner on a mat and said, "Just stay here," and went back into the temple room. I forgot about her, and after his lecture Prabhupada walked out of the temple room, down the hall, right to the classroom where I had put this little girl, and saw this little girl who by then had fallen asleep on the mat in the corner. She woke up, saw Prabhupada, smiled, ran to him and paid her obeisances at his feet. He reached down, patted her on the head, and had a little exchange with her. As I watched this I had a lot of realizations. I was twenty-one or twenty-two and taking care of many small children from before *mangala-arati* – giving them showers and braiding what seemed like endless braids – to after the *gaura-arati* bed-time story, as well as chanting my own *japa* and preparing lessons for the next day. Sometimes I got completely overwhelmed and I wasn't as nice to those children as I knew I could be. Watching Prabhupada, I realized that the only way to teach the children was with love. I hadn't chastised the girl, I'd just taken her out of the temple room and dumped her in the corner, but I could see that wasn't the way Prabhupada related to her. He related to her completely on the platform of love. He loved her and taught her about loving relationships with devotees and Krishna. All of these realizations were coming to me like a flash as I watched Prabhupada deal with this little girl. From that time on I knew I had to change, to be more careful, to be like he was – loving with these children.

That incident showed me that Prabhupada's method was love. Now I knew my spiritual master wanted us to deal with the children with love and compassion and to stimulate them with a loving mood rather than by being strict. So from that time on I always tried to be like that, although it was a strain with the situation being so overwhelming.

Everything about Srila Prabhupada touched me in a personal fatherly way. In exactly the same way that a person would feel the direct reciprocation in their heart when they do something nice for their own father and he appreciates it by smiling, saying something kind, or giving something in loving return, I felt direct internal reciprocation from Srila Prabhupada when in his presence, even if I had no chance to speak with him. When I think back it felt like I was receiving little internal "Aerograms" of support, love, blessings, and needed guidance.

At a certain point, it was not possible for Srila Prabhupada to keep in direct contact with everyone as there were so many of us all over the globe! Since he traveled continuously, we could only hope to see him once or twice a year. Although hundreds of his followers would gather around him everywhere, I never felt "lost in a crowd." Many times Srila Prabhupada glanced at me and I felt him looking within at the real me – like a penetrating X-ray – seeing everything about me. It was extremely humbling and embarrassing, yet loving, and I felt I would never be separate from him. Many of his disciples experienced this and it seemed to us like we were meeting someone from eons past whose love for us was timeless.

Not having direct contact with Srila Prabhupada was something most of us learned to live with right from the beginning, and this gave us the opportunity to learn how to serve him in his absence. Everyone was eager to please Srila Prabhupada, so we learned how to serve his mission together without his presence on a daily basis. We followed his instructions, attended the programs, read his books, heard his tapes, and happily gave our youthful energy to serve his mission. We would ask those senior to us, "How would Srila Prabhupada do this?" Or, "What would Srila Prabhupada say?" Srila Prabhupada had instructed us to "depend on Krishna," and this was the ever-present meditation of everyone. We actually felt invincible and anxiety free – like little children in the care of their loving wealthy parent – and we credited every success to his mercy. He in turn repeatedly credited every success to our participation and the mercy of his spiritual master, "who has sent you all." He made us feel wanted and valuable although we knew we were virtually worthless without him.

While "separated" from Prabhupada we learned to pray for his guidance and turn to him in moments of need from a distance. Especially we would go to the shelf of his books and randomly pull a book off the shelf and open it with deep intent – letting the page fall wherever it may. Miraculously some kind of help or realization would come through. Sometimes we would sit in front of his photo, or later, his life-like image on the *vyasasana* or his beautiful form in his *samadhi* hall, and place all our worries or challenges at his feet. For me, as well as many others, an answer would come, somehow or other, so we felt a kind of extended personal protection from Prabhupada which we accepted as the special mercy of the Lord.

Myself and many others had the opportunity to hear how Prabhupada had touched the lives of many devotees who were leaving their bodies and how they felt safe in his shelter. Near their passing away, many of these devotees had visions of Prabhupada or had some type of message or communication they believed was from him. This gave them peace and hope in their last moments and showed us all that Prabhupada's mercy could transcend time and space to reach out to those who have faith in him.

Krsna Premi devi dasi

In 1970, Krsna Premi and three of her friends went to the Sunday Feast at the Bondi temple. When she heard Upendra play the mridanga and sing, Krsna Premi thought, "This is very familiar, I love this music." When Upendra talked about Prabhupada she felt, "Prabhupada is a very special man." And when Upendra spoke about Prabhupada's teachings she understood, "That's the way things are." She said to her friends, "After hearing this, we need to do something practically." They said, "What!" and went their own way. She moved into the temple.

Every day in the temple we'd play records of Prabhupada's singing. The depth and beauty of his voice took me to a deep place within myself and I'd cry and cry. I knew, "He's my spiritual master." During the day, when we went to the beach on *harinama*, I'd want to run away: "What am I doing here? What am I doing with this sheet on?" The thick sheets we wore for *saris* made me feel like I was in a tent; sweat dripped down me while everyone around was in bikinis eating ice cream. But when we went back to the temple and read Prabhupada's books I'd remember, "Okay, that's what I'm doing here," and chanting made sense again.

I felt connected to Prabhupada by the power of conviction I felt in his singing, his books, his descriptions of the Lord and the material world, and his connection with the Lord in his own heart. Prabhupada had implicit faith and realization that Krishna existed and because he had a close relationship with Krishna, Prabhupada knew we could too. Because he was feeling and living and sharing what he already had, Prabhupada made such an impact on our lives.

When he initiated me, in Sydney in 1971, he said, "She is Krsna Premi because she is always crying for Krishna." Somehow that encouraged me. He saw deep into the soul and fanned whatever was there. Later, when I received Gayatri, I was sitting near Prabhupada in his room and he told me to count with my fingers but I didn't understand. My mind was dead, black, frozen. Then he smacked my hand, "Wake up!" and showed me how to move my fingers and told me what to say. I understood. Prabhupada closed his eyes in thought. He opened them and said, "Take help from your godbrothers and sisters, they will help you." At that point I didn't have friends because people had hurt me, been nasty to me, which was how I had treated them. I had the "pure devotee syndrome," thinking I'd become a saint overnight, and was critical and judgmental. I thought it was just me and Prabhupada and me and Krishna. Prabhupada wanted me to stop being insular. As the years went on, this insular mood lifted and all of us became more kind.

Prabhupada was seemingly angry when things weren't done properly. He wanted to show us the proper standard and wanted us to take things seriously. He was a deeply loving person and his anger was only to teach us.

Prabhupada wanted my husband, Ajit, and me to go to Sweden. He said, "Speak in the universities and schools." We said, "What should we wear, Prabhupada?" He said, "You can wear a long dress and he can wear a suit." He encouraged us to blend in. We asked, "What Deities should we get?" Prabhupada said, "Radha-Krishna or Gaura-Nitai." We were sitting in front of Prabhupada for about ten minutes and he was deeply absorbed. Then he opened his eyes brightly and with a big smile said to me, "Who do you love more, Krishna or your husband?" I thought, "What am I going to say to this?" Prabhupada saw that we weren't compatible, but he encouraged us. He said, "Irrespective of the problem in the marriage, if you go to Sweden on behalf of Chaitanya Mahaprabhu you'll get all His blessings." We created communities in Sweden, and from there the preaching went into all areas of Scandinavia, Russia, and the eastern countries.

We're connected with Prabhupada through his instructions. The Lord and His representative are there for each and every one of us who want to connect with them and they continuously pour their blessings on us. But if our hearts are shut down, if we've been hurt, rejected, abandoned, or pained, we might not feel and receive these blessings. All Vaishnavas need to learn how to feel at a deep level. We can even allow ourselves to feel the negativity within us. Let it come up, hand it over to the Lord, and let Him take it away. He can work in our lives. When we have something unresolved, we can pick up one of Prabhupada's books and find the answer. Prabhupada is our guardian, our ever well-wisher.

Krsnalaulya devi dasi

In 1971, when Krsnalaulya was eleven years old, her oldest brother, Jim, joined the Honolulu temple, which was an old house around the corner from her school. Krsnalaulya would visit Jim wondering, "What's this all about? What's going on?"

I was curious and would go whenever I had the opportunity. My family had a mango tree in our yard and when Prabhupada came to visit, Jim and I would fill a big box with mangoes and Jim would climb over the devotees carrying this box and present it to Srila Prabhupada.

The whole time Prabhupada was on the planet I couldn't understand his accent but he always mesmerized me; when he entered a room I'd burst into tears.

Krishnarupa devi dasi

The Melbourne devotees had been up all night painting the temple room for Prabhupada's arrival and then had gone to the airport to meet him. Krishnarupa, who'd been in the temple two weeks, and a few others remained behind and soon heard a cry that Prabhupada had arrived.

I'd been hearing, "Prabhupada said this, Prabhupada said that, Prabhupada did this, Prabhupada did that," and was worried that I'd be disappointed by Prabhupada. But as soon as I saw him it was like a curtain on a window opened. I knew without a doubt he was a pure devotee sent by Krishna to take us back to Godhead.

Later I was a seamstress in Mayapur and wanted to make something for Prabhupada and hear him praise me, "Oh, this is very nice. Who has made this?" I embroidered a *kartala* bag and when Prabhupada picked it up he simply said, "Thank you." In my heart I laughed, because while making this bag I'd wanted something in return and somehow Prabhupada knew that and responded appropriately. No matter how small our interactions with Prabhupada were – even just a smile – we retain them for the rest of our lives.

The happiest time of my life was when I delved deeply into studying the *Bhagavad-gita* and *Srimad-Bhagavatam* and gave classes to the bhaktins. At first, the statement "women are less intelligent" was a stumbling block for me, but later, when I read that the reason women are less intelligent is because they're ruled by their emotions, I accepted it.

Why were thousands and thousands and thousands of people of both genders, of all ages, and of different races and religions attracted to Krishna consciousness? Due to Srila Prabhupada's purity. Prabhupada is the personification of his books and as we read his books and follow the process of Krishna consciousness, we become purified and our faith deepens.

Krishna sent Prabhupada to establish Krishna consciousness, and Prabhupada is transcendental to all constraints of geography or time. Generations of future devotees can be inspired by Prabhupada and develop their love for him by hearing about him, seeing videos of him, and reading his books. I only know Krishna through him and it's my love for him that keeps me associating with devotees, coming to Mayapur, and praying to him every day. Prabhupada is the center, the lynchpin, of everything.

Krishnavilasini devi dasi

In October 1969, the experimental college at the University of California at Berkeley offered Tuesday and Thursday evening classes on the Bhagavad-gita given in the Hare Krishna temple in Berkeley by Hansdutta. Krishnavilasini attended.

The Quarter lasted nine weeks and since we read one chapter for each session, we completed all eighteen chapters. During the Christmas break I met Vishnujana Swami, who'd been a devotee for about two-and-a-half years. I thought, "If that's what devotees are like, I want to be a devotee."

I moved into the Berkeley temple and experienced such a high taste. I thought, "The person who is giving this must be extraordinary," and felt love for Srila Prabhupada because he was giving me Krishna. I wanted to hear anything I could about Srila Prabhupada.

A month later we drove to the old La Cienega Street temple in Los Angeles and Srila Prabhupada initiated me. I was terrified that I was going to forget the four regulative principles, but when my turn came Prabhupada looked right in my eyes and drew out all my anxiety.

During a lecture in Los Angeles a couple years after that, in his own transcendental way Prabhupada was smashing women, saying they're less intelligent. Then he looked over at the women with an incredibly enchanting smile and said, "So what can you do?" Somehow we women didn't get angry that he belittled us. Another time I went into Srila Prabhupada's garden while he was hearing a devotee read from the *Krsna* book, and felt like I got hit by an atmosphere of intense purity radiating from Prabhupada and filling the whole garden.

Once my then husband said to Srila Prabhupada, "We've been married for six years," and with an oceanic smile Srila Prabhupada said, "Oh, do you fight much?" I felt his smile couldn't be contained in that room, that it should fill the whole universe with its beauty.

I loved Srila Prabhupada because he touched my heart and the hearts of so many people and gave us something pure and transcendental. After he left, at first it was very difficult but somehow in my heart my relationship with him never wavered. I accepted *shiksha-gurus* who had deep love for Srila Prabhupada and helped me increase my love for him.

By following the principles Srila Prabhupada has given and avoiding offending devotees, we'll get a taste for Krishna consciousness and automatically feel love for Srila Prabhupada.

Krodhasamani devi dasi

In 1970, Krodhasamani was studying Eastern religion at a University when she received a Back to Godhead *magazine from a devotee.*

I was interested in yogic life, Vedic life, but I couldn't find anyone, anywhere who could show me how to live it. But after I read a wonderful article by Srila Prabhupada in that BTG, I went to the Cleveland temple and saw the devotees trying to live a life of *bhakti-yoga* day-by-day and moment-to-moment. I was convinced that Srila Prabhupada was my guru. I joined the temple and also got my teaching degree.

In 1972 in New Vrindavan, I saw Srila Prabhupada for the first time. He was walking up a path with the forest behind him. The forest looked like Vrindavan and Prabhupada was glowing. He was the greatest, most compassionate yogi and pure devotee. I stood next to him, amazed and blissful. I'd come home to my real father, my guru. Prabhupada referred to us – his followers – as his children and was happy that we were taking to Krishna consciousness. He saw the good in us, extracted that little bit of good, and made it the main focus of our devotional career. He never really saw the negative.

In my initiation letter he wrote, "Now you must all carefully follow these four regulative principles (1) No meat eating, (2) No illicit sex life, (3) No intoxication, (4) No gambling. Always be sure to chant minimum sixteen rounds daily. Study my books carefully, go for *sankirtana* and engage in Deity worship in the temple. You are all very sincere boys and girls and now I request you to make your life successful for going back to home, back to Godhead." He asked us to please learn the Krishna conscious philosophy deeply so we could preach. Because I knew preaching was important to Prabhupada, whoever I met I tried to tell them about Krishna.

After I married and had children, I felt it was my service to be attentive to them. I found it was good for my boys and good for me, too, to read *Krsna* book. Once, at the L.A. airport, my little son gave Prabhupada a silver ring. Prabhupada laughed, put it on his finger and said, "Thank you very much." My son remembers getting a cookie from Prabhupada and then running back again to get another, and then another. Prabhupada knew what he was doing, but laughed. Prabhupada loved children.

Now my boys are grown. I teach hatha-yoga and try to bring my students to Krishna consciousness. It's my duty to Prabhupada to try to engage everyone as much as possible according to their ability, little by little. Just by developing the qualities of a devotee – enthusiasm, a positive attitude, not lamenting the past but going forward, trying to go to the transcendental platform, trying to see whoever we meet as Krishna's servant – then, if someone knows we're a devotee and appreciates us, they make spiritual advancement.

I always associated with Prabhupada through his instructions, so after he passed away I continued to try to follow his instructions the best I could and continued to feel he was with me. And I still feel like he's with me every minute. *Sadhana, mangala-arati, guru-puja,* are a good part of the purification process he gave us.

I remain grateful every day that I have a guru, Jagat Guru, who plucked me from the ocean of ignorance by his causeless mercy. I try to do some menial service for him.

Krishna Bhamini devi dasi

During the summer of 1967, Krishna Bhamini was guided to devotees singing and dancing around the first Ratha-yatra cart in San Francisco. Immediately attracted, she naturally chanted the Hare Krishna mantra, which would soon change her destiny. The seed of that sweet sound was planted in her heart, but attendance in school forced her to depart. Little did she know that Krishna was directing her to Srila Prabhupada, the pure devotee.

I was from Buffalo and wanted to go to California to experience the "Summer of Love," so I enrolled in some classes at the University of California, Los Angeles (UCLA). Early one Saturday evening, a friend and I decided to hitchhike to San Francisco from L.A..

The next morning, as we were walking towards Haight-Ashbury, we heard this incredible singing and saw blissful young people dancing, and guiding a flower-decorated flatbed truck down the avenue. I looked up and read the banner they were holding which read Hare Krishna Hare Krishna Krishna Krishna Hare Hare Hare Rama Hare Rama Rama Rama Hare Hare. I said to myself, "I don't know what this means, but it is so beautiful." Hundreds of flat breads (*chapatis*) were being thrown from the truck to all the people. Although at the time I didn't know what *prasadam* was, I felt compelled to get into the spirit, went into the nearby grocery store, bought a large bag of popcorn, and began to pass it out. That was my first *sankirtana*!

A year and a half later in 1969, I was a senior at the University of Buffalo, and had the fortune to take a class called "A Study in Vedic Literature" taught by Professor Rupanuga. Again, by Krishna's causeless mercy, Srila

Prabhupada came to the University. The first time I heard Prabhupada speak I knew instantly he was the captain of the ship that I wanted to be on. Little did I know that his ship could carry us over the whole material ocean of repeated birth and death to the lotus feet of Sri Sri Radha-Krishna.

My marriage and initiation ceremony took place on July 10, 1969 at New Vrindavan. Secretly I wanted Krishna in my name. After chanting on my beads and asking me the four regulative principles, Prabhupada asked my name. "Inez," I replied. So he named me Indumati. But there was already a devotee with that name, so he then gave me the name Indira dasi. But there was also a devotee with that name. So Srila Prabhupada, knowing the deepest desire in my heart, said, "I am trying to find something beginning with 'I,' but I cannot. All right then, your name shall be Krishna Bhamini dasi, which means servant of one who Krishna takes pleasure in looking upon." Needless to say I was ecstatic!

My husband, Bhagavan dasa, and I went to Detroit to start the first temple there. We welcomed many new young people who joined us and the temple grew by leaps and bounds. We installed Lord Jagannatha Deities. There, along with our daily *sankirtana* activities and cooking, I was allowed to assist in editing *Krsna* book. Srila Prabhupada wrote us many instructional letters and when I became pregnant, he wrote me saying I should not travel by train or plane in the advanced stages of pregnancy or be too active on *sankirtana*. Always like a loving father, he named our son, the very special name, Vaishnava dasa. We outgrew that temple and secured a lovely, much larger, temple.

Srila Prabhupada visited and we participated in all the preparations and decorations for his auspicious arrival. He was so sweet to my son, as he was one of the first children born in our newly established Society. Frequently he would offer him mangoes from his plate which Vaish devoured greedily. One morning after Prabhupada finished chanting the *prema-dhvani* prayers, Vaishnava, still in diapers, was playing the *kartalas* in perfect rhythm. Prabhupada said, "Just see. He is taking up where he left off in his last life. Otherwise, how would he know how to play these at such a young age." He then proceeded in giving the *Bhagavatam* class that morning based on the verse in *Gita* where Krishna confirms that whatever spiritual progress one makes in this life is never lost. In Detroit 1971, I gave birth to my daughter and Srila Prabhupada wrote me a beautiful letter offering his blessings to my new child, Manjari devi dasi and stating, "Have a feast, perform fire *yajna*, offer her a garland, and announce, 'Our spiritual master has given her this nice name.' So now your first duty should be to see that your children develop nicely. There is no doubt they are advanced souls, so simply being in the association of their parents and other devotees, they will very quickly make advancement."

We moved to Paris in 1972 to help Srila Prabhupada with his mission there. After some time we were able to acquire a fabulous center in the heart of Paris with an elevator. There he meticulously and lovingly installed Radha-Parisisvara and enlivened so many. One day, Prabhupada interrupted *Bhagavatam* class to tell me I should get bitters for my son's thumb so he would stop sucking it.

In 1975 we were able to secure our beautiful farm community three hours south of Paris called La Novelle Mayapur which was a large chateau of eighty hectares. At one point we had three hundred devotees living there including one hundred children. When Srila Prabhupada visited, we prepared, and cleaned his wonderful quarters. He allowed me to fan him during an entire *Bhagavatam* class, clean his rooms, teach his children, go on *sankirtana*, cook and dress the Deities, sew for the Deities, work in the flower and vegetable gardens, and so many other services. The beautiful Deities of Krishna-Balaram were installed there by Srila Prabhupada in 1976. My third child, Gauravani, was born there. Srila Prabhupada told us all in a class, at a time when I was undergoing much personal stress and difficulty, that our most difficult times in Krishna consciousness are really much better than the seemingly temporary happiness in the material world. This instruction went deep in my heart and has helped me throughout the years during difficult times.

When Srila Prabhupada visited Bhaktivedanta Manor in England, we all went there to see him.

Because I was always with my young children, I didn't have much opportunity to render personal service and Prabhupada's visits were rare. Although I wasn't much of a seamstress, I was determined to sew a *kurta* for him. I obtained some nice silk and labored all night in the sewing room while my kids were asleep. Just before 5:00 am when I thought I was finally finished, I turned it inside out and to my horror saw that the underarm inserts had been put on wrong and they were sticking out like long cones. Just in the nick of time the only other lady in the sewing room helped me fix it and I was able to give it to Prabhupada's secretary Srutakirti. He told me Prabhupada put it on and spun around like a dancer, kindly accepting my imperfect effort. I felt such loving reciprocation. During that same visit, I wanted to attend his class on the lawn, but my young son was crying. I was advised by some of my godsisters that if Mother Yashoda could tie up baby Krishna, maybe I could put my son in the open peacock shed so I could go to the class. Sound traveled and Srila Prabhupada was disturbed by my crying son, Vaishnava, and said, "What mother is neglecting her child!"

I was so embarrassed and ashamed that I immediately scurried away like a dog with my tail between my legs to rescue my little boy. Both the chastisement and praise of the spiritual master are equally important in their lessons.

I was so blessed to be able to live with the devotees in the temples for close to twenty years, serving our exquisite Deities, attending so many classes, distributing Srila Prabhupada's transcendental literatures, and spreading the holy names on the streets of Paris. We practiced serving selflessly and tolerating many austere conditions, as well as learning patience, getting along with so many people from diverse backgrounds and walks of life. We all came together under the umbrella of Srila Prabhupada and Krishna. By the mercy of Srila Prabhupada and the Vaishnavas, three generations of my family are now all endeavoring to continue on this path of devotional service. In such a short time, Srila Prabhupada sacrificed so much to make the most unfortunate, fortunate, following in the footsteps of Lord Nityananda. How can we ever repay him? I have hope and faith that one day some of the transcendental drops of nectar will pierce my heart, like they did when I first heard the *maha-mantra* over fifty years ago, and my natural affection for Sri Guru and Sri Sri Radha-Krishna may manifest in this hard heart.

Krsna-lila devi dasi

Krsna-lila was born and grew up in a Vaishnava family in Bengal and later married Murari Hari, who was from a Gaudiya Vaishnava family in Bengal. Three months after Murari Hari came to Mayapur he called Krsna-lila to join him there. She came in December 1974 with their two sons and their seven-month-old daughter.

My father passed away some time before I came to Mayapur, and when I saw Srila Prabhupada I immediately felt affection for him as a father. Later, on Janmashtami in 1976, he initiated me and so became my spiritual father.

In Mayapur I was quite busy cooking in Radha-Madhava's kitchen, but most mornings I'd offer Prabhupada a flower during *guru-puja* and take some *prasadam* from his hand. I had no chance to speak with him, however. At that time the Mayapur leaders, Bhavananda and Nitai Chand, would tell me and some others, "Oh, you Bengali mothers, why are you coming to see Prabhupada? Not now, not now. Go, go, go." Sometimes those leaders didn't even want me to attend *guru-puja* or to go on *parikrama*. They'd say, "Just take care of the Deity kitchen. You have to cook for Guru Maharaja and Radha-Madhava." They were so heavy I was afraid to go near Prabhupada and I lamented. I thought, "I don't speak English so I cannot express myself to Bhavananda and the other leaders, but my Guru Maharaja speaks Bengali. I want to speak with him." Finally I thought, "My older godbrothers told me to simply cook. So what can I do? Srila

Prabhupada is sitting in my heart and I will pray to him to please accept my humble service." Although I was anxious to talk to Prabhupada, I believed that if I did *seva*, then that was also having his darshan – in fact, a better darshan. Prabhupada had told us, "Cook in such a way that people will be satisfied by the taste and the quantity," and the devotees in Mayapur were happy with my cooking.

Once Bhavananda said to my husband, "Murari Hari, Prabhupada wants to see you!" Murari Hari was happy to see Prabhupada and the first question Prabhupada asked was, "Where is my mother?" Murari Hari couldn't understand what Prabhupada meant and Prabhupada said, "Why aren't you answering? My mother, Krsna-lila, where is she?" Then my husband understood. Murari Hari said to Prabhupada, "Guru Maharaja, Krsna-lila is cooking in the Deity kitchen. She is preparing *bhoga* for Radha-Madhava." When I heard this, I understood that Prabhupada knows our heart.

I took care of Prabhupada's sister, Pishima, and she told me many wonderful stories about and instructions from Prabhupada, which attracted me more and more to him. She also told me, "Your Guru Maharaj likes *bati charchari, kachori, puri, beguni* (eggplant coated with chickpea flour and fried)." After I heard that I would make those dishes for Prabhupada's pleasure.

Now when I hear a recording of Prabhupada speaking, when I listen to the morning or evening shenai that Prabhupada liked, and when I hear Prabhupada chanting *japa* or singing – especially the Prayers to the Six Goswamis – in my heart I feel, "Oh, my Prabhupada is here, my Prabhupada is still here!" Yet at the same time, whenever I think about Prabhupada, whenever I hear his voice, I feel some burning in my heart because Prabhupada is also not here. If he were here I could wash his feet and offer him *prasadam*.

Even though many of us did not get personal contact with Prabhupada, by serving him and by his mercy Krishna will recognize us. Prabhupada is Krishna's best friend and he is our Guru Maharaja. By his kindness we can know that Krishna is our friend too; we can recognize Krishna. Otherwise, Krishna's position is so high that it is not possible for us to recognize Him.

We are thankful that Prabhupada can accept our love and our *puja*. Our condition is so fallen that without him it would be not possible for us be engaged in Krishna's service. Without Srila Prabhupada it never would be possible. People everywhere should know who Prabhupada is, why we lament his absence, and why we serve and worship him. They should inquire and then they will also become Krishna's devotee. All over the world places are illuminated due to Prabhupada's mercy – even in India, even in Mayapur.

I feel, "I am doing my service for Prabhupada, for Radha-Madhava," and

I want to sleep less and serve more. In my family, each and every day before we eat any grain of foodstuff we first offer that food to Srila Prabhupada and to the Lord. We never take anything without first offering it to them. That is our vow. We are keeping that vow all these many years and I hope to keep it up to my last day, my last breath.

Krsnavesa devi dasi

It was the sunny London summer of 1972 when Krsnavesa first encountered the Hare Krishna devotees–those wonderful, spiritually intelligent, people who had answers to all life's important questions and ignited in her a profound, joyful amazement. She was an English school girl, fourteen years old, enjoying her summer holiday.

A year later, in the summer of 1973, I was swept up in the newness, dizziness, and excitement of George Harrison's gifting Bhaktivedanta Manor to ISKCON, and the coming installation of Radha-Gokulananda. I slept over one night as a guest at the Manor when Prabhupada was in residence, blessing the whole beautiful happening with his presence.

Early in the morning I went to my first *guru-puja*. As I danced and sang with all the devotees before the *vyasasana* in the temple room, Prabhupada walked in from the grounds through the side door to the left in front of me, and for the first time I glimpsed him, taking in the golden brightness of his body clothed in saffron, and the surprising smallness of his form. It was as if a little sun traversed the pathway from the entrance to the throne of Vyasadeva while all the disciples bowed to the ground, and I along with them.

By January, 1974, I was clear in my mind that I wanted to join ISKCON. For one reason or another, I came to the decision to run away from home to a temple in Germany. While I was there, Prabhupada came to visit, and I had the honor of being able to accompany him, with other devotees, on a morning walk. As everyone was gathering to commence the walk, I found myself standing quite alone a few feet from the car Prabhupada was sitting in with his window rolled down. He saw me and made eye contact with me. I told myself, just try to keep your heart open – and then I held the eye contact for a few more moments. No words, smiles, or frowns were exchanged. All I knew was that he'd seen me, and that now he knew me. And that was enough.

Before I'd run away from home, I'd written Prabhupada a letter. I'd wanted to tell him what I was planning to do, to explain why I felt I needed to do it, and to ask him if it would be okay. Three months went by, and I did not hear back from him. Things at home had come to a head, and so at a certain point I took matters into my own hands and flew the nest. After I'd been in Germany a little while and had my first initiation, unexpectedly one day a devotee brought me a letter from Prabhupada in reply to mine. I had given up on hearing from him, and now that my situation had moved on, I feared complications as I opened his letter. My hands were shaking.

Sure enough, in his letter to me, Prabhupada told me to stay at home in spite of the difficulties, to chant sixteen rounds every day, follow the four regulative principles, and finish my education. With a good education, he said, I would be able to do some valuable service for Krishna one day in the future. There is no material impediment to becoming Krishna conscious, he wrote, and gave the example of Prahlada Maharaja who was a great devotee despite having a demoniac father (who, by the way, was a good many times more demoniac than either of my poor parents).

For a while I kicked myself for having made a choice that turned out not to be Prabhupada's preference. Now I celebrate the events that gave rise to Prabhupada's issuing that instruction to me, because in spite of my miscalculated actions, his guidance has made me wiser in the long term, and the opportunity that arose through these events for all of us to hear Prabhupada's position on the issue of a minor running away from home created a precedent that others in similar circumstances may refer to.

A nice incident took place involving Prabhupada while I was actually in the act of running away from home. Besides running to Krishna, I was also running away from a difficult family situation, and had been planning my getaway for months. Attached to my meagre collection of material possessions, I had contrived to keep two or three large cardboard boxes packed full of belongings – clothes, tape player, and such – hidden beneath a bedspread in my room ready to be mailed off to the temple. How I imagined I would get these things out of the house without transportation, or that my parents would fail to notice what I was up to, I have no idea. That's the mind of a child for you. In any case, close to the date I had planned to leave, my parents did figure out what was happening. Once I knew it was all over for me unless I acted quickly, I decided to leave that very night. At three o'clock that cold January morning in 1974, I got up from bed, dressed, hoisted one of my large cardboard boxes into my arms (one was better than none), stole out of my bedroom and slowly began to descend the stairs to the front door, which was always kept locked at night. When I'd made it to the third step, my parents' bedroom door burst open, and my father came charging out in his pyjamas roaring at me. I stumbled as quickly as I could down a few more stairs, clutching onto my box, and knowing I'd have to do something instantaneous and drastic. I turned to face my father, threw the box down on the steps that remained between him and me, and began running as fast as I could down to the front door. The moment the box hit the steps, the jolt triggered the start button on the tape player inside, and suddenly Prabhupada's powerful, melodious voice came booming out of the box, singing at an incredibly high volume, and an incredibly fast tempo.

"Hare Krishna, Hare Krishna, Krishna Krishna, Hare Hare; Hare Rama, Hare Rama, Rama Rama, Hare Hare," the voice belted out at the crescendo of one of his famous recorded kirtans. It was as dramatic a moment as one can imagine. By some miracle the front door was not locked. I opened it with ease and flew out into the night with nothing but the clothes on my back and the Hare Krishna mantra on my tongue. The rest is history.

After some months in Germany, I returned to England to serve at Bhaktivedanta Manor. One morning when Prabhupada was visiting and had given a *Bhagavatam* class, he asked if there were any questions. A question had been on my mind for a little while, and so I thought, why not take the opportunity to have an exchange with my spiritual master? I raised my hand and, to my shocked surprise, I was called on. What I wanted to know was if Krishna always speaks *Bhagavad-gita* to the same person, Arjuna – and if He speaks it always in the middle of the same pastime, counselling Arjuna before the battle of Kurukshetra. But suddenly all that seemed much too complex to put into words right there and then to such a great and important spiritual master – and in front of all those hundreds of devotees! So what came out of me instead were the words, "Does Krishna speak *Bhagavad-gita* on the hellish planets?"

It was as if all the atoms in the room stopped moving for a split second as everyone present paused to consider the wackiness of my question. I was wishing the ground would swallow me up. And then Prabhupada answered, "Yes, this London is a hellish planet, and Krishna's speaking *Bhagavad-gita* here."

Suddenly, all the devotees laughed. Prabhupada's answer had been factual, intelligent, witty, and funny – a perfect answer to the question asked.

After being at Bhaktivedanta Manor a few months, a bewildering political situation arose between two parties of leaders there. Some of the devotees were lobbying to replace the existing temple president and governing body commissioner with another candidate for each post. I was confused by the situation and wrote to Prabhupada for guidance. An excerpt from the letter he wrote back to me reads as follows: "My request to you is that you try to follow the authorities there, the temple president, the GBC, etc. Co-operate nicely with them. Our Movement is based on love and trust, so if we do not co-operate, then how is that love and trust?"

I soon came to embrace this instruction of Prabhupada's as the primary spiritual challenge of my life. Our ability to work cooperatively with each other was extremely important to Prabhupada. In fact, as he came close to departing this world, he said that his disciples would show their love for him by how well they cooperated after he left. But I was not born with the cooperative gene, and it has been a long, eventful journey to personal transformation for me.

The relationship between the guru and disciple is bittersweet. There are the bitter, smarting wounds to the false ego that the guru's incisive words produce as he sculpts us into purified versions of ourselves. And then the sweetness that arises from the bitters as the disciple surrenders and takes up her personal nuanced journey of many years to self-improvement. As I look back on my life I am humbled that Krishna blessed me with the chance to become Prabhupada's eternal disciple, and happy that in the smallest of ways I somehow succeeded in placing my head at my master's lotus feet.

Krsnanandini devi dasi

When Krsnanandini was seventeen, she received a full scholarship to attend the University of Chicago. She attended this prestigious university for a year and then left as a student in good standing to get married. At nineteen, in 1971, her mother (later to be initiated as Bhumata devi dasi) came to visit her and her new husband and left her a Bhagavad-gita by Srila Prabhupada, without much comment or fanfare. Krsnanandini quickly read the book and somehow knew that "Prabhupada is my guru, Krishna is God, and I am meant to serve them." Though she had not met any Hare Krishna devotees, Krsnanandini soon felt impelled to join her mother in Cleveland, Ohio to practice Krishna consciousness in earnest. And so, she and her little two-year-old daughter and a friend went from Chicago to Cleveland, with a promise from her husband to come later.

In mid-1971, my mother, a metaphysics teacher and Christian evangelist, had rented a large house near the Cleveland Hare Krishna temple where some of her children and former students were practicing Krishna consciousness. We were chanting sixteen rounds of Hare Krishna *japa* a day, studying *Bhagavad-gita* and *Srimad-Bhagwatam* (the few volumes that were available) and we endeavored to attend the local temple.

It wasn't long before we were challenged. Batu Gopal, the young temple president discouraged us from adopting the Vaishnava practices of wearing *tilaka*, *shikha*, and calling each other by spiritual names. In her zealousness, my mother had given her children and other students Sanskrit names. The temple president said she could not do these things without being initiated first. While Bhumata had no objection to being initiated, she was enthusiastic to take up the spiritual practices immediately.

There ensued an increasing conflict between the temple president, my mother, and our group of aspiring devotees. My mother and I wrote letters to Srila Prabhupada, who was in India, even though we had not met him yet in person. In our letters, we surrendered ourselves as his disciples and informed him of some of the difficulties we were having. Srila Prabhupada's welcoming and compassionate mood was evident in his letter. He said we were welcome in all of his temples. So we returned to visiting the temple.

But Batu Gopal had given wooden sticks to the temple devotees to fight us off and was having the Deities removed from Their altar, presumably to protect Them in the upcoming conflict. Then he called the police. What a strange scene! My mother and one of her students were arrested for disorderly conduct! I was pregnant with my second child and this experience shook us to the core. An article was published in one of the local Cleveland newspapers about the incident. We were firmly convinced, however, that Srila Prabhupada was not in agreement with this kind of behavior. Still we were at a loss. Where could we go? Krishna consciousness was so new that there were few temples in the U.S. In our own Christian family there was much tension as they already considered that we were involved in a terrible "cult."

This was a time for deep faith. We wanted to go somewhere where we could practice Krishna consciousness. Where could we go? We chanted and prayed for a few days. My mother was guided with the idea to leave Cleveland and head west. We had no idea where we were going but we packed everything up and drove west.

It was touch and go for several days but eventually we ended up in Dallas, Texas, home of the first *gurukula* in ISKCON. There are so many details to this mysterious story but we knew that somehow Srila Prabhupada had directed us to Dallas because the day after we arrived, he came to Dallas! We thought he was in India!

Five members of my family were initiated on Radhastami, September 12, 1972. My mother, Bunsier, became Bhumata devi dasi; stepdad Roy became Rupchand dasa. My two brothers (Arthur, fourteen) and (Soloman, twelve) became Asutosh dasa and Subhanu dasa. I became Krsnanandini devi dasi! That same day Srila Prabhupada installed Their beautiful Lordships Sri Sri Radha-Kalachandji. Srila Prabhupada initiated us despite protests from some of his senior leaders because in his own words, "Whenever I see a spark of Krishna consciousness, I must fan it."

Years later, Batu Gopal Prabhu sincerely apologized for the ways he had treated us. But we held no malice. Though we couldn't see it at the time, his negative treatment of us had resulted in such a blessed outcome.

I only had *vapuh* association with my beloved Gurudeva four or five times. But my real connection with Srila Prabhupada came when it was revealed that I had to find him in my heart. This heart connection with Srila Prabhupada has sustained my devotional life.

Srila Visvanatha Chakravarti Thakura, one of the wise *mahajanas* in our disciplic succession, has emphasized that "just as one cannot separate the body from the soul while in the conditioned state, similarly the disciple cannot separate the instructions of the spiritual master from his or her very life." In other words, following the instructions of the spiritual master means life and not following means death.

One specific instruction that I received from Srila Prabhupada is to be an instrument to show people all over the world how to have a real Krishna conscious marriage. I have dedicated my life to doing this.

I see Srila Prabhupada's loving hands and guidance through all the turmoils, reversals, and setbacks on this path of bhakti. He has allowed me to associate with a fantastic team of Vaishnavas of the Grihastha Vision Team who are committed to strengthening and supporting "healthy marriages, happy families, and a strong community."

As a senior minister in the Cleveland Nama Hatta program for over twenty years, we've had steady, regular programs, *sankirtana*, *prasadam* distribution, and festivals in the greater Cleveland area. Only because of Srila Prabhupada have I been able to raise ten biological children, many other spiritual children, and be married to a Muslim gentleman for almost thirty years. As a couple, we are like a bridge between different religious communities. We established the Dasi-Ziyad Family Institute to implement spiritual principles in the secular community as well. This is all by the grace of Srila Prabhupada – because he fanned that spark.

Throughout the years, Srila Prabhupada has continuously fanned the spark of my Krishna conscious life through his example, his books, his disciples, and through the personal instructions he has given me in letters and dreams. I pray to be able to serve under his direction and for his glorification for the rest of my eternal life.

Ksama devi dasi

Ksama dasi first met the devotees at a Hindu temple in Birmingham, England, in 1970. Though still in high school, she attended the temple weekly. Her parents were very disapproving, and so she could not move into the temple, but ended up running away and joining the Amsterdam temple. She later moved back to England.

Srila Prabhupada's room in Bury Place was on the first floor. Any time you wanted to go anywhere in the temple, you had to pass by Srila Prabhupada's room. He used to come out of his room and cross the landing in the hallway to go to the bathroom. The door would open and sun would stream through. Srila Prabhupada's skin looked golden. He looked so beautiful, very effulgent and golden. We were sitting there at the bottom of the stairs, because Srila Prabhupada was coming out, and we were looking. I was showing Bhakti Kirtan [Kishori's son] how effulgent and golden Srila Prabhupada was. When he came out, he looked at Bhakti Kirtan with a big smile and said, "This boy will be big kirtan leader." Because he looked just like Brahmananda–very big and strong, and he had very strong Dutch features.

Prabhupada was very active and seemed very relaxed. The door to his room was open all the time, except for when he was taking rest or having a massage, and any number of visitors would just walk in and sit down, many Indians especially. Nearly all morning long and in the afternoons people would come in for darshan. Prabhupada would be sitting in his rocking chair and speaking and the people would just sit.

He did many engagements while he was in London at that time. In Kshirodakshaya Prabhu's home Srila Prabhupada installed Radha-Krishna Deities. He did a seven-day reading of *Srimad-Bhagavatam*. Prabhupada held a fire sacrifice there and I received Gayatri initiation. Prabhupada got angry at Pradyumna half way through the fire sacrifice, because Pradyumna was chanting some of the mantras incorrectly.

Every day I rose at 3:30am to prepare the *mangala-arati* offering. Srila Prabhupada was very sick at that time, so I was be careful to be very, very quiet. It was very dark because we didn't dare put any of the lights on. Afterwards, I tiptoed down the stairs to sit by Srila Prabhupada's room. After about thirty seconds later the door opened and Srila Prabhupada stuck his head out. He asked me what I was doing. And I explained that I was up early chanting. He looked around, and then he looked back at me, and in a very puzzled tone said, "But where is the light?" From that day on I've never chanted *japa* in the dark.

Another time I was outside his room "guarding" him. We were a little naive then. We couldn't imagine anyone could possibly want to hurt Srila Prabhupada so anyone without special qualifications used to take turns. It was lunchtime, so another devotee and I were taking *prasadam* while sitting outside Srila Prabhupada's room. Prabhupada came out and walked past, so we bowed down to offer obeisances to him. But he chastised us. He didn't want us to offer obeisances while we were honoring *prasadam*.

When I went to get my Gayatri mantra I had some presents for Srila Prabhupada. We knew about *guru-dakshina*. I had bought a little tin of macadamia nuts, which were very, very expensive. I covered the tin in red velvet and glued on jewels and trim. And I got a very big ripe mango. I had these in my hands and I went in.

Srila Prabhupada was sitting behind his desk on a big cushion, and the other cushion was kind of tucked underneath his back. His desk was in front of the windows, so Srila Prabhupada had his back to the window, and he was kind of half lying down. I paid my obeisances, and as I got up he looked at me. He was peering over to see what I had in my hand. He looked just like a little child. He said, "Oh? What do you have?" So I handed him the mango, and he looked at it and he opened his eyes really big, like a little child, and then he patted his tummy and he said, "Oh, mango." And he took the little tin of nuts and he shook them to hear what was in there. He asked me what it was, then put them down on his table.

Srila Prabhupada was saying the lines of the Gayatri and showing me on the paper as he went and how to count on the fingers. When he got to the line, *klim krsnaya govindaya*, he stopped. I really didn't know what to expect, so I just sat there, and he closed his eyes. The way he was just sitting there was indescribable. It was in the afternoon, and the sun was coming through the window shining on Srila Prabhupada. He was wearing a pale orange, very soft wool sweater, and he was kind of half lying, and all this golden sunshine was coming in. He had this blissful look on his face, and he was gently stroking his stomach with his left hand, and it seemed like ages that he sat there like that.

Suddenly he opened his eyes and said, "What is next?" And I said, "I don't know. You didn't tell me yet, Srila Prabhupada." So he looked at the paper and carried on with the last line. I expected that before he left that he'd ask me some very esoteric question or something to make sure I was ready for Gayatri, but the only question he asked was, "Do you chant sixteen rounds a day?"–which is really the most important question. But I was very surprised because I thought that was a simple and basic question, that you had to chant in any case.

When Srila Prabhupada was in London, he always seemed very relaxed. He would pose for pictures any time you wanted to take a picture of him. For instance, he'd be coming down the stairs, and he'd see someone with a camera, so immediately he'd stop and he'd stand there facing you, and he'd put a big smile on his face. And you'd take the picture and then he'd carry on.

But the thunderbolt quality was also there. One time this boy fell asleep in *Srimad-Bhagavatam* class. And Srila Prabhupada got very angry, stopped the class, shouted at him, and he told him to leave. Of course, the boy hesitated. He thought Prabhupada was just angry and he wanted him to wake up, but that's not what Srila Prabhupada wanted. He told him he should leave the room, he didn't want him there any longer, and he should go upstairs and sleep. He'd also get angry at Pradyumna because Pradyumna would come late to *Srimad-Bhagavatam* class, and Srila Prabhupada would always ask where he was.

One time Prabhupada came into the temple for darshan. We'd made these new clothes for the Deities. We had heard that Srila Prabhupada liked balloon skirts. You know those big puffy ones which are like a balloon that we make for Lord Jagannatha. Unfortunately, it was for Lord Jagannatha that he liked them. So we'd made these new outfits with lots of layers of netting underneath Radharani's skirt.

He said this was very nice, "But not like this." And he made this motion with his hands to show the skirt coming out full from the waist. He said,

"It is like this," And made another motion to show going smooth from the waist and coming out at the bottom. He told us that Radharani looked pregnant the way we made these skirts. So he said they should be more smooth and then full. So that night, Lilasakti, I, and Bala Gopala, stayed up all night long to fix all these outfits.

On another day he told us that there had to be two little thrones inside the Deity room, on either side of the altar. One was for Narada Muni and one was for Lord Brahma. We were to receive them. Mahavishnu stayed up all night to build these two little thrones. They were not even three foot high, maybe 2 1/2 foot high at the most. We upholstered them overnight and decorated them so that they could be there the next day for Srila Prabhupada to see.

One time we had this huge flower vase. It was almost as big as the Deities, maybe two thirds as tall. It was put it in between Radha and Krishna and Srila Prabhupada said it should be moved. He explained that nothing ever comes between Radha and Krishna. There's a famous picture of Radha and Krishna and there's a cow in the middle. But Prabhupada said that's not bona fide because nothing comes between Radha and Krishna, not even a cow.

The next time I saw Srila Prabhupada was in Dallas in 1974. I was a teacher there then. He came again in July 1975. The temple owned a house right next door to the temple building, and it had a nice garden. At least we made it nice, and we put all these *tulasi* plants in it. It's very, very warm at night there in summer. It doesn't get cold at all. The nights are very hot, and Srila Prabhupada would sit out in the garden in the evening. We'd take his rocking chair out there and an electric fan, and Srila Prabhupada would have someone read *Krsna* book. Now and again Srila Prabhupada would comment, and we would ask questions.

In any case, Prabhupada told us about his childhood, when he was learning to play *mridanga*. How his father would let him learn to play *mridanga*, and he wanted to be a famous *mridanga* player, and his mother was always very unhappy.

Jnanagamya Prabhu asked, "How can we ever repay you, Srila Prabhupada?" And Srila Prabhupada said that you can never repay the spiritual master.

Nandarani couldn't cook for Srila Prabhupada for some reason, so I was cooking his breakfast at that time. And then Nandarani couldn't cook lunch, so I started cooking lunch also. I remember Srila Prabhupada didn't like that it was changed–that first someone was cooking for him, and then someone else was cooking. The first day that I helped Upendra cook lunch and I took the plate in to Srila Prabhupada, he asked, "Where is Nandarani?" He was extremely patient, though.

I'd make his breakfast while he was giving *Srimad-Bhagavatam* class, and Srila Prabhupada would come upstairs to take breakfast. The offering would finish just as Srila Prabhupada came up the stairs, and someone would run down the stairs and grab the spoon and the cup from one of the Deities' plates and run back up, so that we could use it to take in Srila Prabhupada's breakfast. One day the boy who was meant to go fetch the spoon forgot, and so we brought in Srila Prabhupada's breakfast tray and set it down without a spoon. Prabhupada just sat there patiently. He showed no sign of anger at our gross incompetence.

I wanted to make him *choody* noodles to take on the airplane in his tiffin. He was leaving straight after *Bhagavatam* class in the morning and he would take breakfast on his flight. I stayed up late that night after I put all the children in my ashram to bed, and I had made them by hand. I was thinking that I was really going to please Srila Prabhupada. I had rolled out all these thin noodles and cut them up and fried them. I hadn't spiced them, put in peanuts or anything. I wanted to finish them the next morning. I covered them with tinfoil and asked Vamanadeva, who was guarding Prabhupada's room, to put them up in Prabhupada's kitchen. As Vamanadeva was walking there, Srila Prabhupada came out of his room and asked him what he was carrying. He took one out and said, "Too big," and he rejected the whole thing in a second. So that was it. Ego deflated.

Kulangana devi dasi

Kulangana was born in Poland and met devotees in London in 1972. The first time she heard the sound of sankirtana it struck her that it was transcendental sound from beyond this world.

All my successes in Krishna consciousness completely depend on the mercy of the Vaishnavas. My godsisters, who were already initiated, were helping me. Sarvamangala invited me to go to Ratha-yatra in 1972. Mondakini, Yamuna, and Malati all went. I was so impressed that they didn't have any material desires. I realized they were pure devotees. And Dhananjaya Prabhu and Bala Gopala. I depend completely on the mercy of these Vaishnavas. I am in this Movement only by their mercy.

After I took initiation in 1974 I had great opportunities to serve Srila Prabhupada by cooking. When Prabhupada came Bury Place one time, the president asked me to offer cashews to Srila Prabhupada. He meant raw cashews. But there was so much love in my heart for Srila Prabhupada, that I prepared raw cashews, fried cashews, raw almonds, and fried almonds. The president chastised me. He said if the guru asks for a glass of water you shouldn't give a glass of milk. This was the first lesson: offer what the guru asks for.

One time when Srila Prabhupada came I had become recognized for cooking feasts, especially at the Bhaktivedanta Manor. Mondakini asked me to make *gulabjamons* for Srila Prabhupada's lunch. I put everything into making those *gulabs*. Srila Prabhupada accepted them. The next day she sent for *gulabs* again. But Prabhupada said, "They are so hard, I can't eat these *gulabs*." I saw how difficult it is to cook for Krishna. I was very disappointed.

One time I cooked lunch for Srila Prabhupada and George Harrison. Mukunda Maharaja suggested what was best to cook. I made *kulfi*. I didn't know what it was but I had read about it in a book. I put all my time into making this *kulfi*. I added some mango to it and put it in the cooler. Srila Prabhupada liked this preparation. Prabhupada asked who had made it because it was very good.

Another time, I made custard. I was completely absorbed in the thought that Srila Prabhupada was coming. For a day and a half I wasn't able to eat or sleep, and I was cooking this custard in a very ecstatic mood for a feast for the devotees. The feast was served to Srila Prabhupada and he said, "I like this custard very much. Please give me more." But it was finished. They asked me to cook more custard because he wanted more. That was quite fortunate–not like the *gulabs*.

The last time Srila Prabhupada came to Bhaktivedanta Manor I was distributing books every day. I cooked breakfast for Srila Prabhupada in the morning and then went out. In the evening, Prabhupada would ask how many books we had distributed. He told Tamal Krishna Maharaja, "These *sankirtana* mothers, they are very dear to me. Please gather them together and tell them that Srila Prabhupada is a young boy." For me it was very important to hear that. Every day I meditate about his message. He's such a great personality, such a serious person, so educated, so learned and he says he is a young boy. I just realized that I am not this body, definitely. Srila Prabhupada helped us by sending this message.

Srila Prabhupada sent an instruction through Vicitravirya Prabhu who was temple president at the time. He said we shouldn't waste even a drop of milk. Prabhupada said we should put a little bit of water in the bottle, rinse it around, and get all the milk out of it. Prabhupada didn't want to waste a drop of milk.

This I remember every day because I am engaged in the service of cooking *mangala-arati* sweets. So after I take the churn I put a little water and rinse to be sure that each drop of milk is taken out from this churn. Wherever I am cooking *mangala-arati* sweets–actually nearly every day–I remember this instruction because Srila Prabhupada didn't want to waste a drop of milk.

One time, devotees offered milk to Srila Prabhupada but it was only warm. So Srila Prabhupada rejected this milk. Devotees made very, very hot milk. Srila Prabhupada was sipping this milk with a little spoon. It was so hot. He said that he wanted sugar in the milk. He said warm becomes urine, and hot milk goes to brain. So I drink a lot of milk because I never had a brain before.

I remember his first lecture in Bury Place. I was attached to Lord Jesus Christ and I studied the Bible every day. I used to sit in churches and pray to be sent somewhere as a missionary. I was a physiotherapist and there was a war in Korea, so I was thinking it would please Lord Jesus Christ to be sent to Korea to help handicapped people.

But I didn't have knowledge. The priests in the Catholic Church didn't say anything substantial, so I didn't even know that God was with me in my heart. I didn't know that God is a person. I thought God must be very old.

Then Prabhupada spoke about God. He said that God is a person. It struck me so much. Then he said, "You should be like a swan. A swan can take water from milk. You should only drink milk, not water." This was very important for me, especially these days, when there are so many different instructions and devotees don't actually follow Srila Prabhupada's instructions. Srila Prabhupada never makes mistakes and is nondifferent from God. Therefore whatever he says should be completely followed. Devotees should follow exactly what Prabhupada wanted.

So I think, "Kulangana, only milk, no water." This is why I'm not so much affected by different changes because I try to drink only milk like Srila Prabhupada said. Milk means only Srila Prabhupada's instructions. I am never disappointed. Prabhupada never disappointed me, because whenever I obey his instructions, I can see that I'm able to make some spiritual progress and advancement.

Kulapriya devi dasi

At fourteen, Kulapriya was attracted to a chanting party in Berkeley, CA, in the summer of 1970. A year or so later, a small group of devotees from the L.A. temple gave a talk at her high school in her comparative religions class. Again, she was attracted and intrigued. But it wasn't until early 1974 when she read the Bhagavad-gita As It Is, that her real relationship with Srila Prabhupada began.

Although I was fortunate enough to see and hear Srila Prabhupada on a number of occasions in person, my main relationship to my spiritual master has always been through reading his books and letters, listening to audio lectures, through service, and by grace.

The first glimpse I had of Srila Prabhupada's person was when he visited New Dwarka in June of 1975, which was just a month after I had moved into the temple. I was among a large group of devotees who had gone to LAX (the Los Angeles aiport) to greet him. In those days, of course, you could go right up to the arrival gate. I was toward the back of the crowd. When I saw Srila Prabhupada, he looked like he glided or floated rather than walked, and his effulgence was so bright and immense, it seemed literally tangible. It was definitely clearly visible, even to me. I know many other devotees have described almost this same kind of experience, but it is uncommonly true. I am a very reserved person, at least in public or with people I don't know well, but I was so overwhelmed by seeing His Divine Grace. I started crying quite hard. The more I tried to pull myself together and regain my composure, the more uncontrollable the crying became. I'll never forget that first vision of Srila Prabhupada for as long as I live. As far as I was concerned, Srila Prabhupada had just stepped off an airplane that came directly from Krishnaloka. He was obviously not of this world.

The following experience may have been that same visit, or it could have been in June 1976 when Srila Prabhupada again visited Los Angeles. Srila Prabhupada was sitting on the *vyasasana* in the L.A. temple room. I was sitting downstairs kind of midway between the temple room doors and the *vyasasana*, pretty much right in line with Srila Prabhupada, so I had a really good view. Srila Prabhupada was chanting "Jaya Radha Madhava" prayers and casually looking around at the assembled devotees in front of him as he did so. I was looking at Srila Prabhupada, whom I already had a great deal of faith in and devotional feelings for, but then my mind took off. Honestly I don't remember what passed through my mind at that moment. I would tell you if I knew. Whatever it was, it wasn't completely horrible, but it was definitely "off." Srila Prabhupada's head turned very quickly to the side and his eyes immediately locked right on me. Our eyes met, and it was a thunderbolt-to-the-heart experience for me. It happened very quickly, but it was quite profound. There was no malice at all coming from him, but whatever I was thinking, it needed to be purified. That is what I felt – purified and chastened. Krishna showed me that He was working through Srila Prabhupada as the Supersoul of all.

The only other close encounter I had with Srila Prabhupada is a bit silly on my part. This occurred in 1975 or 1976. I was on the cleaning team for Srila Prabhupada's quarters in Los Angeles. When Srila Prabhupada would visit, we would clean his rooms when he went for his morning walk. One morning he came back quite early, and the three or four of us who were cleaning had to quickly leave his quarters. There wasn't even enough time to make it down the stairs, so we all hid in the walk-in supply closet that was at the end of the hall. When we thought the coast was clear, I was the first one through the door, only to bumble out, face-to-face with Srila

Prabhupada about five feet away. He had stepped into the hall unbeknownst to us. As surprised to see me as I was to see him, he said "Hare Krishna" in his deep voice. But I was so flustered, I don't think I said anything. I just immediately offered obeisances. I didn't lift my head from the floor until he had turned to go into another room, but, when I did stand, I saw that the other women were still hiding in the closet. So I not only got to be a fool in front of my spiritual master, but, by sharing this story, I get to be a fool in front of all the Vaishnavis as well.

I can't imagine any life without having come into contact with Srila Prabhupada. It would have only been another turn on the wheel of *samsara*, another illusory dream sequence. Whatever success or happiness I may or may not have experienced would ultimately only end in death. I now have real life. I am in the process of reviving my dormant relationship with Lord Krishna. I have started on the path back to Godhead and my present as well as my future is very bright indeed. I can never thank Srila Prabhupada enough. His mercy is truly all I am made of. *Jaya* Srila Prabhupada, Hare Krishna.

Kumkum devi dasi

Kumkum, anxious for truth and in complete dismay at having any prospect of finding it in college, dropped out. She stayed in the university town trying to arrive at truth by constantly posing questions to philosophers, historians, and anthropologists. One day she felt, "There is no truth," and questioned her theism. That day she received a Back to Godhead magazine.

This was June 1971, and I kept turning the magazine pages, knowing that I was going to find an answer. When I read Prabhupada's "Markine Bhagavat Dharma" prayers I was struck with the fact that Prabhupada knew the Lord – how to talk to, pray to, and approach Him. I was convinced by Prabhupada's utter humility and his excitement and enthusiasm to go forward with his mission.

From then on I had to meet Prabhupada. In the Atlanta temple the devotees presented the truth to me nonstop, and their enthusiasm connected my heart to it. I dived in, followed the devotees, tried to cooperate, to serve, and found out how much I'd gain every moment, by every thought, every word, and everything my hands and legs contributed.

When Prabhupada came to Atlanta I sewed a cushion for him, thinking, "If I'm going to do something for the person who is giving me God, then I'll do the finest thing I can." My heart burst with happiness to see him. Later, in Dallas, Srila Prabhupada wrote many letters about how he wanted the children to be happy and educated and to learn everything about the glories of growing up in Krishna consciousness. When he visited,

Prabhupada was full of love and appreciation and at that time Sri Sri Radha-Kalachandji arrived. To our astonishment Srila Prabhupada said, "I'll stay and we can install Them." One devotee thought the Deities should be repainted and was making all sorts of changes to Them. Srila Prabhupada sweetly and kindly chastised this devotee, but when she said somebody else had done this in another temple, Srila Prabhupada raised his cane high over his head and loudly said, "Why you are not asking me? I am right here!" He was taking care of things for God. Srila Prabhupada did the first *arati* for Radha-Kalachandji and left the next day. We could hardly believe that in only three days we had gained so much. Everybody was coming forward trying to enthusiastically and properly follow all the new things that needed to be done for the Deities.

Even though we're separated from Prabhupada on the physical level, as his followers we have the heartfelt understanding we'll be in union with him when trying to spread what mattered so incredibly much to him. It's not that he ever turns away from us, even slightly. If our hearts are sincerely open, if we're anxious for his instruction, at all times there's a flood of grace coming from him. That's my feeling all day every day; it's simply up to me to want that. Prabhupada's always present. He's my unceasing guide.

Kusha devi dasi

Kusha joined ISKCON on May 1, 1969 in Hawaii and was later initiated in 1970 at the Honolulu temple.

Jayasri and I nursed the first *tulasi* plants in our Movement from seeds Srila Prabhupada gave Govinda dasi. And Govinda dasi had us plant them in the front yard. I was very interested in finding *kusha* grass and was researching the local university. When my initiation letter and beads arrived I was very moved. My name was short and sweet and he had sent the exact type of *tulasi* beads I had wanted. This penetrated my heart because Prabhupada read my mind. I shivered realizing the kindness and compassion of our beloved guru!

I moved to the San Francisco temple mid-1972 and Prabhupada came. As Srila Prabhupada was entering, I was finishing up some sewing. Prabhupada said, "Please bring something to wash the legs. If the legs are washed, one's whole body feels refreshed."

That night, Jayananda drove us to Telegraph Avenue, for *harinama sankirtana*. He brought a 55 gallon container of popcorn and had popcorn bags printed with the *maha-mantra* on it. Srila Prabhupada came by in the car and the kirtan party went wild and Jayananda Prabhu handed Srila Prabhupada a bag of popcorn. Prabhupada ate all of it and said, "I like popcorn very much!" But the following day, Srila Prabhupada remised that perhaps popcorn was not so good for his health.

In December 1973 my son, Atmarama was born. When he was almost one, his father decided to take a second wife and divorce me to marry a lovely underaged seventeen-year-old girl. I was confused and saddened. I had no idea how to act in this circumstance. So Jayatirtha Prabhu encouraged me to write to Srila Prabhupada. In his reply, Prabhupada said this wasn't our philosophy, that I should not associate with such a person, and that I should increase my hearing and chanting and always live in the association of devotees.

I cooked for Prabhupada during this period and I over salted Srila Prabhupada's *raj bhoga*. He told me not to salt anything and he would add it. The next morning in *Bhagavatam* class, he used over salting as an analogy for over endeavor. He said over endeavor destroys everything, just like over salting. I thought I would die, but I never forgot that instruction.

When my son was two weeks old, we were living at the temple at Moana Loa Loop in Hawaii. Srila Prabhupada came to Hawaii and we were daily going on the morning walks. I had Atmarama bundled in a blanket as the morning air was crisp and chilly. Srila Prabhupada turned to me and said, "Can he walk?" I said "No, Srila Prabhupada," shaking like a leaf. Srila Prabhupada saw my nature was so mothering that he needed to warn me against being overprotective in a kind of predictive way. Twenty years later I am finally realizing how hard that instruction has been for me to follow. Srila Prabhuapda really sees right through us.

Srila Prabhupada came to Hawaii on this occasion to save the temple. The whole temple had blooped. Srila Prabhupada sent a party of eight devotees, including six *sankirtana* devotees to collect for and care for the Deities. He reclaimed Them. To bolster our waning spirits, Srila Prabhupada walked around the garden identifying plants that could be used as food. There were things growing there with which we were entirely unfamiliar. Srila Prabhupada gathered such things as squash blossoms and parval to prepare us a feast. I was sitting in back of a curtain stealthily watching Srila Prabhupada cooking and cleaning us as he cooked. He made chickpea *kachoris* – we had never had such delights. He thrilled us with transcendental cookery. Our spirits soared. Srila Prabhupada saves us again and again.

My son was well behaved and daily gave Srila Prabhupada a garland over the years. Again and again, Srila Prabhupada had a twinkle in his eye and would lovingly give Atmarama one of his garlands in return. The interchange was a daily affair. Three times, Srila Prabhupada said, "This boy is a great devotee," or "This boy is a big devotee." He also said he was a kirtan dancer from a previous life.

One day, Atma was at Srila Prabhupada's side as he took *charanamrita* and he sprinkled his wash water on Atmarama's head.

I did *pujari* work, book distribution, cooking, and different types of *seva*, but I was most personally rewarded by seeing Srila Prabhupada's attention on the second generation and how much love and light he basked upon them. He very much adored our young folk.

We were new to sprouting beans and seeds and whatever we did, we wanted to offer that to Srila Prabhupada. So we put sprouts on his plate. In his infinite compassion he said that each individual sprout should be offered and honored and none wasted.

Knowing how much Srila Prabhupada liked mangoes, we were accustomed to sending them wherever he was. We marked each box "Fragile Photographic Equipment," so they would be treated carefully. One box of mangoes arrived safely in Mayapur, and delighted Srila Prabhupada ate them. He handed the seed to Tapamoya and told him to plant the seed. That seed became a huge mango tree that grew in Mayapur for decades. It was only just removed to make way for TOVP.

Srila Prabhupada oversaw most everything we did. We were worshipping Srimati Tulasi Devi using sparklers for *tulasi-puja* instead of ghee wicks. Srila Prabhupada nipped it in the bud, saying, "You westerners are so inventive. But follow my instructions, don't invent."

We asked what to do with the *tulasi's* that were overgrowing the walkway. At first, he said, we could duck down to get through the *tulasi* hedge. She was six feet tall and very wide. Then he said we could tie her back with rope and he told us, "Do not step on her shadow."

We landed in Vrindavan on Thanksgiving Day in 1976. At the last minute, Govinda dasi was trying to cancel the trip. I retorted, "If you cancel, I will never speak to you again, I am going anyway." This became the last three months we spent with Srila Prabhupada, and it was a great adventure traveling with him in India.

We went immediately to Srila Prabhupada's quarters and gave our *guru-dakshina*, while Bhagatji mused about Vrindavan's glories. Srila Prabhupada was greatly entertained as Bhagatji bragged about him and glorified the *dhama*. He told us about the time he made a bet with Srila Prabhupada that he couldn't cook for one hundred men in one hour. He said, "I gladly lost the bet." Srila Prabhupada always soundly defeated him. Srila Prabhupada's wide eyes sparkled. Then Bhagatji went on to say that Vrindavan *dhama* is such a special place that every grain of sand says, "Hare Krishna, Hare Krishna, Krishna Krishna, Hare Hare," on it. Every drop of Yamuna water says, "Hare Krishna, Hare Krishna, Krishna Krishna, Hare Hare." That the bones of the saints are made of the *maha-mantra* too. He said the fish in the Yamuna stay exclusively in the Yamuna and if by chance they get close to the Ganga, they make sure they turn around and only swim in the Yamuna.

Srila Prabhupada asked Bhagatji to take us around to look at safe real estate around the temple. Bhagatji knew how dangerous it was to live outside of ISKCON. He took us all over Vraja too.

Next thing you know, we were on a train to Bombay in the coupe next to Srila Prabhupada! He swept us up to Bombay. When we arrived so many devotees were sick. Visvadevi became our best of bestest of friends. She really knew her way around.

Srila Prabhupada's health was not so good, so the devotees were carrying Srila Prabhupada up and down the corridors in a palanquin. When he would alight from the palanquin, he would get into one of those beautiful Ambassador cars with flag-festoons flapping in the breeze. The look was so noble. Gopal Krishna Maharaja's son would sit on Srila Prabhupada's lap and ride with him in the car. One morning, he was not there. So my son uncharacteristically started a ruckus. He wanted to go with Srila Prabhupada. I was a nobody, so I said, "Please quiet down." But Srila Prabhupada heard him and said, "Come on!" Again my joy knew no bounds. These little moments endeared me for lifetimes of loving *seva*. Prabhupada stroked his silky blonde *shikha*.

There were no trains, planes, cars, taxis, or buses available to go to Allahabad for the Kumbha Mela. Everything had been booked for months. Still Srila Prabhupada wanted to see what his disciples were doing for this momentous occasion. Abhirama Prabhu knew the head of the train station in Bombay, Mr. Gupta, who added two cars on the already-full train. One first class car and one second class car. We were in the coupe next to Srila Prabhupada. At various stops, we bought fruit and sent my son, Atma, in to Srila Prabhupada with fruit gifts.

Srila Prabhupada had told Govinda dasi that this particular Kumbha Mela was the most auspicious in one hundred and forty-four years. He said many yogis would come from the Himalayas and all over to grace this festival with their association. He had said to Govinda dasi, "I will take you!"

That is the moment we both realized that Srila Prabhupada has *vac siddhi*, that whatever he says comes true, or is true. He said that if you take cold bath, follow the principles, and chant sixteen rounds a day for twelve years, whatever you say will come true.

We got down in pitch blackness in Allahabad to make our way toward the camp site. It was chaos, as the train station was filled with pilgrims of all sorts. Srila Prabhupada was not impressed with the location of our campsite. He sent us out on *harinama*. When they served *prasadam*, Srila Prabhupada asked that we invite the public. They did not have enough *prasadam* and Srila Prabhupada admonished the organizers, "We must do *prasadam* distribution."

People there were gawking at us and calling us *mlecchas*. We didn't care because we were with Srila Prabhupada. Throngs would gather around my little Atmarama, as a result, he lost his gold bracelets.

At 11:27 am, we took holy bath. Buckets of water were brought from the river for Srila Prabhupada to take bucket bath as he was too weak to endure the intense crowds. I lashed my son to my body, so there was no chance of him getting separated from me. It was an incredible rush into the *triveni sangam*. It was dangerous and anyone could easily drown in such a crowd.

On the way out of Kumbha Mela, one of our *sannyasi* godbrothers was trying to get our first-class coupe for an important devotee instead of us. Mr. Gupta told us this was happening and we worried we would be stranded at the Mela. Srila Prabhupada, admonished our godbrother saying, "They are the most important devotees." So the plot to throw us off the train was foiled under the protection of Srila Prabhupada!

Srila Prabhupada was on the train platform unprotected, unguarded. Govinda dasi got very perturbed and put her arms out to protect Srila Prabhupada. Then Ramesvara Maharaja put his danda sideways as if it was a guard rail. She inspired Ramesvara to protect Srila Prabhupada.

In Mayapur, I met Pishima, an astounding perfect female version of Srila Prabhupada. She equally adored young ones, so Atma got her attention. We lived very austerely. Pishima walked with only her *gumcha* wrapped like a man around her waist. Some godbrother's started complaining to Srila Prabhupada about his own sister, who was extremely old. I thought if they had the audacity to complain about Pishima, then what can be done? They're going to complain about anything about any woman. I can't take any of this seriously. This is not personal and has nothing to do with me. If they can complain about Pishima, they just will have to grow up some time, hopefully soon.

Again we found ourselves on a train to Bhubaneswar with Srila Prabhupada. He was going to visit Gour Govinda dasa brahmachari, who had just acquired some land. They reserved a nice hotel room for Srila Prabhupada but he preferred staying in a mud hut on the property. When I think of it now, I realized Srila Prabhupada was sanctifying the place, preparing it to become the glorious temple.

Srila Prabhupada was mystical living in his Bhubaneswar mud hut. He gazed over the fields saying, "We have enough devotees now. We need to simply boil the milk." This was nectar to our ears, hearing that Srila Prabhupada wanted to concentrate on concentrating our *prema-bhakti*. Srila Prabhupada was protecting us and saving us over and over again.

We scouted on ahead, as Srila Prabhupada wanted to go to Puri, and we met Bhagawan Singhari from the Singhari family written about in

Chaitanya-charitamrita. I was Lord Jagannatha's *pujari* in Hawaii, and I wanted to get some Deities carved. Mr. Singhari was arranging for everything, including daily Jagannatha *prasadam* and flag raising. We brought him to meet Srila Prabhupada. They had a lively exchange in their native language. Bhagavan Singhari was impressed with Srila Prabhupada's divine grace.

Govinda hatched a plot to try to sneak in to the temple. The *chaukidhars* spotted her, ripped off her *chadar,* grabbed her cane, and started hitting her with it. She fled for her life. Rushing out the gate in a huge panic she collapsed into my arms. We went immediately to Srila Prabhupada, whose eyes were as big as saucers, listening raptly to her every description. He kept saying *"Accha,"* as if to say, "Really?" He was thinking deeply on how to protect his adventurous devotees.

Wherever we went Guru Kripa Maharaja's and Gargamuni Maharaja's party were there. They had Mercedes vans and they would almost run us off the road. We stayed as far from them as possible, but they loomed everywhere. Our godbrothers were so frequently a challenge. Srila Prabhupada remained our shelter and protector.

The next day an invitation arrived from a Puri Temple *panda.* He was holding a *pandal* program, not far from Haridasa Thakura's *samadhi,* to dedicate his new book, and he invited Srila Prabhupada to be the keynote speaker. Prabhupada arrived with about thirty devotees in tow, and the *panda* gave him a copy of his book. Srila Prabhupada put it to his forehead, blessing it, saying, "I have not read it." He proceeded to tell them that Jagannatha is not Puri Natha or Orissa Natha, but He is Jagannatha, Lord of the universe, and that devotees from all over the universe were coming to get His darshan. If they would not Jagannatha's devotees get darshan of Jagannatha, then Jagannatha would pack His bags and move in with us."

With that, Srila Prabhupada raised his hands and a wild celebration of the holy name loudly proceeded down the beach to Haridasa Thakura's *samadhi.* The kirtan was so empowering that everyone was three feet off the ground. We knew Srila Prabhupada was taking us all the way back to Krishna, no matter what the caste *brahmanas* had to say about it. Prabhupada's kirtan was so uplifting. It was forever astounding. Bhagavan Singhari said, "I've never experienced any kirtan like it." The next morning, Bhagavan Singhari rushed to see Srila Prabhupada. He reported that a vote was held in the Puri Management. The *panda* whose book was to be glorified, spoke that foreigners should never be allowed in. Still we all knew, it is a matter of time, if Srila Prabhupada wants it. Just see how he is constantly protecting his disciples.

Srila Prabhupada is our inspiration, our protector, our guide, and our master, keeping us safe amongst the abounding crocodiles within and without. We live in Prabhupada's grace. He gifted us a joyful life of blissful Krishna-*seva*.

Lalita devi dasi

Lalita devi dasi was initiated in Montreal in 1974 on Govardhana-puja. She had joined about nine months earlier at nineteen.

When I was fifteen, I used to distribute newspapers early in the morning. I'd come home and eat cereal while looking through the newspaper. There was a photograph of the devotees at the Montreal temple, all prostrated on the floor. Later, on the Pierre Berton talk show Ishan and Bibhavati were interviewed.

My father got me a job at the Canadian National Railway, where he had worked his whole life. This to-become-friend, Ann, walked over to my desk, put the *Bhagavad-gita* on it, and said, "Do you want to go to the temple?" So we made arrangements to go to the temple together.

I had a dream where I bowed down to Srila Prabhupada with my mother to my right. It was very, very powerful dream. I didn't have a clue really what a spiritual master was. But I went out and got a picture of Prabhupada and spent $40 to frame it.

Later, I had joined up with a *harinama* party and went back to the temple with them. Someone asked me if I'd hem some *dhotis,* and I really freaked out because somehow, in that moment, I knew what surrender meant. I knew I had to give up everything and leave.

Thus I was becoming pulled by Krishna and Prabhupada. I mentioned to someone at work that I had many cats. They came that night and took every one of them. We got a notice in the mail that they were going to rip down the place where I lived with a boyfriend. Everything was opening up. I had my mom, dad, and brothers come to look over my possessions and take anything they wanted. I took the rest to the temple.

It was very, very wonderful at that bowling alley. We used to wash our feet before we went into the temple room. The *brahmacharini* room was to the left of the temple. Sadhvi was there, she was a great influence. She once told me that the spirit soul is embarrassed by this body. I still had a hippie consciousness about the body, but she was a very pure soul.

Chandra devi was the head cook. She made a preparation when I first joined. She placed a layer of deep-fried eggplant in the pan and she salted it lightly. Then she put a layer of curd that was mixed with saffron and sugar, and then another layer of eggplant, another layer of curd, and then she baked it. I felt like I left this world when I ate it, it was very powerful for me.

Then I got to see Srila Prabhupada in New York. That experience was sort of overwhelming because there were so many devotees. The energy was incredible being in the temple room with Prabhupada giving *Srimad-Bhagavatam* class. You just felt that you weren't in this world, you were transported. We were completely infected with this ecstatic emotional feeling of reuniting with the most dear. Srila Prabhupada – so beloved to us. It was so obvious to us that when we lived in a temple, followed the principles, chanted sixteen rounds, got up for *mangala-arati*, did services, and went on *sankirtana* that we were going back home. There was no question.

Then I got to go to see Srila Prabhupada in Toronto. I met Rukmini devi dasi and Srikari was there. All the *matajis* were hanging their *saris* on the stairwell. Everyone was young and beautiful. I felt like I was in the spiritual world.

When Prabhupada came to Montreal, it was kind of mysterious to us. We were running around getting everything ready. They reupholstered the *vyasasana*, and I dressed Kartamasha and made Srila Prabhupada's garlands. I was in the kitchen, and I made my mother's recipe for apple crisp for Srila Prabhupada.

Ultimately I didn't get the personal association that other *matajis* got, but I got the benefit of getting their association.

I went through many hardships. I was in a serious car accident. Despite the fact I hadn't chanted for so many years, the whole time the car was rolling I was chanting, "*Krishna Chaitanya, Krishna Chaitanya, Krishna Chaitanya!*" It landed on the roof, and it was raining. It was a very dramatic moment. I remembered that Prabhupada had engaged me and introduced me to Krishna, and then I realized They didn't forget me and They didn't let me forget the holy name. It was so powerful to have that near-death moment and have Krishna on my tongue. It gave me tremendous strength. I had to reconcile the past and understood that even though we're chanting, unless we have strong association, it's very difficult.

Then I was given blessings to join the *sankirtana* party and again try to serve with my whole heart. So despite all of the reactions or karmic issues I didn't die. The process is eternal; it doesn't end. Even as a very young child, I remember looking up at the sky and wondering where God was. Krishna says that even without seeking He sometimes come. You know, she put the *Bhagavad-gita* right on my desk. So Krishna is very kind.

I just keep praying that I learn to hear the holy name and do service with sincerity and maybe someday understand what humility is. But the fact is I keep seeing one *anartha* after another dropping from my husband. It's so powerful to see, and it's so powerful to see the clarity of his vision on his attachment. In fact, in this past Karttika we took the vow to chant *Bhagavad-gita* every day, and it was originally just for Karttika. But then we decided just to continue on. And one night I was exhausted and I had to lie down and he came and said, "Well, when should I wake you up? We still have to do the *Bhagavad-gita*." So it's very wonderful.

He's so proud that I was initiated by Srila Prabhupada. He always says, "My wife's initiated by Prabhupada." He's just is so thankful, and he says that all the devotees are so sweet. Srila Prabhupada reaches out beyond the limits of time and place.

I'm also very thankful that I got to serve in Berkeley *dhama* because of taking care of the Deities thirty-five years ago. I remember having pneumonia and I'd still get up every day and go and dress Them. I was rescued. Even though the temple was in disarray in many ways, I felt, "Wow, I can touch God! I can put *tulasi* in Radharani's hand. I can make Krishna's turban, and this is by Prabhupada's mercy."

Lalita Madhava devi dasi

Lalita Madhava was about twenty-eight when she started thinking, "What's life about? Why are so many people dying of cancer? Why are they taking so many drugs?" She began to study philosophy and read the Bible again.

I heard a wonderful man was coming to Melbourne and thought, "Well, I'll go with an open mind." A couple of friends and I went to the exhibition buildings where the devotees looked like they'd come from another planet. The flowers and incense made a lovely environment. All of a sudden a beautiful elderly man walked like a swan down the center to the stage, where he sat on a beautiful chair. He was glowing in his robes, his face was effulgent, and he said, "Everyone is looking for God. I can show you God. His name is Krish-NA." I was captivated and shaking so much my friends had to hold me. I thought, "Wow, this is beautiful!" Prabhupada went on to talk about the *Bhagavad-gita* and Krishna's message to mankind.

My eighteen-month-old daughter and I started going to the Krishna temple on Sundays to eat beautiful food and have a wonderful time in what I thought was the epitome of the dream I had – a world of love and transcendental existence. Then we went to Mayapur and while I stayed in the back feeling lowly, my blonde-haired daughter walked right up to Prabhupada who said, "Who is her mother?" and I was presented.

Now I'm aware that the next big ceremony in my life is going to be my funeral and I do not want to come back to this planet. Prabhupada gave us the regulative principles to save us from the pains of this material world. By accepting the philosophy and living under the tenets Srila Prabhupada has given, we live in a beautiful way and have the best chance not to repeat birth and death.

Lalita-sakhi devi dasi

Lalita-sakhi met devotees in Philadelphia. She took up chanting japa and offering her food at home in her senior year of high school. She left home to live in the temple just after her seventeenth birthday in 1972.

At thirteen years old, I walked with my mother in downtown Philadelphia. A small group of young people dressed in robes sang and played small hand cymbals on the other side of the street, and when I looked across, a girl made eye contact with me that pierced so deeply that I remember it over five decades later. I had unknowingly made first contact with my oldest and best friend, His Divine Grace A. C. Bhaktivedanta Swami Prabhupada, my eternal guru, through the mercy of his devotees.

A year or so later, again downtown but on my own, a robed young person handed me a card that read "Chant these names of God and your life will be sublime – Hare Krishna, Hare Krishna, Krishna Krishna, Hare Hare / Hare Rama, Hare Rama, Rama Rama, Hare Hare." At home I tried the chanting but wasn't sure how to pronounce "Hare." Was it like the rabbit? or like Harry? The card sat in a drawer forgotten. But Srila Prabhupada hadn't forgotten me.

In my last year of high school, a seminar teacher gave us an assignment to make a presentation on anything we wanted. I chose the Hare Krishnas, went downtown to find them, and spoke for hours to one devotee, who then had to take public transportation back to the temple, because he spent so much time with me that he missed his ride in the *sankirtana* van. A few devotees came to my class, chanted and talked, and distributed buttery Simply Wonderfuls. I bought the *Krsna* book and stayed up all night reading, mesmerized by the beauty of reality. I felt the power of Srila Prabhupada's bhakti in his book and in his followers, to whom I am deeply indebted. The idea of Krishna consciousness took over my life at that point and temple life soon followed, with long days of enthusiastic service and short nights of rest.

I saw Srila Prabhupada only a few times and never spoke with him but, like all the devotees, worshiped him and served his mission. After a few months in the temple, we traveled to New Vrindavan for the big 1972 Janmastami festival, where I was to be initiated. One morning I was sent with a group of other girls to clean Prabhupada's house while he gave *Srimad-Bhagavatam* class. While we were cleaning, we saw Srila Prabhupada's car returning and quickly ran out the front door and into our van to go back to the temple house. But we'd all left our shoes at Prabhupada's back door, so I ran back through the house to gather all the shoes. Just as I got to the back door Srila Prabhupada was entering. I'd never seen Prabhupada in person before. He was beautiful and quite small. I offered my obeisances, and when I rose Srila Prabhupada folded his hands and said, "Thank you very much." I gathered the shoes and made my way back into the van, pretty much in shock. How could anyone that empowered, so much bigger than life, so in touch with reality, possibly be embodied? It was hard for me to understand the combination of divinity with humanity.

When Srila Prabhupada initiated me he said, "Your name is Lalita-sakhi." Then he stared at me, as if he could see straight to my soul, and he said forcefully, "dasi." He also said, "Chant at least sixteen good rounds on your beads daily." This is the only direct personal instruction I ever received from him. That one instruction has been my lifeline and the foundation of my *sadhana*. Since that day it's been my most important practice. Srila Prabhupada *could* see to my soul; he knew what I needed. I'm still trying to understand what it truly is to become a servant of the Vaishnavas rather than a servant to my mind and senses.

I was blessed to go to India for the Mayapur festival in 1976. Srila Prabhupada would daily circumambulate Sri Sri Radha-Madhava in the temple room, and he would ring the large bell as he came past the altar. Amidst hundreds of devotees chanting in kirtan, Prabhupada, surrounded by *sannyasis* and *brahmacharis*, emerged on the path from behind the altar and pulled the bell's rope. The kirtan went wild. I was standing in the first row of devotees at the end of that pathway, directly facing Srila Prabhupada. Oh, I wanted to dance, but was unsure if it would be appropriate, being influenced by the gender-consciousness prevalent at the time and the sea of saffron and *dandas* approaching. I was looking at Srila Prabhupada, who was beaming, and as he walked closer he extended his hand, palm up, and lifted it a few times. I was certain he was indicating, "Dance!" And I did, happily.

Through the enlivening times of hard work and blissful festivals, gorgeous Deities, and Their all-encompassing service, cooking special preparations for the temple president to take to Srila Prabhupada when he went to visit him and later hearing how Prabhupada liked the treats, and from publishing Prabhupada's books, to the nightmare of abuse by those in trusted positions, the subsequent pain and absence of support, and the scars that remain throughout life, Srila Prabhupada was and is my anchor to spiritual reality because of the knowledge and philosophy he gave that spurs my *sadhana* on and the tangible glimpses of spiritual reality I've experienced by his grace that keep the fire of hope burning.

After Srila Prabhupada left this world, when I was unable to comprehend how such horrible things could happen in his Movement, I prayed to him for understanding and he appeared to me in a dream to instruct and encourage me to carry on. My dreams are my own of course, so only proof to myself, but I think others also have this experience.

As a naïve sixteen-year-old, I thought spiritual life would be peaceful, that life's problems were now solved, and all questions had answers. In *sadhana-bhakti*, life still happens. As one godsister said to me in greeting after many years since we'd last met, "We're still standing." And that is by Srila Prabhupada's mercy. It took some time to realize that the *sadhana-bhakti* Srila Prabhupada introduced to me isn't the goal but just the beginning of a long road ahead over many lifetimes. Srila Prabhupada has guided me through this lifetime by his instructions and his life's example of the firmest faith in and love for Krishna and his devotees. I've been a poor student, but I aspire to become that faith-imbued "dasi," servant, to which he so pointedly drew my attention. He's given the means to do that. As he said in that famous pastime about how to get his mercy, "Here! Take it!" I have to take the burden of responsibility and do the hard work to get his mercy. He's an excellent guardian to bring me to that point.

Years after Srila Prabhupada's departure when I felt increasingly bereft of spiritual guidance and prayed to him for help, I soon recognized, without a tinge of doubt, Srila Prabhupada coming to me again through other Vaishnavas. So, full circle. In this life I first met Srila Prabhupada through others carrying him in their hearts. He was and is always there in my heart since he accepted me as his disciple. After he left this world, when I needed him most, he manifested through another's heart more strongly than I could access him from within my own heart. It seems spiritual life is a world of friends. Srila Prabhupada becomes increasingly dear to me the more I see him in others. I pray that I will have the opportunity to recognize my oldest and dearest friend in every life to come and that I will earn and be blessed with the role of servant to my Gurudeva, Srila Prabhupada.

Lalita Sakhi devi dasi

Devotees were having kirtan at the Catonsville Community College outside Baltimore and had a table with prasadam and books. Lalita Sakhi tasted the prasadam and sometime later began attending the devotees' vegetarian cooking classes. Her first Krishna conscious book, Sri Ishopanishad, was alive for her. Through that book she felt a heart-to-heart connection with Prabhupada. She was initiated in June 1976, at New Vrindavan.

I was living in the Baltimore temple when Srila Prabhupada visited Washington, D.C. in 1976. We stayed up all night painting the Potomac temple to prepare for his visit. The morning Prabhupada was to come, I made him a petal garland. In Baltimore we competed to make the prettiest petal garlands for Nitai-Gaurasundara. That evening for the darshan, I brought my *Srimad-Bhagavatam* with me–I thought Prabhupada would like that. In his room I saw the garland I had made offered to *tulasi*. It was endearing that Prabhupada had put it there.

During his class in Baltimore, a fly was bothering Prabhupada, who commented, "Problems will come. Even though you don't want them, they will come." That stuck with me, how problems are going to come whether or not we want them. One morning in Potomac, Prabhupada was walking around the valet area with some disciples. I waved my hands and said, "*Jaya* Prabhupada!" He turned and looked at me, raised his arms, and smiled.

Over the years I've always been doing service, and although I've had lots of challenges I've always chanted sixteen rounds. I've never missed a day. They're not the best rounds in the world, but completing my rounds is something I feel strongly about. I feel peace with chanting, and I feel a lifetime commitment to it. Some devotees feel more strongly about some other aspects of Krishna consciousness, but I feel strongly about completing my sixteen rounds. I also read Prabhupada's books every day, at least some verse and purport.

The books and the chanting are my strongest connection with Srila Prabhupada–a heart-to-heart connection. With all the confusion in the material world and all the situations that come to us either by our own doing or someone else's, Prabhupada's books and chanting the holy names of Krishna are definitely the boat to carry us forward.

Lavangalatika devi dasi

In 1968, Lavangalatika, twenty-eight, was living in a teepee in the hills near Sante Fe when she read Bhagavad-gita As It Is and found it was simple and straightforward and made more sense than all the other books she'd been reading: Zen, Sufism, the Mother. At the Santa Fe temple Harinama Prabhu said to her, "Come. We're meeting Srila Prabhupada in Los Angeles."

My hair was tangled and I was wearing a *sari* Indumati had put on me when I saw Srila Prabhupada. He looked absolutely wonderful, and I was dumbstruck because I'd never seen such a pure personality. My son was wearing cowboy boots, and his beads were dangling from his hand. Prabhupada took away the beads, saying, "Give them to him later. He's too young and will spoil them." Then Srila Prabhupada asked me, "Do you have any questions?" I couldn't speak, but Indumati had told me, "Please ask Prabhupada what Krishna is like," so I did. Srila Prabhupada became serious and seemed to emanate displeasure. He pointed to a picture of Krishna next to him and said, "Here is Krishna." He then pointed to another picture,

"There is Krishna." I understood I have to be pure to know what Krishna is like and it was wrong to try to find out about Him before I'd served my spiritual master.

After I'd lived in the temple a month or two, I said, "Srila Prabhupada, I'd like to get initiated." He said, "The love is already there. You are serving, so just keep serving and one day you'll get initiated. It's a formality you don't have to worry about." And the next month, in February 1969, I got initiated. Srila Prabhupada laughed when he gave me my name, which means "cloves." Before I joined the Movement I hadn't taken care of my teeth and I used to chew cloves.

My son and I went to New Vrindavan, but Hayagriva didn't want me there and said, "Srila Prabhupada, does she have to stay?" Srila Prabhupada said, "You can tell a tree by the fruit it produces. Her son is chanting, she is chanting. What's the problem? They're both chanting."

We women slept in the temple room, and at about two I'd wake to hear the transcendental sound of Srila Prabhupada chanting *japa* floating down from his room. My mind bathed in his chanting, and all my anxieties, *maya,* and karma were washed away. Every morning Srila Prabhupada would come for *mangala-arati,* standing before the Deities in the dim light.

Once I asked Srila Prabhupada, "What is my service?" He answered, "Your service is your son. See that he never takes birth again in another womb." Since I didn't have a husband, another time I asked, "Srila Prabhupada, should I shave my head?" He said, "No, no, don't do that." He didn't want me to be a false renunciant.

Once Satyabhama said, "Srila Prabhupada, I had a dream about you." He said, "No, no. If the spiritual master is present, a dream has no meaning. Only after he's left is your dream significant. While I'm here, don't pay attention to it."

Srila Prabhupada gave me *brahmana* initiation at New Vrindavan. By mistake I said *goruh* instead of *guroh,* and he corrected me: "No, *guroh.* The spiritual master is not a cow."

Once my son Dwarakadisa was crying because the horse passed stool on his little Jagannatha Deities in a box and he didn't know what to do. We asked Srila Prabhupada if we should clean the box with *gobar* (cow dung). Srila Prabhupada said, "No. You can just show Lord Jagannatha the *gobar* and everything will be clean. You don't have to actually rub the Deity with *gobar.*" When he was twelve Dwarakadisa received first and second initiation from Srila Prabhupada.

Srila Prabhupada was compassionate toward the animals at New Vrindavan. He said, "The animals are not ordinary; they're very fortunate and the devotees will never harm them."

Once, Srila Prabhupada saw me distributing books in Los Angeles and gave me a quick look that seemed to say, "Be careful, don't bother people too much." He was gentlemanly and I immediately understood I should also behave nicely.

I was happy to do my service and didn't speak much with Srila Prabhupada, but I did write him a letter. He wrote back saying I had been a devotee in my last life and I should take care of myself and take care of Krishna and I would always be happy. I know how much Srila Prabhupada wanted cow protection, and now I'm protecting cows. Prabhupada said, "This rascal modern civilization based on cow-killing and technology is doomed," and, "Maharaja Parikshit stopped Kali from killing the cow, and now Krishna wants to see what we will do, how we will do." He's left it up to us.

Laxmimoni devi dasi

Laxmimoni, twenty, had friends who were attending Rupanuga Prabhu's classes at the University of Buffalo, and by her friend' influence she started chanting quite a bit. In April 1969, she saw Prabhupada for the first time and was shocked to see the devotees bowing down to him. Still, within a year she had joined them, been initiated, and was married to a devotee.

Jagadisa, my husband, and I went from Buffalo to Detroit and then opened a temple in Toronto. In January 1974, Bhadra Priya and I went to India to shop for the Toronto Deities and, when we were in the Delhi temple, arranged to make a *vyasasana* for Prabhupada. But the *vyasasana* came out all wrong. We stayed up nights trying to alter it, and by the time Prabhupada came I was a wreck. When Prabhupada sat on the *vyasasana*'s soft pillow, it made a *"whoo"* noise. When he stood, the pillow filled with air and went *"whoo."* Prabhupada sank into the pillow like he was inside the bottom of a clamshell, we couldn't see his knees! Suddenly he smiled broadly, looked at me, and said, "Thank you very much." I was tremendously relieved. Prabhupada was amazingly tolerant.

In Delhi I cooked for Prabhupada and he told me, "Everything is very nice. Only I would have liked some *shukta*." At that time I didn't know what *shukta* was. Again Prabhupada knew I was unqualified and a nervous wreck, but he kindly accepted what I offered. On Nityananda's Appearance Day I went into his room and presented him with a fuzzy orange mohair *chadar* I had bought, dyed, and added a button and buttonhole to so he could easily keep it closed. He buttoned the button and then slipped it over his head. It fit. He thanked me and asked, "Is Jagadisa coming to the GBC meetings?" I said he was. He asked, "Is he bringing your son?" I said no, he wasn't. "He should bring," Prabhupada said. So I called Jagadisa and told him Prabhupada wanted him to bring our four-year-old Nirmala. Prabhupada was kind, friendly, warm, and merciful to Nirmala and me. In Mayapur, when I was pregnant with Nitai, he arranged for all the pregnant and nursing women and all the children to get hot milk every day. He was careful and caring. I always found Prabhupada kind, accessible, willing to hear, to speak, to address, to reciprocate.

In 1972 we were in Toronto when Prabhupada asked for a volunteer to become GBC of India. Jagadisa volunteered. I was pregnant with Yugala at the time and furious that Jagadisa was going to India. I got in a car, drove from Toronto to New Vrindavan, marched up Prabhupada's stairs and into his room and said, "How can Jagadisa go? I'm going to have a baby. How are we going to live?" Prabhupada said to the devotees present, "Yes, she's right. Jagadisa will have to get her a nice apartment in Bombay. Otherwise it will not be possible for her to stay." Prabhupada was concerned that the women were taken care of. Around that time I was sitting on the floor playing *mridanga*. Prabhupada sent me a message, "You shouldn't play *mridanga*, because *mridanga* is hard work and a pregnant woman shouldn't do any hard work."

Once in his room in Mayapur Srila Prabhupada said men should always think of women as mothers. Pusta Krishna said, "You know that verse, Prabhupada, 'When I think of women, I spit on the idea'? The men think, 'When I think of women, I should spit on them.' " Prabhupada thought for a second and said, "First let them become free from sex desire, and then let them spit." When Gurukrpa was serving *prasadam* in Prabhupada's room after darshan, Prabhupada said, "Women and children should receive *prasadam* first." And in the Dallas *gurukula*, Prabhupada saw the children regularly and was always kind and involved with them.

Jagadisa was Prabhupada's secretary when Nirnasha was dying of leukemia. Jagadisa told Prabhupada, "Nirnasha's parents would like you to encourage him to get chemotherapy so he can have a normal life." Prabhupada said, "Normal life? Normal life is life without death. Can they give him a normal life?" We'd see compassion in one way and Prabhupada would immediately turn it around. Ultimately, his compassion was spiritual. Nirnasha was convinced by a devotee to go to a cancer clinic that used alternative medicine and later died of his leukemia.

Prabhupada was strict about us following the four regulative principles and getting out of material life. He gave us a sense of urgency and made us determined to go back to Godhead. And he tried to keep us living simply, working together, and focused on preaching. Now we talk about more esoteric aspects of spiritual life than we ever did when Prabhupada was here, but our lifestyle is much less urgent. At the same time, Prabhupada was extremely fatherly, compassionate, and caring about children, women, and people in general. He wanted all of us to be happy on all levels. Prabhupada balanced being a rose with being a thunderbolt and was able to laugh with children and joke with women and men easily. He could see both sides of an issue and figure out when to draw a line and when not to. About Deity worship he was inclusive and gave us simple instructions–basically keep it clean, keep it punctual, make the Deities beautiful, and have nice flowers. He didn't focus on the complexities of worship and he didn't make worship exclusive. He wanted the Deities to look so gorgeous and be so attractive that no one could take their eyes off Them.

Once in Los Angeles Prabhupada asked, "Is everybody chanting sixteen rounds?" No one answered. Prabhupada said, "Is anyone not chanting sixteen rounds?" Again no one answered. He said, "Is anybody fibbing?" A few hands went up and he said, "You must chant sixteen rounds. You do not have to go looking for *maya*. *Maya* is the backside of Krishna. As soon as you do not see Krishna, immediately *maya* is there. Chanting sixteen rounds it not difficult. You can chant one hour in the morning and one in the evening, but somehow you must chant sixteen rounds."

Bhakta Dasa said, "Prabhupada, I'm working hard to make Krishna's temple beautiful. Sometimes I only sleep four hours a night." Prabhupada immediately said, "Then sleep two hours. But somehow or other chant sixteen rounds." He didn't ask much of us: the four regulative principles, sixteen rounds. But he wanted us to do those things.

Lila Avatara devi dasi

Lila Avatara was nineteen and already initiated when Prabhupada came to Venezuela in 1976.

I was very wild. I had fingernails painted different colors, and when Prabhupada glanced at everybody, his glance returned to me and he just stared. I couldn't keep looking at him. I looked down and started taking my nail polish off. I looked up again and he was still looking at me. I felt like a fool, "What am I doing? I got initiated, I know spiritual life is what I want, and I'm still acting wild." In his glance he made me see that I want Krishna consciousness, as if to say, "Where have you been? Where are you coming from?" When I see Prabhupada's *murti*, I see the same look that he gave me then. If I'm feeling misguided or confused, I see his *murti* and he reinforces his message.

In Venezuela, one day, I was so proud to bring in the plate of fruit for Srila Prabhupada. Srutakirti returned the untouched plate to me and said, "He wants every peel of the tangerines, all that white skin out. Then cut them in half and take out all the seeds." It was meticulous work, and it took me a while. I was crying and very nervous and Prabhupada was waiting. Then Srutakirti took the plate back to Prabhupada, and Prabhupada accepted it, asking, "Who cut the fruit?"

In 1976, a lot of devotees went to New York Ratha-yatra when Prabhupada was there. We weren't allowed to use the temple elevator, but I was with a chubby *mataji*, so I said to her in Spanish, "Maybe we should say you're pregnant so we can get on the elevator." Then I heard someone clear his throat slightly. I turned around and there was Srila Prabhupada. He understood what I was saying in Spanish. I never went on that elevator again.

Also in New York, once, everybody was pushing to get into the *prasadam* room. The *matajis*, mainly Latinos, were in the back. Prabhupada stopped and everybody stopped. He held the door open and said, "Ladies first." After that, of course, somebody else came and held the door open. But Prabhupada was such a gentleman that he held the door open first.

I was sixteen when I first met the devotees. I started reading *Easy Journey to Other Planets* and thought, "Srila Prabhupada wrote this." But he was humble. His classes and his look and his gentle preaching made me want to be near him. He had that attraction.

I am not so learned in scripture, but I think that if Prabhupada had never come to the West and sacrificed the way he did, how would the most precious holy name have come into our lives? Every morning and night I dress the Deities at New Talavan. I love dressing Them, putting ornaments on Them, and changing things around to make it look like They're dancing this way or that. I don't have the words or eloquence to say it beautifully, but I am eternally grateful for Srila Prabhupada and to all my godbrothers and godsisters.

Some of my godbrothers and godsisters are special souls whom I'm attached to. Brahmananda Maharaja gave me good advice when I got divorced. I couldn't understand that if I'm a dedicated *pujari,* why did the divorce happen? Certain people have the power to make you feel like you're worth it and you're here to spread Lord Chaitanya's movement and to surrender to Srila Prabhupada.

I clean houses, take care of people, walk dogs. I do what I have to, to maintain. But my real service is at the temple. Prabhupada's enthusiasm to serve Krishna has stayed with us.

Lila Katha devi dasi

Initiated in 1976, Lila Katha never got to meet Srila Prabhupada personally, yet she felt a direct link to Srila Prabhupada at her initiation.

I joined the temple in Montreal in 1976 and I was initiated the day before the deity installation of Radha-Manohara. The elder devotees had seen Srila Prabhupada many times when he visited Montreal, Toronto, and New York, and had taken initiation directly from him. At the time of my initiation, the new devotees received an acceptance letter with our initiated names, and never actually received the blessing of Prabhupada's personal association.

I found my new Sanskrit name to be quite amazing! *Lila Katha* means to speak the pastimes of Krishna and His devotees. *Lila* means "pastime," and *katha* means "to speak." I found that quite interesting. The joke was that Srila Prabhupada knew that I never shut up. Although I never got to meet Srila Prabhupada personally, by giving me that name I felt that he knew who I was. So immediately I felt I had a direct link with Srila Prabhupada.

I moved to New Vrindavan and served the Deities with a very special *mataji* named Hladini. Hladini showed me a huge amount of letters she had written to Srila Prabhupada. Through those letters I witnessed how Srila Prabhupada was very personal with his replies. In those letters to Srila Prabhupada, Hladini had written down all of her questions and doubts. In his replies, Srila Prabhupada addressed her as "Dear beloved Linda, my dear daughter" and explained the meaning of the spiritual name he had given her. It was really amazing to see the love Srila Prabhupada showed as he patiently answered every single detail. It was just so sweet. I gave these letters to Mother Yamuna when she wrote her book.

Compassion, patience, and all those beautiful qualities we get from Srila Prabhupada. He has taught us how to free ourselves from envy, lust, and crazy material desires by showing us an even more beautiful love. I feel that it's only through Srila Prabhupada's mercy that we got to experience that. And his books are still there, every sentence.

A few years ago I got a chance to go to India for the first time. I traveled to Jagannatha Puri, and later Mayapur. When I returned from India the feeling that Srila Prabhupada loves us was even more strong. If Prabhupada would not have come here I would never have imagined going to India. Before meeting Srila Prabhupada I was very close to the American Indians, so I would have been worshiping trees or the beautiful sun or whatever. I would never have imagined worshiping Krishna! Srila Prabhupada really gave us such a gift. His love is so deep.

Lilasakti devi dasi

Lilasakti didn't know who God was, and was looking into different religions, and interviewing people at different churches looking for Him. She read the Back to Godheads devotees gave her and understood, "Wow, so this is God!"

I was a book distributor and daily went out feeling connected to Srila Prabhupada by knowing I was one of his soldiers. Every night Prabhupada was pleased to hear our book distribution results and all of us were happy to give him our report.

In New Dwarka in the early 1970s, it didn't matter what we wanted or didn't want, we did what Prabhupada wanted. Although I wanted to devote my life to Krishna and be done with material relationships, since Prabhupada thought all women should be married, I agreed to get married. But I continued living in the temple and distributing Prabhupada's books. After a year-and-a-half, my husband, Madhukara, said to me, "Lila Shakti, I want to have a family," and he wrote Srila Prabhupada a letter saying if we weren't going to have a child, then he wanted to take *vanaprastha*. Prabhupada wrote him a long letter back:

> I know your wife Lilasakti, and I know that she is very serious and advanced disciple. But now you are married to her, there is some obligation according to our Krishna consciousness or Vedic system. These things cannot be taken so lightly, otherwise the whole thing will become a farce. Simply get married without considering what is the serious nature of married life, then if there is little disturbance, or if I do not like my wife or my husband, let me go away, everyone else is doing like that. So in this way the whole thing is becoming a farce. You say that your "association together was hindering your advancement." But Krishna consciousness marriage system should not be taken in that way, that if there is any botheration that means something is hindering my spiritual progress, no. Once it is adopted, the grhastha life, even it may be troublesome at times, it must be fulfilled as my occupational duty. Of course, it is better to remain unmarried, celibate. But so many women are coming, we cannot reject them. If someone comes to Krishna it is our duty to give them protection. Krishna has informed us in *Bhagavad-gita* that even women and sudras and others inferior class of men can take refuge in Him. So the problem is there, the women must have a husband to give protection. Of course, if the women can remain unmarried, and if there is suitable arrangement for the temple to protect them, just like in the Christian Church there is nunnery for systematic program of engaging the ladies and protecting them, that is also nice. But if there is sex desire, how to control it? Women are normally very lusty, more lusty than men, and they are weaker sex, it is difficult for them to make spiritual advancement without the help of husband. For so many reasons, our women must have husband. That's all right, but if once they have got a husband he goes away so quickly, that will not be very much happy for them.

"Now I do not know the situation in your particular case, I am simply giving you the general policy or background understanding. We should never think of our so-called advancement as being conditioned by or dependent upon some set of material circumstances such as marriage, vanaprastha, or this or that. Mature understanding of Krishna consciousness means that whatever condition of life I am in at present, that is Krishna's special mercy upon me, therefore let me take advantage in the best way possible to spread this Krishna consciousness movement and conduct my spiritual master's mission. If I consider my own personal progress or happiness or any other thing personal, that is material consideration. If there was unhappy adjustment for becoming married, why you got married at all? Whatever is done, is done, that is a fact, but I am only pointing out that once before you did something without proper study of your real responsibility, now you are contemplating again some drastic action in a similar manner. Therefore consider it carefully in this light. There is one verse from *Bhagavad-gita*: *yasman nodvijate loko lokan nodvijate ca yah/harsamarsa-bhayodvegair mukto yah sa ca me priyah*, "He for whom no one is put into difficulty and who is not disturbed by anxiety, who is steady in happiness and distress, is very dear to Me." (12.15) One mistake of judgment often made by the neophyte devotees is that any time there is some disturbance or some difficulty they are considering that the conditions or the external circumstances under which the difficulty took place are the cause of the difficulty itself. That is not the fact. In this material world there is always some difficulty, no matter in this situation or that situation. Therefore simply by changing my status of occupation or my status of life, that will not help anything. Because the real fact is that if there is any difficulty with others, that is my lack of Krishna consciousness, not theirs. Is this clear? Krishna says that His dearest devotee is one who does not put others into difficulty, in fact, who puts no one other into difficulty. So try to judge the matter on these points, whether or not you are putting either your wife or yourself into some difficulty.

The right understanding of *Bhagavad-gita* is Arjuna's understanding. In other words, Arjuna came to the conclusion that he must perform his occupational duty, not as a material obligation, for reasons of wife, family, friends, reputation, professional integrity, like that – no. Rather he must conduct the functions of his station of life only as a devotional service performed for Krishna. That means that devotional service is what is important, not my occupational duty. But it does not mean that because occupation duty is not the real consideration, that

I should give it up and do something else, thinking that devotional service may be carried on under whatever circumstances which I may whimsically decide. Krishna recommended Arjuna to remain as he was, not to disrupt the order of society and go against his own nature just for convenience sake. Our occupational duty is not arbitrary, that means once we have taken up some field of action, if we are advanced in our understanding, then we shall not change it for another. Rather our devotion is the important factor, so what does it matter what I am doing so long my work and energy are completely devoted to Krishna? Just like Krishna, He is the Supreme Personality of Godhead, He has no work, neither He has anything to do, still He comes here to teach us this lesson. He accepts not only His occupational duty as cowherd boy, royal prince, but also He accepts married life, He enters politics, He is philosopher, He is even chariot driver during a great battle. He does not give example of Himself avoiding His occupational duty. So if Krishna Himself is exhibiting by His own conduct what is the perfection of existence, then we should heed such example if we are intelligent. Even supposing there is wife at home, with children, that does not matter, that is no hindrance to our spiritual life. And once we have accepted these things, occupational duties, we should not lightly give them up. That is the point. Of course, our occupational duty is as preachers of Krishna consciousness. So we must stick to that business under all circumstances, that is the main thing. Therefore married, unmarried, divorced, whatever condition of life, my preaching mission does not depend on these things. The varnashram-dharma system is scientifically arranged by Krishna to provide facility for delivering the fallen souls back to home, back to Godhead. And if we make a mockery of this system by whimsically disrupting the order, that we must consider. That will not be a very good example if so many young boys and girls so casually become married and then go away from each other, and the wife is little unhappy, the husband is neglecting her in so many ways, like that. If we set this example, then how the thing will go on properly? Householder life means wife, children, home, these things are understood by everyone, why our devotees have taken it as something different? They simply have some sex desire, get themselves married, and when the matter does not fulfill their expectations, immediately there is separation – these things are just like material activities, prostitution. The wife is left without husband, and sometimes there is child to be raised, in so many ways the proposition that you, and some others also, are making becomes distasteful. We cannot expect that our temples will become places of shelter for so many widows and rejected wives, that will be a great burden and we shall become the laughingstock in the society. There will be unwanted progeny also. And there will be illicit sex life, that we are seeing already. And being the weaker sex, women require to have a husband who is strong in Krishna consciousness so that they may take advantage and make progress by sticking tightly to his feet. If their husband goes away from them, what will they do? So many instances are already there in our Society, so many frustrated girls and boys.

So I have introduced this marriage system in your Western countries because there is custom of freely intermingling male and female. Therefore marriage is required just to engage the boys and girls in devotional service, never mind distinction of living status. But our marriage system is little different than in your country, we do not sanction the policy of quick divorce. We are supposed to take husband or wife as eternal companion or assistant in Krishna consciousness service, and there is promise never to separate. Of course if there is any instance of very advanced disciples, married couple, and they have agreed that the husband shall now take sannyasa or renounced order of life, being mutually very happy by that arrangement, then there is ground for such separation. But even in those cases there is no question of separation, the husband, even he is sannyasa, he must be certain his wife will be taken care of nicely and protected in his absence. Now so many cases are there of unhappiness by the wife who has been abandoned by her husband against her wishes. So how can I sanction such thing? I want to avoid setting any bad example for future generations, therefore I am so much cautiously considering your request. But if it becomes so easy for me to get married and then leave my wife, under excuse of married life being an impediment to my own spiritual progress, that will not be very good at all. That is misunderstanding of what is advancement in spiritual life. Occupational duty must be there, either this one or that one, but once I am engaged in something occupational duty, then I should not change that or give it up, that is the worst mistake. Devotional service is not bound up by such designations. Therefore once I have chosen, it is better to stick in that way and develop my devotional attitude into full-blown love of Godhead. That is Arjuna's understanding.

Hoping this meets you in good health,
Your ever well-wisher,
A.C. Bhaktivedanta Swami

After we received this letter, my husband and I went to a motel once a month, chanted our fifty rounds and I conceived a wonderful son, Manasa

Chandra. He's caused me no problems. He's given me a wonderful grandchild, and I have no regrets about performing that service.

Prabhupada gave us God, Krishna; he told us who God is, where He lives, and what He looks like. If we want to, at any moment we can touch Prabhupada's unbelievable, cherished gift. It doesn't get more special than that.

Lila Shakti devi dasi

Lila Shakti was always searching for something higher and had many questions the minister in her parents' Christian church couldn't answer. When she was nine, she realized that life was mostly suffering. Later, after one of her schoolmates died in an accident, she thought, "I wish it was me. She is now free. When you die, things must be better." After she graduated from college and before going on to higher education, she decided to take a year off to go to London. A few days before she left, she heard the Hare Krishna mantra on the radio and found the chanting amazing. Lila Shakti is one of triplets and one of her sisters, Inga, came with her to London.

In October of 1969, Inga and I were walking down Oxford Street when we saw devotees and heard them chanting the same melody as on the radio. We ran up to them and said, "What are you doing?" A new *brahmachari* said, "It will purify the dust from your heart accumulated from years together," and gave us a leaflet to go to Conway Hall.

In Conway Hall I met Ishan and asked him, "After you die, before you take your next body, do you go somewhere else or do you just go straight from one body into the next?" Reincarnation already made sense to me. Ishan was honest and said, "I don't know the answer to that question. But birth, death, disease and old age–there is nothing but suffering here. The secret is to get out." I thought, "At last! Someone's thinking the way I've been thinking all my life. This is a place of misery. We have to find a way to get out."

I was attracted to the devotees' chanting but was put off by seeing Prabhupada sit on a high table and the devotees bowing to him. The second time we came, Saraswati run up to him and he stopped talking to this big hall full of people to smile at her and give her some attention. That let me understand, "He's not an arrogant guru; he's different."

Prabhupada's personality was overpowering. He's as good as Krishna and knew what you were thinking. After Prabhupada gave me my Gayatri, he picked up *The Teachings of Lord Caitanya* and said, "Do you read this book?" I said, "I do, but I find it difficult to understand." He said, "If you don't understand, then ask the older devotees here. But as long as I'm here, come and ask me."

In 1971 Bala Gopala and I were worshiping Radha-Londonisvara and decided we needed to ask Prabhupada some questions. We went to Prabhupada's room in Bury Place and asked about the Deity offerings. Prabhupada said, "Big plates, plenty of variety. Krishna is the Supreme Enjoyer." And he put his arms all the way out, as if the plates were to be a meter wide.

Another time I was outside Prabhupada's room when I heard devotees one floor above loudly laughing, joking, and noisily singing devotional songs and playing guitars. Prabhupada heard it too, came out of his room, looked at me and said, "Are the Deities resting now?" I said, "Yes, Prabhupada." He was angry that they were being so noisy while Krishna was resting. He said, "Stop them."

As a *pujari* I struggled a lot. I'd think, "Do I really want to stay? Is this where I want to be?" But Prabhupada came about once a year, and just his nod and smile would make me think, "Even if nobody else knows, Prabhupada knows what's going on." In 1976, some German devotees came and said, "Women cannot be the head *pujari*! They cannot be in charge!" Whenever Prabhupada came into the temple he always popped into the temple room to see the Deities, and one day I was the only one there. I was standing next to him and he was looking at the Deities like he was talking to Them. Then he turned to me and said quietly, "Are you in charge?" I said, "Yes, Prabhupada." He said, "That's very good." That kept me going.

Once Prabhupada came for a short visit and I gave him some pictures of Radha-Londonisvara with a note, "Here's some pictures of my Krishna." In his letter back to me, Prabhupada wrote, "Thank you very much for the pictures of your Krishna."

At one point we made a glittery, green polyester-satin outfit covered in shiny white and gold sequins with a gold lame backdrop. That was the first of that kind. Prabhupada came into the temple room, stopped halfway, raised his arms and said, "*Aahh*! This is Krishna. Every time I come here, the Deities are so beautifully dressed." He was so pleased with the way They looked. Later in a letter he wrote: "I am so happy to see that the Deities are decorated the best. You are all working so hard and this will not go in vain. This is to your eternal credit."

When Prabhupada arrived in 1971, we were sitting in his Bury Place room when Malati came to the door with Saraswati. Prabhupada addressed her as "Malati Prabhu," and he addressed Saraswati as "Saraswati Prabhu," with a glint in his eye. When I joined this Movement everyone was a Prabhu. Now this has become an issue and devotees seemed to forget that Srila Prabhupada himself addressed women as Prabhu. I never heard Prabhupada address any of his women disciples as *mataji* or *mata* or mother. Prabhupada instructed us by his example, and because it came from him it meant a lot to us. I'm not attached to being called one thing or another, but I want to follow Srila Prabhupada's example and standard.

Lilamrita devi dasi

Lilamrita moved into the Vancouver temple just before Gaura-Purnima 1976. A few weeks later the temple president asked her if she would like to be initiated. He asked, "Do you know what it means to receive initiation?" She said she didn't. "It means you can never leave," he said. She told him that she couldn't imagine ever wanting to leave Krishna consciousness. "Fine," he said, "I will add you to the list."

Soon, a letter came back. Srila Prabhupada had accepted us as his duly initiated disciples. It was the most important moment in all my sojourn in this material world. One year later I received second initiation. In my beginning my main service was book distribution, and my favorite prayer was the one Srila Prabhupada wrote onboard the *Jaladuta*, which I would recite daily for inspiration to preach.

My association with Srila Prabhupada has always been through reading his books, listening to his lectures and *bhajanas*, his *japa* tape, watching videos of him, and whenever possible associating with those fortunate disciples who had his personal association. Hearing about Srila Prabhupada's loving exchanges with his disciples has always been a great motivating force for me. If somehow or other I can keep trying to take shelter at his lotus feet through following his instructions to the best of my ability, I too will attain such good fortune. It is my greatest hope. It is like the principle of advertising that one must hear about something in order to develop a desire to obtain it.

In November 1977 I was in Anchorage, Alaska distributing books at the airport with Radhika devi dasi. When we received the news of Srila Prabhupada's disappearance we returned to the Vancouver temple to be with the other devotees. It was a very difficult time. From that time on I was away from the temple much of the time, traveling with one other devotee in a van throughout the northwest Canadian provinces. In our van we had a bookcase with all of Srila Prabhupada's books and a small altar on top, where we had a small brass *murti* of Srila Prabhupada. We would be away for weeks, sometimes months, phoning the temple once a week. Our shelter was reading Srila Prabhupada's books, listening to his lectures, serving his *murti*, and doing our service. Politics and problems happened back at the temple, but we never heard about most of them until they had come and gone. There was no internet back then. Srila Prabhupada's mercy was available and real and kept us going. Krishna consciousness was real for me. The problem for me only came when I allowed the problems of others to disturb my own practice. So, while I was dependent on devotees and leaders, I found that if I maintained my main connection to Srila Prabhupada even when over time some devotees had difficulties or even left Krishna consciousness, I was able to keep going. I feel that by continually hearing from Srila Prabhupada the understanding has come to me that the biggest problems I have to face are my own shortcomings and my own inability to surrender to Srila Prabhupada's instructions.

Once, a few years ago, a guest asked me what it was like to be in Srila Prabhupada's company. I replied that I had not actually meet him; I had received initiation through a letter. Afterward, my mind became disturbed and I began to think, "Am I less of a disciple because I didn't met Srila Prabhupada?" That night I had a dream. A small group of book distributors from different countries were gathered, and Srila Prabhupada came into the room. I was crying tears of happiness, and when I came before Srila Prabhupada after offering obeisances, I said, "Oh, Srila Prabhupada, I am so happy to meet you!" Srila Prabhupada was standing there, smiling so beautifully, and then I noticed what he was wearing. It was a hand-knit woolen blanket, exactly like the one I had knitted for his *murti* at the Vancouver temple.

I cannot claim to understand much about Krishna consciousness, but what I do understand is that Srila Prabhupada is most extraordinarily compassionate, and he has given us a way out of this miserable material world. I recently read in one *Srimad-Bhagavatam* purport a beautiful sentence. Srila Prabhupada simply stated: "Krishna is lovable." Srila Prabhupada, Krishna's pure devotee, is also lovable. In my eyes, those devotees who are attached and dedicated to serving him are lovable, and I long to have their company and some opportunity to serve them.

All glories to Srila Prabhupada!

Lokadristi devi dasi

In Thunder Bay, Ontario, Lokadristi would sometimes ask her hatha-yoga students, "Why do you need a guru?" When she heard their ridiculous answers she thought, "Why do you need a guru for that?"

After my husband, Kamsahanta, read *Bhagavad-gita As It Is*, he bought all the other books Srila Prabhupada had written: the First, Second, and Third Cantos of *Srimad Bhagavatam*. We had no devotee association but Kamsahanta took every word in Prabhupada's books like they were as good as God.

We hitchhiked to the Toronto temple where someone opened the door and said, "Come in, it's Radhastami!" Urvasi sold me a *Hare Krishna*

Cookbook and explained how this was an ancient science that goes back thousands of years. Impressed, I thought, "That makes so much sense."

Then we went to Bhaktivedanta Manor and somehow arrived the same day as Srila Prabhupada. I was three months pregnant and fit from teaching yoga, and wound up washing pots in ice-cold water till midnight. I slept on the bare floor in the *brahmacharini ashram* until 3:30 am when someone said, "Get up for *mangala-arati*." My body wouldn't do it. At 6:30 someone said, "It's time for our spiritual master's greeting, you have to get up." I saw Srila Prabhupada sitting on the *vyasasana* and thought, "That's such an ugly seat. If they love their guru so much, how can they offer him such an ugly seat?" Years later I heard that on seeing that *vyasasana* Prabhupada said, "Oh, are you expecting Lord Shiva?"

While Kamsahanta went on traveling *sankirtana*, I ended up in the Toronto temple where I'd cry at night, "What am I doing here?" Nobody cared I was pregnant and there was hardly anything to eat. But Cintamani saved me. She told me stories about Prabhupada and we'd laugh until midnight. She put a personality to the person and connected me to Srila Prabhupada.

The Toronto temple was in a bad area and had a twenty-four-hour Deity watch. During my time, an hour-and-a-half in the morning and an hour-and-a-half in the afternoon, I read the *Nectar of Devotion* and *Krsna* book and was drawn into Prabhupada's words. Laxmimoni had asked me to make an outfit for the Deities and I also meditated on how to do that. Reading Prabhupada's books and making that outfit were the two things that made me a devotee.

I've gone through a lot of difficulties within ISKCON and people have told me different things about how to raise my child, how to do this, how to do that. Srila Prabhupada was compassionate, logical, and reasonable and if what I was told wasn't, I'd question it.

My husband and I never had the opportunity to serve and interact closely with Prabhupada, but we were always close to him in heart. Prabhupada blessed us by giving us the opportunity to connect to Krishna, and I want to share Prabhupada with others and give them the opportunity to do devotional service.

Madan-Mohan-Mohini devi dasi

In August 1966, Madan-Mohan-Mohini, a recent high school graduate, was in New York City when she heard ping-ping-ping, ping-ping-ping and saw strange-looking persons with flowing robes chanting. She said to her friend, "New York sure is a weird place. Let's get out of here." But she kept coming in contact with devotees year after year.

In 1970, I went to the Madison, Wisconsin temple and when I saw Prabhupada's picture on the wall I immediately felt, "This is my father." I felt this is a person who would never let me down and felt a kinship with him and protected and sheltered by him. The devotees' love for Prabhupada made me even more attracted and connected to him and I became serious about Krishna consciousness.

In the early summer of 1972, I joined the Hamburg temple and was satisfied and happy. Through the years I used to make garlands and put them on Prabhupada. Making and offering beautiful garlands meant so much to me; I wanted Prabhupada to have them, and Prabhupada kindly fulfilled my desire. He'd humbly fold his hands and nod his acceptance of my small, insignificant service. There was never any question of "I'm a woman, I can't do this." Prabhupada never discriminated between men and women. I'd put garlands on him in front of *sannyasis*. In the early days, we were a big family absorbed in trying to please Prabhupada through our service.

When I was initiated Prabhupada explained, "Madan is a name for Cupid and he's so attractive, he can attract everybody. Madan-Mohan is a name for Krishna, and He's so attractive that He can even attract Cupid. But Madan-Mohan-Mohini is the attractor of the attractor of Cupid or Srimati Radharani, the one who enchants Krishna." I floated away. I felt Prabhupada knew me through and through and felt his deep, wonderful care and love.

I've always engaged in Deity worship and now worship my own Deities. Prabhupada wanted us to be responsible in our Deity worship and was pleased by a high standard of worship. He also wanted the devotees to be well taken care of, to eat well.

I've had lots of personal association with Srila Prabhupada through dreams. When I wake up from these dreams, I feel a deep satisfaction that Prabhupada is here and knows my heart and what I need when I need it. For example, he told me not to be disturbed when things change in my life, which is something I'm still working on.

My fortune in coming to Krishna consciousness is beyond my understanding; it baffles me. It's inconceivable.

Madhuryalilananda devi dasi

Madhuryalilananda was living in Boulder as a hippie and was miserable. Everyday she'd pray, "I just want to be happy, that's all I want." One hippie was always chanting and one day he said to her, "You know, you're not that body." She said, "Oh, my God, that is such a relief to know!" He gave her Srila Prabhupada's Bhagavatam, and Nectar of Devotion, The Teachings of Lord Chaitanya and a Krsna book. The books were so good that after she finished reading them she moved into the temple.

I joined in Denver in the spring of 1972, a month or two after my twenty-first birthday, and the next fall was initiated by letter. In my initiation letter Srila Prabhupada wrote, "Chant sixteen rounds and you'll get rid of hazy consciousness." At that time I did feel that my consciousness was hazy. Then the next spring I went with the other Denver devotees to New Vrindavan for Janmashtami and first saw Srila Prabhupada at the Pittsburgh airport. His smallness surprised me and his presence and demeanor was something I'd never experienced before.

For Janmashtami, everybody stayed up until midnight reading *Krsna* book in the temple room and everybody was exhausted and falling asleep. Finally after midnight Srila Prabhupada said, "It's time to take *prasadam*," and everybody said, "*Jaya! Jaya!*"

When Prabhupada visited Atlanta, the temple room was packed. It was a wall of devotees, and Srila Prabhupada was looking at every single one of us. I thought, "Oh, my God, I'm going to be next, he's going to look at me!" I felt like ducking down and running, but I didn't. Sure enough, he looked straight at me, and I had a feeling that he knew exactly what was going on with me, he was looking straight to my soul.

Srila Prabhupada was the center of our life. Everything we thought and did was for him and Krishna. We were totally absorbed. By Krishna's grace I never had any major problems. I always felt Krishna protected me and put me in a situation where I could do some service.

Srila Prabhupada said, "Chant sixteen rounds daily" and I do that, although sometimes I don't remember why. I think, "I'm doing this because Srila Prabhupada told me. I might not have a lot of attraction, but I'm still doing it. And somehow I'm still here after all these years."

Madira devi dasi

In July of 1971 when she was seventeen years old, Madira went to New York City with all the other Buffalo devotees. She had been waiting for two years to get initiated and so received both first and second initiation.

During the initiation, Prabhupada was joking with the initiates. Many of the names he gave were hilarious. There was one devotee from Buffalo named Peter, who became Kusakrata and was a translator in L.A. for years. Prabhupada asked him the four principles and Peter remembered three. Prabhupada said, "Which one do you like the most?" Peter said, "Oh, intoxication, Srila Prabhupada." Everyone was responding to Prabhupada's good mood and humor. When he handed me my beads, Prabhupada said, "Your name is Madira. This means intoxicated." I said, "Oh, boy." Then he smiled and said, "By chanting Hare Krishna." I was young when I came to the

Movement and had never taken any intoxication but I loved to chant in kirtan, so when he said that I could understand my name was appropriate.

Later, when I went to get Gayatri mantra from Srila Prabhupada, I felt inept. I couldn't figure out the finger movements Prabhupada showed me. Finally Prabhupada took my thumb and put it in the right place and then I understood. It wasn't really difficult, but in Srila Prabhupada's presence I was awestruck. His presence was state changing; it was like stepping into Vaikuntha.

Just before I was initiated, I married Tejiyas and moved into the Buffalo temple. Tejiyas and I promised my parents that we would stay in Buffalo, but I was initiated in July and Tejiyas and I moved in September.

Tejiyas and I served in Delhi and when Srila Prabhupada came, I'd be doing Deity worship, cleaning the temple, cleaning Prabhupada's room, and cooking for Him. It was wonderfully intimate to bring Srila Prabhupada his *prasadam*. Once at an evening kirtan in Delhi, I thought, "Well, there's nobody here," so I sat next to Srila Prabhupada and played the drum while he played the *kartalas* and led the kirtan. When devotees heard the kirtan they started coming. Prabhupada, seated on the *vyasasana*, looked at me, and sped up. I sped up. Then he sped up more and I kept up. By then the room was full of devotees. Prabhupada closed his eyes, completely immersed in the kirtan. He was okay with my drum playing.

Once, when I was nineteen, Tejiyas said to Prabhupada that he wanted to take *sannyasa*. Prabhupada said, "Why?" Tejiyas said, "She doesn't do what I tell her to do." Srila Prabhupada said, "Well, you have an intelligent wife. If she doesn't do what you tell her to do, then you do what she says to do." I felt good about that answer but it didn't happen and Tejiyas didn't take *sannyasa*.

When we had a daughter, Prabhupada said, "Tejiyas has had a daughter, so her name is Tejasini," and laughed. He was kind to the children and would often play with Tejasini. Once we were on the rooftop of the Delhi ashram when my daughter had measles and was crying. Srila Prabhupada was about to come for his massage and Hari Sauri saw us there and dramatically pointed at me and pointed at the door. I got Tej packed up, left, and I saw Srila Prabhupada coming up the stairs. He looked at us and said, "Where are you going?" I said, "We're going to go to the temple, Srila Prabhupada." He said, "You don't have to leave." He was exuding kindness.

Once in Vrindavan the Radha-Syamasundara Deities had just arrived from Jaipur and Prabhupada wanted to see Them. When They were uncovered, Prabhupada looked at Radharani and then looked at Yamuna and said, "She looks like you. You've been going to Jaipur and the carvers saw you and made Her face look like yours." We laughed, and then Prabhupada looked at me and said, "No, She looks like you." It was a beautiful, loving exchange.

One evening we were at Radha-Damodara temple when a very pious man, Brijmohan Janiwala, came from Delhi to Vrindavan to have Prabhupada's darshan. They were speaking in Hindi and after a while Prabhupada started playing the harmonium and chanting a *bhajana*. It was one of those absolutely wonderful, rare experiences where Prabhupada swept the whole room away to Goloka.

Once in Vrindavan he asked me if I was taking good care of my husband. I did take care of Tejiyas in sickness and health, but inside I didn't care for him. I didn't like him much and didn't get along well with him, so I didn't know how to answer Prabhupada's question honestly. I said, "Yes, Srila Prabhupada," but with that element of not deeply caring.

During the Delhi *pandal* in the LIC Grounds in Connaught Circle, Yamuna had jaundice. We were all staying in a Delhi *dharmshala* and Prabhupada came to see Yamuna and how she was being cared for. Prabhupada was concerned that the devotees had proper *prasadam*, that they had a clean place to stay.

Prabhupada took us to visit the holy places in Vrindavan and afterwards, when we went back to Delhi, Pakistan and India were at war. Every night we blacked out the windows, used candles, and while warplanes flew overhead, Prabhupada spoke. He told us how during the Second World War everybody was leaving the city but he stayed. They also had blackouts and all the lights would be off except for the one he had so he could make *kachoris* for his little Deities. He said, "The bombs were dropping, and I was making *kachoris* for Radha-Govinda."

In Jaipur Prabhupada did the *sannyasa* ceremony for Tamal Krishna Goswami. Prabhupada seemed serious and the event was somber and shocking to me. Our crew of women was small and tight, and my heart went out to Madri, Tamal Krishna Maharaja's former wife.

Once in Delhi, Mrs. Bakshi, a generous donor, invited Srila Prabhupada and all the devotees to her home. We were sitting in a long row taking *prasadam* when a few of us realized the chickpea dish had onions. Disturbed, we turned to Srila Prabhupada. Rather than embarrass the hostess, Prabhupada commented, "I am not eating onions. I am eating chickpeas." In that way we learned the proper etiquette for this particular moment. This woman was gentle and a genuine well-wisher to the devotees and Prabhupada didn't want to hurt her. We tended to be dogmatic and zealous.

At different places in India Prabhupada would often call on Yamuna and some other disciples to speak. He appreciated how the devotees spoke from their hearts as well as the philosophy they conveyed. Srila Prabhupada accepted our service so graciously. His kindness always struck me.

Maha Bhagavat devi dasi

Maha Bhagavat's friend hung a picture of Srila Prabhupada on the wall of her house and sometime later showed her how to chant japa.

As my friend started chanting *japa*, something happened in my heart and I had a wonderful realization that the person in the picture was my spiritual master. Not only was he my spiritual master, he was *jagat-guru* – he was everyone's spiritual master. I realized I'd been a huge fool all my life and I was fortunate to find Srila Prabhupada. These realizations were such that I felt I'd never doubt Srila Prabhupada. The next day I moved into the Portland temple. It was 1975 and I was thirty-four.

In the temple, Srila Prabhupada was a looming presence for me but I didn't feel love for him. Then, over the years, I started having dreams of Srila Prabhupada that made huge changes in my life. This so-called reality that I'm in right now is not nearly as real as my dreams. In one dream I looked at Srila Prabhupada's face and for the first time in my life I felt satisfied. In another dream Krishna told me, "Don't doubt Srila Prabhupada, not a word he says. He will never cheat you." The day after I've had such dreams I'm filled with happiness, vigor, and joy and feel a personal connection with Srila Prabhupada. These dreams keep me going. They remind me of the importance of chanting *japa* and following the four regulative principles and they remind me to never give up. They are my shelter, my personal time with Prabhupada and Krishna. I have yet to fully recognize and appreciate Srila Prabhupada's greatness, but now I do love him to some degree.

Mahadevi devi dasi

In 1970 George Harrison released "My Sweet Lord." That song changed Mahadevi's life, leading her to Srila Prabhupada and his devotees. After high school, she moved into a house of musicians in Georgetown, D.C. One day, the harinama party was chanting and dancing down Q street in Georgetown. Mahadevi's loyal Labrador named "Peace" followed the devotees with her to the temple on Q street. Damodara dasa was the temple president then and friendly Mankumari devi dasi gave them both a plate of prasadam.

I was instantly drawn to the spiritual feelings and the photo of Srila Prabhupada on the *vyasasana*. Mankumari told me many wonderful things about Prabhupada. "Prabhupada describes the divine formula for freedom and peace from the ancient *Vedas*. Freedom from this bodily identification is the real peace." The next day, my band known as "The Simple Truth," traveled for a big gig in Key West, Florida. We hitchhiked twelve hundred miles with Peace. This was a crazy, daring experience that was preparing me for the hi-octane adventures in Prabhupada's *sankirtana* mission.

In Key West is a famous nightly festival called "Sunset on the Pier," observed when the huge orange sun slowly goes down. Vishnujana Maharaja was chanting Hare Krishna on the pier every evening for about three weeks along with the very enchanting Radha-Damodara in 1972. I was instantly attracted to Vishnujana's singing, the affectionate way he spoke about Srila Prabhupada, the saintly way he looked while playing his *tamboura,* and the happy feelings that filled up my heart, standing in front of Radha-Damodara.

Maharaja fed Peace and me blueberry *halava* every night, while describing the glories of Srila Prabhupada and the Hare Krishna mantra. He showed me an article in an old BTG of the rolling, green hills in New Vrindavan and convinced me to go visit there.

The very next day, I left the band, and Peace and I hitchhiked to New Vrindavan, West Virginia. When I arrived, there was Mankumari devi! We were so happy to see each other again.

"Krishna's arrangement," she said with a warm smile. "Mary, *sravanam* or hearing is the most important aspect of this bhakti yoga process, so if you put your hair behind your ears, you will be able to hear better." So we tied up my hair behind my ears. Mankumari went on, "Cleanliness is next to godliness. Scrubbing Krishna's pots is like cleaning our hearts. If you could help us with cleaning the sweet rice pots, we would be so grateful. We can give you and your dog free food and accommodations." I had promised Vishnujana Maharaja that I would "try it" there for a month.

I read *Krsna* book to Srila Prabhupada's picture on the *vyasasana* and Radha-Vrindavanacandra in the temple room. *Krsna* book became my favorite book to read and distribute. When George Harrison was doing his concerts in America, we followed him and distributed cases and cases of the blue "trilogy" softbound *Krsna* book, where George had written in the introduction, "All you need is love (Krishna)."

Two weeks later, I distributed BTGs in a Wheeling parking lot and collected fifty dollars. Thus started my life as Prabhupada's *sankirtana* devotee. For six years, twenty-five of us young women were living in Dodge vans (six people to a van) with our sleeping bags. We would sneak into hotel rooms or unlocked dorms to shower. We collected thousands and thousands of dollars for Prabhupada's Palace and later on for Vrindavan.

In the beginning of 1975, I received first and second initiation from Srila Prabhupada. Kirtanananda Swami had told Prabhupada that I was a "*maha* collector" and Prabhupada had said, "Then she will be Mahadevi dasi. She will do great things." Prabhupada is so encouraging.

We went anywhere and everywhere with Prabhupada's books. We would collect between six hundred to one thousand dollars a day sometimes, as we worked the State Fairs, Kentucky Derby, Indy 500, Las Vegas, rock concerts, sporting events, and most of the national airports. We also spent six months in the Puerto Rico Airport. Prabhupada had opened up every town and village for igniting Krishna consciousness. We were always depending on Prabhupada for mercy and successes in our daily lives, as I cried out to him through all our trials and tribulations.

My dear godsister Ragatmika and I were sent to Anchorage, Alaska to start a preaching center there and work the International Anchorage Airport. The pipeliners working in northern Alaska would have hundreds of dollars in their wallet after pay day on their way home. Hundred dollar bills have the face of a picture of Benjamin Franklin on them. So every time we got a hundred dollar donation, we would sing, "*Jaya* Bhakta Ben! *Jaya* Prabhupada!" We felt that Prabhupada was with each of us and all of us just like Krishna is with each individual *gopi*. Although we had never seen Srila Prabhupada in person, we felt empowered by His Divine Grace.

At first, we were happy to be travelling, engaged in exciting adventures for the pleasure of Srila Prabhupada. Then sexual, physical, and emotional abuse began on these women's *sankirtana* parties. It was horrible and really tested our faith. Many of us wanted to leave, but our loyalty to Prabhupada's mission kept us going. I went to jail four times for collecting money and distributing Prabhupada's literatures in illegal places, but we would start kirtans in the jails!

I saw Prabhupada for the first time in 1975 at the O'Hare Airport in Chicago. Srila Prabhupada stopped in his tracks to watch us distribute his books. We had been strictly told not to rush over to Prabhupada although we were yearning to be close to him. We were told that Prabhupada would be *more* pleased if we were to keep engaging souls as he watched us. Prabhupada inundated us with his divine glances and suddenly, he held up his cane very high, waving it in the air, smiling so munificently on us. We all hit the floor right there in the busy terminal and got up quickly so we could see the back of his golden form, which seemed to be barely touching the floor as he walked on, gliding along like a swan. I felt a sublime joy flowing through my heart and doubled my distribution/collection that day due to His Divine Grace.

In New Vrindavan, many of us *sankirtana* women went on a morning walk with Prabhupada when he went to see Radha-Vrindavanath and to visit the "Prabhupada hut" – a simple dwelling made in the old Bengali style of mud and hay. At the Prabhupada hut, devotees offered him the famous, thick New Vrindavan *burfi* on a silver plate. Prabhupada took some bites and indicated that the remnants should be passed over to his *sankirtana devis*, standing outside the window. Prabhupada watched carefully to make sure the remnants reached us! Prabhupada truly did care about us!

When Srila Prabhupada returned to Radha-Vrindavancandra's temple to speak from the *vyasasana,* he called for all his *sankirtana* ladies to accept a cookie from him. I was very troubled at the time, only twenty-three years old. I couldn't understand the abuse going on within our *sankirtana* party, NVSKP. I wanted to leave the party, but I didn't want to leave Srila Prabhupada, book distribution, or his mission. We truly believed that every time someone touched one of Prabhupada's books, that person was being personally blessed by Prabhupada and Krishna's mercy.

So when it was my turn to receive a cookie, tears filled my eyes, and I knew Prabhupada could understand my heart. As I extended my trembling hand, I looked up at his transcendental, beautiful features through my tears, and he smiled. Very distinctly, within my confused heart, I heard Prabhupada say to me, *"I am always with you, do not be fearful."* He filled me with a shelter and solace that I had never known in my whole life. Someone had to nudge me out of the way. I went to sit outside and wept in gratitude.

Those two comforting sentences have carried me through all kinds of challenges in my forty-five years with ISKCON. Later on, I did escape the abuse on the *sankirtana* party and moved to New Dwarka where I served for twelve years as a teacher and *pujari* and I managed the iconic *prasadam* cookie marathons for the pleasure of Srila Prabhupada.

The Prabhupada Prasadam Marathons in L.A. collected thousands and thousands of dollars for Prabhupada's BBT to build Vrindavan and Mayapur *dhamas.* I organized "bake sale tables" in front of thirty stores on a daily basis during the Christmas season. L.A. was flooded with OR, PB, and CC cookies (oatmeal-raisin, peanut butter, carob chip). People would come to our *prasadam* tables and tell us, "Your cookies just taste different, a special taste." Prabhupada says we are the "kitchen religion."

Srila Prabhupada, Sri Sri Rukmini-Dwarkadish, Nitai-Gaura, and Jagannatha would be offered a breakfast plate of cookies every morning and all of Watseka Avenue would smell like a bakery. In the early 1980s, I was teaching at our wonderful New Dwarka *gurukula.* I also woke up Srila Prabhupada and Rukmini-Dwarkadisa on the altar every morning at 3:30am. Vatsala Prabhu and I renovated Prabhupada's quarters, and I started cleaning Prabhupada's rooms, dressing him, and offering him a simple breakfast every day, as well as reading *Krsna* book to him every night. I've heard this daily *puja* is still going on. Staying personally connected to Srila Prabhupada is my life.

One of my services was caring for my mom for eighteen years, eventually changing her diapers when she became an invalid. The doctors said Prabhupada's sacred voice (*shabda*) in the home twenty-four hours a day, seven days a week helped her "become more peaceful." She was diagnosed to live for six months but lived for five more years. Srila Prabhupada and Krishna had a plan for her.

I begged Prabhupada, Krishna and Balarama for months to allow me to bring my seventy-year-old court-certified deranged mother to Vrindavan to leave her body. I was given permission by a country judge and Prabhupada was with me every step of the way. Thirteen days after we arrived in the *dhama,* my alcoholic, drug-addicted dear mother left her body during the sacred Kartikka. Who can understand the inconceivable mercy of Srila Prabhupada and our Lords?

I continue to serve in Sri Vrindavan *dhama* to try and please Srila Prabhupada and our Vrindavan Lords. Listening to Prabhupada's classes daily, *sadhana,* distributing a few books along the way, and serving devotees has kept me close to Prabhupada in my senior years. May we always try to please Srila Prabhupada in whatever we do, say, offer or give away.

Most of us who were initiated by Srila Prabhupada didn't have his personal association. Our connection to Prabhupada was always through hearing from His Divine Grace, our *sadhana,* rendering service, and regularly speaking about his glories. "By his grace, one can cross over the ocean of material suffering and obtain the mercy of Krishna."

Mahaguna devi dasi

In 1971, after Mahaguna's husband had met Prabhupada in Japan and joined Krishna consciousness, Mahaguna started going to the temple.

In early 1972, Prabhupada came to the Takao temple, a huge, beautiful, old, Japanese-style farmhouse in the mountains. Prabhupada liked it. Sudama Prabhu was the temple president and had each person present offer Prabhupada a flower. When I did that, Prabhupada seemed huge to me and I felt awe and reverence towards him. He was clearly an exalted, genuine, and kind person.

Later my husband and I were living at his parents' house in San Francisco and going to the temple every night. One night a devotee said to me, "Prabhupada is giving initiations tomorrow. You should go get initiated." I had no idea what that meant but I said, "Okay, yeah, sure." My husband was already initiated and I had no reason to refuse.

We drove to Los Angeles. This was in 1972 and I was twenty-one. We had the fire sacrifice, and when my turn came to receive my beads, Srila Prabhupada said, "Are you Japanese?" I said, "Yes." He said, "Where is your husband?" I pointed to him and Prabhupada nodded. Afterwards, Prabhupada called my husband and me to his room. Excited, we went in, paid obeisances, and in a jolly mood Prabhupada asked me, "What do your parents think about this?" I didn't speak much English. I said, "I don't have parents, Prabhupada." He laughed and said, "Oh? The stork has brought you here?" My husband said, "Her parents passed away." Prabhupada told my husband, "You should go back to Japan, take citizenship, and your wife can be temple president there." I thought Prabhupada was joking.

We did go back to Japan and from there we moved to Hawaii, where Prabhupada came in 1976 to do a lot of translating. Beautiful jasmine flowers cover the front porch of the Hawaii temple, and their smell is wonderfully intoxicating. One evening we were on the porch when we heard Prabhupada singing and playing the harmonium upstairs. I thought, "The spiritual world must be like this."

When Prabhupada passed away we were in Hawaii. It was traumatic; I felt sober and felt that he had handed us the responsibility to keep his mission going.

Mahamaya devi dasi

When she came to the movement in Boston, Mahamaya, twenty-four, was happy to be in the temple and didn't know that a guru led the movement.

In the beginning I heard, "Chant and you'll be happy." I tried it for a week and was happier. Then I tried it for another week. At some point I knew I wasn't going back to my old life. Then I read the abridged version of Prabhupada's *Bhagavad-gita* five times. Combined with living the temple lifestyle, it changed my life. I developed some trust in Prabhupada and the process he gave, but I didn't imagine that he was living in this world and that I could meet him.

When I finally saw Prabhupada for the first time, all of my deep doubts disappeared. It was like seeing an old friend after a long time. I understood that I knew Prabhupada through his picture. When he initiated me in the Henry Street temple in 1971, I was shocked to hear my name.

Prabhupada said, "Mahamaya. Mahamaya, illusory energy. The illusory energy is not all bad. Just like there are phases of the moon, Mahamaya is a phase of Radharani. For one who does not want to serve Krishna, the illusory energy is there." Prabhupada was personable and human. At the same time, he saw through my uncountable layers of false ego to the real me, the soul.

When I went to India in 1975, I lived in the *dhama*, met lifelong devotees, and met Prabhupada's sister Pishima, who adored Prabhupada. My trust in the process deepened, I became more grounded, reinforced, and committed to serving Prabhupada. I came to another level of reality. I always felt that Prabhupada knew what I was doing and accepted my service. And at the same time he was a person; I understood that his memory and knowledge came through Krishna.

When he came to Juhu after Mauritius, Prabhupada invited us to his room and said, "I was in a car accident. Krishna saved me because just before the accident, He told me to move my cane in front of me, and that braced me. But I hurt my knee." He lifted his *dhoti* and showed us his bruised knee. It was endearing, personal, and sweet, like something a member of your family would tell you, not the guru of the Hare Krishna movement.

Once at a darshan Sarva said, "Srila Prabhupada, yesterday you said a *sannyasi*'s business is to preach, a *brahmachari*'s business is to assist the *sannyasis,* and a *grihastha*'s business is Deity worship. But can *brahmacharinis* do Deity worship?" Prabhupada said, "Yes, you may also do." We were relieved. I wanted to ask, "Can I have my own Deity?" but I said, "Can devotees have their own Deities?" Prabhupada said, "No, it will distract from the temple Deities."

Prabhupada didn't give us a small mandate but a huge mission. Are we using 100% of the power of Lord Chaitanya's army to help fulfill that mission? If we're not hearing women's voices are we working as effectively as we could be? It's only common sense to honor devotee women.

Prabhupada presented us with a process: to hear and chant, follow the principles, think of Krishna, help others become Krishna conscious. And he exemplified that process. As ISKCON's founder-*acharya*, he's in a special position, and every devotee in ISKCON has an important relationship with him. The disciplic succession goes on, but no one will ever replace Prabhupada. Prabhupada was so Krishna conscious that it made being in his presence special. I could feel he was thinking of Krishna, and at the same time I firmly believe we can experience his presence by reading his books and following his instructions. There's every reason to believe that if we follow what he taught us we'll get the results he said we would get, and he'll take us back to Godhead at the end. It's a science.

Maharha devi dasi

Maharha joined in Boston in 1970, and then blooped for about five months. During those months she crocheted a blanket for Prabhupada, although she didn't know how to crochet. The blanket turned out weird. It was about ten feet long and two feet wide, with two different colors and a shrunken center part. She sent it with a little note saying, "I really like you, Prabhupada. I wanted to make this gift for you," and wondered if he ever got it. Years later she opened Prabhupada's locker in L.A. and was shocked and excited to find that blanket. Srila Prabhupada had saved it.

When I went on *sankirtana* in the Port Authority in the early years, I used to be mad at Prabhupada and think, "Why do I have to do this? You never had to do this. This is so hard for me. You probably don't know what I'm feeling." But I couldn't get out of *sankirtana* and in my heart I knew that, although it was painful and I wasn't good at it, it was purifying. I started praying to Prabhupada, "Please help me, I know you want me to do this." Then one day I watched Buddhimanta, who was really good at *sankirtana*. I thought, "I'm going to eat all this *halava* here and get so intoxicated that I'll be able to do it." I did huge and that was it: "Okay, she's good, we've got to keep her out there."

I served in New Vrindavan where we were always collecting money. We didn't spend any time reading and didn't have much of a morning program; we were told, "Work now, *samadhi* later." When Prabhupada was in New Vrindavan I was a nonsense; I didn't take his presence seriously. Many horrible things happened in New Vrindavan and my situation there was horrible.

When I heard that Prabhupada passed away, I felt bad because it didn't affect me much at first. Although I didn't have a lot of attachment for him, I tried to serve him. The hardest thing I had ever known was to go on *sankirtana* but I kept doing it, and every year I got more attached to Prabhupada and felt his presence more. I felt more connected to and protected by him. Like a father, he was helping me. The more a person stays in Prabhupada's Movement, everything becomes revealed. It becomes more and more apparent how fortunate we are and how Prabhupada saved us. If he hadn't come, we'd all still be covered over and miserable.

Now I feel Prabhupada's presence strongly, more than when he was physically present. I love to listen to his lectures, to hear him speak. By listening to him I feel close to him and safe. I read his books when I walk and, gratefully, am attached to reading them. I learn so much from Prabhupada's books and love to talk about them; when I give classes I feel that Prabhupada helps me.

Prabhupada's mercy will help us with any problems we have, anything that we're suffering from, and any attachments we have. Prabhupada is awesome and is powerfully in the life of whomever comes to this Movement. Without his mercy we can't do anything. It's amazing, but he's still here with us and sends us whatever we need. His lectures and books are never old but ever-fresh. I'm fortunate that I'm part of this Movement and grateful for what Prabhupada did for me and for all of us. All glories to Srila Prabhupada!

Mahasini devi dasi

In 1970 Mahasini dasi and her husband Kavichandra dasa (now Kavichandra Swami) were hippies living in a VW bus in the Arizona desert with their one-year-old daughter and two dogs. They met the handful of brahmacharis who had begun a small temple in Tucson and they liked the young men, the chanting, and Srila Prabhupada's writings. They began to help with things around the temple until eventually they re-homed their dogs and drove their VW to New Dwarka.

It was really Kavichandra who was most attracted to the devotees and ISKCON. I was still pretty mired in the hippie-dippie concept of being "cool" by practicing yoga and being a vegetarian. By Krishna's grace alone I came to deeply appreciate the philosophy. My first service, even before initiation, was when I was conscripted to prepare a giant kettle of sweet rice for the Sunday Feast shortly after we arrived in New Dwarka. I had no clue what I was doing but I was twenty-one and kind of fearless to try anything. I have to say it was daunting but Krishna allowed it to turn out wonderfully. Later I became the cook at New Dwarka and prepared countless Sunday Feasts.

When Karandhar, the temple commander, told my husband, "You should get initiated," I piped up, "What about me?" "Okay," he said, a bit grudgingly, "I guess you can too." Srila Prabhupada was in Los Angeles and he personally chanted on all of our beads. I recall he was upset that the beads were not true *japa* beads. The set I got were tiny and round, but he chanted a round on each set and handed my set to me. I cherish those funny little beads. He told me my name means "Great Wife" and is the name of Lord Shiva's wife, who is a great devotee.

My fondest initiation, however, was my *brahmana* initiation. We were each sent individually into his quarters in New Dwarka to receive the Gayatri mantra. I was feeling intimidated and when I reached the top of the stairs I paused and kind of peered into his room. In a very gruff voice Srila Prabhupada unceremoniously ordered, "Come on!" That memory is as fresh as the day it happened.

I do not know how I would have survived my life without Srila Prabhupada's instructions. Although I have not lived in the temple for the last twenty-eight years, my life is governed by his teachings. I am blessed that my daughter has remained a devotee and is bringing up her two daughters as devotees. I am blessed that my godsisters and brothers still tolerate me and that I find welcome in the temples wherever I roam. I am blessed beyond measure.

Mahati devi dasi

Once in the New Dwarka temple room in 1971, Mahati distinctly felt Srila Prabhupada intensely looking at her. Mahati thought, "Familiarity breeds contempt" and, not wanting anything to mar her newly found and wonderful guru-disciple relationship, didn't look at Srila Prabhupada.

Although I had many opportunities to look at Srila Prabhupada's lotus face, in New Dwarka I didn't look directly at him even once.

In 1975, in the courtyard of the new Krishna-Balaram temple in Vrindavan, Prabhupada was present for the fire sacrifice for my second initiation. Such was the mercy of Srila Prabhupada that even a low-born *candala* woman got second initiation from the great *jagat-guru* of the universe. Amazing.

Later that morning, I went alone into his big darshan room to receive the Gayatri mantra. I offered my obeisances and gave Prabhupada a little bowl of sweets covered with a decorated cloth that I'd sewn. Srila Prabhupada was pleased to see the pretty cover cloth, but when he uncovered the bowl his face was stricken with shock. Unfortunately, I'd brought sweets made by karmi sweet *wallas* in town. Prabhupada almost tipped back on his pillows. Immediately he instructed me, "Never offer sweets made in town." I felt awful.

I was sitting in front of his desk, and he instructed me to sit beside him. He said, "You chant Gayatri like this," and he moved his thumb over parts of his fingers to show how it was done. Speaking so softly that I could barely hear him, he said, "You chant in the morning, at noon, and at night." I didn't speak at all. I offered my obeisances, got up and walked across the big room to the door. But I felt guilty, so I turned around and bent down with *pranams* before stumbling out. Prabhupada looked satisfied with my effort; maybe someday I would understand how to properly worship the spiritual master. After that, I fled the room.

Once in Bombay, I saw Srila Prabhupada leave with some of his disciples for his morning walk on Juhu Beach. It was glorious to see the flashing of saffron as he walked off as fast and free as a deer, the young devotees struggling to keep up with him. I offered my obeisances to the glorious caravan.

Prabhupada had open darshan daily at 4:30 in his old Juhu apartment. He was so merciful to all of us in India that even the lowest of the devotees got to see him a lot. Once I sat against the dark wall and listened to him repeat and repeat to an Indian gentleman, "You must chant Hare Krishna." I realized that by saying that, Prabhupada had answered my unspoken question: My problem could be solved by chanting all my sixteen rounds again.

Shortly after that, the room gradually filled with devotees. Prabhupada was engaged in some very serious dialogue with a devotee, and with heavy difficulty, great effort, he pulled his attention away from his important preaching to glance graciously at me. I looked down. A few moments later, we all went to the roof and had some mango that he'd tasted. It was a lovely time in my life.

Srila Prabhupada was beautiful. His graceful movements and the lovely auspicious features of his body were enthusing to behold and sublime satisfaction for my heart. He was so regal he looked like a king. Thank you, Srila Prabhupada, for being you and being so beautiful. May I always remember and never forget your lotus feet, for if I can do that, I'll be happy and peaceful and wherever I may be, I'll live eternally.

Mahavisnupriya devi dasi

It was Hrdayananda Maharaja who said about meeting Srila Prabhupada that, "Just like a dream, he stepped into our lives."

I met Srila Prabhupada in May of 1975. I was materially exhausted and was ready to look in another direction, a spiritual route. I felt that I was at last at the right place, at the right time with the right associates. Srila Prabhupada stepped through the sliding glass doors of the airport terminal and out amongst the throngs of excited devotees, who instantly fell to the ground to offer their obeisances. Srila Prabhupada's aura was emanating from every cell in his body. Everything moved in slow motion.

Srila Prabhupada looked so serene and elegant as he gracefully made his way with palms pressed together toward his vehicle parked at the curb. I had brought a bouquet of gardenias to give him. Just as I was within tapping distance of Srila Prabhupada, out of nowhere, Guru Krpa Maharaja stepped between Srila Prabhupada and I, grabbed the flowers from my hand with one smooth jerk of the wrist. He sneered at me, as if to say, "You Dog, who are you to approach the spiritual master directly?" while turning on a dime and handing the bouquet to Srila Prabhupada, in one graceful almost dance-like movement.

Srila Prabhupada immediately put the flowers to his nose and drank them in as if they were liquid nectar. He seemed to become so refreshed by doing this, his whole countenance softened; he smiled broadly and looked around at all of us gathered there.

One day, I was asked to wash Srila Prabhupada's laundry. I crept into his room silently and began to search for the dirty laundry. Everything was neatly folded and sweetly scented of flowers; how was I to tell the dirty from the clean cloth? I decided to just take everything and to wash it all. I felt that I was receiving a lot of special mercy as I washed these delicate clothes and ironed them. Srila Prabhupada's body was not even of this world, as all of his clothes; such fine silk garments were as if they had never even been worn!

When asked if I would wash Srila Prabhupada's plates, the temple president said, "You can have all the *maha* left over from his plates. It will all be yours." Who could refuse such an offer? But the plates had been picked clean! The bhakta's eyes who helped me got very wide and he immediately paid his obeisances on the floor. "*Maha* salt! *Maha* salt!" he exclaimed with great joy. Yes, Krishna had given us some remnants of salt and we were overjoyed and in bliss!

We saw Srila Prabhupada every morning when he left for his morning walk. The car was brought to the front door under the breezeway, and devotees would line up to pay their respects to Srila Prabhupada, to throw rose petals, offer garlands, and exchange memorable and grateful glances.

When Srila Prabhupada's car was spotted coming back up the driveway, we all assembled with shouts of "*Jaya, Hari bol!*" and encircled Prabhupada's vehicle. Srila Prabhupada would always pay his full prostrated obeisances upon entering the temple room. Then he would get up slowly and with folded hands approach the front of the altar. His eyes would moisten as he looked at the Deities with such love and appreciation. It was as if there were huge volumes of dialog going on between the eyes of Srila Prabhupada and Their Lordships. He would stand there for extended periods. I would always wish that I could be privy to these intensely sweet exchanges. Oh, to be able to hear what was going on, what was being said and expressed. This loving exchange with the Lord would have to be the greatest nectar in the universe!

After greeting Their Lordships, next Srila Prabhupada would take *charanamrita,* pay his obeisances again, and make his way to the *vyasasana* for *Srimad-Bhagavatam* class. Every movement he made was so elegant and graceful. You could not take your eyes off of this unique, riveting, and compassionate individual.

To hear *Srimad-Bhagavatam* from the lips of the pure devotee enriched my heart like nothing else in this world. While I struggled to get my mind around one idea, Srila Prabhupada had covered three more. It was like someone had turned me upside down and shaken me, saying, "This is the right way to see things now."

He told us that all those who come to ISKCON after us would be far more advanced than us. He looked wide-eyed around the room at all of our faces. "As they will understand the pure example without ever having seen it."

One morning while Gurudeva was talking, his words had a particular heavy effect upon me, and I was crying. Tears of joy, gratitude, appreciation, relief, validation, and so many emotions all rolled into one were exploding in my heart. Then all of a sudden, it sounded as if Srila Prabhupada was speaking directly and only to me. He was talking about the great, female devotee saint, Devahuti, and how surrendered she was to give up her palace and riches to live with her husband in a simple hermitage. When out of nowhere, he said, "And the tears are putting out the fire of material existence." He wove these words so effortlessly and flawlessly from the rest of the narrative that he was speaking.

I gobbled up his words greedily, just as a drowning man grabs for safety. When I think of Srila Prabhupada's mercy and kindness and his great sacrifice of coming to our foreign land to save us, at such an advanced age, it helps me to remember that the tears these thoughts provoke are putting out the fire of material existence.

One lady spent great effort and time in creating a cake in the shape of Lord Krishna. She had decorated the cake with flute and peacocks and so many brilliant colors. We thought, she will surely gain good graces. But when Srila Prabhupada saw it, he was profoundly grave, "And what will you do with this? Cut off Krishna's head and eat it?"

Another devotee lady baked Ekadasi cookies for Srila Prabhupada to pass out after his *Srimad-Bhagavatam* class. This devotee had sprinkled sesame seeds on the top of each buckwheat, sugar cookie as a decoration. The large tray of cookies was brought to Srila Prabhupada on the *vyasasana*, who took one look at the cookies and his eyes widened. He stated, "What is this?" "I cannot give this. Today is Ekadasi, is it not?"

Then many senior disciples began trying to convince Srila Prabhupada that the sesames were seeds and not grains. Prabhupada was still skeptical. Pradyumna, the Sanskrit scholar of the day, ran upstairs and grabbed a book. He returned and tried to read to Srila Prabhupada that biologically speaking the sesame is categorized as a seed and clearly is not a grain. This went on for some time, with each senior disciple weighing in on the issue. Finally, Srila Prabhupada relented and said it was okay. It may be that sesame is considered a grain in India and not taken on Ekadasi. But for us, at this one time, Srila Prabhupada allowed the seeds to be eaten.

Devotees loved making garlands to offer to their spiritual leader. One day, I noticed a large tree of gorgeous blooming plumerias. This was an unusual type of plumeria (champaka) as it had very large petals, three times bigger than a normal plumeria. I was so excited stringing the flowers together. My husband and I were competing to see who could make the nicest garland. I thought, "I'll make mine really big because bigger is better, right? Srila Prabhupada is really going to like this garland." My garland ended up being about four and a half feet long. "This will extend to Srila Prabhupada's ankles. This is great!"

I could hardly wait for the following morning for my husband to garland Srila Prabhupada, as he came down the temple stairs, wearing what my mind called, this very special, "prize winning" garland. The next morning, as Srila Prabhupada came down the stairs, my husband was waiting at the bottom. When Prabhupada got into the car, with one elegant movement of his hand, he extricated himself from the garland and flung it upon the shelf area behind him sprawled out from one end of the car to the other. I looked in aghast, "I have made a car ornament!" The whole time I was congratulating myself for making a fabulous garland for my guru, all I really succeeded in doing was creating a car decoration like in a floral parade!

Love means that you offer to the other person something that they really love. You must be thinking only of what is best for the other person. Your offering has to be unmotivated, unselfish, coming from your heart. My garland was so huge. It was so ridiculous to think that he would in any way have worn this lei comfortably.

During *guru-puja,* all the lady disciples would stand in line on the side of Srila Prabhupada's *vyasasana,* waiting to offer a flower to his lotus feet. It was as if Srila Prabhupada would look deeply and clearly into each devotee's soul. I felt that he could read our hearts and minds. I know that at one point, I was praying strongly, "Dear Srila Prabhupada, please see me. Please accept me as your servant eternally." I was offering my flower and I was fervently, pleading for his acknowledgement. Srila Prabhupada gave me this wonderful sidelong glance starting at the top of my head and moving down to my feet. It was as if a long, cool, soothing wave of moonlight spread over me and engulfed me in soothing, radiant energy. It was truly one of the most memorable gifts of Srila Prabhupada's arsenal of mystic treasures ever bestowed upon me. How can I ever repay such kindness to the pure devotee? I could feel each part of my body getting bathed in the cooling moon glow of his glance. Srila Prabhupada was putting out the heat of material attachment for me by his precious, soft, long, and sincere glance. What amazing good fortune!

Over the years, I have had many opportunities to reconsider all the blessings that I have been so fortunately awarded by Srila Prabhupada. These memories are just like great gems of rare beauty that I carry in my heart always. These gem-memories nourish my soul and propel me deeper and deeper into my spiritual life. I cannot express the gratitude I feel in my heart for so much good fortune. This is the bond that I have with Srila Prabhupada. This is the bond of affection that Srila Prabhupada establishes with his disciples and through his disciples to so many others. He was always teaching us in so many different ways how to come closer to the Lord and how to revive our lost relationship with God. But I also know that everyone who had the blessings to be in Srila Prabhupada's association for even a moment also received untold good fortune and treasures of spiritual inspiration and compassionate mercy. How else could so many godbrothers and godsisters still be so much in awe, so dedicated and in enthralled with Srila Prabhupada after all these years? I pray that I may carry these treasures in my heart eternally. Thank you Srila Prabhupada! Thank you again and again!

Mahendrani devi dasi

In 1975 when she was nineteen, Mahendrani got a BTG and a few books from a devotee book distributor in Trinidad. The next Sunday she went to the temple for the feast and a devotee, indicating the murti of Prabhupada on the vyasasana, said, "This is Srila Prabhupada. He's a personal associate of Krishna, and he has descended from the spiritual world just to save us." Those words resonated in Mahendrani's heart. Somehow she knew that this awesome personality had come from the spiritual world to save her.

I was a teacher at the time and didn't join the Movement right away. That summer I spent a week in the temple, and in April 1977 Prabhupada initiated me by letter.

I never saw Srila Prabhupada in person but I never felt a lacking because from the beginning I felt he was personally taking care of me. Every step of my life was so synchronistic, so clearly arranged, I felt he was making the arrangements. When I went on *sankirtana*, I felt him inspiring me, guiding me, telling me he was pleased.

In 1979 I went to the Philadelphia *gurukula* thinking I was going to teach, but instead I became an ashram teacher. I hadn't a clue how to do that. After some months the headmaster told me I needed to be more personal with the children and suggested I read the *Lilamrta* about the early days of ISKCON and see "how personal Prabhupada was with the devotees."

I read how Satsvarupa Maharaja didn't come to the first initiation because he wasn't invited, and how Prabhupada extended a personal invitation to him and said, "If you love me, I will love you." Hearing that, something shifted in my heart. It opened and I understood how to be more loving and personal with the children. After that I felt Prabhupada was using me as an instrument to give love to the children.

I always felt eager to hear the *Bhagavatam* classes because I thought, "What is Prabhupada going to tell me today?" In every class there was something that stood out, a little instruction that Prabhupada was telling me. *Bhagavatam* class is one of the things that keeps me going. In fact, if I relax and get quiet and breathe, whatever situation is going on I say, "Srila

Prabhupada, you know how dull I am. I don't know what to do, please make it clear." And he does.

Sometimes, when I hear the standard of purity of the Vrindavan residents, I think, "Oh, I can't do that!" But then I feel I hear Prabhupada's voice saying, "What small step can you take now?" Over the years, my service and that voice have helped keep me going in Krishna consciousness.

Maithili devi dasi

Before she met Prabhupada, Maithili had a horrible family life. After fighting with her parents about meat eating, she became a vegetarian and ran away at the age of fourteen. She lived as a degraded hippie on New York's Lower East Side where she heard the devotees chanting on Saint Mark's Place. She chanted with them a little but thought them a bit mad.

I wasn't interested in Krishna consciousness but I had depressive end-of-life feelings and started seeing different swamis. I had pictures of swamis on my wall, including one of Srila Prabhupada. I found Prabhupada the most foreboding of all of them; I was frightened of him. But a friend explained to me the philosophy of Krishna consciousness and it intrigued me. He said, "They believe there's a land where there's no suffering, where there's *gopis*, and everyone is satisfied and happy, where you never take birth again. Everyone has a relationship with Krishna, and no one ever feels left out." It made more sense than any other philosophy. I went to the temple on Frederick Street in San Francisco, and there was Tamal, Madhudvisa, and Jayananda.

In 1969 I moved into the temple and was initiated by letter in March of 1970 when I was seventeen.

In the beginning in San Francisco, devotees asked Prabhupada, "What's the spiritual world like? Are there Valentines?" Prabhupada said, "Sure." "Are there lollipops and balloons?" Prabhupada said, "Yes, everything. Why not?" And when reporters asked him, "What do you think of women's liberation?" He said, "Our women are automatically liberated." His answer was clear and to the point, without complications. I always felt affection from Prabhupada in a way that I never conceived was possible from anyone. I felt a deep love from him, and I felt very secure. I never had loads and loads of questions. Krishna consciousness flew right into my heart and stayed there.

I learned Deity worship from Silavati in Los Angeles, and Prabhupada gave us lots of personal instruction. Again and again he stressed that the four most important points of Deity worship are cleanliness, punctuality, beautiful decoration, and nice *prasadam*.

After I'd been in Detroit for some time, the temple president told me, "You can either get married or you can go to India." So I went to India. I arrived in Bombay in May of 1972 when the Deities, Sri Sri Radha-Rasabihari, were in a tiny tent on Hare Krishna Land in Juhu. Their crowns had just been stolen off Their heads and Prabhupada was angry. He said of me, "She does Deity worship, she can do it." So I started serving Sri Sri Radha-Rasabihari.

In Juhu, Prabhupada used to distribute fruit from the evening offering and he'd tease me about liking the watermelon. He liked to pretend to give me watermelon and then switch to an orange piece, then see my face and switch back to watermelon. I was eccentric and Prabhupada found me jolly. When we did *harinama* I would dance like crazy and Prabhupada called me, "The funny one." He'd say, "Put the funny one in the front."

I never thought anybody could completely steal my heart, but Prabhupada did. I never thought I'd surrender to anybody, but I surrendered to him. He empowered me to do the things I did, to tolerate the austerities, like doing six *arati*s a day with boils under both arms. No matter what, I'd jump to do anything he asked.

In Vrindavan, Himavati and Yamuna were arguing and Prabhupada said, "If you argue, offer obeisances to one another. Then Krishna will take away the offenses." They would do that, get up, and argue again. They really didn't get along. Personalities can clash, but you can't deny the amazing nature of devotion. Yamuna made amazing outfits for the Deities, and was an amazing cook. She used to wake us early in the morning – I wanted to hit her for it – but every day she'd bang a whole *Brahma Samhita* verse into us.

Once in Vrindavan Yamuna and I cooked for George Harrison and Ravi Shankar. George gave Yamuna and me a big kiss on the cheek. That's when I realized that something had changed in my heart: Prabhupada was my shining star. I was so concentrated on pleasing him that I didn't care about Ravi Shankar or George Harrsion.

Once in Delhi at one o'clock in the morning, there were bats flying around. Prabhupada said to me, "This is the hour of ghosts and spirits. It's an inauspicious time to be awake." I was never that familiar with him but always in awe and reverence. I said, "Okay, Prabhupada, I'll go to bed now." He said, "But don't you have work to do?" I said, "I do, Prabhupada, we're installing the Deities tomorrow." He said, "Okay, I will keep my curtains a little open and you continue your service." Prabhupada opened his curtains so I could see him lying on his side reading. I felt, "This is what it means to be transcendental to everything."

The next day we installed the Deities. The room was small and tons of devotees came. They were bathing the Deities when the paint came off

Radharani's pupil. Someone said, "Go get some kajjal." I got kajjal, gave it to Bhavananda. Then, in front of everyone, Prabhupada said to me, "You fool! You rascal! Get out! Never do that!" I was shattered. I ran out of the room and stayed on the roof for the rest of the installation. I felt, "My life is over. Prabhupada called me a fool and a rascal." I cried and prayed all night. When Prabhupada came out of his room the next morning, he didn't look at me or say a word. He went down the stairs and Srutakirti said to me, "Prabhupada left something for you in the room." Prabhupada had left me his watermelon. The message I got from him was, "I played with you with watermelon in Bombay every night for months. I know you like watermelon. You are my beloved disciple."

Prabhupada was king of one-liners. I love him for his sarcasm and wit. In one sentence he would make everything clear. One morning walk in Paris, Harivilasa showed Prabhupada the restaurant on the top of the Eiffel Tower. Prabhupada said, "*Ho, ho, ho,* look at me. I am eating so high up."

Mr. Nair sold the Juhu land twice, kept the money he had been given, and tried to sell it again to Prabhupada. But Srila Prabhupada refused to be cheated. Nair paid the police to destroy our temple; they were smashing everything. Most of the devotees were already in the paddy wagon when the police started for the Deities. I closed the Deity doors, put my back on the doors, and said, "No way." Policemen came at me from all sides, started smashing the tube lights and went for Tulasi Devi, who was in the middle of the temple room from the morning *puja*. I went to get Tulasi. Then they grabbed me and started hitting me hard. I locked my arm around a pillar and they beat me hard on the elbow and the head. I had two long braids and they dragged me by one braid and one leg across the whole field with a thousand people standing around watching. Not one person lifted a finger to help me. The police threw me face down into the paddy wagon, and I was spitting. There is not one moment in my life that I have ever experienced Krishna consciousness except for those moments. I did not feel any pain, not a thing. I had no other thought in my mind except Radha-Rasabihari. That's the only blessing, true blessing I've ever had of all the practice, all the devotion, all the *sadhana* I've ever done – those few minutes. I tell people, "It's not me who saved the Deities. That was the moment the Deities saved me." For those moments, I was not in the world. The devotees described to Prabhupada how I was the last one to go and how I was kicking and screaming and biting and fighting. He said, "She'll go back to Godhead kicking and screaming all the way also." That whole incident was a blessing. I didn't do anything special but Krishna stole my heart at that moment. I've been trying to escape ever since, but I can't ever let go of Prabhupada, and he will never let go of me.

On one level I miss Prabhupada. On another level, I don't know what people are talking about when they speak about "living guru" because I still have a living guru. I can still hear his voice. You don't have to play a tape for me. I can still hear his comments. I feel connected to him. Actually he won't let go of me. It's us who let go of him. We try to let go, but he doesn't let go. Prabhupada said, "Just do what I say. I shall never leave you. I shall never leave you." And he keeps his word. I was born to meet Srila Prabhupada and to serve him.

Maladhari devi dasi

Maladhari received harinama initiation at the same time Abhaya, her older sister, did. Maladhari was seventeen and still in high school.

When I was fifteen I started visiting my sister in the temple. Socially it was difficult for me because my girlfriends didn't understand why I was going to the temple, chanting Hare Krishna, and being with devotees, and they dropped me. But I wanted to do these things and when I did my heart was full of joy; I was blissful.

After I graduated I moved in. I never saw Prabhupada but I heard that he once said, "Physical presence is for fools." I thought, "Well, he doesn't want to see me because I'm such a fool, but I still want to see him," but the opportunity never arose. I met him through his wonderful disciples who had had his association, and I got lots of good advice and instruction from them. I felt fortunate and grateful. Akuti was a super-mata who could do the work of ten *brahmanas*. She played the *mridanga,* cooked the whole Sunday Feast by herself, sewed the Lord's outfits and built a house. She was a dynamic woman who was always understanding.

It was a beautiful thing for me to find Krishna consciousness when I was a teenager, to learn values that I've treasured ever since, to learn how to cook nice offerings for the Lord. I was in awe of Srila Prabhupada. What a perfect personality and a brave soul he was to come to the West and teach a motley crew of drug-taking hippies Krishna consciousness. He saved me. He made the joy of wanting to know God on a personal level wonderful. When I read Srila Prabhupada's books, it's like I have personal association with him and with Gauranga.

Malati devi dasi

In 1966, Malati met Srila Prabhupada on a mountain top in the isolated Oregon wilderness where she and her boyfriend were living. Sam was a lookout for forest fires. Mukunda and his newlywed wife, Janaki, surprised them with a visit and introduced them to the Swami and the original edition of Srimad-Bhagavatam, the first canto in three volumes. That introduction determined Malati's fate. They caravanned to San Francisco with an idea to open a temple and invite Swamiji to the West Coast. She had recently turned twenty-one. On January, 17, 1967, Bhaktivedanta Swami arrived in San Francisco on a commercial airline flight from New York, Prabhupada's first-ever ride on an airplane. A few days later, they were initiated and married with a fire yajna conducted by Srila Prabhupada. Malati and Syamasundara departed San Francisco for Montreal en route to the UK in late August 1968.

Upon arriving in Mayapur for the first time, I was excited, bewildered, and a bit overwhelmed, although overwhelm never presented a "stop sign" to me. There was no electricity except for a single light bulb hanging on a cord in Srila Prabhupada's kutir. There was no running water except for the rivers, no proper toilets or bathing facilities, and we had tents for accommodations. The kitchen was an area to squat and cook over a pot or kerosene stove. There were no tables or counters or refrigerators. And the only markets were across the river in Navadvipa! How did one cross the river? We fought and bartered our way onto a boat navigated by a super skinny guy wearing a thin cotton cloth around his loins (gamcha) who sat at the helm chewing on pan.

Since my husband Shyamasundar had become Srila Prabhupada's personal secretary, it was an unspoken arrangement that I would cook, clean, and shop. I had begun these services in Bombay at Akash Ganga, our first official residence in India. There, Their Lordships Sri Sri Rasa-Bihari resided after the Cross Maidan Pandal program. At the time, my kitchen was a little room with an Indian toilet attached that would have been the servant's quarters. Akash Ganga was a very respectable building, but it was still in the process of completion. It had two elevators, one for the residents and the other for tradesmen and their goods. Though we were on the 5th floor, the servants were not allowed to use either elevator.

Srila Prabhupada and his entourage, including my husband, had gone ahead by car to Mayapur. We journeyed from Howrah Station in Calcutta by a wooden-seated train to Krishna Nagar. Then we got in an open-windowed bus with wooden seats. There was only standing room. People piled up on the roof and hung outside of the stairwells. We arrived in exotic Mayapur, the birthplace of Chaitanya Mahaprabhu in deep rural West Bengal. I saw rice paddies all around and further out beyond the little thatched roofed hut that was Srila Prabhupada's majestic quarters, was a bamboo open stage. I wondered what would be happening there. We were introduced to the only source of water on our property: a hand pump. There was no drainage so it was surrounded by mud. The rivers Jalangi and Ganga ran one on either side, although not immediately visible. I had no time to take in much of anything, as I was expected to prepare *prasadam* for Srila Prabhupada and I had no idea how this would happen, given the Spartan situation.

Shyamasundar emerged from the hut smiling. "Not much here," he remarked. Then he showed me the "kitchen" area, which was at the rear of the hut. My metal kitchen trunk was brought over. There were some scraggly vegetables inside the hut, along with some cheap rice, stone-filled dal, and atta. I had brought ghee and spices. There's was a bucket of water nearby. I had not even seen the tent where I would sleep with my daughter and at the moment I didn't even know where she was. Our shared suitcase and shoulder bag were left sitting on the ground while I began to prepare prasadam. Prabhupada was inside, but I had not yet seen him. It was challenging enough to live in Bombay and Calcutta, but this situation showed how inexperienced we were. Right away devotees fell ill, generally with stomach-related illnesses, dysentery, and dreaded boils. Forgetting to boil the water to purify it for drinking was always a major mistake in the cities and here was no exception. In the cities where water supply was limited it was rationed, here water seemed to be endless. But either way, water had to be boiled and cooled down before drinking. But we just could not get that together, so we suffered a lot. I rarely had time to eat or drink, which spared me some of the misery, but even when I did get ill, I had to carry on as if I wasn't.

This was Mayapur and "purifying" became a catch word for almost every question. "How are you, Prabhu?" "Oh, I am getting purified. Big time!" "How's your service, Prabhu?" "Oh, it's really purifying!" Though I didn't used that phrase, I understood what it meant because I was getting purified as I attempted to serve Srila Prabhupada. Even the weather added to the purification by raining. Our leaking tents afforded little shelter and our sleeping bags were soaked with the ground: there was mud, lots of it. With a toddler and a husband who both required clean dry clothes daily, the situation was definitely "purifying."

Although completely ecstatic on the one hand, I had a daily series of opposing elements to combat. It went something like this:

1. Try to take care of daughter and husband.
2. Meet the treasurer to get funds for Srila Prabhupada's *bhoga* before anyone else visited him to minimize the chances he would be in a bad mood and then argue over every *paisa*. We had no personal funds most of the time so if my daughter needed anything, I'd have to beg from the treasurer. I also had to beg and fight on behalf of Srila Prabhupada every day. One time, the treasurer didn't want to give me rupees for a pineapple, which Srila Prabhupada really enjoyed. His reasoning was that he didn't eat the entire pineapple, therefore it was wasted money!

3. Go to Bhaktisiddhanta Road and walk to the boat *ghat*. Have an argument with the men who were not connected with the boat, but stood in the path demanding a "toll." It would have been a lot easier to give them a few *paisa*, but I didn't have enough money for anything beyond purchasing fresh *bhoga* for Srila Prabhupada.
4. Fight with the boat *wallah* about the fare. Being a Westerner, I would get special mercy. Being poor, I fought back like anything. Even Srila Prabhupada once remarked in Bombay, "Only Malati should go shopping because she never gets cheated." I couldn't afford to!
5. Disembark on the other side of the river in Navadvipa and endure another cheater trying to extract a toll to go up the embankment from the boat.
6. Fight with a *rickhsaw wallah* about the fare to go to the *subji* market.
7. Argue with the *subji wallah* over quality and prices.
8. Argue with the fruit *wallah* over quality and prices.
9. Argue with another *rickshaw wallah* over the return ride to the *ghat*.
10. Sometimes, go to a *misty bhandar* (sweet shop) and purchase *rasagulla* or *misty dahi*. Another argument.
11. Confront the fake toll collector on the Navadvipa side to leave.
12. Fight again with a boat *wallah* (who now saw my purchases and thus had proof of my wealthy status).
13. Fight with the fake toll collector on the Mayapur side.
14. Because I now had parcels and needed a *rickshaw*, fight with another *rickshaw wallah*.
15. If my daughter was with me, the entire situation intensified. I had to worry about her. Sometimes these rascals would try to separate us as a way to force me into giving more.

By the time I would get back to our camp, there was no time to do anything else except begin cooking. In spite of all of this, my entire daily meditation was fixed on pleasing Srila Prabhupada. In fact, I would not stop thinking about this from the beginning of the day to the end. As soon as I completed his lunch *prasadam,* I would begin meditating on the next day, keeping in mind any mistakes that I might have made that day. It seemed to me that I was making a lot of mistakes because every day Srila Prabhupada would correct one thing or the other. And no matter how careful I tried to be, there would always be something "wrong," or that needed improvement. Therefore, I was always in anxiety about pleasing him. In addition to pleasing Srila Prabhupada, I was also on call as a mother and a wife and it didn't always flow smoothly.

The almost-final straw was that I only had two fires to cook with. One was a traditional small bucket lined with mud and dung with bars over the top to hold a pot or puff up a *roti*. The other was one of those demoniac kerosene stoves that you had to pump up before lighting. They usually flared up in your face, singeing your eyebrows and hair. I needed them both, but every day Prabhupada's servant took one to heat the water for Srila Prabhupada's bath. That left me with only one fire towards the end of preparing his meal. This was very difficult, and extremely frustrating especially when it came time to cook the *rotis,* which were the last item on the menu.

One day, after a particularly careful meditation and effort to please, a bit of pride crept in. I felt that day as if I finally did my service very well. That mistaken idea did not last for long. Srila Prabhupada called me and asked, pointing, "Why so much salt?" I was to include some salt, pepper, bits of chopped fresh ginger, and a slice of lemon on the side of his plate. At that moment, I suddenly felt defeated. I thought, "I am just not able to do this service properly. I can't give up being a wife or mother, but I could stop cooking. After all," I reasoned, "I am not able to please him no matter what I do, so it would be better to have someone who could do the service properly be his cook." I began to feel some relief. I decided that the next day I would tell him that I would find someone else to cook for him. My burden lifted. I felt as if a big problem had been resolved. However, then next day did not go as planned.

It turned out that some of his godbrothers were coming for lunch. Prabhupada was being criticized, among other things, for having a woman cook for him. I reasoned that he would not want me to cook that day and therefore decided to tell him my plan the following day.

Suddenly, I heard my name called: Srila Prabhupada wanted to see me. Wondering why, I entered his *kutir* and made obeisances. Before I could even raise my head, I realized he was telling me what he wanted for lunch that day. This was not the right time to tell him that I was not going to cook any more, so I just nodded my head in agreement even though I was surprised.

The godbrothers were seated inside with Srila Prabhupada when I finished. As I came to the less-than-elegant burlap sack "curtain" between his quarters and the back end of the *kutir* that served as the servants area, I hesitantly took a peek at the wondrous scene before entering.

It was simply spectacular. The little *kutir* was not well lit, so it was usually very dim inside. On this day, it was luminous. Srila Prabhupada was at the end of the room flanked by three or four of his godbrothers, who were venerable, elderly Vaishnava gentlemen. But the entire attention was on Srila Prabhupada and he appeared as if he were a rare diamond in an exquisite setting. You see, a diamond on its own is undoubtedly gorgeous, but when it is put into a proper setting, its natural beauty becomes even more enhanced. That was how Srila Prabhupada appeared to me at that moment and I became very much intimidated to enter. I pulled my *sari* completely over my head, I went down on my knees and elbows, pulling the *sari* even over my arms. Only my hands were exposed, holding his *thali*. In this way, I crawled in, using my knees and elbows for support. I put the plate down, and made ground-level obeisances and began to retreat, slithering out the same way I had entered, on my knees and elbows.

Suddenly, I heard his voice: "Yes, she cooks for me. And I criticize her. [pause] But she would slit her throat for me and I would do the same for her." He used the word "slit" with a slight accent of an "e" mixed with the "i."

My foolish mistaken attitude was immediately adjusted. Immediately. I clearly saw how he had been reciprocating with my desire to perfectly please him. And I also knew that I had foolishly taken his words as criticism. That was a wonderfully humiliating discovery. I realized that I was being used as an example in this situation. While it appeared as if he were referencing me, he was really talking about the unique relationship that existed between himself and his disciples. I was just a fortunate example. His amazing words were meant for all of us, telling his godbrothers in no uncertain terms of the mutually loving relationship between him and his disciples.

I had no further thought about quitting. The next day was like all the others, except that instead of feeling beaten down and oppressed by the various "battles," I felt exhilarated by the opportunity to serve Srila Prabhupada. I couldn't believe my former foolish mentality and how perfectly Srila Prabhupada had exposed and smashed it. Now, each "argument" was completely ecstatic, beginning with the treasurer to the final *rickshaw wallah*. I felt as if I was flying with my feet on the ground. I just loved this service and my love for Srila Prabhupada increased along with it. Our good fortune knows no limits. Srila Prabhupada *ki jaya*.

Mallika devi dasi

Mallika was attending Temple University when she saw The Nectar of Devotion in the discount bin at the college bookstore. She bought it for 75 cents.

I went to the Philadelphia Ratha-yatra in 1974, saw the Deities, tasted a *gulabjamon,* and got a *Bhagavad-gita*. I was already a vegetarian due to bumping into friends of the Hare Krishnas and I was fascinated with Krishna stuff. When I saw Srila Prabhupada at the Philadelphia Ratha-yatra in 1975, I knew he was the person I was going to surrender to but I was covered over. I left Prabhupada's association to cook steak sandwiches at the bar where I worked.

In Mayapur in 1977 I took photographs of Srila Prabhupada speaking and circumambulating the Deities with his devotees. During *guru-puja* in the roomful of hundreds of devotees, I got his glance. He knew who I was and I knew who he was. I felt ashamed because I'd let him down by trying to enjoy inside a body. I took a photo and then ran outside, waited on the steps, and took another photo in which Prabhupada is looking right at me with his hands folded.

Many years later in my devotional life my husband blooped and I had no male protective energy. I told Prabhupada I was his daughter and needed his protection and mercy but I felt he'd left me and I was alone. Then I looked at that photograph I'd taken in Mayapur and saw Prabhupada was looking right at me, blessing me, and giving me his mercy, and I took shelter of that.

When I was a *brahmacharini*, I'd wake up at 2:30 am, finish my rounds by *mangala-arati*, distribute books all day in the airport, come home to transfer the Deity plates, go to bed with tons of *maha* in my belly and still get up at 2:30 and go distribute books. During that bubble of time Krishna manifested mystic potency. Krishna enabled us to do what we did because He was so indebted to Srila Prabhupada. Krishna blew Prabhupada's mind: hundreds of twenty-five-year-old Western conditioned people looked like devotees. It was absolutely the most wonderful time and now that we have had that taste we have something to work toward – that level of total abandon and service to Prabhupada 24/7.

Temple life facilitated many of us to come to a high level of service and awareness and ability, and now I feel like Arjuna who couldn't protect the queens. But soon Krishna is going to give us that ability back again. We just have to work for it. Whenever I want to please Srila Prabhupada, I ask Krishna because I know He'll help me.

Mamata devi dasi

In the fall of 1970, nineteen-year-old Mamata moved into the Washington, D. C. temple. That spring she went to Brooklyn to type for ISKCON Press, and in July Prabhupada came

I first saw Prabhupada at the New York airport. Both sides of the airport hallway were lined with devotees and as they offered obeisances to Prabhupada, it looked like two lines of dominoes falling. When they looked at him it was like they were seeing God. Prabhupada's presence, his spiritual energy, the love between him and Krishna filled the whole room and filled everybody in it. His energy was waves of spiritual love, and it was palpable and obvious, not at all theoretical. I experienced it directly and it's what convinced me. When Prabhupada spoke, everybody in the room felt he was speaking directly to them. What he talked about, how he answered questions and prayers, addressed whatever was bothering a person, was just right for everyone present. It was extraordinary and incredibly beautiful to see. Prabhupada was the external manifestation of Supersoul, Krishna.

When I got my beads during my initiation, Prabhupada was kind and sweet. When he said my name it sounded like a *mridanga* beat and he put the emphasis on the last syllable, "Mama-TA. *Mamata* means "one who is very affectionate to everyone." The devotees liked that and went, "*Ahhhh*." Prabhupada smiled and looked around the room.

When Srila Prabhupada sang "Jaya Radha Madhava" for the first time in New York in 1971 he said, "You know this song, 'Jaya Radha Madhava'?" We all shouted, "Yeah!" He said, "You think you can follow me?" Again we shouted, "Yeah!" Then he started singing slowly in that beautiful booming voice, "Jaya Radha Madhava . . . " We were blown away by his deep realization and his loving relationship with Krishna. When he sang, all that came across. The devotees were filled with ecstasy, transcendental happiness, like nothing you could describe. No one can get material happiness like that.

In those early years, 1971, 1972, 1973, there wasn't such a distinction between the men and the women. We were a family. We all chanted on the streets together and nobody thought, "Oh, there's a man next to me," or "There's a woman next to me." We were absorbed in Krishna and in giving this gift of Krishna consciousness to others. Later on it became, "Okay, men over here, women over here."

My main connection with Prabhupada was when I transcribed his lectures, morning walks, and room conversations from all over the world. Before I moved in the temple I wanted to travel with him and I thought, "I'll stay here in Washington, work, save some money, and when he travels I'll go to wherever he is." After a couple of months I surrendered and moved into the temple, but Krishna fulfilled my desire by letting me work on the Bhaktivedanta Archives project. By hearing his lectures, room conversations, and morning walks, I got be with Prabhupada much more than I could have been physically.

A transcriber can't space out but has to focus and hear every word. I found that Prabhupada spoke about whatever was disturbing me, making me anxious or bothering me and he'd immediately make my problems and philosophical misunderstandings go away. That happened so many times it was phenomenal.

Prabhupada's not a mundane person of this world. Everything about him was beautiful because Krishna was so present in him. Such a great personality is the most rare thing in this world and seeing him personally definitely reinforced my faith in him.

Mandakini devi dasi

From Jehovah's Witness to Mormonism, Roman Catholicism, and Buddhism, Mandakini was searching for the Absolute Truth. On Adelaide's main street in early 1973, she received a Bhagavad-gita *from Bhutanatha Prabhu, who was friendly and smiling effulgently. Mandakini decided to attend the Sunday Feast.*

At the temple I was impressed with the devotees, the pictures of Krishna, and the smells of cooking and incense. My senses were inundated and enlivened and I could see the devotees were in a good situation spiritually. I moved in and would constantly hear the devotees talking about Srila Prabhupada: "Srila Prabhupada said this," "Srila Prabhupada said that." From that and from hearing recordings of Prabhupada's lectures and his enchanting *japa,* I became extremely attached to him. His books answered all my doubts and questions. Particularly strange was that even the things I didn't agree with on a mental level, I embraced and acknowledged on a heart level.

In 1974, I went with the other Adelaide devotees to Melbourne and at Ratha-yatra saw Prabhupada for first time. I'm a hardheaded realist, but when I was dancing next to Prabhupada, it felt like my feet weren't touching the ground, time stood still, and I was in another dimension. His physical presence transported me to some spiritual space and I was no longer conscious of my body. It was magnificent when Prabhupada stopped walking and, with a look full of love, turned to see the beautiful golden Lord Chaitanya. Then, as he turned back to continue, he caught my eye and looked at me deeply for what seemed like an eternity. I was transported and transfixed. That cemented my dedication to his mission, his Movement, his instructions, his books, and the chanting of Hare Krishna.

In one of his Melbourne lectures Prabhupada talked about chanting Hare Krishna and said everything is contained in it and we should somehow, with our life and soul, chant. I be,came determined to do that: "If I can perfect my chanting, then I can be successful." With pictures of Krishna in front of me, I'd chant diligently and fanatically, definitely in the mode of passion. But I always understood the importance of chanting and prayed, "If I don't do anything else, please allow me to always chant Hare Krishna." I'm grateful that Prabhupada's basic instruction, "Just chant Hare Krishna," is dear to me and sustains me.

Prabhupada came to Melbourne again in 1975, and I was impressed with his beautiful, strong character. He was also gentle, almost like a little boy. That combination of strength and simplicity attracted me and I felt, "This is the person I've been looking for my whole life." I knew without a doubt that I adored and respected Srila Prabhupada, that I would give the rest of my life for him, that my whole ambition was to follow his instructions. I'm an avid, daily reader of Prabhupada's books, and that reading makes me strong. Srila Prabhupada says he's in his books and his instructions and through his books I feel his presence in my heart and in my life, watching and guiding me, talking to me.

Anyone anywhere can embrace Srila Prabhupada's books and be spiritually nourished and sustained. It's even more joyful to embrace them in association with devotees – asking questions, sharing realizations, churning the nectar.

This Krishna consciousness movement is Prabhupada's and he's pleased when we come together to push it on. Very early I decided that before even thinking about it I'd always say yes to whatever I was asked to do and worry about it later. To become anxious to perform devotional service is a natural byproduct of chanting and reading, and I want to be eager for service. This and everything Prabhupada has given is my substance.

Manjari devi dasi

In the summer of 1970, Manjari, sixteen, was living at Krishna Yoga Society (Siddhaswarupa's Hawaii ashram) and chanting Hare Krishna.

One day Siddhaswarupa told us he needed a guru, he was going to surrender to Srila Prabhupada, and we could do that also. So, in November 1970, I joined the ISKCON Honolulu temple. Siddha had impressed on me the importance of accepting a pure devotee – Srila Prabhupada – but I felt unqualified to be Prabhupada's disciple. Govinda dasi said, "Of course you're not qualified. That's why you need a spiritual master. It's not like you come to the guru qualified." That made sense so I wrote to Prabhupada that I realized I needed a spiritual master. Prabhupada accepted me as his disciple from Bombay, May 28th, 1971. He wrote back, "I am so glad to note that you have accepted the importance of the spiritual master for making advancement in spiritual life. Now that you have been formally initiated, you are linked up with all the great Vaishnava *acharyas* via the *parampara* system and so the effect will be there fully. By the mercy of the *acharyas*, the path for going back home, back to Godhead has been made very easy."

In 1972 I first saw Prabhupada in the Honolulu airport, walking like a swan with his head held high. The devotees gave him so many garlands they went up to his eyes. He called for Siddha, who was in the back. Siddha touched Prabhupada's feet and Prabhupada patted his head. I thought, "Prabhupada is so affectionate."

During that visit, Prabhupada installed the Pancha-tattva Deities, gave Siddha *sannyasa,* and spoke every night. He said, "Lord Chaitanya took *sannyasa* when He was young," and he explained why Mahaprabhu took *sannyasa.* One devotee asked, "What do you do when the mind wanders?" I thought, "What a good question! I wish I had asked that." Prabhupada was stern and said, "You don't know?" I thought, "Oh, my God, I'm so glad I didn't ask that!" I would have crumbled and cried, but the boy was sweet and honest and said, "No, I don't know." Prabhupada's mood changed and he said, "You bring it back." And he made a pulling back motion with his hand. Prabhupada's affection with Siddha, his sternness, and his great intelligence revealed how the spiritual master is sometimes as hard as a thunderbolt and at other times as soft as a rose. Prabhupada was charming and captivating.

Later, in New York, I made the long, thick, pretty garland that Prabhupada wore for the classic picture of him standing holding a *danda* in front of a purple, crushed velvet backdrop. Prabhupada preferred light garlands, but he kindly accepted that one.

When Prabhupada was about to depart from the New York airport, Baradraj was leading kirtan and Prabhupada, surrounded by devotees, was sitting with his head down, and his eyes closed. He was weeping. I was shocked. At first I thought there was something wrong but then I felt, "This is beyond me." Prabhupada didn't reveal his ecstasy often; I was fortunate to get a glimpse.

The next time I saw Prabhupada was during the Gaura Purnima festival in Mayapur in 1974. I had married Navayauvana and gone with Atreya and his wife to Tehran. Prabhupada was happy with us because we were coming from Iran, but I was so overcome by shyness that even when Prabhupada spoke to me I couldn't bring myself to reply.

When Srila Prabhupada visited Tehran, my husband told him he wasn't happy and was thinking of going to India. Prabhupada listened and then told my husband how, when he'd crossed the Atlantic on the Jaladuta, the ocean was rough and he'd suffered two heart attacks. Thinking over Prabhupada's response, Nava and I understood that Prabhupada had revealed the sacrifice he'd made and how we shouldn't take our situation lightly. Prabhupada wanted us to understand what it takes.

More and more I've come to understand and love Srila Prabhupada's spoken words, his books, and his videos. What he's given us is for all time. I always follow Prabhupada's instructions: the regulative principles, chanting at least sixteen rounds, engaging in Krishna's business, reading Prabhupada's books. A pure devotee's association is so strong that it touches the heart. But at the same time, unless we're reciprocating from within with our own determination for spiritual life and spiritual advancement, our spiritual life can become sentiment. Sentiment for the pure devotee is wonderful but if we don't do our part, if we don't endeavor, the depth of our love doesn't develop much.

Manjuali devi dasi

Manjuali was traveling when she met devotees in Chicago toward the end of 1970. She visited the Portland and Santa Barbara temples and when she came to New Dwarka in December 1971, she heard, "Srila Prabhupada's coming in March! You have to stay. We need help."

I left all my books – *Be Here Now, I Ching*, Lao Tzu – behind. I had one little backpack, shared the New Dwarka *brahmacharini* room with twenty-two others, and did whatever there was to do: *harinama sankirtana*, Saturday Krsna book distribution, sewing for the Deities, Deity support service, filling bottles of oils, and stacking incense in the incense factory.

When Srila Prabhupada came it was like a demi-being had entered my world, I was in awe of his presence and nobility. On Nrsimhadeva's Appearance Day in May 1972, when I was twenty-four, Prabhupada initiated me. He gave me my beads and said, "Manjuali. *Gopi* name." His eyes were grave, but his smile was a generous "Welcome." It was a rite of passage.

Prabhupada was upset that devotee married couples were not staying married but he approved my marriage to Jayatirtha. My mom came from Chicago and gave us $50 as a gift. After our wedding Jayatirtha and I, tied together, went to see Srila Prabhupada in his New Dwarka garden and I gave Prabhupada my mother's check. I also brought a plate of *prasadam* and a garland for him. Prabhupada, sitting in his lovely seat surrounded by yellow roses, looked at Jayatirtha and said, "She is beautiful," and winked. In class Srila Prabhupada had said, "A beautiful wife is an enemy to the husband, because she'll distract him from his spiritual journey." So I thought, "Oh, my God, I'm an enemy to my husband!" Prabhupada picked up the drink I'd brought and with his little finger out, took a sip and looked at Jayatirtha, "And she can cook." Prabhupada had us sit at his feet like we were his children and he was a gorgeous, wonderful master. We were intoxicated to be in his presence and had a lovely exchange.

He said, "What do your parents think of Krishna consciousness?" I said, "My mother chants Hare Krishna when she does the dishes." Prabhupada's warmth and his caring attention and humanity in asking about my family were peak experiences. He gave Jayatirtha and me instruction about married life, "Attachment comes through service. If you keep Krishna in the center of your relationship, you'll be successful." That was the seed, the guiding light. Jayatirtha and I were a team and with him I had a wonderful opportunity to serve, grow as a human being, learn many skills, and also be absolutely broken in order to come back together again.

Srila Prabhupada taught us how to wake up in the morning, shower, cleanse ourselves, eat, sing, dress – everything. And everything was focused around the Divine, was a gift for the Divine. We were a gift for the Divine. Prabhupada gave the presence of God as His holy name and we became purified every time we chanted the holy name. That Name held the presence of God within us and radiated out. Such gifts.

I didn't have a lot of association with Prabhupada, but that wasn't important. I loved Deity worship and my whole life, my every breath, was absolutely absorbed in Their service. My association with Srila Prabhupada was through Deity worship at New Dwarka because we served the Deities for him. He taught us to do everything with pure intention, beauty, grace, an open-hearted spirit, and as an offering. Our false ego had to step back. Every morning Prabhupada came in, the Deity doors opened, and the "Govindam" prayers played. We had dressed the Deities and were fanning Them with *chamaras,* and it was beyond time and space. Oh, the honor of doing that! Prabhupada would offer *dandavats* and move to the next altar. Then he'd sit on his *vyasasana,* play his gong, and the doors would close for the offering.

Once after class, Prabhupada said to Srutakirti, "Who has dressed the Deities?" "Manjuali." "Bring her to me immediately." "Prabhupada wants to see you immediately." I thought, "Oh, my God." I trembled upstairs, my heart beating, "What have I done?" I went to Srila Prabhupada's room with its blue walls and saffron curtains (he'd told us those were the colors of his boyhood room). The light was shining through the curtains behind Srila Prabhupada, who was sitting on his little seat without his shirt, just his top piece, shiny silk *dhoti,* and beautiful *tilaka.* He had an effulgent aura and was smiling. His smile carried the whole universe. He said, "Thank you very much, you have done nicely. Krishna is looking beautiful and I'm very pleased. When you decorate the Deity, you decorate your heart," and gave me $20 for the Deities. I said, "Thank you Srila Prabhupada. This will go to the next outfit." He said, "Always serve Krishna and this life will be perfect and the next will be perfect for you will go back to Godhead." I couldn't believe it. There was a pause and a presence without words that said everything. The little girl in me, the daughter of Srila Prabhupada, was being acknowledged and encouraged by his mercy, kindness, and generosity of spirit. That moment in time will always be with me.

To please Prabhupada was our lifeblood because Prabhupada was everything to us. We were in love with him and his message. He was our gateway to a sweetness that we didn't know was available to us. He opened a container within us and by his love gave us a jewel, and that jewel is something we can hardly speak about because it's so precious. Sometimes I don't honor it as much as I should, but I feel that the jewel Prabhupada gave us was himself, his love, and his wisdom. Prabhupada could see the big picture and was cent-percent dedicated to the mission and lineage of Mahaprabhu and Krishna.

My stories of Srila Prabhupada are few, but my love affair is deep. Sometimes I think the blessing is so great that we can always be honoring the story, holding its mystery in our hearts, an eternal moment in time. By some grace and blessing, a little hippie girl who was on the road looking for soul connection was picked up and given a jewel. We try to represent the integrity of the gift we've received, but the core of it is a heart connection. Srila Prabhupada touched our hearts, opened our minds, and gifted us with an unconstrained love. Ours is a living, fluid, ongoing relationship that takes focus, an open heart, and grace. It's a dance. It requires ongoing discipline to serve the relationship and not take it for granted. Prabhupada gave us the fellowship of a family of like-minded souls who are seeking a connection with the mystery of the Divine. I'm deeply honored I could be part of the story. He touched my heart and captured me by his unconditional love.

Manmohini devi dasi

For as long as she could remember, Manmohini was looking for this Movement. She was nineteen when she joined the 61 Second Avenue temple in October of 1969, and soon after went to Boston.

I had tried to be a vegetarian over and over, but didn't know what to eat until I found the devotees. I wrote Prabhupada a nice letter asking to be initiated, and in February 1970 I got a beautiful initiation letter back. I love the name Prabhupada gave me – it's a name for Radharani. *Man* means "mind" and *mohini* means "attractor of."

In his letter to me, Prabhupada wrote, "My dear daughter Manmohini, Please accept my blessings. I am in due receipt of your nice letter dated 18th February 1970 along with your beads for chanting and a pair of lovely flower garlands. Thank you very much. I have immediately offered the flower garlands to Radha and Krishna, and they are so nice looking. I am very happy to accept you as my disciple, and I am glad to know that you are praying to Lord Krishna only that you may always remember that your position eternally is to serve and take shelter of His transcendental lotus feet. So I am returning your beads duly chanted by me, and your spiritual name is Manmohini dasi. Manmohini is another name of Radharani, and

Manmohini dasi is the maidservant of Radharani. Now please chant Hare Krishna mantra and be sublimely happy. You know that as my initiated disciple you must chant regularly sixteen rounds of beads daily and follow the four restrictions, namely no eating of meat, fish or eggs, no illicit sex life, no taking of any kinds of intoxications and no gambling or mental speculation. If you stick to these principles and chant the holy name, avoiding the ten offenses in the matter of chanting, you will become steady and rapidly advanced in Krishna consciousness. I am very pleased to note that you are nicely engaged in preparing bhoga at the Boston temple and you are also going on *sankirtana*. Please study very carefully all our books and learn our philosophy with the help of our many experienced students there in Boston, and remain happy in Krishna consciousness under the care and guidance of Sriman Satsvarupa and Sriman Brahmananda as you are their younger sister. I am enclosing herewith one sheet listing the 26 qualifications of a devotee, the 10 offenses to be avoided in chanting the mahamantra, and standard practices for initiated devotees. Hope this will meet you in good health. Your ever well wisher, A.C. Bhaktivedanta Swami"

I was ecstatic to receive this letter. It melted my heart to know somebody so exalted, somebody directly in the *parampara,* cared so much about us fallen condition souls. Prabhupada risked his life to save us. He has such love and compassion and kindness and mercy and patience and tolerance and forbearance. I'm grateful and honored to be linked up with this Movement, and my meager lifetime is not enough for me to repay the debt I owe Srila Prabhupada.

I got married when I was twenty and had one daughter soon after. After I was married, I called my mother to tell her and she said, "Really? What's his name?" I said, "Hold on, I'll ask him," because I didn't know my husband's legal name. My mother said, "You're nuts," and hung the phone up, which she had done before. I thought, "She's got a point." But when I thought about all Prabhupada went through for us, what he did for us, and how he gave us the perfect diet, the perfect philosophy, the perfect lifestyle, I would gladly marry a guy I didn't know and dance in the street wearing sheets, and much more.

My husband and I opened some temples and then he stopped following the principles and left me, left the Movement, and soon after passed away. Srila Prabhupada was in New Dwarka at the time, and I went to Prabhupada's quarters with my brother, Swarupa, who was also a devotee, to see Prabhupada.

Before we entered the room, I heard Prabhupada say, "So, you wish to remarry?" I said, "Not right away, Srila Prabhupada. I just wanted to know if I was prohibited." Prabhupada said, "Prohibited? I will not prohibit. But you are asking my opinion?" I said, "Yes, Srila Prabhupada." He said, "Don't do it." By this time we were sitting down. It was Swarupa, Prabhupada's servant Srutakirti, and me in the room. I was terrified and didn't look at Prabhupada. Prabhupada said, "What is your guarantee your next husband will be different from the first one?" He explained how in Kali-yuga men have no training in *dharma* and women have no training in chastity. I already had one child and I should give all my love to this child. There was no reason for remarriage. At some point Swarupa said, "Srila Prabhupada my sister feels she needs to remarry for protection." Prabhupada's eyes got big, he looked at me and said, "You are not protected?" He looked at Swarupa and said, "You are not protected?" He looked at Srutakirti and said, "You are not protected? Just see, there is no faith." He explained that in relation to Krishna we are all *prakriti,* that Krishna is the only one who can protect all of us, that a husband cannot protect a wife from disease or accidents, old age, death, nothing. Krishna is the only protector, and in relation to Krishna we are all *prakriti.*

This was lofty. We were still new devotees and, as Prabhupada always does, he gave us the absolute truth. At one point I looked up and Prabhupada was beautiful. The sun was shining on him, he was bronze and golden, and was coming from ages and ages past and sounded like the Supersoul speaking. I felt fallen and my heart was beating fast. I was quiet and listened. At one point he said, "Can any man give you a written guarantee?" I shook my head, "No." He said, "Why gamble?" As we were leaving, he spoke directly to me and with so much compassion and love said, "Read my books. I have written so many books. All day long I read, I write, I chant, I take bath. You do like this." I said, "Yes, Srila Prabhupada." Later, Prabhupada saw me wearing white and approved, and I lived to please Prabhupada.

When Prabhupada was at New Dwarka, it was so thrilling I couldn't sleep. I'd stay up at night and make him little presents. Once I made a jar of *rasagullas*. Another time I made a little *tulasi manjari* garland for his Deities. I'd wrap the present in white tissue paper and put ribbons around it tied in a bow that was easy to open and have someone put it on the *vyasasana* next to Srila Prabhupada. At some point Prabhupada would see the gift, open the ribbons, peek inside, and usually be pleased. There were always ways to have ecstatic loving exchanges. When Prabhupada was at the temple it was almost like Watseka wasn't part of the planet anymore.

One morning around ten, I was with two *gurukula* students when I saw Srila Prabhupada walking toward us with devotees on either side of him. Prabhupada came right before us, pointed to one of the students, and said to me, "He's not wearing neck beads. You can take care of this?" I said, "Yes, Srila Prabhupada." Before I could finish that sentence, they were gone.

This was during the book-printing marathon and there was a lot going on. Yet Prabhupada noticed that one of the *gurukula* children didn't have neck beads. It made me realize that every aspect of Krishna consciousness is equally important. After that I became a neck bead fanatic and always made sure all the children had neck beads.

I owe Srila Prabhupada so much. What else is there in life but to try and please him?

Manoharini devi dasi

When she was fifteen, Manoharini's brother gave her a Bhagavad-gita As It Is *and invited her to the temple for the Sunday Feast.*

I became a vegetarian because I figured it would help me understand Prabhupada's books. On a TV dinner table in my home, I made an altar with a big picture of Krishna with a cow. I didn't know about offering food, so I'd cook something, put it in a little container, put it on the altar, and then eat at the same time.

I had one foot in and one out until I had a traumatic experience. A guy in a park went crazy and tried to kill me. He was banging my head and I thought, "I don't know how I can get out of this situation," and the only persons I could think of to pray to were Prabhupada and Krishna. I said, "Prabhupada, I know I'm not pure enough to go back to Godhead, but could you please let me take birth as a devotee in my next life? Then maybe I can get it right." After that the right things came to me to say to get out of that situation. I heard myself telling the guy, "You'd better stop. My brother and my friends know I'm with you. You're going to leave me alone." And he did. I was a mess, with makeup running down my face, tears, scattered hair. I went home, called the temple and said, "I want to move in," because I felt I'd been given a second chance.

I stopped all drug taking and felt safe and happy in the temple. The devotees loved it when I cleaned the bathroom because I scrubbed and scrubbed. I said, "Prabhupada said cleanliness is next to godliness, and I'm scrubbing these tiles as clean as I can." I distributed Prabhupada's books in the Chicago airport, got initiated when I was nineteen, and not long after got married.

When Prabhupada was sick, devotees in all the temples had twenty-four-hour kirtan. My time was early in the morning just before the Deities were woken up. I'd go to the quiet temple room, get the songbook, sit in front of the *vyasasana*, and chant to Prabhupada for an hour with little *kartalas*. It was the most peaceful time of my life. I felt close to him.

Even now I have a small altar at home with Jagannatha Deities, Prabhupada, and the disciplic succession. Every morning I make a little offering and pray to Prabhupada: "Whatever is your will, just show me," and he reciprocates.

Mantrini devi dasi

Mantrini was initiated in Chicago in July 1973. Tamohara (then Tom) and Mantrini first met the devotees in 1972 at a rock festival in Stevens Point, Wisconsin.

We saw a group of men dressed in orange chanting together and assumed that they were Buddhist monks. They came around to the crowd later distributing incense and *Back to Godhead*s. After reading about the American temples in the BTG, and having met some traveling *sankirtana* devotees in our home town, we decided we wanted to visit a temple. I had the quaint notion that you had to be "invited" to visit a temple, so I dutifully wrote to all the temples in the U.S. asking permission to visit. There were only a handful at the time, and the only one that responded was the Seattle temple. We were living in Illinois at the time, so we hopped in our van and drove all the way to Washington State.

After talking at length with the Seattle temple president, Sukhadeva Prabhu, we decided to move in then and there. He cautioned us, however, that there was no "facility" for married couples in the Seattle temple. We had a four-year-old daughter at the time, and he advised us instead to go to the New Vrindavan farm temple in West Virginia, where "all the householder couples" lived. He also told us to get *japa* beads and directed us to the local Tandys store where we bought huge brown wooden beads and painstakingly strung them on yellow cord. We began chanting on beads at that point. Taking his advice about visiting New Vrindavan, we turned around and drove 2,000 miles back to West Virginia! This was a stroke of luck.

After our long trip from Seattle, we arrived in New Vrindavan at dusk. Unbeknownst to us, Srila Prabhupada happened to be visiting New Vrindavan at the time and had just reinstalled Sri Sri Radha-Vrindavanachandra in Bahulavana, an old farmhouse on the property, the day before. As we entered the temple we heard the devotees excitedly whispering, "He's coming, he's coming!" and we became hopeful that they were referring to "the Hare Krishna guru" we had read about. Sure enough, Srila Prabhupada indeed was coming, and to our amazement, he settled himself on the *vyasasana* in the back of the temple room and played the *kartalas* during the entire night *arati* ceremony.

I remember that the temple room was all dark except for the brightly lit altar with all the beautiful Deities shining forth. Srila Prabhupada was chanting intently and had his eyes closed most of the time, but every once in a while he would open his eyes and look at the Deities. It was astonishing, but from his eyes it looked like there were two headlights of light beaming towards the altar. Then he would close his eyes and the light would be gone. This happened again and again throughout the *arati*! It was entirely a mystical experience, so much so that I felt as though we must be with the most important person in the universe at that moment. He was so important that if all the world around us dropped away except for that small plot of land, we would be safe as long as we were with him! He was indeed the spiritual master we had been searching for. I also had the strong feeling that the entire cosmos was represented in that room that night. As we joined the devotees swaying back and forth, chanting and dancing the "swami step," it felt like we were all walking, imperceptibly advancing, towards the perfect goal. We were moving toward the spiritual world with God and His consorts shining forth ahead of us! And there was Srila Prabhupada – the teacher, the guide – powerfully steering us from behind. It was a spiritual "window experience" where the curtain lifts, and you are allowed to see the truth.

After *arati,* Srila Prabhupada gave *Bhagavad-gita* class, of which, unfortunately, I cannot remember a word, but I do remember that a girl chanted the Sanskrit verse, and Srila Prabhupada remarked what a nice voice she had.

From that few hours in the presence of the pure devotee, Srila Prabhupada, along with his instructions in his books, we were both convinced that he was indeed our spiritual master! Although New Vrindavan in 1972 was too austere for our little family, we vowed to join the temple in Chicago. A few days later we drove back to Illinois, and two months later we joined the Evanston Temple.

A postscript to this story is that a few years ago, we were watching one of Yadubara Prabhu's videos of Srila Prabhupada and realized that we were watching a movie of that very night so long ago in the Bahulavana temple room! The camera panned around the room, and we caught sight of our long-haired, hippie selves, as well as many other devotees we now know and love. The camera, however, was not able to capture Srila Prabhupada's "lighted vision" nor the marvelous image of our collective journey back to Godhead with Srila Prabhupada at the helm! We gratefully realized that Krishna had given us spiritual vision that night that was way beyond the scope of a movie camera lens.

Mayapriya devi dasi

As early as twelve years old, lacking the answers to life's deepest questions weighed heavily on Mayapriya's mind. In ninth grade her favorite teacher introduced her to existentialism, which only deepened her sense of the futility of this world. In high school she asked her father to take her to a different church every Sunday to see if any of the various faiths had answers. Nothing helped, so when she went off to college, she immersed herself in the anti-war movement and the counterculture.

After college my boyfriend, Jon, and I moved to South Florida to live with friends. We were all seekers, already tired of the material world at twenty, and together we read every book on yoga and Eastern religion we could find. Nothing really resonated with us, and I remember wondering how one could expect to find a guru in Florida!

One day a co-worker had a *BTG* sitting on his car seat and I asked him if he wanted it. He gave it to me. Jon and I read it cover to cover, and when we acquired Srila Prabhupada's *Bhagavad-gita As It Is*, we felt we had found our teacher. His *Gita* answered all the existential questions that had plagued us and kept us from pursuing material life with the gusto others our age seemed to exhibit.

Jon and I packed up our pickup truck and moved to Cape Cod, where his family owned several houses, so that we could visit the Boston temple. Jon's older brother, Jeff, also read the *Gita* and the three of us would drive to the Boston temple each week to attend the Sunday program. When we walked in, we felt as though we had come home. As weeks passed, we became more committed, chanting sixteen rounds a day and reading what books were available (circa 1973). By Spring 1974, Jon and I got married, and Jeff, Jon, and I decided to move to New Vrindavan because it fit our natures better than the city. Srila Prabhupada accepted us in the winter of 1974, but our formal initiation was on Gaura Purnima, 1975, in New Vrindavan. We received the names Amitacara dasa (Jon), Maharudra dasa (Jeff), and Mayapriya devi dasi.

From the time in 1972 when I received that *BTG* to today, Srila Prabhupada has been my guiding force and, frankly, the most important person in my life. But, sadly, I never was able to have his personal association.

New Vrindavan was very austere, very strict, and there was also a hierarchy of devotees. I was young and a newer devotee. I taught at our little school; I was just a simple servant. One day a paper appeared on the bulletin board that said that the first twelve devotees to sign the paper would get to go to Philadelphia where Srila Prabhupada was going to visit. No one had signed up yet! I looked at that paper and wanted so much to sign it – if I could find a pencil (not an easy thing in NV). As I looked at it, I couldn't help thinking, "Who am I? There are so many devotees who have been serving here longer than me, they should get to go before me. Who will take over my service at the school? And, being a woman, they will probably cross my name off anyway." So I did not sign it, I was sort of afraid to.

I missed my opportunity, and I have regretted it my whole life. I was so young and naive, and I didn't have the confidence, nor did my humble husband, to just strike off, leave our service, and go to wherever Srila Prabhupada was visiting. We had been trained that it was more important to do your service to Srila Prabhupada than to abandon it to see him.

"Never think that I am absent from you. Physical presence is not essential; presence by message (or hearing) is real touch. Lord Krishna is present by His message which was delivered 5,000 years ago. We feel always the presence of our past Acharyas simply by their immutable instructions. I hope you will understand me right and do the needful." (Srila Prabhupada, letter to "My dear Students," August 2, 1967)

But in spite of that misfortune, there hasn't been a day that I do not feel the great good fortune of being one of Srila Prabhupada's daughters, and I feel closer to him with each passing year. We are linked to him eternally, so eventually we will be reunited with him.

We became close friends with Brahmananda dasa, who stayed with us many times and told such wonderful stories. We felt close to Srila Prabhupada through him and others. By reading Srila Prabhupada's books, his conversations, and lectures, and seeing all the videos and photos and, most of all, continually trying to actively serve him, I have always felt very close to him.

After leaving New Vrindavan, we helped establish a center in North Carolina. After 10 years there, we started a center here in Charlottesville, VA, where, for the last twenty-eight years, our main focus has been preaching to students at the University of Virginia. When we hear young people chanting for the first time, we feel close to Srila Prabhupada.

By teaching these new young people, Srila Prabhupada has blessed us with enthusiasm for Krishna consciousness, which is ever fresh and the only real welfare work. Before each program I pray to Srila Prabhupada to be able to nicely represent him and the philosophy. And when I return to my altar after the program, I thank him for using us as his instruments. More than a dozen initiated devotees have come from these programs, and all are Prabhupadanugas, who love Srila Prabhupada as their spiritual grandfather. Hundreds more learned about Krishna, chanted, and honored prasadam—beginning their spiritual journey.

Knowing books are so important to Srila Prabhupada, and being a book designer by trade, we were grateful to design most of the books published by his Archives, and many of Srila Prabhupada's books published by the BBTI. In addition, we have been thankful to be able to work on books by our esteemed godbrothers and sisters. In so doing, we hope we have somehow pleased Srila Prabhupada.

But as the years have passed, and my love and devotion to Srila Prabhupada has reached deeper into my heart, separation from him has become less and less bearable. I pray to someday see him face to face. I hope he remembers me as one of his daughters, who didn't give up, or walk away, but stayed to teach Krishna consciousness to the next generation of innocent souls. I pray that I have somehow pleased him, even while serving my entire life in separation.

Medhya devi dasi

Medhya dasi was born in Montreal to a Catholic family. She prayed to Jesus Christ to guide her. Shortly after, in secondary school, a friend did a project on the Hare Krishnas. Accompanying her friend, they went to the temple with tape recorders and cameras to interview devotees in 1972.

My first impression was amazing. I kept looking around. Everything was just so far out. Devotees were happily cutting vegetables. I liked cooking, so I looked at this round sweet that was being passed around. I thought, "It's not a cake, . . . " That was my first *prasadam: gulabjamon*. It was wonderful.

I worked very hard on the school project and started going to the temple on a regular basis. When I told one of my teachers he said, "Why don't you come to my class and talk about it?" I said yes right away, which surprised me, because I'm very shy. But I was so enthusiastic about Krishna consciousness.

In the summer I got a job working six days a week. I started to visit the temple during the week and really wanted to join, but I was hesitating. I decided to spend a weekend at the temple. It was wonderful. I was sure I wanted to join, but I just couldn't make myself take the step. I was studying to be a nurse and working to pay rent. Three months later, I joined the temple on Park Avenue.

It was an old bowling alley. Inside it was divided by something almost like cardboard. You could put a knife through the "wall" and it didn't even reach up to the ceiling. The *brahmacharis* were on one side, the *brahmacharinis* on the other. The temple room was the other side of the *brahmacharini ashram*. So we could hear the *pujari* put the Deities to sleep and wake Them up in the morning. It was the best time in my Krishna consciousness, because we were like a big family.

I couldn't speak or understand English at that time, and there were no

French books, so that was difficult for me. There was only one French *Easy Journey to Other Planets* and one French *Back to Godhead*. I was trying to read the English *Bhagavad-gita*. It took me about three hours to read one page because I had to look in the dictionary for all the words. But that was the best way to learn, I guess. I learned English. All the classes were in English, most of the devotees spoke English.

We used to pay obeisances when the conchshell blew at the beginning and end of each *arati*. Wherever you were, even if you were not in the temple room, whatever you were doing, like sewing for the Deities, everybody paid their obeisances. If Krishna's plate passed by, we would pay obeisances. I think we were more on the floor than anything else!

I was very shy and reserved, and in those days when you joined you were on the street doing *sankirtana* the next day. So before joining, I used to take a few *Back to Godhead*s home and I used to practice alone on the street where there was nobody. Then I'd see one person and I'd try to go to them. Of course, *sankirtana* in those days was the main activity. You had to go out even if it was just for one hour. Everybody had to go out to distribute Prabhupada's books.

I got my first initiation when Srila Prabhupada came to Montreal temple in 1975. We had just got the temple which was an old church. So when Prabhupada came, there was actually a lot still that needed to be done. And, of course, we didn't sleep for a few nights before Prabhupada's arrival, painting and sewing.

The devotees went to pick up Srila Prabhupada from the airport and I stayed back to do service. Then I heard a kirtan outside, so I knew Prabhupada was right there. It was more or less like a Charlie Chaplin movie: everybody started to frantically finish up what they were doing. Sivarama Maharaja was fixing up Prabhupada's *vyasasana* in the temple room. I finished what I was doing, and quickly opened the door just as Srila Prabhupada was coming up the stairs. I didn't have anywhere to go so I was face-to-face with Srila Prabhupada. I just moved to the side a little bit.

After that, Srila Prabhupada gave a little class and then everybody went to sleep. But I had to cook the next offering, so I went back in the kitchen. I made some date *pakoras* and Prabhupada asked for more. So I made some more but I was very, very tired. Then Prabhupada gave another talk in the afternoon outside, in a little garden on the side. So that was wonderful.

I got *brahmana* in 1976 when Srila Prabhupada came to Toronto. We only stayed for one day, one night. Srila Prabhupada gave a lecture. But I couldn't understand English very much and, of course, Prabhupada's English is even harder to understand.

Srila Prabhupada gave us so much. I'm very grateful that I joined and stayed in the temple. In those days the training was very, very intense and it was like some kind of tidal wave. You just sort of get enthused by everybody's enthusiasm and it just builds up and builds up and builds up, and then you get very fired up.

One devotee had joined three months earlier than I did, so for me she was an older devotee. She would give me instructions and I followed the instructions. There was a lot of training, and *sadhana* that was very strict. We had *mangala-arati* and chanting your rounds in the morning. That was very, very helpful in my own spiritual life. Srila Prabhupada gave certain basic instructions for a reason.

It's very hard to see what has been done, what is being done now. There have been lots of mistakes and there's still mismanagement. People taking advantage of position and power. We've all seen a lot of that. Many of us have been hurt, but the thing is that I learned from it. Every negative situation I can think of gave me something positive.

Mekhala devi dasi

Mekhala was in a miserable state when she first heard Upendra–who was caring, lively, and joyful–talk nonstop about his funny and personal exchanges with Srila Prabhupada.

I decided to join the St. Kilda temple in Melbourne and in 1972 Prabhupada gave me first and second initiation because he was installing Radha-Krishna Deities and needed a team of *pujaris*. When I went into Prabhupada's room to get second initiation I had a strong feeling of belonging to him that I'd never felt with anyone else. I also felt he was my best friend. Reflecting back, receiving Gayatri mantra from Srila Prabhupada was the most important thing that ever happened to me. Prabhupada took my hand and showed me how to chant and I said, "Srila Prabhupada, what does it all mean?" His eyes had such depth as he looked deep into my eyes and said, "You will see." The mantras given by a pure, bona fide spiritual master give us direct transcendental knowledge of who we are – an eternal, loving, blissful servant of Radha and Krishna.

I was touched by the personal exchange Prabhupada had with my dear godsister Chitralekha, whose affection helped me in my early days. Prabhupada captured everyone's heart by his love and always gave me the strength and courage to keep chanting and following. He's my well-wisher and I depend on him for guidance and feel protected, maintained, and nourished by him in all areas of my life.

Prabhupada says that after the spiritual master leaves, his instructions are the pride of the disciple. By absorbing our mind and heart in Srila

Prabhupada's instructions and by developing our faith and surrender, we'll get the guaranteed result of Krishna consciousness: happiness.

Actually Vaishnavas don't die. Srila Prabhupada is above this material existence and I, a soul, am also above this material existence. By following Prabhupada's instructions – chanting sixteen rounds every day and following the four regulative principles – we can cry out to him and he'll be there to help us. Srila Prabhupada planted a seed deep within me that's gradually fructifying. Feeling the power of his presence in my life, I'm eternally indebted to him.

Misrani devi dasi

In 1980, when she was thirty and had been initiated for seven years, Misrani's parents had a Christian woman from Minneapolis "deprogram" her.

During the first part of the six-week ordeal I'd wake up in the mornings and want to be with the devotees, but by the end of the day I was okay with where I was. Then I'd dream about the devotees at night and in the morning again want to be with them. Finally material illusion swallowed me. Yet over the years I always kept a place in my heart for Krishna and Srila Prabhupada. I married someone who's supposedly a Christian, but part of me tried to teach my children about Krishna. Finally I decided it was time to get serious and by the mercy of Srila Prabhupada and Krishna I'm again chanting Hare Krishna.

I joined Krishna consciousness because I was tired of everything material and in need of Krishna's mercy, which came through Srila Prabhupada. After I was deprogrammed I felt angry, "Krishna, why did this happen to me?" but remembering Prabhupada helped me. Prabhupada's mercifully watching over me, there for me when I need him, and someone I turn to. Now I feel my relationship with Krishna and Srila Prabhupada is natural and comfortable.

Material illusion can be overwhelming. Even devotees can be caught up in *maya* and attachments that are hard to give up, and they can have difficulty seeing things clearly. But once we've associated with Krishna, Srila Prabhupada, and other devotees, they're always available for us. No matter what the test, the mercy of Krishna is like an ocean and Srila Prabhupada's grace can pull us to that ocean. Chanting the *maha-mantra* is always available and will give us relief from the anxieties and distresses that come from our material attachments. No matter how low we fall, chanting and the mercy of guru and Krishna are the real safety net. Tests are not a big deal; they're just part of life.

I'm only around devotees a little on the Internet, but throughout my day I try to become more Krishna conscious and bring Krishna into my life more and more. It's fun. Mondays, for instance, I wear red because the Deities wear red on Mondays. And every time I see a bumblebee I think of Radharani scolding the bumblebee.

We should never give up or let material things keep us from Krishna because they can't. Once you've learned the *maha-mantra*, you're a sucker for Krishna. And that's a nice thing.

Mohanasini devi dasi

In 1971, when she met Vishnujana Maharaja chanting in front of a little picture of cowherd-boy Krishna, Mohanasini was twenty-four, had been married twice, and had three children.

I was brought up a Baptist and always felt I needed to serve God every day, not just on Sundays. But I was falling short. I was smashing my head against a brick wall at every turn and was so miserable I didn't know whether to commit myself or kill myself. I also thought, "Maybe I need to be a missionary."

When I met Vishnujana Maharaja, I saw that he was serving God every day and thought, "I don't know who this little blue boy in the picture is, but I've never seen anyone like Maharaja, who has so much love in his eyes. There's got to be something to this." Within a week I moved into the Dallas temple.

When I received second initiation from Srila Prabhupada in Los Angeles in 1973, I didn't know much about Krishna consciousness. I only knew I wanted to be a devotee and I wanted to know what my name meant. I thought, "When I go to Srila Prabhupada's room to receive my Gayatri, I'm going to ask him what it means." I went to his room, offered my obeisances and when I popped up Prabhupada said, "What's your name?" I said, "Mohanasini Dasi, Srila Prabhupada." He said, "Oh, that's a very nice name. *Mo* means 'illusion' and *hanasini* means 'destroyer of.' " I didn't have to ask him.

Once I wanted to take a photo of Prabhupada as he came down the stairs from his room to go for a walk. I got in position, thinking, "I've got to be quick!" As Prabhupada came down the stairs, he stood still to pose for me. I was thinking, "Oh, my God!" I thought he was going to whisk by, but he regally stood on the stairs waiting to let me take a photo. That was awesome.

Another time Prabhupada chastised me. I wanted a good seat to see him give class, so I climbed beyond the balcony railing and sat on the ledge. He sat on the *vyasasana*, looked up and said, "Get down!" I was devastated.

I cried for a half a day. Then somebody said, "You don't need to cry. Even the spiritual master's chastisement is mercy." I was consoled, "Oh, okay, I got some mercy from Srila Prabhupada today."

Once, as Prabhupada passed by, I handed him an apple and my hand brushed his. I cannot describe how soft his hand was. I haven't felt anything like it in my life; softer than silk, than velvet. My daughter, Navadwipa, told me that when she was five and in the Dallas *gurukula,* she wasn't feeling well one day and was crying, and Prabhupada picked her up and patted her to comfort her. Navadwipa also said his hands were incredibly smooth and soft and cool.

When Srila Prabhupada was with us, the norm was that we all did whatever he said. There weren't factions; everybody served Prabhupada. It was a special nectar time that I feel fortunate to have experienced and that can't be replaced by anything. And that time we had with Srila Prabhupada seems much more special now than it did then. But watching videos of him gives a sense of him, as does reading his books and associating with the devotees who have carefully followed his instructions. Those devotees have, to one degree or another, been instrumental in keeping me in the Movement. Since they were following and becoming Krishna conscious, I felt more secure that I was rightfully situated.

When I was young, it was hard for me to realize that this material world isn't where it's at. Now I feel more focused on trying to be a devotee, because what's left for me is old age, disease, and death. In other words, not much. Even though I've fallen into lots of potholes of problems along the way, I know Krishna consciousness is the place to be. I keep trying, and hope I'll get serious before my body is finished. If I have to take another birth, at least in this life I'm rightfully situated and trying to make progress.

My passionate, immature years are finished and I've found a service that I'm happy with and that keeps me inspired. That service is book distribution. I used to be shy and couldn't approach people, but I finally got over that and now that I'm good at book distribution, it's a lifesaver. It's kind of sense gratification for me–it takes me off the material platform, it makes me feel good, I enjoy it. I know I'm doing the right thing, and I feel that Srila Prabhupada is happy. And book distribution makes me realize that I have a lot of things to work on, especially humility. I'm among the top book distributors in the world and I find I'm so proud of myself!

Anyway, in the end I just want to be a devotee. Even if I'm not a very good devotee, I know it's the right thing for me to do.

Moksalaksmi devi dasi

With a dream job with kids that she loved, an apartment, a serious relationship, and business interests in the local hippie shop, Moksalaksmi was in no hurry to drop everything for life with the Hare Krishnas in their blissful but austere Bury Place temple. Visits were enough for her.

Since meeting the devotees in 1969, donating to the cause, and hosting them in my centrally located apartment throughout the early 1970's as they sold their books in the towns of central England, Krishna stepped in and I found myself surrendering everything. It was never my plan, but, hey, I'm not complaining. I have had an amazing life. The best part of the adventure started when I traveled to India in January 1975. Arriving in Delhi, luggage lost, I walked into the warm evening, saw the cows huddling, and immediately fell in love. I knew I was home.

Journeying to Bombay led to the first time Srila Prabhupada spoke to me. I had been cleaning his rooms in his old quarters, mistimed my exit, and met His Divine Grace on the stairway as I hurriedly jumped into a neighbor's doorway. Seeing me he stopped, "So you are chanting Hare Krishna?" he questioned.

"Yes, Srila Prabhupada," I replied. "*Jaya*," he called out and proceeded up the stairs.

Years later it occurred to me that what was important to Srila Prabhupada was that we are indeed chanting Hare Krishna. Everything else is secondary.

During this time I started a small school for street children. These children were very poor with many holes in their ragged clothes. We used to have great kirtans with the children. On one occasion Prabhupada heard the kirtan and inquired who was chanting. Thus he learned about our little school. Benevolently he asked to see the children and invited them to his room. It was such a special treat for the children whom we cleaned and dressed up in new clothes for the occasion. The children drew pictures of Krishna and they presented them to him. Srila Prabhupada looked graciously, even commenting.

On reflection of this delightful pastime, it always astounds me how Prabhupada, with his incredibly busy schedule filled with the rich and important people of Bombay and immersed in building a temple there, had time for the little people of the world. There is no doubt that Srila Prabhupada saw only the soul within the body, not the outer dress, intending Krishna consciousness for everyone.

During my time in Bombay, I received *brahmana* initiation directly from Prabhupada. I had collected some *guru dakshina* and spent some of it on gifts, which I had wrapped in hot pink coloured tissue paper. It was quite a balancing act carrying all of the items into his room and I kind of tipped them all onto his desk. It was as if Prabhupada turned into a young boy opening presents on his birthday. I actually felt motherly towards him, which was strange as I was young enough to be his granddaughter! He inquired about the ones he didn't open; it was a unique few moments of my life. Then just as abruptly as it started, the mood reverted back to one of master and student as Prabhupada taught me how to chant the Gayatri mantra. Years later, it struck me how perfectly Srila Prabhupada lived his teachings. In one lecture, I had heard him say how men should see all women except their wife as mother. Surely I had experienced Srila Prabhupada exhibiting this.

I was lucky enough to travel to Ahmedabad and be a part of the *pandal* program that took place before Jasomatinandana and my dear friend Radha-kunda moved there to start collecting for the construction of a temple. There I saw Prabhupada at his charming best. In an initial program at a life member's house in front of, I am sure, the crème de la crème of Ahmedabad's elite, I saw the marvel of Prabhupada's preaching. He captivated the Gujarati gathering when he told them that Gujarati and Bengali were special births. Krishna's father was a Gujarati, he stated to the smiling and laughing audience.

After his immediate success, Prabhupada asked Jasomatinandana to complete the lecture. Now, one could argue that it was because Jasomatinandana was Gujarati and spoke the language, but I would contend that Srila Prabhupada was all about empowering devotees to do outstanding things. He wanted his devotees to seize the day and push on Krishna consciousness to the best of their ability. He was not one to micromanage, but of course that does not mean he did not correct.

One time he returned to India from Mauritius with a horrifying story. We were all crammed into his room when he told us of a terrible car incident. He had been driving in a car when another car rammed into them. Just previous to the crash, he had put his walking stick in such a position that the weight of his body was braced by it. This had lessened the impact of the collision on his body but he was still hurt, and he rolled up his cloth and showed us his swollen, red knee. He further explained that Krishna had saved him with his walking stick. That was a sad and sobering exchange with my beloved Prabhupada.

Bombay was a wonderful part of my life filled with the arrivals and departures of Prabhupada, which he called his office. The airport was nearby so we would all bundle into taxis to greet or say our farewells to Prabhupada. If he was leaving we would remain until even the plumes of smoke emitting from the airplane had disappeared, remembering how the *gopis* waited until the dust had settled when Akrura took Krishna out of Vrindavan.

Eventually, I was sent to Vrindavan, where amongst other services, I once again got to clean Prabhupada's house. It was a fantastic service. After *mangala-arati* I would slip into Prabhupada's house through his back garden, close any doors that needed closing to separate myself from him, and start cleaning. My dear friend Srutirupa had told me how Srila Prabhupada was not happy with the oil stains on the marble bathroom floor. Determined to restore it to its former glory, I would daily squat down, roll my *sari* around my knees, and scrub away with a hard brush and scouring powder. The floor was beginning to shine. Usually at this point in the morning Srila Prabhupada would be on his morning walk and I was free to clean away. So it was with great surprise that one morning the bathroom door began to open as I was scrubbing away, *sari* around my knees, and a very familiar face popped around a crack in the door.

"May I come in?" he asked as a perfect gentleman. "Of course, come in Srila Prabhupada, come in," spluttered a shocked young girl covered in scouring powder.

The thing that always struck me was how when I left the bathroom and entered the black stone floor of the bedroom I made white scouring powder footprints but Prabhupada, who also would have had to walk over the powder, left none.

Living in Vrindavan in the latter part of 1977 was a rollercoaster of emotions as Prabhupada's health declined. Daily we sought out reports on what Srila Prabhupada had eaten. There was a communal feeling of relief when a juicer was brought from America. Surely now Prabhupada would get the nourishment his body so dearly needed.

Nothing really prepared me for the night he left for London. It was around midnight when he departed. The whole temple was out in the road to wave him off. As fate would have it Prabhupada's car unexpectedly stopped in such a position that I was looking down at him and he was looking up at me, our eyes locked. I hadn't seen Prabhupada for a while and was shocked at how skinny he was, skin and bones really, as he lay on top of some Guesthouse mattresses. This is when I realised how determined a character was our Srila Prabhupada. Nothing could stand in the way of him and his preaching mission.

November 14, 1977 is cemented in my brain forever. Watching Prabhupada leave his body is a forever sobering occurrence. To balance it out, I like to remember when Prabhupada danced through the streets of London at the 1973 Ratha-yatra. I was distributing those special Ratha-yatra magazines to the crowd, when all of a sudden the hairs on my body just stood on end. I turned around and there was Prabhupada a meter away, arms upraised dancing away. Now that's a sight to remember.

Mondakini devi dasi

Mondakini joined ISKCON with her two friends from high school, who later became Jyotirmayi and Ilavati. Mondakini and Jyotirmayi were studying ethnology at La Sorbonne in Paris. They were interested in the conception of God in different civilizations and trying to find out the goal of life. Disappointed with material life, they wanted a spiritual master and were ready for anything.

We met devotees, who looked like pure angels, and were impressed with the *maha-mantra*. The devotees told us, "Our spiritual master is in London. Why don't you go and meet him?" Ilavati was working and couldn't come, but Jyotirmayi and I somehow managed to get to Bury Place.

It was a powerfully spiritual place. The temple was beautifully done and had a mystical atmosphere. We were polite young girls, so when, during kirtan, the devotees all bowed down, we did too. I picked up my head a little and saw two golden feet nearby. I looked up and there was Srila Prabhupada, and I had an absolutely unusual, wonderful feeling. Prabhupada went and sat on the *vyasasana* and led a beautiful, meditative kirtan. When I caught his glance for the first time, tears fell from my eyes, although I didn't understand why. They were not tears of sorrow or of mundane joy; I had a true feeling that this person knew me better than I knew myself, that he could see inside me to who I really was. I felt a sense of eternity beyond my body, and I felt that Prabhupada and I had known each other for a long time. His strength and purity struck me. He looked humble and merciful, but at the same time, he appeared to be the emperor of the universe.

I loved the devotees more and more, but because I was so contaminated by Mayavadi books I had a big problem with the philosophy. Even though Prabhupada answered every single doubt and question we had–even those we hadn't asked–in a clear, convincing, logical, and mystical way, every day Jyotirmayi and I would ask each other, "Do you think Srila Prabhupada is our real spiritual master?" And we'd answer, "We have to wait a little more to know for sure."

One day, after a Sunday lecture, an Indian guest said, "God has no form! Krishna is not God." Prabhupada became red with anger and began to scream at him, "You rascal!" Jyotirmayi and I thought, "The spiritual master is not supposed to get angry." I was crushed and thought, "He's not my spiritual master. He doesn't control his anger. We have to leave. We cannot go on with this just because of affection. I cannot take a wrong path; I'm looking for the truth." We were getting ready to leave when somebody told us, "Srila Prabhupada wants to see you." We went into his room and he asked me, "Do you know how to type?" I didn't at the time. Prabhupada wanted to engage us, and he completely captured my heart with the simple feeling of his presence, love, and care.

I stayed, and our wonderful Yamuna taught me the basics of devotional life in a creative, personal way with enthusiasm. The temple was pure happiness. We were with wonderful, bright, creative devotees. We were never bored, and service was a pleasure, never a burden. We didn't sleep much, and every minute was an inner and outer adventure. Trivikrama Swami, then a *brahmachari*, took us on *sankirtana* in Piccadilly Circus and on Soho Street. He was like a big brother to us. Minute-by-minute, my love for Srila Prabhupada grew and my link with him became more and more established. I felt that every second should be for the joy and the service of the Deities. They were the center of our lives and we felt protected by Them too.

A week went by and Srila Prabhupada was to leave for America. Even before he left, I felt intense separation from him. In his presence, I felt the reality of Krishna and of Krishna consciousness and of the fact I am not this body. Prabhupada opened our hearts. And he opened a window to the spiritual world. At the airport, everybody was crying, and when he finally went off in his aristocratic way, I was convinced that he was my spiritual master.

That strong feeling of separation came again later. He was on the point of leaving us after one month at Bhaktivedanta Manor. I had a strong feeling of loss–that I wouldn't be able to live without his physical presence. He was bringing us directly to the spiritual world, convincing us more and more. Life without him seemed unbearable; it seemed impossible to carry on without his physical presence. But after some time, I realized that I had to resume my service, and by doing so I would be with him. Then by Krishna's grace, I was able to tolerate his physical absence and to feel his presence through devotional service.

We used to send Srila Prabhupada little things like *lugdlus* and scarves that we'd made for his Deities. He would always acknowledge and reciprocate, and that increased the love between Srila Prabhupada and us. It was a competition of love. As we became more and more attached to him, we were also becoming more attached to the lotus feet of Krishna. Once Prabhupada came in the temple wearing a little scarf I'd made and given him the day before. The scarf was too small and looked funny, but he accepted my simple, imperfect offering with love. Prabhupada was expert at increasing the loving exchanges between his devotees and himself, and in strengthening our spiritual link and loving affection.

Srila Prabhupada used to joke with me sometimes: "Oh, Mondakini, you are not married yet?" At this time I didn't want to get married. He laughed, "You didn't find anybody good enough for you? Don't worry, Krishna will send you somebody good enough."

By hearing Srila Prabhupada's lectures and reading his books, I developed a desire to preach. Once I heard that you can progress in spiritual life when the spiritual master asks you to perform a difficult task and when you immediately say yes to him. I prayed, "My dear Sri Sri Radha-Londonisvara, please have Srila Prabhupada ask me something difficult and please remind me to say yes straight away."

Then I heard that Srila Prabhupada was in Russia with Shyamsundara Prabhu. I thought of Prabhupada's bravery. Russia was such a strange and terrible place. I myself would never want to go there. When he returned from Russia, Srila Prabhupada looked at me with a big smile and said, "Mondakini?"

"Yes, Srila Prabhupada?"

His tone was so casual and familiar, like he was going to send me across the street to buy potatoes. He said, "Would you like to go to Russia and to marry this boy Anatoly to help to spread Krishna consciousness?" I quickly remembered my prayer and said, "Yes, Srila Prabhupada!" His smile became huge, and he turned to Shyamasundar, "*Ah,* good. Shyamasundar, you arrange."

That was the beginning of my wonderful adventure in Russia for Srila Prabhupada. I was twenty. Russia was a special blessing. For many years I took it as my heart's service. Prabhupada was always asking me for news and was very thankful that I was going there. He always encouraged us, and was happy with whatever little progress we made. That was the time of the Iron Curtain, and the KGB would follow us around. Preaching there was dangerous. But the Russian people were eager to hear about Krishna and take *prasadam*. I met Russians who were ready to lose their freedom, maybe their lives, in order to gain spiritual knowledge. Any book we managed to bring into the country would be read overnight and passed on to someone else. It was very exciting–absolutely extraordinary. Somehow or other I got legally married to Anatoly, who became Ananta Shanti, and who did wonderful things.

Once at Bury Place, we were sitting at Srila Prabhupada's feet for *Srimad-Bhagavatam* class, when he asked the devotees to recite the Sanskrit verse. When my turn came I felt shy. I was frightened to recite Sanskrit in front of everybody. Srila Prabhupada had this big laugh and said, "Just see, she's not frightened to go to Russia, but she's frightened to speak a Sanskrit verse."

When Srila Prabhupada left this world, I felt separation without union, and that was extremely painful. I was alone. It took me time to find him again in the mood of union in separation through service, through trying to follow his instructions, and through the association of his gemlike family of devotees in all its generations.

Mukhya devi dasi

In 1973 Mukhya was a student at the University of Michigan living with friends in a house in Ann Arbor. One of them had met Srila Prabhupada in New Vrindavan, so when she had to visit three religious places for a World Religions course, he insisted she visit the Hare Krishna temple in Detroit.

It was an other-worldly experience, the smells, the colors, the food! I took home a *Bhagavad-gita As It Is* and sat on my front porch to check it out. I couldn't put the book down and by the time I'd finished the second chapter I knew this is what I wanted to be studying. My boyfriend and I continued visiting the temple, developed friendships with the devotees, and after a road trip cross country where we saw Srila Prabhupada in the San Francisco temple during their Ratha-yatra, moved back to Detroit and into the temple full time. Srila Prabhupada visited the Jefferson Avenue temple the next year. I stood on the second floor window ledge and showered flowers down on him. He was such a giant in my mind and heart but of small stature in reality. Seeing him surrounded by big burly American boys on all sides, the flower petals floating all over them, it was such a transcendental scene.

I had so many adventures during my years in Detroit, my life was full of excitement. I never felt there was anything I couldn't do in service to Krishna and I was always encouraged to do what I wanted to. When we purchased the Fisher Mansion Srila Prabhupada told us to make it a showplace for Krishna, and over the years we were able to do that. My boyfriend-turned-husband traveled all over India for several years buying beautiful artwork to spiritualize the architectural masterpiece that is Devasadhan Mandir. The devotees cleverly created Auto Baron Tours bringing busloads of people to tour our mansion along with the estates of other famous car barons. They learned about Krishna consciousness through the FATE exhibits, the artwork, and the *prasadam* in our Govinda's restaurant.

On one visit Srila Prabhupada was sitting out back on the lawn leaning against a beautiful striped pillow (it's one of the classic BBT photos of His Divine Grace now), looking out at the Detroit River, and he said, "This is one of the most beautiful spots in the world." There were only a few devotees sitting there at the time. I thought, "Yes, wherever Srila Prabhupada is is the most beautiful spot in the world."

I have understood so much more about Srila Prabhupada in the years since his passing, through the recorded memories of his disciples, and the personal realizations I have through continuing to serve him. The relationship has grown deeper and sweeter and continues to do so. I am filled with gratitude to him for giving us the path back to Krishna, and pray that I may always stay on it.

Munipatni devi dasi

Munipatni traveled on a sankirtana party from the day she joined the Los Angeles temple in October, 1975. She was still on that party six months later, when she received a letter from Srila Prabhupada in which he accepted her as his disciple.

As a teenager I had heard of the Hare Krishnas and once, off the top of my head, I told my parents that if they didn't leave me alone I was going to join the Hare Krishnas. But I didn't know anything about them or about Srila Prabhupada. After I graduated high school I was working my way into the corporate realm in downtown Chicago when one day I saw small posters on trees and telephone poles all over the city that said, "Come for a free vegetarian feast," with a picture of Prabhupada and some of his disciples.

I was already interested in vegetarianism and had been asking my mom about it from a young age. When she was cooking our Thanksgiving dinner, for instance, I asked her, "What's this?" And she told me the meat of the turkey was like the muscles in our body. I said, "So does it hurt the turkeys when they're cut up?" I don't remember her answer, but that question sat deep in my mind for a long time. I decided, "When I grow up and I get out of my house, I'm going to be a vegetarian," and the devotees' vegetarian feast posters solidified that.

Once in downtown Chicago I saw three devotees on the other side of the street doing *harinama* kirtan. They weren't wearing *kurtas* and *dhotis*, but bed sheet-like material. I was looking at that from afar and somehow they were eerily familiar. I thought, "Wow, that's so interesting." The clang of the *kartalas* drew my attention and I thought, "These guys must have something going on to look like that." Then someone said, "Would you like to give a donation and read our *Bhagavad-gita*?" I said, "Sure, but I only have three dollars." He said, "Okay, I'll take that," and he gave me the book and some incense. I went back to my office with the feeling that I'd found something valuable. I loved the pages and the look of the book. I loved the look of Prabhupada in the book. He was clean and elegant. The other authors I'd seen had long hair and a crazy smile on their face. Prabhupada looked serious and sincere. That's what impressed me. He looked like a holy man. I was used to Roman Catholic priests and their drinking and their woman hunting, but Prabhupada didn't look anything like that. Back in my office I thought, "All these people can play all their office flirtation games, but I've got this book and I've got this incense." I was happy even though when I tried to read the *Gita* I couldn't understand one word. But I kept it on my mantelpiece at home.

I started to decorate my room with madrases and a popular poster print of Sri Nathji. I thought about spiritual life and when my friends and I were sitting in the back of our garden staring up at the cosmos, I used to tell them, "You know, I bet you there's more people out there. How can we be the only persons? In this whole universe, we're the only ones?" They would think, "Oh, that's her, she's just thinking like a whack again." But, I thought, "They don't know anything. I think that there must be something out there."

So these revelations would strike me from time to time, and I started to pick up books in head shops by yogis that were at the forefront of yogi-ism. I'd read a few pages and quickly put them down and say, "Well, this isn't it." I'd pick up spiritual newspapers and head magazines just looking, looking, looking, looking for the right source of information, and I couldn't find it.

After a few of my friends died from drug overdoses, I thought, "I'm not going to end up like that. I want to go to California where you can even be a Hare Krishna if you want and no one's going to say anything about it." On that inspiration I went to a Catholic church. It was empty, which I was glad of, and I prayed hard, "Whoever You are, I need Your help now. Just guide me to put one foot in front of another so I can go where I need to go." And that night I hitchhiked from Chicago all the way to Los Angeles. Of course, you can't do that anymore – and probably couldn't do it then. I don't know why but I wasn't afraid. I didn't have any money, yet the trip was smooth. Everybody was helpful, giving money and food, and I wound up on the corner of Bagley and Watseka. For a week I stayed with a friend who lived in an apartment on Bagley. When we went by the Hare Krishna temple, which was just around the corner, I'd loudly yell out, "Hare Krishna." I was happy and making fun and having a good time. My friends in the car would say, "What does that mean?" and I'd answer, "I don't know, but I like it."

One day, after I'd been in Los Angeles for a week I ventured into the Hare Krishna community. Pranada was there and she said, "Oh, we have a Sunday Feast going on. Would you like to join us?" She brought me in and showed me the Deities, Rukmini and Dwarakadisha. I looked at Them and loved what I saw. I'll never forget Pranada for bringing me in, for giving me some Sunday Feast *halava*. I ran back to my friends with the *halava* and told them, "Look what I've got! This is so great, it tastes so nice, the smells – everything was just beautiful in there – you guys have got to come!" They criticized it and I thought, "These people don't know." At that moment I cut myself off from my friends because I thought, "If they can't appreciate this, then what am I doing with them?"

The next day I went to the temple and asked, "Do I have to read *Bhagavad-gita* before I can become a devotee? I can't read that book but I want to be a devotee." The devotees said, "No, no, don't worry, you can be a devotee anyway. We'll teach you how to read the book. Gather your things and meet us here tomorrow morning." I said, "Absolutely."

I didn't say anything to my friends. I got all my things together, went back to the temple and met Hasyapriya. He said, "Do you like to travel?" I said, "Yes." He said, "Would you like to go on traveling *sankirtana*?" I said, "Yes, I love to travel." I didn't know what *sankirtana* was. The next day Yudhamanyu scooped me up, and off I went for two years on the road. It was difficult. We went to bed at ten and got up at two every day. We were out all day in winters and summers. And I didn't know one thing about Krishna consciousness. After that traveling *sankirtana* party was over, I went to the airport and distributed big books every day.

This whole time I never saw Srila Prabhupada, I only listened to his lectures during our morning programs. In the beginning, I didn't think too much about him because I was trying to absorb all the things that one has to absorb on *sankirtana*. But eventually I understood that Prabhupada held something valuable and I wanted to know what it was. It was clear that I was now in Prabhupada's realm, and I needed to be patient. Determination took over. I thought, "I'm going to do whatever it takes to join this group." I had been a rebellious teenager so to become a surrendered devotee I had to make a complete turn around. But when the devotees initially accepted me, from way deep inside – so deep that I don't even know where it came from – I knew I was doing the right thing. Although I didn't know anything about Prabhupada, his drawing power was pulling me in.

Even though at first I couldn't understand his words, I felt the potency of his lectures. I listened and slowly understood him and got to know him. Finally, when I became more knowledgeable about Srila Prabhupada I was respectful and grateful, "Thank you so much." Prabhupada did everything with such care. His preaching and the way he spoke from *Bhagavatam* was so direct – no nonsense – but sweet and kind and charming and witty at the same time.

So slowly I became more attached to Srila Prabhupada, and that attachment protected me throughout my life with almost every major thing a person can go through – marriage, children, chanting rounds, sticking with it. When I was young I got so many opportunities to do something else but I always thought, "What would Prabhupada want me to do?" And on that basis I stayed true to him. I listened when he spoke, I prayed to Krishna and to Srila Prabhupada, and my life improved. I wouldn't stick to this process of Krishna consciousness for anybody else, not even for myself. I stuck to it because Srila Prabhupada asked me to. Krishna has His plan and we have to tolerate what He puts our way. We rely on His grace whether He lifts our suffering or lets us suffer for a while. It all works out. When I struggle against His plan, following my mind's dictations and ignoring Prabhupada's compassionate instructions on how to pass through the tides of material nature, I am fooling myself knowingly. So I try to be a little obedient – just a little. And somehow, along with the passing years, as I chanted Hare Krishna and followed the principles and read his books, I got a real sense that I need and want to do what he asks of me. There's no question. So even to this day – now even more intensely – when I see Srila Prabhupada or pray to him, he gives me hope, and so much to look forward to.

Srila Prabhupada has qualities like nobody else. As he said, "Purity is the force." He gave us the shelter of the holy name. His books clearly answered all the questions I had about who I am, where I'm going, why I have this body, why I have to die. His books made me a different person and his presence on this planet changed my life from unfortunate to fortunate.

If you actually think about Prabhupada's contribution, your heart melts. I pray to Srila Prabhupada that I can remember him at the end of my life and be with him always. And I would like to find more fortunate persons who can receive his blessings through his books. There is nothing like meeting wandering persons, joining-up with them spiritually even for a few moments, have them walk away knowing a little more of who they truly are, and being confident that you've given them knowledge from the correct source. My hope is that future generations will respect and admire and love Srila Prabhupada for the way he's drawing us to Krishna and teaching us to depend on Krishna's mercy.

If we stay conscious of Krishna the way Prabhupada kindly taught us to, if we stay pure and simple and thoughtful, our lives will change. We'll be blessed and feel deeply thankful to Srila Prabhupada. Our Movement will thrive – and pivot – on purity. If we struggle for purity and we try sincerely and genuinely to serve Srila Prabhupada, there's no limit to what we can do for him. In his Movement there's no place for impersonalism, but only for trying to follow his teachings. And if we follow we'll get Srila Prabhupada's mercy, we'll understand him, and eventually we'll be with him and with Krishna.

Murti devi dasi

In 1975 in Sao Paulo, Brazil, devotees invited Murti to the Hare Krishna temple where they introduced her to Srila Prabhupada's books. Deeply touched by what she read, Murti felt she had to be in Prabhupada's Movement.

When I was small, my mother used to say, "OK, you have to clean the whole house, and when you're finished the prize will be that you can go to church." I always wanted to go to church to pray but the priests there used to beg people for donations. I'd wonder, "Why don't they give Jesus' bread to the people, why don't they serve the people?" When I read Srila Prabhupada's books and heard about devotees and the principles they follow, that knowledge went deep inside me and I wanted to practice those principles and do devotional service. In the temple, when I saw devotees making garlands, when I smelled the incense, and when I tasted *maha-prasadam*, I thought, "This is my home, I have to stay here." Still, although I heard talks about Prabhupada, it took me a long time to develop a relationship with him.

Now I realize I have a big debt to Srila Prabhupada; he changed my life. I always associate with him in thanks, in gratitude. He taught me that we are not these bodies. We're not women, we're not men, we're not anything material but we are servants of Krishna.

Although most devotees are pious and saintly people, in my thirty years in ISKCON I've had problems with exploitative leaders. They've given me many reasons to leave this Movement but I stayed because I feel faithful and thankful to Srila Prabhupada. Now, thanks to Krishna and Srila Prabhupada, perhaps another generation is coming of more humane leaders, and our generation – the first generation – is advancing in Krishna conscious kindness and humility.

Nabaswati devi dasi

As a child Nabaswati always felt like an outsider in her family. Somehow she never fit in and didn't want to live in her home with her parents. All the time she prayed to find her real home. Srila Prabhupada, like a father, gave her everything she had been lacking: spiritual knowledge, wonderful friends, children, and a husband. Prabhupada and the devotees saved her.

At sixteen, I'd lived in the Bury Place temple for three months, and was disturbed by the friction between the devotees. My sister was studying in London and I started thinking, "I'll go live with my sister now." When Srila Prabhupada arrived and came out of his car, I stood and looked at him. I come from a Muslim background, studied the Koran, and believed in holy men. Srila Prabhupada was a holy man; he had a glow behind him. I bowed down and he touched my head. I looked up at him and cried, thinking, "I've found what I was looking for. That's it. I'm not going anywhere." I had no idea what I was looking for except that I wanted to be happy. I knew there was more than the Koran and what my family was doing and telling me. I used to pray to Allah, "Please get me out of here. Please, there's got to be more," but I didn't know what it was. When I saw Srila Prabhupada I felt, "I've come home," and that feeling has always stayed with me despite everything.

The next day I was sitting outside Prabhupada's room and he said to me, "So where are you from?" and asked about my family. When I told him I came from a Muslim background, his eyes widened and he said, "You come from Muslim background?" Later he told the temple president, "Take care of her."

Sometime later, as I was going into Srila Prabhupada's room to receive Gayatri, Malati Prabhu gave me some yellow roses, saying, "Prabhupada likes them, take them to him." I was nervous and scared to be with Prabhupada but he made me feel comfortable. He said, "Come and sit down." I offered my obeisances but kept holding the flowers. He said, "Are those for me?" I said, "Oh, yes." Prabhupada showed me the finger movements but I got muddled. "No, no," he said, "Not like that," and showed me again. Then he asked, "How are your parents?" I said, "I don't see them much." He said, "But how are they? You must be respectful to them." I said, "Yeah, but they have nothing to do with me." I was so full of zeal I felt I needed to save my parents so I had given them a *Bhagavad-gita*. Srila Prabhupada said, "No. If they're actually following the Koran, they'll make spiritual advancement and be saved." Then he said, "So are you happy?" I said, "Prabhupada, I'm very happy." He said, "If you remain in Krishna consciousness, you will be very happy." Since I was a young girl my whole goal in life was to be happy. Prabhupada knew.

Sometimes he'd notice me and say, "How was it today on *sankirtana*?" I'd say, "Oh, I had a nice day." I would run to give him his shoes. He'd always stop, take them, and look at me. It was personal. I felt he was my father, that he loved me, and he was giving me everything. Prabhupada cared about all of us and made us feel important, that we were somebody, that with whatever little service we did we were helping him.

Despite my frailties and weaknesses, Prabhupada and my godsisters have always been there for me. Magically, Prabhupada has given us everything. I can never repay him and his disciples. I so much needed to be loved, and Prabhupada was the only person I met in my life who never let me down. Whatever he said was to help us progress, become better people, and get out of this world. And he did it with genuine love. He wanted nothing back from us.

Nagapatni devi dasi

Nagapatni saw something special about the devotees who came to the Mystic Arts Store in Laguna Beach where she worked. One of them said to her, "You've got to go to the temple. You'll really like the food." Sometime later she went.

At the feast devotees talked to me about Prabhupada. I thought, "I don't know about surrendering to this one leader." Then I started reading his *Bhagavad-gita*. That was my first experience of Prabhupada. I'd been searching for something that made sense and answered all my questions. I'd read flowery-worded books by impersonalists that sounded cool but made no sense. My father taught theology at Loyola Marymount College and had a lot of philosophical ideas but never had answers to my questions. When I read Srila Prabhupada's books they made so much sense. They had all the answers to all the questions I'd been swimming around in for years about where we are, who we are, where we want to go, where we're coming from. Prabhupada's books went right to my heart, opened it, and let Krishna sneak in. And I loved his analogies.

I joined the Laguna temple in 1969 and every Monday night we all used to go to L.A. to see Prabhupada there. Once Durlab, our temple president, brought me a saffron-colored *sari*, but I had no idea how to put it on. I wrapped it around and around like a mummy. I was hobbling because I couldn't walk and Prabhupada called Sudama's little sister, and said, "Teach her how to put on a *sari* and *tilaka*." That was sweet.

In February 1970 I moved to the Watseka Avenue temple in L.A. Every morning after his walk, all of us would give Prabhupada a flower and he'd give us a flower back. Sometimes he'd touch us – the women as well as the men – on our head and every morning we'd pray, "Please, Prabhupada, touch me on my head." Prabhupada didn't discriminate in any way. At that time, men were on one side of the temple and women on the other. It was divided equally; I never felt sexism.

Once Prabhupada walked around the L.A. temple and asked devotees, "How many rounds have you chanted?" Some devotees said four, some said six, some said eight. Prabhupada said, "Why not sixteen?" Bhakta dasa said, "There's so much service we have to do for you, Prabhupada." Prabhupada said, "You must always chant sixteen rounds," and he called all the devotees and gave a lecture on the importance of chanting sixteen rounds a day.

Prabhupada was simple and personable. I became interested in Deity worship from seeing how much appreciation he had for the way Silavati cared for the Deities. I felt more love from Srila Prabhupada than anyone else and I knew that it was true love, real love. Anything else I ever thought was love was not the same. How do you explain the amount of love he gave everyone? How do you put words to that? I knew that by following him I would truly be happy.

I felt Prabhupada has always protected me and taken care of me, maybe not the way I wanted at the time or what I thought was the best. But because I'm getting older, I can reflect back how things have worked out for the better. I've learned to accept my situation, to surrender. I try to right wrongs but am more concerned about righting my own *anarthas*. I'm happy to read Srila Prabhupada's books and to try to do some service for him.

Nanda devi dasi

Nanda was the head pujari and head cook when Prabhupada came to the Mexico City temple in February 1975. Prabhupada's presence in her life was large and commanding and when she saw him get out of the car in front of the temple, she was shocked at how small he was.

As Prabhupada sat on the *vyasasana* singing the "Jaya Radha Madhava" prayers, he glanced over the packed audience and it was like the sun gradually peeking out as a cloud moves across it. His glance looked casual but I felt its warmth. For the split second his glance caught my eye, time stopped, and he looked deep into my soul. He looked so far into the sojourn I'd taken away from Krishna that I immediately felt a long-forgotten connection with Srila Prabhupada. On him seeing me and me seeing him, tears burst up, and poured down my face. It was mystical. Nothing like that had ever happened to me before and never did again.

One evening Sita and I went to Srila Prabhupada's darshan when Prabhupada was talking with two priests who were representatives of the Cardinal of Mexico. Prabhupada explained the four regulative principles to them and said, "Meat-eating is very bad. You should stop meat-eating. And you should stop bull fighting. Bull fighting is sinful." The priests got fidgety and said, "Thank you very much for your time, it's late now, we have to go." They left and as soon as the door clicked shut Prabhupada chuckled and said, "These are not true Christians. As soon as I said they had to stop meat-eating they left. Jesus Christ couldn't save his followers because his followers were so degraded." Sita asked, "Why couldn't Jesus Christ save his followers if he was a pure devotee?" Prabhupada said, "These people were very degraded. They were low-class people, so he couldn't save them." I said, "If Jesus Christ was a pure devotee, how come he couldn't save his followers?" Prabhupada leaned forward, looked at me, tilted his head, opened his eyes wide, lifted up his eyebrows, and said, "If somebody is a murderer, he's not a very good man, is he?" I said, "No, Srila Prabhupada." Prabhupada said, "These were murderers, they were low-class men." Rohini Kumar said, "*Jaya!* All glories to you, Srila Prabhupada! You are so great that even though we were so degraded, you saved us!" Prabhupada said, "No, no. I am not so great. It is this Hare Krishna mantra that's great." Srutakirti said, "*Jaya! Jaya!* All glories to you, Srila Prabhupada! You are so great that you brought us this Hare Krishna mantra and therefore we are saved!" I was at the corner of Prabhupada's desk, and it appeared that his cheeks got red. He got embarrassed to hear that glorification. He turned his head to the side and said, "Oh, that may be so, but it is this Hare Krishna mantra that is great." It was sweet.

Hanuman had been a *sannyasi* but had married and caused a disturbance. He said, "Srila Prabhupada, you say that we accept Jesus Christ as our guru. Does that mean we should put a picture of Christ on our altar?" Prabhupada said, "I have not told you this. Do not do this." Hanuman said, "Prabhupada, I want to know if you've rejected me like Lord Chaitanya rejected Junior Haridas." I thought, "Now Prabhupada's going to tell him what a nonsense he is." But Prabhupada answered, "No, I have not rejected you. Lord Chaitanya was God, and He could spread this Movement around the world without any help. But I am not God. I am totally dependent on the assistance you have given me. No, I have not rejected you." I was shocked at Prabhupada's compassion and mercy. How low and degraded my attitude was and how pure and exalted Srila Prabhupada's was. Hanuman said, "Prabhupada, we've named our baby Bhaktivedanta." I expected Prabhupada to say something nice but Prabhupada said, "No, you cannot name your child Bhaktivedanta. That's the name of your guru. Sometimes you'll have to chastise your child. 'Bhaktivedanta, don't do this.' You can't do that." Hanuman said, "We'll call him Bhaktivedanta dasa." Prabhupada said, "Then it is okay."

Srutakirti said, "Prabhupada, the evening *arati* started. You have to get ready to give class." We were about leave when Prabhupada held his hand up, "Just a little *Bhagavatam*." While looking straight ahead he casually reached over with his right hand, took a *Bhagavatam* from his bookshelf, put it on his desk, opened it, and said, "You see, it says right here." It was the Third Canto, Fourth Part, where Devahuti speaks about how someone who has chanted Hare Krishna is glorious even if they have taken birth in a low family, a family of meat-eaters. If they've chanted Hare Krishna, they're eligible to perform Vedic sacrifices. Prabhupada said, "You must follow the four regulative principles, chant your rounds every day, and read these books every day." He said, "There are so many Christians, but they don't follow the instructions of Jesus Christ. Don't become like the Christians. You must follow." Then he said, "Even I read my books every day." It was beautiful.

Nandalal devi dasi

Nandalal dasi was initiated in 1970 in Los Angeles. Srila Prabhupada had chanted on her beads and sent them to her.

When Prabhupada was chanting with us in kirtan, it was almost like there was a river of nectar flowing down the rows between the male and female devotees. It was almost like a river of nectar. It's just indescribable how wonderful the kirtans were when Srila Prabhupada was present on the *vyasasana* and chanting.

Prabhupada had taught Silavati how to cook for the Deities. When you tasted *prasadam,* you could almost see the spiritual sky.

I was the only one present in Prabhupada's room when I went up to get my Gayatri. He showed me how to count on my fingers and he chanted the Gayatri mantras. After paying obeisance as I got ready to leave, he said, "Hare Krishna!" That evening in the *brahmacharini ashram,* suddenly a whole cloud of depression lifted off me. It had been so much a part of me actually that I wasn't even aware that I had it. I could feel it going and I was thinking, "Oh, my gosh! Oh, my gosh!" I prayed, "Oh, please, oh, please, don't ever let it come back again!" Then the next day it started to come back, and I thought, "Oh, no! Oh, no! " But suddenly it lifted off again, and it never ever came back. So I really feel that that was Srila Prabhupada's mercy in giving me Gayatri and saying, "Hare Krishna!" It was so purifying that whatever terrible karmas that I had surrounding me lifted off. It was extremely wonderful. It was very vivid.

I was always trying to finagle myself into Srila Prabhupada's room, and I could never get there. Finally I had thought up a question that I thought would be very impressive and it would get me into Prabhupada's room. So I managed to get into Prabhupada's room. I was asking the question, and suddenly Prabhupada said, "Here, you take this Deity with you." He was pointing. There was a small, three-inch high silver Deity of Krishna playing His flute standing on his desk. So I very hesitantly lifted up the Deity.

He said, "So, you take this Deity with you everywhere you go, and you can worship Him anywhere, even under a tree. And when you get somewhere permanent, you can set Him up and worship Him and offer *prasadam* and put some cloth." In fact, that Deity slept with us in the *brahmacharini* room in Los Angeles for a time because I took the Deity everywhere with me. There were times when I was in Vrindavan or Govardhana that I carried the Deity around my neck in a small cloth bag. I was worried that the dacoits might try to take Him away from me because He was silver.

I noticed there was a small tiny hole in the Deity. So I wrote Prabhupada about what I should do. He said, "Simply put some wax in the hole. Plug up the hole with some wax and go on worshiping." Very simple.

Prabhupada was at the entrance to the temple. I think he was going into the temple. He had been somewhere, and I was out on the grounds in Hawaii. When he came, I fell on the ground in an obeisance. I think this was the best obeisance I ever gave in my entire life. I just gave it with all the humility, which I don't have but which I could summon up, all my love for Srila Prabhupada, all my gratitude for everything about him, and all that he had done for us. I put that into that obeisance. Later Srila Prabhupada's servant came out and told me that Prabhupada had commented that just sitting peacefully and chanting was real Krishna consciousness. His servant came down to tell me that, and I know it was directly connected to that obeisance that I paid him.

I was in Vrindavan just before Prabhupada left. Tamal Krishna asked me to clean Srila Prabhupada's quarters. I was thrilled that I was going to get to go into Srila Prabhupada's quarters and clean. I was right near Prabhupada's doors into his rooms, and I heard two devotees talking. They were saying that Srila Prabhupada only had a few more hours left in his body. I noticed then that a lot of the senior devotees and the *sannyasis* were starting to gather in Srila Prabhupada's room, and they were chanting in kirtan.

I went in and stood in the kirtan. We were all chanting and I was the only lady in there. Then I began to notice that all the lady devotees were outside. On the other side of Prabhupada's bed, there was a bank of windows. I was facing Prabhupada's bed looking out through that window, and I noticed all the ladies were gathered outside looking through the windows and chanting out there. About that time, I started to get looks from the men in the room. I noticed they were looking at me out of the corner of their eyes like "*Hmm*, what's she doing in here?" Then somebody was motioning to me, "Come out." I continued chanting and looking at Prabhupada, and they finally gave up. It was clear that they didn't feel comfortable dragging me out of the room or even coming to me and saying, "Mataji, you have to leave the room." So I just continued to stand there, and very shortly after that the ladies outside could see me in the room. I think what they were thinking was, "What is Nandalal doing in there?" So they started to come in, and gradually the room filled up. And as it filled up, it was full of both the ladies and the male devotees, and we all got to be there when Prabhupada left.

I went to Govardhana and I lived there for many years, but I never ever approached any *sadhus* over there because I knew that Prabhupada didn't want us to do that. All that time I really felt that whatever we needed for our spiritual advancement was already there, we just didn't realize it yet, and that when we needed it, it would all be there and that we didn't have to go anywhere else for it. I saw so many devotees going off to other places. It upsets me in my heart because I don't feel like I needed anything else. I chanted my rounds, I read Srila Prabhupada's books, and I just didn't feel any need for anything else.

I did *dandavat parikrama* of Govardhana hill in the 1980s before any other devotees did it, and I was told that I was in *maya*. But I had experiences based on that *dandavat parikrama*, deep spiritual experiences, which confirmed that I don't have to go to anyone else.

I had a small cloth bag which had my extra *sari* in it. I didn't have money, food, any place to stay, a sleeping bag, nothing. But people feed me, gave me a place to stay, showed me where to bathe. I had a dream that I saw Srimati Radharani standing in the cows' pasturing grounds between Aniyor village and Govinda-kunda. She was standing in a lotus flower, and all the living entities in existence were worshiping her so that She could render service to Krishna. The breezes were blowing very sweetly and gently and cooling. The herbs were approaching Her, the different plants that were herbs to be offered, flowers with different fragrances, and forms of beauty and color, all the animals, and all the humans–everything was offering itself so that She could offer to Krishna. This is one of the reasons why I know that we don't require anyone else except Srila Prabhupada. Prabhupada has told us everything. And when we're ready to have the experiences that teach us about the higher aspects of Krishna consciousness, those things will come.

Nandarani devi dasi

In early 1967, Nandarani was eighteen years old. She'd come to San Francisco from L.A. with her boyfriend to check out the hippie scene. There she ran into a friend on the street, who took her to the temple where she had prasadam and in the evening met Prabhupada. From that time, she served Prabhupada's ISKCON for twenty-two years.

The year she turned nineteen she met Prabhupada, helped him cook for her wedding ceremony, opened what later become ISKCON's World Headquarters, and had the first of her three children. Nandarani was one of ISKCON's empowered pioneers.

In early February 1967, she ran into a friend in San Francisco who took her to the Hare Krishna temple. She loved the meal of *prasadam* they gave her, so she brought her boyfriend back that evening. She enjoyed the kirtan, but more than that, she liked the lecture given by the interesting old man from India, Swamiji.

A month later she took initiation from Swamiji, and then in two weeks he married her and her husband, with their families sitting on the floor, listening to the swami chant strange mantras while he poured ghee into a fire that filled the storefront temple with smoke.

For two consecutive days before the wedding, she and the other women had helped Swamiji cook the large feast that she'd financed with a month's salary from her job at the phone company. Swamiji observed her at that time as well as in the coming months as she attended classes and did services in the temple.

In mid-1967, Swamiji wrote her husband, Dayananda, from New York, noting that his wife was very intelligent. He continued: "It is the Grace of

Lord Krishna that He has put me in contact with so many rare souls who are taking Krishna Consciousness in all seriousness, and I am confident that in the future all my student boys and girls will preach this Krishna Consciousness in the western world more successfully."

In August, she, her husband, and Aniruddha traveled from San Francisco to Los Angeles and opened a storefront temple there. A month later, they received a letter from Swamiji, who was in India. He wrote: "I had great desire to have our center in L.A. & by grace of Krishna you have fulfilled my desire."

Then, in November, Swamiji identified her as one of the seven leaders of his fledgling Movement in a letter to Brahmananda: "I wish that you will remain in charge of New York, let Satsvarupa be in charge of Boston, let Mukunda be in charge of San Francisco, let Janardana be in charge of Montreal. Let Nandarani and Dayananda be in charge of Los Angeles. And let Subala das be in charge of Santa Fe."

In February 1968, Swamiji visited his five-month-old temple in L.A. for the first time. During a lecture he quoted a verse by Sarvabhauma Bhattacharya and asked if the devotees knew who he was.

Nandarani said, "He was a great impersonalist who was converted by Lord Chaitanya to Vaishnavism."

Swamiji said, "Yes," and to the other devotees, "Nandarani knows better than you." They laughed, and he continued, "So girls are intelligent."

It was clear that Prabhupada appreciated the work that she was doing in L.A. In April of that year, he wrote to her and her husband: "Nandarani is very intelligent girl, both of you execute nicely and try to bring up your daughter in the same spirit, and live nicely in Krishna Consciousness."

In anticipation of his next visit to L.A., he wrote her a long letter in which he said he appreciated that she was arranging lectures for him. "I am very much pleased with your preaching enthusiasm when you say, 'If people won't come to us here, we will go to them.' And this is the process of preaching, and this is required. I thank you very much for your spirit." He concluded by saying, "I am very glad that you are so inquisitive and trying to understand things in proper perspective. So, I am always at your service, and you are welcome to write and inquire from me at any time."

Than after arriving in L.A., during a lecture, Prabhupada commented on *vatsalya* (parental) *rasa*: "Just like this girl, Nandarani, is raising her daughter, always giving service. The child is accepting service from the parents. Her business is only to accept. Torture and accept service. So, devotees accept Krishna as son so that Krishna may simply torture them and accept service."

The next year, devotees moved to a larger temple, an old church. By this time the Movement had developed so much that Prabhupada was receiving many letters, so he decided to ask Nandarani for help in answering some of the more routine ones. He gave her a letter that asked about the real meaning of Omkara. She wrote, "It is explained clearly in the twenty-first chapter of the *Teachings of Lord Chaitanya*..." Then she gave a detailed explanation.

Prabhupada checked her response and wrote her back a short note: "The answers are all right and you directly write him."

The Movement expanded at a whirlwind speed. She continued to be an important part of it for two more years in L.A., sometimes as Prabhupada's driver, other times cooking for him, and always doing service in the temple. Then she and Dayananda went to London.

From there, she wrote and expressed her desire to be fully surrendered, and he replied: "I am so much obliged to you for your nice sentiments. Krishna will bless you." And in another letter, "I am very much pleased that you are fully engaged in attending Sri Sri Radha and Krishna in London temple and that you are finding great satisfaction by pleasing always Their Lordships." [...] "I am always remembering with pleasure you and your good husband Dayananda, and how you have been with me practically since the first ..."

Her next stop was the *gurukula* in Dallas, and Prabhupada wrote: "I have seen this special Ratha-yatra issue of 'Back to Godhead' written by you, and I am so much pleased that so intelligently you have assorted the matter to completely understand our philosophy in a nutshell. I know that you are very intelligent and educated girl, so fully kindly utilize it for developing the Dallas institution for the benefit of all the children."

After Dallas, she and her husband went to Iran, and Prabhupada wrote her: "Try to publish Persian books as many as possible. That will be a big success. Iranians have very much respect especially for the Americans, and your dealings with them will be very much appreciated."

Later that year, Prabhupada came to Iran. He gave no formal lectures, but his disciples brought interested Iranians to meet with him.

In one conversation, Prabhupada began to speak about the form of God. He said that if Muslims pray, then Allah must hear. "What do they pray?" Nandarani answered, "For glorification of God." Prabhupada said, "Glorification means something about God, His activities, characteristics. What do they say?"

"God is great." "God is great, but how He is great?" She said, "That is not emphasized, how He is great, just that He is great."

"Then there is the proof of less intelligence. God is great, very good. But how He is great? What is the conception of greatness?" [...] "So, if I do not know about God, if I do not know who is God, then where is the question of love?"

On a business trip to New York, Atreya Rsi, who was in charge of the preaching in Iran, met with Prabhupada. During the conversation, Atreya explained that all the devotees were working at regular jobs so that they could stay in the country and maintain the center there. Prabhupada inquired, "And so Nandarani is also working?" Atreya said that she was teaching.

Prabhupada said, "She has got experience."

"Yes, she's very good."

"Both of them are very intelligent," said Prabhupada. "And Nandarani is more intelligent than her husband." He laughed. "I know that." Atreya, who was quite fond of Dayananda, said, "I find that *he* is very intelligent, Srila Prabhupada."

"*Ah*, Dayananda."

"Yes."

"He is intelligent," said Prabhupada, "but Nandarani is still more intelligent." Again, he laughed. "I know that. Both of them are intelligent, but this girl appears to be more intelligent. That's all right."

Nandi devi dasi

Nandi was a new bhaktin when she first saw Srila Prabhupada in the airport in Atlanta, Georgia.

When Srila Prabhupada arrived we were with a huge crowd of devotees and an incredible kirtan was going on. When you see Prabhupada, in one sense he is unremarkable in that he has a small stature and an unassuming attitude. So my first impression was, "This is Srila Prabhupada?" I didn't know what to expect, but even though I clearly had something else in mind I was thrilled to see Srila Prabhupada. I offered my obeisances and we streamed out of the airport with the sound vibrations bouncing off the walls.

In the Atlanta temple Srila Prabhupada sat on the *vyasasana* and began to cry when he saw the Gaura-Nitai Deities. I was new and had never heard about spiritual ecstasies, but I heard the crack in Prabhupada's voice when he tried to speak and was overcome with emotion. I thought, "This is my spiritual master and I'm witnessing an intimate part of his life, of his relationship with Krishna." I knew it was special – and the big brass Deities. Oh! They were truly beautiful, with Their large arms and peacocks embroidered and embellished on Their outfits. I had always been attracted to Deity worship, so for me to see Deities dressed so beautifully was a real treat.

The devotees in Atlanta brought many guests to the Sunday Feast and after Prabhupada's lecture someone in the audience said, "Srila Guru, I would like the name of the tenth *avatara* of Krishna." He was trying to test Srila Prabhupada by asking this arcane piece of knowledge. I was shocked that someone was so brazen, but I also wondered what Prabhupada would say. There was a little pause and Prabhupada began to describe the tenth incarnation of Vishnu, the village that He appeared in, and who his parents were. In time I understood how merciful Srila Prabhupada was to answer a question from someone who was needling him and trying to expose some flaw. Prabhupada could have called that person a rascal, which he clearly was, but instead Prabhupada gave him a different kind of mercy.

The next time I saw Srila Prabhupada was at the Philadelphia Rathayatra festival. There was wonderful kirtan – loud, enthusiastic and long – ebbing and flowing as the heart of the kirtan party came sometimes closer to and sometimes farther away from the cart. I was determined to stay close to the cart regardless of where the kirtan party was moving because this was my first experience and I wanted to be near Lord Jagannatha and His sister and brother, Subhadra and Balarama. I wanted my hand on the rope and I wanted to pull the cart. At some point in the parade route someone said, "Prabhupada is coming. Prabhupada is here!" You think the kirtan can't get any more intense, but it does because Prabhupada is there and the devotees hearts open up even wider and bigger. Without even realizing it you're aware that you're someplace else. It's the same sky and buildings and whatever else is around, but you're seeing these with new eyes because the intensity of the sound vibration of the kirtan transports you to another place. I was pulled to a realm that I have never experienced before.

As Prabhupada approached the cart the devotees parted ways for him so he could have a clear view of the Deities. I was looking at Prabhupada and Lord Jagannatha, witnessing these exalted personalities saying hello to each other. They were so happy to be in one another's presence. I was having the privilege of understanding and seeing that divine meeting, of knowing and believing it. Even today I can close my eyes and I'm there: the sound of the kirtan is deafening but the experience of seeing Srila Prabhupada and Lord Jagannatha meeting together makes even that sound vibration fall away.

I didn't have many close encounters with Srila Prabhupada, and at first I was bitter knowing that I wouldn't be as close to Prabhupada as others had been, but over time I learned to take nectar from many places. One of the great things about Krishna consciousness is that nectar is there in many forms: in reading Prabhupada's books, in associating with his followers, in honoring *prasadam,* in participating in kirtan, in serving in the temple, in hearing about Krishna, in having realizations looking at the Deities. Krishna consciousness is such a full experience.

On the last day that we were at the Mayapur festival in 1976, I heard that anyone could go to Prabhupada's room in the Lotus Building for darshan with Srila Prabhupada. So I brought bananas someone had given me and went to the hallway outside his door where eight to ten devotees were squatting against the wall, waiting in the hot afternoon. As I took my place at the end of the row I thought, "What chance do I have to see Prabhupada?" But at some point someone stepped out of Prabhupada's darshan room and said, "There's room for one more person to come in." I said, "I want to go, I want to go!" and since I was the most eager, I got to go in. Once inside, all of a sudden I had a problem: how do I offer my obeisances with the bananas in my hands? Should I give the bananas to Srila Prabhupada first and then offer my obeisances? What am I supposed to do? In confusion I looked at Srila Prabhupada and saw that he was smiling at me. He was happy to see me. It had been such a long time. I was in Srila Prabhupada's presence and he was happy to see me. Such a simple little thing. At that moment I felt like his daughter and everything was okay. He was happy to see me. It didn't matter that I didn't know what I was doing, that I didn't know what to say or do. He was okay with that. He was happy to see me.

Narayani devi dasi

Narayani first met Srila Prabhupada when he came to Gainesville, Florida, in July of 1971. She had been initiated for one month. When she walked behind him, what struck her most was her sense of belonging, security, and safety. She felt she could follow Prabhupada for the rest of her life.

When Prabhupada initiated me by letter in June of 1971, he'd given me important instructions. He wrote, "Yes, now that you have come to Krishna consciousness, your spiritual life, the real life, has begun. First birth is from your parents but real birth, real life, begins when one accepts a bona fide spiritual master and renders service onto him. Then the path is open for going back to home, back to Godhead, to live eternally in full knowledge and full bliss, and in association with the Supreme Personality of Godhead Himself, Lord Krishna. That is the goal, and the means to attain it are simple. You should strictly follow the regulative principles, chant at least sixteen rounds of beads daily, read and study all our books, attend *aratis*, and go for street *sankirtana*, etc. In this way be engaged in Krishna's business twenty-four hours and your rapid advancement in Krishna consciousness will be certain."

After my husband and I had been devotees in the U.S. for a year and a half, Prabhupada asked for fifty devotees to come to India. Satsvarupa, our temple president, told my husband and I that he was sending us to India.

During our first seven years in India, my husband and I were Radha-Govinda's *pujaris* in the Calcutta temple. I was offering *mangala-arati*, the twelve o'clock *arati*, the four o'clock *arati*, and the evening *arati*, and I was dressing the Deities, putting Them to rest, making garlands, taking care of *tulasi*, and sewing (we made fifty-two Deity dresses). I'd also go out and collect. I slept four hours a day. And the conditions were austere, devotees getting malaria; I got a urinary tract infection and ran a fever of 105°.

Once, when I was offering the ghee lamp during *mangala-arati*, I turned around and Prabhupada was four inches behind me. I was so shocked I almost dropped the ghee lamp. I didn't know what to do. Should I offer the ghee lamp to him from his feet up? I don't remember what I did, but I thought, "Wow! I should think that Prabhupada is right behind me watching every move I make for my whole life."

In India, Prabhupada didn't discriminate between men and women. Women did Deity worship in Bombay, Delhi, Hyderabad, and Calcutta – in every ISKCON temple in India except Mayapur. Women were doing all kinds of services: cooking, *harinama*, leading *bhajanas*, preaching, purchasing Deities for the temples. It was innocent in those days, informal and friendly, like a family. Godbrothers and godsisters were so enthusiastic to chant and preach, so dedicated to Srila Prabhupada, we never thought about mixing together improperly. The feelings we had toward each other were not ones of hatred or inferiority or superiority but of mutual respect. I joined because we all felt that Srila Prabhupada was our common father.

I saw Srila Prabhupada in Vrindavan in 1972. Every day, after his evening lecture, we would pack into his small room for darshan. The first thing he said was, "Don't associate with the *babajis*. It's called *markata vairagya*. Just like the monkeys, they're renounced, they wear no clothes, they're vegetarian. But they have many wives. One monkey, twenty wives. So don't associate with the *babajis*." At another darshan, a monkey ran into the room, grabbed some bananas, and ran out. Srila Prabhupada said, "See how intelligent he is. None of you would dare to do that! But the monkey is intelligent for eating, not for other things."

Once in a darshan he said to me, "My sister Pishima told me that you speak *Bhagavatam* very nicely." I was bewildered because I had never spoken *Bhagavatam* in my life. What was he talking about? Then I remembered that Pishima was present on Janmashtami when I'd read the *rasa-lila* chapter from *Krsna* book. She didn't speak English, but I got into the reading and she got into the mood and cried.

Pradyumna knew me from Boston, and when he saw me in Calcutta in 1973, he said, "Do you want to come to Mayapur with Prabhupada?" I said "Yeah." So he said, "Learn how to read Bengali. We're leaving tomorrow. We want you to type the *Chaitanya-caritamrita* for Prabhupada." He gave me a Bengali book and I learned.

The first building in Mayapur, the Lotus Building, was being built even while we lived in it. There were no windows and the doors didn't close. Prabhupada liked to see what the devotees were doing, and when he looked in the window of my room, I was sitting with earphones listening to a recording of him speaking Bengali verses and typing the English transliterations with a huge Bengali book in front of me. Prabhupada said, "Oh, you know Bengali?" I said, "Yes, Srila Prabhupada," although I'd just learned the alphabet the day before. Then Srila Prabhupada called me into his room and asked me to learn how to type in Bengali script on a Bengali typewriter. Then he said that we would do many books together. His words were prophetic, because thirty years later I started writing books by Srila Prabhupada's inspiration. I wrote *Srimad-Bhagavatam at a Glance*, which has a picture for every verse of *Srimad-Bhagavatam*, and *Bhagavad-gita at a Glance*. Within two months in Mayapur I typed *Adi-lila* chapters 13 – 17. Then I returned to Calcutta to become the head *pujari* there.

Once, in a *Gita* class in Calcutta that Prabhupada was giving, we were studying 9.11. I chanted the verse from memory. Prabhupada, surprised and happy, gave me a look that I'll never forget, like, "Wow, you know the verse!"

Because we couldn't manage things well in India, Prabhupada often stepped in. Once, he became our GBC, another time our temple president. He was also our temple commander, telling us to clean this and that. When the Deity ghee lamp was dirty, he angrily said to me, "Who has done this?" I was shaking. I wanted to disappear into the floor, but I couldn't, because I was face-to-face with Prabhupada. Sometimes we had to take it from him. Another time, after he'd taken darshan of Radha-Govinda, Prabhupada was appreciative. He thanked my husband and me. While we were offering our obeisances after that, a *sannyasi* told us. "Be blessed." Then I felt, "I got Prabhupada's blessings. My life is perfect." The next day, though, I understood that I have to try to get his blessings every day.

If we were hesitating and afraid in our spiritual life, Srila Prabhupada would push us to take the next step. That's the quality in him I most appreciated.

Nari devi dasi

Nari was twenty-two when she joined the Pittsburgh temple in October of 1972. Prabhupada initiated her in April 1973.

The month before I joined the temple, Prabhupada visited Pittsburgh. He was so potent and had so purified the atmosphere that it carried over. Not long after Prabhupada's visit I met a *brahmachari* on the street carrying a

BTG. He handed it to me and said, "If you water the root of the tree, all the leaves will benefit, but if you water each leaf separately, the tree will die. Therefore, when you serve Krishna, you'll be totally happy and you'll also be nourished." He was repeating Srila Prabhupada's words, and Prabhupada's potency came through him. This devotee also said if the hand holds the food and doesn't feed the body, the hand will suffer, but if the hand feeds the body, the whole body is nourished as well as the hand. Similarly, if you serve Krishna, then you will be nourished and completely happy.

I asked the devotee where he had meetings. He told me where the temple was and how the devotees had *mangala-arati* at 4:30 in the morning. I took the BTG and read it from cover to cover, memorized the Hare Krishna mantra, and the next morning, I went to *mangala-arati*. The devotees were jumping up and down and dancing to Nitai-Gauranga, Nitai-Gauranga. It was ecstatic. I could see how the devotees were in ecstasy in love of God through Prabhupada's potency, so I stayed. From then on, Prabhupada's potency kept me in the temple.

I first saw Srila Prabhupada and prayed at his lotus feet when he came to New York. After that, I saw him in Mayapur during the 1975 festival. In Mayapur, after Greeting the Deities, Srila Prabhupada circumambulated Them with all the devotees following behind. I thought, "I'll stand to the side, and as Srila Prabhupada comes around, I'll be able to see him from the front." When he walked by, I was looking at him and praying to him. The third time he came around I wanted to be sure he saw me, so I looked up at him and he looked right into my eyes. In my heart his look felt like it lasted forever. He planted something in my heart and it's still there: the Hare Krishna mantra, the importance of associating with devotees, Deity worship, the *dhama*, everything is just so special–the topmost *jagad-guru* gives his mercy to everyone.

Later, I wrote to Srila Prabhupada that I was having difficulty in my marriage. He replied, "The problems you write of indicate that your spiritual foundation is very weak. To make advancement in Krishna consciousness one must decide whether he is going to be serious or not. If one is actually serious, then by chanting Hare Krishna 16 rounds daily, following the four regulative principles, and reading my books, certainly you will make advancement, and these problems will fall to the side. I therefore request you because you are an initiated devotee to take up Krishna consciousness seriously as you promised at the time of your initiation, and be happy in Krishna consciousness."

In another letter, I asked Srila Prabhupada if I could stay in Vrindavan. He wrote, "You must follow the principles that I have given at all times, under all circumstances. Without these four principles, there is no spiritual life. Even it may be very difficult you must follow. You should reject anything or anyone who advises you to break these principles. Association with such persons is worse than poison. If you like, you may come to Vrindavan and live for some time."

Srila Prabhupada gave us everything. He gave us the Hare Krishna *maha-mantra*, which is Radharani and Krishna. There's nothing higher. We can associate with Prabhupada by reading and studying his books. We can chant and dance, take *prasadam*, be happy, and do a little service.

We can also take the association of the devotees. Without the association of devotees, what are we? We're nothing. We can serve the devotees. Little by little we can do everything only to please Prabhupada, and that will please Krishna. We can't please Krishna without pleasing Prabhupada. It's impossible. The two go hand-in-hand.

Nartaka Gopala devi dasi

Nartaka Gopala first saw Srila Prabhupada in Miami in 1975, again the following year when she and four other Miami book distributors went to the Mayapur festival, and then again at the 1976 New York Ratha-yatra.

Srila Prabhupada came to Miami in February 1975. Our temple was on Kumquat Street in the Coconut Grove area of Miami, on a rented property with several acres of banyan trees. Srila Prabhupada gave the lecture one evening outside under the banyan trees. It was an astoundingly beautiful atmosphere.

I was fortunate in that I was making his garlands every day. One garland was a petal garland: carnation petals in a design with roses and mango leaves. I made it super long and when Prabhupada put it on, he double looped it around his neck, and it still came to his waist. Later for a few years our photo of Prabhupada on the altar was of him wearing one of my garlands.

We took Srila Prabhupada around on a tour of the property and he actually stepped into our walk-in cooler, which was about nine feet square. One wall was completely stacked with small flavored yogurts. Prabhupada's eyes got big when he saw them, and a devotee explained to him that the stores donate the yogurt once it was past the sell-by date. Srila Prabhupada remarked, "Yogurt never goes bad."

I went to India for the first time in 1976. We arrived in Calcutta and immediately took the bus to Mayapur, put our bags in a room, and went to look for some service at the temple. Sukhada devi dasi and I were decorating the umbrella-like *chatri* above Prabhupada's *vyasasana*, when Srutirupa devi dasi told us that our temple president, Abhirama Dasa, wanted to see us upstairs. We went up the stairs and suddenly people were whispering, "Quiet!" We found ourselves in front of Prabhupada's door. Prabhupada was sitting inside. I offered my obeisances and thought, "Prabhupada, can we really come in to see you?" Prabhupada looked over and nodded his yes, so Sukhada and I went in and sat next to Pishima. The darshan lasted forty-five minutes. Everyone was speaking in Bengali. Prabhupada didn't speak to us and we didn't speak to him. But Sukhada and I were in ecstasy just to be near him–all our desires were fulfilled. We had devoted our lives to his service, so just to be in his presence on this rare occasion was the perfection of our lives.

Afterward, we served Srila Prabhupada's sister, Pishima. Being with her was so much like being with Prabhupada because she looked so much like him. Even though she didn't speak a word of English, there was always someone around to translate for us. She taught us a lot about the Vedic standards of etiquette and cleanliness. Pishima's love and admiration for Srila Prabhupada was infectious.

After Mayapur, we traveled with Prabhupada to Calcutta, then to Delhi for a five-day *pandal* program, where we distributed books while Prabhupada spoke to hundreds of people. When the *pandal* was over, it got around that Prabhupada wanted twenty book distributors to go on traveling *sankirtana* with Prabhupada. Sukhada and I went–first to Modi Nagar, and in some of the Vyasa-puja books you can see photos of Srila Prabhupada in a huge, elaborately carved, solid silver *vyasasana* there. The head of the town, Mr. Modi, had a brass band waiting to greet us when we arrived.

Srila Prabhupada traveled by car while our bus of twenty-one devotees followed him. Aligarh was next, and we had a fantastic *mangala-arati* on the roof of the house where Prabhupada was staying. All of us were running around in circles, dancing and chanting, with Lokanath Swami leading.

Finally, we went to Sri Vrindavan, where Prabhupada gave me second initiation. There was a huge *yajna* in the *mandir,* with over forty devotees receiving first and second initiations. There were so many devotees getting *brahmana* initiation that Prabhupada had to give the Gayatri mantra in small batches. I received mine probably three or four days after the *yajna.*

A few months before, during my daily lunch break while distributing books at the Miami International Airport, I'd carved Srila Prabhupada some beautiful wooden shoes with gold leaf along the edges and a toe peg shaped like a lotus flower with a jewel in its center. They were his exact size, as I had carefully measured his lotus feet on our *vyasasana*. I made a velvet bag for the shoes and embroidered his name on it. I'd been carrying them all over India, waiting for a chance to give them to him.

So in Vrindavan, Prabhupada, with a transcendental Vaikuntha radiance, was sitting at his desk in his quarters. He gave me and the four other women with me the Gayatri mantra. One woman couldn't get the finger movements correct, so Prabhupada told me to show her how to do it. Then the others left, but I hadn't given him my gift. I was alone with him and said, "Prabhupada, I made these for you," and I handed him the bag. He opened it, took out a shoe, held it up, and said, "Thank you very much." Then I gave him flowers and left. In my heart I felt satisfied that I had a little bit of one-on-one time with my beloved Guru Maharaja, to whom I had dedicated my life.

During the ten days we were in Vrindavan, I cleaned Prabhupada's quarters with a group of women every morning. We did the cleaning when he was out for his morning walk, before Greeting the Deities. We each had our own area to clean—bedroom, bathroom . . . It was my service to clean his desk and darshan room. Srila Prabhupada would leave his previous day's garland in that room, and somehow or other I had the mercy to get it every day. What ecstasy! Also, I loved cleaning his desk, as the personal items he traveled with were all set out there: his *tilaka,* his silver *acamana,* a silver mirror a devotee had made for him in the shape of a compact with Krishna and Balarama carved in silver relief on the cover. . . . When I went to clean his darshan room the morning after I gave Srila Prabhupada the shoes I had made, I saw that he had placed them on the mantel.

One day, I went with all the other devotees on *parikrama* to Radha-kunda. There were several buses of male devotees, and the women had their own three buses. When we finished our *parikrama,* the men left, but one of the women's buses wouldn't start. We decided that all the women with children should go back on the two good buses, and the rest of us would wait until the third bus got fixed.

It was getting dark and we were stuck. Back at the Krishna-Balaram Mandir, Prabhupada asked, "Where are all the ladies?" He was told that no one knew and that a group of us had never come back. Prabhupada said, "What! Immediately tell the Chief of Police." We had felt abandoned, but when we heard how Srila Prabhupada cared about us, our hearts were touched.

The Tenth Anniversary of ISKCON was celebrated in Washington, D.C. in 1976. The devotees made a huge cake. There's a now famous photo, taken by Visakha devi dasi, of Prabhupada cutting the cake. I made the garland he is wearing in that photo from marigolds grown on our property in Miami. Our temple president at the time, Narahari Prabhu, had gone to Washington to see Prabhupada, so I asked him to offer my garland.

When it was time for the cake-cutting, the temple authorities in Washington said: "Oh no! We don't have a garland for Prabhupada!" They had had one for *guru-puja* and *Bhagavatam* class, but now they wanted to offer another one. Narahari Prabhu heard this and remembered to offer my garland.

The New York Ratha-yatra in 1976 was the last Ratha-yatra Srila Prabhupada attended in his physical manifestation. It was the last for Jayananda Prabhu as well. It was also the first Ratha-yatra in New York that traveled down Fifth Avenue, which Srila Prabhupada had called "the most important street in the most important city in the most important country in the world." There were three huge, gorgeously decorated chariots, and hundreds of devotees chanting and dancing. Ten of us *sankirtana* devotees had flown up from Miami to attend. The parade started without Srila Prabhupada—he said he would come after everything started. We had gone about a mile. I was dancing in front of Subhadra Devi's chariot, and when I looked to the left, down the small side street, I saw Srila Prabhupada walking toward us. He got on Subhadra Devi's chariot and we began dancing in a frenzy. It was so exciting!

When I look at the many blessings I've had, the greatest blessing in my life has been distributing Srila Prabhupada's books for so many years. It makes you feel like he is standing right alongside you. Now I do *shashtra-dana*. I buy his books and give them to other devotees to distribute. As Srila Prabhupada once remarked: "If you want to please me, distribute my books."

Nartaki devi dasi

Although Nartaki is from Germany, she met Vaibhavi and Caru in Australia in 1971.

From the beginning Vaibhavi and Caru were wonderful leaders. At that time the temple was a storefront where people would walk in for our programs, which mainly consisted of chanting and reading from *Bhagavad-gita*. People were attracted by the dancing, chanting, feasting, and happy life.

On Sundays we'd go to Domain Park, which was a replica of London's Hyde Park. People would stand on boxes and speak and a group would gather around to listen. There were political groups, youth groups, hippies. But as soon as we came, everyone would leave the other speakers and gather around us as we chanted and danced. We'd move around and the crowd would follow us, and finally we'd give a little speech and invite everyone to come to the temple for the feast. People were attracted and the Movement started growing very quickly.

We'd distribute BTGs by holding the magazine out and waiting for curious people to ask about it and buy a copy. Only when Buddhimanta arrived did we learn how to distribute big books.

Caru invited Prabhupada to come to Australia and was surprised when Prabhupada replied, "Yes, I will come." We rushed to get everything straightened up and clean. When Prabhupada came we were so happy to receive him. It was like our father had come; it was like we knew him all along. We were also afraid because we thought we'd do something wrong.

Upananda was our cook, but he was regularly burning the chaunce, which made everyone in the temple cough. When Prabhupada smelled the burning chaunce he said, "What is this?" The devotees said, "Upananda is cooking." Prabhupada went to the kitchen, watched, and said, "No, you don't burn the chaunce. You wait till the seeds pop, then the flavor is released, and then you put the *dal* or vegetables in." Prabhupada taught Upananda how to cook.

When Prabhupada came to Australia he brought the Radha-Gopinatha Deities with him. He hadn't been with us long before he said, "We should install Radha-Gopinatha and we should have initiations." None of us knew how to set up the fire *yajna* or what to do for the installation. It was really difficult but somehow or other we managed. Vaibhavi ran to the store to get thread to make sacred threads for the *brahmanas*, and somehow she made them. Prabhupada installed the Deities and we learned how to dress them. I was fortunate from the beginning to have the service of making Deity clothes.

The devotees must have told Prabhupada I was always dancing in the *arati* because at the time of initiation when Prabhupada gave me my name, he said, "Your name will be Nartaki devi dasi. That means you should dance for Radha-Gopinatha."

Narmada devi dasi

In 1974, Narmada was introduced to Krishna consciousness by her former husband Mahabhagavata dasa, who is now a sannyasi and guru in ISKCON. While he was being trained at the temple in Mexico City, he regularly went to Narmada's house in San Salvador, El Salvador along with a small group of sankirtana devotees.

I used to take care of them nicely, but I didn't have any interest in their beliefs. They were very dedicated to devotional service, prepared daily meals to Krishna, and made sure to feed me *prasadam*. They always played "Cintamani Prayers," and I used to listen attentively. Gradually I started to feel an attraction for Srila Prabhupada's sublime voice. More and more I became attracted, but I couldn't understand why, it was like magic.

Around 1975, a group of *sankirtana* devotees from various countries around South America visited me. They brought two gorgeous posters of The Universal Form and The Rasa Lila Dance. I was captivated by them. I became inspired and started chanting two rounds a day.

With great enthusiasm these devotees invited me to go with them and meet Srila Prabhupada in Mexico City. They preached very strongly and convinced me to go. Due to having such good association and seeing Srila Prabhupada, from that day on, I increased my chanting to sixteen rounds daily for over forty-five years now.

It was very impressive when I saw Srila Prabhupada for the first time. My eyes were bewildered and I couldn't believe that I was seeing such a special and exalted person on earth. I felt a lot of mixed emotions and realized he was a truthful and bona fide spiritual master. I immediately knew he had the power to satisfy anybody's desire who wanted to inquire about the Absolute Truth.

I felt I was in front of a sublime soul showing all perfections. His upright presence was extremely awesome and his gracious celestial smile was incomparable, bewitching any soul. I was asking myself if he was from the spiritual world. Could he know and speak about who God was? Yes! In his classes he showed how illumined and wise he was. There was no doubt that I'd found what I was looking for. Without knowing, Krishna had been preparing me, because I had been a vegetarian for two years and had taken initiation from a deceitful yogi-guru who induced me to worship Lord Sankarsana, but I never felt satisfied. When I met Srila Prabhupada I immediately understood he was a bona fide guru.

When I was at the temple in Mexico City, I was invited, along with some other devotees, to have darshan in Srila Prabhupada's room. A representative of the Great Universal Brotherhood was also present, which was a cultural and non-governmental organization founded in Caracas, Venezuela. I was full of joy and appreciation for being close to such an exalted person. In Srila Prabhupada's sweet tone of voice I understood that he could give what I had been hankering for for a long time and could resolve all economic and social issues of the world. During this time in Mexico, Srila Prabhupada was widely acclaimed. Many people came to see him because they were eager to receive benedictions. Srila Prabhupada commented that many aspects of Mexico were reminiscent of the Vedic culture, such as the people's eating, parades, natural fruits, and archeological art work in temples.

In 1976, I was initiated at the same initiation with Guru Prasada Swami at the Costa Rica temple. Before that, I was doing *sankirtana* distributing hardcover *Srimad-Bhagavatams* six days a week by the causeless mercy of Srila Prabhupada.

In 1978, I visited the Guatemala temple where Mahabhagavata dasa was temple president, and I became the women's *sankirtana* leader because I was regularly in the "first place" as a book distributor. One Christmas marathon I was told to distribute all the books in a room filled with boxes all the way to the ceiling with transcendental literature. It was done in four weeks through the power of Srila Prabhupada. Devotees used to say that I was the "Mulaprakriti of Latin America."

In 1979, Mahabhagavata and I opened the first ISKCON temple in El Salvador in Central America. In that way I had the opportunity to uninterruptedly serve my spiritual master, Srila Prabhupada. In 1982, I moved to San Francisco, California where I remain active in devotional service at the ISKCON Berkeley temple and at home. I continue rendering devotional service to my installed Deities at home and love to feed *prasadam* to Vaishnavas.

Srila Prabhupada changed my life completely and by his divine grace and unlimited mercy he empowered me to serve him. At the same time he always made me feel humble with his teachings and all the love he gave to his spiritual daughters. For that I am indebted to him forever. I continuously pray for Srila Prabhupada's unlimited compassion and ask him to continue helping me follow this precious and incomparable path that he revealed to us. Hare Krishna!

Nataka Chandrika devi dasi

In early 1974, Nataka Chandrika, twenty-three, was living in Boulder when a friend told her to visit the Denver temple.

All the devotees were in the *prasadam* room, which was in the basement, watching "The Hare Krishna People." I watched it too and realized, "Wow, this is out of this world. This is different and very strange." I started crying and wanted to leave because I knew this was the truth but didn't want to admit it. I took some sweet rice and drove back to Boulder, all the time crying while I was drinking the sweet rice and feeling, "I don't know what's going on, but this has deeply moved me." Afterwards I was completely bewildered as to what to do with my life because I realized that I'd found what I'd been looking for.

Devotees mailed me some unbelievably intoxicating *laddus*. I was in ecstasy. I went to the temple again and sat in the lobby with Ananda Vardana Prabhu, who answered every question I ever had about anything by quoting verses from the *Bhagavad-gita*. I felt, "I'm defeated, what can I say?" I went through a whole box of tissues and knew this was something I had to do.

A couple of weeks later, in April 1974, I told my fiancé, "All my life I've done what my parents asked and I've done what you asked, and now this is something I want to do for me." I told my boss at the newspaper where I worked, *Boulder Daily Camera*, "After this week I'm quitting." He couldn't believe it and I couldn't either. I cut the ties to my previous life and left with my little red 1966 Volkswagen bug, which I loved dearly, loaded with one box of clothes and my sewing machine, moved in the temple, and never left.

I lived in the one-room *brahmacharini ashram* with twelve others. Mamata and Puja were the bhaktin leaders and we were up every morning at 2:45 and would take rest at 9:45 or 10:00. I was happy and felt I hadn't made a mistake, although my parents were ready to kidnap me. The few times my fiancé came to see me I gave him *prasadam*. Then in the summer of 1974 all the Denver devotees went to San Francisco. When I saw Srila Prabhupada my feelings were confirmed: "This is my eternal spiritual master." My link with Srila Prabhupada was established from that time on.

In 1975, Srila Prabhupada came to Denver. Receiving him at the airport we threw flower petals, offered obeisances, cried, and chanted together as one big happy family oblivious to the whole world. Srila Prabhupada was beaming. When he sat on the *vyasasana* I wanted to watch him speak and watch his aristocratic and perfect gestures forever.

Srila Prabhupada would sit in his rocking chair and read Volume One of the *Krsna* book in the evening in the backyard of the duplex where he stayed. Once a few of us ladies peeked around the corner and saw him with the *Krsna* book on his lap, laughing and making comments, with a lot of *sannyasis*, temple presidents, and *brahmacharis* sitting at his feet. Srila Prabhupada beckoned us, "Come on," like "Why are you over there? Come closer. You can hear *Krsna* book too." We did and I was in another world.

I was part of a small group of women who traveled to distribute BTGs and Prabhupada recognized and encouraged our service. While he was in Denver he wrote a letter to Jusaniya, Ramatulasi, Trpti, and me dated July 2, 1975, "My dear daughters, Please accept my blessings. I am in due receipt of the nice silver gift box which I have already put to my personal use. I thank you very much for your taking seriously to this Krishna consciousness movement by spreading this Movement of Lord Chaitanya's here in Denver. I am sure that Lord Chaitanya will benedict you and that this will be a great success for Krishna consciousness in Denver. I hope that this meets you in good health. Your ever well wisher, A.C. Bhaktivedanta Swami."

Nidra devi dasi

In the early 1970s, after reading Bhagavata Gita As It Is Nidra understood Srila Prabhupada was her guru. Then with much prayer, Nidra felt guided by Prabhupada's internal direction to quit her teaching career and join an ashram. She surrendered to his mission at ISKCON Denver, Colorado, USA.

My first pilgrimage to Mayapur was 1977 for Gaura Purnima. Only once was I fortunate to attend darshan in Srila Prabhupada's room. When I paid my obeisances at the door, I understood that my long cherished childhood desire to know what it would be like to have the association of Lord Jesus and his disciples was fulfilled. My whole being was ecstatically enlivened. Srila Prabhupada, our dear *shaktyavesha-avatara* spiritual master, was present for me for the first time in his *vapuh*. There were no words exchanged outwardly, but in my heart I understood all that he wanted me to do, which was to eternally serve the *sankirtana* mission.

Srila Prabhupada has impacted my entire existence by his love. I aspire to serve the servants of his servant's servants. If those servants bless me, perhaps I can help some souls become more connected with his love. He is always there as we engage the conditioned souls. May we all share that love as much as possible, life after life. There is no other essence for me. Basically, I live in separation from his presence and therefore his books, followers, and service are the only solace.

Nikunjavasini devi dasi

When Nikunjavasini's second brother, who was a devotee in Amsterdam, gave her the Isopanisad, *it was a spiritual "Wow!" for her.*

I'd been confused. I couldn't figure out what I was supposed to be doing and drugs had made me more confused. The *Isopanisad* gave me relief. It completely convinced me and still convinces me now. Back then I was working and buying the *Bhagavatams*, *Chaitanya-charitamritas*, and other books from my brother, who also brought me a picture of Prabhupada, saying, "He's a holy man." I put the picture inside my leather jacket thinking, "It will purify my heart." English isn't my first language and, although I couldn't understand what he was saying, I'd play the cassette tape of Prabhupada reading the *Krsna* book and think, "This spiritual sound vibration will purify me." I stopped taking drugs, my friends disappeared, and my brother said, "Why you don't join? You have nothing in common with your friends any more."

In 1971 Prabhupada came for the installation of Lord Jagannatha in

Amsterdam and my family and I squeezed in to the crowded temple. A film crew had television lights on and it was so hot, sweat dripped down our faces. Prabhupada was upset by the inadequate arrangements for the Deities. He was giving instructions we couldn't understand, and all the devotees were running around to please him. I thought, "This is real spiritual life." My older brother, who was my hero, was following Maharaj ji, the young boy with a big smile, and I was attracted to that too because it sounded easy. But when I saw Prabhupada I thought, "Don't fool yourself." Somehow or other I followed my second brother because what my older one offered wasn't logical. Yet Srila Prabhupada was so stern I thought, "I'll be Krishna conscious in my next life. I want to enjoy and be happy now. I'm not going to follow somebody who's upset."

My second brother kept visiting me but three years passed before I went to the temple again, in February 1974. I did some devotional service and after a while didn't want to leave. That June, when I was twenty, we went to Rettershof in Germany and Srila Prabhupada initiated me.

Prabhupada was strict at the initiation. Each man and woman had to pay full *dandavats* at an angle to the *vyasasana* and if somebody didn't do it properly Prabhupada corrected them. I did my full *dandavats,* said the regulative principles, and Prabhupada said, "Your name is Nikunjavasini. It's a very nice name. It's a *gopi.*" I was happy.

In 1976 we all traveled to New Mayapur where Adi Kesava asked, "In the *guru-puja* song, we say, 'You are my spiritual master life after life.' So, Prabhupada, if we don't make it this time, will you come back to save us?" Prabhupada banged his fist on the table and said, "You make it this lifetime! Don't make me come back!" Prabhupada also told my husband, who passed away in 1977, "Follow the regulative principles, chant sixteen good rounds every day, follow my instructions and for sure you will go back to Godhead in this lifetime."

I've been doing Deity worship for decades, but when I lived in the temple the social life distracted me and I forgot the essence. I had to separate myself a bit to focus on my needs and concentrate more on Prabhupada. Now Deity worship maintains me. When I'm on the altar I'm with Krishna, He takes care of me, and I'm completely happy.

For me, God is on the altar, Radha-Gopinatha [in Radhadesh]. Prabhupada's great gift is that he gave us the Absolute Truth and brought Radharani and Krishna to us in Their personal form. Prabhupada is everything for me. His instructions are a strong life force, a line we can hold onto like a rope. I want to chant, I want to hear, I want to concentrate on Srila Prabhupada and Radha-Gopinatha.

Nirakula devi dasi

Sometime in 1972, Nirakula was watching a black-and-white television show at a friend's house in Brooklyn when Srila Prabhupada came on the news. He was arriving at a local airport and was surrounded by a throng of devotees.

I was seventeen. I'd heard of Hare Krishna from George Harrison's Bangladesh concert, but I didn't know about Prabhupada's books and I hadn't seen devotees. A couple of months later a few friends and I went to the temple where I saw a picture of Prabhupada and realized he was the person I'd seen on TV.

On February 23, 1973, I moved into the Los Angeles temple and Prabhupada came in mid-April that year. I was terribly excited to meet him. A few of us stayed up all night in the temple room upholstering and decorating his *vyasasana*, cleaning, and making gardenia and rose garlands. Finally, when Srila Prabhupada was physically present, I was overwhelmed. All the devotees were feeling sheer joy.

In Los Angeles on May 15, 1973, Srila Prabhupada initiated me. When he gave me my name he said "*kula*" means to be confused, and at that moment I felt like my brain was bouncing in my head. I was the epitome of confusion. Then he said, "*Nira* means 'not.' So Nirakula means 'one who is not confused.' Fixed up." The devotees were laughing as Srila Prabhupada gave me my beads.

I helped clean his quarters in the mornings. I cleaned with awe and reverence. I felt like I was on the altar, dressing the Deities. His room was never dirty or dusty and nothing seemed out of place. I could see that he'd been using things, but everything was where it was supposed to be. Three days a week we'd change the flower vases in his room. Once Srila Prabhupada noticed that there were fresh flowers in the vases although the flowers that had been there were still good. Prabhupada said the old flowers were still all right and it wasn't necessary to spend *laksmi* for new ones. He said we should keep the flowers until they die. I realized that we could be wasteful even if we were using everything in service to Prabhupada and Krishna. That made an impression on me. Everything I know – cleanliness, etiquette, basic human functions – I owe to Srila Prabhupada and those who were trained by him. I relearned everything after meeting the devotees.

Madhudvisa used to lead wonderful kirtans in the L.A. temple. When he left the *sannyasa ashrama,* Prabhupada gave very specific instructions that Madhuvisa was part of our family and he should feel welcome in the temple. He was not to be ostracized. Prabhupada wanted him to come back and do service. It was a very loving, a very fatherly moment. It was like teaching young children how to behave. In those days we were so neophyte and fanatical we could be fearful and judgmental and lose our humanness in dealing with each other.

Since the BBT was in New Dwarka and because Prabhupada did a lot of translating in New Dwarka, the importance Prabhupada placed on reading and distributing his books got instilled in me. Prabhupada took a personal interest in everything that was going on. He would go to the artists' studios, or he would go to the FATE museum and see the work being done. He enlivened all the devotees. If you just happened to be outside, unannounced, Srila Prabhupada might come walking across the street or up to the artists' studios or to your apartment.

I never felt I lacked an intimate relationship with Prabhupada, maybe because I was setting up his plate and doing his laundry and cleaning for him. My connection felt personal. Prabhupada was personal with all of us and we felt close to him. He was teaching us lessons, correcting our imbalances and the fads we'd take up, like drinking only juices instead of honoring *prasadam*. Prabhupada would immediately have a solution for our disagreements and problems or put an end to our lopsidedness or encourage whatever good we did. His word was the final word.

There was the time Srila Prabhupada was there for Srila Bhaktisiddhanta Sarasvati's disappearance day. He gave the lecture, and got really emotional when he started to thank us all. He said that we had all come to help him in his service to his Guru Maharaja. It was overwhelming. Everyone began to cry. It was like we weren't even breathing to see Prabhupada so grateful.

Prabhupada taught me gratitude. And real humility. He was the example of what to strive for, and that day he expressed his deep humility. Everything he did was an example for us, and to hear him, to watch him, to see him. It satisfied every one of our senses.

Here we are, so many years after his departure, and the proof of our spiritual connection to him is obvious. Although we were young then and we had his company for such a short time, we're so fortunate.

Nirguna devi dasi

Nirguna was fourteen in 1971 when she started going with her parents to the Calcutta temple. She was immediately attracted to Radha-Govinda.

The first time I met Prabhupada I began to weep uncontrollably. I knew that meeting him was the most important thing that had ever happened to me.

My father was an intellectual and had met many spiritual leaders and been around many spiritual groups, but when he met Prabhupada he was transformed. He used to say, "There is no pretension about Prabhupada.

He's so straightforward, so down to earth, so real." When Prabhupada was in Calcutta my father and uncle would follow him everywhere and I'd go too. With his contemporaries, Prabhupada was relaxed. He was tremendously interested in what they said and would lean forward, ask questions, and sometimes discuss politics. But he had an amazing way of bringing any conversation back to Krishna. If somebody went off the topic he would skillfully turn the conversation around without being abrasive. These conversations were light, but never trite. They were always meaningful. Prabhupada never posed as the *acharya* or guru in front of his peers. He would say, "Please help me. You have so much to give. You can teach this aspect, that aspect. Please come with me, help me train these young boys and girls." His mood was always extremely friendly and he never acted like he knew more than anybody else.

I saw Prabhupada dealing with many different kinds of people in different ways. Even when he would say "rascal," he was affectionate and would say it with a smile, never condescendingly. He was calling a spade a spade and nobody could take offense.

At my initiation, after I said the four regulative principles Prabhupada said, "But there is one more." I thought, "Which one did I miss?" He smiled and said, "The most important one is to always remember Krishna and never forget Him."

Once Shumana, who was twenty-four, went to Prabhupada when he was in his thatched hut during the first Mayapur festival, and said, "Prabhupada, I don't want to get married." He said, "Okay, it will be difficult but all right, you don't have to." Prabhupada was broadminded; he didn't make the same rules for everybody. He told me, "You have to live with your parents. You have very good parents and you must always do what they say." After my initiation, my parents and I were in Prabhupada's quarters in the evening and my mother said, "So now what is next for her?" My mother wanted me to go to college and I didn't want to go. Prabhupada said, "Oh, she doesn't have to go. No more studies." My parents were so accepting of Prabhupada they didn't argue. Srila Prabhupada always made me feel special and cared for.

Nirmala devi dasi

Nirmala became a vegetarian at the age of twelve or thirteen. When her sister, Rangavati, sent her a Bhagavad-gita and a lot of lugloos and laddus, she didn't understand much of the Bhagavad-gita but ate all the lugloos and laddus.

I was in my last year of high school in Ann Arbor and fearful because I didn't know what to do with my life. I wasn't an intellectual type so university wasn't appealing and I knew working a nine-to-five job wouldn't satisfy me.

I deeply prayed, "Dear God, whoever You are, wherever You are, please send me a sign." Two days later I got a letter from my sister, who was in the Detroit temple an hour away, inviting me to visit her. I drove my little car there.

The temple was extremely clean and glowing and I immediately felt it was my home and the devotees were my people. Everybody was vegetarian and the *prasadam* was phenomenal. The next day devotees asked me if I wanted to go on *sankirtana*. I said, "All I know is that you call God Krishna and He's blue and He plays a flute." My sister said, "That's great, you know so much! Let's go distribute these magazines." I stood with a case of *Back to Godhead*s, Krishna took over, all the *Back to Godhead*s were gone, and I had a pile of *laksmi*. That was my first service to Srila Prabhupada and through it I had a deep connection to him.

After a few months in the Detroit temple, I decided to move to New Vrindavan and drove there with a few others. When Srila Prabhupada came there and I first heard him singing "Jaya Radha Madhava" I started shaking and crying, which had never happened before in my life. Prabhupada scanned all the devotees and when his eyes touched my eyes for a few moments, I felt he saw me to the depths of my being – the good, the bad, the ugly. I was stripped of everything. He saw it all. I'd never had an experience like that before and I was shaken but satisfied. I knew that he was my guru, my teacher, my everything.

Prabhupada always paid attention to and was gentle towards all the children. And I loved how he did so much but was never in a hurry. He was personable, thoughtful, caring, encouraging, conscious and conscientious, and yet he accomplished so much.

In July of 1974 Prabhupada initiated me. He doubled my beads, held them with his thumbs, handed them to me and said, "Your name is Nirmalaaaaa dasi." I still have those beads, they're the most prized possession in my life. Every morning I chant on them and Prabhupada gives me strength.

At one point I thought, "I want some reciprocation with Prabhupada, I wish he'd say something to me." Every morning in Mayapur he came from his quarters to the temple room, and I'd stand where he could see me but he'd see everybody except me. That happened for three days and by the fourth day I felt awful. He was obviously ignoring me. That evening my consciousness shifted. I realized, "Oh, my gosh, I have a service that I can go back to, and that's distributing Prabhupada's books." The next morning I stood in the same place, but this time Prabhupada looked me in the eye, folded his hands, and bowed his head. It was a huge awakening: I realized that he knew my heart. He wanted to see my desire to serve, my change of consciousness. That moment is one of my strongest remembrances and the strongest connection I had with Srila Prabhupada in the physical form.

Whether we spoke or didn't speak to Prabhupada, whether we had his personal association or not, no service done for him in the right consciousness goes in vain. Prabhupada sees and appreciates it all. My service was book distribution, which wasn't easy, but because Prabhupada loved that service his desire gave me strength.

Without Prabhupada I wouldn't have a life. He's given me a life, he leads my life, he's here always with me in my life, and he'll always continue to be in my life – and beyond. I'm eternally grateful. I'm an unworthy disciple, but I pray to someday be worthy.

Nitya-trpta devi dasi

Before Nitya-trpta became a devotee she realized that photography was a powerful communication medium and was what she wanted to be involved in but felt, "I have nothing to say." Later, when she became a devotee, she knew she had a lot to say with photography and soon became "queen" of the Photography Department at the Bhaktivedanta Book Trust in Los Angeles.

My first experience with Srila Prabhupada was when I first came to the temple. At that point I'd only read a bit of the *Bhagavad-gita* and I'd talked a bit to devotees. But that morning in the temple I was so enlivened by *guru-puja* that I offered my full, prostrated, surrendered *dandavats* in front of Prabhupada's *vyasasana*. I was attracted to Srila Prabhupada, that "Here is the great man who can teach me everything I need to know." Gradually, by listening to his lectures and by reading his books, I got a feel for his message and began to understand how we can live in a way that's neither detrimental to ourselves nor to others but is positive – is karma-free. I thought, "Oh, yeah, that's it. That's what I want to know." Through his lectures and books, Prabhupada helped me understand how this material world works and how to function in it, as well as how to be solid in my own abilities in Krishna consciousness, whatever they may be.

I also tried to understand what Prabhupada meant when he spoke and wrote about women being less intelligent. For one thing, I noticed that Prabhupada also criticized men. He compared men to dogs, hogs, camels, and asses. Prabhupada just called women less intelligent, but he likened men to lowly animals. He also said that everyone in Kali-yuga is less intelligent. So I don't take it seriously that women are less intelligent because everyone in Kali-yuga is less intelligent. And the important thing is, as Srila Prabhupada repeatedly explained, that we're not these bodies.

If we identify with being a woman or a man then we may be affected by Prabhupada's criticisms. It depends how we want to take it. Part of the problem is that false ego gets in the way of understanding. Generally intelligence is gauged by one's ability to use reason and logic, which men are often good at. However, there are aspects of spiritual life which require empathy, compassion, and understanding, and women tend to have more of those qualities.

Since women are often more empathetic and emotional than men, those feelings can cloud intelligence and interfere with rational decision making. So with that understanding I agreed that women can be less intelligent. But the woman's empathy is good because as a mother she needs to be empathetic to the child, the crying bundle that doesn't know how to take care of itself. Otherwise, without seeing the situation from the child's eyes, how can a person tolerate it? In Krishna consciousness there are a lot of pluses and minuses that are balanced. If someone is not respectful, if someone treats us as less intelligent, we can avoid that person just as we avoid that person who wants to induce us to do something wrong. But for me the women's issue was a non-issue because I was determined and did what I wanted; I was in charge of the Photography Department. Perhaps that was my karma and I tried to use it for Krishna.

Before Prabhupada came to Berkeley for the 1975 Ratha-yatra, I was cleaning his *vyasasana* and thinking, "A representative of Krishna will soon be sitting on this seat giving us knowledge of Krishna." Similarly, although I took great pleasure in hearing about Srila Prabhupada from those who had his association, for my whole devotional life my relationship with Srila Prabhupada has been through meditation and prayer. When you get so involved in your service to Krishna and Srila Prabhupada that you feel quivery, emotional, almost teary – when you feel like you're connecting – it's a certain kind of spiritual high, a kind of ecstasy. It has nothing to do with material gain because I don't get paid, I basically get what I need. So my drive doesn't come from, "Yes, I'm going to make a profit or get fame and recognition." My drive comes from my relationship with Prabhupada, which has always been one of prayerful service. I pray to Srila Prabhupada, "Please allow whatever intelligence I have to be sufficient for what I'm doing so I can understand how to do my service for your glorification. Please allow me to understand how I can please you by what I'm doing. Please allow these pictures to inspire devotees." And my meditation and prayer is the same today as it was then when Srila Prabhupada was here with us physically.

Omkara devi dasi

Omkara was twelve years old in 1966, and one afternoon, her mother was bringing her to their family dentist on Second Avenue, on the Lower East Side of New York City. That was the first time she saw devotees. She was immediately attracted to these people with their saffron-colored robes and shaved heads. She knew they were spiritually-minded strong, saintly souls. She wanted to be just like them. It was love at first sight.

Our family dentist had his office almost right next door to the Hare Krishna temple on Second Avenue. I couldn't wait to go back to the dentist, because it meant, just maybe, I would see a Hare Krishna once again in his saffron-colored robes. And when I grow up, I thought, I can be one of them! There was no doubt in my mind. I knew, somehow, that this was for me. I felt deep inside that I had lived a devotional lifestyle before. I wanted so much to just go back to the dentist so I can maybe see another Hare Krishna. That was me at twelve years old.

The years went by and I finally turned seventeen. One day, while riding the subway, I noticed a magazine lying on a seat and picked it up. It was *Back to Godhead*. Someone had left it there. I was overjoyed. I was so happy to see the faces of Lord Krishna and Balarama in the Vrindavan forest! I took this precious BTG and embraced it, for this was my long lost love coming back to me. This abandoned magazine had been meant for me, was waiting for me to pick it up.

That very day I started chanting the Hare Krishna mantra and became a vegetarian.

My mother was upset. I taped the Krishna-Balarama picture to my bedroom door and prayed each and every day to this picture. I looked at it for hours, hoping that I could go to the temple and become a devotee soon.

I remember vividly when I finally decided to go to the Brooklyn Temple. I took the subway there alone and walked right into the middle of a Sunday Feast lecture. Srila Prabhupada was speaking. I was amazed and overtaken by his presence. I had never seen anyone like Srila Prabhupada before. I could tell by looking at him – his features, his stature, his movements, his reflections – that he was no ordinary person. Srila Prabhupada exuded something I had not seen before. I could see such sincerity, such spirituality, and yet such simplicity. I felt touched, purified on the spot; blessed and immensely gratified just to be able to come before him. And when I looked around and saw the blissful faces of the young devotees – they were so happy and looked on Srila Prabhupada with such devotion. I thought, "Just chant Hare Krishna and perform devotional service." Seeing Srila Prabhupada felt welcoming and nurturing. He was my real spiritual father, and after the lecture I told the devotees I had come to stay. I wanted to be a devotee. They dressed me in a *sari*. I knew I was home. I knew that this practice was going to become my life and soul.

One day, I was exiting the *pujari* room. It was usually quiet during the day, since most of the devotees were serving at ISKCON Press or out on *sankirtana*. As I paused I heard a strange noise – a *thunk, thunk, thunk*. All of a sudden, I saw Srila Prabupada coming down the stairs, all alone. It was his cane that was making the noise. I was speechless. I was still only seventeen, and now alone with Srila Prabhupada. Srila Prabhupada came closer, he smiled at me, raised his cane, and said so very nicely, "Chant Hare Krishna!" I felt spiritually electrocuted, on fire.

Another time, Srila Prabhupada was coming to the Brooklyn temple. It was a dismal, gloomy day, drizzling slightly. As Srila Prabhupada's car pulled up and he stepped out of it, Kirtiraja lifted a canvas umbrella over his head. He looked so beautiful with his flowing garlands that hung almost to the floor. Srila Prabhupada folded his hands and smiled. He looked at each of us. I noticed with amazement how he was glowing golden. It was almost blinding. The glow was all around his body.

Srila Prabhupada's quarters weren't far from the reception area. One afternoon, I heard Srila Prabhupada singing and playing the harmonium. His singing was quite audible. He was singing the *bhajana*, "sava avatara sara siromani," and I listened very carefully. Suddenly he stopped singing and began to cry. I could hear him sobbing for a few moments. Then he began singing and playing the harmonium again. He was singing with such love for the Lord. This stopping and starting happened several times. I felt fortunate and was also crying to have had this darshan of a pure devotee. I revere those moments.

One morning it was *guru-puja* time and Srila Prabhupada was handing out sweetballs. I was watching the clock because I had to be in the kitchen to set up the Lords' plates for their offering. I was in great anxiety because I really wanted a sweetball from Srila Prabhupada. The temple room was packed. This specific day, to my eyes, it seemed especially packed. There were too many *sannyasis, brahmacharis*, visiting devotees from San Diego, Laguna Beach, San Francisco, and Berkeley – all crowded around Srila Prabhupada. I was trying to figure out how to get my sweetball and get into the kitchen in time for my service.

At one point, Srila Prabhupada started throwing the sweetballs into the air. This made everyone wild. They were jumping in ecstasy and started really crowding in around Srila Prabhupada. In those days, when Prabhupada gave out cookies or sweetballs, the women and children went first. Even then, I still did not have enough time to get a sweetball and make it into the kitchen. So when it started to look hopeless, I disappointedly began to offer my obeisances at the back of the temple room. As I was offering my obeisances, my forehead just a few inches off the floor, I looked up and saw rushing toward me a whole, uncrushed sweetball! It was a perfect sweetball for Omkara, special delivery from Srila Prabhupada.

I remember with great fondness how Srila Prabhupada would oftentimes come to New Dwarka and greet the Deities. I know he had deep affection for Sri Sri Rukmini-Dwarkadhisa. I used to pay particular attention to Srila Prabhupada and watch him during *guru-puja*. There were so many times when he would stand with folded hands and look lovingly at the Deities. His eyes would glow, lit up like two beams of light.

When Srila Prabhupada left his physical body in Vrindavan *dhama*, I was in New Dwarka and had not been feeling well for days. I was incredibly sad, because Srila Prabhupada was ill, and everyone was talking about how he might leave his body. I attended *guru-puja* and saw everyone crying. A devotee told me Srila Prabhupada had left his body. I too cried. This made me terribly sad. However, I knew at that point I had to transcend into another spiritual platform of understanding Srila Prabhupada's presence and our relationship as guru and disciple. I knew that Srila Prabhupada would never leave me, and that a pure devotee of the Lord is always present for his disciples. I learned to be happy and love Srila Prabhupada in his books, his *murti* on the *vyasasana* in the temple, and in my heart. He was always with me, and I could still talk to him each day. I could still see and be with him. I still felt his association and comfort. I never got lonely. This was a special gift that I could cherish and treasure.

Prabhupada taught me that when you chant the Hare Krishna mantra, Krishna "dances on your tongue." You are directly associating with Krishna. This is the same with your guru. When you pray to your guru, your guru is with you. The present gurus are initiating on behalf of Srila Prabhupada. They are carrying on their devotional service and love for Srila Prabhupada and helping spread his Krishna consciousness mission. I know that Srila Prabhupada is pleased with this service, since ISKCON is so important to him. Prabhupada came to the West on the order of his own Gurudeva, Srila Bhaktisiddhanta Sarasvati Maharaja, to preach Krishna consciousness. He came to give *krishna-prema*.

It is my desire to go back to Godhead in this lifetime. I believe in Srila Prabhupada. I have wholehearted faith that he loves his disciples very much. In my initiation letter, he writes that simply by following the four regulative principles, chanting at least sixteen rounds a day, and preaching in the best way one can, in this very lifetime we can have the golden opportunity to go back to Godhead. I pray each and every day to my Gurudeva, my beloved Srila Prabhupada, to please bless me and take me when I leave my body. I want to surrender fully and offer service. This is my commitment to Srila Prabhupada. I owe him so much. Thank you, my dear spiritual master, for your endless blessings.

Padyavali devi dasi

One day in Vancouver in 1971, Mahesa, a devotee book distributor, emerged from a crowded sidewalk and hollered to Padyavali, "Hey you! You meditate, don't you?" She had just registered with Maharishi Yogi and gotten a mantra. Mahesa said, "You have to read these." Padyavali said, "What are they?" He said, "It's the Vedas, the Bhagavad-gita and the Srimad-Bhagavatam." Padyavali didn't understand what he was saying. It sounded like Greek to her.

My husband was a librarian and for ten to twelve years of our marriage he fed me many books. I read everything from Buckminster Fuller to Socrates to all the greats in literature. I was looking for the Absolute Truth and used to ask everybody, "Do you know the Absolute Truth?" I bought the devotee's books and spent months trying to read them. I was a voracious reader, but I fell asleep trying to read the *Gita*. Finally I finished it and then started it over. I read it three times in three months and each reading was on a deeper level. I was excited. I was dancing from understanding something about the *Bhagavad-gita*. I said, "I knew it! This place isn't our real home. We're not doing what we're supposed to be doing with the human form of life." I found everything I was looking for in the *Bhagavad-gita*. It answered all my questions and gave me great hope. Then I realized that the next book, the First Canto of the *Srimad-Bhagavatam*, started where the *Gita* ended.

I sent for more books and for two-and-a-half years read Prabhupada's books. I loved them. His were the best books I'd ever read. I admired his writing style and every word he wrote was like a diamond, with different reflections of depth and truth. Not only that, but I knew Prabhupada by reading them and they revealed the Absolute Truth spoken by Krishna. I was in ecstasy. I didn't know about temples until I found a *Back to Godhead* magazine in a ditch. Then I visited the Vancouver temple and found it effulgent from kirtan. The devotees graciously welcomed me and gave me garlands and lots of *prasadam*. I moved in.

If I want to see Prabhupada, I read his books. That's where I'll find him forever. Presently I'm reading *Nectar of Devotion* over and over. It's stupendous. I go deeper and deeper. Prabhupada said he lives forever by his divine instructions and the follower lives with him. We live with him by reading his books and doing what he says to do.

I can't believe my good luck in meeting Prabhupada and I feel connected to him. His ISKCON is a successful place: it's elevating the devotees' consciousness. And if that's going on, then everything else is all right.

Palini devi dasi

Palini devi dasi was initiated in November 1974 in Los Angeles when she was twenty-three. She was already a vegetarian and chanting sixteen rounds before moving into the temple a year earlier.

When we did the *Chaitanya-charitamrita* marathon to publish seventeen volumes in two months, I was proofreading and ran across the word *phalini*. It means "almost fruitful." So when people ask me, "What does your name mean?" I tell them, "bearing fruit of love of God."

When I first saw Srila Prabhupada in 1973 it was a little bewildering. I hadn't really ingested the concept of guru. I was very excited to find out that God was a little blue boy who played a flute, but it took me a little while to get used to the idea of Srila Prabhupada as guru.

Krishna consciousness was what I had looked for all my life. Ever since I was a little girl, I was looking for Krishna, his holy names, and devotees. When I saw the devotees on television in 1972, it was an immediate recognition. I said, "I want to be with these people. I want to be like them, and I want to locate them."

Later I received *Teachings of Lord Chaitanya*. All the way home I read and read. Every day, all day long for many days, I read and that freaked out my mother. She thought I had gone off my rocker and took the book away. It was quite a fight to make my first few baby steps in Krishna consciousness.

When I finished reading the book, I had such an emotional experience that I bowed down and put my head on my bedroom floor. To pay obeisance came naturally. After that, I became very serious about finding out these people and live with them.

So I went down to the Denver temple. One devotee handed me a broom and said, "You need to do some service. Why don't you try sweeping?" So I swept the sidewalks around the outside of the temple. I approached Kurusrestha Prabhu, who was the temple president at the time, and I told him I really want to live with the devotees. He said, "Well, because you have a little child and there are no children here, you should probably go to a temple where there are small children." He suggested New Vrindavan or Los Angeles. In the end, I went to Los Angeles. When I first got there, it was so scary and new. But at the same time, I was totally convinced that this life was for me.

When Prabhupada was going to arrive, we cleaned our apartment until there was not a single speck of dust in hopes that Srila Prabhupada would maybe stop by, because the devotees told me that sometimes Srila Prabhupada would visit someone's apartment. We cleaned the temple room, got his *vyasasana* all clean and pretty, and his rooms upstairs were *pukka*.

He came to Los Angeles so many times that I don't remember the exact circumstances of the first time he came. But I just remember how blissful it was when Srila Prabhupada used to come, and we would be throwing flower petals on him and paying obeisances. He would stop and pat a child on the head or speak to one of the *matajis* and smile. Everybody just loved him so much that it was contagious. I just fell in love with him, too. He was irresistible. He was just so amazing.

When he would sit on his *vyasasana* and give *Bhagavatam* class, I would scoot up as close as I could to the *vyasasana* and be right at the bottom of it and looking up at him. I just felt so happy to be in his association.

Tusti gave me the nice service of polishing the flower vases in his quarters. When Srila Prabhupada was there, he would come down the stairs from his quarters, stop on the landing, and then go out the door to the alleyway and get in the car to go on his morning walk. One morning we all happened to be waiting for him and we were all lined up along the wall. Everybody who was involved in cleaning his rooms, we were all waiting.

He came down the stairs with his cane and he stood on the landing. He looked at each one of us in the eyes and said, "*Jaya!*" and shook his head from side-to-side like they do in India when they say yes. And that "*Jaya!*" meant everything to me, that he approved of our service that we were trying so eagerly to render. I was very happy about that.

One of my favorite things was when Srila Prabhupada would come out for his morning walk. He would come out of his door and go down the little flight of six concrete steps, and then he would turn to the left, and get in the waiting car. When Prabhupada would come out, there were always a few devotees there. Somebody would hand him a flower, somebody would hand him a garland or put it on him, or offer some prayer or some glorification. Srila Prabhupada was so personable and so kind. He would look in our eyes and smile and make us feel so special. Then when he would climb into the car and the door would close. He would hold up his cane as if he were paying respects to us, giving us a blessing, or acknowledging us. He would do that little gesture where he would lift up his cane. So those were very, very special relishable times when Srila Prabhupada would come out of his door and get in the car.

One of my favorite things was when Srila Prabhupada would come down through the door of the temple room and come in. He would go up to the Deities and pay his *dandavats* after praying with folded hands to each of the altars, first Sri Sri Gaura-Nitai, then Rukmini-Dwarkadisa, then Jagannatha, Baladeva, and Subhadra. He would offer *dandavats* three times with his *danda*, and then he would gracefully come around and ascend the *vyasasana*.

For one *Bhagavatam* class I was standing up in the corner of the room listening. I was in a bad mood that day. He looked straight over at me and said, "We are all more or less *asuras*." It was like a shaft into my heart. He really chastised me because I had a morose mentality, and he just snapped me out of it with that sentence.

In one dream, Srila Prabhupada was sitting and I was crying with my face in his lap. I could feel his *dhoti* getting wet. He was mercifully stroking my head and my back over and over again, and he spoke sweet words to me. Those kinds of dreams really, really cement one's relationship with one's guru. He's our spiritual father and a father has that prerogative to stroke his daughter's head and back. He's so wonderful. Dreams are the thing that I treasure in my heart the most. And, of course, his books are a personal letter to each of his disciples that can be read every day at any time of the day. I get so much strength and enthusiasm from Srila Prabhupada's books. I'd say those are the two things that made the most impact on me.

Paramrta devi dasi

At the Melbourne airport in 1975, Paramrta was about fifteen feet away from Prabhupada while he waited for his plane to leave. Prabhupada was sitting and observing. She wasn't extroverted and was never a book distributor, but she knew that Prabhupada had said the cruelest thing is to keep people in ignorance and he pushed devotees to distribute his books.

I felt, "Can't I distribute some books for Prabhupada? He's given me my life. Can't I try?" I picked up a pink-covered *Nectar of Devotion* and stopped a young businessman who looked at me, smiling, "Yes?" I didn't know what to say and my eyes flooded with tears. The man left. Prabhupada's flight was called, he walked to his gate, stopped, turned around, gravely looked directly at me, put his palms together, bowed, turned, and left. Prabhupada appreciated and was grateful for the effort, not the result.

In the *Gita*, Prabhupada writes that if we're not able to follow this process, if we simply have faith then the time will come when we can follow. No one is restricted from associating with Prabhupada because we associate with him by following his instructions and his instructions are in his books. He hasn't left, he's still present in his instructions. Everything Prabhupada represented, everything he gave us, everything he taught us is right here, right now. Devotees who hear properly and are faithful and sincere will have Prabhupada's company. He'll direct and reciprocate with us if we're free from pretence. In his humility, Prabhupada's obliged to devotees who are honest and decent.

Parasakti devi dasi

In New York City in 1974, Parasakti was taken by the devotees on harinama and would think, "Someday I'll join them." She got mantra cards, BTGs, books, and knew that Prabhupada was right about not eating meat and not taking intoxicants. Yet she still thought there was something to enjoy in the material world.

For years I wanted to go to the Brooklyn temple but wasn't ready. Finally I got there, met many nice devotees and heard many wonderful classes and kirtans. It was a small temple, yet somehow so many young women and men lived there peacefully. I was enlivened to be with all the ISKCON Press devotees, the artists, and performers like Rasajna, who did plays for Srila Prabhupada's pleasure. She and the other women in the temple were eager for me to join.

Every day I'd go on *sankirtana*, but it was difficult; I wasn't a big collector. Daivi-sakti encouraged me by being fearless and so comfortable with giving all kinds of people Krishna consciousness. And Gauri used to open a book and start talking to a person on the street about Maharaja Pariksit, Sukadeva Goswami, and Srila Vyasadeva. She talked straight to the soul and said exactly what was in the *Bhagavatam*. That also encouraged me but, although I did book distribution for nine years, I always struggled.

One of the most depressing moments of my life was when I learned that Gopijanavallabha, the Brooklyn temple president, wasn't going to recommend me for initiation. I was crying and felt like committing suicide. Then I thought, "I won't commit suicide, I'll think Krishna is trying to make me humble." Sunita intervened on my behalf. She told Gopijanavallabha, "This girl is sincere and is heartbroken that you won't recommend her for initiation. You should talk to her." And Sunita told me, "These are the points to say: You accept that the spiritual master, being the representative of the Supreme Personality of Godhead, is as good as God and is speaking on behalf of God. And you accept that you are a menial servant of your spiritual master and what he says is your life and soul." I said that to Gopijanavallabha and meant it. He said, "All right, I'll put your name on the list." I was so happy. I was initiated in Brooklyn, New York, on January 1, 1975 when I was twenty-one.

From the beginning I was constantly being told that *vani* is more important than *vapuh*. So I always keep in touch with Prabhupada through his books and recordings. When I listen to him he's right there and that's kept me bound to the devotees and to Srila Prabhupada all these years. Plus the *Following Srila Prabhupada* series of videos is like having Prabhupada's association. It's amazing.

Parijata devi dasi

Even as a householder with kids, Parijata's first duty was service. She made garlands and cooked for Srila Prabhupada. She didn't have problems with her mind because she was fully engaged; service was the answer to her problems. "What else is there besides devotional service? It's the summum bonum of all scriptures," she says.

In the early days when I was doing so much service I didn't know what's going on, really. My early devotee life is a haze to me. I didn't attend many classes because I was in the kitchen or on the altar. And soon after marriage I had kids, so service was always there. When Prabhupada came, I cooked for him in Paris and in Geneva. All that service helped to purify my contaminated mind.

Now in my old age, family life and attraction to husband is not there, so I can dedicate my thoughts to Srila Prabhupada more. I always hear Prabhupada's recordings because even though his words don't always register, something stays with me. And his voice is purifying. Now automatically I like to go out on *harinama* and preach – to find some interested people and change their life. I pray for that. But at the same time, I try to be patient and tolerant. I have to give up my plans and surrender to whatever comes and try to learn the lesson from that.

I'm inspired more and more because of the purification of devotional service. That's the process, purification. Even if we don't try hard, it comes automatically by chanting, following the principles, and following Srila Prabhupada's instructions. Prabhupada once told a story about a person who had diarrhea. Somebody suggested he eat ghee. At first, the ghee didn't help. But the more he took ghee, its fat coated his stomach and his disease was gradually cured.

I'm preparing for my next life. *Bhajana kara sadhana kara murte janle hoya.* In a lecture, Prabhupada talks about how we have to learn how to die. How, side-by-side, we need a little determination and full faith in Srila Prabhupada. And we need to endure whatever comes.

I want to preach one-on-one. I want to advise people to first of all become serious about the goal of life and then go to somebody they are inspired by, somebody that has good qualities. And also to admit that this material world is a place of misery. Before I became a devotee I was traveling, looking for happiness in drugs or this or that, but I realized, "There's no happiness there."

My inspiration is Prabhupada's every word, really. Kusha was saying that when she made sprouts for Srila Prabhupada's salad, Srila Prabhupada said, "Make sure every one of these sprouts is offered because they are all individual living entities." That's not fanaticism, that's to teach us that there's a soul there. Krishna is present everywhere and we should think, "Who didn't water these flowers, these trees? Why are they dying? Why are we not taking care of these things?" Similarly the animals under our care. The world would be a better place if we had this consciousness.

As I hear so many Prabhupada stories from everybody, it increases my attachment for Srila Prabhupada. It's amazing how that really helps, to hear all these stories. It seems to me that it's good for the younger devotees to know Srila Prabhupada so they know what a devotee is, how he walks, talks, and how he sits. Then you can have a better idea of who to surrender to. You don't have to have a guru that's on the level of Srila Prabhupada, but at least you should know what a pure devotee is like in his daily activities. It's very important.

If we really want to make advancement in spiritual life, we should disassociate ourselves from the mass of people and also from incompatible people because that association is just an entanglement.

A good saying is *atmavan manyate jagat*, everybody sees everything according to his own perception. Prabhupada said, "Every fool thinks everybody else is also a fool." We can stop and consider that not everything is black and white; sometimes we don't know what's what. This process takes time. Everything takes time, sometimes a long time. But the more we are serious the faster it goes.

Shortly before Srila Prabhupada departed from this world he said, "*Varnashram-dharma,* therefore, is essential, for it can bring people to *sattva-guna. Tada rajas-tamo-bhavah kama-lobhadayas ca ye. Tamo-guna* and *rajo-guna* increase lust and greed, which implicate a living entity in such a way that he must exist in this material world in many, many forms. That is very dangerous." (Bhag.10.13.53, purport) So, if lust and greed are dangerous, then we shouldn't waste time in entanglement.

Prabhupada continues, "One should therefore be brought to *sattva-guna* by the establishment of *varnashrama-dharma* and should develop the brahminical qualifications of being very neat and clean, rising early in the morning, and seeing *mangala-arati*. In this way, one should stay in *sattva-guna,* and then one cannot be influenced by *tamo-guna* and *rajo-guna.*"

Haribol, what else is there to say? I always see this vision of Prabhupada on his departure bed with the microphone saying, "That is very dangerous."

Parvati devi dasi

Parvati had gone to the roof of the Santa Niketan temple in Delhi to take darshan of the Radha-Parthasarathi Deities when she met Srila Prabhupada, who was also on the roof, for the first time. It was sunset and the sky's colors blended with

Prabhupada's saffron cloth. Although she was never trained to do so, as soon as she saw Srila Prabhupada, Parvati offered her obeisances.

It was just the Deities, Srila Prabhupada, and I on the roof and I immediately felt a connection with Srila Prabhupada. After that, I followed all the devotees to Vrindavan where Srila Prabhupada was giving lectures and darshans. I stayed in the Radha-Damodara temple with Yamuna and washed Srila Prabhupada's pots after she'd cooked. I knew nothing about devotional service but I was used to washing things in sand and ashes, and somehow washing those pots was the nicest experience I'd ever had.

When I saw Srila Prabhupada during the Mayapur festival in 1974, I knew he would be the most important person in my life. I didn't understand what it meant to have a guru but I got initiated. During the ceremony I paid my full, prostrated *dandavats* in front of Srila Prabhupada like everybody else did, but I had to get up and do it again because I'd done it in the wrong direction. I was so stunned that when Prabhupada asked me the four regulative principles I could only remember three of them, so he added, "No gambling." After the ceremony I helped cook the feast. I was happy to be fully engaged in serving the devotees, going on *parikrama,* and hearing Srila Prabhupada. From that day I've chanted sixteen rounds.

Later, in Nairobi, while Prabhupada was honoring *sandesh* I'd made, he closed his eyes and said, "She has learned the art." He wrote to me, "Please perfect the making of these milk sweets and offer them to Radha and Krishna, and that will be the perfection of your life." I took that to mean that anything we do, we should try to do perfectly, offer it to Radha and Krishna, and that's the perfection of our life. I've tried to follow those instructions in any service I've done.

When Srila Prabhupada gave me Gayatri, he was calm and pacifying and had me repeat the words until I got them right. He asked, "Do you have any questions?" I had a lot of questions when I went in his room, but they were all answered by his presence. I couldn't wait to get out of his room to finish making *sandesh* so I could give it to him for his trip.

Prabhupada's presence is strong in his *samadhi* in Vrindavan and it's so beautifully made that people comment, "Why did we have to go to the Taj Mahal? This *samadhi* temple is much more beautiful." Every day, all day, I have the wonderful service of trying to maintain and protect his *samadhi* and by Krishna's mercy Srila Prabhupada encourages me in dreams and visions and prayers. My *samadhi* service is all-absorbing and is my saving grace.

If it weren't for Srila Prabhupada we wouldn't have *prasadam*, books, and temples. His followers are obligated and thankful to him. Our service to Srila Prabhupada is our greatest reciprocation with him and serving him in his *samadhi* is the quintessence of service in separation. Srila Prabhupada's *samadhi* is the most important place in the world.

Parvati devi dasi

In 1968, Parvati devi dasi was living in San Francisco. One day she was drawn to a group of devotees who were chanting on a street corner and offered them some dried figs. Shortly after, living in Laguna Beach right next to the temple, she heard mangala-arati, and thought the chanting was very beautiful. One night after the Sunday Feast, the devotees were delivering prasadam to all the homes in the cul-de-sac.

I had never tasted anything so delicious. I went to the temple that evening and was greeted by Rukmini, with her big beautiful smile, and was attracted to everything she was saying. I went to the Colorado temple first but moved to the home of Rukmini and Dwarkadish, where there were more householders. His Divine Grace Srila Prabhupada was very soon to live forever in my heart.

I am in my home in Los Angeles while the world is collapsing around us. Last week while staying in my home because of a lockdown for Covid-19, I heard the kirtan party from the temple chanting down the street. I ran to the door and shouted, "*Jaya* Srila Prabhupada!" Yesterday at 4:00 pm, my smart phone let me know *arati* was beginning in Mayapur. There was a magnificent kirtan and my daughter, Lila, and I were listening while she was cooking dinner. We both chanted. Tonight I am on Instagram, watching a video that a dear godsister made of Rukmini and Dwarkadish while she was on the altar. I was privileged to gaze upon Their Lordships, almost as though I was right there with Them. Kirtan is going on all over the world, devotees are sharing stories, birthdays, and the passing of our dear godbrothers and sisters who are departing from this material world. So much love and compassion we all have for one another. Thank you Srila Prabhupada!

It was such a joyous time when Srila Prabhupada used to come to Los Angeles. We were all so excited gathering our children together and coming to greet him at the airport. The chanting was ecstatic and we looked like we were from another planet as he arrived with his beautiful transcendental smile and fragrant garlands around his neck. At the temple we would see Srila Prabhupada every day during *guru-puja* and his nectarean classes. It was especially wonderful to see all our little children receiving their morning cookie.

One time a cake was offered on Krishna's birthday that was almost as tall as the ceiling. We would dance on big full moon evenings in honor of Lord

Chaitanya's appearance day, and we had contests to see who could eat the most *gulubjamans*. It was an honor to pull Lord Jagannatha, Balarama, and Lady Subhadra's carts as everyone was able to see Lord Jagannatha's beautiful smile. *Prasadam* was served to thousands of people, as we embraced Indian culture through dance and music.

When my daughter Chandra passed away on March 26, 2011, it was the most painful, horrifying moment in my life. One of the first calls I made was to my dear beloved Vrnda, who set up a Vedic altar for her transition. Suddenly, my world was shattered beyond belief, and I had to draw upon the strength and knowledge I had received as Prabhupada's disciple and a devotee of Lord Krishna. I traveled to her home in Tucson, where she had died. The morning that she was to be cremated, I asked if I could see her one more time. I wrote, "Hare Krishna sweet Chandra," and the names of each family member who was sending love to her, all over the box that contained her body. Her face was covered with a white shear veil, and her body was covered with *prasadam* flowers. I prostrated myself on the ground and thanked her for being my daughter. I was becoming weak and faint, and as I was walking out of the crematorium, where I had just pushed a button to send her body into fire, I could feel Krishna's sun on my face. I felt a kind hand on my shoulder, holding me up, and I knew it was my godsister Niscintya, who happened to be in Tucson visiting her mother.

I am grateful to have one video of little Chandi, as a little baby in my arms in her pink hooded coat, reaching her hand out for a cookie from Srila Prabhupada, with a little bangle on her wrist. My childhood friend, Cynthia, who lived in Tucson and made all the arrangements for me, suggested, "Let's take Parvati to the temple." I was experiencing ecstatic symptoms, hearing the kirtan, seeing Their Lordships, and feeling Prabhupada's love. I was dancing like a dervish for a long time. I heard Prabhupada tell me that he was taking care of Chandra. It was Prabhupada's love for me and my daughter, that carried me and supported me at the most sad moment of my life. I am grateful for all the support of my godsisters and brothers.

Pavani devi dasi

Pavani was supposed to see Prabhupada in San Francisco, but and at the last minute the Vancouver temple president asked her and a couple of other brahmacharinis to go on traveling sankirtana instead. Pavani, totally surrendered, said, "Sure, no problem." During the initiation ceremony in San Francisco Prabhupada called Pavani's name three times but she wasn't there.

In April of 1977, our party of *sankirtana* ladies was in Mayapur when Prabhupada walked with all of us from the Lotus Building, where he stayed, to the front gate of the Sri Mayapur Chandrodaya Mandir. His little black Indian car was waiting for him there, but before he got in he stopped to talk to us. Each one of us answered a couple of his questions. When my turn came, Prabhupada looked straight at me, asked me something, and I started crying. I cried and I cried. Srila Prabhupada stood there for some time, waiting for me to stop crying, but I couldn't stop enough to talk to him. Finally someone told him it was time to leave. Srila Prabhupada sat alone in the middle of the back seat of the car with his legs crossed and both hands on top of his cane in front of him. His body looked small but his head looked big. He was peaceful and bright and beautiful and wonderful. I felt he was not of this world and am eternally grateful for having seen him in that way.

I heard that when a devotee said to Prabhupada, "I wish my service could be massaging your feet," Srila Prabhupada told him, "Distributing my books is massaging my feet." My relationship with Prabhupada was massaging his feet by distributing his books and I worked hard to get my name on the *sankirtana* newsletter for book distribution. I thought, "Maybe he'll see my name there."

Prabhupada said that it's better to be like a steady drop of water that wears away stone than to be a tidal wave that comes, does some big service, and then goes. I want to be the steady drop, always staying in Srila Prabhupada's service.

Pavitra devi dasi

Pavitra was initiated by Srila Prabhupada on Janmastami in 1977 in Los Angeles, California. It was the last initiation that Srila Prabhupada gave before passing away.

Since I was a teenager I was searching for the truth, going to different yoga ashrams, listening and watching, and meeting a couple of gurus from India. When I was a hippie runaway in New York City I'd see the devotees collecting money in conch shells on the street in Greenwich Village. I decided to go to the Hare Krishna temple and see what it was all about. Devotees tried to get me to join and I felt pounced upon. I left, swearing I'd never go back. It was too scary. But I was pulled toward the devotees when I'd see them chanting *harinama* in Los Angeles, and after I heard George Harrison's album, I started chanting the Hare Krishna mantra. At that time something came over me. My life was never the same. The mantra drew me closer. It was like the clouds parted and the gates of heaven opened up.

Once I woke up in the middle of the night, looked out the window at the stars and had a profound realization that I didn't have to come back. I said to myself aloud, "I don't have to come back. It's my choice." But I had to find someone to help me get out. I needed an elevator to the top.

One Sunday while my daughter and I were at the temple, I went into the gift shop and said to Pranada, who was behind the counter, "Is there any way that I can end my karma?" I knew that my karma was coming full force and was not good. I was scared. Pranada said, "Yes, surrendering to Srila Prabhupada is an elevator to the top." I couldn't believe that after all my searching someone had answered my question.

My daughter was three and I wanted her in a godly atmosphere and I quickly realized that the Hare Krishna temple was where we should move. I threw out all my books from all other gurus, only kept Prabhupada's books, and we moved into the temple.

I had a lot of mental disturbances when I joined. That's my bad karma in this lifetime. But when I distributed Prabhupada's books, I had no problems. I was in ecstasy. Distributing Srila Prabhupada's books was the greatest experience of my life. I realized that all the knowledge of the *Vedas* was being given to me just by distributing Srila Prabhupada's books.

I'm eternally indebted to Srila Prabhupada.

Payasvini devi dasi

Payasvini was into the drug scene but knew she had to make a change. She visited Siddhaswarupa Swami's ashram in Haiku, Hawaii, where she heard from Teachings of Lord Chaitanya.

Prabhupada's words in that book answered my dilemma of what I was supposed to be doing and helped me make a change. I went back to where I was staying, went to a nearby field to chant Hare Krishna, and the answer was there for me. Eventually I joined Siddhaswarupa and, ultimately, met Srila Prabhupada.

I saw Srila Prabhupada lecture at the Honolulu temple and was impressed with how graceful and gentle he was. Yet he could be strong in his preaching too. He knew what we needed to hear and gave it to us–softly, then strongly, then softly. He was trying to get us to pay attention to what he was saying.

I saw him again in New York in July 1970. My room was upstairs, overlooking Henry Street. Prabhupada stepped out of his car and into the temple room and just seeing him and knowing I was going to have his association was magnetic. Devotees had come to Brooklyn from all around the East Coast. Every day for a week, Prabhupada performed initiations. The temple room was full of devotees making *japa malas* with Tandy Imports beads. I still have mine.

Most devotees collected a little *lakshmi* and offered it to Prabhupada as a gift, but I was pregnant at the time, so I couldn't collect and didn't have any money to offer. Instead, I got some scraps of silk from a *pujari* and made a bookmark about 4 inches wide and 7 inches long for Prabhupada's *Bhagavatam*. When I was called to receive my beads and name, I laid the package with the bookmark on the steps of his *vyasasana*. He smiled at me, then gave me the name Payasvini devi dasi. He chanted the first couple of lines of the *Brahma-samhita: Chintamani-prakara-sadmasu kalpa-vriksha-lakshavriteshu surabhir abhipalayantam*, and said, "Payasvini means one who gives an abundance of milk." I offered my obeisances and walked away, thinking, "I didn't tell him what my gift is for, and he'll never know." I was concerned about that, but everybody was so busy it seemed insignificant to write him a message, so I let it go.

About a year and a half later, my husband and I were in Pittsburgh when Srila Prabhupada was visiting. While Prabhupada was out on his morning walk, I was tidying up his desk and saw my bookmark in his big *Bhagavatam*. He knew what my gift was for. That was my most intimate exchange with Srila Prabhupada.

Sitting on the *vyasasana*, Prabhupada always appeared regal and seemed to know everything. Sometimes I'd be thinking something and the next thing he would say related to what I had been thinking. I had to wonder how he knew everything like that. But he knew everything about us and accepted us as we were, and that was special. I'm happy that I've made it this far with him. I'm not as good as I should be, but I'm trying.

Prachi devi dasi

In 1969 in Griffith Park, Los Angeles, Vishnujana invited Prachi to the temple for a Sunday Feast. Once there, devotees told her that Prabhupada would give the evening lecture. They whisked her in, put her in a sari, and stuck her in front.

That evening, I heard Prabhupada speak about Lord Chaitanya's pastimes. Then the devotees invited my husband and me to attend Ratha-yatra in San Francisco. We went and while everybody else was pulling the carts, we ran ahead and saw Prabhupada arrive to join the procession. Prabhupada looked at me and nodded, then he looked at my husband and nodded. We paid our obeisances. At that moment we knew that Prabhupada was our spiritual master.

When I was going to have my first child, we were in New Vrindavan. I asked if I could have a home birth, and Prabhupada told me that if I felt healthy I could. I felt strongly it would work out all right and it did. Our son was born a little after midnight. After a few hours, Prabhupada sent us a piece of paper with a name for our son–Krishnashtami. Prabhupada also sent us his garland and some *maha-prasadam*. Later, when we took the baby to Prabhupada, Prabhupada was grave and quiet.

When I was in Prabhupada's presence, I felt that he displayed all the Vaishnava qualities he tells us to attain. And I felt I wanted to become pure. I'd been a student of Catholic theology, and was always exploring, challenging, and trying to commit more. From Prabhupada's teachings and writings I got more knowledge than I was looking for. No one I knew had better answers than Srila Prabhupada. What really inspired me was how Prabhupada brought my Catholic teachings to what my inquisitive mind needed. I loved his teachings.

And I loved Prabhupada. He was humbly considerate of me. Once, when he was touring Gita-nagari, he came into our cabin and sat down before our big altar with Jagannatha Deities. Prabhupada said, "Oh, Lord Jagannatha lives here." That was wonderful. He was relaxing, drinking water, and looking around. Devotees kept saying, "Oh, Prabhupada, we have to go, we have to go now," and then they invited me on the tour. I was the only woman and I was nervous. Prabhupada was pleased by the crops.

Prabhupada was also pleased that my husband and I and some *brahmacharis* did door-to-door *sankirtana* and he said others should follow our program. But that program wasn't without risks. I was invited into one house and had a knife pulled on me. Another time a gang of people were about to attack me.

I don't think anyone could inspire us more than Prabhupada did. He's given us everything we need to know. We could be Krishna conscious in one minute if we just applied ourselves. We're all so different, yet he's given us all the chance to cross over birth and death and enter the spiritual world. It's the best opportunity anybody can give. I'm very indebted to him.

Prafullamukhi devi dasi

Prafullamukhi started going to the Berkeley temple in 1969. She had a baby and was living in a macrobiotic commune. She thought the devotees chanting on Telegraph Avenue were so beautiful with their flowing saffron robes.

I approached a young man with a shaved head, and asked what he was doing, what the chanting meant, why he shaved his head. He replied that he had no idea! It was the 1960's!

The first time I saw Srila Prabhupada was at Ratha-yatra in Golden Gate Park of that year. I don't remember much, but I remember seeing the big cart and the large Deities with big smiles.

The next time that I saw Srila Prabhupada was when he came to San Francisco for the 1970 Ratha-yatra. My son and I had moved into an apartment, which the temple had supplied, down the street from the tiny storefront on Frederick Street.

When Srila Prabhupada walked, or should I say floated, into the temple, I was in the back of the group of devotees. Everyone bowed down, and we said our obeisances, but I peeked up because I wanted to get a good look. Srila Prabhupada saw me and smiled. At that moment I realized that no one had ever loved me before. Not really. I was bathed in the warmth of his smile and my life was changed forever. He was offered some sweets, fruit, and water. He popped the sweet into his mouth from about a foot away, and the water "waterfalled" into his mouth as he held his *lota* at forehead height. Amazing. I still spill water when I drink it that way.

Jayananda and the rest of us had worked hard on the three carts that were made for Their Lordships. On the day of Ratha-yatra, we all lined up to pull the carts through Golden Gate Park. I was next to Lady Subhadra's cart where Srila Prabhupada was sitting. Along the way, the mechanism that was to lower the top canopy malfunctioned, and the procession was stalled. Srila Prabhupada got down from the cart and started dancing and leaping in the air, in front of Lady Subhadra. He was ecstatic, with tears in his eyes. It was an amazing sight.

I was initiated by letter, in Victoria Island, B.C. Srila Prabhupada named me Prafullamukhi devi dasi, which means one who always has a cheerful face. We had sent him a picture of our *sankirtana* party chanting in the street. He said he like the cheerful faces of the devotees in the picture. You must have been one of them. He named my son Siddhababa, "servant of the perfect child."

I went to New Vrindavan for the Bhagavata Dharma discourses. I was a *pujari* for Radha-Vrindavanachandra and had been working in the kitchen all day, when the *pujari* didn't show up for her *arati*. So devotees pushed me into doing *arati*, dirt and all. I had no idea that Srila Prabhupada was in the temple room. I've always been shy, so in terror I offered the incense to Srila Prabhupada. When I looked at him sitting on the *vyasasana*, instead of his picture, I had the wonderful realization that he is always sitting there, whether he is physically present, or not. That realization has helped sustain my faith over the years.

My parents were very favorable to Krishna consciousness and had given several donations. They gave a donation for the new temple in the Mission District in San Francisco, and donated the funds for a marble floor for the new temple at Bahulaban. They had a darshan with Srila Prabhupada but somehow I wasn't invited. I was waiting for them outside of the little house in Madhuban, and Srila Prabhupada came out the side door alone. I was alone with Srila Prabhupada! I didn't pay my obeisances or anything. I can empathize with the deer in the headlights: Paralysis. Srila Prabhupada laughed, said "Hare Krishna," and went back inside. My parents never forgot the lecture that Srila Prabhupada gave during that darshan.

My son Siddhababa and I were sitting in the temple room Janmashtami night when Srila Prabhupada read *Krsna* book for hours. I was tired and my legs ached from the baby sleeping in my lap, but I wouldn't have missed it for anything. It was wonderful hearing him read about Lord Krishna's pastimes. You could see his pleasure in reading them.

Sometimes I played with a dog who had wandered onto the New Vrindavan farm and was adopted by the devotees. The problem was that when I threw my bucket of ice-cold water over my head, and got dressed, before taking care of the Deities, the dog would jump on me and I would have to take another cold shower. I would tell him to get away. I'd say, "Go away *muchi*." The name stuck. When Srila Prabhupada was walking around the farm, he saw the dog and said, "Who is that?" "It's Muchi, Srila Prabhupada." Srila Prabhupada laughed and said, "Well, Muchi is a Vaishnava now." Fortunate dog.

I'm not sure if Srila Prabhupada was arriving or leaving the Brooklyn temple on Henry Street, but we were at the airport in a conference room. I was very pregnant, standing on a table, leaning on Visakha's shoulders. I wanted to see and hear, so I was impervious to the danger. Srila Prabhupada was being pestered by the *sannyasis* and other men grouped around him to tell them what is the very best service. Of course, they wanted him to say book distribution, but Srila Prabhupada started talking about a couple who lived in Calcutta. I know I don't have the story completely correct, but he said that the couple would rise, bathe in the Ganga, make *kachoris,* do their *puja,* and go to the market to sell what they had made. He was saying how they did the same thing every day of their lives. The fact that he was talking about a householder couple brought joy to those of us who were not greatly appreciated in the household ashram.

Another time driving to the airport, I was in a car driving directly beside Srila Prabhupada. For some reason I had Parikshit and Bhadra's son, Tulasiananda (I think that's his name), in my lap. He was trying to crawl through the window to get to Srila Prabhupada, who was laughing and shaking his finger at the little boy.

I took care of keeping in touch with the Indian community in the boroughs around New York City. On one visit, Srila Prabhupada was lecturing in the temple room, and I was sitting on the steps leading upstairs. I could see Srila Prabhupada from my position. Some Indian guests came in and the devotees were crowding the doorway to the temple. I was very distressed because I wanted the guests to see Srila Prabhupada. During the lecture, Srila Prabhupada looked at me and said, "What is it?" I pointed to the guests and he had the devotees move aside and let them in.

I had a darshan scheduled with Srila Prabhupada. My new son, Arjuna, and I were waiting to go in, when Arjuna made a baby poop, so of course I couldn't go in. Srila Prabhupada walked by me and said, "Just like the baby is always happy in the arms of his mother, similarly, we are always happy in the arms of Lord Krishna."

Srila Prabhupada was sitting in his rocking chair watching the play "Krishna Kidnaps Rukmini." He enjoyed the play very much, he laughed and smiled a lot. At the end he gave the highest praise. Smiling he said, "This is better than the original!"

Srila Prabhupada came for the Manhattan Ratha-yatra. When he came through the lobby of the large, new 55th Street temple the devotees were lined up to greet him. My son, one-year-old Arjuna, was standing in front of me. Srila Prabhupada headed for the elevator and Arjuna got away from me and ran and grabbed Srila Prabhupada's feet. The *sannyasis* and other men around Srila Prabhupada tried to push Arjuna away. Srila Prabhupada said, "Leave him alone, he is a great soul." This was such music for my ears.

Another devotee, Ishani, and I made a nice rooftop garden for Srila Prabhupada. He was pleased and thanked us.

Because I always had children to watch, I rarely got to go to darshans, when Srila Prabhupada was visiting. I finally was able to leave my son with another devotee one evening. I rode the elevator to Srila Prabhupada's floor, and to my dismay the darshan was completely full with no space. I stood in the door, very disappointed. Srila Prabhupada looked up and somehow the devotees shifted and left me room to go sit close to Srila Prabhupada. Everyone turned and smiled at me as I walked through the large room to sit down. It was mystical.

On that visit, Srila Prabhupada visited Gita-nagari. I made a mango cake and some mango pickle for his trip. His servant told me that he enjoyed them.

I didn't see Srila Prabhupada again. When he left the planet, I was living in Gita-nagari. I was standing at the sink where we washed our eating plates, and Madhuvisha came in and told us the news. I had never really understood about the deep attachment, like a rope, between the guru and disciple. But then I did. I screamed for a while, then cried a lot. I will never recover.

Praharana devi dasi

Praharana dasi became a devotee in Toronto in the fall of 1971. She was studying at the University of Western Ontario where devotees visited and served a feast. She was reluctant to go when she saw how they carried on during kirtan–one devotee had neck beads the size of golf balls. But curiosity and hunger got her to the feast. There she bought a Gita.

I saw Srila Prabhupada for the first time in July 1972 in New York. There were devotees in the hallways, the temple room, everywhere. When Prabhupada came to enter the temple room, everybody threw themselves on the floor in obeisances. I couldn't get down – there wasn't a spare centimeter on the floor! I was in a state of awe as I watched him walk by. He looked at me and I felt touched and blessed, "Wow, he noticed me!"

I moved into the Toronto temple and the Deities arrived from India. Laxmimoni told Srila Prabhupada on the phone that the Deity of Krishna had a little belly. Prabhupada laughed and said, "Oh, that's because He's Ksiracora-Gopinatha. You have to serve Him twelve pots of *ksira* every day." And we've done that every night since They were installed in 1972 on Radhastami.

I was initiated on the same day. There were about seventy devotees crammed into the little house on Gerrard Street East, which was in an unsafe neighborhood. I think being jammed together in that little house was good for us – we were all in our early 20s. We lived in great austerity, sleeping on the cold hardwood floor, fifteen girls to a room, with only cold water in the shower, eating mostly cabbage and potatoes and exactly three chickpeas on wax paper plates. We served flat out from 3:00 am to 9:00 pm. We were so exhausted most of the time that to stay awake during class we used water spritzers.

We shared our clothing, which was orange *saris* made from six yards of orange broadcloth for the unmarried girls and the same in yellow for those who were married. Men and women also shared a number of "moon boots" for winter *sankirtana*. Unfortunately, they were all the same size, and we girls had to shuffle and wear many pairs of socks to keep them on our feet.

Many times the girls would come home from *sankirtana* after very long days in the cold with frozen fingers and toes, and our dear godbrother Ayodhyapati Dasa (now BB Govinda Maharaja) would have steaming hot *burfi* ready for us at the door.

Srila Prabhupada came to Toronto in 1975. Seeing the crowded conditions he said, "You have to buy a building. The BBT will help you. Start looking." So we began to collect money for it, mostly selling lollipops on the street.

I was the head *pujari* during his 1975 visit. After I'd bathed and dressed the Deities, I was nervous, thinking "I don't know what I'm doing. Ksiracora-Gopinatha is going to complain to Prabhupada for sure, 'Save Me from this situation!'" Like most mornings, the men were with Srila Prabhupada on the morning walk and the women were at the temple doing service – cleaning, cooking, and Deity worship.

I started the *arati* at seven am. Prabhupada entered the temple room ahead of the crowd, having arrived in the lead car. Srila Prabhupada, Radha-Ksiracora-Gopinatha, and myself were alone in the temple room.

Prabhupada walked to the altar and with folded hands looked at Radha-Ksiracora-Gopinatha, offered *dandavats,* and then stood about two feet behind me, gazing intensely at the Deities. That afternoon, Ayodhyapati told me Srila Prabhupada told him to tell the *pujari* to get a bigger bell. So that afternoon I bought a big bell in China town.

When Prabhupada was leaving, Visvakarma told the women that we were to stay back and finish our services. We were upset with this instruction. We hadn't had a chance to go on morning walks or to be with Srila Prabhupada privately as the men had. There was a "saffron wall" of visiting *sannyasis* and *brahmacharis* always in front of Srila Prabhupada and we felt we had missed out.

We decided to go to the airport anyway. We took an *arati* tray for *guru-puja* with us, and some sweets we knew Srila Prabhupada would like, and about ten of us piled into a van. As we passed Srila Prabhupada's car on the highway, we rolled down our windows and screamed, "*Jaya,* Prabhupada! *Jaya,* Prabhupada!" The temple president was annoyed that we were making such a scene. But Srila Prabhupada folded his hands and smiled at us.

We set up a comfortable spot at the airport and readied the *arati* paraphernalia. Prabhupada sat down and Visvakarma offered *arati.*

When Prabhupada came back in 1976, we had purchased the building he had seen and liked. He was pleased and directed us how to make the kitchen and altars. I went a few times to Prabhupada's room to hear him speak. Once, he told an Indian couple that they should "help these devotees. That is your job. You are from India. You help these devotees to spread Krishna consciousness." I thought, "Wow, that's a nice thing to say," because we were struggling for money. There were a lot of us, but we bought the temple by selling lollipops day and night. We owed a lot of money.

In 1977, I saw Prabhupada in Mayapur. He was ill and weak. He would circumambulate the altar on a palanquin, wham the bell, and everybody would cheer.

The early days of ISKCON were full of energy, bliss, and huge enthusiasm. However we were young, naïve, and often misinformed about the philosophy. When I experienced prejudice or discrimination on the part of the men toward the women I understood that we women had less preferred bodies and, therefore, had to deal with a less preferred situation. I accepted this idea at that time as a way of trying to be more humble and to basically survive and grow in Krishna consciousness. In that way I could remain enthusiastic in Krishna consciousness.

For instance, in 1975 the women were expelled from the temple on the order of Tamal Krishna Maharaja. Maharaja had thought we should all go to Australia, but that wasn't practical, so we had to rent our own place, do services only if we were not seen by the men (*aratis* in the middle of the day as opposed to *mangala-arati*, for example, dressing the Deities behind closed doors, cooking ...) and we were to give classes to ourselves. Of course, we were expected to continue with "the pick" on the street. We felt bad and wanted to move back into the temple, to be a family again.

After about six months, Uttamasloka, now in Chicago, offered to fly us to Chicago and allow us to live in the temple as "full citizens." We were torn. We wanted desperately to be temple devotees again and to feel less like "low lifes," but we loved Radha-Ksiracora-Gopinatha, and some of us also had strong attachments to certain of the *brahmacharis*.

We arranged a meeting between the exiled women with the temple men. We told them they had a choice: they would marry us and stop this nonsense, or we would leave for Chicago. The men were shocked. However it only took a few days for them to respond. They decided to "surrender to the 'fall down' and get married in order to keep the women."

The women then moved back into the temple again, cramming into a tiny side room with no windows. Still, it was a great victory for us and for our temple, and although a number of us were now married, we continued to live as *brahmacharis* and *brahmacharinis* in the temple. Soon after Srila Prabhupada sent Tamal Krishna Maharaja to China.

In the next few years, the temple rented or bought houses for the householders. Generally each mother and her children would occupy one room, and share the kitchen and bathroom. Some of the men lived with their wives, but many continued to live in the temple. I moved into such a house the day I came home from the hospital with my first child. Living in this house with the other women was wonderful. We were sisters and raised our children together. It wasn't conventional family life, but it was our family, and the children were loved by all of us.

We had a nursery school with three babies, as our babies had been born only a few weeks apart. Each of us would take two mornings a week to babysit so that the other two moms could do service. Our children were like triplets. We nursed each other's babies and did whatever was necessary to continue with our temple services and provide loving care for the babies.

We continued to embrace a very austere lifestyle, thinking that simple living meant owning almost nothing at all and providing only minimum comfort for the body – just keeping body and soul together. Beds were unheard of.

The idea of not being so totally austere wouldn't have crossed most of our minds. We had relationships based on strict service goals and not on love and care. We had visions of achieving Krishna-*prema* within a few years. Now I see Krishna consciousness is a long maturing process. I see the value in the philosophy and in the association of devotees, both of which are part of this process. However painful, every devotee will have challenges. How else are we going to learn to look beyond this world?

My husband left our marriage for another devotee woman during a tumultuous and difficult time in ISKCON. He also left ISKCON. Working under Kirtanananda Swami as our zonal-*acharya* was intolerable and insane, so I don't blame him, really. Also, we had never had a true marriage in the sense of what one generally considers a loving relationship. We were real products of early ISKCON and an arranged marriage. I never entered another relationship because when my husband left I had three children to raise, my youngest being only eighteen months old.

Yet I never had felt resentment toward Srila Prabhupada or Krishna consciousness. I knew that we ourselves had mismanaged the philosophy and were naïve in many ways. Even normal relationships with husband, wife, and children were frowned upon. It was easy for the men to take roles of power, control, and superiority. We were pioneers in "get it done no matter what" mode. No sacrifice was too great. Can we expect that things weren't going to go wrong sometimes? Live and learn – and now we want to use what we've learned to coach the new generation.

One thing I didn't understand as a young devotee was the power of prayer. It's important to reveal your mind to Srila Prabhupada and the Lord, to beg for understanding and knowledge in order to make sense of things and to keep faith. It's also critical to reveal your mind to devotees who care about you, to cultivate devotee friendships, and to serve devotees. Serving the devotees, praying, cultivating a humble mood, and doing devotional services that suit your abilities and propensities is absolutely critical to build strong, healthy, loving families. Without that we have no future. We have to understand that to have affection and care and love for someone is not only all right, it's essential. Until you really learn to love and care for somebody else in a material body, how are you ever going to understand what love for Krishna is? How can we become truly personal rather than impersonal in our realization?

We cannot become Krishna conscious alone. Until I had my first child I had no clue what love meant. Holding that baby and selflessly taking care of him, being completely absorbed in his care, it occurred to me, "Oh, my God, this is just a tiny bit of what it is to love Krishna." That was a big insight.

Pranada devi dasi

At eight years old all childhood play stopped, and a spontaneous prayer took over Pranada's life, "If you show me the books of the Absolute Truth, I will surrender everything." She didn't tell anyone of the prayer. By twelve she was reading prolifically about all religions and spiritual paths and ventured out alone into San Francisco's early 1970's eclectic spiritual marketplace. At sixteen, nearly suicidal due to not finding an answer, she sat down with Beyond Birth and Death and Easy Journey to Other Planets. Tears poured down her cheeks as she placed these little treasures on her lap after reading them. Her prayer was answered. The Absolute Truth and her master had revealed themselves. It was time to surrender.

In the weeks approaching Prabhupada's arrival for his last visit to Los Angeles in 1976, I pictured walking with him on Venice Beach early in the morning with our small group of big book distributors: Mulaprakriti, Lavangalatika, Gauri, Bhakta Priya, Jadurani, Nartaki, Vrndavana Vilasini, Sulaksmana (I'm sure I'm missing someone). Then one of the ladies said that the scheduled walk with the women probably wouldn't happen. "After all," she said, "we're women." I thought, *We're distributing books. Prabhupada would want to meet us, wouldn't he?* But the devotee's words gnawed at me. I wouldn't be able to ask any questions or walk beside him in the small intimate group of my friends. I knew in my gut she was right. In past months we were told to make ourselves scarce during Tamal Krishna Maharaja's visit as he was lobbying to send all the women in the Movement to Australia. I'd sat in the classes day after day as the speaker berated women. Jadurani was stopped from giving her good *Bhagavatam* classes. I stood by sisters as they cried when their husbands mistreated them. Women were not regarded well and we knew it. But I just had to have some personal service, some interaction with the life of my life Srila Prabhupada.

Gopanandakari Prabhu stayed in the *brahmacharini ashram* with me. "Is there any personal service we can do for Srila Prabhupada when he's here?" I asked. After a long pause and much questioning she offered, "I heard he likes it when the ladies oodle."

"You know," she said, "the sound some make at the pitch of a *kirtan*." She held her hand over her mouth, breathed deep, exhaled in a high pitched sound as she rolled her tongue off the roof of her mouth. "Take a big breath" she said, "You *have* to oodle three times and hold each one as long as you can."

It was like an American Indian battle cry. The *ulu dhvani* done by Bengali women is considered an auspicious sound of offering respect and good tidings. And those demure Bengali women let out these sounds that were louder than the *kirtan* singers and instruments combined! Every few days before Prabhupada came I honed my skill during Agnideva's ecstatic evening *kirtan*.

We decided to oodle for Prabhupada when he entered the temple for Greeting of the Deities. He would walk from the far right-hand side of the altar past Jagannatha, Subhadra and Balarama, past the doors of Rukmini-Dwarkadisa's altar, and onto Gaura-Nitai's altar just in time for the altar doors to open and the gorgeous sound of Yamuna's voice led us in the "Govinda" prayers.

Gopa and I positioned ourselves in the middle of the balcony during *japa* and waited. As soon as Prabhupada emerged everyone dropped to the floor saying his *pranams* in a low whisper. Gopa and I oodled with full force. And as soon as we began oodling I got this awful sinking feeling from my throat to my stomach all the way to my feet and I wanted to run. Our oodle was *really* loud; it invaded the hushed temple room and startled even me. The oodling I had done during *kirtan* when *kartalas* and *mridangas* played and many devotees sang in chorus was not obtrusive. Now it overtook the whole large space and bounced off the walls.

Prabhupada held his cane between his folded palms. He slightly furrowed his brow as he reached the front of Jagannatha's altar. My mind raced when he wrinkled his eyebrows. Many devotees below lifted their heads off the ground peering up at us with disgust or disbelief.

Oh, god, I'm such a fool! I thought, *How am I going to finish three long-held oodles? I'm not even through the first one. We should be paying obeisance. What was I thinking?!*

I wanted to stop more than anything in the world, but we had to do *three* oodles and I drew in a second breath. As he reached Rukmini-Dwarakadisa's altar Prabhupada began gently shaking his head from side to side in a "no" gesture. Devotees began to rise from their obeisance. Many turned to face us in astonishment, men unabashedly looking up at us in the balcony, then over at Srila Prabhupada to observe his reaction.

What would be our punishment? Genuine terror engulfed me, but I kept going. *Would Srila Prabhupada understand my heart? I must make this, my only direct offering, at his lotus feet.*

All of a sudden, Prabhupada burst into a huge, broad smile, turned and looked directly at us, and slightly extending his clasped hands he shook them in our direction in a thankful gesture.

A smile. Not a grin, a *huge* smile. He's thanking us! Prabhupada had understood our intentions: to honor him. He accepted our offering. There was nothing else to achieve, nothing was lacking.

In dawn's new light, on a warm mid-summer's morning, sometime between 5:30 and 6:00am I gathered with eight or ten other devotees on the small landing at the base of the stairway leading to Prabhupada's room. We chanted *japa* softly with various offerings in our hands. Prabhupada's car was parked in the alley which bordered the sidewalk where we stood. He would walk twenty or twenty-five feet from the base of the stairs to the car door.

When the door to the stairs that led to Prabhupada's quarters opened, I focused on the first stair at the top. Soon enough Prabhupada's feet appeared. Then his legs, next his torso, and finally his full radiant form. His slow descent into view excited my heart, made it pound, and was the unique feature of waiting for him here. You saw him appear *gradually*, each step increased the anticipation of seeing his smiling face, and standing next to him momentarily. The buildup was short, but it was exciting and full of promise. I had never felt more childlike. Prabhupada stopped in front of our little group and took flowers and gifts, asked how devotees were, walked to the car and was gone.

I returned every day, part of the small crowd, to the sidewalk. One morning I decided to watch Prabhupada from across the alley on the other side of Prabhupada's car. That way I would see Prabhupada's loving exchanges from a different angle. I stood twelve to fourteen inches from the car door on the opposite side where he would enter.

I immersed in joy watching Prabhupada exchange a few words and receive flowers and small gifts from the little band of, mostly, women. The concrete walkway, alley, and the drab two-story buildings became luminous by the shining hearts, colorful flowers, and the warm mixture of love and respect. It ended much too soon, and though I was wholly, deeply satisfied I wasn't satiated. Seeing and feeling Srila Prabhupada can make you a little wild, thirsty, inside. It was my constant state while Prabhupada was visiting.

Prabhupada slid into the backseat. Something got his attention. At first, I didn't realize it was me that caught his eyes. He leaned forward to see me, palms folded together, and looked me in the eyes. It's difficult to explain all that happened in the seconds he looked at me. Words can't sum it up. The thing is, my whole life can't sum it up.

When Prabhupada looked at me, and I looked back at him, there was no car, no people, no alley. I wasn't in a body. Time didn't exist. He wasn't uncomfortable to stare into my eyes. This so deeply surprised me, I almost gasped.

I thought I was tucked away hiding in the overhang, instead I might as well have been sitting next to him in the back seat. For the first split-second this rattled me and I was self-conscious. But this sense melted under Prabhupada's glance and was replaced by thoughts about how I was to respond to his look.

The need to respond wasn't the kneejerk response of being in an awkward situation; it was that his eyes spoke to me. They had a message, he deserved a response, and I needed to respond with something *significant*. His look didn't demand, but encouraged me in the most loving, kind, deeply thoughtful manner. Indeed, it seemed his eyes pleaded with me.

I was trying to learn the language of his eyes and decipher what they were saying in split seconds. My eyes stayed fixed, but I was frantic to make sense of what was transpiring. I'd never had a discussion with eyes and the longer I looked the more important it was that I respond. *What was it that I needed to say?*

All of a sudden it was perfectly clear. I felt Prabhupada was my friend–a long, lost friend. He was looking at an old friend whom he was seeing again after a long – very long – absence. At first this was so contrary to my understanding of our relationship that I felt I was just an observer of the exchange. But so full and welcoming were his eyes that I thought, *Surely I am his dear friend and he's reminding me of our love for each other and our long-time bond.* In the next flash I didn't think this thought, I *knew* this truth – as sure as I was looking at him, and he at me – *we* were profoundly connected, there was no distance between us. Everything had been bridged. His look penetrated whatever it is in the world that keeps souls apart. I knew my eyes lit up, because the whole world brightened and I glimpsed eternity in our relationship coming from a long time back and moving forever forward. I saw eternity.

For the first time in my life I was sure. Sublimely sure. Sure my childhood prayer was true and answered; sure I had made the right decision to stand here; the right decision to join the temple; the right decision to take initiation. My search was over, unequivocally. I could rest, absolutely sure I belonged with Prabhupada. I was his and he was mine, and this was so forever. I would never leave him. I said *that* with my eyes, and relaxed into the love of his. So long I had been alone on my journey. So very alone. So long I had waited in seeming darkness. Then the entire matter was sealed and I felt emotion pitching inside, *My friend, my friend. My long-lost friend. My master!*

His smile grew larger, and he gently shook his joined palms in a gesture that said thank you. Then the car began moving. Tears welled in my eyes and I shuddered involuntarily against the connection that at once demanded everything and gave more than I had ever imagined. I stood on the spot for a long time.

Srila Prabhupada's equanimity, compassion, kindness, and spiritual *shakti* are uncommon even among exalted saints. How could a "simple" look put me into direct touch with my soul and eternity, and in a flash of a second, and so powerfully that I've been held by it my entire life during my darkest nights, my deepest emotional despair? Prabhupada was infused with the potency of Krishna's *svarupa-shakti* and he touched us with it. He changed us with it. Extraordinary. Causeless mercy. I beg to be given a spot in eternity in his service.

Prsnigarbha devi dasi

In 1972, Prsnigarbha was a twenty-six-year-old legal secretary who was having difficulties in her marriage and was looking for something more in life when she met devotees selling incense on the streets of Seattle.

Some devotees came to my office to get Articles of Incorporation drawn up for the Seattle temple. I'd phone them about the Articles and there was a silence behind the devotee speaking that was inviting and called to me. Years later, when I read in the *Bhagavad-gita,* "of secrets Krishna is silence," I thought, "This is cool, it comes together."

I started going to the temple to sing and dance and look at the paintings, and once I saw a film of a man in orange dancing and floating with his arms waving. I was transfixed and knew immediately and without a doubt that this person was from another planet. I started reading Prabhupada's books and couldn't stop. I didn't understand them, but I'd read as much as I could whenever I could.

I went to Portland to hear Prabhupada lecture and felt, "This person is going to get our culture and society on track." When I bowed down before him and he walked off, for a split second, it felt like a million butterflies of love were washing over me.

Before I was initiated I was going through the lowest of low times, and I started praying to Saint Jude. After I met the devotees I continued praying to Jesus and Saint Jude. I wrote a letter to Prabhupada asking him about this and he wrote back, "I am very glad your Christian background has led you to Krishna consciousness. However, Krishna says in the *Bhagavad-gita mam ekam,* 'only onto Me.' " I was satisfied. I asked for initiation and Prabhupada accepted me. Financially and in other ways my life was falling apart. I walked into the temple, left my old life behind, and all my problems vanished. I was sewing clothes for Lord Jagannatha and Sukadeva, our temple president, sent pictures of the Deities wearing dresses I had sewn to Srila Prabhupada. He wrote back, "I have seen the pictures of the Deities of your temple. They are very nice. I am very, very pleased." Sukadeva read that to me and said, "We have perfected our human life."

Once I was standing in the temple room when Srila Prabhupada came in surrounded by a horde of men. All of a sudden through the huge horde, Srila Prabhupada turned his head a little, looked inside me and showed me that my desire and ability to be a devotee was practically nonexistent. I realized a huge horde of people between me and a pure devotee does not limit that pure devotee.

The last time I saw Prabhupada I was standing next to my friend Pavani. She saw Prabhupada smiling and beaming. Standing by her side at the same time, for me Prabhupada was sober and quiet.

Puja devi dasi

Puja had been going to the Hare Krishna temple in Denver for awhile. One evening in late August 1973, she went there, and without any plans to do so, spent the night. With thoughts to return to her parents' home where she lived, every day there seemed to be a good reason to stay just one more day. Seems like Krishna had a plan for her. Now, more than forty-six years later, she is sharing her most cherished memories of her experiences with Srila Prabhupada.

I was in the Dallas temple when Prabhupada came there. I was a pretty new devotee, I had only been there a little over a year. I was *so* excited to finally get to see him in person! The devotees lined up in the hall outside the temple room. I was holding Kaulini's two-year-old son Ramachandra by the hand. When the car pulled up, and Prabhupada got out, I was amazed to see him. To me, he didn't have an efflugence around him, he literally *was* the efflugence! I immediately got teary-eyed, and was disappointed that I had to pay my obeisances, as I wanted to keep looking at him. When I stood up, still holding Rama's hand, Prabhupada was right there, and patted Rama on the head. I was so happy to be so close to him!

I was asked to make the *charanamrita* the next day. I had heard about the woman in L.A. who had made it once with salt, and Prabhupada was naturally so displeased. I knew I was making it with sugar, but still had that fear and anxiety, that what if accidentally it *was* salt! There were so many devotees there, I had to stand on my tip toes and try to see when it came time for Prabhupada to take the *charanamrita*. Prabhupada took some, and then literally shrugged his shoulders, and put his palms upward, as if to say it was okay. I was astounded as I felt Prabhupada had done that to appease my nervous mind. It was amazing to me.

I knew the time spent with Prabhupada was so valuable and wanted to figure out another way to see him. So I "borrowed" Jagadish and Laxmimoni's two-year-old daughter to get a cookie from him upstairs in his quarters. I was standing in line with the mothers and their kids. Little Yugala Priti was running around so I didn't know if my plan was going to work. Much to my happiness, she did cooperate long enough to go into the room and get her cookie. A devotee told me to go and get a cookie too. Prabhupada's hand touched my hand, and I felt like I had never felt anything so soft.

I was helping to clean the house where Prabhupada was staying, across the street from the temple. I again wanted to see Prabhupada, and had my sneaky plan! The other few women there were all rushing around and then one of them said Prabhupada was coming and we had to leave out of the back door. But not me. I just had to see him again, so I said I wasn't quite finished with whatever I was doing. When Prabhupada came in through the front door, I was again amazed, as it seemed as though he was already looking at me, and not just noticing someone was standing in the doorway of the kitchen. I folded my hands, and said "*Jaya* Srila Prabhupada" and paid my obeisances. In Vrindavan, there was a bus for many lots of the women to go on a *parikrama*. The bus broke down, and we were stranded for quite awhile. We got back to the temple late at night. The next day a devotee man came up to a few of us and told us that Prabhupada wouldn't go to sleep until all of his daughters were safely back. That is a story that brings tears to my eyes every time I tell it. So much love we received then, so much love we receive now.

Years after Srila Prabhupada departed, I was in the Los Angeles temple room. I had been going through a very difficult time. I was upstairs in the balcony, chanting my rounds, and I said prayerfully, "Oh, Srila Prabhupada, please don't forget me!" Then I heard Prabhupada say in a very stern voice, "Don't *you* forget *me*!" I was so shocked, I leaned over the balcony to see if anyone else was in the temple room and heard the same thing. But it was mid-morning and nobody was there. For me, it was a wakeup call. Sometimes I believe we have a tendency to think of Srila Prabhupada as always kind, loving, and merciful. Which he is, of course. But the voice I heard was also Prabhupada's kindness, which can be by receiving chastisement.

I know how very, very fortunate I am to be one of Srila Prabhupada's disciples, who he lovingly referred to as his "sons" and "daughters." I know how very fortunate we all are that he came to us, and spread Krishna consciousness all over the world! I am grateful beyond words. Even though material life gets in the way, and worldly fears and anxieties are plentiful, I know that I always have Prabhupada's shelter. *Jaya* Srila Prabhupada!

Purnamasi devi dasi

Purnamasi was among a group of twenty devotees who saw Srila Prabhupada for the first time in New York in 1975.

We were so excited. We were running around the New York *brahmacharini* ashram saying, "Prabhupada's here, Prabhupada's here – and we're here too, we're here too!" A little later we heard, "*Bang, bang, bang!*" We opened the door and the devotee standing there said, "Srila Prabhupada is asking, 'Would the white elephants please stop jumping?' " Prabhupada was on the floor beneath us! We almost fainted. The first thing we'd done was disturb Srila Prabhupada.

When Prabhupada came to Toronto in 1975 everyone in the temple went to meet him at the airport except Ayodhya-pati Prabhu, who was cooking, and me, the *pujari*. Later the devotees were returning to the temple when Praharana told me, "Prabhupada's water is warm." The water in Prabhupada's little sterling pitcher that was next to his *vyasasana* should have been cold. So I got the pitcher, filled it with cold water, and was going back to the temple room when the door opened and there was Srila Prabhupada with five or six *sannyasis* behind him. I froze. Then I bowed down, "*namah om visnu-padaya . . .* " Prabhupada went into the temple, greeted the Deities, sat on his *vyasasana* and gave a short welcome address. Devotees from six different temples had come to Toronto to see Prabhupada and our temple was packed. There were so many devotees that there was no way to stick a toe in that room. I stood by the door with Prabhupada's pitcher wondering what to do and then somehow I arranged to pass the pitcher from devotee to devotee until someone near the *vyasasana* got the pitcher and filled Prabhupada's cup. Prabhupada lifted the cup, poured the water into his mouth and then looked straight at me, standing in the doorway. It was a little thing, yet it was personal. I didn't know much scripture but I knew *patram puspam phalam toyam*.

Sometimes I think, "Prabhupada is really accepting our offerings. It's amazing how he will accept even a little service." But then again, with Srila Prabhupada a small thing is a huge thing.

Racitambara devi dasi

In Racitambara's great desire to find the absolute truth, she traveled throughout Europe, Canada, and the United States studying different religions. Finally, she gave herself fully to God, knowing He would surely help her.

I was twenty-two and it was November 17, 1972 when I left home with only the clothes on my back and the prayer, "Please, God, help me find You." After about two hours of praying and walking in Vancouver, Canada, I was standing on the corner of Georgia and Granville when Bhakta John said, "Hey, little lady, would you like some incense?" I said, "No, thank you, I'm looking for God." He said, "Well, you've found Him!" He opened the *Bhagavad-gita* and showed me the picture of Gopal with His arm around a calf and said, "God is a blue boy with a flute." I said, "Man, you're crazy. I've studied many different religions, but no one's told me God is a blue boy with a flute!" He opened to Srila Prabhupada's picture and said, "This is our spiritual master and he believes it." I looked at Srila Prabhupada's picture and thought, "This is the wisest, most all-knowing person in the world. If he believes it, it must be true." I bought a *Bhagavad-gita*, wandered down the street, and met a friend who let me stay with her.

After that I met devotees every day–Bhakta John who became Chaitanya Simha Dasa and Bhakta Roger who became Riddha Dasa–and each day they gave me a gift. I started attending the Sunday Feasts and then moved into the temple. I never left and later married Chaitanya Simha. After a short time we moved to Los Angeles.

In December 1973 Srila Prabhupada arrived at the L.A. airport greeted by a huge kirtan. I was at the back of the crowd with two youngish businessmen behind me, also excitedly looking on. Suddenly there was Srila Prabhupada, and when I offered my obeisances it was like a tidal wave welled up from my inner being and poured out and I cried and cried. It was so purifying. When I finally stood I saw the two businessmen had tears pouring down their faces, too.

One of my main services was to make the cookies Srila Prabhupada gave to the children after class. We called them "Prabhupada cookies," and they were made of butter, flour, and sugar in a simple ratio. I wouldn't have dreamed of making anything but these type of cookies. I would run home after *mangala-arati*, make the cookies, arrange them neatly on a tray, and bring them in time for *guru-puja* and place them behind Prabhupada's *vyasasana*.

Once, Prabhupada was coming to Los Angeles from Hawaii. Rameshvara Prabhu, our GBC, told us that Srila Prabhupada was gravely ill and wouldn't be coming to the temple to see the Deities. "Are there any questions?" he asked. I said, "Should I make the cookies?" In front of two devotees, Rameshvara said, "Stupid woman! I just said how sick Prabhupada is and how he's not coming to the temple, and she wants to know if he's going to give cookies to the children!" I was so shocked by what he said that I wanted to be like Sita and let the earth open and swallow me. I slinked home, crying, and my husband, trying to make me feel better, said, "Service is absolute. You should make the cookies, and later you can offer them to a picture of Srila Prabhupada and give them to the children in the playground." I made the cookies, and the next morning Prabhupada, supported by two devotees, came into the temple room and offered his obeisances before each of the three altars. He took *charanamrita* and said, "There must be *guru-puja*." He was so weak he had trouble getting onto the *vyasasana*. After *guru-puja* he said, "There must be class." He could hardly hold himself up, and even though he was speaking into the microphone, it was hard to hear him because he was so weak. Still, he gave a short class. After the class the devotees wanted him to return to his room, but Prabhupada said, "No, where are the cookies? The children are waiting for cookies." Rameshvara said, "Cookies!" in an odd voice, and I said, "I have the cookies!" I was so pleased that I had done my service and I later thanked my husband for inspiring me.

Once, when I found a cow cookie cutter, I thought, "How wonderful!

Srila Prabhupada will remember the Vrindavan cows!" I made beautifully decorated cow-shaped cookies and took them to Srila Prabhupada. Palika offered the cookies to Prabhupada, and later told me, "Prabhupada said, 'They think I will eat the cow?'" I threw the cow cookie cutter away.

Once, I made carob-mint ice cream for Srila Prabhupada. I gave it to Prabhupada's servant and said, "Please, can you take it to Srila Prabhupada?" He said, "Prabhupada doesn't eat carob." I said, "I worked so hard to make this. Please!" I was almost crying. "All right," he said, "I'll take it in." The servant came back a few minutes later and said, "Do you have more of that ice cream? Prabhupada ate the whole bowl and would like another."

For the 4 o'clock offering I used to cut the grapes in half and take the seeds out. Once Prabhupada sampled the offering and said, "Tell the cook that sometimes Krishna likes to suck on the seeds. She doesn't always have to take the seeds out of the grapes."

Srila Prabhupada's window overlooked an alleyway that was quite scary at night. It was the time of John F. Kennedy and Martin Luther King, Jr., and I was always afraid someone would take a shot at Prabhupada. I'd get up about 1:00 am and chant my rounds in the alleyway looking up at him. He was always before me. His window would be open and I'd hear him either chanting his rounds or translating. I felt I was somehow protecting him. Of course, what could I have done?

In June 1976, Prabhupada told my husband, "We've just purchased a thirteen-story building in New York. I want you to go and rewire, replumb, reorganize, and paint it. When do you think it can be ready?"

My husband calculated and was about to say they could have it ready in a year when Prabhupada smiled and said, "I am scheduled to be in New York in six weeks." My husband came home and said, "Pack up. We're on the first plane to New York in the morning." I never went back to Los Angeles.

Prabhupada said something and we did it. I don't remember sleeping for six weeks. I painted, and my husband was everywhere at once with work crews ripping this and doing that. It was a wonderful marathon, and six weeks later the temple was finished. It was astounding. When Srila Prabhupada's car drove up, the devotees lined the walkway from the road to the front door, each with a gift for him. My husband, who'd been doing last minute things, came running out, and saw that everybody had a gift but him. He ran back in, found an old blackened rose, and came out again. Srila Prabhupada glided along wonderfully slow and regally with his head held high, looking at the temple. Devotees gave him garlands, *chadars*, fruit, flowers, and Prabhupada kept handing them to his servant. When he was in front of my husband, Srila Prabhupada stopped, waited, and put his right hand out like he was expecting something. By now, my husband had hidden the blackened rose behind his back, thinking it unworthy of being offered, but now he slowly brought it out and put it in Srila Prabhupada's hand. Prabhupada wrapped his two hands around the rose and said, "Thank you very much." Prabhupada was pleased with everything in the temple.

In Juhu, Srila Prabhupada asked my three-and-a-half-year-old daughter, "Would you like to ride in my car?" It was like one child with a wonderful idea speaking to another. My daughter looked at me for permission, and then said, "Yes, Srila Prabhupada." She got in the back with Srila Prabhupada and they drove to his apartment. That happened every day for two weeks, and each time it was like a brand new idea, child-to-child.

In early 1977, when Prabhupada came to Juhu for the last time, I was at the back of the crowd thinking, "Oh, Srila Prabhupada, you have so many disciples. I'm also your disciple, but do you know me?" Srila Prabhupada got out of his car and instead of sweeping into the building as we expected, he stopped, looked over the crowd, and saw me. He looked deep into my eyes, into the soul, gave me a smile as if a million suns had come out at once, and nodded his head. I clearly heard him say, "Of course, I know you. We have an eternal relationship." Since then I've always felt Prabhupada is with me and knows me, for we have an eternal relationship.

Then Prabhupada went inside and got on the elevator. I offered my obeisances with my little daughter next to me. But when I stood up, my daughter was gone! I called out, "Has anyone seen my daughter?" Someone said, "Didn't you see? Prabhupada called her into the elevator!" I ran upstairs and there she was, sitting at Prabhupada's feet. Prabhupada picked out a piece of pineapple from a huge tray of cut fruit and popped it into her mouth. How did he know that pineapple was her favorite fruit? The last six months of my pregnancy I ate a pineapple every day because I craved it–it was her craving. She still loves pineapple. Out of so many varieties of fruits, Prabhupada picked out and fed that one to her.

Later, my family was living at the farm in Hyderabad when we heard that Srila Prabhupada was sick in Vrindavan. We purchased cheap train tickets, traveled sitting on our suitcases with the chickens and the goats, and arrived in Vrindavan to have Bhavananda tell us, "You can't go in to see Srila Prabhupada. He's not seeing anybody." We said, "You have no idea of the austerity we went through to get here. Please, let us see Srila Prabhupada one last time!" But he said it was impossible. So the three of us went out and stood in front of Prabhupada's long French doors, knowing that he was just on the other side, in bed. We were saying our last prayers to Srila Prabhupada when suddenly the curtains and doors opened and we saw him. We offered our obeisances and felt satisfied. Bhavananda later said, "Those curtains and doors hadn't been opened for months, but Srila Prabhupada had told his servant, suddenly, to open them." Srila Prabhupada knew. He just knew.

Radha Kunda devi dasi

Radha Kunda's marriage was arranged; she and her husband didn't know each other beforehand. After the ceremony, when they went to Prabhupada's room for his blessings, Srila Prabhupada looked at her with sympathy, took a beautiful gold ring with a sapphire off his finger and gave it to her saying, "Here, take this ring." It was large so she put it on her thumb.

Once in Bombay, I was pregnant, sick, and miserable. When Prabhupada gave *Bhagavad-gita* class I sat in front of him crying. I wanted to tell him, "I can't tolerate these miseries any more," but I realized Prabhupada understood my suffering. The next day he called my husband and me to his room and said to me, "In the Vedic culture, a pregnant woman lives with her mother. You should live with your mother until the baby is born. And six months after the birth, come back and live with your husband." I thought, "Wow! Prabhupada knows my mind." Tamal Krishna Maharaja said, "Prabhupada, Radha Kunda's doing a lot of *pujari* work. There's no way we can send her to her mother's house." My husband said, "Her mother is a demon. She can't go and stay with her." They were arguing and Prabhupada butted in, saying, "May I say something? I think we should send her to her mother's house." I flew out of Bombay realizing Prabhupada knew my heart.

Each time Prabhupada arrived in Bombay, we'd sit with him in an intimate family-like way and he'd tell us about his travels. Once he was reminiscing about the Bowery and how he lived with derelicts, drunkards, and reprobates, and how his typewriter was stolen. We were crying to hear about it. Prabhupada said, "Why are you crying? I didn't look to the right or left. I walked straight through hellfire to go and get you all." Who has a desire like Prabhupada's? If he hadn't put his lotus feet on the Jaladuta, we would have never understood the purpose and goal of human life and how many millions of lifetimes we've passed through. We can't repay Prabhupada for his causeless mercy and compassion. Without him, we'd never have heard of Krishna, Krishna's devotees, and Krishna *prasadam* – coconut *burfi* and *halava*. We'd never have heard of *Bhagavatam* and *Bhagavad-gita*. We'd never have dreamt that human life was meant for developing love for Krishna. Prabhupada transformed our lives and gave us so much to live for.

He wanted us to get out and do something. Once in L.A. in 1973 he was crying and saying, "My spiritual master begged us, 'Please go and preach.' Today I am begging you, please go and preach, distribute books and your life will be a success." All of us would go out for twelve hours a day seven days a week. That was the best time in my life. By distributing books we please Prabhupada, Srila Bhaktisiddhanta, Bhaktivinoda Thakura, the whole *guru-parampara,* Pancha-tattva, Krishna-Balarama, Radharani. So of course we're going to be happy.

Once during a Juhu *Bhagavatam* class, I was absorbed in what my daughter was doing when Prabhupada said, "The attraction of the mother for the child is natural. The mother doesn't artificially have to try to love her child. In the same way, the attraction of the spirit soul for Krishna is completely natural. It's not artificial. We don't have to be forced to love Krishna." Every day while Prabhupada was giving *Bhagavad-gita* class I'd cook the evening offering and do the *arati* for Sri Sri Radha-Rasabihari in Juhu. And afterwards I'd give the *maha* plate to Prabhupada and he'd distribute the *prasadam* from the *vyasasana.*

Today I heard Prabhupada say, "If you read Rupa Goswami's Nectar of Devotion, you associate directly with Rupa Goswami. And if you follow the instructions of the Nectar of Devotion, you worship his lotus feet." So when we read Prabhupada's books we have a relationship with Prabhupada and are associating directly with him. And by following Prabhupada's instructions, we worship his lotus feet. Everyone in his Movement has an opportunity to have a wonderful loving relationship with Srila Prabhupada. We should tell everyone throughout the world who Prabhupada is and what he's done.

Radhanarupini devi dasi

Radhanarupini was initiated in Honolulu temple in February 1975. She had met the devotees when she was fifteen in the Philippines. She wanted to be a nun, but her sister had met Siddhaswarupa's devotees, and began chanting and reading the Bhagavad-gita.

My sister showed me the *Bhagavad-gita* and I started reading it. It had everything that I didn't get as a Catholic: an understanding of the soul–all these different things. Then she gave me beads, and I started chanting.

When I was seventeen, my whole family moved to Honolulu because my father became in charge of Philippine Airlines. In Hawaii, I was feeling so much separation from the devotees because really they didn't want me going to ISKCON. But I was just so sad. My brother took pity on me and took me to one Sunday Feast. It was 1974 or 1975 at the new temple in 51 Coelho Way.

I started going to the temple, and I was very happy to be around the devotees, even if they were ISKCON devotees. I started doing service at the Govinda's restaurant, being a waitress there. On my eighteenth birthday, when I woke up, I packed my clothes and then I went to school and work. Afterwards, Lila took me to my parents' apartment. I went upstairs to get my clothes, and my father was so upset. "What are you doing?" I said, "I'm moving into the Hare Krishna temple." He was smoking up a storm, but I was eighteen. I would come home every weekend and my mother came to see Srila Prabhupada.

I was a *brahmacharini* in the ashram there, which was an old greenhouse with a screen on it. We put tapestry on the walls so the wind wouldn't come through. Srila Prabhupada came. I can't really explain but I had an immediate connection. I knew when I first saw him that I did the right thing.

He would stay in Honolulu for the mango season also. The environment and weather was conducive to his health. I got a picture of Krishna playing the flute and put it on a nice carved piece of wood and wrapped it in silk. During *guru-puja*, I went up and gave it to Srila Prabhupada. And he opened it and his face was like, "Wow, what a wonderful present!" And he touched my head.

When you come in Coelho Way on the right-hand side there's this guava tree or something that's kind of bent, and then there's a stone wall. Mahavisnupriya, Lila, and I would sit there at two o'clock in the morning, and watch Srila Prabhupada in his room stand up, walk around, chant, sit down, go here, go there, and we were just looking. And we would see the people, servants or whoever. Or sometimes we'd go really close, and we could hear him dictating. It was just so sweet.

Dhrtavrata and I went to Vrindavan. We moved into a room at the *goshala* because we heard that Srila Prabhupada didn't want householders to live in Krishna-Balaram Mandir.

My service was to go to the market, pick up twigs and stuff for the fire to cook. And I did laundry by hand with well water. Every morning we got up to the sounds of the Sita-Rama temple, took our bath with the cold well water, and then walked to the temple for *mangala-arati*. Then we went home, did our service, and went back for evening. Both programs Prabhupada would be giving classes. It was so nice, and I'd make garlands for the Deities.

One day, I was wearing this puke green sari that circumstantially I hadn't washed. I had my *tilaka* on with a red dot. I felt like a Christmas tree. I was in a squatting position facing the Krishna-Balaram Mandir within the temple grounds, on the left-hand side where Srila Prabhupada's *samadhi* is. I was chanting and I heard a ruckus going on. I saw Srila Prabhupada standing there, and he was with a group of devotee men. So I thought to myself, "If I pay my obeisances and stay down long enough, he'll pass by and not even notice me."

I still had my head on the ground, and I thought, "Okay, that was pretty long, I'm going to sit up now." So I sat up, and Prabhupada came right in front of me. And he looked me, smiled, shook his head, and then he left.

I found out that Prabhupada had said, "Who is she?" They had said who I was and that I was the wife of Dhrtavrata. Prabhupada said, "And where do they live?" "They live in the *goshala*." And Prabhupada said, "I am pleased with her." And I think he said that because he was happy that we were following his instruction and were living outside.

Dhrtavrata went to Srutakirti and said, "I would like to ask you if my wife, Radhanarupini, could get her second initiation." Srutakirti recommended me to Srila Prabhupada. And because of that, Srila Prabhupada said, "Yes, tomorrow have her come at this certain time." So he didn't even do a fire *yajna* for me. I was the only one that got initiation at that time.

We didn't have any money but I had a pearl that my sister had given me. With money I got from selling the pearl, I bought an open-faced basket like a plate and I was walking around buying fruits to put on my plate for my offering. I was going to put the rest of the money in an envelope as *dakshina*. I was in la-la land thinking about seeing Srila Prabhupada and getting my initiation, when a monkey attacked me. I ran after him because he had the bananas. The *walas* there told me, "No, no! Don't worry!" I was crying because I had no more money, and they all gave me fruit.

I walked into Prabhupada's room. He was sitting directly across from the door on one of those really nice small *vyasasanas* on the floor in front of his table. I paid my obeisances, careful that the fruit wouldn't touch the floor, and then put the fruit on his desk. He said, "Is this for me?" I said, "Yes, Srila Prabhupada." He said, "Oh, nice!" There were pomegranates.

He said, "I am going to give you *brahmana* initiation, and I am going to teach you how to chant. Come here," and he tapped his hand on his pillow right next to him.

He showed me how to count, the way we count when we chant Gayatri. First he did it, then he wanted me to copy him. But I was so nervous. So he stopped and in the sweetest, kindest way said, "Don't be nervous." I said, "Okay." He read the whole mantra, then had me repeat it. He told me, "Now you have to chant this three times a day." Then I paid my obeisances and I said, "Thank you, Srila Prabhupada," and I left.

Prabhupada was walking, and there was this old Indian woman in all white. Prabhupada was surrounded by his entourage of devotee men. This old woman was walking towards Srila Prabhupada. With his hand he made a gesture to make way for her. She came and paid her obeisances. He held her hand with his two hands as if they knew each other for a long time and they spoke. It was very nice, very sweet.

Prabhupada just loved the kids. His smiles would be from ear-to-ear with the kids. And when the women came up, his eyes were just so kind. It's none of this "you woman." It's more like there was this love and affection and protection. I always felt this protection that I never felt from anyone else with Srila Prabhupada. He really wanted to protect the women. That's what he wanted for us, but we didn't get the protection.

In Vrindavan, one man was asking, "Can I get a wife?" and the next thing you know, "Can I get *sannyasa*?" Boy, Prabhupada was just roaring like a lion, he really didn't like that. He wanted to see that the women would be protected and taken care of.

The very few times that I was around him, I felt that when Srila Prabhupada looked at me, he never saw my body, he just never did. He saw who you really are inside. He saw who you were, the spirit soul, the servant of Krishna.

I really felt like his daughter. He was very loving. He was never angry or chastising. Even when he told me, "It's okay, don't be nervous," it was so sweet. He wasn't impatient with me. He wasn't like, "What's this woman? She's so unintelligent, she can't even count on her fingers, and she's taking up my time." But no. Unbelievable. He was just so patient, so calm, so kind, wanting to explain, making it clear, giving it with love.

In my first dream about Srila Prabhupada I was in New York and I was astral traveling one night. I saw my husband sleeping in a sleeping bag. I saw my body in my sleeping bag, and I was just lifted out of my body. I could see the room we were in. Then I saw Srila Prabhupada and I said, "Oh, my gosh, Srila Prabhupada, it's you! Am I leaving my body?" He said, "No, you are not leaving your body, not now. You have to go back in your body. But when you leave, I will be there." He told me that. Then I was back in my body.

I also dreamt about him right after he left and he was crying. My ex-husband and I were looking for him, and we found him in the back of a house. We asked him, "Why are you crying?" He said, "Because a lot of my disciples will be leaving." And he said, "Please don't leave."

I started craving Srila Prabhupada's association a few months ago and I was thinking, "Where are you?" And, "I miss you." I started reading, oh, my gosh, the Purports were screaming at me. They would just come alive. I'd come home from work, and the first thing I'd want to do is read because I felt like by reading I was associating with him. I was getting direct instruction from him. And I think it's following his instructions that way. He's there. We're so lucky we have his Purports.

If you want to be close to your spiritual master and if you want to feel that heart connection, then you have to go towards him, then you have to go towards him and tell him. I feel like Srila Prabhupada is here and he's somehow or another guiding me because he is my *shiksha* and *diksha* guru. I feel like I also have many other *shiksha gurus* like older godbrothers or other very advanced godsisters or other advanced Vaishnavas.

How do I repay him for what he's done? And the only answer to that is do the best you can in your service, do the best you can in your chanting. Walk the talk. Be kind to people, see Krishna in their heart. And when the opportunity comes, tell them about Krishna or give them *prasadam*. How else do you repay your spiritual master? He's given us something. Some of us have fallen and come back, some of us have stayed with it. But that's the best thing you can do to repay him is try to make advancement in your own spiritual life.

Radhapriya devi dasi

In 1972, two months before she turned eighteen, Radhapriya ran away from a beautiful home and a wise father whom she loved too much.

I'd been visiting London's Bury Place temple since I was sixteen and when I knew I'd soon be legally free to join Srila Prabhupada's Movement, I did. The mood of bhakti was the most beautiful thing I'd ever known and it pulled me in. I understood that we should be in a service mood and was always willing to serve; I was submissive and did everything I was told. In 1972 Prabhupada initiated me, four months later I got married to somebody I didn't know, and six months later I received Gayatri. To get the Gayatri mantra I went to Prabhupada's room in the Manor where he was sitting on a low cushion on the floor, and he tapped the spot beside him indicating I should sit there. I did and he was gentle, loving, and totally accepting. Krishna's love poured over me. I felt like a teeny insignificant speck engulfed by an ocean of unconditional gentle love.

Once during *guru-puja* somebody gave me flowers to offer to Srila Prabhupada. I was so shy, nervous, and sweaty I squeezed them into a horrible sticky mess that I couldn't offer. But the next day I did offer flowers to him and felt powerfully bathed in and softened by his unconditional love.

Every part of his being and whatever his movements, Prabhupada was always gracefully dancing for Krishna. To have a bona fide spiritual master and to give your life to that person and to Krishna is the greatest blessing anyone can ever have. Apart from not being able to please the spiritual master, when you're with that person there's no fear of anything in the whole universe.

I used to dress Radharani and Rohininandana, my husband and the head *pujari*, used to dress Gokulananda. I had no idea of ever doing anything else for the rest of my life. Except for Ratha-yatra I didn't even want to leave the Bhaktivedanta Manor grounds. It was the most blessed time. Those seconds just before the curtains open, knowing that Srila Prabhupada was going to see the Deities after I'd dressed Them, was one of the most mystical times imaginable. Everything felt exquisitely perfect and the last split second, when the conch blew, the curtains opened, I ran to the temple room, the "Govindam" prayers started, and I threw my whole body down on the ground in full *dandavats* at the feet of my guru and the Lord. It was the most perfect experience in all the universes.

At the feet of my spiritual master I felt utterly complete. I felt that any good things I might have done in all my past lifetimes and anything that I might ever do in all my future lifetimes culminated when I sat at Srila Prabhupada's feet. I had completely arrived. I'd pray, "Please, my dear Lord, I'm ready to leave my body at this moment. There's nothing more that I could ever achieve from everything I've ever done and will do."

The last time Srila Prabhupada came to the Manor he didn't have any inhibitions about being seen in such a sick condition. He showed the vulnerability of a child and to teach us gave himself to the Lord and the devotees. To see his softness was touching.

Now I appreciate Prabhupada more and his presence is stronger in my life. Daily his words make more sense. He taught us how to wake up early in the morning, chant Hare Krishna, run to greet Radha and Krishna, offer obeisances to Them, and sing beautiful songs for Their pleasure. He taught us to how to love and fully surrender our total being through the mood of bhakti.

Radhika devi dasi

Sometime in the 1970s, Radhika received a Krsna book from brahmacharis in New Westminster, British Columbia. They said, "This is the Indian Bible." She said, "I don't have enough money with me to buy it." But they strolled with her for three or four blocks and she finally gave them the five dollars reserved for her bus fare. She walked home.

I appreciated the *Krsna* book but didn't read it much. Every year my family and I would meet devotees and I started taking *prasadam* and participating in kirtan, although I didn't know what it was.

I got two little books, *Easy Journey to Other Planets* and *The Perfection of Yoga*. I sat in a little café on Fourth Avenue with my customary pot of green tea and started reading. I had a Master's Degree in English, was a literary critic, and considered myself quite learned. Other books I'd read never made the mark but these small books impressed me. After one or two pages I understood that this was the absolute truth I'd been looking for. I thought, "These are the best books I've ever encountered in the world, and this person, A. C. Bhaktivedanta Swami Prabhupada, is the true guru." I was overwhelmed. I read *The Teachings of Lord Chaitanya* and was elated that there was such a personality as Mahaprabhu and Srila Prabhupada had given so much information about Him.

In 1976, on the 17th of September – the day that Prabhupada had arrived in America – my two children and I joined the Hare Krishna Movement. The temple president asked me if I was going to stay my whole life and I said, "Yes, yes." Almost as soon as I joined, my son, Kaliya Krishna, was sent to Vrindavan and Prabhupada initiated him there in 1977. My daughter, Lingini, went to *gurukula* in Seattle. Meanwhile I was hiding in the temple, reading the *Srimad-Bhagavatam* and ecstatic about discovering this wonderful literature. After a few months I started distributing books and did that for about ten years.

Srila Prabhupada's teachings are the most astounding thing on the planet. By reading his books, one's eyes are opened with the torchlight of knowledge: *om ajnana-timirandhasya jnananjana-salakaya*. Not only are one's eyes opened, one's heart is also opened. And not only is one's heart opened, one's head spins. In the *Chaitanya-charitamrita* Ramananda Raya said, "What is the use of a bowman's arrow or a poet's poetry if they penetrate the heart but do not cause the head to spin?" Prabhupada's books are such a delectable experience we want to give them to others.

I never met Srila Prabhupada, but Prabhupada says hearing, *vani*, is more important than *vapuh*, the physical presence. I always try to give a little bit of Srila Prabhupada's teachings to others, whether via his books or his quotes or an article. In the U.S., when I lecture on the philosophy of yoga I always chant Hare Krishna and acknowledge Srila Prabhupada.

Srila Prabhupada's power is amazing and his books are time bombs. For those who are a little pure at heart, who are not envious, Prabhupada's mercy is there for the next 10,000 years.

Ragatmika devi dasi

For about eight months of 1970, Ragatmika, her husband, and their one-year old son were traveling in India. On their return to their native Australia, her husband, who was searching for a guru, began corresponding with the Melbourne devotees and eventually Ragatmika, her husband, and their son moved into the Melbourne temple.

When Prabhupada came to Australia in 1973, my son Janaka was about three years old. Sometimes Janaka used to sneak into Prabhupada's room through Prabhupada's long French side windows and he would spend time with Srila Prabhupada in there. And on a couple of morning walks, Prabhupada held Janaka's hand in his pocket and squeezed his hand tightly. Prabhupada walked quickly and Janaka and the rest of us had to almost run to keep up with him.

Prabhupada was more than a spiritual father, he was also like a real father. He was kind to young children, he showed tolerance and compassion and playfulness. Prabhupada taught us how to dress, how to eat, how to do so many things, and how to be parents also. He is our ever well-wisher and our eternal father.

Rama devi dasi

Rama devi's boyfriend's best friend's brother was Smarahari dasa. Smarahari gave Rama devi a "Govindam" single record that she played over and over until she literally wore it out. After that, all day long Rama devi would sing the "Govindam" prayers.

In 1972, three or four days before my seventeenth birthday, I was invited to the Edinburgh temple for lunch. During *prasadam*, which blew me away although it was just potatoes and carrots with cumin, Kisora showed me a picture of Prabhupada's face and said, "This is my spiritual master." That picture was my first experience with Prabhupada and to this day I can see his face in that picture. His smile was real and I could see that he had no agenda, that he had nothing hidden. It was the first real smile I'd ever seen.

At the time only four devotees were in the Edinburgh temple and Tribhuvanatha was one of them. The first instant I saw Tribhuvanatha I thought, "Wow!" And immediately I had my first experience of Supersoul, who gave me the thought, "No, this is not a person to fall for. He's out of bounds." I adored Tribhuvanatha; he was extraordinary and for me he was a direct connection to Prabhupada.

In July 1972 Prabhupada came for the London Ratha-yatra. When he arrived in Bury Place he had garlands up to his ears and down to his knees and he was so happy he was beaming. I'd never seen anyone that happy and that otherworldly. Prabhupada walked inside, took darshan of the Deities and thanked Lilasakti for taking nice care of Them. Later on, during the Ratha-yatra, Prabhupada sat on the *vyasasana* on the Ratha and I danced nearby. I didn't take my eyes off him the whole time. I didn't have a spiritual big bang, he just fascinated me.

We had no money in the Edinburgh temple but Prabhupada was going to visit and we had to prepare. Sarvamangala made friends with a department store salesperson and he gave us a roll of pink nylon lining on credit. My first direct service for Prabhupada was to make curtains for his room out of that pink nylon lining. I also went to see my mum, who wasn't speaking to me because I'd joined the temple, and I borrowed sheets and blankets from her for Prabhupada. From a junk shop we got an old table and cut off its legs to make a desk for him.

After Prabhupada visited Edinburgh we all went with him to a program in Woodside Hall in Glasgow where someone said, "I am God," and

Prabhupada said, "No, you are dog." It was interesting to see Prabhupada in a strong mood. When he was leaving the Hall, Sarva and I dashed into the room where he had been sitting and grabbed his *maha* oranges and were chomping on them when Prabhupada unexpectedly came back in the room, looked at us, and laughed. We were standing with orange peels in our mouths like complete idiots.

The following year Prabhupada danced the whole way on London Ratha-yatra. Just watching Prabhupada dance was mesmerizing and it seemed that no one's feet touched the ground during that Ratha-yatra. Oftentimes the cart – there was just one in those days – would stop and Prabhupada would turn around and see it far behind. Prabhupada would indicate for Jagannatha to come and then the cart would start moving again and when it caught up we'd go on. The police kept telling Srutakirti, "You're blocking traffic. Tell your leader to keep moving. You can't do this." Srutakirti said to the officer, "You tell him," and the officer backed off. There was a Vaikuntha bubble around Prabhupada protecting everyone who was with him. It was wonderful; amazing. And Prabhupada never showed a hint of tiredness. Actually none of us felt tired even though it was more than a forty-five-minute walk on a hot, sunny day and we didn't have drinking water. Some Vaikuntha energy sustained us all.

I was young and didn't know what was going on, I only knew that for the first time in my life I was happy. Once, at the Manor, Prabhupada paid his obeisances with his feet toward me. I paid my obeisances right behind his feet and as he stood up his heels brushed the top of my head. I'm convinced that most of the reason I'm still here today is the fact that Prabhupada's feet touched my head, just like the mark of Krishna's feet protected Kaliya from Garuda. The other reason I'm still here is the kindness of the Vaishnavas. Except for these two, there's no reason I should be here.

I never understood what Krishna consciousness was all about. I never realized how serious it was – the initiation process, the chanting, the reading. It just was something I was doing. I like devotees; I like the service, the excitement and creativity of the festivals, the exotic locations, and the travel. But also I've realized that there's nothing else – nothing else comes even remotely close to the richness that we have in Krishna consciousness. And I've realized that if I want to make spiritual progress I've got to please Srila Prabhupada. Srila Prabhupada captured me and now I'm spoiled for anything else. Rupa Goswami says if you want to maintain your material life, whatever you do, don't hear Krishna's flute, don't see Him standing in the moonlight on the banks of the Yamuna because if you do, you're captured by Him. That's what Prabhupada has done for us; I would die if I went anywhere else. There's no sustenance anywhere else in any way, shape or form. And what's sustaining us is love and is knowing that even if we're not on the path, our foot is above the path and at any moment we could put our foot down and start walking. And what's sustaining us is the safety of the philosophy. You can't argue with it, it's so logical, and we have *prasadam* and the sounds of kirtans. It's all Prabhupada's legacy and the potential that he's left for us. Ultimately our sustenance is the hope that he's given us. If anyone just applies themselves they can follow the process he's given and be sustained.

I'm inspired by Prabhupada's disciples, like my heroes Jananivasa and Pankajanghri, and I'm inspired by his grand disciples like Bhaktipurusottama Maharaja, Naru Gopal – such a quiet, humble soul – and the *brahmachari* Nitai Prasada. Sitala Prabhu is a Prabhupada person through and through. Murari Gupta has complete faith in chanting; he never misses his rounds and he really tries to chant them well. And Siddhi, a simple, humble devotee, loves to polish and clean. Siddhi sits for hours listening to *Chaitanya-charitamrita* lectures while curling Pancha-tatttva's hair and she has no agenda, no fear.

These devotees are how I experience Prabhupada. For me, the devotees are Prabhupada's representatives. Prabhupada is in the devotees who have taken his instructions to heart. I can't experience Prabhupada directly, I feel so far away from him, but I experience Prabhupada in his devotees. They're practicing and the process is working. They read, they chant, they hear, they attend the programs, they do service to their capability, they have their priorities straight. Many of them have had many difficulties, but they take shelter and they carry on. I'm grateful that I'm still around, that I'm allowed to take part and breathe the same air as such saintly persons.

I don't like to think of Prabhupada in his *samadhis* in Vrindavan or in Mayapur. I prefer to think he's in his Los Angeles garden reading *Krsna* book, he's preaching to the sages at the Kumbha Mela, he's scratching the cows' necks in New Vrindavan. I don't know where he is now, but for me he's preaching somewhere.

Ramaniya devi dasi

Ramaniya liked helping people. When devotees told her, "By giving people knowledge of the soul, you can really help them. You'll help them get out of this material world," Ramaniya thought, "Wow, this is it!"

I read On the Way to Krishna and Ishopanishad in Dutch. Other books I'd read about yoga or religion weren't giving a full answer, but Prabhupada's philosophy was simple, satisfying, and complete. Immediately I wanted to distribute books to help people find this path. Before Srila Prabhupada initiated me, which was in 1976 in New Mayapur, I tried to distribute as many *Bhagavad-gitas* as possible, and I was number three in book distribution.

When I saw Prabhupada in New Mayapur, he looked outstanding, bright, and dominant. I couldn't keep my eyes off him. Prabhupada sat on the grass and, since it was hot, devotees held a red velvet umbrella over him. Prthu Putra Maharaja, a new *sannyasi* from France, was playing the *mridanga* and sweating. Prabhupada said, "Put the umbrella over him." Prthu Putra Maharaja said, "No, no, put the umbrella over Prabhupada." Prabhupada said, "No, no." It went back and forth twice. It was beautiful to see how the disciple and the guru cared for each other.

When Prabhupada took darshan of Krishna and Balarama, I saw that he had a beautiful personal relationship with Them. Although he was sick at the time, Prabhupada was elegant, and offered his obeisances like a swan. On the day of my initiation, Prabhupada sat in a red palanquín under a shady tree. When the first initiate came to get his name and beads, he bowed down while on his knees. Prabhupada said, "This is not proper. When you come before the spiritual master, you must give full *dandavats*." I was next and I offered my prostrated obeisances – full *dandavats* – before Srila Prabhupada. The grass was sticky, and I moved slowly. When I looked at Prabhupada, he had a big smile. He was pleased.

When Prabhupada left New Mayapur, I thought, "Why can't Prabhupada stay?" and I ran after his car until it went too fast and I was left in the dust. Then I felt such emptiness. My determination to make him happy by distributing his books increased. Now I feel that when I read his books, he speaks to me. He replies to my questions through his books or the devotees. He's caring for me, guiding me, not leaving me alone. He tells me what I need to hear, and whatever he says has potency and truth behind it. I've always stuck to the simple program of going to the morning program, chanting sixteen rounds, not speaking *prajalpa*, preaching, and having a simple Krishna conscious life. I try to stick close to Prabhupada's principles in every way. If I don't, I become weak and get into *maya*.

As we go on with the process, inside we become richer. Every class we hear gives us new insights, every time we chant the holy name and see the Deities we get new experiences. Outwardly our activities seems the same, but inside there's variety and nectar.

I'm not a good speaker, but I'm determined to give others this simple life of Krishna consciousness and speak my realizations about the *Bhagavad-gita*. It enlivens me. The most important thing is that we understand the goal of life: to develop love for Krishna. Prabhupada is helping us develop this love. If we sing and dance for Krishna, we'll forget about our worldly problems, become attached to this most beautiful little boy, and be happy. Krishna reciprocates more than any worldly friend. He is there day and night. Prabhupada is opening our hearts for Him to enter. And as we go deeper, it will be more beautiful. There's no limit to the beauty that we can experience in our relationship with guru and Krishna. And the more we understand that there's no limit, the more we become eager for the unlimited nectar that awaits us.

I never thought I'd leave Mayapur; I lived there happily for twelve years, but I had a burning desire to share this life. I prayed to do something more for Prabhupada, and an opportunity came for me to go to South Africa to preach Krishna consciousness. I want others to feel the happiness that I experience in spiritual life. By Prabhupada's mercy, I hope I can help take people out of this rotten world and bring them into the holy atmosphere of Prabhupada's Movement. I'm happy to have this chance.

Rambhoru devi dasi

Rambhoru, a religion major, went to Heidelberg to do an ecumenical year abroad and met a devotee selling books on the street. Rambhoru was fed up with religious movements on the streets and wary of a Hare Krishna with books. But this devotee was not eager to sell her a book, and that puzzled her.

The devotee didn't have that same vibe as the born again Christians I'd met. She said, "Well, you don't want this book, it's too bad." I got a book and visited the Heidelberg temple where Hansadutta spent four hours answering my list of one hundred questions in ways that the university didn't answer. And he told me Prabhupada was coming soon.

At the airport the devotees – who had come from France, England, and other parts of Europe – treated Prabhupada like a VIP. Arrogantly, I thought, "If I could get up close to this person, I'll be able to tell if he's genuine." But there were so many people I couldn't get close. I was astonished how short Prabhupada was. He had an aura around him so he looked like he wasn't touching the ground. As I tried to penetrate what he was about I realized I had no entry there.

Devotees were laughing, crying, and screaming. I hid behind a couch with my head sticking up but that drew more attention. Prabhupada was probably wondering, "Why is this crazy person behind the couch?" When he looked at me, I felt like the sun was pulling the impurities out of a piece of stool. My heart broke – it cracked – it was a feeling that had a sound. I began sobbing. I understood this person is bigger than I could imagine. I had been a Christian looking for the original Jesus, reading the Dead Sea Scrolls, and felt the devotees embodied a grassroots spiritual movement. In my humility and brokenness I joined them. That was a profound moment.

After that my relationship with Prabhupada was through my husband. I thought of my service to my husband as the way I connected to Prabhupada. That was a strength but also a downfall when, after thirty years of having that expectation, I realized it was idealistic to think that anybody else could fill Prabhupada's position. When my life with my husband started falling apart, I was bitter for a while. Sometimes I was angry that my husband wasn't more of an example as a householder and sometimes I was angry at ISKCON.

But I believe that my experiences – marriage, training, cooking, living simply – have helped me. Prabhupada is my guide. When I see another movement or guru I think, "Okay, they sound good but what are they eating? What are they doing?" If I didn't have Prabhupada's teachings I'd have no checks and balances. His teachings are my practical measure of what's authentic.

I went back to school and the pastoral care I've learned could be useful in Prabhupada's Movement: Prabhupada's calling me to care for the devotee community, to selflessly listen to another's heart. My vision is that Prabhupada wants me to nurture the community of devotees by listening, counseling, and training others.

I came to the Movement to do something as a soul, not as a woman. Through the clinical pastoral education and work I do, I've learned what it means to be a community and I'd like to bring an understanding of community to ISKCON.

Rangavati devi dasi

Rangavati, twenty-five and a 2nd grade school teacher, had decided to go to Europe to search for the truth when, at an Ann Arbor art fair, Dravanaksa Prabhu gave her a card with an invitation to the Detroit temple and the words, "Chant and make your life sublime." Instantly she felt connected.

On a lovely summer day I ventured to the Detroit Sunday Feast program in my hot rod GTO. Govardhana was the president and the temple was clean and inviting, beautifully painted in blues and yellows. I smelled the incense and saw the altar filled with flowers and garlands and the Deities magnificently bedecked with jewels and a beautiful sequined outfit. At the feast, held outside, I never experienced anything like the ice-cold strawberry sweet rice Narottama dasa had made. I was captivated. The devotees said, "You should spend the night." I thought, "OK, I'll stay until Wednesday." I started chanting sixteen rounds, going to the temple programs, doing service, and ended up staying.

Overnight I stopped my old habits and my parents frantically wanted to get me out of that situation. They said, "What are you doing?" I said, "It's fine, I'm happy." I invited my parents to join me and the other Detroit devotees to see Srila Prabhupada at Ratha-yatra in Chicago in July 1974, which they did. After the festival my parents and I crammed into Prabhupada's room for darshan. Prabhupada was sitting on the floor at his desk and the room was silent. Looking at him I could understand what everyone was excited about and why they were determined that I should meet him and be part of this Movement. Prabhupada saw the puppet I was holding and said, "What is that?" I said, "Srila Prabhupada, it's a puppet. We've been making puppets in Detroit." He said, "We shouldn't be going around like this. People will think we're worshiping dolls."

Toward the end of the darshan Prabhupada was saying how there's no need to pray to God for our daily bread because God is supplying everything. He said, "Just like the Communist brothers give food and say, 'Now who is giving you food, God or us?' " My father raised his hand and objected and to my shock Prabhupada immediately said, "What are you knowing?" and quieted him down. My father was a proud, macho, Navy veteran but when Prabhupada roared at him it was no contest. My dad didn't pursue it. When the darshan ended I bowed down and my mother hit me and said, "Get up, get up! Why are you bowing down? Don't bow down!"

During the Mayapur festival in 1975, in the morning Srila Prabhupada greeted the Deities in a genuinely humble, sweet, and unassuming way from his realization that, "I'm the servant of the servant of the servant of the servant. I'm just one of God's servants here." Then he gave class and preached like a lion, with no fear, no hesitation, no reservations, only clear and forceful conviction and truth. We listened with rapt attention and open ears and hearts. There was no denying who he was and what he came for. I'd watch his every move and was completely satisfied and filled with a deep sense of gratitude that I was with my spiritual master who meant everything to me.

After class Prabhupada would circumambulate the temple and ring the bell. That simple movement of his arm and that smile on his face as he rang the bell was so surcharged with spiritual energy it was like ringing for eternal life. He was a small boy calling all his friends to come to Krishna and play. Watching his face and being a part of that was utterly divine. He transported us to the possibility of another world and showed us how easy it is to connect with Krishna. Around and around we'd go. What does that bell mean? With open-heartedness the Deity is summoning us to please come to Him.

In Vrindavan I helped take care of Manisha, who was dying from Hodgkin's disease. One night a little before the 6:30 pm *arati*, Manisha, her mother Antardhyana, and I went to see Prabhupada, who was sitting behind his desk in the main darshan room putting on *tilaka*. We sat toward the back of the room and Antardhyana said, "Srila Prabhupada I don't want to bother you, but I'm so upset Manisha's dying." Earlier, Srila Prabhupada had told us to keep Manisha as comfortable as possible but at this time he became stern and chastised Antardhyana. In a loud and strong voice he said, "We're all dying! Maybe you today, maybe me tomorrow, but we're all dying." I was expecting empathy but this was as if Prabhupada was saying, "Haven't you been listening to me, to what my books are about, to why I've come here? Don't you know yet? She's dying, you're dying, I'm dying, everybody's dying. What are you thinking? Why are you coming to me whining, 'Oh, she's dying,' like it's a surprise? There is no surprise." Manisha was having a hard time chanting sixteen rounds and said, "Prabhupada, what will happen if I don't chant sixteen rounds?" He said, "You will come back in an aristocratic family with wealth and beauty. But chant Hare Krishna." It was short and powerful and then Prabhupada left for *arati* as if to say, "Now go do these things." Manisha tried hard and did chant and passed away in the Mathura hospital.

Through the years I had a close relationship with my father and he was a strong figure in my life. But since I first knew Srila Prabhupada and to this very moment he is my real father. I'm anxious to see him again.

Rasalila devi dasi

By the fall of 1973, Rasalila devi had become curious about yoga and about Eastern thought and religion. Coming of age in the 1960's meant living in a time of social upheaval and a shattering of norms. For some, it also meant finding answers to life's most persistent questions in all sorts of new and unusual places.

I first met His Divine Grace early in 1973, through the *Back to Godhead* magazine. After reading just two paragraphs from the Founder's Lecture, I felt certain that I must meet the author, A. C. Bhaktivedanta Swami. The contents of those short, yet eloquent paragraphs resonated with me like nothing else I had ever read or heard before. It was truly mind-altering and, ultimately, proved to be life-altering as well.

Before that year was over, I was guided to go to the closest ISKCON temple which, at that time, was located in Coconut Grove (Miami), Florida. The devotees were welcoming and being there felt strangely familiar. The days turned into weeks and the weeks turned into months. I stayed on, hoping to meet A. C. Bhaktivedanta Swami, whom the devotees called Srila Prabhupada. I had been informed that there was a chance he might be visiting there soon.

In the meantime, I became absorbed in service and study. I began to feel a new-found sense of satisfaction. Learning about and practicing a lifestyle based on spiritual and philosophical principles had been previously unimaginable to me. I feel so very blessed to have had such an opportunity.

Six months later, I had been recommended, and accepted, for first initiation. Although I had some hesitancy, I chose to go forward. I still had not met Srila Prabhupada, but through his disciples and his teachings, I understood just enough to know that this was my path.

Change was in the air, in more ways than one! After being married, we decided to move to the New Vrindaban community. There, in the hills of West Virginia, my cherished desire would be fulfilled. I would finally get to meet Srila Prabhupada, whose words had transformed my entire world! I would finally get to meet my most beloved spiritual master, for the very first time. It would become my great fortune to be initiated there during Srila Prabhupada's visit in July of 1974.

I felt overwhelmed with many different emotions. I felt happiness, elation, awe, disbelief, and also trepidation. Was I ready for such a grave responsibility and commitment? Probably not, but, if I were to intellectualize too much, I might never feel ready. Such momentous decisions can never be made by the head alone, one must also consult with the heart and the gut. Some might call it intuition. Appropriately, I felt a fool, but, as the saying goes, "Fools rush in, where angels fear to tread."

Standing in the presence of Srila Prabhupada, I was overwhelmed by his purity and potency. It was a mystical and otherworldly type of experience, the likes of which can change your life on many levels and in ways that you cannot even begin to imagine. His extraordinary example of loving, devotional service continues to inspire me to honor the commitments that I made upon taking initiation. It enables me and empowers me to remain fixed in the ideal of service, with all its wonderful and practically unlimited possibilities. And it all started with those two short, yet eloquent, paragraphs that opened my window to the spiritual world!

Rasangi devi dasi

After she'd graduated from New York University, Rasangi, a vegetarian and hatha yoga practitioner, lived in New York City in 1969 and 1970 at the ashram of Swami Satchidananda. Then for about a year she studied Sanskrit under Dr. Ramamurti S. Mishra, who Prabhupada had preached to when he first came to America. Rasangi would see and hear devotees throughout New York City but she looked down on them, as they seemed odd.

At the Valencia Street temple in San Francisco I had *prasadam* for the first time and a light bulb went off in my head. For seven years I'd eaten Indian vegetarian food, but something in *prasadam* was unlike anything I'd ever eaten before. That was my first connection with Srila Prabhupada and a profound experience.

I married Dharmadhyaksa and we visited the Q Street temple in Washington, D.C. where I met the amazing devotees Antardhyana, Mamata, Rupamanjari, Varuna, and Damodara, and didn't want to leave. I moved in with my five-month-old son Maitreya and was happy.

I first got Srila Prabhupada's gaze in Los Angeles and at that moment I felt loved for the first time in my life. We'd all pile into Prabhupada's room for darshans, and it was so crowded we couldn't all fit. Once I came when there was no room and Prabhupada told some men to move aside to let me in. Prabhupada cared for me like a daughter and instructed the men to be gentlemen. When Srila Prabhupada spoke I felt he was talking to me. I listened deeply and felt connected to him. My energy would soar – I was on a high.

Rasarani devi dasi

Rasarani felt different from her parents and didn't have much of a bond with them. She started asking questions, begging the universe for answers, and praying to whomever was out there to please save her. Two weeks later she met the devotees and a couple of months after that, in May of 1971, Prabhupada came to Sydney.

I felt like an alien around my father because he was distant and never understood my philosophy. But at the temple I felt at home. Prabhupada provided me with a home and surrounded me with sisters and brothers who understood me and had food – *prasadam* – that I liked. Prabhupada was more of a father to me than my birth father.

I was always curious. I'd ask, "What's this, what's that, and how does this happen?" Nobody could give me answers until Prabhupada and his books came along. His books were amazing because they had fantastic, mind-boggling stories about the things I'd been curious about. Prabhupada spoke of spiritual lands of bliss, eternity, and knowledge where there were flowers, rivers, fun, and games. And these were not fairyland tales but magical and real places where we could go. It was like I'd hitched my wagon to a star. Nothing could touch me; I was safe, I was on the train back to the Promised Land, so to speak, and I was totally excited and happy. Prabhupada saved me in every way that a person can be saved and I was grateful to him for all his gifts.

In the temple there were only five or six of us, so it was intimate and we felt personally responsible to serve Prabhupada. Whatever Prabhupada asked, we'd do to the best of our ability even though we might lose sleep or have physical pain. There was no question of "I can't do that." I felt Prabhupada had chosen us to help him. And when we think that Prabhupada was Krishna's friend, a *shaktyavesha avatara* who descended to rescue living entities, to serve him was an extreme privilege. And yet with tears in his eyes Srila Prabhupada would sometimes say to all of us *mlecchas* with our faulty service and strange desires, "Thank you very much for helping me serve my spiritual master, Srila Bhaktisiddhanta Sarasvati Thakura." Prabhupada was humble and grateful. He would behave in different ways according to the time, place, and circumstances, sometimes commander-like and angry, and at other times childlike, playful, and funny. I thought, "The denizens of the spiritual world must have so many dimensions to their natures."

Prabhupada was concerned about all his disciples, both men and women. Sometimes the men's neophyte understanding of the philosophy made them think women weren't important and act in mean ways. But Prabhupada didn't think that way or have that mood. Prabhupada was always kind, caring, and fatherly toward the women.

I can never forget Prabhupada or lose my link with him. Materially as well as spiritually he was everything to me. Whichever part of Prabhupada's energy we touch, it's potent and dynamic and can change our heart.

Rasesvari devi dasi

At the end of 1972, Rasesvari and her friend traveled overland to India as hippies and somehow ended up in Vrindavan, which they knew nothing about. They asked, "Is there anything interesting to see here?" They talked to some Krishna devotees, wandered around for a couple of hours, and then left.

My boyfriend and I finished our travels, came back to England, got married, and one day he said, "Start packing. We're moving into Bhaktivedanta Manor." I thought, "I can't do this, I can't leave everything. This is my home." But I wanted to be with him and he was adamant.

At the Manor everything was alien. I didn't know anybody, nobody took care of me, and I felt so lost I cried. Then Jagaddhatri invited me into her room, "Oh, welcome, come in, come in!" I thought, "Now that's different. She's the first person to say that." She said, "Do you need some help with your *sari*?" I thought, "Yeah, I really do," and I said, "Actually I need help with everything." She laughed and ever since I've been fortunate that she's always there for me. When I went through lots of troubles, the whole time I kept in touch with her. There are other devotees who helped me, but she is absolutely special.

The first time I saw Srila Prabhupada was during Janmashtami at the Manor. I was on the grounds when a little earthquake-like ripple reverberated through the devotees: "Prabhupada's at the window of his room! Prabhupada's at the window!" Like a tidal wave all the devotees came to see Srila Prabhupada and somebody started a kirtan. I'd seen lots of famous, important people in my life, but nothing prepared me for seeing Srila Prabhupada. Just standing at that window he emanated so much; my feeling of being lost disappeared altogether and the pieces of the jigsaw – all the information and instruction I'd been getting – began to come together. I still didn't know the philosophy or the songs, but I knew that being Krishna's devotee was the right thing to be. Until that point I'd been doing everything because my husband wanted to do it, but when I saw Srila Prabhupada I knew Krishna consciousness was what I wanted to do.

I next saw Srila Prabhupada when he came to the Manor in 1977. It was out of character, but one day in the temple room I sat by his feet. I had to be there. That spot is serene and being there reinforced everything that brings me back to Krishna again and again. I know that whatever happens, Krishna consciousness is right.

Now I have an amazing job, enough money, a house, wonderful children, but I don't have the association of devotees, and so I actually have nothing. To me the important thing has always been the devotees – Jagaddhatri and my other godsisters.

By Prabhupada's grace Krishna has given me some service. In my work I attend interfaith forums as a Hare Krishna devotee as well as the manager of a charity. Everyone understands and respects my beliefs. Remembering Prabhupada at the Manor window, being with him in the temple, I feel he's there for me, and I pray that that's where he'll always be.

Ratna Vrinda devi dasi

Ratna Vrinda was a pious girl who was raised by the Sacred Heart nuns. She never went to public school or read a mundane book; her uncle was a Roman Catholic bishop. In 1971 in Balboa, Ratna Vrinda was on the edge of a precipice when she saw a poster of the Lord in the heart and was overwhelmed by His beauty. She asked a devotee, "Who is this? Is this a boy or a girl?" The devotee said, "This is the Lord in the heart." At that moment Ratna Vrinda thought, "I'm saved, I'm okay now," and knew without a doubt that she would become a devotee and spend the rest of her life serving that Person. On March 16, 1972, when she was fifty years old, she moved into the San Diego temple.

The first day I moved in, I was on my hands and knees scrubbing the floor of the temple room when I first heard the recording of the "Govinda" song.

I cried. I prayed to God, "Oh, my Lord, please cleanse me. Please, my Lord, please make me pure so I can see You."

Two months later, Srila Prabhupada came to San Diego for the first time and seven or eight of us went to the airport to meet him. When I saw his head at the plane door, my hair stood up. I felt, "There's the person who's going to teach and guide me." It was a wonderful moment.

In the spring of 1973 Prabhupada came back to San Diego and stayed in our apartment close to the temple. I was taking care of him, making his bed every morning. The temple president was a wonderful devotee, Bhakta dasa, who, eager to please Srila Prabhupada, had somebody paint the Hare Krishna mantra on the temple steps. Prabhupada said, "What is this? Are we going to walk on top of Krishna?" Right away the devotees painted it over.

My husband and I would regularly see Srila Prabhupada when he was in L.A. Concerned about devotees' bickering, Srila Prabhupada told us that whatever happens we should stick to our devotional service. Later, I was ill in bed and my husband went to L.A. without me. At that time Srila Prabhupada initiated both of us and sent my beads to me through my husband.

Since my husband passed away, I've had the chance to completely dedicate every day of my life to follow my Gurudeva and, without complacency, to accomplish what he expects of me. *Maya*'s big weapon is complacency. Every single joint in my body is contaminated with arthritis, but where there's a will there's a way. I stick to Prabhupada's instructions, never letting them go, and this makes me fortunate, blessed and at peace with myself. I know that I'm doing what Srila Prabhupada expects of me.

We're fortunate to have Srila Prabhupada as our spiritual master and have to hang on to all the immensely valuable instructions he gave us; we cannot let them go.

Rucira devi dasi

In 1970, Rucira was fourteen and still in high school when the devotees starting visiting the hippies who had a commune and health food store next to her home in St. Louis.

My parents had chickens that ran around in our yard, and once, when I was about twelve, I was sitting on the back porch watching the animals when I suddenly felt like I was one of the chickens. I felt what the chicken felt by not having any arms and having to bend down to eat. It was weird and I didn't know where the feeling came from. Later, when I read the *Bhagavad-gita*, I understood that we've been in this world in different forms, and I thought, "That's why I can relate—I've been here as a chicken!"

I became a vegetarian when I was thirteen, and my parents flipped out about what I would eat. A normal midwestern American meal was all meat. Luckily the hippies next door became vegetarians, and I could go to their place and help them cook and then eat with them.

When I got a BTG and saw a picture of Srila Prabhupada, something about him reminded me of my grandfather, and I immediately felt attracted and started chanting. I knew Sundararupa Prabhu before he was a devotee, because he used to come to the hippie commune to teach yoga. Then he quit university and joined the temple and a few hippies from the commune also became devotees. I was stuck at home feeling that I wanted to be a devotee, too, but I didn't know if I could be austere enough.

When I got Prabhupada's small blue *Gita,* the one with Lord Vishnu on the front, it made so much sense. Then I got *Sri Ishopanishad.* I loved that book because it was almost a mixture of the impersonalism I'd been hearing about and personalism. I read *Krsna* book at least five times. I loved *Krsna* book. I felt that personal relationship with God was missing in the Catholicism in which I was raised. There was a lot of ritual in it, but I didn't like that as much.

I was also very attracted to Prabhupada. I got the "Happening" album at the St. Louis temple. I would play Prabhupada's talk about the *maha-mantra* over and over. My mother even started chanting Hare Krishna because that record was on all the time. Then, when they closed the St. Louis temple, the devotees gave me a *tulasi* plant, which I worshiped at my parents' house. My father thought I had gone totally nuts. "Why are you dancing around a plant?" When the St. Louis devotees came back to St. Louis, I started going to the temple all the time. The devotees told me I needed to get married, so my parents wouldn't have any sway over me anymore. So in 1974, when I had just turned twenty, I married a British devotee (not Adi-karta Prabhu) and moved to England.

Not too long after that, Srila Prabhupada came to the Manor. I was very pregnant then, and *grihasthas* had to live outside as there was nowhere for us to stay in the temple. We were living in Norwich, and we went by train to see Srila Prabhupada at the Manor. It was a dream come true to actually see him in person after hearing so much about him.

But it was hellish living away from the devotees, and very austere. Finally, one day I got on a train–my baby was a few months old by then– went to the temple, and said, "Please let me stay!" They agreed. My husband was always coming and going, and then he left ISKCON altogether. But I stayed and did whatever service I could, and luckily I got to take care of Srila Prabhupada's rooms.

Once, when Prabhupada was sitting in his Manor room along with many devotees, he immediately saw that someone had put their bead bag on one of the steps leading into his bathroom. Srila Prabhupada said, "Get your bead bag off the floor." The devotee was looking around. Prabhupada repeated, "Take your bead bag off the floor." The devotee said, "But it's not on the floor, Srila Prabhupada, it's ..." Prabhupada said, "We step on those steps. Take your bead bag off the floor." I still see devotees putting their bead bags there, and I always say something because I heard that.

Once, I went on a morning walk, and as we were walking through the fields around the Manor, someone asked Prabhupada, "In Krishna's time, weren't they digging for gold and gems? Because everyone wore ..." Srila Prabhupada said, "No. When Krishna was on the planet, Bhumi wanted to give to Krishna, so she put all the jewels in the streams or on the hills. The people would take them and make jewelry." That was amazing, because I'd never even thought about how they got all their gems.

I helped Mondakini cook for Srila Prabhupada a few times. Once Prabhupada sent word that she should taste everything before she sent it to make sure it had the right amount of salt.

Srila Prabhupada was always very kind to Himavati. Once, when Srila Prabhupada was leaving by car, he turned to her and said, "Himavati, are you coming?" She said, "Yes, Srila Prabhupada!" She ran to the shoe room to get her shoes, and Prabhupada made everyone wait and made sure there was room for her in the car.

When I first joined I thought, "I want to try this and see." Then after practicing and seeing the results, that's what's made me stay. The proof is in the taste of the pudding. By getting in there and practicing, not just on the surface but actually diving into your *japa,* your *sadhana,* your service, your reading of Prabhupada's books, that's what keeps you going. That gives you juice in life, and that's what's kept me going the whole time: "I can see I'm making some advancement. I can see material desires and attachments dropping off. And I can see Krishna is a real person and that He's always there. I can see that Srila Prabhupada is always there, even when physically he's not. But he's definitely still there to help me along this path."

Why wouldn't I have the faith to carry on? That's definitely what keeps me going, and it's probably the same for most devotees. It's indebtedness. I feel very indebted. We want to please Prabhupada because we owe him so much. Prabhupada has given us something no one else could have given us. He sacrificed for us.

I think, "We've been here so many lifetimes. What's one life to sacrifice?" And what is the sacrifice, really? We're getting so much more than what we're giving. That's what keeps me going too. Plus who can eat better? Who can have better association? And there's so much wonderful service to do. This life is perfect. Really, we have our whole life to be grateful. Every single thing we do is because Srila Prabhupada showed us how to do it:

how to dress, how to keep clean, how to eat, how to live our life, how to get up, how to even take a shower, and go to the bathroom. It's amazing.

When my father was dying, I went home to see him. Looking at my family members I thought, "I could never have lived this life, just in ignorance." Prabhupada opened our eyes to see reality.

In my initiation letter Srila Prabhupada wrote, "We can never repay the spiritual master. But by doing service and trying to spread this Movement, that will do good for you and to all others." I was thinking, "How could you ever repay someone who has given you everything and is freeing you from this eternal cycle of being bound up body after body after body?"

I'm definitely one to speak out if I'm in a situation where I question what devotees are doing. But if I'm not in a situation to speak out, I just carry on. We all have a personal relationship with Srila Prabhupada and with this Movement. So whatever happens I carry on practicing what Prabhupada taught us.

We're all getting old, we're going to be gone soon, so we need to enthuse the younger generation to take up Krishna consciousness seriously and move it forward. It behooves us to show the example and to enthuse them to keep going because they're going to be the ones left. We have to install them in our place. What I want to do with the rest of my life is to try to encourage and train the younger devotees, if there's any possibility of doing that. If they'd like to know something I know, I'd like to help them know it.

Rudrani devi dasi

When she was eleven, Rudrani became a vegetarian and started meditating and practicing yoga. Two years later she got Krsna book and began chanting Hare Krishna.

In high school I only read Prabhupada's books because I thought all other books were useless. I was chanting, skipping my classes, and reading Prabhupada's books in the library. I didn't associate with other students and, although I didn't study, somehow managed to get a B+ average. In May of 1973, when I was sixteen, I came to the Toronto temple with my suitcase and said to Vicaru, who opened the door, "I'd like to move into the temple." He asked if I was chanting and following the four rules and regulations and I said yes. He told me I could move in. I joined the *harinama* and *sankirtana* parties. Those were the happiest days of my life.

In January 1975 my parents had me kidnapped. I was held in a hotel room, sent to Nova Scotia, shipped to San Diego, and then to Ohio, where they forced opened my mouth and put meat in it. I spit it out. For six months abductors who blasphemed, shouted, screamed, ripped up books in front of me, broke my beads, and drew horns on Prabhupada's head shipped me around. Ted Patrick warned that he'd sleep in a bed with me for a month if I went back to the temple. I was scared, but I took shelter of Krishna and my faith got stronger. I didn't want to associate with nondevotee meat-eaters and blasphemers; I wanted to be with devotees and live devotionally. Something kept drawing me back to Prabhupada.

When I was young, my life's pursuit was to find life's purpose. I was searching for a guru. My whole life I had followed the principles, and devotional service was natural and familiar. It felt like something I was continuing from before. I had faith that if I kept doing what Prabhupada wanted, I'd advance. Prabhupada directed me to Krishna and showed me that I was supposed to serve and develop my relationship with Krishna.

I put my heart and soul into book distribution, knowing it pleased Prabhupada, and was one of the top book distributors in Toronto. While I distributed I prayed to Lord Chaitanya and to Prabhupada and thought, "I have a responsibility to Srila Prabhupada." I wasn't trying to prove anything. I just wanted to serve. By reading his books, chanting, and serving, my bond with Prabhupada was strong.

Krishna consciousness is simple. We serve while following Prabhupada's straightforward, easy-to-follow instructions that work and bring joy. I've had hardships and many people have tried to break my faith, but in my heart I always felt, "Plow right through and go for the essence." For thirty years I've been serving and meditating on the Radha-Krishna Deities I worship. Prabhupada gave so much and his mission is about giving, about selflessly helping others in any way possible – through *prasadam*, book distribution, education, Deity worship.

Rukmavati devi dasi

From the age of eight or nine, Rukmavati was wondering who she was, what the world was, and what life was about. When she read the first two paragraphs of Srila Prabhupada's article in a Back to Godhead *magazine, all her questions were answered.*

My bond with Prabhupada began when I read those two paragraphs. And that bond was something that Prabhupada, through his causeless mercy, implanted in my heart. I reread those paragraphs thinking, "I'm a spirit soul, Krishna is God, this is the material world, which is like a prison house. The aim of life is to chant Hare Krishna, get out of this world, and go back to Krishna." I'd been tormented by not knowing the answers to all my piercing questions, so I was eternally indebted to Prabhupada for giving me this knowledge. The way Prabhupada touched my heart is not something of this world; it comes directly from Goloka Vrindavan.

When I met Prabhupada at Burnett Street in St. Kilda, I couldn't wrap my intelligence around him. I couldn't categorize or measure him or grasp who he was. He wasn't like anybody else, and I realized I had no idea what a *sadhu* was or how that person interacted in this world.

On one morning walk, Ramaniya and I positioned ourselves behind Srila Prabhupada and she spent the whole time looking at the back of his feet and chanting *japa*. For most of us, Ramaniya's *japa* was annoying and disturbing. With a funny smile on her face she'd froth at the mouth as she loudly chanted. At one point on the walk, Prabhupada stopped, turned around, and looked at Ramaniya. She folded her hands and stepped back with her head bowed. I thought, "He's going to tell her not to chant *japa* like that." Prabhupada said, "This chanting is very good." The smile on Ramaniya's face, with froth in the corners of her mouth, went practically to her ears.

Prabhupada gave me the faith that Krishna consciousness is the reality and that I can capture this reality through the process he gave. Every day I rise early, chant, worship Giriraja Govardhana, sing *bhajanas,* and always try to focus on the goal. Like unceasing waves, life's happinesses and distresses will come and go. We can't change that, but we can always remember the goal. Prabhupada can give us an intense, real relationship with Radha and Krishna.

In the same way he touched me through his *Back to Godhead* article, Prabhupada can touch someone who is coming to Krishna consciousness now. But ultimately, each person has to find someone who can give him or her bhakti. There's a living disciplic succession. We can't think that Prabhupada is the last pure devotee that Krishna is going to send. Bhakti can only come from bhakti; only someone who has bhakti can give it.

Rukmini devi dasi

Rukmini was sixteen years-old when she first met Srila Prabhupada, whose first words to her were, "Where are your parents?"

When I was initiated, Prabhupada beautifully encouraged me. Maybe I reminded him of Rukmini because he told the story of Rukmini and then he said to me, "You are a beautiful girl and now become more beautiful within also." Those words were such a profound, life-long instruction. Prabhupada also said, "Krishna can accept any number of beautiful girls. Your name is Rukmini and some day Krishna will kidnap you." Prabhupada saw me in some far-distant perfected stage and he was encouraging me to take the steps I needed to take to get there. He had faith in his disciples and he was patient with us.

Once in 1968 when Prabhupada was in his quarters at 26 2nd Ave in New York he was looking at every single devotee directly and deliberately and he said, "I want each one of you to open a temple somewhere." At that time I was still sixteen and impetuous, so I said, "Even the girls, Swamiji?" Prabhupada said, "Yes, there is no difference between the boys and the girls when you are preaching Krishna consciousness." That was a thrilling and important instruction.

Once my parents came to the Sunday Feast in New York and the temple room was so crowded that by the force of the crowd they had to bow down with everyone else. Afterwards I told Prabhupada and he said, "Yes, this is the goal of our Krishna consciousness movement: just get them to bow down before Krishna."

The next year, 1969, my husband and I came to see Prabhupada and he thought I looked thin and I didn't look happy or healthy. At that time Prabhupada said that my husband and I should live separately. It was shocking, but on his order I stayed in New York working with the altar and Baradraj went back to Boston where he was painting. Then I asked Brahmananda, the New York temple president, if I could go to Los Angeles to learn Deity worship from Silavati. He agreed so I was in Los Angeles for about a year learning Deity worship. It was wonderful. During this period, my then husband met Prabhupada and tried to explain himself to Prabhupada but Prabhupada ignored him. Finally Prabhupada looked directly at him and said, "I have given you my daughter and you have not taken care," and then looked away.

After that Prabhupada traveled and was gone for a long time to London and Germany and when he got to Boston he looked at my husband and said, "Where is your wife?" My husband said, "You sent her away Prabhupada." Prabhupada smiled and my husband said, "Should I send for her?" Prabhupada said "Yes, husband without the wife is only half, wife without the husband is only half." So I was in Los Angeles when Prabhupada was in Boston, and when I went to Boston, Prabhupada went to Los Angeles. Twice I was going to miss his darshan. I was feeling sad that I wasn't going to see him so I made a big batch of *bundi luddus*. Prabhupada had told us, "If you can learn to make *luddus* and *kachoris* I will bless you. I only want to go to Krishnaloka to get Krishna's luddus and kachoris." So I made a big batch of these *luddus*, wrote a little note to Prabhupada, and asked the devotees to give it to him.

After a week or so Upendra, Prabhupada's servant, called and said that Prabhupada liked the *luddus* and wanted me to make some for him every fortnight and send them to him. So I started making and sending *luddus* to Prabhupada every fortnight, and each time I would also send a little letter and a little prayer. And every time Prabhupada would reply with a sweet and grateful letter to me. But these were the days when we were asked not to write letters to Prabhupada because we were disturbing him. I thought, "Okay, I should send *luddus* without writing a letter." I sent the box without a letter and then at the bottom of a letter Prabhupada wrote to Chandanacharya, Prabhupada wrote, "I have received a box of *luddus* and I think they are from Rukmini devi, so please thank her and give her my blessings." That was a great and sweet lesson about service in separation. I didn't get to see Prabhupada personally, but it was more meaningful to do that service and I received more reciprocation than if I had been there.

Devotional service is extremely personal. We are serving a person who is really there, observing us, hearing our prayers, tasting our offerings. When our service is tinged with love, with longing, with ardent prayer, we will experience the reciprocation for which we are longing. In this story, I was unable to be there with Srila Prabhupada, and I was so much wishing that I could be there. But through the tiny service I rendered, even in separation, I had more reciprocation with him than if I had personally been there. This is the mystic quality of devotional service.

In Los Angeles I'd learned Deity worship from Silavati, who had a beautiful standard. Then I went to Boston and tried to introduce the things that I learned in Los Angeles, but the response I got was, "That may be the way they do things in Los Angeles but we are not really interested in what you have to say. This is the way we do things here in Boston." After that I had a dream that the Radha-Krishna Deities were on the altar, the curtains closed, and then opened and the Deities were gone! Everyone was lying on the floor in the temple and saying, "This is how they do things here," and no one was doing anything. In the dream I was distraught and went to Prabhupada and said, "I think it's my negligence that the Deities disappeared." So later, in my disturbed waking state, I wrote a letter to Prabhupada saying, "I heard that you said that Deity worship without *bhava* is idol worship." Because of my negligence I felt the Deities had disappeared and we were worshiping idols. Prabhupada replied with a beautiful letter in which he said, "Deity worship means to be very, very clean. The Deities should never be approached without one having bathed first and changed to clean cloths. Keep teeth brushed, fingernails clean and trim. Be sure that your hands are clean before touching anything on the altar or the Deities. And cleanse the Deity room, altar and floor daily thoroughly. Shine the various aratrik paraphernalia after aratrik. The idea is summit cleanliness. That will satisfy Krishna. So you should never be negligent. Always be careful, then in due course you will feel bhava."

Rukmini Priya devi dasi

Rukmini Priya first met devotees in late 1972 in Delhi, India, on the "Magic Bus," a bus company that went from London to Katmandu. Bitter, cold winter was coming and she was on her way to Manchester to visit her father. Rukmini purchased books and befriended two devotees who had just left Vrindavan and were on their way to start a temple in Israel.

I always feel grateful towards Srila Prabhupada, I even appreciate the name that Srila Prabhupada gave me. Way back in summer 1973, at the opening of Bhaktivedanta Manor, the devotees were preparing for the upcoming fire *yajna* and the intiations. My name was Ruth Sweetman. I was thinking telepathically out loud, what name beginning with "r" I would like. I said to myself, *"I would love the name Rukmini, but I will never get that name."*

So when at the initiation ceremony, after I had walked up to receive my beads, and I was bowing my head to the ground, I heard Srila Prabhupada say, "Rukmini was the first queen of Krishna," I was so happy.

Srila Prabhupada's gifts are boundless and we have no way of repaying these gifts. As we evolve all we can do is our duty and follow Srila Prabhupada's desire and not diminish and water down his instructions to us.

Saci devi dasi

Saci devi was initiated on Easter Sunday in 1969 when she was nineteen years old. She first met Srila Prabhupada in Los Angeles.

Being there was otherworldly. There were probably sixteen or eighteen devotees so it was very small and intimate. After Srila Prabhupada gave his lecture he circumambulated the room as kirtan began. Stopping at each picture on the wall, he would hold up his hands and sway very gently. In the back of the room sat two little old ladies. They had on short flowered dresses and stockings. When he got to the back of the room, very gently smiling, he motioned with his palms up to get up and dance with everyone else, and they did.

While paying obeisance, I saw Prabhupada's feet coming and his saffron socks. His feet stopped by my head, and my heart was just pounding, pounding. Prabhupada asked Tamal, "So when will she be initiated?" Tamal said, "The next one, Srila Prabhupada, it's on the 25th." So Prabhupada walked on and I met him on the stairs again. His head was golden with a background of beautiful blue sky. Prabhupada looked at me with a big smile, "So you are happy now?" This world just disappeared, it just kind of blanked out, and Prabhupada adopted me as his daughter right then and there. He was my eternal father and my guru forever. It was an intrinsic and very sweet connection, and I felt that he cared about me so much. He cared that I was happy, and he noted that I was especially happy, I was very jubilant.

Kausalya, Rohini, and myself, went to Prabhupada's quarters. We were seventeen, eighteen, and nineteen, just little girls sitting at the lotus feet of Srila Prabhupada. He was being very fatherly. He held up his palm and he said, "You should never see the fingernails over the fingertips because then they are not clean, they are too long." Then we went for a walk with him, the three of us walking behind Prabhupada like little ducklings. He stopped to talk to someone who was watering his flowers, "Good morning. These are my disciples, and I have come to teach them how to serve God." The man was very friendly and receptive. It's one of those memories of just pure joy to be with Prabhupada. There was no discussion, but just to be with him and to feel his protection and his shelter.

For the 1969 Ratha-yatra the procession was from the temple on Frederick Street down to the ocean, which was six miles. So there was a lot of time to focus and to be with Srila Prabhupada. At one point he got up and put his arms up in the air. He was just so happy, so ecstatic. Literally we all practically fainted. There was just something about the moment. Prabhupada was infusing us with so much, and he was so pleased to see so many hundreds of people there following the cart.

A little bit later I was married to Karandhara just after the temple on Watseka was found. I remember the day that we met Prabhupada over there when he saw it for the first time. And, oh, he was so pleased. His smile was from ear-to-ear and he was looking at it and he said, "This is the mercy of my Guru Maharaja."

The temple room was painted for Srila Bhaktisiddhanta's disappearance day. Srila Prabhupada put his Guru Maharaja's picture on the *vyasasana* and worshipped him. Then Prabhupada sat down on a cushion on the floor. He had made the list for the feast, and now he was managing all the servers. When he saw that someone had finished their *gulabjamon* or *samosa* he would call the server over to that devotee for more. It was the first time that I became aware of Srila Prabhupada's reverence for his Guru Maharaja. It was a lesson to us how to honor Prabhupada.

The next year, Prabhupada was there for Srila Bhaktisiddhanta's appearance day. I was in decorating the *vyasasana*. Gopavrindapala came in with a picture of Srila Bhaktisiddhanta. You couldn't see Gopa because the painting was quite large. Someone asked a question and Gopa responded from behind the picture. Prabhupada laughed, "See, my Guru Maharaja is always speaking to me." So we all had a really good laugh.

One morning, Prabhupada came in and took *charanamrita* as usual. That day it was very rich, thick, and sweet. Prabhupada turned around–you could see the whites of his eyes they were so big, "This is so good, I could eat the whole thing."

Another morning there was salt in the *charanamrita*. I had never seen Prabhupada more angry. You could have heard a pin drop, everyone was just frozen. Prabhupada said, "Who has done this?" And Sucitra, "I did, Srila Prabhupada." And he chastised her for being careless in serving Krishna. But the depth of his voice, it was deeper than usual, so serious and somber that I don't think we even breathed. I think we were just stunned. She was very brave to raise her hand.

In those days, Prabhupada was always giving instruction. If a child wasn't sitting right in the temple and their feet were towards the Deities, he would correct that. He would look around and watch. If a child didn't have neck beads on, he would say, "Why doesn't this child have neck beads?" He would see *tulasi,* he would give an instruction about Tulasi Devi. He would tell Silavati something about the Deities. So every morning it was a surprise: What are we going to learn this morning? What are we going to hear? What is Prabhupada going to do? We were very lucky in Los Angeles to have him there sometimes six months at a time.

I was taking care of *tulasi*. One morning there were two *tulasis* flanking his *vyasasana*. He leaned over to Karandhara and said, "Before a *tulasi* plant is a year old, if she is younger than a year, don't allow the *manjaris* to go to seed because it's too taxing on the plant."

I was probably six months pregnant and I was dancing. Prabhupada leaned over to Karandhara and said, "Tell your wife she cannot dance like that anymore, she is too far along." After six months, no dancing and no traveling.

When I was pregnant, Karandhara sent me to San Francisco to be the head *pujari*. I was getting up at two o'clock in the morning to do vases and make sure the brass was polished, etc. I was very distraught because I was ill with the pregnancy but trying to be dutiful. I wrote a letter to Prabhupada saying, "I could go to my parents but they're not devotees. I can't go home while I have this child. I'm forlorn, I have no shelter." And I sent it with Kanta devi who was going to Los Angeles. As soon as Prabhupada got the letter, he called Karandhara in and very sternly said, "You send for Saci devi right away."

So I was back in Los Angeles the next day, and Prabhupada called us in. Prabhupada was sitting on his cushion on the floor with his desk in front of him. He was upset with Karandhara. And Karandhara could not give an explanation of why he sent his pregnant wife away. Prabhupada was so upset, it was kind of hard for him to speak. He would say, "Why have you done this?" Karandhara: "I don't know, Prabhupada. I don't know." Prabhupada said, "She is pregnant, she must be blissful. You must look after her and make sure she is cared for. She is carrying a child. I can see by her face she is a nice girl. Why won't you take care of her?" "I don't know, Prabhupada, I don't know."

So Prabhupada said, "She must stay here. You don't have to talk to her, but you must make sure that she has *prasadam,* that she has nice accommodations, and that she has everything she needs." Prabhupada rescued me from a very difficult, stressful situation, and gave me shelter.

Prabhupada would always approach me in the temple or outside and say, "How are you doing? Is everything okay?" Or if he didn't see me at the temple he would ask where I was. When Bhakta Rupa was born, Prabhupada would always give him flowers or touch him on the head. And he would say, "Are you happy now?" Of course, I was very fulfilled being a mother. So that just solidified my affection for Prabhupada and my indebtedness to him. Married life was not real easy for me, it was a constant difficulty.

Someone threw a cherry bomb in the temple one afternoon. Nagapatni was pregnant, and there were several of us in there. Of course, this was the first instance of such antagonism and danger–the first danger that we really experienced in the Movement. When they told Srila Prabhupada, he said, "As the Movement gets stronger, the demons will retaliate. They will be more threatened." It was very, very frightening. We already were singing the *tava kara kamala* prayers. But when he came down the following morning he taught us the *namaste narasimha* prayers and told us to chant them after every kirtan.

Prabhupada began distributing cookies to the children. There were so many children at that time, and they all hovered around Prabhupada's *vyasasana.* Bhakta Rupa was about two years old then, and he was standing next to Kulasekhara and he wanted his *kartalas,* but he couldn't get them so he started to cry. Prabhupada leaned over and handed me his *kartalas.* Bhakta Rupa stopped crying and his eyes widened and he was just in shock. He stood still like, "What do I do?" So I handed the *kartalas* to Bhakta Rupa.

Before the first fall and winter, we built a beautiful redwood-framed screened-in *tulasi* house. You could walk in. Maybe six people could stand in there comfortably. It was probably eight feet tall. So we had all the *tulasi devis* in there, and Prabhupada invited us to come in because he was so pleased. He was always pleased when *tulasi devi* was thriving. It was very clear how important that was to Srila Prabhupada. So we sat down around him, and Prabhupada became reminiscent about his mother. He said that the *tulasi* house reminded him of his mother who loved plants. You know, he said, in India their roofs are generally flat and then there's a kind of wall that goes around. She had a lot of potted plants up there. He was remembering his youth and how plants were so important to his mother.

When we moved into Watseka there were pews in there. Prabhupada liked them. He wanted people to be comfortable so he wanted them to be able to wear their shoes into the sanctuary and sit in pews that they were used to in going to church. So we kept the sanctuary for that.

At one point, Karandhara Prabhu wanted to take *sannyasa*. Prabhupada did not want him to take *sannyasa*. I had just had a child, he was an infant. In those days, it was glorious to be a *sannyasi*. You got to be with Prabhupada a lot, and naturally young men aspired to that. It was a position of respect and a lot of close service to Srila Prabhupada. So Karandhara was kind of badgering Prabhupada and Prabhupada said, "No, you are more than *sannyasa*, you are householder. I want you to stay in Los Angeles and be the GBC and continue to develop the zone, open temples, and manage what you have."

But after a while, Prabhupada gave in because he was so insistent. And Dayananda wanted to take *sannyasa*. So Prabhupada called Nandarani and I in. I had little Bhakta Rupa in an infant seat. We were going to go to Dallas and they were going to take *sannyasa* two days later. When I got to Dallas, and before even the initiation, Karandhara had sent me a telegram and asked me to come back. He just said, "This is foolish, I'm not ready." I was twenty-one or twenty-two. He was maybe twenty-three.

Sacimata devi dasi

Sacimata dasi met Srila Prabhupada at a program in a park in 1970 in Calcutta when she was sixteen. Prabhupada suggested she come to meet him at noon the next day.

I hesitated a little because I was a little scared. I didn't know ISKCON and I am from a conservative family. So without saying anything to my parents, I went to meet him but I was a little late. Syamasundara Prabhu was Prabhupada's secretary at that time. He said I might have to come the next day, as it was now Prabhupada's lunch and then he would take rest. I explained how hard it was for me to get away from my family. So I went in and Srila Prabhupada was in his *gamcha* getting a massage. He corrected me for coming late and asked what kind of *seva* I liked. I said cooking and then he called for Kausalya. I met Malati and her daughter Sarasvati at that time, too.

When Prabhupada came back a year later, the devotees told me I could get initiated and I was so glad. Then Srila Prabhupada asked me to come to Mayapur, which was barren land at that time. There was one hut that Srila Prabhupada stayed in. We stayed in *pandals*. Prabhupada used to go for a morning walk with all the *sannyasis*.

All my godsisters and godbrothers were receiving nice names when they were initiated. I thought I would like to have a name from *Mahabharata* or *Srimad-Bhagavatam*. I was the last one to get *harinama* from him that day. He said, "Your name is Sacimata," and I was a little annoyed. I wanted a name from the *Srimad-Bhagavatam*. He made a joke, "Sacimata is not married yet, I will find a nice Jagannatha Misra for her." And everyone laughed.

In 1972 Prabhupada asked me to come to Vrindavan. It was a transcendental year for me at the Radha-Damodara temple. Prabhupada gave me second initiation, along with Lokanatha Maharaja. Three times Prabhupada showed me how to count with my fingers, but I kept making mistakes. Prabhupada was very angry with me. He said, "You are not sincere. Go away. I'm not going to give you." I just grabbed his feet. I said, "Prabhupada, please, this is the last time you will have to teach me. I will be serious now." I was a little sleepy, and he could understand that I wasn't paying attention. So he was refusing me and I was almost crying. Then Prabhupada was merciful. So he showed me how to count again and I could catch it nicely. Then Prabhupada said, "Okay, be careful from now on. Every day you chant this Gayatri mantra. Three times, okay?" I said, "Okay."

I was very anxious about cooking but Yamuna Mataji wouldn't allow me in the kitchen. So I went to Srila Prabhupada because he was like my father. "Prabhupada, give me some service because they don't allow me in the kitchen." Prabhupada said, "Okay, you clean my room every day."

When I would come to clean he would leave with a bucket and a towel. He would say, "Sacimata, close the door, okay? There's a monkey." I said, "Okay, Prabhupada." Every day he would remind me and every day I would forget. One day a monkey entered, grabbed the *laddus,* and ran away. I thought, "What will happen now? He will chastise me." I was crying and praying to all the demigods. The monkey was sitting on a tree and one *mataji* was making *capatis*. So she offered a *capati* to the monkey and he threw the container down, but all the *laddus* were gone. I was really, really scared and my heart was beating.

Pishima was always with me and Prabhupada would tell me, "Take care of my sister," and I would do that. So Pishima was sitting in the same room at the Radha-Damodara temple. Prabhupada came back and said, "Why do you have that expression on your face? What happened." She said, "I saw something happen." Instead of scolding me Prabhupada laughed. He laughed a lot. I was surprised. Then he gave me ten rupees and told me to go and get *jalebis* and distribute them among everyone.

In Calcutta, Palika came to my house. She said, "Go and get *parval* from the market. Prabhupada wants soup." Prabhupada told me how to cook the soup. I made a whole nice feast for Prabhupada but I cooked the rice first. Then I sent in his *prasadam*. After five minutes Bhavananda said, "Prabhupada wants to see you."

Prabhupada was good and angry. He said, "Who cooked?" "I did, Srila Prabhupada." He said, "You don't know any *guru seva*? Why is the rice cold? You made the rice first, yes? Rice should be hot. How you will serve Krishna? How you will serve all the elder *sadhu* Vaishnavas? You are not serious at all." And then he said, "Go and make *capatis* for me. I don't want this rice." And then I made some hot *capatis* and brought them.

In the afternoon at 4:00 he called me into his room and said, "Okay, Sacimata, now you understand how to do *guru seva*?" I said yes. He said, "I'm sorry. I did not want to scold you, but I wanted to give you a lesson." I said yes, and tears were coming, but with a lot of love in my heart for my Guru Maharaja.

My father was a heart patient and my three brothers were in school so we had financial problems. Gargamuni said, "If you don't come to the temple every day, then you are not allowed. Go and stay with your family. You cannot work outside." I didn't know what to do. Should I keep my Krishna consciousness or work? I was attached to my family, they were pious. I wrote Prabhupada. He said, "You earn for your family. Make them a happy Hare Krishna family. Let them be Krishna conscious. I don't have any objection." Then Gargamuni allowed me to work outside. I was so happy.

Sadhvi devi dasi

Sadhvi dasi joined the temple in April 1972 and was initiated in Montreal on Govardhana-puja in 1973.

There was a spiritual fair in the basement of a church in Montreal. I went and there was Guru Maharaj ji, Sri Chinmoy, Yogi–Bhogi Yogi–so many different kinds of gurus. Then I heard the holy name, and I told my friends, "That's it! That's it!' That's it!" Then I started reading *On Chanting* that a devotee had left at the health food store where I was working.

I was constantly hungry, which was difficult. But when I read *On Chanting*, immediately I felt at peace. My senses and mind became completely controlled and peaceful. Immediately I knew this was my spiritual master, because no one else could do that.

I began reading, but it was very difficult because I only spoke French. But Srila Prabhupada reciprocated with my little endeavors because one night I had this wonderful dream. I used to live on the second floor of the Sri Aurobindo Ashram in Montreal near the health food store where I was working. That's where I became a vegetarian. But I didn't like their mood so much, because everyone was walking around thinking "I'm God." When I first saw the devotees bowing down, I thought, "This is more like it."

One time some devotees sold some posters to the Ashram's little store where I was working. There was a poster of Lord Indra with the elephant and Lord Krishna with the cow. Lord Indra was offering obeisances. Then there was the poster of Lord Brahma with the cowherd boys and Krishna. I bought these two posters. At that time, I wasn't sure if God existed or not. I was in ecstasy putting those two posters on the wall, thinking, "He exists, He exists!"

At that time I had a dream. There was a corridor that led into my room on the second floor. Srila Prabhupada was standing on the stairs. I came out of my room and Srila Prabhupada was standing in the corridor on the right. I recognized him from *On Chanting*. Srila Prabhupada was standing there coughing. A blizzard had opened the door. I ran downstairs and closed the door. Then I went back upstairs to see Srila Prabhupada and he coughed again. The door had opened again, so I ran downstairs and again closed the door. Then I went back upstairs to see Srila Prabhupada. But then the door opened a third time. By then I was angry. I took a two-by-four and stuck it in the door so no blizzard could open it. Then I went upstairs and looked at Srila Prabhupada. There was a silence. I knew in my heart what I wanted the most in my life. Of course, he knew, because he had so kindly come. He signaled with his head. I knew in my heart–it was not even formulated into a sentence–that I wanted the holy name. I bowed down and he smeared his lotus foot on my head.

I always felt that Srila Prabhupada really wanted his books distributed and my service was to assist the book distribution in whatever way I could. That was the greatest mercy for the whole world. So I took that instruction in my heart, and I always pray that wherever I am, whatever I am doing, I can always be an instrument for him for the distribution of his books.

In 1975 I went to India. By then Srila Prabhupada had a lot of *sannyasis* around him. I was nobody. But when I saw him, even though his entourage was there and I couldn't come close because I was just a little *brahmacharini*, I could feel very, very strongly the purity of his heart, and I could see that my heart was so dirty. Because of the difference, I just couldn't stop crying. I was looking at him and crying and crying. It was so wonderful because it felt so purifying and ecstatic, actually. That was very special.

I was in India for five weeks. We couldn't serve Srila Prabhupada directly, but I got to clean his room. I got to chew on his neem toothbrush–I wish I had kept it! I went to his classes, of course, and he was ringing the bell in Mayapur. It was ecstatic. By then I could understand enough English, though his accent was a little difficult.

My relationship with him is very much there because I did many years of *sankirtana*. Whenever things would be too difficult and the modes of nature were too intense, I would sit down wherever I was and write a letter to Srila Prabhupada. Of course, I never sent the letter–we were discouraged because Srila Prabhupada was very busy. But he answered in many different ways. He *always* answered. The next time I opened the book the answer was there. He answered through devotees. And he gave me the strength to go on and to try to assist him in whatever way he could.

I also had dreams of Srila Prabhupada at different times when guidance was needed. I was so aware of his protection–very aware of his protection. He sends people to guide my devotional service. I feel very protected. Sometimes when I offer obeisances I feel like I'm his little puppy. He pats me on the head. I'm just there to make him smile, make him laugh.

One time, on his disappearance day, I made an offering to him. I said, "Srila Prabhupada, I just want to make you smile. That's all I want. I want to make you smile." That night, I had a dream. Srila Prabhupada was in Los Angeles giving a class. He came down from the *vyasasana* and he had all these devotees around him, but he turned around, looked right at me, and he gave this beautiful, big smile. I was very happy. What a reciprocation.

He's very much here. He's here every day. I would never have been able to stay in this body if it wasn't for Srila Prabhupada. It was too difficult in the material world. But he gave us so much: so much knowledge and protection.

Sailendriya devi dasi

Sailendriya told her mother, who wasn't favorable to Krishna consciousness, "I'm the person I am because I met Srila Prabhupada. He brought out all the good things in me and taught me how to be a proper human being. Without him in my life, I don't know what kind of person I'd be."

Prabhupada infiltrated everything we did, everything we thought, and the way we conducted ourselves. Just experiencing his humility, his wisdom, his knowledge, his affection for his disciples, and his encouragement, especially for the women, inspired us to try to be conscious of Krishna. If we saw an animal, we'd want it to hear the holy name because Prabhupada said that would make the animal fortunate.

Srila Prabhupada encouraged women to do Deity service and taught us in detail how to do that service, as well as how we should bathe, dress, apply *tilaka*, and what state of mind we should have when we're in the Deity room. Although I was always busily serving in the background, Prabhupada's influence was always there in my approach to what I did and how I thought.

When Prabhupada was personally with us it was an affectionate, warm, and wonderful time. The women supported and cared for each other. Everything was such a rush. There was no time for nonsense and we were new, didn't understand many things, and had to adjust and learn. But that wonderful feeling is also present through Srila Prabhupada's books if we read them with an open mind and a humble attitude. We'll never have read them enough because every time we read Prabhupada reveals himself to us more and we understand more.

Now I'm a public schoolteacher and I feel compassion for the students. Kali-yuga is increasing. Srila Prabhupada needs devotees in every part of society so people all over have some contact with Krishna consciousness. I'm also a scientist, and sometimes people say, "How can you be religious if you're a scientist?" I say, "The more I see of the natural world, the material world, convinces me that there's an amazing designer behind it. It's too perfect. Just because you're taking something apart doesn't mean you can't wonder at the whole of it." Prabhupada is there in everything I think about.

Samapriya devi dasi

Samapriya devi dasi was initiated in Berkeley, California, in July 1975, the day after the Ratha-yatra festival.

I sat with my daughter in my lap along with the other devotees who were to receive initiation in a circle around the fire *yajna*. I had made a bouquet to give to Srila Prabhupada. When I was called, my small but determined child wanted to come with me. I convinced her to wait by the fire pit. I was the last of about forty devotees to received initiation that day. Srila Prabhupada was humming as he waited for me to come up and offer my obeisances.

When I got up after paying full *dandavats,* I handed Srila Prabhupada my bouquet with my left hand while extending my right hand to receive my beads. Jayatirtha dasa, who stood next to Srila Prabhupada, called out with great force, "Don't give Srila Prabhupada the flowers with your left hand! Offer them to him with your right hand." I immediately transferred the bouquet to my right hand to offer to Srila Prabhupada and extended my left hand to receive the beads. Again he called out, "Don't take your beads with your left hand! Take them with your right hand." I transferred the bouquet back to my left hand and offered it to Srila Prabhupada, extending my right hand to receive the beads. Beside himself with frustration and obviously disturbed by my lack of intelligence, Jayatirtha once again attempted to correct the situation.

At this point Srila Prabhupada, who was witnessing this absurd exchange, turned to Jayatirtha and said with the utmost compassion, "It's all right." Kindness personified, Srila Prabhupada handed me my initiation beads and accepted the bouquet. I don't remember exactly which hand did what in the end, but he told me that my name was Samapriya devi dasi and then said "That's all."

As I reflect on these small jewels of eternity, which have shaped my life, it seems that Srila Prabhupada is always telling me, "It's all right." If we are doing the best we can with a sincere heart, endeavoring to please Krishna and His pure devotee, then it is most definitely all right.

One day in Los Angeles, Srila Prabhupada went to Golden Avatar Studios to do some recording. I prepared a fruit plate that we placed next to the spot where Srila Prabhupada was to sit. It was mid-morning, and only a handful of devotees were standing outside anxiously awaiting his arrival.

Finally, a car pulled up. We all offered our obeisances and stood up. A *brahmachari* stepped out of the car and opened the car's back door for Srila Prabhupada. The sidewalk was about eight inches above street level, so when Srila Prabhupada tried to get out of the car, he had to pull himself up by holding on to the door handle. It was an awkward stretch, and it looked like Srila Prabhupada, appearing as an elderly gentleman, was struggling to do it.

I held my breath at the inconvenience the curb presented to my spiritual master, and prayed deeply from within my heart as loud as I could, hoping the *brahmachari* would hear my thoughts to help Srila Prabhupada out of the car. To my dismay, he did not hear my thoughts and did not extend a hand to assist Srila Prabhupada. I felt terrible. I should have run to the aid of my guru and accepted this fortunate service, at that moment available to only a few. None of us did anything.

Srila Prabhupada remained inside the Golden Avatar Studios for a few hours, and again I stood outside, waiting for him. I wanted to apologize for my great negligence in not helping him get out of the car. I knew I could not live with myself if I was not absolved of this deviation of proper conduct. When Srila Prabhupada came out of the studio, I walked up to him and with heartfelt regret said I was sorry for not helping him get out of the car. He looked at me in wonder. Then he looked at the *brahmachari* and asked, "What is she saying?" The *brahmachari* said, "Oh, it's nothing Srila Prabhupada."

Beside myself and not understanding how the *brahmachari* could call this nothing, I said. "Yes, it is something, Srila Prabhupada. I am so sorry for not helping you get out of the car when you arrived here. It looked like you needed help and I did not help you and I beg your forgiveness."

Again Srila Prabhupada looked at the *brahmachari* and asked, "What did she say?" And again the *brahmachari* said, "Nothing." By now I was on the brink of tears, and in great turmoil, almost whimpering, I said, "Yes, Srila Prabhupada, it is something. I am so sorry for not serving you by helping you get out of the car."

Then, Srila Prabhupada turned to me with a gaze full of compassion and said reassuringly, "It's all right." I felt like I had been holding my breath, suspended in a timeless zone. With those three words, Srila Prabhupada gave me life again.

I wanted to make a present for Srila Prabhupada. I was engaged in jewelry making, and decided that a necklace of *tulasi* beads would be the most appropriate and worthy offering for my spiritual master.

Bending silver wire to create spirals and bordering *tulasi* with silver beads, I created a symmetrical pattern. When it was finished, I carefully packaged it and sent it to Srila Prabhupada in Dallas.

Shortly after mailing my package, I heard that Srila Prabhupada did not like the devotees to wear *tulasi* beads separated by stones, beads, or silver. I was devastated. What had I done? I had given a gift to my spiritual master, and it was just what he instructed us not to wear. In great anxiety I prayed for forgiveness from Krishna for having offended His pure devotee.

During this time, *Chaitanya-charitamrita* was being released. Srila Prabhupada's books are a treasure for all his followers. Every time a new book was printed by the BBT, we immediately found a way to secure a copy. The latest book was the eighth volume of the *Madhya-lila*. There was always a beautiful photograph of Srila Prabhupada in his books, and the devotees anxiously waited to see if the picture would be one they hadn't seen before.

When I got the new book and opened it to the picture of Srila Prabhupada, I saw that he was sitting on the *vyasasana* in Dallas. I could not believe what I saw. It looked like Srila Prabhupada was wearing my necklace! I found a magnifying glass and carefully examined the photo. I saw the spirals and the silver beads. I was sure it was the same pattern I had made. It looked like my offering to Srila Prabhupada. He had not rejected it, but was wearing it in the photo. I was very grateful and very relieved that Srila Prabhupada was so kind to accept my humble offering.

Sanatini devi dasi

Sanatini and her husband had come to a part in their lives when they were wondering, "What happens next?" When she saw the Jagannatha Deities at Bury Place, Sanatini thought, "I've finally found what I was searching for. I'm home."

When I learned that Jagannatha was God it made complete sense. When I first had a Simply Wonderful it was simply wonderful, and when I paid my obeisances to Srila Prabhupada it felt natural and normal. Prabhupada had a presence like a father. He knew the situation of each of us, and what we needed to hear and didn't need to hear. He'd put us in our place or comfort us.

My husband and I were Life Members and moved into the Manor with our son, Prahlada. After Prabhupada passed away I felt very alone and had a dream I was in India when Prabhupada's body was being taken around. As he walked past me, he put his hand on my shoulder and said, "I will be always with you." I don't think you can ask for anything more than that.

Sandamini devi dasi

In Cincinnati in 1973, a devotee picked up Sandamini, who was hitchhiking.

This devotee, Satsangananda, had a shaved head, was wearing a *kurta*, had a kirtan playing and incense going, and had posters of Krishna, Shiva, and Lord Vishnu in his Volkswagen van. I thought, "I got in the wrong car," but became interested when Satsangananda preached to me. I was just out of high school and had registered for the University of Cincinnati and, to the dismay of my parents, I packed up and went to California where I saw Srila Prabhupada at the San Francisco Ratha-yatra.

I moved into the San Diego temple. When Prabhupada came I was on the roof with everyone else, throwing flowers. Someone had painted the Hare Krishna mantra on a private sidewalk and as soon as Prabhupada saw it there was a little commotion and we heard, "Prabhupada said the holy name should be taken off immediately." He didn't want anyone to walk on the holy name.

In San Francisco in 1975, Prabhupada told us that when he was on the plane the pilot asked him, "If God is all-good, why did He create evil?" Prabhupada explained that just as you create a shadow when you turn your back to the sun, so when you turn away from God you create evil. Then with pure-hearted innocence he said to us, "Was that all right?" He really wanted to know if we thought his answer was good.

Once in Mayapur in 1976 I was very sick. When Prabhupada circumambulated, he looked right at me and with his hand indicated, "Chant, dance, and be happy," and that gesture lifted me up from horrible dysentery pain and let me dance. By Prabhupada's potency, that was one of the few times I was off the bodily platform.

At that time the Movement was very big and who was I? But Prabhupada's love came through, so I never felt without his loving embrace, shelter, and protection. I felt he was empowering me and by his mercy I could do any service with anyone at any time and in any circumstance. I never felt I couldn't do something because I was a woman or wasn't as sharp as someone else. I was given all facility to preach and utilize my full potential to help Srila Prabhupada spread Krishna consciousness. The only thing that held me back was my own mind and senses.

We're here for one purpose: to serve Srila Prabhupada in whatever way we can, to help as many souls as we can along the way, and simultaneously to try to purify ourselves of material desires so we can go back home, back to Godhead. I'm grateful for the association, strength, input, and endeavor of all the devotees who are serving Prabhupada. And I have implicit faith in Prabhupada's promise that if we follow the principles, chant, and serve sincerely, he'll take us back to Godhead. At the time of death he'll be there for all of us and arrange for us to happily serve him again somewhere.

Sangita devi dasi

In 1970, when she was fourteen years old, Sangita saw brahmacharis distributing BTGs at Fisherman's Wharf in San Francisco. She asked her older sister, "Who are they?" Her sister said, "Oh, they don't have any sex." The next Sunday her sister dragged Sangita to the Sunday Feast. Sangita didn't like it. She was an impersonalist, chanted Om, did drugs, and was looking for God in all the wrong places.

After *arati* my sister came out of the temple room and said, "I feel so high!" I thought, "I don't get it." I left and went to a Scientology meeting but I didn't like that either.

I lived with my parents in Philadelphia and for two years every time I went to town I'd see Hare Krishna devotees. They'd give me the same four items–a *Back to Godhead*, a Spiritual Sky strawberry incense stick that didn't smell so great, a Simply Wonderful, and a mantra card. I'd give them fifty cents and think, "Oh, here they are again." At sixteen, I moved into a house with hippies and college students. A couple who were also living in that house, Mangalamaya and Madhupuri, used to wrap me in a *sari* and drag me to *mangala-arati*. One day after *mangala-arati* I got a *Krsna* book for a dollar. I read it from cover to cover; I couldn't put it down. I thought, "This is for me. I really like this philosophy. I don't know why I've been running from it for two years."

I wrote Prabhupada a letter to introduce myself and ask him two questions: how I could serve him and why devotees thought there's a difference between living inside and outside the temple. Prabhupada wrote back, "I am very encouraged that you want to join this Krishna consciousness movement for the perfection of your life." He told me to chant sixteen rounds, read his books at least two hours a day, rise early, cleanse, and attend *mangala-arati*. He said, "You are right that there is no difference between devotees living inside the temple and devotees living outside the temple. The idea is that you follow the principles, chant, and make your home a temple." I hadn't written it in my letter, but I'd been feeling uncomfortable about all the rules. Prabhupada wrote, "You are frustrated about the rules and regulations, but without the rules and regulations there will be more frustration. So follow the rules as you know them," and he reiterated what to do. I thought, "This is my guru, he knows my heart. He knows everything about me. He knows my questions and anxieties." That was it for me.

A little later I turned seventeen, moved into the Los Angeles temple and got initiated in September of 1973. Six months later I got second initiation and became a *pujari*.

I thought I'd automatically become a pure devotee and didn't understand why my mind was still reeling. So I wrote to Prabhupada, "I've taken a lot of LSD and my mind thinks so many things I can't concentrate when I'm chanting my rounds." He wrote back a two-page philosophical letter about chanting Hare Krishna and cleansing the mirror of the mind. In the last line he said, "So there is no better solution that I can tell you for your problem. Simply chant Hare Krishna and everything will be all right." And it was and is all right. Prabhupada was sweet and pure and personal, and that's what I needed – a father then and now and always.

When I was nineteen I was a *pujari* for the Pancha-tattva Deities in Honolulu when Prabhupada came for a month. One morning while Prabhupada was walking at Ala Moana Beach Park, he pointed to the surfers and called them "sea sufferers." Someone said, "No, Prabhupada, they're surfers." He said, "You call them surfers, I call them sufferers. They will all take birth as fish."

I'd been beaten down and harassed by the *sannyasis,* but they were not going to keep me from my guru. When Prabhupada took his first walk around the temple grounds, I went too. Prabhupada was sweet to the girls because he knew what we had to put up with in his Movement; he knew how much we had to persevere and gave us special mercy.

That walk didn't end well. Prabhupada saw birds eating the rice and *subji* remnants on the paper plates left in the *prasadam* room. He got angry and said, "If you waste, you will be in want," and walked to his room.

I was shy, tiny, and unnoticeable. One evening in *Bhagavad-gita* class I prayed to Prabhupada, "If you could give me eye contact once my whole life would be perfect." I was standing alone in the back of the *pujari* room when, as he left, Prabhupada stopped, turned toward the *pujari* room, folded his hands, and nodded with a sweet smile as he looked right at me. Tears immediately came down my face. Prabhupada hears our prayers.

One afternoon I was running to wake up the Deities as Prabhupada watched me from the balcony. I paid my obeisances, stood up, and looked at him. He folded his hands and smiled and there was eye contact for what seemed like an eternity, although it was probably three seconds. He saw through me – who I was, my eternal relationship with him and with Krishna, the awful things I was going through, what I had been through in my life – and I knew everything was going to be okay. It was an incredible moment, "You'll be okay."

Prabhupada is always looking out for us and making arrangements to help us. He speaks through devotees and nondevotees; now and forever he somehow tells us what we need for our spiritual life.

Saradiya devi dasi

Saradiya devi dasi was initiated at the beginning of January 1968 at the Sri Sri Radha-Krishna temple on 518 Frederick Street, San Francisco, California. Her name means, "Servant of the goddess of autumn."

Having grown up in San Francisco, I would sometimes explore the city. The Haight-Ashbury district was particularly intriguing in those days. Around February 1967 I saw a card on the sidewalk that stopped me in my tracks: "Chant this mantra and you will stay high forever: Hare Krishna, Hare Krishna, Krishna Krishna, Hare Hare/ Hare Rama, Hare Rama, Rama Rama, Hare Hare."

By immeasurable great fortune, the mantra attracted me and I began to chant it, although I didn't realize that it was a collection of names of God. I could feel the uplifting effect so I would chant the mantra on many occasions while walking or riding the bus.

During that 1967 "Summer of Love," as I found myself jostled by the throngs of tourists on the main street running through Haight-Ashbury, I noticed an intriguing poster about a July parade festival of Lord Jagannatha. At the Psychedelic Bookstore I was drawn to the blue mimeographed magazine *Back to Godhead,* although the esoteric articles were beyond my understanding. In another shop, I bought a wooden flute decorated with a picture of the face of a pretty blue boy.

That autumn, I received a copy of the *Bhagavad-gita*. Although I couldn't fully comprehend the teachings, I was inspired to stop eating meat. It seems that I was getting ready to meet someone who was actually a devotee.

Not long after Thanksgiving, I was invited to the temple. As the door opened, I heard the melodious singing of the *maha-mantra*!

The temple had rich red carpet and freshly painted white walls. On one wall was a painting of beautiful blue Krishna sitting on a rock and playing His flute. It was a feast for my eyes. The air was sweet with the aroma of incense and delicious *prasadam*. Lord Jagannatha, Subhadra, and Balarama stood on the altar at one end of the temple room. I was very impressed by the tranquil atmosphere and sincere followers who told me about their guru, Swamiji.

After that visit, I purchased Swamiji's "Happening" album, and thus I was introduced to him through transcendental sound vibration. While gazing at his photograph on the back cover, I began to cry. Not fully realizing it, my connection with Swamiji began even before I met him in person.

A few weeks later, Swamiji (now Srila Prabhupada) returned from India. His face and body was surrounded with a golden aura. Hearing him personally chant the *maha-mantra,* the *Bhagavad-gita,* and *Srimad-Bhagavatam* was nectar to my ears. Two weeks later, he kindly accepted me as his disciple. Although I was only sixteen, I had enough wherewithal to realize that my initiation was a significant turning point in my life and was to be taken seriously.

I was extremely blessed to have had Srila Prabhupada's association on the West and East coasts of the United States and in Canada, India, and England. Srila Prabhupada took a special interest in each of his disciples, and lovingly encouraged us in various ways. I'd like to mention a few memorable incidents to highlight his compassion, concern, and direct involvement in the lives of his disciples, both female and male.

On numerous occasions Srila Prabhupada encouraged me in my attempts to follow this path. The main program at the San Francisco temple took place at 7 pm on Mondays, Wednesdays, and Fridays. The temple room was a renovated storefront; although it was not very large, it was sufficient for the number of devotees and guests who attended.

We would eagerly wait for Srila Prabhupada's arrival from his nearby apartment. When he entered, one devotee would blow a conchshell (I enjoyed doing this) and everyone else would prostrate themselves. Devotees and guests would then sit facing Srila Prabhupada's *vyasasana,* with the Jagannatha Deities to their left.

Prabhupada began the evening programs with the *"vande 'ham"* prayers and then a Hare Krishna kirtan. The kirtans were ecstatic, and people would sit or stand, facing the Jagannatha Deities. We would dance slowly, moving our feet from side to side and raising our arms as Srila Prabhupada had taught us was the proper way to dance before the Deities.

On one occasion, Gurudasa recorded Srila Prabhupada and the kirtan with a video recorder. Srila Prabhupada indicated to Gurudasa that he video the two women devotees dancing in the kirtan who were dressed in new *saris*–this was Ali Krishna devi dasi and myself. Ali Krishna and I were friends from high school and I had introduced her to the chanting and the temple. She and I were initiated on the same day.

A few blocks from the temple, Srila Prabhupada lived in an apartment with a couple of *brahmachari* assistants. He held darshans there on Tuesday and Thursday evenings. On one such evening, as a dozen devotees sat in front of his low desk, Srila Prabhupada personally and instructively began to say our names with a lesson in mind: "Saradiya, nice *tilaka;* Krishna dasa, no *tilaka,*" and so forth for every devotee in the room. We learned from this of the great importance of wearing *tilaka* on one's body.

Srila Prabhupada usually took his daily walk at Stowe Lake in Golden

Gate Park, and we took turns going with him, usually in small groups of three or four. Devotees sometimes asked him questions, but we were satisfied just being in his presence. On one particularly cooler morning, I was wearing my long coat and a turquoise shawl. Like a concerned father, Srila Prabhupada asked if I was sufficiently covered.

Occasionally, the *brahmacharis* relayed messages to me from Srila Prabhupada. He told me I should finish high school and that I shouldn't have boyfriends. Since I was still attending high school, this protective directive helped me to focus on my high school education along with my spiritual practices.

These examples illustrate how Srila Prabhupada was concerned for our welfare, both spiritually and materially. There was no indication that he preferred either his female or male disciples. As our spiritual master, he encouraged us in following his instructions; as our spiritual father or grandfather, he looked after us in his caring, personal, and compassionate manner.

Later that year, Srila Prabhupada came from Montreal and arrived back at the first temple he began in New York City at 26 Second Avenue. It was the auspicious occasion of Radhastami. The devotees were eagerly awaiting his arrival and anxious to hear his transcendental message. After he settled onto his *vyasasana,* he graciously thanked the artist who had painted the beautiful Radha-Krishna painting that was hanging in Montreal. Then he said that all the women should learn to paint.

In addition, he said "These women are all goddesses of fortune, and you should not think of them as objects for your sense gratification." Srila Prabhupada compared his female disciples to the goddesses of fortune in order to encourage them, but also to remind both men and women that they were not ordinary women. Because his female disciples were engaged in devotional service according to his direction, they were to be treated with dignity and respect. He also suggested an engagement that would please both him and themselves, as well as Radha and Krishna.

On several occasions, Srila Prabhupada said he needed paintings to illustrate his books as well as for ISKCON temples worldwide, so I took up the service wholeheartedly. Wherever I traveled, I made it my service to paint a few paintings to beautify the temple, and so my paintings have found their way to the United States, Canada, Trinidad, South America, India, Germany, and England. I was also able to contribute a few paintings for Srila Prabhupada's books and his *Back to Godhead* magazine.

Later that day in New York, the devotees went to a local park to hold kirtan and hear Srila Prabhupada talk about Srimati Radharani. He said that the reason people are attracted to forests and parks is because Radha, Krishna, and the *gopis* are engaged in an eternal *rasa* dance in the forests of

Vrindavan. Our natural longing for these places is from that original attraction on the part of the Lord. Srila Prabhupada pointed out that the highest pleasure for the eternal soul is to engage in pastimes with Lord Krishna and the *gopis*.

The next year, in May 1969, I participated in the first Vedic wedding in Boston at the Radha-Krishna Temple on Glenville Avenue. The occasion was reported in the local papers. Jahnava dasi and Nandakisore dasa, Rukmini devi and Baradraj dasa, and me and Vaikunthanatha dasa got married. Srila Prabhupada performed the fire sacrifice and gave us his blessings. After the ceremony, while Srila Prabhupada was sitting on his *vyasasana* and taking *prasadam* with all of us, he looked over at me and asked, "Saradiya, now you are happy?"

The next morning, Vaikunthanatha and I took a walk with Srila Prabhupada and his servant. Srila Prabhupada remarked to me, "You are no longer 'Miss Saradiya'; now you are 'Mrs. Saradiya.' " Prabhupada kindly graced me with these encouraging words. From this particular instance I realized that since I had become "Mrs. Saradiya" didn't mean I was losing myself or my individuality because I had gotten married. I was to remain myself, and I felt that he was reminding my husband of the same. He wanted his female disciples to get married, and the householder couples to then help him spread Krishna consciousness around the world.

From the end of 1970 until the spring of 1972, Vaikunthanatha and I pioneered the Krishna consciousness movement in the Caribbean islands of Trinidad and Tobago, near the coast of Venezuela and Guyana. I traveled all over Trinidad for a year, going to outdoor markets, door-to-door, and various temples on the small island, meeting people of different ethnicities.

From Georgetown, Guyana, we wrote Srila Prabhupada asking him to give Vaikunthanatha *brahmana* initiation so we could worship Deities as I had been given Gayatri initiation previous to marriage. In his return letter, Srila Prabhupada said that any *brahmana* could perform the ceremony and give Vaikunthanatha Gayatri. He said Saradiya, or any *brahmana* could do it. So I performed the sacred fire sacrifice before a few dozen guests and visitors. This service helped me feel very connected to Srila Prabhupada, and I realized that he was being extremely merciful to me. I was humbled that he had allowed me to carry out his direction. Although thousands of miles from him, I felt closer than ever before as I sensed he was pleased by my attempt to assist him with this preaching.

Srila Prabhupada confirmed my feelings in a letter he wrote me, saying that the *grihastha ashram* would be served by preaching this philosophy as he had taught us. Later that year, in the fall of 1972 in India, when I again saw Srila Prabhupada, he mentioned me in his welcome talk to the small audience gathered at Srila Rupa Goswami's *samadhi*.

During the Gaura Purnima festival in Mayapur 1973, many of Srila Prabhupada's godbrothers were in attendance. During the main program, Srila Prabhupada asked a couple of his female disciples to speak, mainly Kausalya and Malati. Then he turned to me and asked, "Saradiya, you would like to speak something?" I nodded, thinking I would have a few minutes to think of what to say, since Kausalya and Malati were going to speak first.

When it was my turn to speak, I stood up and said that we are all like Jagai and Madhai and therefore we need to take advantage of the holy names. I must have said something humorous because the audience laughed, so I think my little talk went over all right.

A few months later, I moved to England. Srila Prabhupada continued to shower me with mercy and kind words as he encouraged me in my new role as mother of a newborn daughter, Brajarani. When he came to the Bhaktivedanta Manor in the spring of 1974, Brajarani was just over a month old. All the devotees gathered in his room for darshan. I sat with my daughter on my lap. When Srila Prabhupada looked in our direction he said, "That is a beautiful child." He acknowledged her as beautiful in her own right, and I felt that she belonged to Krishna while I was her fortunate caretaker for the time being.

On another occasion, near the end of 1974 in Los Angeles, Srila Prabhupada was walking with a group of devotees, touring the various departments of ISKCON Press. I was holding Brajarani and walking nearby. He gave us both a loving smile and asked, "Is your daughter walking yet?"

On the occasion of the ISKCON Berkeley temple opening, just before the 1975 San Francisco Ratha-yatra, Srila Prabhupada posed with a large group of devotees in front of the temple. His room was accessed from the outside, so afterward, he got down from his new *vyasasana* and walked past the devotees to head toward his room. I was sitting on the ground in the front row with my daughter in my lap when Srila Prabhupada stopped for a moment, looked down at us, and asked, "Is your daughter still sleeping?" He then continued toward his quarters.

So this, and many other such personal encouragements have endeared Srila Prabhupada to me eternally. I am forever indebted to his lotus feet and I pray that someday I can repay what he has given me. No doubt this will take many lifetimes. I hope to assist him in spreading Krishna consciousness throughout the universe, as he desires.

Sarvamangala devi dasi

Sarvamangala first saw Srila Prabhupada sometime in 1971 when Shyamasundara brought her to the Bury Place temple. Sarva doesn't like to recall that time, however, because she was on LSD and painfully aware that she was in a pure environment but with unclear consciousness. A week or so later her consciousness cleared.

I went to the airport with all the devotees to see Prabhupada off and everybody was crying. I realized then that I had missed a great opportunity, so when we returned from the airport I wrote Srila Prabhupada a letter. I copied his *pranam mantra* and, writing each word carefully, I told him I felt bad that I hadn't really been able to see him and I was worried that I'd never see him again. He wrote back and said, "It is nicely written, correctly spelled, which shows that you are a very intelligent girl and you can use your talent and intelligence for serving the Lord. Young boys and girls are sometimes agitated in mind but if we follow the regulative principles and chant Hare Krishna mantra regularly the onslaught of material nature can be checked." And he also wrote, "Some way or other if we are able to keep in the transcendental position by devotional service we remain completely untouched by the contamination of matter. By the grace of Lord Chaitanya things have been reduced to a very easy operation: by chanting Hare Krishna, Hare Krishna, Krishna Krishna, Hare Hare, Hare Rama, Hare Rama, Rama Rama, Hare Hare." He was encouraging and everything he wrote in that letter was prescient. Although they may seem general, his words were completely relevant and personal.

When Prabhupada glanced at us we felt he knew us – our spiritual identity, who we actually were. His glance held more than compassion: he saw us as spiritual personalities and from his glance we had more of an understanding of our spiritual identity. In Prabhupada's association we got knowledge of ourselves. His glance informed us that we weren't this body and it brought us into the spiritual world because Prabhupada brings the spiritual world with him since he's with Krishna. This feeling wasn't just sentimental (although there's nothing wrong with sentiment if it's directed to Prabhupada), but Prabhupada knew that we're not this body, that we're in the spiritual world, and every time we saw him to some extent we experienced these transcendental truths.

When Prabhupada installed Radha-Gokulananda I was standing behind him, and as he shimmered the peacock fan from side to side while he offered it to the Deities I was in total wonder. I thought, "Oh, that must be how a peacock dances." It felt real; it reminded me of Krishna's pastimes and it felt like Prabhupada was caressing Krishna. After the *arati* Prabhupada called us all into the Deity room. He invited us into the spiritual world to circumambulate the Deities and then he gestured for us to dance. Prabhupada's feet didn't touch the ground and our feet didn't either. That was the most transcendental, profound experience in my life. As the kirtan went to another level I had an understanding that we are in the spiritual world now. It's not some place we go to, but it's being in transcendental association. The experience wasn't just a mental thought process, it was experiential knowing, and that's why it penetrated. To have Prabhupada's association and to be with the Deities and to hear the Hare Krishna mantra with all the devotees, that was the spiritual world.

In Juhu, Prabhupada was more accessible than in London and when I was there bit-by-bit he engaged me. Every night I'd cut some fruit, give the guests *prasadam*, put night queen flowers on his pillow, and shut his shutters. Then I started cutting fruit for Prabhupada's breakfast; it was lovely to do this as well as I could, to carefully cut the ginger and put the lemon juice on it. To peel the grapes, cut them in half and take out the pits. I'd take his plate to him, have a little exchange with him, and learn what he liked. Once I was daring and ridiculous and made cauliflower with white sauce and offered it to him on his break fast plate with the fruits. When he asked for seconds of the cauliflower I was happy.

I used to get little opportunities to serve in Juhu because other people weren't around. Once Prabhupada woke up from his nap and rang the bell but nobody came – his servant had gone to Santa Cruz. So I took the *chandan* and the garland in and Prabhupada indicated that I should put the garland on him, so I did. And he indicated that should put the *chandan* on his forehead, so I did. Then I gave him his fruit and a dob and asked him if he would like more dob. He said "Yes," so I ran like crazy to buy another one. In those moments it was like nothing else existed.

Another time I annoyed Prabhupada by asking a silly question. I said, "Srila Prabhupada, can we pray to Lord Balarama to give us the spiritual strength to serve you?" He said, "Don't pray to Krishna to serve me. I am Krishna's servant." He didn't like me asking Krishna for the strength to serve him. Of course, I still do, but he didn't like to hear it.

When I ironed Prabhupada's clothes, I could smell the massage oil mingled with his bodily fragrance and I understood that being in relationship with Prabhupada is not just cerebral, it's an experience in which all our senses become purified. Being in his vicinity, smelling his clothes, and seeing his beautiful form awakens our senses and introduces us to how to be in relationship with Krishna; it's personal. Our relationship with Krishna is like that too – we touch him, we smell His garlands. If Prabhupada hadn't purified and engaged our senses how would we be able to follow the regulative principles? It's not just a philosophical point, "engage your senses," it means we get to use them, we get to be in relationship through our senses as well, hearing and seeing Prabhupada, tasting his *maha-prasadam*. The first time I had Prabhupada's *maha-prasadam* – outside Prabhupada's room at the Manor Srutakirti gave me a piece of orange – I couldn't believe it. I was naïve and innocent like a baby and had no preconceived idea about Prabhupada's *maha* except that it must be amazing. The taste of that orange tingling in my mouth felt like an explosion.

I remember being on the top floor in Prabhupada's old quarters in Juhu, looking down the stairwell and seeing the top of Prabhupada's head coming up the stairs, seeing his beautiful, golden form, and then as he came closer, seeing his face. It was an ecstatic, transcendental experience to see Prabhupada coming into view and just remembering it I get the same feelings I had then.

When I saw Prabhupada interacting with people in his room I learned to be attuned to what was appropriate and not appropriate, to be aware of the time, and to notice if Prabhupada was tired. In one sense we were like children the way we adored Prabhupada, but at the same time Prabhupada's presence was so grave and commanded such respect There was such depth in his exchanges that he was like a king amongst *sadhus*. Prabhupada was so regal that by comparison everyone else seemed puny. When the Birlas and other wealthy people came to see him, Prabhupada didn't ingratiate himself to them and, although we served them nicely, we never thought, "Oh, we've got to have a special arrangement for people who are going to give money." Those people knew that Prabhupada was a great personality and that they were privileged to meet him.

I used to dress Radha-Rasabihari in Juhu, and do Their *arati*. After his walk Prabhupada would take Their darshan. That was fantastic. And when the new temple was going up, at any moment we'd suddenly see Prabhupada walking around to look at how the construction was going.

In April or May of 1977 I was the temple president's secretary in Vrindavan and I had a room overlooking Prabhupada's back veranda where he slept and translated. Prabhupada wasn't well then and one day the Loo was blowing while Prabhupada translated. When the Loo comes people keep their windows closed and no one goes outside because it's dangerous and unhealthy. But Prabhupada kept trying and trying to translate, to keep the pages of his book from turning, to work his dictating machine. At that time the leaders were strict about who could see Prabhupada, but I realized that you can't legislate intimacy. Any time in the night I woke up I could see Prabhupada.

Srila Prabhupada's rooms are like a *tirtha;* Prabhupada is personally present in them and by serving his rooms and becoming his *pujari*s we can come closer to Prabhupada and feel his presence in his rooms. There is no dichotomy between the experience of serving Prabhupada's form, serving in his quarters, and serving him when he was physically here with us. Once we get a taste for relating to Prabhupada in his rooms we'll love it. His rooms are a stepping stone, an access point to him. His rooms are not some concept or ritualistic place. There's nothing that Prabhupada taught us that's just a ritual. His rooms are where we practice being a servant again.

After he passed away we didn't have enough time to grieve for Srila Prabhupada. I was a *pujari* in Bury Place at the time and I put my head on Radha-Londonisvara's feet and prayed to never forget Srila Prabhupada. It seemed like the end of the world to me because I wouldn't be able to see Prabhupada's transcendental form anymore. His form gave me the most beautiful experience a person could ever have. In my heart I feel that he accepted the little things I did for him and that, by his transcendental potency, he extended himself to me. Whatever little service I did and however insignificant I was, I know Srila Prabhupada touched me forever.

Sarvani devi dasi

By fifteen years Sarvani had been greatly influenced by Beatlemania, Christ consciousness, and she was examining the similarities and differences between Western and Eastern philosophies. Autobiography of a Yogi, *by Paramahamsa Yogananda, served to introduce her to the magic of India and awoke within her a long-lasting desire that one day she would be mystically led to a "bona fide" spiritual teacher who was still physically manifest and accessible on this planet.*

My first introduction to A. C. Bhaktivedanta Swami Prabhupada was in 1967 listening to him chanting the Hare Krishna *maha-mantra* on "The Happening Album." After hearing this record album I became attracted to chanting the Hare Krishna *maha-mantra*. My sister Srila dasi eventually joined the Hare Krishna temple and soon thereafter I did as well. I moved into the Laguna Beach temple in 1972 at nineteen, along with my one year old daughter. I was initiated in October of 1973.

The day Srila Prabhupada arrived in Los Angeles to stay at the New Dwarka temple was indeed memorable. The devotee's excitement was palpable as we prepared for an airport arrival.

I caught my first glimpse of Srila Prabhupada approaching from a short distance away. While I bowed down to pay my obeisance I was swiftly kicked in the head by another devotee rushing past me. I remained focused on reciting my prayers and when I looked up Srila Prabhupada was standing there with his cane, smiling, and looking down directly at me. He had stopped the procession and was waiting for me to finish my obeisances. In that moment, as I encountered his dignified saintly presence, time stood still and that initial personal exchange remains forever cherished within my heart.

As the devotees proceeded through the airport, surrounding Srila Prabhupada on all sides, I found myself pushed forward and about to go through a turnstile that allowed only one person to pass through at a time. Devotees were rushing past and it was very chaotic. As I turned to avoid both myself and my young daughter getting slammed into the metal gate by another devotee who was diving towards the turnstile, I found myself facing Srila Prabhupada who stood, smiling, directly in front of me. As I stepped aside to allow him, and the rest of the procession to pass through the turnstile, I felt transfixed and joyfully sanctified by his holy divine presence.

I recall his profound class lectures, his kirtans, his beautiful heartfelt singing of "Jaya Radha Madhava," his handing out *prasadam* cookies to the children, following him and his entourage of disciples as he walked about New Dwarka, and when my little daughter handed him a flower on the steps leading to his quarters.

One day Srila Prabhupada tearfully spoke of how grateful he was that his young disciples were helping him to fulfill Lord Chaitanya's mission of spreading Krishna consciousness throughout the world, and that by doing so we were helping him serve his own beloved spiritual master, Srila Bhaktisiddhanta Saraswati Thakura. We were all deeply moved and shedding tears.

I was privileged to be able to associate with a few devotees who served Srila Prabhupada closely. For their association I am eternally grateful and indebted.

As I look back upon my early years of being a young fledging female disciple, what I find to have been truly valuable to me was sitting and listening to my senior godsisters tell me of their personal history and pastimes with Srila Prabhupada. Their stories always revealed his kind fatherly demeanor, his light-hearted humor, his endearing personal guidance, his serious concern for their spiritual well-being, as well as their physical and mental health, and how he motivated them to fully utilize and develop the natural talents and abilities that were suited to their own unique individual natures, in service to Krishna.

Most importantly for me, and for future generations to hear, was that he viewed his women disciples as spirit souls, above and beyond any material body designations, and how he provided them with many opportunities to actively serve side-by-side with their godbrothers in helping him spread Krishna consciousness throughout the world.

My obeisance to those devotees who continue to write of their own experiences and share the valuable contributions and personal pastimes of Srila Prabhupada's spiritual daughters. How truly innovative, wise, and merciful Srila Prabhupada was in adopting the term *brahmacharini,* and allowing women, such as myself, to take shelter at his lotus feet. All glories to His Divine Grace Srila Prabhupada!

Satarupa devi dasi

After becoming Miss Denmark, Satarupa went to London as a model and three months later – when she was twenty-two – was on the cover of Vogue, Elle, and other major magazines. She modeled all over the globe for three or four years.

I was going out with a famous photographer who met George Harrison and started chanting Hare Krishna. I said, "Chanting Hare Krishna, why not? Let me chant Hare Krishna." I also became a vegetarian, but since this photographer was taking drugs I left him; I didn't like drugs.

Once I went alone to the Manor and sat in a darshan, and when Prabhupada asked, "Any questions?" I asked, "If we're all spirit souls, how come we're born as men and women?" Looking at me nicely he said, "Desire." That word "desire" went into my heart and allowed me to understand. I said, "Thank you very much." In the corridor after I left Prabhupada's room I burst into tears and cried like a madwoman in separation from Prabhupada. That day I got beads.

In the summer of 1973, by chance I visited the Paris temple while Prabhupada was installing Sri Sri Radha-Parisisvara. From the *vyasasana* Prabhupada looked around, saw me, and said, "*Hmm*, bead bag." He acknowledged my bead bag. I listened carefully during his lecture, trying to find some faults with what he said, but I couldn't. It was all too good to be true.

I loved *prasadam* and soon started happily making Krishna's garlands. After awhile Bhagavan said, "Why don't you give up modeling and move in?" I said, "Yeah, why not?" I called my agent, Johnny Casablanca. He came to the temple and said, "I've lost a lot of girls, but I've never lost one to God. You have two months of solid bookings, you can't do this." I said, "Yes, I can. I'm working tomorrow; cancel the rest." He said, "Please!" I said, "No, I'm finished."

A couple of days later Prabhupada went to Geneva and I went with Parijata to help cook. Yogesvara, said, "Srila Prabhupada, this is Ann. She's a famous model," and went on and on. Prabhupada was looking right into my eyes and with my eyes I was trying to tell him, "I'm not a famous model any more, I gave it up. I'm a devotee now. Please don't listen to him." When Yogesvara finally stopped, Prabhupada, looking like a five-year-old with tinkling eyes, a beautifully lit-up face, and a fantastic smile, said, "Chant Hare Krishna!" I said, "Yes, Srila Prabhupada," and fell on the ground.

I lived in the temple and did my service and sometimes I'd think, "I was famous. Why doesn't the press come and ask me what I'm doing?" When they didn't come I thought, "Forget it. I'm not here to talk to the press, I'm here to serve Krishna." And then the press came: *Paris Match,* newspapers from America, Denmark, India. *Paris Match* did a nice interview and put me on the cover with the lead article "She left everything for Krishna." Bhagavan showed the article to Prabhupada in Bombay and for a week Prabhupada showed it to all his guests, saying, "She gave up everything for Krishna, you should do the same thing." Prabhupada told Bhagavan, "Right now she's a little bit of a Maya-devi, but later on she'll do some tangible service."

I hope that tangible service is coming now. I don't have any great powers and I don't know what to do or where to do it, but I pray that Krishna and Prabhupada will inspire me. I'm ready to go wherever Krishna wants and to do whatever He wants. I want to do some tangible service.

Saucarya devi dasi

Saucarya was nineteen and attending college in Hamilton, Ontario when devotees came to the campus to distribute big buckets of halava prasadam along with Prabhupada's books. The devotees had answers to every question she asked them: "If God is good, why is there suffering in the world?" She was relieved to learn about the laws of karma. She asked, "What's the purpose of life?" They said, "To develop your loving relationship with God." She thought that was wonderful because she'd always wanted to be a nun, but her father wouldn't allow her to go to the nunnery. He had said, "You don't have the personality to be a nun. You're too funny. You have too much love for life."

When Srila Prabhupada arrived in the Detroit airport I saw him for the first time and was overwhelmed with love and appreciation. Srila Prabhupada was so happy to be with us he was beaming. I'd never seen a person like that in my life. He was gliding across the carpet, elegant, regal, and beautiful. I thought, "I'm going to give my life to him. He knows all the answers."

For Prabhupada's Vyasa-puja in 1972, we went to New Vrindavan. Srila Prabhupada was asked, "Why is *maya* so strong?" He said, "*Maya* is not strong, your purpose is not strong." That was a brilliant answer. Krishna is stronger than *maya*. But even though Krishna is stronger than *maya*, unless we choose Krishna we will be bewildered and decimated by *maya*. Our vows, our determination – we'll forget everything unless we stay close to Prabhupada's lotus feet and pray to him for the strength to maintain our vows and our commitment to serve.

Srila Prabhupada's mood was loving, gentle, and accepting. Mayapur was difficult because the devotees didn't understand the importance of protecting women; they so easily let my husband, Hiranyagarbha, take *sannyasa*. But I always felt protected by Srila Prabhupada, and I would always get solace from his books, especially his purport to *Bhagavad-gita* 18.66, "One should be confident that in all circumstances Krishna will protect him from all difficulties. There is no need of thinking how one should keep the body and soul together. Krishna will see to that. One should always think himself helpless and should consider Krishna the only basis for his progress in life." I often read this purport and think how Prabhupada is protecting us. No matter what our karma, we have to take shelter and pray for the purity, strength, and wisdom to do our service for Srila Prabhupada and to make progress in going back to Godhead. Death may come at any time and we have to be prepared. I feel Srila Prabhupada's personal presence in his books, especially the *Krsna* book. After a hard day I come home and make a little offering and read *Krsna* book. The pages become a wonderful interactive film in which Srila Prabhupada explains the pastimes and philosophy. *Krsna* book is reality TV. I'm so grateful that Prabhupada's given us a higher taste and a positive alternative to living in the material world. By opening the pages of his books and listening to what he's saying we can live in the spiritual world. He's brilliantly giving us himself in every word of his books.

When we preach, Prabhupada gives us a more clear understanding of his mission and how to help him in his mission. Don't ever let yourself get down, just come back to Srila Prabhupada's books and understand how we're in the material world and how our life is a flash in eternity. It's Srila Prabhupada's profound mercy that we know who we are, where we're going, and how to cross the ocean of birth and death. The dearest friend is someone who helps you, who shows you how to cut the chains of the material world – the cycle of birth and death that we've been in since time immemorial.

I'm a fool, I've made so many mistakes, but I'm grateful to Srila Prabhupada and feel his presence. In a beautiful letter he wrote to me, which I got when I was twenty years old, Prabhupada asked me to read his books an hour a day and I try to do that now. In the last line of that letter he wrote, "So just always try to please Krishna and no material circumstance can cause you any difficulty. I hope this meets you in good health. Your ever well wisher, A. C. Bhakivedanta Swami Prabhupada." No matter what circumstance we're in, the perfection of our life is trying to please Krishna and the spiritual master. That's how we're preparing to go back home, back to Godhead.

The last time I saw Srila Prabhupada was in 1977 in February in Mayapur. In class Prabhupada was looking at all the devotees individually. When he looked at me, in his glance he gave me love and affection and communicated, "I'm yours, you're mine, and I'm bringing you to Krishna." I could see he had been there for me for many lifetimes and he was saying, "Please come back to Krishna." It was like a glimpse of the spiritual world.

The moment Srila Prabhupada left the planet I felt pain, but he came in my heart. I sat down and wrote him a poem, "Prabhupada, how will anything go on without you?" But we have his books and tapes and videos. Srila Prabhupada was an expert manager, had delightful communication and personality skills, and was expert in every realm. Now his Movement, the International Society for Krishna Consciousness, is flourishing because Srila Prabhupada humbly followed his spiritual master and brought Krishna consciousness to people all over world. He is touching the whole world.

Every year I love to read his Vyasa-puja books because the offerings are from all over the world, including remote corners. Devotees write, "Srila Prabhupada, we're running this temple for you. We're increasing our preaching. We have *prasadam* distribution. We've attracted many youth." People everywhere are dancing to Srila Prabhupada's instructions, and those who follow his instructions live with him because the spiritual master is eternal. It's glorious that Srila Prabhupada's Movement is blossoming. It can't be stopped. The love of Srila Prabhupada for his spiritual master and the whole disciplic succession and Lord Chaitanya has cast the floodgates wide open, and the flood will continue. Everybody will be touched by Krishna consciousness.

Prabhupada did and does so much for us. We've met the most beautiful personality.

Saudamani devi dasi

Saudamani had been chanting Hare Krishna for a year and a half when she saw Srila Prabhupada for the first time in July 1971 when he was arriving in the New York airport. Tears came from Saudamani's eyes as if, on their own, the tears were offering obeisances to Srila Prabhupada.

My first impression of Prabhupada was how beautiful he looked. His features seemed perfect – all the details were well made. He did not look like he was any ordinary living being, yet I didn't anticipate that I could perceive his transcendental nature with my gross senses, with my eyes. The devotees had brought a *vyasasana* to the airport and after Prabhupada sat down they gave him a big fruit tray. He was giving devotees fruit from the tray. At one point he began feeding my four-year-old daughter Emily little pieces of fruit, popping them into her mouth, and he kept patting her on the head and smiling at her. The next day the New York newspaper carried a picture of Srila Prabhupada with Emily. There was a concession stand nearby with magazines and candies, including big lollipops in different colors that looked yucky sugary-sweet, but Emily spontaneously took a lollipop and gave it to Srila Prabhupada. Srila Prabhupada accepted it and it was distributed as *prasadam*.

The next day, the 21st of July, ten devotees were initiated, my husband and I among them. The ceremony started at nine in the morning and went to noon and when it was my turn to come forward I felt intimidated. I went up and Prabhupada said, "Do you know the regulative principles?" and I said "Yes, sir," but I didn't say what they were. I took my beads, offered my obeisances, sat back down, and had to ask my husband what my name was. Immediately after the ceremony we were sent in a van to Wall Street to collect *guru-dakshina*. We were asked to collect *guru-dakshina*. We all told people the same thing: "We have just been initiated and we're collecting alms for our guru." Alongside us other devotees had a *harinama*. The Hare Krishna tune that they sang, led by Bhakti-jana was a popular one at the time; it sounded like a cross between a Broadway show and a minstrel.

After our initiation, I wrote Srila Prabhupada a thank you letter and Prabhupada wrote back saying, "The expression Saudamani has made proves that you are an intelligent girl. Your intelligence can be used in Krishna's service. Both of you are good souls. So try together to preach this sublime gospel, Krishna consciousness, and surely you will have Krishna's blessings."

In India in 1976 I was on the Vrindavan *parikrama* when the women's bus got caught in the sand in Varsana near Radharani's garden. It got later and later. There was a huge argument between our bus driver and another bus driver. Our driver was afraid he wouldn't get paid if we went on the other bus. We took shelter at a nearby Durga temple, waiting until we were found. We were stranded and didn't get back to the temple until close to midnight, when we found out that Prabhupada was in anxiety. He had hired many taxis to go looking for us. He'd yelled at the leaders, "Why did you send the ladies off by themselves with no one to protect them?" He said that the men hadn't taken proper care of his daughters.

Once at the Philadelphia airport my daughter Radhikaika (Emily), who was eight, sat by Prabhupada while he was waiting to go on the plane. Radhikaika was wearing different types of bracelets that my husband had brought back from India. She must have had sixteen bangles on each arm and Prabhupada was going over each bracelet with Radhikaika. Prabhupada turned to my husband and said that Radhikaika should marry a *kshatriya*, but after Brahmananda had Radhikaika chant some *Bhagavad-gita* verses for Srila Prabhupada said, "No, better she marries a *brahmana*."

We had gone to Mayapur in 1975 with the idea of arranging for Radha-Krishna Deities for the Philadelphia temple and I was disappointed when the GBC said, no, first we had to get Gaura-Nitai Deities. I then was thinking maybe we could arrange for Radha-Krishna and Mahaprabhu like in Mayapur. On Gaura Purnima day that year, in his lecture Prabhupada explained how we can't worship Radha-Krishna unless first we worship Lord Chaitanya and that we shouldn't think that we can worship Lord Chaitanya without first worshiping Nityananda and we can't worship Nityananda unless we follow in the footsteps of the Six Goswamis and it's impossible to follow the footsteps of the Six Goswamis unless we surrender to and worship the spiritual master. I felt like his lecture was aimed personally at me; I felt put in my place. It was a nice feeling to be put in my place because it meant that I had a place amongst the devotees. And I recognized my neophyte, humble position.

We always heard people were leaving the Movement, especially people that were close with Prabhupada, and when Srila Prabhupada was sick in Vrindavan in 1977 I wanted to write to him to tell him how many devotees and disciples were following him, following the principles he had set forth, and chanting. Many of these people hadn't had his personal association and I wanted Prabhupada to know that there were sincere devotees who were carrying out his will to the best of their ability. But we were discouraged from writing because so often devotees would write about their problems.

Prabhupada's disappearance made us heartbroken. At that time in Philadelphia we were moving from one temple building to another. Four days after Srila Prabhupada's disappearance we moved. The Deities had a temporary altar in a room on the third floor. We would all go to that room for *mangala-arati* and it was very intimate, with big Balarama and Jagannatha and Subhadra and little Gaura-Nitai. It was as if the Deities were among us to give us solace.

Now I feel Prabhupada is present in his Deity form. And I feel Prabhupada's presence in his purports. As I endeavor in devotional service I sometimes think, "Oh, now I understand what that purport means!" These experiences bring me closer to Prabhupada; they're personal. It's like when I was sitting in the huge Mayapur temple room listening to Prabhupada's Gaura Purnima lecture, I understood that he wasn't speaking just for me, but it seemed like it was just for me.

Srila Prabhupada wrote books for us, his disciples, and he was concerned that we read and understand them. He was trying to save us. In that sense our bond with him is very personal. Sometimes his big entourage, the thousand people who are jumping up and down in front of him, make him seem far away, but when you're chanting or thinking of him, or serving his Deity or reading his purports, there's no block or impediment. In his purports Prabhupada is revealing his heart to us, and as I make advancement I'll have realizations about his words. I don't feel distant from

Srila Prabhupada at all. He gave us everything, *prasadam*, the association of devotees, the Deities, everything.

Saumyarupa devi dasi

When Saumyarupa found pieces of a ripped up BTG, she put them together and read that she was not this body, she was a spirit soul. That was the knowledge Saumyarupa had been looking and waiting for.

For some time I tried to avoid the devotees because I was attached to my own ideas and I didn't like the bedsheets they wore. But I was suffering. I tried everything – drugs, whatever was there – and nothing helped. Then I went to the temple in Germany in the summer of 1975, and found the devotees shining and enthusiastic, the kirtans refreshing and enlivening.

I stayed at Rettershoff and was very happy. Somebody told me, "You're so happy you have stars in your eyes." I liked everything about Krishna consciousness except that the devotees worshiped an old man. At that time, I didn't know Prabhupada, what to speak of have faith in him. Prabhupada was far away.

I got initiated because everybody had a nice name except me, and because I wanted to wear three strands of neck bead. In his letter to Chakravati accepting me and others as his disciples, Prabhupada wrote, "So you are the president there at Schloss Rettershof, it is your duty to see that the standards of Krishna consciousness are always maintained, especially chanting sixteen rounds daily, observing the four regulative principles, no meat, fish, eggs, no intoxication, no gambling, and no illicit sex life. The students must all attend morning and evening *arati* and classes. If we follow this simple program along with regular *sankirtana*, distributing the books and preaching, then there will be no fall down. Just like if one keeps himself clean and properly nourished by eating regularly, he will not infect disease, but if there is neglect, then there is room for infection, he becomes weak and falls prey to disease. So Krishna consciousness is the medicine for the material disease, and chanting Hare Krishna mantra sincerely is the basic ingredient of that medicine." I keep those instructions in my heart. I got them from Prabhupada, and they've protected me and kept me going my whole life.

When I think about how stupid I was to think, "Why should I worship *him*?" How I was full of envy thinking that Prabhupada was an old man, and how Prabhupada mercifully initiated me anyway, I cry. But he did initiate me and he gave me such nice instruction. Now I listen to Prabhupada often and feel his mercy. He's full of compassion.

Sharanagata devi dasi

Sharanagata first met devotees in Austin, Texas, in January, 1972. She was sharing an apartment with a young Mormon woman who had a child about her own daughter's age: eighteen months old. She had left her daughter's father in the mountains of New Mexico to visit a friend who attended the University of Texas Graduate School.

As fate would have it, I never returned to him as Lord Krishna had other plans for me. After my arrival in Austin, a *sankirtana* devotee came to my door and asked me for a drink of water. I invited him in and he spoke to me about the suffering in the material world and Lord Krishna and he mentioned his temple. I was suffering because I had lost my beloved mother. She passed away at age forty-six of Hodgkins' Disease in 1966 and in 1968 my three-month-old son had died from Sudden Infant Death Syndrome.

I asked the devotee to write the temple address down for me and I borrowed a quarter from my roommate to buy a *Back to Godhead* magazine. A few weeks later I rode a bicycle with a baby seat on the back to the temple. It was all uphill and at one point, I almost gave up as it was hot and the hill was steep. I managed to maintain my determination. It turned out to be Lord Chaitanya's appearance day and the devotees invited me to take the feast with them. I began regularly attending the Sunday Feast and other programs. I was given a bead bag and *japa* beads and I began chanting Hare Krishna. I stopped eating foods in the mode of ignorance and offered my food at home. In the summer of 1972, I hitchhiked from Austin to Moundsville, West Virginia to see Srila Prabhupada in New Vrindavan.

The first time I saw him in person was at the Pittsburgh airport. He was effulgent and very beautiful wearing a number of lovely flower garlands around his neck. He was smiling and the palms of his hands were together. In my heart, I knew right then and there that I wanted him to be my spiritual master.

Later that year, I moved to Los Angeles with my young daughter and got an apartment near the temple. I was initiated by Srila Prabhupada the following April 3, 1973. He was personally present and he chanted on my beads. He asked me to say the four regulative principles and told me, "Your name is Sharanagata." He corrected Brahmananda Prabhu, who had not pronounced my name to Srila Prabhupada's liking. Prabhupada said "No, no, your name is Sharanuhgatah, gatah." This means one who has surrendered to Krishna." Then he said "servant, servant."

The following December 3, 1973, I became Srila Prabhupada's second initiated disciple. Srila Prabhupada was again personally present at that time and I got to go up to his quarters to receive the Gayatri mantra from him which was sheer bliss. Srila Prabhupada was sitting cross-legged on the white tile floor looking resplendent. As I entered the room he motioned for me to sit across from him on the floor, which I did after paying my obeisances to him. He gave me a sheet of paper on which the Gayatri mantra was printed. After we chanted the Gayatri mantra together I started to get up to leave, but hoped he would ask me something about myself.

He said "Where you have taken your birth?" I answered, "In Chicago, Srila Prabhupada." He then said, "And your parents, they are still there?" I replied, "My mother left her body in 1966 but my father, he is still there." He said, "All right." For those minutes in time I was there with Srila Prabhupada, just he and I. Our meeting took place at noon that day and the sun was streaming brightly through the window in the room. It was a beautiful day.

I was blessed to go to Vrindavan for the first time in 1974. The temple was a construction site. I was given the service of washing and ironing Srila Prabhupada's clothes. I hung them on the steel reinforcing bars of what was to be Krishna-Balaram Mandir. His garments were saffron silk and dried very quickly in the Vrindavan sunshine. I had to watch them carefully so they wouldn't blow down and fall on the ground. When they were dry I ironed them in a very confined space with an Indian iron that had a cord so short that the plug kept popping out of the wall socket so that the temperature of the iron kept fluctuating. I was frustrated but persevered to get Srila Prabhupada's clothes ready for him.

Over the years, I was blessed to see Srila Prabhupada many times, especially in India. At various times I got to do personal service for Srila Prabhupada. I even cooked for him once in Los Angeles on an Ekadasi. I made him Gouranga potatoes and carrot *kheer*. I later asked Nanda Kumar Prabhu if Srila Prabhupada liked what I had made for him. He said, "Srila Prabhupada didn't say anything. He just ate it."

I knew Prabhupada was departing from Vrindavan for Hyderabad on an early morning in November 1976. I rushed over to the side gate of the temple near his house and almost bumped into him in the pre-dawn darkness. He had just emerged from his house to go to the black Ambassador car waiting at the side gate for him. I got down and paid my obeisances to him. He waited for me to rise. When I got up, I looked at his face and he looked at me for what seemed to be a long time. I felt he was trying to communicate something to me. The very next thought that came into my mind was "Don't forget me." Srila Prabhupada knew it would be the very last time we would meet. I treasure that last time I had a few minutes alone with Srila Prabhupada. His Divine Grace Srila Prabhupada's face and memories are engraved within my mind and heart. All glories to Srila Prabhupada forever.

Shaktimati devi dasi

In a letter dated 28th May, 1971, Srila Prabhupada wrote: "Your name is Shaktimati devi dasi. Shaktimati means one who has spiritual strength."

In 1976 my husband, Turya dasa, was head *pujari* at the Berkeley temple when he was invited to come to Vrindavan to be head *pujari* at Krishna-Balaram Mandir. We had brought small Gaura-Nitai Deities from our preaching center in Santa Cruz and They were on the Berkeley altar while we trained some devotees in the standards of Deity worship. I was insistent on bringing Gaura-Nitai to Vrindavan because I suspected that I wasn't going to be able to do any Deity worship in Vrindavan. I was clinging onto Their lotus feet because I wanted to have Them as my service.

When we arrived in Vrindavan, I was asked to go to Jaipur to make dress patterns for the Bombay Sita-Rama Deities that were being carved for future installation. We were living in the Krishna-Balaram Guesthouse and Gaura-Nitai was in one of the cupboards as Their house. When I returned from Jaipur a week or two later, I saw two dried up garlands hanging on the handle of the closed cupboard. I was immediately suspicious. "Where are Gaura-Nitai?" I opened the door, and They were gone!

Lokanatha Swami had heard about our Gaura-Nitai Deities. Prabhupada wanted a traveling bullock cart party, called Padayatra, to carry Gaura-Nitai Deities from village-to-village with kirtan. Instead of going to the market and purchasing new Deities, they wanted Deities complete with all dresses and crowns. Actually Gaura-Nitai just wanted to go. They didn't want to stay in the cupboard in Vrindavan. They were showing the example that preaching is important. So They got on the bullock cart, and we used to hear reports: "Gaura-Nitai are in this village. Now They are in this temple. Wherever They go They enliven the people." The Padayatra was supposed to go up the Yamuna to the Kumbha-mela and then return with Gaura-Nitai.

The Kumbha-mela was a huge success. Srila Prabhupada went that year, and thousands of people had Gaura-Nitai's darshan. Srila Prabhupada was very pleased with the Padayatra, but somehow Gaura-Nitai didn't come back to Vrindavan. They kept going.

After the Kumbha-mela, They followed the Ganga and ended up in Bhubaneswar on Their preaching tour. To secure the land in Bhubaneswar, Srila Prabhupada went there and installed our Gaura-Nitai. For ten years They were in a grass hut while the temple was being constructed, and the devotees lived there under tremendous austerities. Devotees told us that the Deities were literally the heartbeat of the whole project and it was so difficult there that without the inspiration from Gaura-Nitai, no one could have gone on. They are still there installed on the ISKCON Bhuvaneswar altar.

Right after I came back from Jaipur and found out the Deities had "taken *sannyasa*," I was broken-hearted. Then the next day or two we got a message that Srila Prabhupada said that in connection with my husband, I could go on the altar and serve Krishna-Balarama to assist him. Prabhupada also mentioned that Srila Bhaktisiddhanta Saraswati let the women do Deity service behind closed doors. After that blessing from Srila Prabhupada, I began daily dressing Baladeva while my husband dressed Krishna.

In those days in Vrindavan, it was as if Srila Prabhupada was the temple president. He personally had an interest in every aspect of the temple management. There was a daily struggle with the people who delivered flowers. Prabhupada would say, "They are cheating you." They were putting stones in among the flowers and He warned us to be vigilant that they weren't tipping the scales with rocks to get more money.

And Srila Prabhupada tricked us all, too, with the flower garlands. When we first came, devotees were buying garlands for the Deities. But he thought we should be making the garlands. Purchasing the flowers was okay, but he wanted the devotees to string the flowers. Himavati was there at that time, and Prabhupada told her to get the women to make the garlands. Day after day she was trying to get people interested, but nobody was very inclined to do it. Then Prabhupada told Himavati, "You tell all the ladies that I am going to show them how to make flower garlands." So everyone got excited. Prabhupada is going to show us how to make flower garlands! We were to meet not in the temple but on Srila Prabhupada's own upstairs veranda. And did Srila Prabhupada come? No! We were all sitting there waiting for Srila Prabhupada, and then Himavati comes upstairs and sits down with the flower baskets and says, "Okay, now we are going to make the garlands!" He completely tricked us but from that day on, the ladies were stringing the Lord's flower garlands.

The Deities had no new clothes since the temple opening in almost 1-1/2 years so we promptly set up a sewing room in the basement under the altars and were able to make twelve sets of outfits in twelve months. The temple had very little money in those days but we did the best we could, often creating Deity dresses from ready-made *saris*. Many talented godsisters from all over the world would come and help me when they visited. It was the best service to have Srila Prabhupada come in each day and take darshan of Krishna-Balarama after our efforts of sewing and then dressing Their Lordships. Daily He would sit in front of Krishna-Balarama while the *gurukula* boys sang and that gave us the greatest happiness.

One day while we were in Delhi and a phone call came in from Vrindavan that Prabhupada was in seriously weak condition and the *kaviraja* didn't think he would make it through the night. They said that all the devotees should come immediately to Vrindavan.

According to the timetable, there were no more trains to Mathura that day. We couldn't afford taxis, so that was completely out of the question. There were just a few of us in Delhi thinking, "What are we going to do? How are we going to get to Vrindavan?" It seemed like there was no way to do it because there were no trains. And just like some kind of Vaikuntha airplane, a devotee pulls up in a van and stops right in front of the temple driveway. His name was Ravi, and he was one of the traveling *sankirtana* devotees. He had just had new tires and a complete tune-up done. He pulled up right in front of the driveway where I was standing, and I ran up to him and said, "They just called. Prabhupada is leaving." He said, "Let's go!" Everybody piled in the van, and I had the misfortune of not having a seat. I was in the back luggage part, and the road was very torn up and rough. There was nothing to hold onto, and I was being thrown around. But Ravi literally flew over that road. I don't know how fast he was going, but he had it going as fast as that machine could move. I never saw Ravi again. I still don't know who he is. I don't even know if he exists on this planet! I offer him my *dandavats* because he drove like a maniac, but safely.

When we got there, Ravi stopped the van right in front of the temple gate on the main road and everyone jumped from the van and ran into Prabhupada's house.

Srila Prabhupada left at 7:20 p.m., and it was right about seven o'clock when we arrived. We were there just in time to be present for Srila Prabhupada's departure. And the beautiful chanting. I was struck when I came in thinking, "We don't usually sound like this!" Honestly, you can't hear it on the video. It seemed that the demigods were singing along with us. Never had I ever heard kirtan done like that. Some of the devotees were singing Hare Krishna and some other devotees were singing "*Jaya Gurudeva*" all together at one time, and it was so beautiful I couldn't believe it. Most of the devotees had been there chanting all day, and it was so close to the last few minutes so it was very intense.

But no one knew it was coming to an end. It was just happening, and then all of a sudden it felt as if the ceiling had opened up. It was like there was no ceiling, no material boundary. The doors of the universe had opened to us and the Vaikuntha angels were all there. They were there for Srila Prabhupada to come and get him. I looked up and it was like the denseness of the atoms of material energy were insignificant. Material energy was no obstacle for this divine energy to pass. Prabhupada's eyes had been closed, and he opened his eyes and looked at everyone for the last time and said, "Hare Krishna." And then he left.

Then all of a sudden a few voices starting wailing. The next thing I knew, Tamal Krishna Maharaja shouted, "Everybody out!" and the devotees just started leaving the room.

For some reason, my husband didn't move. Since he was head *pujari* there, they let him stay and he was given directions to change Prabhupada into fresh clothing, the clothes he wore in his *samadhi*.

Srila Prabhupada was put into a palanquin and they circumambulated the temple with kirtan three times and brought Prabhupada into the temple room and placed Him on the *vyasasana*. He sat on the *vyasasana* all night long, and there was kirtan throughout the night. We could see ecstatic symptoms – hairs standing on end, and colors changing on his body.

When the sun rose, he was again put on the palanquin, and we went through Vrindavan town on *parikrama* of the seven major temples.

As we walked, everyone from all the temples and all the shops came out. We stopped again and again as they all did *pujas* to Prabhupada in the street, offering flowers, and *tulasi*. When we came back to the temple the ground had been prepared and as soon as we came back in the gate, they lifted Srila Prabhupada's body and lowered him, sitting in full lotus posture, right into the ground. Then they did a special ceremony and built a little brick house over the burial spot.

Someone took a flower garland off of Srila Prabhupada and handed out some of the flowers to those of us who were present. The rest of the flowers were then taken to Sri Dhama Mayapur and were placed in the ground there as the basis for the Pushpa Samadhi that we see in Mayapur today. They built that huge palace over the flowers, and we have the same flowers on our home altar in a copper pot with Vrindavan sand packed around them. After the ceremonies concluded in Vrindavan, a Los Angeles devotee friend of ours offered to take us with him to Mayapur for the ceremonies there for the Pushpa Samadhi. So we had the good fortune to attend the Mayapur ceremony as well. His Holiness Tamal Krishna Maharaja led the ceremonies, and he spoke so lovingly about Srila Prabhupada. It was unimaginable on that day, standing in a completely open empty field while red ants bit our feet and ankles, that such a magnificent palace would manifest there in time. I felt very blessed to be at both occasions.

Siladitya devi dasi

Everyone told Siladitya she had a promising acting and singing career on Broadway. But, typical of those days, she became a drugged-out and spaced-out hippie. Her relationship with Srila Prabhupada began before she joined the temple.

People told me I was ruining my life. I said, "What do they know? I'm seeing the light, I'm picking up wonderful wisdom." Then one day I was on a New York City subway when the doors between the trains flew open and a woman came out with orange sheets blazing all around her, hair flailing in the breeze, and shouting, "We've got an emergency here! People are dying in Bangladesh!" I didn't know what was going on. She came with a bucket for donations. I gave a quarter, and she gave me a *Back to Godhead*. I thought, "That's cool. *Gee*, I wonder what it is?" I flipped it open to an article by Srila Prabhupada and read, "Those who are taking LSD are living a hallucination." I slammed the magazine closed and said, "What does he know?" Everybody else had told me the same thing and it didn't affect me, but when Prabhupada said it, his words haunted me. Until I finally joined the temple in Buffalo I kept thinking, "What does he mean, living a hallucination?"

When I joined the temple, I had an illusion that I could talk directly to God and didn't need anybody else. One devotee, Bhaktanidhi, picked up my mood right away and said, "Srila Prabhupada is number one, do you understand?" There are benchmarks in our Krishna consciousness that set us on course, and after she said that I started paying more attention to Srila Prabhupada and to serving him in separation.

Prabhupada didn't come to Buffalo so we went to New Vrindavan and Toronto to see him, but both times there were so many crowds I didn't experience Srila Prabhupada. Krishna was showing me that seeing Srila Prabhupada wasn't the most important thing and I had to find him in other ways. I most felt Srila Prabhupada when I was sincerely meditating on him, looking in his eyes in a picture, speaking my heart out to him, begging for his mercy, watching that picture glow right in front of me and feeling his love.

Prabhupada instructed Baradraj and other devotees to make "dolls" or sculptures to use in diorama exhibitions depicting our philosophy. I was in L.A. helping with this project when lots of temples were requesting *murtis* of Prabhupada. My service was to sand the seam along the side of the *murti* after it was molded. I was in a room full of Prabhupada *murtis* that needed sanding, and my meditation was that I was massaging Prabhupada's body. I felt Prabhupada intimately and relished that service.

It was a jolt when Prabhupada left, but there was a continuum in my Krishna consciousness. It wasn't a drastic change for Prabhupada to "leave" because I was never dependent on his physical presence. I felt that if I focused on Srila Prabhupada and my relationship with him, he was there and still is. I feel blessed.

Silpakarini devi dasi

As a young teenager, Silpakarini investigated communism, Amnesty Inter-national, and missionary service. When she was sixteen, she became a vegetarian.

Often, on the street in Hamburg, I saw the *harinama* devotees sitting on a carpet playing instruments and singing. In early 1970, after my brother got a *Back to Godhead* magazine, I went to the Hamburg temple for the Sunday program. I couldn't figure out what it was about, but I was attracted by the *prasadam* – *puris* and Simply Wonderfuls. For the next few years, I mentally chanted the Hare Krishna mantra in all kinds of situations and felt some inner protection.

I liked reading the *Autobiography of a Yogi,* but I couldn't understand how to meditate on nothing. Devotees invited me to a festival program and, as I listened to them, I found that they were answering all the questions I had, questions that I had never found answers to anywhere. I was happy and the chanting was so enlivening that I danced on the stage with the devotees! After the program, the devotees gave me Prabhupada's garland, a big plate of *prasadam* and a cassette of the "Govindam" album.

I started listening to Prabhupada's lecture and *bhajana* recordings. There were so many realizations in them, I felt they were directly from the spiritual world. Everything fell into place and was clear. I thought, "I want to go to the temple and serve." I went home, got my sleeping bag and told my mother, "You can call the school and say I'm not coming anymore. I'm moving into the Hare Krishna temple," and that was it. It was a *brahmachari* temple, but one other woman and I moved into the shoe room, which was four feet by eight feet. We lay underneath the jackets and that was perfectly fine.

I received second initiation at the Schloss, and was sent into Prabhupada's room. I paid my obeisances and stayed squatting by the door. I didn't know what to do. Prabhupada looked at me and said, "Come closer." I scooted forward a bit and he said, "Closer." I scooted forward again and he said, "Sit here," which was right next to him. I sat next to him and as he held a paper with the Gayatri mantra, he pointed to each word, said it, and I repeated it after him. Then he showed on his fingers how to count the mantras. Prabhupada was sober and I felt wonderful in his presence. I felt his force and was trying to be sober and pay attention. I paid my obeisances and he said that he had a headache and needed some sandalwood pulp. We didn't have sandalwood for the Deities, but Himavati had some sandalwood beads. She grated some of the big beads and made emergency sandalwood for Prabhupada.

When Prabhupada visited the Manor in 1976, I washed his clothes, although there was nothing dirty about them – they were beautiful, with a mustard oil smell. I rinsed them, hung them up, and watched while they dried so nobody touched them. Once, I was in Prabhupada's view while I swept his floor. Prabhupada was sitting cross-legged with his *dhoti* high up, and he looked young, sober and beautiful. While I finished the rest of his room, he put on *tilaka* and said Gayatri. I really relished those moments of taking care of his room while he sat there.

Sranti devi dasi

Once, in the Clearwater-Largo area, a friend of Sranti's had taken a hallucinogenic and seen on his ceiling the Universal Form with Krishna in the middle. Later this friend got a BTG from a brahmachari at a streetlight, and as soon as he saw the pictures he was attracted. He sent away for cookbooks, cooked, and offered dishes as best he could, and he and his friends, including Sranti, started reading BTG.

I'd read many different yogi books and none of them made any sense. But in BTG I read an article about chanting – how to chant, what chanting meant, how it purified us – and thought, "Here's something practical. I don't have to pay a bunch of money. I can chant Hare Krishna."

My friends – Garuda Pandit and Bhranti – and I became absorbed in the *Bhagavad-gita*: we'd read a couple verses and meditate on them and on Prabhupada's purports. I became convinced, started following, and chanting my rounds, and in February of 1975 we drove to Atlanta to see Prabhupada. When we arrived the kirtan was so uproariously ecstatic and the temple room so crowded that we had to dance because the whole group of devotees was moving in unison. After Prabhupada's lecture, somehow the devotees made a little opening and we walked the length of the temple room to get a cookie from Prabhupada. As I walked up it was like everyone but Prabhupada disappeared, and Prabhupada was seeing straight to my soul.

After that the four of us – Branti, Garuda Pandit, my then husband Akincina Krishna, and I – moved into the Gainesville temple. Kaulini was my mentor and I started doing book distribution. Although that service was austere and it was sometimes hard for me to control my mind, I felt connected with Prabhupada and part of his army. I'd meditate on how much Prabhupada did for his spiritual master and how distributing books was much simpler than what he did.

My prayers for strength to do book distribution were the essence of my relationship with Prabhupada. I never felt a lacking, I never felt, "I want to speak to Prabhupada," because I spoke to him constantly. When people were angry and mean I took shelter of him and of Krishna. Once in the

Jacksonville airport a businessman hit me with his briefcase. All my books went flying and I fell. As I picked up the books, tears were coming. I prayed, intensely begging for shelter: "I don't mind what I have to go through, but if you could send me one person who wants to be Krishna conscious, it will be worth it." Slowly I replaced my books, stood up, and approached another businessman. As he took a *Bhagavad-gita*, his eyes welled with tears, and he said, "I've been looking everywhere for this." He bought one of every book I had. Prabhupada had responded to my insignificant prayer.

Book distribution wasn't natural for me but I knew Prabhupada loved it, so I was cent percent sold out to distribute his books whatever the weather and however I was feeling. Because I was doing that service for Srila Prabhupada, it was a personal exchange, like the spider who helped Lord Ramachandra. All the austerity of book distribution was worth it for me to somehow please such a pure devotee.

Sri Kama devi dasi

Sri Kama first met Srila Prabhupada in 1974 in Geneva, Switzerland. She had been reading Prabhupada's books and chanting.

I walked into the garden and Prabhupada was performing a fire sacrifice. At that point, he looked over at me, straight into my eyes. I felt how contaminated my whole being was. I just wanted a hole in the ground to open and swallow me up. I felt naked, subtly, totally bare. Along with this incredible shame of all my sinful activities I knew one hundred percent that he was my spiritual master. Totally and utterly was aware of that. It was clear. It was an amazing revelation actually. I would have probably moved into the temple but nobody talked to me: they all talked to the boy I was with.

Later I met a devotee who is quite a notorious devotee, but I didn't know that at the time. What I saw when he walked into my life was that he was a servant of Krishna. I just saw this wonderful *brahmachari* in orange. I thought this person is pertaining to Krishna and I was longing for Krishna, but somehow I didn't have the courage to just go forward. But this person was abusive and I wasn't with him for long. I got pregnant and came back to be with my mother.

I came down to the Bhaktivedanta Manor to see Srila Prabhupada in 1975 and I went on a morning walk. I was really large, very pregnant, but I didn't want to miss this opportunity. The party was walking out the front gate of the Manor and I was waddling behind. Prabhupada and the devotees were chanting. I was floating along there. The sound vibration was incredible. I felt as if my feet weren't there on the ground at all.

Then I got involved with the Edinburgh temple and eventually got initiated. In 1976 they shut down the Edinburgh temple and we all shifted to the Manor. My daughter was a couple of months old and then Prabhupada came to visit. We practiced for a play to do for Prabhupada on Janmashtami. I was so disappointed because he was sick and he couldn't come.

Rasa Lila was just a little toddler. She was very cute and I was very shy, so I gave her a yellow rose to give to Prabhupada. He smiled at her and took the rose. I got the mercy indirectly. We ladies always stood close to Prabhupada. He was looking at the Deities and chanting. It was ecstatic. Suddenly he looked at me right into my eyes. Of course, I felt wonderful but his gaze was a very penetrating gaze. It was another one of those intense looks. He was very grave. I wish I had been more clear, I might have got a message there.

Srilekha devi dasi

Srilekha's first experience with Srila Prabhupada was when she got initiated in 1974 in Australia. All the initiates were going up one by one by one to get their name and japa beads. When she went up she waited to receive her name, but for some reason Prabhupada didn't have a name ready. Finally he looked at her and said, "I will call you Srilekha," and gave her the beads. Srilekha is a name for Radharani meaning "one who writes beautiful love poems for Krishna."

Later, in Bombay in 1975, Prabhupada gave me Gayatri, repeating the mantra for me and showing me how to count on my fingers. Then he said, "Is there any question?" The men were pressuring me to get married and I didn't want to. I wanted to ask, "Can I please not get married?" I was looking at Prabhupada and he was looking at me with those big brown eyes and that soft face, and I just couldn't ask such a mundane question to such a beautiful spiritual person.

Through Srila Prabhupada's teachings, through devotees who are following Prabhupada's teachings, and through the guru-disciple relationship, Prabhupada's there for everyone even now. By understanding that he's a beautiful person inside and out – his skin was like gorgeous folds of velvet, his face, his eyes, they were like deep, dark brown pools of love – our appreciation of him will grow. I've always remembered how Prabhupada is beautiful in every way, and I'll never forget that, never.

Srimati devi dasi

Srila Prabhupada came to Seattle, near where she was living, in September 1968. The devotees had just moved into town, and had posted flyers on telephone poles to advertise Prabhupada's arrival.

The small living room of the rented house Upendra and Gargamuni set up as the Seattle temple was so full that people stood outside, poking their heads in windows and doors. Tamal Krishna told me that Srila Prabhupada had inquired about me and he told Prabhupada I had come to stay. Srila Prabhupada said, "Oh! Very good."

Prabhupada instructed Harsharani how to do a full *arati* ceremony, with incense, camphor, ghee lamp, water conch, handkerchief, flower, and fan. Prior to this we were only doing *dhupa aratis*.

Vishnujana had given me some large black beads, made from a type of seed, that he called "Krishna bullets." Srila Prabhupada named me Srimati dasi, saying Srimati was another name for Srimati Radharani. The next day, six *brahmacharis* and I headed to L.A. in a van to help Dayananda and Nandarani. Each night we chanted and danced on Hollywood Boulevard. On Sunset Strip *Hair* was playing. The hippies had very long hair in those days, and they thought we were chanting "hair" when we were actually chanting "Hare."

The Hollywood Boulevard temple closed and Srila Prabhupada asked regularly when we would find a new temple building. Tamal Krishna met a woman on *sankirtana* who offered her garage for Srila Prabhupada's preaching. It was in a nice neighborhood, and the double garage was clean. We put up madrases on the walls, hung pictures over them, and built an altar for Jagannatha and a *vyasasana* for Srila Prabhupada. Incense filled the space. Jai Gopal was out front ready to blow the conch as soon as Srila Prabhupada arrived. Though it was a garage, Prabhupada walked in majestically, took his seat on the *vyasasana,* and began kirtan. His lecture attracted the curiosity of the neighbors and guests, who went home with magazines and *prasadam*.

Srila Prabhupada was anxious to establish a permanent temple so he gave up his morning walks to look for a building himself. He liked a church for sale on La Cienega and told Tamal Krishna to buy it. Though we couldn't afford it Prabhupada insisted. The building seemed so large but it was soon filled with visitors.

One day, after Srila Prabhupada's Sunday Feast lecture, we invited him to watch a puppet show. I managed to sit right next to him. "Srila Prabhupada," I asked. "Yes?" He spoke even that one word with such presence in his voice that I was startled into joy. "How do you say Hare Krishna?" He replied in my ear, "Hare Krishna." I melted hearing him say the words, and my happy grin remained throughout the evening. I still relish that moment, recollecting it.

One time, I went to see Srila Prabhupada and sang and danced during the *arati* for his Deities. Afterward, Srila Prabhupada talked to me about my husband and children, who were not part of my life at that time. "Srimati, take Krishna for your husband," he said and told me to continue to make dioramas as Muralidhara, Vishnujana, and I had been doing. He told me to make one nice face and make a mold of it so many other faces could be made out of clay, and he drew me a picture of how they should look. He asked me to bring clay and he would show me how to do it. I brought clay, newspaper, water, and clay tool into his room. "What is this?" he wanted to know, and I reminded him. "Oh, yes!" Then I set out the materials on his desk and he began sculpting a small head. Next he asked me to make crowns for his Deities, and he handed me a jewel to use. Seeing the finished crown he exclaimed, "Srimati, generally Krishna is so opulent that He doesn't need jewelry, but this crown makes Him all the more opulent!"

Once I was in Srila Prabhupada's room cleaning. I had made his Deities new wigs and asked him if They looked all right. He said Krishna's hair was too long and I should cut it. I sat Krishna on Prabhupada's desk, and was gauging just where to cut. Srila Prabhupada suggested a length, but just as I went to cut, he said, "No! Wait, Radharani likes it."

One time Prabhupada said, "It is the intention that counts," as we were not doing well making *chapatis*. Another time he said, "I have used my intelligence; now you use yours."

Jayananda and I were then sent to start a temple in Berkeley. Missing Srila Prabhupada, I sent him part of a poem I had read from Bhaktivinoda Thakura. I wrote, "Srila Prabhupada, you are everything to me: mother, father, lover, son, lord, preceptor, husband." Srila Prabhupada wrote back saying these sentiments are meant for Krishna; as your spiritual master I am your eternal father."

When Srila Prabhupada returned from his morning walk, I came late as he began to walk toward the temple. Seeing me he greeted me and said, "Srimati, is everything all right?"

"Yes, Srila Prabhupada, everything is all right."

"When are you coming to India?"

"As soon as I collect the money, Srila Prabhupada." I closed my gaping mouth into a smile and followed along with the rest of the devotees.

My first experience in India was the New Delhi *pandal* program. There was a war between Pakistan and India at that time, and blackouts were in effect in New Delhi. We had to keep all the windows covered and only use candles for light at night. But every night we would have these ecstatic kirtans and Srila Prabhupada would lecture. Srila Prabhupada did not seem concerned about the war, but he followed it in the newspapers.

Before coming to India, I had passed through New York, and Rukmini asked me to purchase a black marble Krishna and a white marble Radharani for the temple there. So Kausalya and I went to Jaipur to find Deities for the New York temple.

We liked Jaipur a lot and had kirtans every night. Kausalya could sing and play the harmonium well; I accompanied her on *karatalas*. We were nicely taken care of by the many persons who remembered Srila Prabhupada from when he had stayed with a family there. Then we were invited by the town of Jaipur to put on a festival. There were only two of us, and we were young women trying to make our way alone in India, but we saw it as an opportunity to please Srila Prabhupada.

We set up a huge *pandal* tent. The New York Deities were in the middle of the stage, Prabhupada was on the right and devotees chanted on the left. Srila Prabhupada had come in a palanquin on top of a decorated elephant. Many colorful flags waved as we chanted through town. The *pandal* was constructed behind Rupa Goswami's temple, and Rupa Goswami's Deities faced a large garden. Across from them was the palace of the former king and queen. It was all very old and opulent.

This program went on for eight days. After the program, Srila Prabhupada called Kausalya and me into his room and said, "You girls are carrying on Lord Chaitanya's movement so nicely. Just see, even without husbands, you go on preaching." He was especially pleased with P. K. Goswami for hosting us in his guest room. Srila Prabhupada warned us constantly not to be alone on the streets at night, but P. K. Goswami gave us shelter while we were in Jaipur.

After getting Deities for New York, other temples asked me to send them Radha-Krishna Deities. So Malati went to Jaipur with me. There was a large, black marble Krishna being used as a doorstop in one of the stores. I knew this was the Deity for the Texas school children. He was just so impressive. I had a Radharani Deity made and she was much smaller.

In the meantime, Malati and I were going to the Radha-Govinda temple every morning. Srila Prabhupada had asked us to observe everything and write to him. We told him that Radha-Govinda were dressed in night clothes each night, that their dress was changed twice a day, and how eager everyone was to receive Their *prasadam,* how the *pujaris* offered perfume on cotton-tipped sticks, and how they passed back many garlands once they were offered. Srila Prabhupada said these were all practices we could do for our ISKCON Deities.

In Calcutta, Srila Prabhupada called for me. He said I should take one Bengali girl with me and go to a small town near Mayapur called Gourni. He wanted me to find a teacher there who could instruct me in clay deity making. I was to invite the artist to Mayapur so Srila Prabhupada could meet him. If he was expert, Srila Prabhupada would hire him to teach me how to sculpt with clay. Srila Prabhupada told me the artists in Gourni were so skilled that the fruit they sculpted looked edible.

I found a young man named Mohan in Gourni, who was the son of a sculptor and lived with his many relatives in a village of sculptors. Some of them made demigod forms that were thirty-five feet tall. Those demigods were parikramed around town, then taken to the ocean. Every month there was a different demigod's festival, so these sculptors were busy.

But Mohan came with me. As Prabhupada spoke, Mohan sculpted a bust of Srila Prabhupada that pleased him. So he was hired and came to the Mayapur temple every morning to teach me. Srila Prabhupada told me "make and break" is the way to learn.

Baradraj, Rukmini, and a few other talented devotees came to India to also learn. Baradraj in particular is a born artist, inheriting his talent from his Russian father. He scuplted Lord Nrsimhadeva and Prahlada, with Hiranyakashipu being torn apart on Nrsimhadeva's lap. I did Mother Yashoda looking into baby Krishna's mouth and seeing all the universes. I made a 12 – 16-inch set of Pancha-tattva dolls for Srila Prabhupada. He had them set on the shelf above him in his room in Mayapur and told Tamal Krishna that they were "Srimati's Deities."

After Gaura Purnima, Srila Prabhupada went on to Vrindavan, which now had the beautiful Krishna-Balaram Mandir. We all gathered on the roof and stairs of that building for a group picture, which was later published on the cover of *Back to Godhead*.

The next year during Gaura Purnima Prabhupada was meeting with his godbrothers. Devotees were onstage chanting in their L.A. or New York styles, and Srila Prabhupada sent one *brahmachari* to tell them to change their tune to the ones he had taught them. I guess they were a little too rocking for his godbrothers.

I left India to reunite with my children. Three months later, I went to the San Francisco Ratha-yatra. After Srila Prabhupada's talk, Tamal Krishna told me that Srila Prabhupada wanted to see me. Prabhupada said, "Srimati, why are you not in India?" I let him know that I was missing my children and that I felt bad I had disappointed him.

Srila Prabhupada always made it clear that he was present in his books and that what he taught in his books was what was most important for us. All glories to His Divine Grace A. C. Bhaktivedanta Swami Prabhupada.

Srisa devi dasi

By the late 1960s, Srisa thought she'd achieved all her goals. She had the teaching job she always wanted, was living in Laguna Beach, which she thought was paradise, had enough money, and was having fun.

I was twenty-seven and in my third year of teaching when I called my parents and said, "I'm not happy. I need to figure out who I am, what life's all about, and what we're supposed to be doing. If I keep going I'll probably have a breakdown." I quit my job and, with my husband, Yugadharma, moved into a hundred-year-old adobe house without running water in a hippie commune in the New Mexico mountains. Everybody there was smoking pot, following all kinds of different yogis, and chanting all sorts of things. In my heart I wasn't comfortable with all that. I had a baby to take care of, which made me more responsible.

A devotee visited and left us a *Bhagavad-gita,* some *japa* beads, a songbook, and the Radha-Krishna album. From listening to the album and reading the songbook I memorized the *samsara* prayers. Then at some point someone told us, "The spiritual master is coming to L.A. and you need to meet him." We packed our Toyota Land Cruiser and went to the L.A. temple with our six-month-old daughter. I was in the back of the temple when Prabhupada came in and on seeing him I thought, "He's not fake. He's real, he's doing what he says he doing. This is the truth and I'm going to do what he says." I had no doubt that Krishna consciousness was what I was looking for and was happy. The hippies had been saying the way to be spiritually realized was to get stoned and someone who didn't get stoned was a straight creep. After I'd seen Prabhupada I had the strength to tell them, "I have a spiritual master and he says not to get intoxicated."

My husband and I didn't have much association but we were convinced. We traveled a bit and ended up living near the Laguna Beach temple. I loved *mangala-arati*. I'd wrap our two babies in blankets and take them with me, then spend all day at home, and in the evening go back for *sundara-arati*. I was chanting my rounds but because of my children I couldn't go to class, read, or serve in the temple. Before Prabhupada came, though, I managed to make a red and gold pillow for his *vyasasana*. I was grateful, "Finally I have some service." One morning when Prabhupada was about to give class I was leaving so my kids wouldn't disturb him when Prabhupada indicated to me that I should stay. He wanted me to hear.

Somehow I got Srila Prabhupada's causeless mercy. As far away and ignorant as I am, he's my spiritual master forever and he's never going to give up on me. How special is that? It makes me happy even though I don't really understand the power of it.

Srutirupa devi dasi

A devotee sold Srutirupa's mother some of Srila Prabhupada's books in 1970 and invited her to the Sunday Feast. Her mother said, "My daughter is vegetarian," and she later brought fifteen-year-old Srutirupa to the Miami temple.

In 1973, I was eighteen years old and traveling in Europe, reading the books my mother had given me three years earlier. My childhood friend from Key West, Kathy (who later became Kanti), was with me reading the same books, and she and I decided to visit the Paris temple. There, during a *Bhagavatam* class, I looked over at Kanti and mouthed, "I'm not leaving." She mouthed the same back to me. From then on, Srila Prabhupada pulled the strings of my life's journey.

My friend Kanti may have told the temple leaders that I had money, because they asked if I would like to purchase what was needed for the upcoming installation of Radha-Parisisvara. I was overjoyed to be able to help. So not long after I moved into the Paris temple I accompanied Bala Gopala dasi and her husband Dhananjaya to London to shop for Krishna. On our arrival, I was utterly surprised to learn that Srila Prabhupada was at the Manor. The first morning I walked into the temple room he was singing "Jaya Radha-Madhava," and the sound of his voice just struck me down. Hearing those hypnotic sounds and seeing the expression on his face, I became motionless and tears started to flow from my eyes. In that moment I knew that this was what my life had been leading to and that I was now home, safe, and forevermore Prabhupada's daughter.

Aside from the shopping in London, I managed to take on a few kitchen duties during our time at the Manor. In Paris, I was also in the kitchen to assist in preparing the devotees' breakfast and lunch, and a few weeks later, when Srila Prabhupada came to Paris for the installation, Bhagavan asked me to make Prabhupada's afternoon offering of fresh juice along with sandalwood paste for his forehead. So in the first few months of being a devotee I served Srila Prabhupada personally and I knew it was what I wanted to do forever. From 1973, the desire to personally serve Srila Prabhupada became my constant and daily prayer and meditation. I was absorbed in such thoughts until they came to fruition in 1975.

After my time in Europe I moved into the beautiful Miami temple, which was in a grove of banyan trees on three acres of lush tropical gardens. When Srila Prabhupada visited, two special types of Florida oranges and tangerines–Honeybells and Mercots–were in season, and I made his afternoon juice by combining these two beauties. After Srila Prabhupada tasted the juice, he asked Srutakirti Prabhu about it and then asked to see me. This was the first time that I understood how refined Srila Prabhupada's palate was. He immediately recognized and commented on the quality of the fruit. In all things he appreciated good quality, and good quality became the standard we all sought to achieve in every aspect of his service and in our own consciousness as we served him. Srila Prabhupada made us rise to the highest standards of service, and if we couldn't maintain that, we would find ourselves inevitably having to leave his personal service. To serve Srila Prabhupada was a joy unknown in this world; a joy that I'd never known before and that I have never experienced since.

I'd become attached to being near Srila Prabhupada, so in the summer of 1975 I joined him in Vrindavan for the four months of Caturmasya, where I again focused on serving him personally. Daivi-sakti Prabhu was in charge of his quarters and cooking and was preparing to leave for Tehran, so she trained me in all areas of Srila Prabhupada's service: cleaning his quarters, cooking for him, taking care of his clothes, caring for his *tulasi* gardens, and so on. Now that I had real entry into Srila Prabhupada's personal service, my desire for it intensified. I wanted only to be near him. I couldn't escape this feeling. When I was not directly doing some service, I was meditating on serving him, and strongly desiring to do something for him.

At the beginning of 1976 I moved to Calcutta, where Abhirama, my husband then, was temple president. In India I had many opportunities to travel with Srila Prabhupada, to have many wonderful exchanges with him, and to again engage in his personal service.

My intense desire to be near Srila Prabhupada never left me, and in different situations I was able to be in his presence, all the while absorbed in his daily life, his every word, and activity. It was another universe and I was happy to be a part of it. What he awakened in me forever changed me, and I could not return to anything less. The day-to-day life with Srila Prabhupada and how he interfaced and responded, all now remain a voice in my head, and I cannot separate from it. This was the blessing and great fortune that we had by having Srila Prabhupada's personal presence in our lives. I was only twenty or twenty-one years old, and looking back I'm amazed at how it all happened and how life shifted into this alternate universe. It was certainly a time that was completely mercy-driven.

In the summer of 1977, Srila Prabhupada's health was declining, yet he decided to leave India and go to the West. As Abhirama was Srila Prabhupada's personal servant and assistant secretary at the time, I traveled with Srila Prabhupada to London as his cook. When we arrived at the Manor, Srila Prabhupada told me he had no appetite and that I should bring him only what the Deities and the devotees were eating–he wanted to see what it was. Each day I would do that for his breakfast and lunch, but I'd also always make something I knew he liked in the hope of awakening his appetite.

Each morning at the Manor I'd gather the *maha* sweets and breakfast offering while Srila Prabhupada greeted the Deities and the devotees offered him *guru-puja*. Before I returned to his quarters to prepare his rooms and breakfast, I'd greet the Deities and see Srila Prabhupada for a few minutes. Standing alone in the back of the temple room, with folded hands I'd spontaneously pray the same prayer, as tears ran down my face, every day it was the same. I would beg Srila Prabhupada for his mercy and service, saying "Srila Prabhupada, please let me serve you, I beg you, please do not kick me away, please let me serve you."

One day Tamal Krishna Maharaja asked me to buy some sunglasses for Srila Prabhupada, because the light was bothering his eyes. So the next morning I left whatever duties I had with Abhirama and went into London to look for sunglasses. I spent the whole day looking. Finally, at 5 pm, I found something I thought was dignified enough to offer him. He wore my sunglasses the next morning but said nothing. Then Abhirama told him, "Srila Prabhupada, my wife has given." Immediately Srila Prabhupada turned and said, "Oh, if she has given I must accept." Tamal Krishna Maharaja said, "Srila Prabhupada, she can return them if you don't like them." Srila Prabhupada said, "No, if she has given, I must accept. She very much wants to serve me. Tell her thank you and be blessed."

At that very moment I felt the most amazing mercy and never again prayed as I had been doing daily, for I knew now that Srila Prabhupada knew my prayers and how much I wanted to serve him. And I realized for the first time that Srila Prabhupada would be leaving this world. After that, each morning I continued my quick darshan, but now I began to pray, "Srila Prabhupada, if I cannot always be with you, please bless me that I will always feel your presence near me."

It is these moments and experiences that carry me every day of my life.

Subhangi devi dasi

In 1974, Subhangi and her boyfriend, both students, enjoyed wonderful prasadam and music at the Sunday Love Feast in Hamburg. Later, when they read in a famous German magazine, "The dangerous and fanatic Hare Krishna sect is forcing money from old people," they decided to avoid devotees. But when Sacimata Prabhu gave them an Ishopanishad *and said, "You have to have this book, it will change your life! It's free!" they started reading it daily.*

We were both Christians and wanted to give our life for God. After reading the *Ishopanishad*, we became vegetarian. In early 1975 we moved into the Schloss Rettershof and that summer got initiated and married. Before I joined, I'd studied dance in Paris and thought I had to give up that attraction, but "Subhanga" is the name for Lord Chaitanya when He was dancing in ecstasy in front of the Jagannatha Ratha in Puri in seven groups simultaneously. I got the name of the biggest dancer in the universe and understood that Srila Prabhupada knew me through and through.

Once, during *guru-puja* in Delhi, everyone was singing and one by one lovingly offering flowers, and Srila Prabhupada was giving each of us a flower back when my son crawled on the *vyasasana* and threw all the flowers on the floor so Srila Prabhupada had none to give the devotees. The *pujari*, Omkara, pulled my son away, threw him in my arms, and said, "Get out of here!" Srila Prabhupada said, "What you are doing? Let this child play!" I was a helpless mother being bossed around, but Srila Prabhupada understood the difficulty and diffused the tension this devotee created.

Once in Vrindavan, I was sitting in the back with my child on my lap during Srila Prabhupada's class. My son started to scream and Srila Prabhupada said, "A devotee should scream to Krishna in the same way this baby is screaming to his mother." Everybody looked at me; I flushed and rushed out of the temple.

In a private darshan in Delhi in 1976, Srila Prabhupada encouraged us, saying "Your son will be very intelligent, don't worry." My husband, Sarvabhavana, and I asked, "Why are there so many fights going on in a spiritual movement like ISKCON?" Srila Prabhupada said, "It's a spiritual movement, you are right. But we are all conditioned souls. So we have to be patient with each other." I asked, "How can we understand fighting amongst devotees who are trying to serve one mission all together?" Srila Prabhupada said, "Both parties are wrong. The one who gives the insult or slap is not right and the other one who doesn't take it humbly is also not right." That consoled me.

Subuddhi devi dasi

Subuddhi dasi joined the Toronto temple in 1971 and was initiated in 1975.

The *gurus* I had seen were mostly impersonalists. They gave some mantras from here and there. They didn't show us the direct line. It was confusing. When I was three or four, one *mataji* guru, Satchitananda, gave me a mantra. But I wasn't touched by that. As soon as I heard Prabhupada talking about Krishna and the disciplic succession it touched me, especially Chaitanya Mahaprabhu.

I was working at the cash register at the Your Pantry grocery store in Victoria Park. A devotee, who was purchasing a little package of milk, had a *Krsna* book in his hand. I said, "Krishna in Canada?" and I grabbed the book. He said, "Oh, you want to come to the temple?" I was thrilled because we'd been worshiping Krishna since I was a child.

My husband and I went to find the temple. "Oh, this is a small street and there is a small little house. This can't be the temple." He knocked on the door and Saucarya opened it with a big smile. She had on beautiful *tilaka,* a bindi, and a piece of material–not a proper *sari*–but it was really beautiful. Ksiracora-Gopinatha were there in that small little place. Something really touched my heart, I felt connected.

My daughter was 2½ years old. And one son was seven and the other one was eight. They really loved it. Ayodhyapati, B.B. Govinda Maharaja, used to sit with my boys and talk to them about Krishna. The devotees' loving exchange and caring touched our hearts.

We started going regularly. The children loved it: the kirtan and especially devotees' loving exchange. Then I began making garlands.

We would listen to *Krsna* book and Prabhupada's lectures every night. This started clearing my heart. And meeting Prabhupada also, but especially the association of the devotees was very wonderful. They were very caring and that kept me going.

After two years or so Prabhupada was going to come. Everybody was so excited and the devotees from Montreal and Buffalo also came. We went to the airport and waited at the gate. There was an announcement that Prabhupada's gate had been changed. So all the devotees ran towards the other door. I saw Prabhupada coming out. He had a saffron sweater and a big smile. He was holding a *danda*. Someone pushed me so hard I fell on Prabhupada's feet. I said, "Oh, no! They told me not to touch Prabhupada's feet! Now I'm here at Prabhupada's feet by force." I held onto his lotus feet for a few seconds. I was crying. That was amazing, Prabhupada's mercy.

At the temple, we had a big *guru-puja*. My two boys were dancing in front of Prabhupada in very nice *dhotis* and *kurtas*. Prabhupada had about five or six garlands on. He started taking a garland off, and with his finger pointed, "Come on, this dancing boy." Jagadisa brought him close and Prabhupada gave a garland to my son. My son always says, "I am Prabhupada's disciple. Prabhupada gave me a garland."

My husband took me to India and then took my passport and return tickets and disappeared. Only after much endeavor and with my parent's help, was I able to get a new passport and returned to Toronto.

I used to go house-to-house distributing magazines to collect money for the new temple and I was teaching. Then Viswakarma said, "I want her to get initiation from Prabhupada." When I went to get my *japa mala* from Prabhupada's hand, Prabhupada said, "What are the four regulative principles?" I said, "No meat-eating." Then I just started crying. I couldn't say any more, I was just shivering. I couldn't believe that I was getting initiation from Prabhupada. Then Prabhupada said all three of them, he said them for me. So it was so amazing connecting with Prabhupada.

Prabhupada stayed in the upstairs room and I was underneath that room. I used to make *parathas*. When anyone would go upstairs, I asked, "Please take my *paratha* to Prabhupada." Nobody would take it, because they were all *sannyasis*, all these big, big devotees. In the end B. B. Govinda Maharaja was going up and I said, "Please take." He said, "Yes, yes, I will take it." So I always say people like my *parathas* because Prabhupada ate it.

Life has completely changed under Prabhupada's shelter. He gave me so much and his mercy is unlimited. *Seva* gives me so much pleasure.

I am very thankful to Prabhupada and ISKCON. The leaders and devotees lovingly and devotedly serve. I always pray to Krishna, "Please, till the last end of my life give me this body working so that I can serve You." There is nothing out there, nothing out there. Do your duty but at the same time keep your anchor here. We are only on the first step, but we are on the right path. Prabhupada gave us the right path, keep going. One day Prabhupada will open the door for us. He is sitting there waiting, isn't it? He is waiting.

Suci devi dasi

At her religious school, Suci received a prize for her knowledge of scripture. Her fondness for the Beatles led her to meditating and wondering about life.

Once, on Late Night Line-Up, I heard Prabhupada saying, "Don't die like cats and dogs. Don't waste your life. Do something with it!" I wrote the *maha-mantra* on my bedroom wall and used to dance to the Radha Krishna Temple album. The devotees, who seemed to be glowing, attracted me. I bought the *Teachings of Lord Chaitanya* and the *Krsna* book. Krishna's story, I found, was like Jesus's story.

In 1972, when I was twenty, I was desperate to join. I knocked on the door of the Edinburgh temple and said to the devotee who opened it, "I'm here!" I'd given everything I owned away and hadn't even brought a sleeping bag with me, as I thought that would be *maya*. The temple was poor but my life there was lovely. Six months later I was initiated.

When Prabhupada arrived at the Manor in a helicopter in 1973, my husband, Svayambhur, and I were there, and my expectations of Prabhupada were high. As he walked past me, I waved my arms to get his attention. I ran up the back stairs and stood on the landing, thinking, "Where's his effulgence? I can't see anything!" Prabhupada looked through me and walked past. I shouldn't have expected his attention, but I wanted it and lost enthusiasm. Although devotees told me that Krishna was making me humble, I was bothered. I felt rejected and my mind filled with doubts. Prabhupada had had such a stern look that I couldn't see the humility devotees talked about; he seemed proud. I doubted that he was in his picture and was watching over me.

I could relate to Prabhupada's books, but unfortunately, I had a problem with his *vapuh*, his physical presence, and I avoided him.

When I went into Prabhupada's room to receive the Gayatri mantra from him, at first he seemed to be very fatherly. He patted the cushion for me to sit down. Then he became stern. He didn't look at me but looked ahead. He and I were alone in the room and I thought, "He's setting a proper example." But that experience compounded my hurt feelings. After he showed me how to chant Gayatri, I looked at him and wondered what was next. All he said was, "Go!" Ever since then I've thought, "What did I do wrong? He didn't like me." After receiving Gayatri from Srila Prabhupada, I should have felt wonderful but instead, I struggled with that experience. As a child, I'd fantasize about meeting Jesus, so I had high expectations of Prabhupada.

I was in Nairobi in 1975 when Prabhupada visited, and when he left, I felt closer to him and wrote him a note saying that I'd miss him. On November 4th, 1975, he wrote to me: "You have rightly said that the best way to associate with the spiritual master is to follow his instructions. There are two ways of associating, by *vani* and by *vapuh*. *Vani* means words and *vapuh* means physical presence. Physical presence is sometimes appreciable and sometimes not. Therefore we should take advantage of the *vani*, not the physical presence, because the *vani* continues to exist eternally. *Bhagavad-gita*, for example is the *vani* of Lord Krishna. Although Krishna was personally present 5,000 years ago and is no longer present physically from the materialistic viewpoint, still *Bhagavad-gita* continues. So you have correctly concluded."

Sucirani devi dasi

Sucirani was born and raised in Bangladesh. Every day, after putting her ten children to sleep, Sucirani's mother would listen to Bhagavatam class and would worship Radha-Krishna. After Sucirani had grown up and had a family of her own, she would visit her brother in his house in Shantipur and it was there that her son, who was eleven, heard about an ISKCON temple nearby. The boy told his mother, "There's a nice temple in Mayapur, why don't you take me there?" Sucirani did that and then started coming almost every day.

Vrindavani Prabhu was cooking for Radha-Madhava and when she noticed me coming regularly she said, "Please come and help, Seva." My name was Seva then. I did some kitchen service, washing, and cutting, and after some time she told me, "Now you must become a devotee." I said, "Okay, I will." Later Srila Prabhupada initiated my husband, our two sons, and me.

I did a lot of service for Prabhupada. Every morning and evening I'd cut a dob (green coconut) for him; everyday I'd grate five coconuts and make *lugdoos* for him to distribute to his guests; sometimes I'd cook his lunch (he was satisfied with my cooking); and every day I'd wash a mountain of pots. I also served the Western devotees who were visiting. The leaders asked me to do these services and my heart told me, "You must serve Prabhupada, you must serve his followers," so what I heard from outside and from inside coincided.

I liked to serve Prabhupada and even now, at age seventy-eight, I still serve him because I can't sit in my room idle. That's not my nature. I have to do something. Nobody asks me to serve but after I chant my rounds I often help in the big kitchen. One day I'll make a *subji,* another day I'll make *chapatis,* another day I'll cut vegetables. I can't be idle.

My sons and other relatives don't come to see me, but sometimes my brother invites me to his home in Shantipur. In truth I don't feel like going there or anywhere else. I stay in Mayapur because here I feel connected with Prabhupada. At any cost I never want to leave this place. Prabhupada helped me come closer to Krishna and Mayapur is Prabhupada's place; he is present in Mayapur. I want to stay in his place, I want to take shelter of him. If I let life's material aspects distract me my mind won't remain fixed on Prabhupada. By staying here I'm forced to fix my mind on Prabhupada.

Now I'm not even able to eat – I can only eat a tiny bit. But I don't want to bother the devotees. If they take care of me or if they don't take care of me, it's okay. If I return back to Prabhupada, that's enough for me.

Sudevi devi dasi

When she was eighteen and had just graduated high school, Sudevi was visiting her aunt and grandmother in Buffalo, her native town. One day while shopping downtown, she saw people in beautiful orange robes. She got a little closer and heard the mridanga, the karatalas and the melodious harmonium. When she saw the men's bald heads with pony tails she thought, "How beautiful, but who are they?"

I went up to them – the devotees didn't come up to me – and asked, "Who are you?" They said they were teaching love of God and were into yoga. I was soul-searching. I wasn't happy. I knew that there was more to life than getting up in the morning, having breakfast, going to school, coming home, doing your homework, having dinner, watching TV, and then going to bed. The devotees said to me, "Would you like to come to our temple?" I said, "Yes, okay." When I first walked in I saw Lord Jagannatha. I didn't know who He was but He blew me away.

I tasted the *prasadam* and thought, "I've never had anything like this before. It's so good!" I realized that the devotees had an answer for every question and thought, "This is nice!" As I kept visiting, I knew that Krishna consciousness was what I was looking for. I moved into the Buffalo temple and hung out in the *pujari* room making ghee wicks, making the Deity plate, and transferring the Deity plate. I felt at home in the *pujari* room and wanted to become a *pujari*.

In 1971, I was initiated in Detroit, Michigan, and the next day I received *brahmana* initiation. I was happy to finally be Gaura-Nitai's and Lord Jagannatha's *pujari*. I started doing *aratis* and dressing and bathing the Lord.

In those days, everything was ecstatic. We *brahmacharinis* were always singing or telling Krishna stories. It was a happy, blissful time. In 1972, I went on a *japa* walk with Prabhupada in New Vrindavan. I'm emotional and get deeply involved, and as we walked I was only looking at Prabhupada's feet. I couldn't look up because I felt very fallen and insignificant before him.

Prabhupada is a pure devotee of the Lord and, although I'm not deserving of it, I was in his presence, having his darshan. I was so fortunate to have such a wonderful experience. As Krishna says in the *Gita*, out of thousands of people, only one will be interested in spiritual life, and out of thousands of those, only one will be a devotee. How rare a devotee is and how fortunate we are that we saw Prabhupada, were in his presence, walked in his footsteps! We owe everything to Prabhupada.

Sudharma devi dasi

1974 was a time of trying new things, of questioning the purpose of life, of looking to understand life from a new perspective. Sudharma was at San Francisco State University at that time, where that type of thinking was very much in vogue. For her, as for many others, such thinking wasn't a fetish but something real. She used to sit with good friends and talk about philosophy, which prompted her to explore further, because she and her friends had such limited information.

I think each of us has in our core existence remnants of former devotional service we've performed that carry from one life to another. It's something that helps guide us. I clearly remember sitting in someone's dorm room and picking up Srila Prabhupada's *Bhagavad-gita*. I only needed to read one sentence before I said, "*Ohhhh,* okay. Finally! This is the book I was looking for." I'd read other translations of the *Bhagavad-gita* and found them confusing and lacking substance. Prabhupada's *Gita* was the opposite.

In 1975 I went to the San Francisco Ratha-yatra with a few friends. At that point, I didn't know anything about Srila Prabhupada. But when he got off the cart at the Ratha-yatra, I was standing in the crowd as he walked down to the stage. I remember thinking that this was not what I had expected. As he walked by quite close to me, he nodded, and while I understood that this was a nod for the group, it affected me in a personal and direct way; I was very affected by his presence. I wasn't looking to feel a connection with him, but I did.

Then he sat on the stage, and there were so many elements to his presence that were new and different. Here we were in Golden Gate Park with thousands of people engaged in so many different ways, including groups of Christians trying to shout down the devotees, but Prabhupada was unperturbed and unmoved. The world quieted the moment Srila Prabhupada sat on the stage, and as I gazed at him, I felt a stillness pulling me in. He was somehow completely unaffected by everything around him, even the wind. He looked toward the Christians and said, "Tell them to be quiet," and they were. Then he spoke, and I remember him saying, "You are not the body." I could see that this was right, and that he was realized and that he was living it.

I never thought I would become a Hare Krishna because those were the people who wore bed sheets, walked on the backs of their shoes, and looked funny, but the *Bhagavad-gita* resonated with me and I thought I should go to the temple and check it out. That was how I came in contact with the devotees, and when I finally settled into the temple, it seemed to me to be the end of a long journey of searching.

I had almost no association with Srila Prabhupada, although I did have the blessing of being initiated by him. My connection has always been through the devotees, books, and service. Srila Prabhupada told us everything was in his books and I believe him. The more I practice devotional service, the more genuine and valid the process has been for me, and the more this very real process connects with every fiber of my being – the more I realize how important, deep and genuine this process is. I want to have every drop of it I can have and to share it, no matter how much I may have to struggle with everyday existence. The more service you give, the more your heart softens. A soft heart lets you stay in devotional life continually, despite the many ups and downs life throws your way.

No matter who or where we are, we each have the right to perform devotional service to our fullest capability. In my experience, Krishna reciprocates with the attempt to do just that.

I've had the kinds of incredible experiences you can have only by depending on Krishna. Once I was traveling across the Philippines with a small group of eighteen- and nineteen-year-old girls. One day a boat dropped us on an island, where we found ourselves in the middle of a sugarcane field. The sugarcane was so tall that we couldn't see where we were. When we finally got to a road, the locals spoke a different dialect than we did, and we had trouble communicating with them. As we walked along the road, the sun started to set. We came to a beach and walked along it as the sky darkened. By this point we figured we'd sleep on the beach, but we saw some lights in the distance, so we kept walking until we finally came to a small fishing village. A small group of people, led by the mayor of the town and his wife, were standing on the beach waiting for us with lanterns and blankets. They gave us hot milk, a vegetarian meal, and shelter in a school for the night.

In the morning, the whole village came to visit, and we chanted Hare Krishna together, had a *Bhagavatam* class, and then, along with about a hundred villagers, took a *japa* walk along the beautiful, very white beach. The villagers were chanting, too! Although the sun was shining, there was a sprinkling of rain followed by a beautiful rainbow. Our mood was already jovial, when atop a white sand dune appeared a white wild horse. He looked down on all of us, ran down the dune, circumambulated the entire group, ran up the dune, and disappeared. We completed our walk, and then the townspeople graciously directed us to the city we were trying to reach.

It was an incredible experience, but one of many such experiences I've been honored to have during this lifetime. Like so many of my godsisters, I've been able to do wonderful things in a renounced, fully dependent preaching mood – and I also got to be the mother of three children.

Really, there are no limits in devotional service. If we each were to decide that we shouldn't use whatever abilities Krishna gave us, then our Movement will be a small percentage of what it could have been. People want to do the best they can, and they want to be appreciated for the things they do. That's perfectly natural.

If we want to think in a spiritual way – something we have the option of doing at any time – that means we want to see everybody take another step toward Krishna.

Sujana devi dasi

When, as an eighteen-year-old hippie, Sujana saw devotees on the streets, she'd avoid them because she didn't want to talk to guys who wore dresses.

My husband would take the devotees' magazine, bring it home, and talk about what was in it. Then, in 1969, when my husband and I were living in Vancouver, B.C., some *brahmacharis* asked us for a place to rent. We gave them our spare room in exchange for *prasadam*. They moved in, fixed the room, set up an altar, cooked for us, and preached to us. In the evenings, we'd have programs with hot milk, cut up fruit, and Simply Wonderfuls. At one point I said, "Okay, this is exotic, but why is the old man's picture on the altar?" Although Srila Prabhupada was the cause of all the mercy that I've experienced in my life, in ignorance, I questioned what he had to do with it. Of course, the devotees explained who he was.

In July, 1971, we were waiting at the Detroit airport in great anticipation of Srila Prabhupada's arrival, and as soon as he appeared, everybody burst into tears. We all went crazy and had a wild, out of this world kirtan.

As Prabhupada went down the escalator, he seemed to be floating like a heavenly being, and I had so many tears I could hardly see him.

Later on, I was having a rough time because I got initiated, but my husband didn't and was uncooperative, which made things awkward. I wasn't getting much association and felt useless and uninspired. When my husband's parents came for a visit, I left the children with them and went to see Prabhupada in Portland. As Srila Prabhupada walked through the crowd of devotees at the airport, I handed him a beautiful saffron rose and said, "All glories to you Srila Prabhupada." He took my flower, looked at me, and said, "Thank you very much." I felt satisfied that I could offer him a symbol of my appreciation and that he appreciated it. At the temple, I did every service that I could for him – helping with the flowers, washing and ironing his shirt, *dhoti*, and *kaupinas*. I'd made a tan-colored wool cape with beautiful saffron silk lining for Prabhupada, but felt too shy to give it to him. When he was in his quarters about to leave for the airport, Jagadish gave my cape to him. As Srila Prabhupada walked to his car, Jagadish said to me, "Do you see?" Prabhupada was wearing my cape! He kindly gave me the satisfaction of accepting my gift. At the airport, as Srila Prabhupada waited for his flight, he took off his big, beautiful garland of roses, put it on his lap, broke the string and distributed the flowers. I cried seeing Prabhupada's merciful and compassionate gesture of love to us. He saw us mourning his departure and wanted to reciprocate with and encourage us.

I was in Vrindavan when Srila Prabhupada came in 1977. His presence was exciting and thrilling and fulfilling, yet bittersweet too, because he was ill. Once, when Srila Prabhupada was sitting in his rocking chair, gazing at the Deities, my oldest daughter, Kaumini, who was eight, wanted to see him, so she sat in the middle of the open aisle in front of him. Devotees tried to get her to move, but she wouldn't. Srila Prabhupada raised his hand and said, "Leave her alone. She's not bothering." Not long after that, in August of 1977, Kaumini told me her head hurt. The next thing I knew, she collapsed on the floor and turned completely blue. I was alarmed and couldn't imagine what was wrong because she was fine the day before. I chanted, "Hare Krishna, Hare Krishna!" and she left her body. I was totally distraught and inconsolable. When Srila Prabhupada heard about Kaumini's passing, he said that it was mysterious and that, since she'd died in Vrindavan, she got personal liberation. He also said that because she was only eight and still pure, her body should be wrapped in a cloth and floated on the Yamuna.

I was so devastated, I couldn't think properly. When her body was on a palanquin and we were gathered outside Prabhupada's quarters preparing to do a *parikrama* through Vrindavan, Prabhupada sent us his garland saying, "Put this on top of her body." At that moment, a huge weight left my body and mind. I felt Srila Prabhupada knew my heart and cared deeply about me and my daughter and was blessing both of us. We took her body through Vrindavan and floated it down the Yamuna, and I danced ecstatically the whole time. Because Srila Prabhupada had made that one seemingly small gesture, he turned that incident into an ecstatic experience for me. He lifted an immense weight that I thought I needed to carry. And he's done that for me my whole life: he picked me up from the depths of ignorance and placed me at Krishna's lotus feet. Who could be more merciful?

Then, the ultimate gift that Prabhupada gave me was that I was allowed to be in Vrindavan three months later, when he left the planet. The emotional experience of being in the same room with him and with all the devotees chanting so intensely was powerful and devastating. I thought, "This can't be happening, Prabhupada's going to pull through. How can I go on without him?" But he left and everyone was crying. A lot of us were wondering, what do we do next? How do we go on? I went to my room and played a recording of Prabhupada chanting. Many devotees stayed in the temple room all night chanting and crying.

When Prabhupada's body was in the *samadhi*, I was standing over the hole watching devotees place salt around him. The salt was getting higher and higher, covering his shoulders, his neck. Then the hated moment came when his shining, beautiful head was covered. Afterwards we started a twenty-four hour kirtan at his *samadhi*, and every day Sitala, Arundhati, and I chanted for a couple of hours before *mangala-arati*.

Experiencing Prabhupada's departure was the closest I've ever come to feeling real spiritual emotion. Despite ups and downs and different material situations, that spiritual emotion tightly bound me with Srila Prabhupada. I'm grateful for having been given the opportunity to be there.

Sukhada devi dasi

Sukhada heard about Krishna consciousness from her college friends, Mukhya and her husband Vrajendralal, and when she walked into the Detroit temple with them she instantly felt peaceful and at home.

Growing up I was enthusiastic about life. I'd anticipate an event – whether Christmas or New Years, turning sixteen or turning eighteen, getting married or graduating from college – and my anticipation so much exceeded the event I was always disappointed. But that changed when I met Srila Prabhupada. The first time I saw him, Prabhupada was arriving at the Miami airport and Nartaka Gopala and I were backing up as he walked, putting rose petals in a path before him. Finally I experienced an event that far exceeded my anticipation. In fact, it was better than anything could ever be. Feeling how great Srila Prabhupada was yet how approachable and unguarded he was – qualities we never see in the material world – was amazing.

Before I met him, Srila Prabhupada's books excited me because they were clear. He gave a wealth of information about who we are, our destination, the different planetary systems. I loved the personal nature of the knowledge. Even though it was called mythology by some, I had more faith in the knowledge in Prabhupada's books than I did in the Big Bang theory and other theories because the knowledge in Prabhupada's books was backed up by the authority of the original scriptures.

From the second day I came to Miami I became fast friends with Nartaka Gopala and she and I were daily *sankirtana* partners. After that, during the summer of 1975, I went with a group of devotees on traveling *sankirtana* up and down the East Coast following Srila Prabhupada. When we were in Philadelphia for Ratha-yatra my husband, Suvrata, and I were initiated. Inspired and happy to have my name, I rededicated myself to Prabhupada's mission by continuing to distribute his books, for I knew he wanted that. By Srila Prabhupada's potency many people I met were transformed and later would come to me and say, "Oh, do you remember me? I met you in such-and-such a place." And if I ever became forgetful on *sankirtana* and felt like I was the doer, Krishna and Srila Prabhupada would immediately remind me of the fact that Krishna is the doer and that I was His instrument.

Whatever else happens in my life doesn't matter because during the New York Ratha-yatra down Fifth Avenue I showered Srila Prabhupada with flower petals and pulled Subhadra's cart while he was on it. I was in Vaikuntha – without anxiety – just by being in his presence. I'm sure I could have appreciated Prabhupada more, but I never took him for granted. I knew he was the most special person in my life, I knew I was willing to give up everything for him, and I knew devotees were the people I wanted to be with and to be like. For instance, although I was attached to my husband and although my husband was interested in Krishna consciousness, he wasn't as interested as I was. So I prayed, "Krishna, please either make him a devotee or break my attachment," and Krishna kindly helped him become a devotee.

Once in India in 1976, on the way back from Radha-kunda the women's bus broke down, and Srila Prabhupada stayed up late at night until we got back. He knew the importance of the nurturing factor, of the invaluable service women offer, and was concerned that when he was gone the women would not be properly protected.

Another time in India I was feeling ill but I was still distributing books when Srila Prabhupada came by in his car, folded his hands, and bowed to me. I was shocked. Srila Prabhupada was grateful for whatever smidgen of service we did.

I'm unqualified to see Krishna; the only way it will happen is that, when I'm ready, Srila Prabhupada will bring me to Krishna. Srila Prabhupada is my connection and I like that. That's how it should be because I would never know anything if it wasn't for him. I have no complaints about anything. Whatever mercy or benefit I've received from his institution, ISKCON, so far outweighs any injustices done to me or mistakes made that I can overlook those injustices and mistakes and move on. I know we're correcting ourselves, we're getting better, and going forward.

I love reading and hearing about Prabhupada because it's important to know his character and what he did; it lends a brilliant light on how we should act. Prabhupada was a perfect gentleman, treated the children beautifully, was kind and personal, never discriminated between his disciples, and when devotees were sick Prabhupada was concerned and would ask questions and give advice. All I ever felt from him was the greatest love.

Whatever our economic or cultural background, whatever our race, whether we were ruffians, motorcycle people, mode of goodness people or business people, Prabhupada brought us together. And he's still here to bring us together. In one sense he hasn't left, and in another sense we can't experience the same kinds of exchanges with him as we had when he was present. I miss those exchanges and hanker for them. The only way I can deal with Srila Prabhupada's departure is by keeping close to his lotus feet, reading his books and dedicating myself to his children. Now thirty-year-olds tell me about the positive experiences they had when I was their elementary school teacher, and as I see them – the next generation – taking up Krishna consciousness, I have hope for the future of Prabhupada's mission.

Sukhada devi dasi

The first weekend of September 1970, at seventeen, when Sukhada was in her senior year of high school, she went with a few friends to the Beacon Street temple in Boston.

Seeing the shaved heads of the men and the robes that both the men and women were wearing, the bright colors of the temple, the altar, and the blissful chanting and dancing made me smile and want to find out more about this group of happy souls. As we walked up the porch steps, an angelic looking devotee was there holding a bunch of flowers. He smelled the flowers and said, "How can one say there is no God?" I thought, "Wow, this is already far out. There might be something interesting going on here." After a short lecture explaining what Krishna consciousness was about we were served a wonderful and tasty feast.

We continued to attend the Sunday Feast programs, and that fall two of my friends moved into the temple.

My parents were upset that I was going to the temple and tried to forbid me, but I kept going. That January I turned eighteen and in early June moved in. What surprised me most after moving in was the strictness of daily life. I had difficulty with the lack of sleep, full day of worship, cleaning, and the many hours of *harinama*. Most difficult for me was dealing with the stress associated with the low status assigned to the women. Although I felt overwhelmed, what kept me going was knowing that Srila Prabhupada was coming to the temple in March 1971. Somehow I hung on, even when his visit was delayed until July.

The months before his arrival the devotees were excited and eager for their chance to spend time with their spiritual master. I kept thinking about how wonderful it was going to be to sit with our small group of devotees and ask Srila Prabhupada questions and to hear him speak. It would be so intimate.

Days before his arrival, devotees from other centers started to arrive and fill the temple up beyond capacity. Although at other times I would have loved to have the association of other devotees, at this time their arrival caused me much stress and anxiety, because now I realized that the time I had imagined to spend with Srila Prabhupada was not going to happen.

Most of the devotees went to the airport to greet Srila Prabhupada and the kirtan there was ecstatic. Srila Prabhupada gave a short lecture there at the airport and when he got up to leave I realized that this might be the only chance I would have to be close to my spiritual master. As he was leaving we all bowed to pay obeisances. From this position I turned my head and watched him approach to pass by me. Just before he got to me, I jumped up to be as close to him as possible. As I stood side-by-side with him I thought how fortunate I was that I was given this opportunity to be so close to a pure devotee and I was overwhelmed by such a blissful feeling. Maybe a small thing, a quick moment in time, but a moment of great happiness that I have always cherished.

The temple was in such bad shape that when Prabhupada came that summer Satsvarupa reserved a hotel room for him. But Prabhupada wouldn't stay in a hotel. Instead the *brahmachari*s moved all their things and Prabhupada stayed in their quarters. The women's bathroom was opposite the men's bathroom and once, about 2:00, 2:30 am, I ran into Prabhupada as he was coming out of the bathroom. I offered my obeisances and stayed down until he walked by and then scurried into the bathroom.

At that time Prabhupada held initiations and installed the Deities. I was supposed to get initiated, but spent the whole time cooking. After Prabhupada left, Satsvarupa said, "What name did Srila Prabhupada give you?" I said, "I didn't get a name because I've been cooking for days; nobody came to get me." He said, "Oh, no, you were supposed to get initiated!" He immediately wrote a letter telling Prabhupada about me and Prabhupada wrote back, "Sukhada, one who gives pleasure to Krishna." Later I had a fire sacrifice.

Over the ensuing months, the difficulties with the increasingly poor treatment of the women devotees in Boston resulted in my going home a couple of times, but Srila Prabhupada and Krishna always drew me back to the temple. Finally, the situation became unbearable and I left with another *brahmacharini* who said the Pittsburgh temple was a wonderful place. In Pittsburgh I was immediately given great services and the temple's devotional family atmosphere was a wonderful revelation after the discouragements I had experienced in Boston. Also in Pittsburgh in 1973, I met and married my husband Mahendra dasa.

In 1976 we moved to the Los Angeles Temple community for Mahendra's work with the BBT, and I was very fortunate to spend time in Srila Prabhupada's divine presence on numerous occasions when he spent about a full month in Los Angeles later that year.

I have always known myself to be a very insignificant devotee. Our first child was born in 1974 in Pittsburgh and from that point on I have always considered that my most important service is to be a good mother. Our second child passed away at age 2-1/2 and that pain of losing her was nearly unbearable; only our philosophical understandings that Srila Prabhupada has given us kept my despair at bay. I have been blessed with four wonderful and successful children along with eight grandchildren (and counting) and I am so thankful for all that Krishna has blessed me with. Through our struggles encountered for several years after leaving the ISKCON institution, we can only stand in appreciative awe of what Srila Prabhupada sacrificed and endured in coming to the West at such an advanced age to bring Krishna to us.

My realizations have always come from Prabhupada's books because I didn't have any one-on-one contact. For me, his physical presence wasn't what kept me linked to him, so after he left I never felt lost or bewildered. He left us so much I never felt I had to search out somebody else to take his place. He's written so many books with so much nectar in all of them, sometimes I think, "Which book should I read now?" I want it all.

It's humbling to think about what little I've done to help him. He was always kind to us, always concerned about our welfare. He signed every letter, "Your ever well-wisher."

Sukla devi dasi

Sukla had just finished high school, had been reading all sorts of spiritual books, and was desperately praying to the full moon for a spiritual master. Then her brother came with a bead bag around his neck and said, "Guess what? The leader of the Hare Krishna Movement is coming in one week."

At the time I didn't realize my brother was into Krishna consciousness. He said, "You can go to the temple." I said, "Okay, very cool." The next day I went to the Melbourne temple and started sewing Deity outfits. A couple of months later I moved in.

A year later, January 1973, Prabhupada was going to install beautiful big marble Deities, Radha-Vallabha, in Melbourne. About an hour before the installation Madhudvisa summoned a few of us and said, "You're to receive first and second initiation in one go. But you have to understand that you're going to be serving the Deities here forever. If you accept it, then okay." I thought for about five minutes and said, "Yes, certainly."

Prabhupada said to me, "Your name is Sukla. Sukla is pure and white and the full moon; Krishna is the full moon amongst many stars," And I'd been praying to the full moon. It was like I'd known my name from lifetimes. Prabhupada told me to always take care of the Deities nicely. After that, my mother, who had been in a rage about my getting initiated, met Prabhupada and he calmed her down.

For *dakshina*, I made Srila Prabhupada a gold beaded *karatala* bag. I paid my obeisances, Prabhupada smiled and said, "So what have you brought me?" I said, "Oh, it's just a little *dakshina*, Prabhupada." He loved it. He said, "Bali Mardan, Srutakirti, come see what she has made me," and he showed them the *karatala* bag.

The day after my initiation was rainy and Prabhupada came from his walk early. I was cleaning and had buckets and mops in my hand. I flew into a side door and closed it thinking, "I hope he didn't see me." All of a sudden Prabhupada opened the door and said, "So I have tricked you this morning." I said, "Oh, yes, Srila Prabhupada I wasn't expecting you back so soon." He said, "It is raining." I said, "Yes, Srila Prabhupada." He laughed, said, "Hare Krishna," and walked back into his room. The following day he came back early again, but I was prepared. He said, "You were ready." I said, "Yes, I was ready."

Ramaniya used to chant fast and wildly, and we thought, "Ramaniya needs to learn to chant properly." On a morning walk Prabhupada turned to her and said, "Very nice chanting." From then on we were quiet about her chanting.

Once Srutakirti asked me to take Prabhupada his lunch. I was at Prabhupada's door with his plate and I could hear him banging his fist on the desk and yelling at someone, "You will never make advancement while you're envious of the spiritual master!" I thought, "Do I have to knock on the door now?" But I knocked and Prabhupada said, "Come in." I opened the door quietly and Prabhupada broke into a big smile, "Hare Krishna, *ah, prasadam*," so sweet. I put the plate down. Prabhupada said, "Thank you very much." I said, "*Jaya* Srila Prabhupada," paid my obeisances and left. As I closed the door I could hear Prabhupada banging his fist on the desk again. He wasn't really angry but was making a point.

The last time Prabhupada came, May 1976, I was at the bottom of the stairs waiting. Prabhupada looked down, saw me there with a flower, walked down the stairs, took the flower out of my hand, and walked back up the stairs. During that visit I asked Prabhupada, "What is most important, hearing, chanting, reading, or remembering?" Prabhupada looked at me and said, "Hearing." I thought, "Okay, I got it."

Prabhupada was loving and compassionate, wonderfully warm and caring like no one I'd ever known. Every word that came out of his mouth was full of love and purity. Whenever he saw me, he always had a big smile. He was so grand and royal he made me want to always do things properly. He was also mischievous and playful with me.

Whether someone meets Prabhupada or not, his instructions are there and the more they hear, their relationship with him will directly develop on a spiritual level, as well as through Prabhupada's disciples. By hearing about Prabhupada, a person can know him well. If we open our heart Prabhupada is there, ready to give us spiritual life.

It was the philosophy, the instructions, and the scriptures that brought me and holds me to Krishna consciousness. My sweet relationship with Prabhupada enhanced those things, but I can't have that affection without the scriptural knowledge and instructions. A lot of people have sentimental relationships with gurus, but unless there's philosophy and instruction and seriousness behind it, it won't last or be beneficial.

Sumati devi dasi

When she was living on New York's Lower East Side in 1968, Sumati heard the maha-mantra on the radio from the musical "Hair." She had no idea the mantra was names of God, but it became her favorite song and when she sang it while hitchhiking around Europe in the summer of 1970, it made her feel protected.

When I came back to Maryland I heard about the local temple, knocked on the door there, and a beautiful effulgent girl answered and said, "Hi, my name's Mary, and all you have to do is bring your toothbrush and you can live here and be happy for the rest of your life." I went in and instantly my heart felt happy. I felt like I was home, and I had never felt that way before. The next night I packed my knapsack, went to the temple and said, "Can I live here?"

I helped Tosan Krishna in the kitchen and he suggested I write to Prabhupada, which I did. Prabhupada immediately wrote a handwritten letter back, thanking me for the bookmarker I'd made for him and saying he was using it every day in his *Srimad-Bhagavatam*. I felt, "Here's a person who has some feeling for me even though he's never met me," and that was the beginning of my feelings for him.

January 1st, 1971, I moved to Boston, which was wonderful because Satsvarupa, the temple president, talked about Prabhupada all the time. When he got one of his many letters from Prabhupada, he'd call us all together, "We got a letter from Prabhupada!" and read it to us. I had a sense that now I had a family, which I'd never felt before.

Before Prabhupada came, which was in the middle of July, we didn't sleep for days. We were cleaning, decorating, painting, and trying to make everything perfect and beautiful. When I saw Prabhupada step out of the airplane it was like seeing the sun suddenly rise. He was effulgent, had the most beautiful smile I've ever seen, and warmly greeted the devotees he knew. He spoke at the temple and then Satsvarupa asked him if he wanted to go to his hotel. Prabhupada said, "Hotel? The brothel and the liquor store are in the mode of ignorance, the city and the hotels are in the mode of passion, and the country is in the mode of goodness. But the temple is Vaikuntha. I will stay in the temple." He was happy in his simple room in the temple. The next morning he bathed and dressed Radha-Gopivallabha and installed Them.

Through a Northeastern University communications major we used to do weekly radio show dramas of *Krsna* book stories. I was Mother Yashoda, and when Prabhupada heard me screaming on seeing Krishna wrapped in the coils of Kaliya he asked, "Who's that crying?" Satsvarupa said, "That's Sumati." Prabhupada said, "She should always cry for Krishna like that." When I chant *japa*, I try to remember that instruction and it helps me stay connected to Prabhupada. I pray that in some lifetime I'll really cry for Krishna, be a real devotee, and do some real service for Prabhupada.

Sunita devi dasi

One day when she was coming back from work, Sunita heard the devotees chanting the maha-mantra in Boston Common. She had just returned from a visit to India, her homeland, and never imagined kirtan would be going on in the West. The devotees were sweet and kind to Sunita and invited her to visit the temple. Sunita was attracted and never stopped visiting. She joined the movement a year later in Boston in 1971.

When I went to the Boston temple for the first time I saw a picture of Prabhupada sitting, with his hand in his bead bag and wearing many *chadars*. I was brought up in Vrindavan where the *sadhus* wore no clothes, had a beard, and were practically naked, and when I saw Prabhupada with all those clothes and was told that he's the guru, I said, "He's the guru? What kind of guru is he?" I didn't understand.

In July 1970 Satsvarupa (he was not Maharaja at that time) took me to see Prabhupada. When I saw him and had a conversation with him, there was no doubt in my mind that he was no ordinary man. He was from Vaikuntha; he was a Vaikuntha man. I was with my husband and in Hindi Prabhupada asked me if I was from Bengal, and I answered in Hindi that I was from Agra. Prabhupada said, "Oh, you're from a Vaishnava family. So make your life successful, don't waste time in this life."

Prabhupada continued, "So it's very nice that you both are coming," and to my husband he said, "You're an intelligent person. If you take to Krishna consciousness you can impress a lot of people. We want intelligent Indians to come forward." My husband was about to say what he said to me all the time, that "These Americans don't know anything about Krishna, they have to practice. But we Indians, we already know, it is in our blood." Three times Prabhupada interrupted him and I thought, "Prabhupada knows his heart, he knows what my husband is about to say." Prabhupada told him, "Don't be one of those Indians who think, 'Oh, I know Krishna. I can worship Krishna any time. I can take to Krishna consciousness at any time. Let these Americans do it because they don't know.' Don't think like that. Learn from these people how to worship Krishna, how to take to Krishna consciousness."

That impressed me. I admired the devotees, and after Prabhupada told us to learn how to worship Krishna from them, I felt submissive to the devotees, but my husband was a smoker and a drinker and not very interested in Krishna consciousness. Then Prabhupada told us a story. He said that there was a man in Jagannatha Puri who would bring water to Lord Jagannatha every day but he never saw Jagannatha, because he thought, "Oh, I can see Jagannatha any time, let the pilgrims see Lord Jagannatha, they have never seen Him, but I come here every day, I can see Jagannatha any time." Then that man died never having seen Jagannatha. So Prabhupada said, "Don't be one of those Indians who thinks that you know Krishna and you can take to Krishna consciousness at any time."

My husband gave Prabhupada $100 and left. Prabhupada was thankful for the donation and asked Satsvarupa, "Where is he going?" Satsvarupa said, "Oh, Prabhupada he probably went to smoke. He's not very interested in Krishna consciousness. His wife is more sincere about Krishna consciousness than he is, she comes here often. Her husband mistreats her and is very bad. She wants to leave him." Prabhupada said to me, "Oh, no, you should not leave. You should stay with your husband. Be sincere and remain strong. If you remain strong and sincere, then your husband will turn around and become strong and sincere himself." Then he said, "Though a woman is an insignificant part of the society, if she remains strong she can turn the whole society. Just like ear," and he pulled his ear. "The ear is such a small part of the body. But if you pull the ear, the whole head comes. So in the same way, if you remain strong your husband will come to the right path."

But my relationship with my husband became more and more sour because he didn't really want to surrender to Krishna and I wanted to. I was very impressed with the devotees, their lifestyle, their austerities. I thought the devotees were really going somewhere. My life was empty and miserable; I wanted to do something exciting and I knew that Krishna consciousness would lead me to something more.

My husband was becoming impossible and I didn't want to stay with him. Although it's not acceptable in Indian society for a woman to leave her husband, I decided that I would have to leave him. There was no way I could stay with him, and devotees encouraged me, "Yes, you should leave him and move into the temple, Prabhupada won't mind." When Prabhupada found out about it, he said, "Oh, no, if she can't get along with her husband then she should go back to India, she should not come and live in the temple." When Satsvarupa told me that I said, "What?! I can't go back to India. If I go back to India I will never be able to be a devotee." Satsvarupa said, "I don't know what to tell you, maybe you should write a letter to Prabhupada."

So I wrote a long letter to Prabhupada, the first and last letter I ever wrote to him, saying, "You have accepted so many boys and girls. What is wrong with me? Why can't you accept me? What have I done wrong? You're telling me to go back to India, but if I go back to India my parents will never let me join the Movement, or even if I get married again I will never be able to worship Krishna the way you want your disciples to. You know how things in India are, everybody will spit on me because I left my husband, the social pressure is so strong. I feel like you are kicking me out, you don't accept me." I appealed to him severely. When Prabhupada read that letter he said, "All right, let her come. But she has to get married again." At that time I was so fried with married life I didn't want to hear about it.

I was Prabhupada's first Indian woman disciple and Prabhupada didn't want Indian people to think that he was breaking up families. But out of his kindness Prabhupada let me join, and a couple of months later I got initiated.

Once Bali Mardan told Prabhupada, "This Indian disciple of yours, she's a very good cook." I don't know why Bali said that – I didn't know about cooking, although I used to cook the Deities' evening offering. Prabhupada said, "Oh? So she should teach others how to cook. Every night there should be one lady with her learning to cook." Then Bali said, "Prabhupada, she's a good *pujari* too." Prabhupada said, "She should do that too." "Prabhupada, she's also a good book distributor." Prabhupada said, "She should do a little bit of everything." So I took that seriously and always had varied temple services.

In Vrindavana in 1977 Prabhupda was sick and devotees would see him in his room. At that time Prabhupada said, "Krishna is eternal, the holy name is eternal, and we are eternal. You chant Hare Krishna and you all go back to Godhead. That's all I have to say, I have nothing else to say." We were completely sad, thinking "Oh, my God, what's going to happen?"

During those weeks a couple of times I had eye contact with Prabhupada. He would always recognize the fact that I was there – his sense of awareness was amazing. Once Vaikunthanatha, one of Prabhupada's early disciples who had blooped for quite a while, came and was sitting at the back when we were in the courtyard having kirtan. The rest of us didn't even know that Vaikunthanatha was there, but Prabhupada saw him and asked him to come close. Vaikunthanatha sat at Prabhupada's feet. I was thinking how kind Prabhupada was. I remember one devotee didn't have *tilaka* on and he was sitting way back in the crowd and Prabhupada looked at him and said, "Go put *tilaka* on." We couldn't believe it, he was so aware in all these matters.

It was the month of Sravana and once Prabhupada was sitting in front of Krishna and Balarama while we were having kirtan inside in the temple room when a bunch of Rajasthani ladies, with big traditional skirts and jewellery, completely blocked Prabhupada's view of the Deities. These ladies were not aware of what was going on. Tamal Krishna Maharaja told me to tell them to move. I started to do that but Prabhupada gestured to me not to do it, to let them have darshan. He said, "No, don't stop them, let them have darshan. Why are you stopping them?" I said, "Tamal Krishna Maharaja told me to." But Prabhupada did not want it. It reminded me of the incident of the lady who stood on Lord Chaitanya's shoulder to take darshan of the Deity. Lord Chaitanya's followers were saying, "Oh, don't do that, you're committing offenses," but Lord Chaitanya said "No, let her be. She's so anxious to see Lord Jagannatha."

I have small kids and my husband has to work outside to support the family. The way I can remember Prabhupada is if I chant my rounds, follow the four regulative principles, give donations to the temple, and do some service for the Deities and for the temple. I distributed books for fifteen years. I distributed lots of books in my life and I have read those books. Now I want to live those books. We want to show to the world how we can also live a perfect life as a devotee, with Krishna in the center. We can set an example of how to live a good Krishna conscious *grihastha* life. I think this is one thing missing in our Society and in our lives, that we haven't shown to the world how we can live in Krishna consciousness. It's the most important preaching. I take care of my kids, and as much as possible I give them Krishna consciousness, and I think Prabhupada would be pleased with that. I see so many families breaking up in our Krishna conscious society and children taking drugs. It's disheartening. If I can make my kids Krishna conscious and continue with my devotional service, I think that's the best thing I can do and that's how I keep my link to Srila Prabhupada.

Once Prabhupada started to lecture about a prayer of Kunti Devi, the one about Mother Yashoda tying Krishna with a rope, and I was thinking, "Oh, now we're going to hear the nectar from Prabhupada." But Prabhupada talked about, "You're not this body." As a neophyte I used to think, "Oh, my God, this is so dry." But that's how Prabhupada preached. Prabhupada never told us about *gopi bhava* or *rasa* with Krishna, or *rasa* with the *gopis,* or what is my position as a *gopi*. Personally I don't want to say anything that's not in Prabhupada's books and I don't want to do any thing different from what Prabhupada has said. Prabhupada told us, "I've said everything that's got to be said in my books." To tell the truth I don't even like to read any books besides Prabhupada's. If we just keep praying to Prabhupada, remaining indebted to him, Prabhupada and Krishna will help us.

When I chant, I think, "Just see, every time I mention the name of Krishna, Krishna is hearing and it's pleasing Him. And chanting and kirtan are going on all over the world. Devotees are singing the *mangala-arati samsara* prayers in Florida, in New York, in Los Angeles, in India. Prabhupada has this vibration going on all around the world. I pray to

Krishna that when I die, I'm completely surrounded by devotees and I'm chanting the holy name. That's all I pray, that I'm not somewhere in the street with nobody around. I'm very afraid of this material world, because it's such a bad place, but I'm constantly praying to Krishna to get me out of this world and I hope that I don't have to take birth again.

Over the years when I see how devotees have died, I see that Prabhupada taught us how to die. We don't realize how much we are indebted to him.

Postscript: While floating down the pristine Itchatuknee River in Florida, Sunita devi dasi suffered a major heart attack and passed away peacefully on the river bank, surrounded by devotees who were chanting the holy names of Krishna.

Surabhi devi dasi

In Amsterdam in 1971 Surabhi, who was from Australia, met the devotees. There used to be beautiful paintings on the wall, one of Prabhupada and one of Bhaktisiddhanta and Surabhi would chant and look at them. By the time she met Prabhupada, she already loved him because the devotees talked so wonderfully about him. Everyone emanated love for Srila Prabhupada, so it just rubbed off.

We went to London in August 1971 and devotees from all over Europe had come to see Srila Prabhupada. I became very, very attached to him because he was so kind to us all the time. Every part of Europe had come there because they had all been waiting. The devotees in Amsterdam had been waiting about eight months to get initiated, and I had only been in the temple for two months. So it was amazing how I got that opportunity.

Me and Kishori used to talk about being initiated, and Kishori used to say, "What name would you like to have?" I said, "I really like the pictures of Krishna with all the animals. I'd like to be one of Krishna's animals." She said, "Oh, I really like Krishna and the *gopis*. I want to be one of Krishna's *gopis*." Every few days we'd talk about it. Then I said, "We shouldn't really care what kind of name we get. Srila Prabhupada will give us a name that's a nice name anyway."

On my initiation day, all the Holland devotees got initiated. I was a bit afraid because I wasn't really confident in large crowds and when I was in that room, there must have been over a hundred devotees. Prabhupada said, "So your name is Surabhi devi dasi, the name of the transcendental cow, the giver of abundance of milk." And then he looked at me because I was just sitting there. I had my hands folded and I was looking up and he said, "Don't be afraid. If you follow this process, you will go back home, back to Godhead at the end of this life." He said it in such a kind way, looking at me so kindly like a father.

One morning I was going on the morning walk with him in the little park nearby. A devotee said, "Do you see that Srila Prabhupada is glowing?" and I said, "Yes." He's got kind of like an effulgence around his head, and when we were walking in that park you actually could distinctly see it. There was an effulgence around him.

When it was time for us to go back to Amsterdam, Prabhupada called us all in his room and told us to keep distributing magazines and spreading Krishna consciousness.

About two years later Prabhupada came to France at Fontenay-aux-Roses. Devotees had a room on the ground floor which was used as the temple room, and we were all there with Prabhupada. We didn't worry about men and women, we just stood naturally anywhere. So I went as close as I could to Srila Prabhupada and sat down. We had never read the Sanskrit during class before. Prabhupada pulled out the *Bhagavatam* and read the Sanskrit. Then he said, "Okay, you're next," and he gave the book to a man. I thought, "Oh, my God, the ladies are probably going to chant." And then I thought, "Oh, my God, they're going to give it to me because I'm the closest! Oh, no!" I felt like crawling under the carpet. Anyway, someone gave me the book and I tried to read the Sanskrit for the first time in my life. Prabhupada was so caring and sweet and just like a father. He was encouraging me and reading it with me. Half the time he read it, and in between I was reading it. Then at the end he said, "Very good." He was so merciful because he could see I was so nervous. He was so kind like that. Even if you could just sweep the floor well or wash the temple, he would be saying, "You are doing such wonderful service," even if you couldn't do anything much. He would encourage you even if it was only a little thing.

In 1973 Prabhupada went to Amsterdam and he offered *arati* to the newly installed Deities. I saw the tears come down Prabhupada's eyes–tears were flowing down his eyes–and I thought that was so amazing. At the installation, Prabhupada was really angry because they didn't have any flowers or yogurt and the altar was too short.

I thought, "Prabhupada's so mad, I've got to do something. I used to live here, I know where the yogurt man is." So I ran down the road to the yogurt man and I said, "Have you got some yogurt?" He said, "No, the devotees bought it all." Then I ran down the road to another place, and I think I might have got a little bit and I brought it all the way back. I just didn't want Prabhupada to be upset.

In Germany, 1973 or 1974, we got to go out on the morning walks with Prabhupada. One day he had been out on a morning walk and he came in and it was so, so quiet, you could have heard a pin drop. I thought, "Oh, someone should be doing kirtan." So I started a kirtan and as soon as I did,

Prabhupada turned around and he nodded at me. For me, Prabhupada was the kindest person I've ever met, just like a real loving father.

The *sankirtana* devotees would go out on the big VW buses. Prabhupada asked Hamsaduta, "What are the devotees eating on *sankirtana*?" At that time, we were buying bread because we'd be away six days a week. He said, "They have bread, and they make something." Prabhupada said, "Well, the bread is *karmi* bread. The devotees shouldn't be eating that. See if they can try to make it themselves." So then after that we didn't take bread anymore. We made our own bread. We would make it with a little baking powder. We'd make loaves of bread and cook ourselves.

I went traveling with some devotees as part of the Hare Krishna Festivals in a large van that carried all the props and cooking equipment. In Sweden, Prabhupada came and said, "What have you made?" and then looked at all the *prasadam*. He said, "Oh, what kind of drink is this?" And they said, "A strawberry drink, Prabhupada." He tried it and he said, "Oh, very nice, but the strawberries aren't fresh." They said, "No, we took the strawberries from cans." Prabhupada said, "Try to always make fresh."

Every time I remember this pastime I cry. Prabhupada circumambulated the Mayapur temple and rang the bell. When everyone circumambulated around to the other side, I'd run to the opposite side so I could be there and see Prabhupada ring the bell. We were all chanting, "Prabhupada! Prabhupada! Prabhupada!" The more we said, "Prabhupada," the more he rang the bell, and the tears were just flowing down our eyes. We were just ecstatic. It was the most amazing experience. Each time he'd come around, he'd ring the bell more. Then on the last time, he just rang it and rang it and rang it and rang it. The devotees called out, "Prabhupada! Prabhupada! Prabhupada!" and his smile was getting bigger and bigger and bigger. He was ringing that bell for the pleasure of the devotees because the devotees were just going wild–all going wild. The more we were reciprocating with him, the more pleasure he was getting and the more pleasure we were getting. And he just kept on ringing that bell because he could see it. It was so amazing. There was so much love coming from him and so much love coming from us seeing him do that. That was such a wonderful pastime. It was just so beautiful. That's my favorite pastime of Srila Prabhupada. Every time I see the film of this moment, it's so heart-wrenching.

I traveled with Srila Prabhupada on the train to Hyderabad. We stayed in the Surabhi Hotel and we had *surabhi* cows outside and we had Surabhi dasi inside. That was funny. Prabhupada came out of the room and was talking to a few devotees, and he kept on looking over at us (women disciples) and commenting to a few. When we were going back on the bus each woman said, "Oh, Prabhupada looked right at me like he was talking to me." And I said, "Yeah, Prabhupada did that to me, too. Each woman felt Prabhupada was looking at them, and it was very nice.

Srila Prabhupada was always very kind to us. He didn't see our woman's body. He just saw us as spirit souls and that we had come to him and taken shelter of him and we wanted to go back to Krishna. That was all he was interested in. He didn't see us as women, and he never treated us unkindly. He always treated us very, very nicely and made us feel cared for and loved. We always remember that and we want that it can be like that again, that Prabhupada's mood is still there and that ladies get treated nicely like he used to treat us.

Svarga devi dasi

In the early 1970s, Svarga walked away from her old life and wholeheartedly took up the process of Krishna consciousness that Prabhupada provided within his temples. By living in the temple she received what this extraordinary person, Srila Prabhupada, was giving and made rapid progress. Krishna consciousness, she felt, was a great but not easily understood blessing. Her family thought she was seriously ill.

Prabhupada planted the seed of bhakti in me that totally shaped my life. My relationship and connection to Prabhupada is through *bhakti-yoga*. The process of bhakti and Srila Prabhupada are practically integral, and whatever bhakti I've imbibed is what I'll carry with me after I leave this body. Prabhupada's level of love is so complete it enhances my trust in him and acceptance of the process he gave. By his grace he makes me receptive to his gift of bhakti.

After many years, I deliberately dismantled my institutional identity because I was identifying with the institution more than the process of bhakti. Now, rather than sacrificing my self to imbibe bhakti, I include my self in imbibing bhakti. An important aspect of bhakti is being aware of yourself because it's yourself that you're surrendering. In other words, I see my shortcomings, my inglorious aspects, and accept them. I use the lens Prabhupada gave me for seeing life and, because I continue to grow in the process of bhakti, I feel internally connected with him. He continues to provide the basis for my spiritual advancement.

When you're growing up, at some point you have to leave home and figure out for yourself what nourishes you. In Krishna consciousness I have to give myself the room and space to reassess, "Okay, what's surrender?" As I move on my perspectives change, my emphasis changes. Today, the values Prabhupada gave me are the values I choose to adhere to still. Prabhupada's teachings are as beneficial as knowing him as a person: What he said is as important as his personality. We need to follow his teachings carefully.

I want to develop a consciousness of appreciation and I find the strength to do that in japa.

Syamasundari devi dasi

In 1975, at a Hare Krishna program near Johannesburg, twenty-year-old Syamasundari watched "The Hare Krishna People" movie and looked at Srila Prabhupada's books.

When I first saw Srila Prabhupada's picture on the back of the *Krsna* book I was attracted because he looked completely different from other swamis that had visited South Africa. Immediately I became a Life Member and from then on started practicing: reading, offering *prasadam*, eating separately from my family, and visiting the Johannesburg temple.

When I saw Prabhupada humbly offered *pranams* to audiences in South Africa, I was attracted by his humility. He left such an impression on me I couldn't get him out of my mind. I only wanted Krishna consciousness in my life, but my relatives were trying to get me married and giving me an extremely difficult time. I moved in to the Yeoville temple and the devotees, excited to have an Indian girl, took care of me. I was a young *brahmacharini*, and from *mangala-arati* until I took rest I'd make Life Members, do school programs, and sell BTGs. Sometime later Prabhupada initiated me and I married Riddha Prabhu.

I've brought up five children and three of them are initiated. Chanting the Hare Krishna *maha-mantra*, serving, and studying Prabhupada's books have kept me going through the years. Srila Prabhupada inspires me and every day I pray to the Deities to keep me close to him and to never let me leave ISKCON.

Prabhupada planted many seeds. He left us valuable devotee mentors – advanced souls who are good examples – and he left us his books. We can all study Srila Prabhupada's books, take shelter there, and maintain the traditional standard he gave us.

Tadit devi dasi

Tadit, along with a friend, drove from Denver to San Francisco to attend Ratha-yatra. The rath carts, Jagannatha, and the twelve-foot Lord Caitanya Deity overwhelmed her. When a devotee threw the huge rose garland from the Lord Chaitanya Deity, thousands of people wanted it but Tadit caught it. She took that garland home and kept it in her room, touched that Krishna would let her get it.

I had met the devotees in Denver and was chanting sixteen rounds, but it took me over a year to move into the temple. Once I moved in, things moved fast. Three months later Prabhupada initiated me; he said Tadit, a name for

Radharani, meant, "lightning over the Yamuna River." Four months after I'd moved in I got married; I was twenty-one, and my husband, Svavasa, the *sankirtana* leader, was also twenty-one. A year after I'd moved in I received *brahmana*.

In 1975 I missed seeing Prabhupada in Atlanta and I missed him in Denver, but when we were in Atlanta we had had an unbelievable, world-famous *sankirtana* day where we distributed three thousand big books in the airport. It was mystical, as though Krishna took over the airport. The next day they closed down the airport. I wrote Prabhupada telling him we were concentrating on distributing his books, asked if I could name our son Acharya, and sent him a little gift. Prabhupada wrote back that he enjoyed the slippers and *kaupina* and was happy about the book distribution. And he said, "Yes, the name Acharya is approved by me, this is a very auspicious birth."

The more I observe what Prabhupada did and the more I try to understand who Srila Prabhupada is, the more I'm amazed. Each year I realize a little more how carefully and brilliantly he introduced this perfect process, how he constructed it like a lotus flower that's opening up, and how this process could uplift every living entity on the planet. There's not a half hour of a day that goes by when I don't think of Prabhupada. I have a craving, a yearning, to know about him that leads me to different aspects of understanding and serving him.

Prabhupada gave everything to us: how to discriminate, what proper action is. I want to do the right thing, especially when I'm dealing with devotees, so I consult Prabhupada's books almost every day and try to use what little intelligence I have to understand his mood. The more I understand, the more I can deal properly and Prabhupada's books are my only real reference. He took care to give us the perfect thing, and I don't want to mishandle it.

In this process, I have an ongoing appreciation of this soul. How in the world did we get the mercy to contact him? It doesn't matter who you are and what you're doing, because Prabhupada touched you, you touch me, I touch somebody else, and in that way Prabhupada has touched everybody. That's how profound this process is, and all we have to do is pass it on without messing it up. Prabhupada's intelligence is beyond anything. And he is the embodiment of humility.

Taruni devi dasi

Taruni was living in New York's East Village when she saw Prabhupada and the devotees chanting in Tompkins Square Park. She chanted along and then went with them to the temple.

I had learned the *maha-mantra* from hearing Allen Ginsberg chant it for an hour in some hall in New York so I was chanting before I met Srila Prabhupada, but the devotees' charisma was attractive. I spoke with them about eating whole grains and their mood gave me an uplifting feeling.

My husband, Yadunandana, and I moved to Athens to be with nature. He worked at the Student Union where someone told him, "I've invited Swami Bhaktivedanta to lecture. Could he stop in your home on the way to get some refreshments and use the bathroom?" My husband said, "Sure." Srila Prabhupada sat in our front yard and his disciples sat in a semi-circle around him. I was bringing out a bowl of fruit salad for them when I saw Srila Prabhupada and he saw me. The moment his spiritual eyes penetrated my heart, I fell in love. I felt some exalted thing, like there's a lot more than I'm aware of within my own self, and wanted to fall on the ground but I had the bowl so I had to walk.

After the refreshment, Srila Prabhupada came in our house, which was clean and simple, and seemed pleased. He sat in the rocking chair, looked around, and said, "See, we have no need for couches." He was regal and beautiful and his mood, his demeanor, his energy, was loving, sweet, and giving. He lectured at the college, walked out, drove away, and there went my heart. It was nighttime and the devotees chanted on a college green outside the hall and the mantra penetrated my heart. I felt like the heavens had opened up and all the love in the world that I could ever imagine was coming down and opening up my heart. Through some remarkable transcendental energy that Prabhupada carried and gave, I got great satisfaction in chanting so others could hear. Prabhupada had captured me. Yadunandana was also intrigued and happy.

In June 1969 we went to New Vrindavan when Srila Prabhupada was there. The ladies threw a *sari* on me and said, "Come quick, Prabhupada's having darshan upstairs." Srila Prabhupada was sitting at a little desk and the devotees piled in against the wall. He led a kirtan and gave the mantra to us, the wonderfulness, fullness, and beauty of Krishna. I was ecstatic. I wanted to get up and dance but I was afraid of my *sari* falling off. Prabhupada hooked me to the holy name.

Later he sat under the persimmon tree. I was stunned by his presence and couldn't believe the import of what he said: he answered all our questions and made sense of the mystery of life. His presence was kindly, inviting, stable, and giving, and his mercy was powerful. From my little association with him I knew the proper mood.

I loved to see Prabhupada in this natural setting and feel his wonderful, simple, intimate mercy. The way he would hold his *dhoti* up or skip down the steps was sweet and fatherly. I felt his majesty. Once I asked him,

"Would you marry us, Srila Prabhupada?" He said, "*Ohhh*? You are not married?" His eyes got big, and he looked gorgeous. I got flustered and said, "Yes, yes, but we would like you to marry us." He graciously said yes. He married us and it was peaceful and homey sitting in that farmhouse temple room while Prabhupada did the fire sacrifice. I felt safe under Prabhupada's protection and shelter. His presence surcharged everything and I knew I was rightly situated. When I didn't see him again personally, I felt his presence when I smelled the camphor, saw the Deities, heard the mantras, and associated with his sincere followers. His happiness was the joy of my heart, his displeasure the destruction of my heart.

Once Srila Prabhupada wrote me, "You have enough milk, you have enough fresh produce, you have good association, you have fresh air, you have spiritual life. Practically speaking, the needs of your life are fulfilled. Now keep it nice." Sometimes I'd be in the throes of despondency and his fatherly nature, his love and care and all wrapped up with his instruction would penetrate my heart. Then I'd think I needed to be stronger, try harder and go on.

In another letter he wrote,

"My dear Taruni dasi, Please accept my blessings. I beg to acknowledge receipt of your letter dated 21 January 1970, and your writing encourages me that if you try you can write some articles for BTG. I want that every one of my disciples should engage in reading and writing about Krishna consciousness. Every one of you must have sufficient engagement 24 hours. Otherwise your mind will be attracted by Maya. The greatest allurement of Maya is sex urge, and therefore I have recommended most of my students to get married. Not only marriage can pacify restless living entities, but he or she must have sufficient working engagement for Krishna. Please try therefore to read and write on Krishna consciousness and take care of your child. I understand that on account of your going away outside of the temple there was some misunderstanding between you and your husband. But I know your husband is very good boy, sober your husband. So whatever is done is done. Forget both of you. But henceforward you shall always be engaged in some work. Do not be disturbed. So those kinds of things, Chaitanya Mahaprabhu's advice is not to be agitated. One has to become humbler than the grass, more tolerant than the tree and thus chant Hare Krishna mantra. Live peacefully and chant Hare Krishna. There is no problem. Husband, wife, child, good place, good association, so everything is there. Don't be disturbed in mind. I hope this will meet you in good health."

That always stayed with me, this idea that if there's a misunderstanding there's to be tolerance, there's to be engagement, that it's largely my responsibility to keep things on an even keel. Srila Prabhupada's presence always loomed in my life. He was always very practical and always a gentleman. When he left us, he kindly left his mercy behind.

Tilaka devi dasi

Tilaka first met the devotees in Washington, D.C. in 1969 when she was seventeen. Then, during her Christmas vacation, she visited the Frederick Street temple in San Francisco.

The devotees welcomed me and encouraged me to take Krishna consciousness seriously and when the temple got a women's ashram I moved in. In 1970 devotees from all over came to San Francisco to meet Prabhupada at the airport, where we offered him a beautiful gardenia garland. After the San Francisco Ratha-yatra, during a meeting between Srila Prabhupada and the West Coast temple presidents, I overheard a devotee say, "Jaya Prabhupada!" and Prabhupada say, "Don't just say 'Jaya Prabhupada,' glorify me by your activities."

It was ecstatic to see Prabhupada, hear his lectures, do the most menial service for him, or taste the remnants of his food. To be seen by Srila Prabhupada felt very special because his vision was infused with Krishna's mercy and he saw us as eternal servants of Krishna and not the material body. Because of that vision of seeing *jivera svarupa haya nityera krsna dasa*, he was able to relate to people from many different social and cultural backgrounds.

In Juhu in 1974 I was part of a group of devotees that went on a morning walk with Srila Prabhupada. On returning to the temple complex, one of Prabhupada's Western women disciples was talking with an Indian man inside the gate and Prabhupada said, "Just see. She is not an ordinary woman, she is preaching." Prabhupada was proud of his disciples.

On the day of the grand opening of the Krishna-Balaram Mandir, many high-class Brijbasis were sitting comfortably on chairs in a sunny section of the temple courtyard. Srila Prabhupada sat with them, smiling, relaxed, and obviously relishing the conversation, which was interspersed with verses from his books. That very special day that Prabhupada had waited so long for was filled with brightness. Later Prabhupada offered the first *arati* to Krishna and Balarama.

My husband was president of the St. Louis temple in 1975-76 when the Radha-Damodara Party, which was crisscrossing the country, would often stop there. Devotees on that party gave discouraging and often embarrassing classes to the *brahmachari*s about women and householders. It became unbearably uncomfortable and oppressive; women were treated like ghosts. Later I was in Mayapur when Tamal Krishna Goswami discussed the householders and women with Srila Prabhupada. Tamal Krishna Goswami said, "Well, what should I do, go to China?" Srila Prabhupada said, "Yes, you can go to China." We women were thrilled that Prabhupada had come to our rescue.

By hearing Srila Prabhupada's *bhajanas* and lectures and associating with devotees we can remain enthusiastic. The special mercy of Kali-yuga is the technology of the personal tape player because every day we can go about our activities and at the same time hear Srila Prabhupada, who had so much feeling in his voice. We're fortunate to have Srila Prabhupada's books and these recordings. The facility that we have to hear is a first in Vaishnava history.

Titiksa devi dasi

When Titiksa first saw Srila Prabhupada he was sitting on the ratha cart at the Chicago Ratha-yatra. She thought, "I know the most important thing is to serve Prabhupada."

I looked at the devotee fanning Prabhupada, and he looked at me and held up the fan as if to say, "Do you want to fan him?" I said yes, climbed up on the ratha cart and fanned Srila Prabhupada.

During Prabhupada's famous Atlanta visit, I dressed Gaura-Nitai every day. By then I'd been Gaura-Nitai's *pujari* for a couple of years. When Prabhupada first walked in the temple room, he greeted the Deities and then sat on the *vyasasana* and cried. He could see that Lord Chaitanya was personally there in the Deity – in Podunk Atlanta. Some of Prabhupada's servants said, "Wow, we're so fortunate because Prabhupada doesn't display such ecstasy very often."

In Atlanta Prabhupada played the *mridanga* while he sang "Parama Karuna." He asked, "Are you recording?" and someone said, "Yes." He said, "Play it back," and the devotee played it back. Prabhupada played along with the tape and taught all of us "Parama Karuna."

At a Sunday Feast somebody asked, "Prabhupada, what pleases Krishna the most?" All the book distributors were thinking, "He's going to say 'distribute my books.' " But instead he said, "That you love Krishna." We were all delighted because Prabhupada's answer included everybody.

When I went to India in 1976 I prayed, "I need to talk to my eternal guru. Krishna, when I'm in India please make an arrangement so I can see and talk to Prabhupada." In Mayapur, I got dried fruits and nuts for Prabhupada. Sukhada and I arranged them on Prabhupada's heavy stone plate. We took it in to Prabhupada, who was in his room having a darshan with Indian guests. I put the plate on Prabhupada's desk and said, "Prabhupada, this is from your disciple, my husband Gadi dasa. He's sending it with his devotion." Prabhupada smiled in acceptance and then distributed the dried fruits and nuts to all the guests.

After Mayapur we went to Vrindavan, where one day I was one of the first devotees to go into Prabhupada's room for darshan. Himavati, whose husband, Hamsadutta, had just taken *sannyasa* in Mayapur, was sitting next to Prabhupada and Prabhupada was taking care of her like a daughter. He was talking and laughing with her, giving her total shelter and love. Whatever bad feelings I had about Hamsadutta taking *sannyasa* melted away when I saw how sweet and fatherly Prabhupada was with Himavati.

A Life Member at a preaching center Gadi and I started couldn't accept that Lord Chaitanya is nondifferent from Radha and Krishna. So in the darshan, when Prabhupada said, "Are there any questions?" I said, "Srila Prabhupada, there's an Indian gentleman who asked me to ask you how Lord Chaitanya is the same as Radha and Krishna if He doesn't play a flute?" Prabhupada said, "Who is this nonsense!" He told Adi Kesava to get the *Chaitanya-charitamrita*. While Adi Kesava was getting the book I said, "Prabhupada, if we worship the Deity of Gaura-Nitai, will we get the same liberation as those who worship Radha and Krishna?" He said, "Yes. And what is this liberation? Isn't chanting Hare Krishna enough?" Inside I was thinking, "No," but I said, "Yes." Then Prabhupada nodded at Adi Kesava to read the verse "*sri-krsna-caitanya radha-krsna nahe anya*," and the purport. Adi Kesava read for twenty minutes, not only for my benefit but also for the benefit of the many Indians in the room.

Tripti devi dasi

Tripti dasi started visiting the temple in Portland, Oregon in 1973. About a year later she moved into the Denver, Colorado temple and received initiation in 1974.

I was in high school and had met the devotees. I would get ready for school while listening to Prabhupada's lectures. One time my mom came into the kitchen while I was making breakfast. She stood there for a few minutes and said, "Can you understand this?" "No, most of it I can't, but it doesn't matter." I just kept listening and trying to hear.

During that same period I incorporated studying Prabhupada's books into my school curriculum because I had an independent study program. I read the *Bhagavad-gita* over and over. I didn't understand it, but I knew that I had to read it.

The first time I saw Srila Prabhupada was at the Ratha-yatra in San Francisco in 1973. Prabhupada danced on the stage and threw flowers out to the crowd. I was too far from the stage to catch one, and I was really disappointed about that.

In 1975 at the Krishna-Balaram Mandir all the women who were receiving second initiation went to Srila Prabhupada's room. We each had a sheet of paper with the Gayatri mantra on it. Prabhupada went over it word-by-word with us collectively. I was sitting right next to him on his left. He had everyone hold up their hand to demonstrate that they were understanding how to count.

In Mayapur, we would circumambulate the altar and Prabhupada would always ring the bell. He was always so delighted. It just seemed like he had much energy when he would do that. As he would go around each time he would stop and ring the bell. It seemed to tickle him, like he was having so much fun doing it.

Distributing Prabhupada's books gave me impetus to continue with Krishna consciousness. I had to always be vigilant about my state of mind, to hold onto my Krishna consciousness, or it didn't work. You knew immediately if you were off track by people's response to you. Book distribution was almost like an addiction because it forced me to focus on Prabhupada and Krishna to avoid the pain of people's responses being negative!

Somehow by Prabhupada's mercy I have been able to hold onto the awareness that Krishna consciousness is the highest, greatest gift, and that I have no idea how fortunate I am to have come in contact with a spiritual master. Many people's intelligence gets taken away and they don't remember this. They criticize the Movement or they criticize Srila Prabhupada. By Prabhupada's grace that hasn't happened to me.

I remember sitting in Prabhupada's lectures or in his room when he would have darshans and different people would come. It didn't matter if it was a formal class or an informal setting. I would close my eyes and become aware of how hearing Prabhupada in person was no different from hearing him on his cassettes. I understood it was the same. I never felt bereft. Like some devotees say, "Oh, I never got to see Srila Prabhupada," or, "I never got to do this or that." I think, "Well, of course you did. Every time we read his books or listen to his tapes we have his association."

I've had two exceptional experiences with Prabhupada's presence. Both of them were life and death situations. One time I thought I was going to drown–really thought that that was imminent. Instead of panicking, which is common, I got a sense of calmness and peacefulness. Prabhupada was there with me. The lifeguard reached in–I was out in the ocean–and grabbed me. I remember saying, "Prabhupada, I'm not ready for this."

Another time I was reading the verse in the *Bhagavad-gita* where Krishna says that the devotee doesn't have to fear anything. At the end of this verse he says, "Do not fear." As I reached that point in the verse, I actually audibly outside of myself heard Srila Prabhupada say, "Do not fear." Then I was okay.

So those two experiences–along with everything else–has given me some long-standing sense of the authenticity of Krishna consciousness. Personal experience, I guess is the phrase. The *Gita* describes that a devotee has an experience of the Absolute Truth. That's what it is–you experience the Absolute directly.

Tushita devi dasi

Tushita first came to the Los Angeles temple on December 10th, 1975 when she was sixteen.

In June 1976, Srila Prabhupada came. Waiting for him at the airport, I said to myself, "I'm not going to get emotional – it's not like he's Jesus Christ." I thought Prabhupada might get puffed up if I over glorified him. Then when he arrived, I immediately felt flat on the ground saying, *namah om visnu padaya krsna presthaya bhutale* like my soul was crying out. I realized that Prabhupada deserved all the glorification he got.

Later, in the balcony of the temple room, I was sitting on the far right side thinking, "If Srila Prabhupada is really a pure devotee, he'll look up at me in the balcony." The whole eleven days he was there he never once glanced or smiled at me. After he left I realized that I was very noticeable in the balcony – it was almost impossible for him *not* to see me. I felt he didn't look at me on purpose because he understood that I wanted recognition.

Prabhupada's room was upstairs from the *pujari* room, and he used to walk through the *pujari* room to go to his garden. Once, as he came through, he stopped in front of us, looked at us while we were making *tulasi* garlands, and said, "You are all fully engaged?" We said, "*Jaya!* Yes, Srila Prabhupada."

It was easy for me to be personal with Prabhupada because I washed his plates, and every time he walked I'd collect his dust, put it in an envelope and write on it, "Prabhupada's Dust." I had access to oceans of Prabhupada's remnants – flower garlands, toothbrushes, toothpaste, soap.

When Prabhupada left his body, I knew that it didn't mean he was going to leave me because he'd left me so many books. I was only nineteen, and really didn't know what love was. I felt that my pangs of separation from Prabhupada would increase as the years went by – that I'd understand more as I got older. And it's true – as the years go by, my attachment to Prabhupada gets stronger. He is protecting me from sinful activities by always engaging me in Krishna's service like following Ekadasis, attending the morning programs, hearing lectures, chanting Hare Krishna, and by his example of purity. Because of my devotional service and his example,

I don't go to the bar, I don't have illicit connection with the opposite sex, I don't take drugs. Srila Prabhupada is the rock and roll star, guru, teacher, and father that I was always looking for. By his instructions, he's telling me and every living entity how to live life. It seems every conditioned soul would want to know what Srila Prabhupada is saying.

I'd like to follow him and take shelter of his pink lotus feet wherever he goes, whether in the spiritual world with Krishna or in the material world preaching. I'd like to follow him birth after birth after birth.

Urmila devi dasi

From the time she was four, Urmila was looking for God. If somebody said, "What do you want to do?" She'd say, "I want to be spiritually perfect. I want to find God." They'd say, "Don't you want to get married, have kids, have a career?" She'd say, "Nope, I don't want any of that. I just want to find God."

My first contact with Prabhupada was in 1967 when I was twelve and would listen to him chanting on the Happening Album playing in Alan Coleman's shop on the Lower East Side. I'd ask, "What is this record? Who is this?" My next contact was through the Radha Krishna Temple album, which I heard on the radio. Prabhupada's picture was on the album and my initial response to it was negative. I didn't like the whole idea of a guru and thought someone who says he's a guru must be proud. I thought, "Prabhupada must be very proud." When I'd play the record, I'd skip the "Gurvastaka" prayers.

Through getting a *Bhagavad-gita* I decided to move into the temple but I didn't want to get initiated. Soon after I moved in I got married; my husband was already second initiated and in his association I started thinking, "How am I going to be able to find God and become spiritually perfect without a spiritual master?" Gradually my relationship with Prabhupada developed.

When Prabhupada first came to Chicago in the summer of 1974, a little more than a year after I'd moved in, I was expecting a mystical experience. Prabhupada was sitting on the *vyasasana* giving class and I was fanning him. I felt, "Prabhupada has always been here because playing a tape of Prabhupada lecturing and listening to him lecture in person is exactly the same." I was hearing him directly but I felt like I was listening to a tape. I thought, "I want something different."

Later that morning my father, husband, and I met Srila Prabhupada in his room and I got to know him as a person. He was funny, laughing, casual, jovial, and exchanging affectionately with my father. I understood he cared about me personally, as an individual, and I felt a loving relationship with him.

My father asked why we give people *prasadam* and Prabhupada said, "Just like if you eat the food of a sick person, you will get their disease. If you eat Krishna's food, you will get Krishna's disease." My father thought he was only supposed to come to the temple if he was a devotee so he asked, "Can I come to the temple just to see my daughter and son-in-law?" Smiling, Prabhupada said, "They are loving Krishna. Chanting and dancing are symptoms of loving Krishna. You are loving them and they are loving Krishna, so two things equal to the same thing are equal to each other." Prabhupada's mood was light but I felt, "Prabhupada said I love Krishna, so it's just a question of time. Someday I'll love Krishna." That meeting changed my life. And it moved my father. He said, "Prabhupada's a genuine holy man." He enjoyed Prabhupada's company and became somewhat of a devotee.

Some years later my son Madhava, who was a baby, and I saw Srila Prabhupada off at the New York airport. Prabhupada was sitting on a couch in the VIP lounge talking with Satyabhama, Kirtanananda, Jayadvaita, and a few others while I was a couple feet away holding Madhava. I felt left out and was jealous of those devotees' intimate connection with Prabhupada. I thought, "They really know Prabhupada well," but it was also a very relaxed time getting to be with Prabhupada as a person again. During the kirtan Prabhupada transported everyone to the spiritual world. I forgot that I had a body and that I was in New York. Prabhupada was meditating on chanting and I thought, "Prabhupada is chanting for his guru." It was incredible. Then at some point in the kirtan my awareness flooded back: I was in New York holding a baby.

For about a year-and-a-half I dove into Srila Prabhupada's books and lectures and that deepened my relationship with him as much or more than when I personally saw him. Then in the summer of 1975 I went to Philadelphia for Ratha-yatra and to get Gayatri. At class one morning, the devotee reading from the *Bhagavatam* manuscript said, "Ajamila cried out three times loudly, 'Narayana! Narayana! Narayana!' " Prabhupada said, "What is this three times? I have not said three times. Once is sufficient." It was life-transforming for me to hear him say that calling out Krishna's name just once in helplessness is enough.

That same morning my father, husband, and I met with Prabhupada again. When he saw us, Prabhupada's whole face lit up as if we were his favorite people in the world. Like he was meeting a dear old friend he said to my father, "How are you now?" My father responded with similar exuberance and joy. As we were leaving Prabhupada said, "Good father, good daughter." Prabhupada saw something good and worthwhile in me; he was pleased with me.

When I got Gayatri mantra my husband was carrying Madhava and Prabhupada's attention went to Madhava. Prabhupada said, "He's laughing. He's very intelligent and fortunate." Prabhupada had me repeat the mantra and I thought, "I don't want to say it perfectly because Prabhupada will think I'm puffed up." To try to be humble I purposely made a mistake when I repeated the last line. Prabhupada looked utterly disgusted. I thought, "*Oop*, that wasn't the right thing to do." I said, "Prabhupada I want to preach and please you, but I have this little baby. It's hard to go out on book distribution." He said, "You must take care so you may not go out." The feeling I got from Prabhupada was, "This is really a stupid question."

The next time I saw Prabhupada was in the summer of 1976 when he came to New York for the Ratha-yatra. Again my father met Prabhupada. At one point Prabhupada pointed to me, my son was about a year-and-a-half. He said, "Just like this mother is loving her son without any expectation of return. In that way, you should love Krishna." My father said, "Will loving her son help her love Krishna?" Prabhupada said, "No, but loving Krishna will help her love her son." If we have Krishna as the center and are attached to Him, then we can love everyone else. If we love people on a mundane level, it doesn't help us love Krishna – it takes away from that love.

Somehow what Prabhupada said when I was with him was just what I needed to hear. His words changed me.

Urvasi devi dasi

Once, in the very crowded Sri Sri Radha-Damodara temple in Vrindavan, a pujari *was giving the Lord's garlands to some of the hundreds of devotees present. As Urvasi thought, "I want to bring a garland to Srila Prabhupada," the* pujari *walked straight to her and handed her a garland. She then brought it to Srila Prabhupada.*

Before I left for India, I was visiting my family in California when my mother, who's not a Hare Krishna devotee, said to me, "What can I give you to take to your spiritual master?" I wasn't sure, so I asked her what she thought. She said, "What if I made some guava jam from the fruit on my trees and you take that to him?" I agreed.

Once I arrived in Vrindavan I gave the jam to someone to give to Srila Prabhupada. Later on, that devotee was looking all over for me. He told me, "Srila Prabhupada was so happy to receive the guava jam. I told him it was from your mother, and he said that his mother used to make him guava jam." This was in April of 1975, when hundreds of devotees were present for the opening of the Krishna-Balaram temple, but Prabhupada had asked this devotee to get my mother's name and address, and later that day Srila

Prabhupada wrote my mother a letter thanking her for the jam. He also wrote, "Your daughter is doing nicely. Don't worry about her. I'm taking care of her, and she is engaged in the topmost devotional service for the Lord."

About seven years later, my mother's health declined. I was cooking and offering her meals, reading *Bhagavad-gita* to her, and talking to her about Krishna. Her passing was auspicious. During her final moments I put headphones on her and she passed away listening to the songs on the beautiful Srila Prabhupada Krishna Meditations album. I'd given her *tulasi* and holy water and I was chanting *japa* aloud to her at the time. I hope I have one fraction of that mercy when I pass away. I attribute her auspicious passing to her little bit of devotional service to Srila Prabhupada. Such is the potency of serving the pure devotee.

Uttama devi dasi

Uttama devi dasi would occasionally see devotees chanting on the streets, and would cross to the other side, so as not to be accosted. One day though, her husband, Partha dasa, took a Bhagavad-gita As It Is and Krsna book, Part Two out of the library. She relished the stories in the Krsna book, starting with the Shyamantaka Jewel, an awesome soap opera-like saga! Her husband wrote a letter to the nearest center, and in a seven-page reply, received an invitation to visit.

My husband and I joined the Krishna consciousness movement because we didn't want a mundane life. We married young and went on a spiritual quest. Very soon, we discovered Srila Prabhupada's books in a library, and after one visit to a temple, knew we had found our home.

A few months later, in December of 1973, Srila Prabhupada visited Los Angeles and so almost the whole Vancouver *yatra* drove there to see him. During *Srimad-Bhagavatam* class one morning, Srila Prabhupada was discussing the annihilation of the Yadu dynasty, and how in an intoxicated state, they fought with each other. He described that one could make a very nice wine out of rice! I was just about to vow never to take intoxication so I figured I would file that comment in "To be Understood Later."

The next day, after making my vows, Srila Prabhupada said, "Your name is Uttama dasi. Uttama means beyond this material world. Krishna is *uttama*. So, you are servant of, maidservant of Uttama, Krishna."

I quickly became absorbed in being a maidservant of the Deities and sewing outfits for the Lord. Who could ever imagine sewing clothes for God? Hopefully in a previous life, I wasn't sewing clothes for Kamsa.

My main relationship with Srila Prabhupada has been through his association in his books. They inspire me, guide me, answer my questions, and help me filter the misunderstandings of others. Like when there were two *brahmana* threads in mine and my husband's brahminical initiation letter. Some said, if Srila Prabhupada sent it, you should wear it and chant on it. Just don't let the men see it! I understood from reading Srila Prabhupada's books, and listening to many, many of his recorded talks while sewing, that probably, a secretary simply counted the names and put a matching amount of threads in the envelope.

Srila Prabhupada once commented that if one doesn't read all his books, they may fall down, back to material existence. I have found that the whole perspective I gained by reading them all, is invaluable. I gained a sense of Srila Prabhupada's person. His loving nature. Therefore, I have never been negatively triggered by reading that women are less intelligent. I have always felt valued by the important men in my life and have felt protected by them. So, when I read that women are less intelligent, my understanding is that, yes, sometimes I do make emotional decisions, and at those times, I may need the more rational perspective. If a person with a desire to control me in some way, were to tell me that, would I accept? No! Intelligence, Srila Prabhupada said, refers to the power to analyze things in their proper perspective.

Srila Prabhupada personally taught me how important the association of devotees is. Especially at the time of death. Srila Prabhupada requested that devotees come and be with him in his last days, and so our temple president offered us a ticket to Vrindavan. By this time, Srila Prabhupada was not able to come out, but my husband was able to go into his room every day, all day, and I was able to relish nectarine tidbits of pastimes shared by those fortunate souls in the rooms.

Then, one day during lunch *prasadam,* it was announced that the *kaviraja* estimated Srila Prabhupada only had hours left before he would leave his body. The men all flocked to Srila Prabhupada's room and the ladies assembled in the temple to chant and make sandalwood pulp for Srila Prabhupada. I have never been expert at grinding sandalwood, but I pray that somehow a few drops of my efforts were able to reach the body of His Divine Grace.

Quickly, someone arrived and said the women should also come in Srila Prabhupada's rooms. I pray Srila Prabhupada, that somehow, you also accepted a few drops of my chanting for your pleasure. You are so potent that even a few drops of devotional service accepted by you, is enough to grant one a place in the spiritual world. Now it's up to me to take advantage of that.

The singing was subdued, with us somehow all chanting in unison, one tune for hours.

I was so hoping you would just sit up and say, "Thank you very much" like you do at the end of every lecture and tell us you are well now. But it's me that needs to thank you! I am well, now, after lifetimes of suffering in a mundane existence.

Vajresvari devi dasi

Vajresvari was initially disappointed when her darshan with Srila Prabhupada was cancelled. What she thought was her misfortune turned out to be a gift.

In 1976, Srila Prabhupada was visiting New Vrindaban. I had been at New Vrindaban for Prabhupada's 1972 and 1974 visits, and the closest I'd gotten to him was offering flowers at his *guru-puja*. My daughter, Rati Dasi, had been born in January of that same year and was too young to receive a *prasadam* cookie; she wasn't six months old yet, and not supposed to be eating grains. I considered *prasadam* from the guru's hand an exception to that rule so I wasn't going to pass up this opportunity to come close to him again. In my eagerness for any possible contact with Srila Prabhupada, I stood in line holding Rati dasi, along with the other mothers who also had very young children. When I nervously stepped up to Prabhupada's *vyasasana,* my baby daughter, who was seeing Srila Prabhupada for the first time, was apparently having her own experience of it, and would not reach out to accept the cookie! So, I held her little baby arm with my hand and extended it toward the cookie Srila Prabhupada was offering. But she still wouldn't open her hand! I continued to extend her hand toward the cookie, but she was not cooperating. I was embarrassed. After a few moments Srila Prabhupada placed the cookie in my hand.

The next time cookie distribution happened I eagerly waited my turn. As I approached the *vyasasana,* instead of attempting to get my daughter to take the cookie, I extended my own hand. This time Srila Prabhupada seemed to know that Rati would take it herself. Without any hesitation Prabhupada offered Rati the cookie and she immediately accepted it. Prabhupada's actions showed that he knew exactly what was going on. I felt like a fool; once again I had not understood the mind of my daughter. Yet, feeling like a fool felt good knowing that his teaching was always out of love.

In the summer of 1976 I was still at New Vrindaban. Srila Prabhupada was visiting for about ten days. All the New Vrindaban residents were scheduled to attend small darshans, as there was about a hundred of us, so we were divided up alphabetically. Because my name, Vajresvari, began with the letter V, I was scheduled on the last day of his visit. I looked forward to this darshan every day, all day long. This would be the first time I would be with Srila Prabhupada in a setting more intimate than the temple room. I kept my hope to see him close to my heart.

Traditionally, flowers are offered at such darshans, but being poor I couldn't buy any. That morning I walked through the New Vrindaban woods and pastures and found the most exquisite tiny blooms! They were weeds, really, but I gathered them into a bouquet and tied them carefully together with a long piece of grass. I thought they were lovely. We all rode up from Bahulaban to the house where Prabhupada was staying. When we arrived, someone in saffron told us the darshan had been canceled because Prabhupada wasn't feeling well. I was devastated. We all were.

After a while, a car came to take us back. I placed my little bouquet of flowers on the fence and hoped he would see it. Everyone piled into the car, but there wasn't room for all of us. I was left standing with a few others to wait for the car to drop the first load off and return for us. I decided to walk the two miles instead as I was too upset to simply stand there. I walked quickly, trying not to cry. This was the worst day of my life. I thought, what bad karma I have, I missed my opportunity to see Prabhupada. I didn't know what to do with my feelings. Should I be angry at Prabhupada for not being able to be present for me? But how could I be angry with my guru? He had thousands of disciples and had just held darshan consecutively for days in a row, taking karma from so many of his devoted students. Was the messenger in saffron responsible for making the decision that had deprived me of an opportunity to see my spiritual master? I somehow got through the day.

The next day I rose early, as usual, and had all sixteen rounds of *japa* done before *mangala-arati*. By 7 am, the time Srila Prabhupada would give class, I even finished my temple *seva* of doing laundry for over a hundred devotees in a big industrial washing machine. I went to the temple, and Srila Prabhupada was singing "Jaya Radha Madhava." Everyone was already seated and it was very crowded. I could have gone inside, but I needed to be available to check on my baby daughter who was sleeping in my room nearby. As soon as I saw Srila Prabhupada on his *vyasasana* I bowed down in the doorway of the temple room. When I stood up, in that crowded temple room of over a hundred devotees, I received my intimate darshan. We were communicating through our eyes! Srila Prabhupada must have seen me walking down the road, known how heartbroken I was, and that I didn't know what to do with my thoughts about the cancelation. I was uncomfortable even remembering it, because I had wanted to blame someone for my misfortune. And then, he seemed to ask me how I wanted to serve. I knew I wanted to live an independent life away from the ashram, live in the mainstream, and be Krishna conscious. Prabhupada tilted his head back and forth the way Indian people do when they are saying "Okay, no big deal." And then he left my glance.

So my misfortune turned out to be a gift. I felt so close to my guru, so understood, so completely embraced and accepted for who I was, so loved for whatever I was able to be in that moment. I have recalled these moments over and over for years. They have brought many tears of release of pain, and of the blessings of my enlightened teacher.

Varuni devi dasi

Varuni first saw Srila Prabhupada in New York in the summer of 1972. She was from a temple of twelve devotees and in New York she was overwhelmed to be among five hundred devotees.

I joined the Movement when I was sixteen and I'd always worshipped pictures of Srila Prabhupada, but when I saw him in New York, there he was: a pure devotee who was a person with feelings and everything else that comes with being a person. It was a far out realization that made Krishna consciousness even more relishable. Seeing him in New York put everything together for me.

Srila Prabhupada taught us everything. Laxmimoni, my temple president's wife, told me: "Srila Prabhupada's your friend, your father. Everything that we know we've learned from him." I was raised a Catholic, and no one in the Church could answer my doubts and questions, but when I started studying the philosophy of Krishna consciousness, it all made sense and attracted me. Since I was taught that God is a person it was easy for me to accept Krishna as the Supreme Person. I assumed that in a short time the whole world would be Krishna conscious. Then I found out that Krishna consciousness is like a diamond: diamonds are rare and not everyone can afford them. That's what keeps me enlivened in Krishna consciousness.

My husband and I both work. He has a big poster of Srila Prabhupada in his office and I have pictures of Krishna on my desk. Everybody knows we're devotees. Every Saturday my husband preaches in Indian people's homes. We stay in touch with many families – Nama Hatta families – and each weekend we visit a different family and do a regular temple program with kirtan, a lecture, and *prasadam*. In our home we worship Gaura-Nitai, offer all our *bhoga* to Them, chant our rounds, try to associate with the devotees in Los Angeles as much as possible, and have devotee guests in our house. Srila Prabhupada's our life.

When Srila Prabhupada left it didn't really affect me that much, because to me Srila Prabhupada was always his instructions in his books and in the association of the devotees, and those things didn't change. It was just a question of hanging on through the weirdness because eventually that went away and Krishna consciousness came shining through.

For me the most important Krishna conscious instruction is to follow the basic things that Srila Prabhupada taught: chant sixteen rounds a day, follow the four regulative principles, and associate with the Vaishnavas. Everything else will come from that. If we don't do that, we won't have control of our minds to do anything.

I dream that one day I'll become a pure devotee, that I'll lose my material desires and increase my spiritual desires. Preaching is important for all devotees because by preaching we not only preach to others but we also preach to ourselves. Everything Srila Prabhupada did was preaching. One day I'd like everything I do to also be preaching!

Vedamata devi dasi

One morning after guru-puja at the Honolulu temple in the winter of 1976, Srila Prabhupada was about to give class when Kamini, Lajjavati, and Vedamata started walking past the vyasasana to leave the temple.

Gurukripa told Srila Prabhupada, "These girls are from New Vrindavan. They're going to the airport to distribute your books." With our book bags, long dresses, and covered heads, we stopped in front of Prabhupada, seated on the *vyasasana*, and he looked at us. Time stood still. Prabhupada folded his hands on his chest, shut his eyes, bowed his head to his hands, and then raised his head. I was shocked to see how much awe and reverence Prabhupada had towards our service and us. Book distribution and book distributors meant so much to him. Then and there I made the commitment that whenever I gave Prabhupada to a person, I would do it with dignity and respect and without trickery or tomfoolery. That morning as we drove to the airport all three of us had tears rolling down our eyes, and for months we were walking on air.

After the Ratha-yatra parade in New York City in 1976, I happened to see Kirtanananda sneaking Prabhupada away. Premaka and I ran at fullback speed to Prabhupada's limo where Prabhupada and Kirtanananda laughed and smiled as Premaka and I jumped up and down on the side of the limo chanting, "*Jaya,* Srila Prabhupada!" Prabhupada, covered with garlands, looked at me with a huge smile. I thought, "I'd love to have one of those garlands." Slowly Prabhupada took a garland off and with affection in his eyes played a game with me until, just seconds before the *brahmachari* kirtan party arrived, he leaned over, motioned to me, and handed me his garland through the partially opened window. Tears ran down my face from Srila Prabhupada's loving glances.

Vedanghi devi dasi

When Vedanghi first saw Prabhupada, at the New York airport in 1971, she immediately felt he was not of this world and she cried in happiness. Prabhupada looked angelic and, in some ways, innocent and childlike.

Before I met the devotees my life had no meaning. I was unhappy. As a Christian I had a vague concept of God, that He was the supreme, judgmental, formless being off in the sky somewhere. School and society had taught me I was supposed to get married, have children, and settle down in a house surrounded by material acquisitions. I thought, "If I'm not successful materially, then what's the purpose of this world?" It was Prabhupada who defined a spiritual purpose for me and for all of us. He said the human form of life is a rare opportunity that shouldn't be misused; that it's meant for a higher spiritual purpose. We should develop our consciousness and try to go back to the spiritual world. All material things should be used in the Lord's service and in that way purified. Prabhupada made Krishna consciousness a direct personal experience of God who is a definite being with a form and pastimes.

In a letter, Prabhupada explained my name means "one who is always studious of the *Vedas*." He wrote that Krishna is not obligated to accept anything from us and that I should continue to chant my rounds every day, perform service for the Lord, and develop my love for Him.

Once in Brooklyn in 1972, Prabhupada was giving *Bhagavatam* class when he said, "I have a song I want to teach you," and he started singing "Jaya Radha Madhava." We all repeated after him and learned that song. Another time, by Prabhupada's request, I made *chapatis* for him using milk instead of water to make the dough.

Prabhupada was a *paramahamsa*, a pure devotee, and his association was powerful. Although he's not physically present, we're fortunate to have his association through his teachings. If we follow, the potency is there, but still there's some difference. When Prabhupada was physically present, there was definitely more potency in our Movement and if there was some problem we could receive instruction from him. Quite frequently while we were drinking evening milk our temple president would read us an encouraging letter from Prabhupada, a letter that would always end with, "Your ever well-wisher."

I feel that Prabhupada is still present in my life and in all of our lives as long as we follow his instructions and perform devotional service. *Guru-puja* is significant, to have darshan with Prabhupada either in the temple or our home because our home can be a temple, too. The material energy is powerful in Kali-yuga, so we need each other's association. I go as much as I can to have Srila Prabhupada's and the Deity's darshan, and I maintain some service in my home.

Vegavati devi dasi

Vegavati didn't have any verbal exchanges with Prabhupada. In his presence she had memorable exchanges of glances or feeling experiences.

I had been very moved by Prabhupada's books, had given up sinful habits, and had been following his instructions, and practicing Krishna consciousness for a couple of years. Then, during a *guru-puja* in the Honolulu temple, the kirtan hall was filled with devotees dancing in ecstasy. I was in the back of the room, singing and dancing in the kirtan, when I looked at Srila Prabhupada and his glance came on me and penetrated to my soul in a way that I had not previously experienced. Because he was seeing me as a soul, his glance made me, for the first time, clearly aware of myself as a soul. And since he was also seeing a whole array of petty qualities in my heart, hypocrisies, and prejudices, I was thereby able to see those for the first time, and that completely mortified me.

I was so embarrassed and humiliated by these qualities that Prabhupada saw in me that I looked away in shame. But the kirtan was going on, the holy name was there, and after some time his magnetism made me look at him again and his glance was again right there. This time I could understand two things: I have this pettiness but in spite of it, Prabhupada loves me. Still I was embarrassed and looked away, and the kirtan kept going on. Then I looked a third time and this time I understood that Srila Prabhupada sees and loves me as a pure soul. He conveyed to me, "That conditioning will fall off in time because it's temporary. You don't have to relate to that aspect." He brought me to a higher level, a level that's my real home, and I know I will get there by becoming purified by following his instructions. Practically daily I still see in myself examples of ridiculous, stupid jealousies, envies, selfish thoughts.

Prabhupada related to everyone in a deep personal spiritual way. Someone may not take an experience like mine seriously, but it's real. If one person has tasted honey but another has only seen the outside of a jar, that second person will have no idea honey is something real.

Another time I felt Prabhupada's glance on me with my entire being. I was completely enveloped by love as if I were in the spiritual world. Prabhupada carried that Vrindavan intimacy of souls loving Krishna without prestige or politics or gender tension. He treated everyone as a soul and brought us closer to Krishna. No matter what difficulties come, I can't forget the relationship Srila Prabhupada introduced me to. My memories are very real and deep.

Every morning when I first get up I relish reading Srila Prabhupada's *Bhagavatam*. He's always been there for me in his books. Many times I'm going through something and then I pick up one of his books and a page or two into it I find my questions answered or some guidance. Srila Prabhupada is really in his books and I find him there.

Prabhupada gave us this Movement so we could associate with each other, talk about his books, have kirtan, and honor *prasadam* together. Every day I'm grateful that I eat *prasadam*. Who else can we thank for our great riches but Srila Prabhupada? By faith in him and by following his order, as we become qualified everything will come.

Venudhara devi dasi

Before hearing about Srila Prabhupada and his teachings from a friend, Venudhara, yearning for insight and direction, had called out to whatever was there.

When I heard Krishna's words in the *Bhagavad-gita* and started going to the Adelaide temple, suddenly, like a withered garden that's been watered, what had been dried up and withered inside me started coming alive and blossoming. The natural proclivity of the soul stirred.

I moved into the temple but on a material level wasn't comfortable with a lot of things. I said to myself, "I know what Prabhupada says is touching the truth in the core of my heart and I have faith that the devotees will become more perfect, I'll become more tolerant, and everything will fall into place." I was strongly appreciative of the gift opening before me and served eighteen hours a day thinking, "I'm doing this for Srila Prabhupada." I wanted to make Prabhupada's effort worth his trouble and my faith in him made me more tolerant than I naturally was.

I longed to see Prabhupada but always felt he was with me, especially while I was distributing books and offering others what had so delighted and lifted my heart. I was sickly and those long, punishing days with too little rest were agony but I continued because it pleased Prabhupada. I'd pray, "Prabhupada, please, I need help, I'm failing here."

When Prabhupada passed away I was devastated to lose the person that changed my world and had given me everything. Then the sense that Prabhupada was with me all the time came strongly again. It's my responsibility to keep that sense alive; Srila Prabhupada is waiting for me to turn fully around and face him. Sometimes I haven't prioritized Prabhupada as much as he deserves and my heart longs for, but I try to live as he would want and tell others about him, and that keeps him close to me.

Devotee men endured a lot, but we older women have a unique position in Krishna consciousness that is still unsung and unrecognized. We raised children, contributed full-time service, and endured being marginalized, being made lesser than we are, and not expressing ourselves. Motherhood wasn't given proper credit and its huge social impact wasn't recognized. Yet we thought, "If these are the terms necessary to have this rarest of gifts, then I'll tolerate." New devotees, male or female, should seek out and hear from these women.

We can love, serve, and respect devotees, understanding that we're all on a path to the same thing. Sometimes the journey is interrupted, but once Prabhupada has touched our heart we don't look at anything like everybody else does. The cataracts are removed and we see everything clearly and from another perspective and move through the material world differently from others. Who could possibly dream of having this knowledge given to them?

Vidya devi dasi

Vidya and her husband were looking for a spiritual master and the Absolute Truth in Costa Rica when they met a couple who'd recently seen Srila Prabhupada and were chanting japa *and reading Prabhupada's books.*

When this couple gave us a *Back to Godhead,* I had a fearful feeling, "Oh, no, now our lives are going to really change!" But my husband said, "We're going to examine everything. That's why we're here." Reading an article by Hayagriva we found that he, like us, was desperately searching for something more than material life. When my husband saw Prabhupada's photograph in the magazine, he thought, "There's my spiritual master."

We went to the Miami temple and after a few days, took a midnight flight to Los Angeles to help out with the *Chaitanya-charitamrita* marathon. The next morning we saw Prabhupada.

The sight of a pure devotee is beyond description. On seeing him, my heart became completely opened, as if rays of light were entering my soul and mind. I felt a joy, confidence, and ecstasy that I'd never before felt. Prabhupada's beauty was not so much in his physical features as the magnetic and electric power of his being. His qualities permeated my tiny being. I was so overtaken that I wanted to hear every breath he uttered. I almost fell into a trance because this potent spiritual being was more than I could bear.

We attended the San Francisco Ratha-yatra, where, halfway through, Prabhupada joined us and sat on Subhadra's cart. The procession was already ecstatic, but after he came we were floating. Before, when I'd seen devotees chanting I'd thought, "They're pretending, they can't be that happy." But on this Ratha-yatra with Srila Prabhupada, I understood that the devotees' smiles were genuine.

When Prabhupada entered the Los Angeles temple when he visited the following year, I was on the temple balcony with a few others. We threw flower petals down on him and again I felt an incredible, indescribable fullness. Light radiated from him, and I felt such ecstasy in my heart that it was as if I was in a transcendental body. I'll never forget that feeling.

My husband and I decided to devote our lives to Prabhupada. We gave away our possessions and moved to India. Although I didn't speak with Prabhupada, several times he looked at me and asked internally if there was anything I needed. I was embarrassed and internally answered, "I am perfectly all right. Thank you, Srila Prabhupada."

Once, in Vrindavan, when Prabhupada wasn't feeling well, he was sitting in his rocking chair in front of the *tamal* tree. I was sitting in front of him with another devotee, when a mentally challenged girl sat down almost on top of us. The girl next to me pushed her out of the way harshly. Prabhupada looked at me with the heaviest look I'd ever seen. I thought, "Prabhupada, I didn't do it!" But he kept looking at me just as harshly as he looked at the devotee next to me. I understood, "I didn't try to make that sweet child feel better; I let it happen." I felt bad.

In November 1977, my husband and I were at the Vrindavan *goshala* when we heard that Prabhupada had only a few hours left to live. The devotees were almost hysterical, and Prabhupada's room was filled with people. I felt such a heart-rending, horrible emptiness. I had a lump in my throat. I couldn't swallow or breathe. The thought that Prabhupada was leaving us was horrific.

Before this, each time there'd been an emergency in Prabhupada's life, we'd all pray and he would lift the consciousness of the whole Movement to a higher level. This time was different. As the hours passed, the kirtan became more and more gloriously angelic and transcendental and fully vibrant. I thought, "Even the demigods are here!" Then I realized, "My voice is here, too!" My voice was so strong and lovely that it didn't sound like my voice. Everybody's voice was enthusiastic and exalted. I felt as if I wasn't in my body anymore, that we were rising up and up. Then all of a sudden, "*Tung!*" I was back on the ground again. Prabhupada had gone.

They brought Prabhupada's body to the temple on a palanquin. He took darshan of the Deities, circumambulated the *tamal* tree three times, and sat on the palanquin on the *vyasasana* as the kirtan went on into the night. All of a sudden I realized that I didn't have to stand in the back. I went up and stood right beside Prabhupada. I understood that we could be with Prabhupada any time and as much as we wanted just by having the desire, by thinking of him, by remembering him. He'd always been there for us in those ways, but I hadn't realized it before. Every time we read his books, he's with us, giving instructions.

Vimala devi dasi

Brought up a Christian, Vimala had reservations about Deity worship and the philosophy of Krishna consciousness. But her husband used to wonder, "Who am I, where am I going, and what am I doing here?" and became interested in Krishna consciousness. Vimala wanted a nice, happy suburban life, and was hoping her husband's interest would wear off.

In 1974 my husband went to the Melbourne temple and came back with *prasadam* and books and said, "Yep, this is what I want to do with my life, but the good news is you can come, too." I was attached to him so I thought, "Okay, I'll come along." In the temple I was a fraud. I'd chant mechanically and go to class every day but my heart wasn't in it. At one point I decided to leave. I got my bags and went to the bus stop thinking, "I'm going to go back into the material world," but then Krishna gave me a vision of what the material world was like. It looked horrible, raw, and unfriendly, and I had never experienced that before. After that I was flying a bit on my own.

Prabhupada came in 1976, and my husband and I were initiated. Later I went back to school for three years and got qualified to be a teacher and now I teach full-time at the *gurukula*. It's absorbing and keeps me very busy. To give Krishna consciousness to children is a privilege I love; it's wonderful.

My relationship with Prabhupada has been through service. I like multi-tasking and have always been fully engaged. Krishna has given me a lot of mercy and taste. For the last few years I've been studying Prabhupada's books more to get an in-depth understanding of the philosophy, and my husband and I have a preaching center on the North Shore of New Zealand to help families come to Krishna consciousness together. I made many mistakes in bringing up our son and daughter, but by Krishna's kindness they are devotees. We can learn from our past mistakes and help others not make them.

My husband was searching for knowledge but my taste came through practical devotional service. I'm grateful to Prabhupada because if it weren't for him I'd have been a frustrated suburban housewife trying to make a perfect family life, which never could be. Krishna consciousness gives answers to all of life's dilemmas and I'd like to give Krishna consciousness to others.

Vinode Vani devi dasi

For one college term–from January until May of 1970–Vinode Vani worked at the University of California Hospital in San Francisco. Every day on her way to work she walked past the Frederick Street temple in Haight Ashbury.

I was into Buddhism and fasting and never stopped at the temple but used to buy incense and *Back to Godhead* magazines from devotees on Market

Street. Later, in Houston, my husband bought two *Back to Godheads* from Dharmabhavana, who was distributing door-to-door. Those magazines attracted me; a light went on. I went to the Houston temple the next day and a few days later my husband and I joined.

About a year-and-a-half later my husband and I moved to Dallas and when Prabhupada came I cooked *urad dal bharats,* cauliflower *pakoras,* tomato chutney, and other dishes for him. He liked them. Sometimes I also dressed Radha-Kalachandji and Prabhupada commented that They were dressed better than the Deities in many temples in India.

In Dallas, the children and adults memorized one verse of *Bhagavad-gita* a day and knew ten chapters by heart. We showed off for Prabhupada but, interrupting us, he asked one of the children to stand up. Prabhupada recited a verse and said, "What is the meaning of this verse?" The child didn't know. Prabhupada said, "Better you know the meaning." He didn't want us to simply parrot the Sanskrit. Prabhupada took great pride in the children. He was protective of them and loved them like a grandfather.

Parents from Los Angeles made hundreds of *rasagullas* for the children and presented the *rasagullas* to Prabhupada. Prabhupada said, "I will distribute them. Call the women and children." A hundred and thirty children filed into his room, paid obeisances, and got two *rasagullas* each. Then Prabhupada said, "Call the women." One by one we went in. When my turn came I paid obeisances and began to cry. Prabhupada, smiling, affectionate, and accepting, put two *rasagullas* in my hand. He never considered women lesser; he loved us and was comfortable around us.

Rukmini-Dwarakadisa's worship in Los Angeles was unparalleled. Every day They had full rose garlands, exquisite outfits, and a clean altar. Sometimes I dressed Them, and to open those doors and see Prabhupada standing there, his eyes filled with tears . . . it was wonderful to serve him and have him acknowledged my service.

I've associated with different offshoots of ISKCON and I keep coming back to Prabhupada, because what he gave is a practical, sustainable form of Krishna consciousness that I can maintain and isn't esoteric but relevant to my life. If we follow what Prabhupada set down – *mangala-arati*, sixteen rounds, the regulative principles, reading his books, doing service – we get the result: we become ecstatic and our mind becomes peaceful and free from doubt.

Prabhupada was a genius to create ISKCON. The process he gave us is scientific. It's like a complete diet and by following it we get spiritually sustained and nourished. I hope future generations have a chance to practice Krishna consciousness just the way Srila Prabhupada gave it to us. No one can beat that.

Visakha devi dasi

As one of Srila Prabhupada's personal photographers, for six years Visakha devi dasi sometimes traveled with Srila Prabhupada in India, the U.S., and Europe. Here she reflects on her experience of Srila Prabhupada's teachings, how he practically applied those teachings, and the result of that application.

Srila Prabhupada's teachings caused me to reflect that "I" – the person called "Visakha" – was connected to a deep truth, namely, that I'm a spiritual being who is temporarily inhabiting a woman's body. By its constitution, that body (and mind and intelligence) could do certain things and couldn't do others. But whatever my bodily and mental gifts and limitations, I was everlastingly a servant of God who was meant to end all bodily identification and enter His company. The whole focus of the ideal Prabhupada upheld was single-minded: for me and for each and every individual to understand our deepest identity and to function in that capacity.

Gradually it became evident to me that for Prabhupada, the purpose of tradition, of society, and of life itself was to make progress in bhakti, devotional service to Krishna. When tradition helped that progress, he promoted it unreservedly, and when tradition didn't lead to progress in bhakti, Prabhupada disregarded it. Thus I spent months away from my husband and around Prabhupada constantly, using my camera in devotional service: to photograph him and his followers.

Prabhupada's promotion of tradition baffled some people, but I could see that when tradition was illumined by bhakti, it was beautiful; it didn't fit into a hackneyed stereotype but was dynamic and unbinding. (In Chicago, when asked if a woman could be temple president, Prabhupada had immediately replied, "Yes, why not?") For Prabhupada, bhakti, not gender or any other bodily consideration, was consistently the issue. The whole idea was to keep the goal, bhakti, clearly in view and to steadily move toward it. That made complete sense to me. In fact, it thoroughly delighted me.

Prabhupada was the maestro conducting a full orchestra in a complex classical composition. To my ears, some of the sounds were discordant, but the overall effect was beautiful. And the way that music flowed in Prabhupada's character was irresistible. From the moment I'd met him, all I'd experienced – and was still experiencing – was his encouragement. He aroused in me a spirit of voluntary, enthusiastic service. He generated an atmosphere of fresh challenge and I enthusiastically agreed to rise and meet it. He drew out my spontaneous loving spirit of sacrificing my energy for Krishna. He appreciated my efforts. He wanted me to be all I could be for Krishna. I never sensed a smidgen of male chauvinism or misogyny, superiority or self-righteousness, hubris or haughtiness in him. Neither a whiff of desire to exploit, oppress or repress women or anyone else.

Prabhupada was prying open gates to allow the holiness of natural feminine softness and courage and confident devotion to flow. He was putting me in touch with my uniqueness; he was speaking of a graceful, harmonious, spiritual dynamic in relationships in which all parties benefited and were deeply fulfilled. He spoke of things that were difficult to relate to, given my and most people's background. I couldn't say that I'd deeply experienced the potency of dependence and vulnerability and surrender, but I did appreciate his vision.

The joy of this path of devotional service to Krishna was lucid for Prabhupada. He said,

"These boys and these girls, they are no longer thinking that they are American or European or Canadian or Australian or Indian. They are equal. So if you want equality, fraternity, friendship, love and perfection, solution of problems, all problems, economic, political, social, religious, then come to Krishna consciousness. Come to this platform. Then all your ambitions will be fulfilled and you will be perfect."

Prabhupada's ambition was to help me realize that I was not my body, mind, or intelligence. His method – Krishna's method – was bhakti, which was for everyone equally. Whether man or woman, bhakti, devotional service to Krishna, took precedence. He said:

"My only concern is that people shall not waste their valuable human form of life. After so much struggle they have got this human form, and I do not want that they should miss the opportunity. As for me, I cannot discriminate – man, woman, child, rich, poor, educated or foolish. Let them all come, and let them take Krishna consciousness, so that they will not waste their human life. It is not an artificial thing. It is not a material thing. Chant and follow the four rules and pray to Krishna in helplessness."

Prabhupada's teachings were a continual out-of-body experience that he lived from moment to moment. Being around him made me amazingly eager to also have an out-of-body experience. To be in Srila Prabhupada's presence was to be aware of another dimension where the predominating feeling was unfettered and ongoing joy.

Visalini devi dasi

Visalini appreciated a Nrsimhadeva's appearance day festival in a San Francisco park, but the devotees seemed weird to her. Later, however, she heard a Bhagavad-gita class in the temple.

The philosophy made more sense to me than anything I'd ever heard and at the end of the class I asked, "Can I move in?" Later, when Prabhupada came to Los Angeles in 1972, my husband and I brought him a box of mangoes.

I was shy but Prabhupada would chitchat with me. When I went to his garden for darshan he asked, "How long have you been here?" "Do you like it here?" and I gave one- or two-word answers. He was pulling more and more out of me and I quickly became attached to Him. I was twenty-one and realized the most significant relationship of my life was and always will be with Srila Prabhupada. My relationship with him guides, soothes, and inspires me. I have complete trust in it and there's nothing that compares to its quality.

I desired love and Prabhupada taught me what love is. Love is there day or night; it's boundless and isn't subject to this world, only to my intent and choices. Prabhupada taught me that the greatest love and the Supreme Person are accessible by chanting the *maha-mantra,* and chanting has been my lifeline. I learned from Prabhupada that there's no higher occupation than engaging in *bhakti-yoga* and developing love for God and guru. Whatever I do I try to keep bhakti, service to Krishna, in the center and I feel privileged to do any service. Once I said to Prabhupada, "I want to take your every instruction as my heart and soul." Prabhupada replied, "Do this very thing and your journey back home, back to Godhead is assured."

One year in Vrindavan I was in the hospital for months with bacillary dysentery but I was determined not to miss Prabhupada's darshan. I went to his room with my husband, paid my obeisances, and was trying to get up when Prabhupada said to me, "How are you now?" My husband said, "She's so ill if she doesn't get better, she's going to die." Prabhupada was in a beautiful relaxed pose. He looked at me and with a big smile said, "You are maidservant of Radharani. Maidservant is Radharani. You are Radharani." I felt my father was calling me a princess and got better almost immediately.

I was eight months pregnant in Vrindavan when my young child passed away. That was a great test. If my values or belief system had been flimsy they wouldn't have carried me through, but the philosophy Prabhupada so painstakingly gave did carry me through. His instructions eradicated my fear of death. Prabhupada saw through the eyes of *shastra*. He was always firmly planted beyond the boundaries of this world and could refocus others so they could see through his eyes to a bigger picture of existence based on a different reality. By taking shelter of God and guru, I felt safe even while in this temporary, unpredictable world.

Srila Prabhupada's eyes were not diseased with material contamination; he didn't relate to us as males or females. Like rain pours on the ocean indiscriminately, Prabhupada had equal love and affection for, and faith and trust in, both his male and female disciples. He continually attempted to train his male disciples in appropriate manners, respect, and caution in dealing with his female disciples. He wanted all of us to be generous in heart, to realize we're not these bodies, and to see our contact with Krishna consciousness as our greatest investment in life, one that will make us immune to death.

Srila Prabhupada wanted us to act as if our guru was watching us at every moment. He wanted us to take responsibility with integrity and to be accountable for our personal behavior. His personal example and qualities proved to me that there's so much more than my deadened eyes can see. I take everything he said verbatim because of the example and conviction I was privileged to glimpse in him. He was the purest and greatest example of life's purpose; any dilemma can be eradicated by taking shelter at his lotus feet. I believe Krishna is the Supreme Personality of Godhead because of the love I've seen Srila Prabhupada manifest for Krishna.

Visesa devi dasi

When she was nineteen, Visesa and her boyfriend started visiting the Montreal temple. She liked the Sunday Feasts and the devotees but never thought she was going to become one of them.

In 1974, my boyfriend, daughter, and I lived at the Manor, where I was a teacher at the preschool because that was my training as a *karmi*, and I started to like Krishna consciousness more and more. We also lived in the Amsterdam temple where I became friends with Visvadevi, Jyestha, Maithili, Nikunjavasini, and Nabhaswati. I cleaned the temple room and respected everything. My boyfriend was chanting sixteen rounds, reading the *Gita*, preaching to guests and, later on, translating Prabhupada's books.

When I saw Srila Prabhupada in Paris in the summer of 1974, I knew he was from another world. Coming from an atheistic French background, I wasn't inclined to spirituality, but after seeing Prabhupada I decided to try to be a devotee. I wanted to give my child the best and I no longer liked hippie life. So I got initiated. *Visesa* refers to a quality of Krishna – that He's extraordinary. My boyfriend was also initiated and we married.

I wanted my child to live in the country so my family and I moved to New Mayapur in 1975. First I taught preschool there, then was the bhaktin leader, and then became head *pujari*. I took care of the Deities when I was pregnant and when my kids were small and when everyone left the farm, and I've had many experiences with them. Although my husband left Krishna consciousness in the early 1980s, I'm still in New Mayapur serving the Deities. Eventually I remarried.

But at some point I had a nervous breakdown and lost my taste for life, materially and spiritually. I could not sleep or eat. I questioned my faith. I've dressed the Deities for thirty years so I feel guilty when I think: "Does

God exist? Is Krishna really God? What I am doing? Am I happy? Do I want to go back to Godhead?" Such thoughts are constantly in my mind and it overwhelms me to see myself thinking like that. I feel so bad. I think I'm crazy and cry sometimes. Some say this dark night of the soul is normal and I should never stop praying. So I keep on chanting and serving. I'm scared where stopping my rounds could bring me, but I always feel ashamed and guilty. To be in front of Krishna and to doubt Him is very hard. Sometimes I don't want to live anymore because I wonder, "Live for what?" I pray that all my doubts go away and I wait for grace.

Now my children have grown up, all my kids and grandchildren are devotees, and my house is empty. I've done lots of service but even after all those years I have not read all of Prabhupada's books. I'm trying to now and am taking shelter in that. I have the best guru and should accept what he says. I pray to Prabhupada and reveal my mind to trustworthy, understanding people. I need friendship, love, care, and encouragement to continue. I can't get out of this state by myself.

Nothing happens by chance. When the mind goes crazy it's a karmic disease. Some people get a physical disease and I have a mental disease. I find solace in thinking, "I'm getting purified. I must have made people unhappy and now I'm unhappy. The day I've paid for that, it will end."

Visvadevi devi dasi

Visvadevi didn't know what she wanted to do with her life. Even when she joined the movement, she couldn't see what service she could do. The first time she went to a temple, however, was during a Deity installation and from her earliest years in Krishna consciousness to this day her service has been Deity worship. She likes to see it as her eternal constitutional position to have Deities made and to make clothes, jewelry, and simhasanas for Them.

The windows in the Paris temple in Rue le Sueur were rounded and about four o'clock in the afternoon sunshine was coming in from those windows. Prabhupada was sitting in the room's peach glow and I sat next to him to receive Gayatri initiation. Prabhupada read the Gayatri mantra to me, made me say it after him, and showed me the finger movements. Then he told me to do it on my own and I did it right. He said, "Good," and I became proud. He told me to chant Gayatri before sunset, before sunrise, and at noon, and then asked me to chant it again. This time I got it wrong. He corrected me by taking my thumb between his fingers and moving it.

Before the Krishna-Balaram temple opened in Vrindavan I helped Kishori make a set of clothes for each day of the week. When Prabhupada looked at the clothes and jewelry we'd made he thought they were beautiful and said, "Those outfits will be worn for twenty years." I was just over twenty years old and it seemed like an incredibly long time for Deities to wear an outfit.

Prabhupada wanted his disciples who were living in India to learn Hindi and in Vrindavan we had lessons every afternoon, learned the alphabet quickly, and started to read. Once during Prabhupada's darshan I said, "Srila Prabhupada, we have a good Hindi teacher, we can all read." Prabhupada said, "Can you speak?" I said, "No." He burst out laughing and said, "You can read and you can't speak, what's the good of it?"

Every morning Visala used to recite *shlokas* as Prabhupada left the temple for his walk. One day Prabhupada said, "Do not show off in front of the spiritual master." While Prabhupada walked on Chhatikara Road, which is now Bhaktivedanta Marg, he'd ask about every aspect of the temple: how much we spent on the Deity *bhoga* and how much profit we made from selling *maha-prasadam*. He wanted the Deity department to be self-maintained and was strict and rigorous about finances. He asked how many times we go to Loi Bazaar and when I told him we went once a day (at the time it cost one rupee to go to Loi Bazaar) Prabhupada said, "No, make a list and go once a week." A retired Indian man named Pranab was living in the Vrindavan Guesthouse with his wife. Pranab loved Prabhupada and Vrindavan and the Deities, and he loved his wife. Prabhupada insisted that he and his wife live separately and asked relentlessly about this. One morning Pranab said he had moved out. Prabhupada said, "Where?" Pranab said, "Across the hall." Prabhupada laughed and said, "Not good enough."

Prabhupada saw Krishna in everything and wanted us to use everything for Krishna. Whenever Prabhupada entered the Krishna-Balaram Temple he used to check everything. Once water was coming down the steps from the kitchen and he asked, "What is this?" He was meticulous.

The afternoon in May 1977, when Srila Prabhupada arrived in Vrindavan from Hrishikesh, he repeatedly said that the disappearance of the body is not important. He said, "I have explained everything in my books." The idea that Srila Prabhupada would not be physically with us became a constant dark cloud hanging over our heads and I felt crushed by its weight. Everything was dark and gloomy. Although Prabhupada appeared frail and weak his transcendental body had a molten gold coloring and his skin was smooth. He never appeared sick.

We lived on a day-to-day basis, not knowing whether Srila Prabhupada would leave or stay. Then on November 14th, 1977 the Kaviraja said that Prabhupada had five hours left. I found myself at the foot of his bed and stayed there for hours, standing up straight, my hands folded in prayer, intensely focused on Srila Prabhupada's body. Prabhupada and his bed were covered in Deities garlands. Pishima was sitting on his left. As the time approached, we all sang the *maha-mantra* in unison and with an increasingly intensified rhythm. Then when Srila Prabhupada departed, it was like time stopped forever. There was no past, present, or future. For once in my life my mind did not stray and was wholly in one place. Whenever I think back on Prabhupada's disappearance, it is like yesterday with every detail impressed in my brain and heart.

Later, when we took Srila Prabhupada's transcendental form to have darshan of Krishna-Balarama, I kept looking from Srila Prabhupada to Krishna-Balarama. In the face of what seemed to be a tragedy of monumental proportion – devastating beyond endurance – I was shocked to see Krishna smiling. I felt that Srila Prabhupada was with Krishna. I realized that on the transcendental plane the appearance and disappearance of the *nitya-siddha paramahamsa* are the same and Srila Prabhupada is always with Krishna. It became a glorious moment. Until that point I had been dumbfounded and had stopped singing or chanting but after that I found myself chanting and even smiling, putting my arms in the air, and dancing with the devotees.

We sat Srila Prabhupada on his *vyasasana*, had kirtan for the remainder of the night and offered *guru-puja* to him. By then everything had taken on a dreamlike quality. In the early morning we went with Srila Prabhupada on procession around Vrindavan. Everyone was lining the roads, bowing down, and throwing flowers as Srila Prabhupada passed by, the kirtan reaching a crescendo of magnitude as more devotees participated with more *mridangas, karatalas,* and speakers. We reached the Radha-Damodara temple and the *brahmanas*, the *sannyasis,* the *pujaris* showered Srila Prabhupada with garlands and *maha* flowers. And so it went at every temple. The whole of Vrindavan offered their respect. Srila Prabhupada's body was soft and flowing, gracefully sitting on the palanquin, gently swaying. It was of momentous significance that his body, being holy and completely transcendental, did not undergo rigor mortis. To glorify His dearmost eternal associate, Krishna arranged for all the inhabitants of Vrindavan to witness and recognize this. It was a magnificent testimony to Prabhupada's transcendental nature.

I understand to a small degree what Prabhupada meant when he said that there are two kinds of association, *vani* and *vapuh*, and that *vapuh* is sometimes appreciable but *vani* exists eternally. But the thought that I will not behold Prabhupada's transcendental presence anymore is devastating.

Visvadhika devi dasi

Visvadhika first saw Srila Prabhupada in the Henry Street temple in New York.

I was reading and chanting regularly. The purification process had begun. In many ways I was bewildered by the changes in myself. Of course, the relief from material entanglement brought very swift and intense joy and peace to my heart. Simultaneously I was beginning to become aware of the depth of my material entanglement. Around this time I had dream in which Srila Prabhupada came and told me, "You have a very big false ego." Really! I was ready to argue the point, but then realized that this reaction only proved my spiritual master's comment.

Srila Prabhupada gave class one morning. On the material level, I was nobody in that room, just Joanne sitting in the corner, with my "big false ego," trying to hear. But as Srila Prabhupada was speaking, I became very enlivened because it seemed that His Divine Grace was speaking directly to me. "How can that be possible?" I thought. Yet I could not deny that he was addressing exactly my concerns. Many devotees have had similar experiences. Krishna has a personal relationship with every single infinitesimal *jiva*, no matter how innumerable we are. As Krishna's pure devotee Srila Prabhupada was manifesting that same capacity for personal encounter even in a crowded room with hundreds of devotees.

During this same visit, I had a 30-60 second encounter with Srila Prabhupada that continues to inspire me. I had the fortune of being on the team of women (we were not "Matajis" in those days) who cleaned his quarters while he went for his morning walk. On this one day, he did not go out. We were told we could clean but if he entered the room where we were working, we should leave. So, I was cleaning the floorboards in the hallway. They were spotless, but I was happy to be there!

I felt someone had entered the room, so I looked up and there stood Srila Prabhupada. He said a "Thank you very much." I offered my obeisances in awe. In loving fear I looked up but His Divine Grace was gone.

That was it. One moment of association!

In one purport Srila Prabhupada says that one moment of proper association with the pure devotee can make one's life perfect. By Krishna's mercy in that one moment of encounter with Srila Prabhupada, I was serving and not engaged in nonsense. I am so fortunate to have had this one moment.

Unfortunately for some years I left the association of the devotees. By the mercy of devotees, I was able to come back. In 2011, Malati said to me, "You want to serve the devotees, by offering homeopathic medicine. Great idea. Come to the Festival of Inspiration." I could not understand how spiritually inspiring homeopathy would be. But I went. By her mercy and the mercy of many wonderful godbrothers and godsisters in New Vrindavan, I am again in the association of devotees. Though I have always lamented that I had extremely tiny personal association with Srila Prabhupada, I understand now that he has given this insignificant devotee the greatest blessing. He has taken me again into his service through the mercy of his disciples. Thank you Srila Prabhupada.

He is truly a manifestation of Krishna's divine grace as evidenced by so many accounts of his interactions with disciples when we were blessed with his association. That divine grace is still manifesting, even though we cannot see his presence today, and though many of us are granddisciples and great granddisciples.

Vrnda devi dasi

Vrnda devi dasi was reading Bhagavad-gita As It Is while floating on Wascana Lake in Regina, Saskatchewan in a dingy, when she heard the sound of devotees chanting Hare Krishna. Parking the boat, she ran, in her bikini, in the direction of the transcendental sound and climbed aboard a blue sankirtana bus full of sannyasis and brahmacharis. She was welcomed, handed a chadar, and asked to please cover herself. Already a vegetarian yogini familiar with bhakti-yoga, she soon moved into the Toronto temple.

After a letter arrived from Srila Prabhupada, accepting me as his disciple, naming me Vrnda devi dasi, I travelled to New Vrindavan in West Virginia for initiation in 1972.

We gathered flowers, leaves, and branches to decorate Prabhupada's outdoor *vyasasana* for the initiation. We sang as he arrived, walking with a cane, to grace us with his presence. When he asked me to recite the four regulative principles, I managed to get the words out. He smiled and handed me my beads. I was now twice born and had a spiritual father.

My second initiation was in Chicago, where I observed Prabhupada's saffron book bag looking quite tattered. I told his servant that I could sew, and would be honored to make a new one befitting my guru. I was instructed to make it identical with all the pockets for his *karatalas*, books, etc. I took a bus to a fabric store to buy the saffron-colored raw silk, but was not able to procure the amount I needed, so bought some cream-colored fabric to be used as lining. When complete, I was invited to Prabhupada's room to present it to him. I felt him looking intently at me with loving eyes. His penetrating gaze knew my heart and my struggles. I felt unconditional love pouring from him. When I handed it to him, he said, "Very nice," and thanked me. Then he looked inside the bag and said, "But why not all saffron?" So I explained to him my saga. He smiled and said it would be fine.

I later picked a bouquet of flowers, hoping to give them to Prabhupada. As I handed them to him, I felt his hand slightly brush mine. He smiled and thanked me.

After moving to the Winnipeg temple, a letter arrived inviting all artists in ISKCON to move to Los Angeles to create the First American Theistic Exhibition. I heard that Prabhupada had a vision of a three-dimensional representation of the *Bhagavad-gita,* to be used for preaching. I knew, therefore, it was already done, but if I chose to be of service in manifesting it on the physical plane that would be my good fortune! And indeed it was!

Being engaged as a sculptor for the FATE Museum allowed me to dovetail my artistic propensities into the service of Radha-Krishna – the highest use of my God-given talents.

It seemed like we were always on a deadline. Prabhupada was inquiring about our progress and was planning a visit. We would begin work at 4:30 am right after morning *arati*. We listened to *Bhagavatam* class over speakers in our cold, but inspired workspace. *Prasadam* was brought in and we worked until late each evening. It was a form of meditation – engaging all of my senses – bringing two dimensional drawings into 3-D spiritual forms. We had carved our sculpting tools out of bamboo and offered them before using them. I often experienced a trance-like state, as though my hands that were using straw and clay, were being guided and empowered in service to create forms and Deities that furthered Prabhupada's mission. My life had purpose and direction. I was inspired, filled with joy and gratitude for this spiritual opportunity.

With a kirtan party to greet Srila Prabhupada at the Los Angeles airport, I experienced his commanding, energetic potency overflowing, as his small stature walked quicker and with more intention than those of us decades younger than him. He was on fire with a desire to please his Guru Maharaja, and that fire was contagious and put a spring in my step!

Arriving at FATE's work space, Prabhupada gazed at the forms with appreciation, making comments and smiling. His vision was being manifested and he was pleased. We served him water in a silver goblet, some *prasadam,* and listened to him speak about the importance of what we were doing. He described it as potent preaching work.

On the day Srila Prabhupada left his body, I was given that silver goblet. I put it on my altar and have offered him water in it ever since.

While pregnant, I recall cleaning Prabhupada's room, and then going home to take a nap, during which I received very clear instructions in a dream. He was pleased with my service, but mentioned specific things to avoid, to protect the baby I was carrying. They were words from a concerned spiritual father to protect his daughter and child in the womb.

In hosting vegan potlucks and educational health gatherings, I have always made a point to put Krishna's plate out on the table and invite participants to put a sampling of their preparation on His plate. Then I explain that although the food we are about to partake of is in the mode of goodness, it still binds us karmically to the material world. Therefore, in taking a moment to offer the food to Krishna, it spiritualizes it, freeing us from the karma and benefiting us spiritually. Krishna just wants our love. Often, someone will ask if they can observe the offering and want to hear more.

As an Iyengar yoga teacher, I have woven the philosophy and Vedic teachings imparted to me by my lifetime teacher Srila Prabhupada into my classes. His words endure decades later.

Vrindavani devi dasi

When the Manor opened in 1973, Vrindavani, who had been visiting the Bury Place temple for a couple of years, moved in. She was sixteen.

The day I stepped in the Manor door, the first person I saw was Srila Prabhupada, who was just going in to the lecture room to give the *Bhagavad-gita* class. As soon as I saw him I paid obeisances.

At a darshan at the Manor that summer, an Englishwoman said to Srila Prabhupada that she was married to a person who wasn't a devotee and what should she do. I expected Srila Prabhupada to say, "Oh, you've married a demon. You must give him up. Move into the temple and serve Krishna." But from that day to this, I'm amazed at Srila Prabhupada's answer. He said "There is no impediment to Krishna consciousness."

Srila Prabhupada has said Krishna consciousness is our birthright and if we really want Krishna there is no impediment. Whenever I point the finger or blame circumstances, I know I have to look a little more inward.

Prabhupada spent a long time at the Manor that summer. Later I went to India and saw Srila Prabhupada in Juhu for many days. I was helping with secretarial work, *pujari* work, and cleaning Srila Prabhupada's rooms. In the late afternoons I'd go to the roof where Srila Prabhupada would regularly have informal darshans and many devotees and guests would sit and listen. One day I went up, opened the door and immediately paid obeisances. As I was getting up, Brahmananda indicated that I shouldn't be there and said, "What are you doing here?" I said, "I'm sorry. I thought Srila Prabhupada was speaking." Prabhupada said, "You wanted to speak to me?" I said, "Oh, no, Srila Prabhupada, I came to hear you speak." For whatever reason, that afternoon he wasn't having the darshan. But I got the feeling that Srila Prabhupada was always there for the devotees. He hadn't reacted in any sort of negative way. It was as if someone had turned up and he said, "Oh, you want to speak?" It seemed as if he had all the time in the world, and if I needed to speak to him, he was there. That's always stayed with me; it's always been my comfort.

At another of those darshan times in Bombay, Srila Prabhupada was reading about Dhruva Maharaja, and said there's a Vaikuntha planet within the material universe. I couldn't get my head around that at all. I was trying to bring the mundane into the transcendental. I asked Srila Prabhupada about it. Srila Prabhupada said, "You have to be pure." Since then, whenever I've had any difficulty in my spiritual life, I always come back to that instruction from Srila Prabhupada: that you have to be pure. I'm not pure, and that's why this difficulty is there. Spiritual life is a cleansing process.

There were a lot of women and children in the Vrindavan Guesthouse but it wasn't an ideal place for them, and Prabhupada suggested that they go to Mayapur, which would be better. One morning I had to leave Vrindavan to help out in Hyderabad and had my bags packed ready to go when Srila Prabhupada returned from his walk. I offered obeisances and Srila Prabhupada said, "Oh, do you have somewhere to go?" I said yes, I was going to do my service in Hyderabad. Srila Prabhupada's reaction was always so natural and he was so easy with us. There was no awkwardness. Although there were so many devotees, he was concerned about and observant of us individually.

Another time, in Srila Prabhupada's Mayapur room, one of the *gurukula* boys was feeling a bit chilly and Prabhupada was concerned that he had a jumper, that he was warm.

In January of 1977, I went to Kumbha-mela and happened to be on the same train as Srila Prabhupada. Even though I'd been a devotee for years by then, I used to think, "Oh, what's the point of a marriage ceremony? What's in a marriage certificate? It's a piece of paper." At the Kumbha-mela, Srila Prabhupada said there has to be a ceremony for a marriage. The whole community should know that this man and this woman are husband and wife. That was a lesson for me. One could say, "Why did you have to learn that? You were already a devotee and knew these things," but sometimes it takes years to catch on to something. Whatever Srila Prabhupada said always made so much sense. It wasn't difficult to accept. He made everything acceptable and understandable and meaningful.

Sometimes what Srila Prabhupada said was hidden and sometimes it was something that we had to understand as we became purer. Sometimes Prabhupada said one thing and we could understand it in one way at that time and years later we'll understand it in another way. Of course, as the years go by we understand in a deeper way.

Vrndavana Vilasini devi dasi

Vrndavana Vilasini was attached to her independent hippie life but was suffering dreadfully. Everywhere in America she met devotees, heard the holy name, and took prasadam. Finally she ended up in Seattle, Washington, her hometown.

The Seattle temple president, Makhanlal, said to me, "Do you want to meet someone who loves God more than anyone else?" I said, "Sure!" So June 8th, 1972 we drove six hours to the Portland, Oregon airport. The moment Prabhupada came to the door of the plane, even though I was far away, my deep bond of love with him began. His heart said to my heart, "I love you, I will never leave you." My heart replied, "I love you, I will never leave you." It was an unbelievable internal bond of love and affection. I was in total shock from it and for two or three hours I experienced the whole world – every radio, person, blade of grass, everything – chanting Hare Krishna. Ever since that day I always feel Prabhupada is with me. He's my life and soul, my best friend, and more close to me than the air I breathe.

After Portland I flew to L.A., joined the temple and never left. I was happy. Three months later, on Balarama's appearance say, Prabhupada initiated me. I wanted to make him happy, so after I said the regulative principles I looked up at him like a little kid and added, "And always remember Krishna and never forget Krishna." Prabhupada laughed and said, "Your name is Vrindavana Vilasini devi dasi. It's a name for Radharani, the one who enjoys in Vrindavan." Then for seventeen years, day in and day out, I tried to please Prabhupada by distributing his books, and after his departure I moved to Vrindavan. Now I live on the bank of the Yamuna.

When people asked Prabhupada about women being less intelligent, he said, "If you think you're a woman, you're always going to have troubles. Don't think you're a woman, think you're a spirit soul, a servant of Krishna." He never made women feel inferior, unequal. We had equal opportunity for service: women dressed the Deities and cooked for Them.

Prabhupada's a real, transcendental personality. He's still glancing at us and sending us personal letters through his books. If we can offer our *bhoga* to a picture of Prabhupada and it becomes *prasadam*, how is it we can't talk to him? How is it we can't get his glance? Why not? It's a matter of faith. We have faith that our *bhoga* becomes *prasadam*, so why don't we have faith that he can talk to us? He's alive and well, he never dies. When we make Sri Guru our life and soul and serve him with love and affection and gratitude, he'll reciprocate. It's a matter of faith.

Prabhupada gave me the desire to serve and please him, and that's the real bond. It's his mercy that I'm enthusiastic, that I have a taste. When I first read that if you have firm faith in guru and Krishna then you will know all the imports of the *Vedas,* I thought, "I don't have that firm faith, but I'll pray for it and get it." I had faith in the process and followed as best I could. Krishna consciousness is simple, but we have to be patient and tolerant.

Vrndavanesvari devi dasi

In 1971 Vrndavanesvari dasi, eighteen, traveled with her boyfriend (now husband) to Los Angeles to visit his brother, who happened to live across the street from the Los Angeles ISKCON temple. Before long, they were eating prasadam *and bought a* Krsna *book and the* Bhagavad-gita.

Our next travel took us up to Northern California, where a large group of hippies lived. They lived a degraded lifestyle. My daily ritual was to read the *Krsna* book, and Madana read the *Bhagavad-gita.* We left that place and I began chanting two rounds daily, which dramatically changed my perspective and faith in Krishna consciousness.

We went back to the Los Angeles temple, living in our van. I attended all the temple functions, increased my chanting to eight rounds, and worked at the incense factory all day, listening to the beautiful Radha Krishna Temple album every day.

About three days after I moved to Los Angeles, a bunch of devotees asked me if I would like to travel with them up to San Francisco for a festival. I agreed. Then fourteen woman sat cross-legged on the floor of a van to go north for an adventure. A sweet devotee named Mary befriended me, and we spoke throughout the drive. When we stopped for a picnic of what I thought was unusual food, she explained what everything on my plate was and practically fed me with her sweetness. She was motherly and imbibed how a devotee should be. I think her kindness had a very big influence on me. Later she was initiated as Manjuali.

Two weeks later I felt impelled to move into the ashram and become a full-fledged *brahmacharini.* I was enthralled by the atmosphere. It was intoxicating to enter the temple room with billowing frankincense and myrrh. A few feet away from the temple room was the kitchen, with all its exotic smells, blending with the smell of incense. The temple room itself was a riot of colors and joy.

I immediately bonded with the devotees, like I'd always known them. There were so many devotees there in New Dwarka, teaching by their example. Everything was first class. All the intensely sweet bonds and attachments I made with my godsisters softened my heart and brought me a happiness I had never experienced, and I still feel close to those devotees even after so many years and miles have separated us.

It was magical to offer obeisances with your head on the floor while saying exotic prayers and then everyone yelling out "*Jaya!*" It was glorious. In the first couple of weeks at the temple, whatever I had been speculating was the purpose of life, my questions, were answered. I had been infatuated with death, and when the devotees explained that we're eternal, I felt that a lot suddenly made sense. Within the first two weeks, I felt I was reborn.

In May, word got out that Prabhupada was coming. There was so much excitement that devotees were going nuts. I was excited but didn't really know what to expect. I went to the airport with who knows how many devotees, and we were so excited that we screamed and jumped and chanted like we were in another realm, oblivious to everybody around us. We were out of this body because Prabhupada, who had saved us with this knowledge and the *maha-mantra,* both of which had given us bliss, was coming to be with us.

Prabhupada deplaned and glanced around at everyone with such apparent pleasure. He saw all the new devotees along with the ones who had already dedicated themselves to him, and he gave us this loving smile and glance. I immediately felt a transcendental connection with him; Prabhupada was my eternal father. He made me feel at home and that I was doing the right thing. Seeing a regal and sweet pure devotee, I was in awe.

Every Sunday, all the *brahmacharinis* and *brahmacharis* went into the kitchen for about six hours. Men at one table and women at another, we rolled *puris, samosas,* and sweetballs for the feast. It was ecstatic service. Again, there was such a bond between the devotees. There wasn't any difference between men and women in service.

Prabhupada was there for two months. I observed his grace, his humility, his loving glances, his appreciation of many small things. Once I stood near him when he was taking *charanamrita,* and saw the boyish grin on his face as he said, "This is so nice, I could eat this all day." It was so sweet.

Prabhupada reciprocated with his devotees, and never discriminated between the men and women. All the women paid full *dandavats* and Prabhupada certainly approved. When he toured the apartments, some of us followed him, and felt how he cared for, appreciated, and was concern about all of us. He reciprocated with us.

Once in San Diego, a TV reporter interviewed Prabhupada and I was with Prabhupada when he watched the interview on TV. Prabhupada found the interview funny and laughed so much he fell back on the couch. The air was so thick with his ecstasy and laughter I felt the demigods were laughing; every atom was full of joy.

Once a woman asked, "Why do you shave your head?" In a heavy way Prabhupada said, "Why do you shave your legs?" There was silence and then lightheartedly Prabhupada said, "Better to have a cool head than cold legs." Everyone laughed from the change of mood. By saying the right thing at the right time Prabhupada could control a situation.

At times in his lectures in a pleading way Prabhupada said, "Krishna wants you back home! What is the difficulty?" I thought, "Wow!" and became excited. That statement made Krishna consciousness easier. Prabhupada was moved by his disciples' attempts to serve. He was a real and a sensitive person and when he glanced upon us, we felt his love and compassion.

Once I heard him say, "If you chant your sixteen rounds, your deathlessness is guaranteed." Prabhupada was in his mid-70s and wasn't in the best health but he danced.

One of my strongest remembrances is Prabhupada sitting on the *vyasasana* in the packed, small, old temple room. There were devotees from all over the world there, and Prabhupada was singing "Jaya Radha Madhava" ecstatically. I was completely absorbed. He was playing the gong with his little hammer, raising his arm up like an orchestra conductor and motioning for everyone to dance–and everyone danced exuberantly. I used to think, "I'm going to touch the ceiling!" I was so high from the energy that I really felt like I was going to float up and touch the ceiling. In that ocean of devotees I was thinking, "Prabhupada, look at me," because I wanted his special attention. And suddenly through this ocean of devotees, heads all around, I realized that Prabhupada was gazing right at me with this intense look. At the moment I felt guilty and foolish, but I didn't care. I felt ecstatic that Prabhupada picked up on my energy, and we had this eye contact that lasted several moments. And I went crazy, dancing more.

I think it is the lessons and causeless mercy of Prabhupada that keep me going. I have some attraction to chanting. I wake up and chanting is in my head. At night it's my lullaby for sleeping. I was fortunate to have many years of sincere service to the devotees, which I think is very important–to recognize the importance of giving to Vaishnavas. They are not ordinary people. I think having a strong foundation in service is really important. Krishna consciousness is not just reading and chanting; it's physically doing something, because that connects you. In the spiritual world, everyone is actively engaged all the time.

In a lecture in L.A., Prabhupada said two things that have always stuck with me. He said there are three ways to transcend this body–by chanting, by dancing, and by playing a musical instrument. Sometime later he said, "Even if you don't want to dance, force yourself to dance, and the bliss will come." That was amazing. Dancing is not an ordinary thing. It was a special benediction given by Lord Chaitanya, given by Prabhupada. So many times

I feel ill or my back hurts or my foot hurts and I'm dragging, I wear my orthopedic shoes in the temple, but this is a special benediction. When we dance, we transcend the body. Dancing was important to Prabhupada.

I am eternally indebted to my guru, His Divine Grace Srila Prabhupada, who has so kindly entered my heart, opened my eyes, and given purpose to my life, with song, dance, and a smile.

Yamuna devi dasi

In September of 1966 Yamuna was in New York for ten days to attend the wedding of her younger sister, Janaki. During that time she heard Srila Prabhupada tell the story about love and lust called "Liquid Beauty." That story was like a punch in the solar plexus for her. She cried and thought, "Yes, it's true. In the material world there's so-called love, but it's nothing like the real love that Swamiji speaks about."

After New York I left with Janaki, who was the first woman Prabhupada initiated, and her husband, Mukunda dasa – who was one of the first eleven male disciples Prabhupada initiated. We went to San Francisco and picked up two old friends – Sam Speerstra and Melanie Nagel, who turned out to be Shyamasundar dasa and Malati devi dasi. With their help and the help of a few more interested people we started the San Francisco temple in January of 1967. Srila Prabhupada came to encourage and guide us and when he went on his daily morning walks anyone could go with him. So I was walking with him one morning and I said, "Swamiji, do you think sometime you could allow us to go to Vrindavan with you?" Prabhupada turned around and said, "Yes, I will take you to Vrindavan one day, and I will show you Vrindavan on foot." I thought that was the most hopeful thing I had ever heard in my life. I was just waiting for that time to come.

In 1968 August we went to London to try to start the British *yatra* and about a year later Srila Prabhupada came and, on the invitation of John Lennon of the Beatles, stayed with his disciples in John's Tittenhurst Park estate. After his morning walk on the estate, Srila Prabhupada would sit alone in his little greeting room, take off his socks, and sing prayers while he played the harmonium or the drum or a pair of *karatalas*. One morning I was sitting silently on the stairs outside his room listening to Prabhupada singing. I don't know how he knew I was there but when he'd finished he called me. I went in and he said, "What are you doing?" I said, "I'm listening, Srila Prabhupada. Your singing is beautiful." He said, "Do you want to come in and listen?" I said, "Yes, very much." He said, "You can play drum and I will play harmonium and Purushottama can play *karatalas*." Then for several mornings we recorded Srila Prabhupada singing a prayer by Narottama dasa Thakura, *Vijnapti, Hari Hari Bifale*:

hari hari! bifale janama gonainu
manusya-janama paiya, radha-krsna na bhajiya,
janiya suniya bisa khainu

When I heard Srila Prabhupada sing this I said, "What does this prayer mean?" because we didn't have songbooks at that time. He explained the meaning to me, that "Oh, Lord Hari, I have wasted my life. Although I have taken a rare human birth, like a miser I have not served Radha and Krishna and thus I have knowingly drunk poison." When Srila Prabhupada sang this *bhajana,* he went so deeply into the mood of this prayer, that "I have not served Radha and Krishna," that he repeated this line eight, nine, ten times.

Then he sang the next verse eight or ten times, going deep into its meaning:

golokera prema-dhana, harinama-sankirtana,
rati na janmilo kene tay
samsara-bisanale, diba-nisi hiya jwale,
juraite na koinu upay

"The treasure of divine love in Goloka Vrindavan has descended as the congregational chanting of Lord Hari's holy names – Hare Krishna Hare Krishna, Krishna Krishna Hare Hare, Hare Rama Hare Rama, Rama Rama Hare Hare. Why did my attraction for this chanting never come about? Day and night I'm burning in this dark world without working to make the correction."

After he'd sung this song Prabhupada said, "So Yamuna Prabhu, what is your favorite prayer?" I only knew the prayer from the introduction to the *Srimad-Bhagavatam,* so I said, "I like the *Shikshashtaka* prayers." He said, "That's very nice." I said, "Swamiji, what is your favorite prayer?" He said, "This prayer, *Hari Hari Bifale.*"

A party of about twenty devotees – a third of them women – arrived in India on October 4th, 1970, and until March of 1972, several traveled throughout India with Prabhupada serving together and chanting the holy names on a *nagar sankirtana* like a close family. By Prabhupada's mercy he allowed women close proximity to him on his personal *sankirtana* party. In our Vaishnava history this was revolutionary, and the effect it had in India was profound. In fact, it shocked India. Every place we went the front page of the newspaper would have an article on the dancing white elephants of devotees who were going through the streets chanting the holy names.

At the Magh Mela in February 1971 Srila Prabhupada was speaking from the Sixth Canto for the first time, the story of Ajamila. Everyone in our party lived just to hear Prabhupada. To be with Prabhupada was one thing but to hear his *Bhagavatam* class every morning, we would run for that. I would sit right next to his *vyasasana* at Prabhupada's lotus feet. In my early years of Krishna consciousness Prabhupada was so open and merciful to the ladies that he never gave much stricture of separation. But at this Mela Achyutananda Swami, who had been living in a Gaudiya Math temple for some time and who was aware of etiquette, told me, "Yamuna, have you noticed where all the other women are sitting?" I said, "Yes, I have." The other ladies were way in the back. Achyutananda Swami said, "You should be sitting there too." So the next morning I sat way in the back. Later that morning Prabhupada called me. I went into his tent, paid my obeisances, and before I got up he looked at me with plaintive eyes and said, "You don't like to hear from me anymore?" I burst into tears and said, "I love to hear from you more than ever, Srila Prabhupada. More than anything in the world, all I want is to hear from you." Prabhupada said, "So why you weren't sitting?" I said, "Achyutananda Swami told me that it was the etiquette that I sit far in the back with the ladies." Prabhupada was quiet. Then he said, "Yes, that is etiquette." I said, "Srila Prabhupada, how many times were you with your Guru Maharaja?" He immediately said, "Since I met him I have never been away from him, not for one second." But I was a little forceful, I said, "But how many times were you with him physically?" Prabhupada said, "Very few, maybe five or six times, but they were intimate and meaningful to me." Then he said, "Many of my godbrothers were big *sannyasis* and thought that associating with the spiritual master personally was most important. But in some cases, they are no better than mosquitoes on the lap of the king. And what is the business of mosquito? It is simply to suck blood. So don't think that that's the only way to associate with the spiritual master. You try to hear." For me this was a tremendous learning moment. Up until then, I couldn't conceive of being separated from Prabhupada or that he would die. But at this time I realized that there would be a point in the future when I would be physically separated from him and I would have to come to terms with that.

In March of 1972, my husband and I were stationed in Vrindavan to help to start the Krishna-Balaram temple. Srila Prabhupada wanted Vrindavan and Mayapur to be places for pilgrims to come from around the world to "hear in the *dhama* and to taste the beauty of the *dhama*." He wanted an international guest center with vibrant Krishna conscious activities going on, and he wanted *prasadam* distribution. He said, "Especially in Vrindavan, you won't be recognized so much for your scholarship. But if you distribute *prasadam* nicely and if you worship the Deity nicely, you will be respected."

Prabhupada mercifully revealed Vrindavan to us, sometimes with encouragement and sometimes with chastisement. While we were trying to do the Vrindavan project Prabhupada gave us lots of chastisement.

Chastisement is a special relationship that one has with the spiritual master and sometimes it's difficult to appreciate its potency when you're being chastised, but in retrospect it becomes relishable mercy that we continue to learn from years and years later. When you get chastised, you feel your energy change and sometimes it takes a long time to put the beauty of that chastisement into perspective.

Once Srila Prabhupada was in Delhi when I came from Vrindavan and joined him there. Although he knew that I was part of the Vrindavan project and was just visiting the Delhi temple, Prabhupada said to me, "How could you have let this happen?" I didn't know what he was referring to. Prabhupada said, "You have left Krishna sitting on the fence post." I tried to explain, "Srila Prabhupada, I'm just visiting. I don't have anything to do with the Deity program here." But Prabhupada chastised me, because it's the disciple's duty to try to preserve what the guru has given. He said, "I have trained you in Deity worship," and he felt that I should extend myself to the Delhi temple also. He also said to all of us, "You may think that this is a stone statue, an idol, standing before you and you may think, 'Let me give this rubbish garland to this stone statue, and Krishna will not mind.' But if you do that Krishna will remain a stone statue for you forever. So please take care." He made it clear how important it is to be attentive in our service to Krishna and in our service to Krishna's devotees. Under the merciful instructions of the spiritual master and in a loving way we're supposed to help each other go back to Godhead. That's a glorious thing to explore because there's no end to it. As long as we're breathing, there is no end to the potential of helping each other become Krishna conscious in every minute of our existence by following the instructions of our spiritual master.

In the beginning of the Vrindavan project I was the only woman in the party. All the others were men, and all of us had important roles. My role was the Deity department and Prabhupada's rooms. When we made the temple, we made every mistake you can make and one really big mistake was the floor in Srila Prabhupada's room. It was an amalgamate floor with the wrong mixture of black so that when it dried the black color continued coming off it and nothing we did stopped that black color from coming off that floor. Prabhupada said, "Who has done this?" I made the ridiculous comment, "Srila Prabhupada I am not sure what to do." He said, "No intelligence, there's no intelligence there." "That's very true, Srila Prabhupada. Do you have any suggestions how I could better take care of the room?" He said, "No. You figure this out." It took many months before that floor was clean.

Prabhupada was strict with me about cleaning. When he went for his morning walk in Vrindavan we had a whole cleaning system so every surface in his room was cleaned twice. One morning Prabhupada came back from his walk, sat down at his desk, took his mini staple gun out of its plastic protective sleeve, opened the staple gun so it was flat, rubbed his pinky finger in the space between the knob and the staple, and said, "Dust. Who has cleaned my room?" I said, "I did, Srila Prabhupada." "Haven't I trained you how to clean the room?" "No, Srila Prabhupada, I'm so dull that I never ever thought to look there for dust." "*Asara*, useless."

Prabhupada was strict with me in many ways but I treasure that today, I treasure that dust in Prabhupada's staple gun because when the spiritual master is strict, it helps us to be conscious of what conditioning means. Otherwise conditioning is just a word. The statement "I'm conditioned from time immemorial" is hard to wrap your mind around. Conditioning is a huge thing. Unless the spiritual master trains us, how will we get out of our conditioned state? So when the spiritual master chastises us by giving us instructions on simple things, it's helpful.

Srila Prabhupada came in and out of Vrindavan many times in 1973 because we Western disciples had no knowledge of the language, of anything to do with business, of the many social customs of the holy *dhama*, but we were trying to build the Krishna-Balaram temple. We had to accept the obstacles that Krishna put in front of us to help us learn how to get out of this material world. And Srila Prabhupada had to come many times to help us move the project forward in a timely fashion.

Once Prabhupada came for a short time and afterwards Tejiyas, Gurudas, Shyamasundara, and I brought him to the Delhi airport. His plane was delayed and we were sitting in a little group waiting when we heard this *click, click, click-clack, click-clack* coming from a twenty-year-old girl with tall high heel shoes, black stockings, and a mini-dress. Shyamasundara said to Prabhupada, "We're not in Vrindavan anymore, Srila Prabhupada." Prabhupada looked at him and said, "Yes, we are in Vrindavan. This is not Vrindavan?" That made a light bulb turn on in me that yes, you leave Vrindavan, but Vrindavan is also in the heart. We can drink in Vrindavan using all of our senses and when we leave the *dhama* of Vrindavan, we can bring its atmosphere with us wherever we go.

Every time I remember these defining moments with Srila Prabhupada I learn from them. Prabhupada once made the simple, obvious comment that "In order to remember, you must hear and chant." He said, "Your remembering will become less effective to the degree that you hear less and chant less." So those three things: hearing, chanting, and remembering, which are part of the nine processes of bhakti, are also the core of my relationship with Prabhupada. Hearing about and remembering Srila Prabhupada are the two most important things in all my spiritual life. Hearing and remembering are Srila Prabhupada's beautiful gifts to us and I am deeply grateful for this transcendental mercy.

Yasasvini devi dasi

Yasasvini was brought up a Christian and always had the desire to go back to the spiritual world, the kingdom of God. The only time she didn't care for going back to Godhead was when she sat in Srila Prabhupada's presence. Prabhupada's association was perfect and evoked a sense of complete satisfaction in her.

I had gotten a *Back to Godhead* magazine along with an invitation to visit the Bury Place temple in London. I went to the temple and was in a room with students and Indian people when Srila Prabhupada came in and sat down. A devotee also came in and paid his obeisances, which I had never seen before. It was an amazing way for one living entity to treat another. While everybody was waiting for Srila Prabhupada to speak, he sat silently for three to four minutes. I was struck by how comfortable he was and thought, "If everybody was waiting for me to speak, I'd feel obliged." Normal social pressure didn't affect Prabhupada. He had unusual strength and complete confidence in what he believed. When he finally spoke, he asked our names, and where we came from and then gave each of us a piece of *burfi*.

When Srila Prabhupada stayed in Bhaktivedanta Manor for the summer of 1973, he gave class every morning, and we had amazing kirtans. It was like being in the spiritual world. His strength made everybody strong. I was one of a few women who was doing full time *sankirtana* and once, when I went in his room, Srila Prabhupada sincerely thanked me very much. He fully realized what we were doing and was grateful that somehow, even in our conditioned state, we were giving our energy to help him spread this mission for the pleasure of Srila Bhaktisiddhanta.

It wasn't my nature to do *sankirtana* so I found it difficult and had problems with my mind. Once, when Prabhupada was giving a general talk, his eyes fixed on mine, and he said, "You cannot change your nature." He paused and said it a second and then a third time, "You cannot change your nature." He seemed to be speaking to me: "Be what you are for Krishna," and it helped me.

Prabhupada never liked to waste energy; his every movement had a purpose. He carefully thought out and put together what he wrote. His lectures were basic and simple. When I joined, Prabhupada lectured for eight days on 'you are not this body.' One boy asked, "We hear every day we're not this body. Can we go on to something else now?" Prabhupada said, "Have you realized you are not this body?" The boy said, "No." Prabhupada said, "We will continue then."

Now, after many years, I'm beginning to realize how wonderful Srila Prabhupada is, how we need him, and how important he is in our lives. My relationship with Srila Prabhupada is developing. He's become more of a reality. We shouldn't take what he said lightly. As time goes on my realizations are getting deeper and Prabhupada is more present now than when he was physically present.

Yasodamayi devi dasi

In the summer of 1974, Amarendra and Gayatri told Yasodamayi, then a newcomer to the Gainesville temple, that Srila Prabhupada would be attending the upcoming Philadelphia Ratha-yatra.

I felt that if I was taking some interest in this group, I should meet its leader and learn about him. So five or six women jumped in my small motorhome and we drove to the Ratha-yatra where I met Srila Prabhupada.

At this first meeting I thought I'd have an epiphany or something amazing would happen; I thought there'd be at least a few sparkles, if not fireworks. But, due to my mundane vision, all I saw was a nice, elderly gentleman from India. I didn't see a pure devotee because unless you're a pure devotee yourself, you can't recognize a pure devotee. With mundane vision a pure devotee looks like a regular guy. Later on, as I became more familiar with the philosophy, I understood you don't actually see a pure devotee with your eyes but with your ears. Hearing his teachings, reading the philosophy, learning as much about Krishna consciousness as you can – then you begin to recognize that a person is a pure devotee and not someone ordinary who's making up his own philosophy.

Everything about the Movement was so new to me; it was shocking to be in Philadelphia with the hundreds of devotees who had come from all over the East Coast. Yet at the same time I was impressed with everyone's devotion. After the Ratha-yatra we drove to New York, where Srila Prabhupada was going next. After Srila Prabhupada's lecture there everyone went up and got a cookie and I personally received one from Srila Prabhupada. Just to get that cookie was amazing. I gobbled it down immediately.

Mostly my interaction with Prabhupada was through his books. Gradually I gained a better idea of the philosophy and at some point felt that the philosophy made sense, it really was the Absolute Truth. It answers the question of why bad things happen to good people – without karma and reincarnation there's no explanation for it.

I realized that we are actually all servants. We all serve our bodies or our children, our boss or our society as a whole – everyone's a servant of someone or something, and the ultimate goal of life is to be a servant of Krishna. That realization had a profound effect on me. The ultimate goal of life was simple: to serve Krishna. It made complete, total sense. From that point on I felt Krishna consciousness was a legitimate philosophy and goal.

No other philosophy tells you who you are and who you're not. It makes sense that God is a person and is personally involved with His devotees' lives, as they are involved with His life. And there's plenty of Krishna to go around for everyone.

My whole life led up to the moment when I came in contact with Krishna consciousness. Meeting Srila Prabhupada positively affected the rest of my life. It never occurred to me that there might be a better philosophy, or maybe I made a mistake and wasted all those years. On the contrary, no one can ever take away the service in our spiritual bank account. It's there eternally. I've also realized that it's easy to offer lip service to the philosophy but hard to actually live it.

Yasomati devi dasi

In 1971, Yasomati was visiting the Montreal temple when she heard Isana crying as he read a letter he had received from Srila Prabhupada. Feeling Isana's special love for Srila Prabhupada was the beginning of Yasomati's relationship with him

I was sharing Srila Prabhupada's teachings at high school but my situation at home was difficult. The temple president told me, "Maybe Srila Prabhupada should hear your situation." By then, I felt Srila Prabhupada and Krishna were so big and I was so insignificant that, although I tried every day for a week, I couldn't write to Srila Prabhupada. It seemed inappropriate. My relationship with Srila Prabhupada was always in his absence and I felt he answered my letter through my seniors.

I traveled from Montreal to Vancouver and the following month Srila Prabhupada was in Portland, Oregon. I went there, was able to serve Srila Prabhupada by making his garlands and doing his laundry, and Prabhupada initiated me. He said, "Your name is Yasomati, mother of Krishna."

From the beginning, I was happy with Srila Prabhupada sending me instructions through others. When I pray for instructions they come somehow, through someone.

Sometimes my godbrothers, godsisters, and even juniors seem to have emotionally-laden love for Srila Prabhupada while my relationship is more formal. That bothered me. I'd think, "Maybe I don't love Srila Prabhupada the same way others do." So I asked Srila Prabhupada about it. Then someone – I can't remember who – quoted Srila Prabhupada saying, "As much as you love me, I will love you." I got my answer. I show my love for Srila Prabhupada through my service and he loves me equally. I'm insignificant, but I still have a personal link to Srila Prabhupada and it's revealed by the service I choose to do for him.

List of Srila Prabhupada's initiated daughters

Abhaya devi dasi	Portland	2	1975
Acintyasakti devi dasi	Caracas	4	1976
Acyutapriya devi dasi	New York	4	1976
Adija devi devi dasi	Frankfurt	6	1974
Adisakti devi dasi	London	9	1973
Aditi devi dasi	London	8	1970
Aditi devi dasi	Mayapur	3	1977
Aditya devi dasi	Dallas	1	1973
Agni devi dasi	LA	6	1972
Aha devi dasi	San Diego	1	1972
Aharada devi dasi	Amsterdam	12	1975
Ahoula devi dasi	Sydney	5	1971
Aja devi dasi	San Diego		1972
Akara devi dasi	New York	7	1977
Akhilesvari devi dasi	Miami	3	1977
Aksunnasakti devi dasi	London	12	1974
Akuti devi dasi	Houston	7	1971
Akuti devi dasi	Montreal	9	1977
Alarka devi dasi	New Vrindaban	9	1972
Ali Krsna devi dasi	Paris	7	1972
Ali Krsna devi dasi	San Francisco	1	1968
Aliptavani devi devi dasi	Edinburgh	7	1974
Amara devi dasi	Ann Arbor	6	1976
Ambhoda devi dasi	Montreal	12	1975
Ambika devi dasi	Sydney	4	1972
Ambudhara devi dasi	New Vrindaban	6	1976
Amekhala devi dasi	London	6	1974
Amitasakti devi dasi	Caracas	7	1976
Amohamoha devi dasi	Germany	12	1975
Amohamoha devi dasi	Italy	12	1975
Amrta devi dasi			
Amrtakeli devi dasi	Toronto	9	1977
Amrtaprada devi devi dasi	New Vrindaban	2	1975
Amrtavilasini devi dasi	Berkeley	7	1976
Amsumala devi devi dasi	Germany	11	1974
Anaghasuri? devi dasi	Toronto	9	1977
Anala devi dasi	Vancouver	1	1973
Anandacinmayi devi dasi	Miami	3	1977
Anandamurti devi dasi	Brazil	7	1976
Anandavidya devi dasi	LA	10	1973
Anandi devi dasi	London	9	1973
Anandini devi dasi	Caracas	3	1977
Anandini devi dasi	Philadelphia	5	1971
Anangamanjari devi dasi	Gainesville	7	1971
Ananta devi dasi	Chicago	7	1974
Ananta devi dasi	New York		1967
Ananta devi devi dasi	Chicago	7	1975

Name	Location		
Anantarupini devi dasi	France	9	1977
Anarta devi dasi	New Vrindaban	7	1977
Anasuya devi dasi	New York	10	1970
Anasuya devi dasi	New York	4	1973
Anavadyangi devi dasi	LA	9	1973
Andharupa devi dasi	Miami	1	1976
Anjana devi dasi	London	3	1975
Anjanasuta devi dasi	Caracas		1977
Annada devi dasi	Paris	11	1972
Annada-priya devi dasi	Brazil	3	1977
Annadasri devi dasi	Mayapur	3	1977
Annapurna devi dasi	Detroit	3	1977
Annapurna devi dasi	LA		1968
Antardhyana devi dasi	New Vrindaban	9	1972
Anumati devi dasi	Montreal	9	1976
Anuradha devi dasi	Denver	8	1972
Anuradha devi dasi	LA		1970
Anuttama devi dasi	Seattle	2	1977
Anuttara devi dasi	Mayapur	3	1977
Aparajita devi dasi	Melbourne	4	1976
Aparajita devi dasi	New York		
Apsara devi dasi	Mexico	6	1972
Aradhya devi devi dasi	Paris	6	1974
Araudra devi dasi	Boston	1	1973
Arca devi dasi	Sweden		
Arcamurti devi dasi	Toronto	9	1977
Arcana devi devi dasi	Nairobi	3	1974
Arcanasiddhi devi dasi	Washington	10	1977
Arci devi dasi	Atlanta		
Ardra devi dasi	Amsterdam	8	1976
Ariya devi devi dasi	Frankfurt	6	1974
Artiha devi dasi	Rome	12	1975
Arundhati devi dasi	Boston	1	1969
Aruni devi dasi	Melbourne	2	1973
Arya devi devi dasi	Vrndavana	4	1975
Asalata devi dasi	Toronto	1	1976
Asanga devi dasi	Germany	8	1976
Astasakhi devi dasi	Denver	4	1976
Astasakhi devi dasi	London	8	1972
Asurani devi dasi	Vrndavana	4	1976
Ati Candra devi dasi	Berkeley?		1973
Atigarvita devi dasi	Toronto	4	1973
Atitagamana devi dasi	Amsterdam	12	1975
Atitaguna devi dasi	Australia	4	1976
Atmamaya devi dasi	San Francisco	7	1974
Atmarama devi dasi	St. Louis		1975
Atmasakti devi dasi	LA	11	1973
Atmavana devi dasi	San Diego	1	1972
Atri devi dasi	Sydney	2	1973
Atura devi dasi	Philadelphia	6	1974

Name	Location	Month	Year
Bahubhavini devi devi dasi	LA	7	1975
Bakula devi dasi	Trinidad	12	1976
Bala Gopala devi dasi	London	1	1971
Balai devi dasi	New York	12	1967
Balavati devi devi dasi	Dallas	2	1975
Ballabhi devi dasi	Atlanta	7	1971
Ballavi-devi devi dasi	Chicago	7	1975
Barhismati devi devi dasi	Toronto	7	1971
Bedangi devi dasi	Philadelphia	4	1971
Bhadra devi dasi	New York	5	1971
Bhadra devi devi dasi	Melbourne	4	1975
Bhadrakrti devi dasi	Caracas	3	1977
Bhadramurti devi dasi	Mexico	10	1973
Bhadrapriya devi dasi	Toronto	9	1975
Bhadravati devi dasi	Rome	3	1977
Bhagamalini devi dasi	Mexico		1974
Bhagavatasakti devi dasi	Miami	12	1973
Bhagavatcitta devi dasi	LA	3	1973
Bhagavati devi dasi	Fiji	4	1976
Bhagavati devi dasi	St. Louis	7	1971
Bhagyavati devi dasi	Washington		1972
Bhaismi devi dasi	Germany	4	1974
Bhaja Govinda devi dasi	Gainesville	7	1976
Bhakta devi dasi	Buenos Aires	10	1973
Bhaktanidhi devi dasi	Buffalo	10	1973
Bhaktapriya devi dasi	Denver	10	1973
Bhaktavasya devi dasi	Toronto	10	1973
Bhakti devi dasi	Houston	7	1976
Bhakti? devi dasi	?		
Bhaktilata devi dasi	Denver	8	1972
Bhaktilata devi dasi	Detroit	9	1977
Bhaktilata devi dasi	London	8	1973
Bhaktilata devi dasi	N. Varsana	7	1977
Bhaktilila devi dasi	Berkeley	11	1976
Bhaktilila devi dasi	Washington		1973
Bhaktinidhi devi dasi	New Vrindaban		1975
Bhaktinistha devi dasi	Buffalo	10	1976
Bhaktiprema devi dasi	Vrndavana	6	1977
Bhaktirasa devi dasi	Buffalo	10	1976
Bhanutanya devi dasi	Dallas	6	1972
Bhavanasini devi dasi	Buffalo	10	1973
Bhavani devi dasi	London	9	1973
Bhavani devi dasi	St. Louis?	11	1977
Bhavatarini devi dasi	Bombay		1975
Bhavatarini devi dasi	Dallas	6	1972
Bhavatarini devi dasi	LA		1972
Bhismaka devi dasi	Vrndavana	9	1977
Bhogavati devi dasi	LA		
Bhogini devi dasi	Paris	9	1973

Name	Location		Year
Bhrama-karika devi devi dasi	LA	7	1975
Bhranti devi dasi	Gainesville	4	1976
Bhumata devi dasi	Dallas	9	1972
Bhumi devi dasi	New York	4	1973
Bhutamata devi devi dasi	Brazil	6	1975
Bhuvanapavani devi dasi	Miami	12	1973
Bibhavati devi dasi	New York	2	1969
Bidhibhakti devi dasi	New York		1972
Bijoy Laksmi devi dasi	Boston	11	1971
Bimala devi dasi	New York	7	1971
Biramala devi dasi	Dallas	1	1972
Brahma-vadini devi devi dasi	Cleveland	6	1975
Brahmajanani devi dasi	Edinburgh	5	1973
Brahmani devi dasi	LA		
Brahmapatni devi dasi	Auckland	1	1976
Brahmaraksi devi dasi	Frankfurt	7	1976
Brahmi devi devi dasi	Toronto	7	1974
Brajavanesvari devi dasi	New York	4	1977
Buddhi devi dasi	San Francisco	4	1976
Bundhya devi dasi	LA	6	1976
Caitanya devi dasi	LA	4	1970
Caitanya Lila devi dasi	LA	9	1977
Caitanya Lila devi devi dasi	LA	7	1974
Caitanyavani devi dasi	Auckland		
Cakrini devi dasi	Paris		1976
Camari devi dasi	Melbourne	3	1974
Cancala devi dasi	New York	4	1973
Candi devi dasi	Hawaii	8	1977
Candra devi dasi	New York		1973
Candra-lila devi dasi	London?		1976
Candrabali devi dasi	San Francisco	3	1967
Candranibha devi dasi	San Francisco	5	1973
Candrarekhika devi dasi	New Vrindaban	1	1974
Candravamsi devi dasi	Laguna	5	1976
Candrika devi dasi	Dallas	6	1972
Candrt devi dasi	Gainesville	3	1974
Caranti devi devi dasi	Houston	1	1973
Caroni devi dasi	New York	7	1971
Catura devi dasi	LA	4	1975
Cekitana devi dasi	Sydney	4	1972
Champakadevi devi dasi	LA	11	1973
Chayadevi devi dasi	New York	7	1971
Cinmayi devi dasi	Denver	7	1973
Cinmayi devi dasi	LA	5	1973
Cintamoni devi dasi	Columbus	5	1969
Citisakti devi dasi	New York	7	1971
Citraketu devi dasi	Buffalo	6	1973
Citralekha devi dasi	LA	1	1970
Citraratha devi dasi	New York		

Name	Location		Year
Citraratha devi dasi	Paris	8	1976
Citrarupini devi dasi	Rome	11	1975
Dainyahrt devi devi dasi	Baltimore	12	1974
Daivi devi dasi	Washington	7	1976
Daivi-sakti devi dasi	Philadelphia	8	1970
Daksayani devi dasi	Detroit	5	1973
Daksi devi dasi	Boston	10	1977
Daksina devi dasi	LA		1972
Daksinavari devi dasi	St. Louis	7	1973
Damadamini devi dasi	France		1975
Damagrahya devi devi dasi	New Vrindaban	2	1975
Damayanti devi dasi	London	8	1971
Damayanti devi dasi	Vrndavana	4	1976
Damodara Priya devi dasi	Dallas	7	1975
Danakeli devi dasi	San Francisco	7	1975
Danasila devi devi dasi	Chicago	2	1975
Dandakesi devi dasi	Paris	3	1974
Danta devi devi dasi	St. Louis	3	1975
Dantadhara devi dasi	Philadelphia	6	1974
Dapena devi dasi	Philadelphia		
Darpana devi dasi	Germany	4	1974
Darubrahma devi dasi	Berkeley	6	1976
Darumurti devi dasi	Montreal	3	1977
Dasarathi devi dasi	Seattle	10	1976
Daya devi dasi	Montreal	7	1976
Dayamayi devi dasi	Edinburgh	11	1972
Debraja devi dasi	New Orleans	2	1973
Desan Punanti devi devi dasi	Seattle	1	1974
Deva devi dasi	Brazil	12	1976
Devadarsana devi dasi	Melbourne	4	1972
Devadeva Priya devi devi dasi	Sydney	11	1974
Devadidhiti devi dasi	New York		1973
Devahuti devi dasi	Calcutta	3	1977
Devahuti devi devi dasi	Boston	4	1976
Devahuti devi devi dasi	LA		1969
Devaki devi dasi	Atlanta	4	1976
Devakulya devi dasi	Vancouver		1977
Devamata devi devi dasi	LA	10	1974
Devavani devi dasi	Siddh	3	1977
Devayani devi dasi	Boston	7	1971
Devayani devi dasi	Gainesville	8	1977
Devi devi dasi	Florida	1	1971
Devidarsana devi dasi	Sydney		
Dhanasri devi dasi	Seattle	5	1974
Dhanistha devi devi dasi	San Francisco	7	1974
Dhanurdhari devi dasi	LA	1	1974
Dhanvantari devi dasi	Indonesia		1972
Dhanya devi dasi	Brazil	7	1976
Dhara devi devi dasi	Atlanta	7	1974

Name	Location		Year
Dharini devi devi dasi	Vancouver	4	1975
Dharmada devi devi dasi	LA	6	1975
Dharmakala devi dasi	New Vrindaban		1974
Dharmapatni devi dasi	Brazil	9	1976
Dharmarupa devi dasi	Paris	12	1975
Dhatreyi devi dasi	LA	12	1973
Dhenumati devi dasi	Detroit	1	1974
Dhenuvati devi devi dasi	Edinburgh	7	1974
Dhira devi dasi	Miami	7	1976
Dhira-sevi devi dasi	LA	1	1974
Dhrti devi dasi	LA	10	1975
Diksa devi dasi	Miami	7	1976
Diksavati devi devi dasi	LA	10	1974
Dinadaya devi dasi	Cleveland	8	1976
Dinadayadri devi dasi	Detroit	2	1970
Dinasarana devi devi dasi	Germany	11	1974
Dinatarini devi dasi	Dallas		1972
Dinesvara devi dasi	LA		
Dirgha-devi devi dasi	Paris	6	1974
Divya devi dasi	LA	1	1974
Divyadrsti devi dasi	Berkeley	2	1977
Divyasakti devi dasi	Dallas	7	1976
Divyasakti devi dasi	London	8	1972
Draupadi devi dasi	London	9	1969
Duhkhahantri devi dasi	New York	8	1973
Duhsala devi dasi	Gainesville	8	1977
Duravanya devi devi dasi	San Diego	11	1974
Durgadevi devi devi dasi	Chicago	7	1974
Dvarakavasini devi dasi	Laguna	5	1976
Dvijapatna devi dasi	Washington		
Dvijapriya devi dasi	LA		1973
Dyuti devi dasi	Dallas	3	1974
Ekabuddhi devi dasi	New York	7	1976
Ekadasi devi dasi	France	6	1976
Ekanga devi dasi	Brazil	7	1976
Ekanti devi dasi	Germany	9	1976
Ekayani devi dasi	New York	12	1967
Gandhari devi dasi	New Orleans	2	1973
Gandhari devi dasi	Portland	7	1974
Gandharvi devi dasi	Mayapur	3	1974
Gandharvika devi dasi	New York	7	1971
Gandharvika? devi dasi	Johannesburg	8	1977
Gandini devi dasi	Mexico	9	1977
Gandiva devi dasi	Bombay	10	1972
Ganga Gati devi dasi	Vrndavana	4	1976
Gangamayi devi dasi	London	8	1972
Garudi devi dasi	Paris		1976
Gati devi dasi	Montreal	9	1977
Gaura devi dasi	Chicago	3	1977
Gauranga devi dasi	Cleveland		1973

Name	Location		Year
Gaurangi devi dasi	Sydney	5	1971
Gauravani devi dasi	Auckland	4	1976
Gauri devi dasi	New York		1970
Gavisi devi dasi	Vrndavana	1	1976
Gaya devi dasi	Hawaii	8	1977
Gayatri devi dasi	Gainesville	7	1971
Girija devi dasi	Montreal	9	1977
Girindra Mohini devi dasi	New Vrindaban	9	1972
Girisuta devi devi dasi	Mexico	2	1975
Girvani devi dasi	Frankfurt	7	1976
Gita devi dasi	Vancouver	1	1973
Gokularani devi dasi	London	3	1975
Gokulavasini devi dasi	Colombia	3	1977
Golokavasini devi dasi	Hawaii	1	1974
Gomata devi dasi	New Vrindaban	4	1973
Gopa Kanya devi dasi	Detroit	8	1975
Gopala devi dasi	Sydney	2	1973
Gopala-sakhi devi dasi	London		1976
Gopalasya Priya devi dasi	New Vrindaban	11	1975
Gopamatrika devi dasi	Baltimore	11	1976
Gopanandakari devi dasi	Denver	9	1975
Gopanandini devi dasi	New York?	4	1976
Gopanandini devi dasi	Paris	12	1975
Gopapatni devi dasi	Gainesville	4	1976
Gopi devi dasi	Heidelberg		1972
Gopika devi dasi	Berkeley	7	1971
Gopika devi dasi	Vrndavana	4	1975
Gopimata devi dasi	London		1977
Gopinatha devi dasi	Philadelphia		1973
Gopipriya devi dasi	Auckland	4	1973
Gopipriya devi devi dasi	London	1	1975
Govardhana devi dasi	Edinburgh	5	1973
Govatsa Rakhala devi dasi	London	4	1977
Govinda devi dasi	San Francisco	2	1967
Govinda Mohini devi dasi	Mayapur	9	1977
Govinda Mohini devi dasi	San Diego	9	1977
Govinda Mohini devi dasi	Sydney	5	1971
Govinda-vallabha devi dasi	Boston	12	1973
Govindanandini devi dasi	Brazil	3	1977
Govindanandini devi dasi	Sydney	5	1971
Govindarupini devi dasi	St. Louis	7	1973
Gunamayi devi dasi	LA	8	1971
Gunaraja devi dasi	Edinburgh		1973
Gunavati devi dasi	Melbourne	6	1974
Gunyarupini devi dasi	New Vrindaban	4	1973
Guptalaya devi dasi	Paris	8	1974
Guru Carana Padma devi dasi	Chicago	9	1977
Gurubhakta devi dasi	Amsterdam	8	1976
Haladhara devi dasi	San Francisco	2	1967

Name	Location		Year
Hamsarupa devi dasi	Mayapur		1975
Hamsini devi dasi	New Orleans	7	1973
Harakanta devi dasi	Boston	10	1977
Haranetrani devi dasi	New York		1973
Hardajna devi dasi	Philadelphia	7	1975
Harestanu devi dasi	Miami	1	1976
Hari devi dasi	Melbourne	11	1976
Harikanta devi dasi	Dallas	7	1975
Harilila devi dasi	Vancouver		1976
Harinama devi dasi	Chicago	7	1974
Haripriya devi dasi	Hamburg	4	1970
Haripriya devi dasi	London	3	1973
Haripriya devi dasi	Washington	7	1974
Haripuja devi dasi	Pittsburgh	6	1972
Harirani devi dasi	Montreal	3	1977
Harisevaka devi dasi	LA	1	1974
Harsarani devi dasi	San Francisco	2	1967
Harsita devi dasi	Nairobi	3	1977
Havirdhani devi dasi	San Francisco	3	1973
Hemalata devi dasi	Washington	7	1971
Herapancami devi dasi	LA	8	1972
Himavati devi dasi	San Francisco	5	1967
Hiranmayi devi devi dasi	Geneva	2	1975
Hiranyangi devi dasi	Sweden	2	1977
Hladini devi dasi	Detroit	3	1970
Hladini Sakti devi dasi	London	9	1973
Homavatsala devi dasi	Paris	8	1974
Hrimati devi dasi	Hamburg	4	1973
Hrtkamalaya devi dasi	Germany	8	1976
Iccha devi dasi	Stockholm	4	1974
Icchagati devi dasi	Boston	2	1976
Icchamati devi dasi	Detroit		1970
Ila devi dasi	New Vrindaban	3	1977
Ilavati devi dasi	Hamburg	1	1970
Indira devi dasi	Germany		1973
Indira devi dasi	New York	12	1967
Indrani devi dasi	Hamburg	7	1970
Indriyani devi dasi	Baltimore		1971
Indujyoti devi dasi	Berkeley	7	1976
Indukanthi devi dasi	Frankfurt	7	1976
Indumati devi dasi	Brazil	12	1976
Indumati devi dasi	New York?		1968
Indurekha devi dasi	Bombay	5	1974
Indurekha devi dasi	Mexico	6	1972
Iravati devi dasi	LA		
Isa devi devi dasi	New York	9	1974
Isani devi dasi	New Vrindaban	9	1972
Isesvari devi dasi	Caracas	3	1977
Isvarapatni devi dasi	Germany	8	1976

Name	Location		
Isvari devi dasi	London	9	1973
Jagaddeha devi dasi	Philadelphia	7	1975
Jagaddhatri devi dasi	London	3	1975
Jagaddhatri devi dasi	Seattle	8	1973
Jagadisvari devi dasi	Seattle	1	1973
Jagajjanani devi dasi	Denver	12	1976
Jagamohini devi dasi	LA	12	1971
Jaganmata devi dasi	New York	6	1975
Jaganmata devi devi dasi	Montreal	4	1975
Jaganmayi devi devi dasi	Ann Arbor	2	1975
Jaganmurti devi devi dasi	Buffalo	5	1975
Jagannatha Puri devi dasi	Berkeley	11	1976
Jagannathesvari devi dasi	Vrndavana	4	1976
Jagarini devi dasi	LA	5	1973
Jagatam devi dasi	Philadelphia	4	1976
Jagatikanda devi dasi	Toronto	4	1973
Jagatkarana devi dasi	LA	9	1977
Jagatkirti devi dasi	Paris	3	1974
Jagatpriya devi dasi	Sydney	8	1976
Jagattarini devi dasi	Hong Kong		1971
Jahnava devi dasi	Boston	2	1969
Jahnavi devi dasi	Caracas	3	1977
Jahnavi devi devi dasi	Chicago	7	1974
Jaladhosa devi dasi	Mexico	8	1974
Jalangi devi dasi	Gainesville	3	1975
Jalapriya devi dasi	Paris	8	1974
Jalasayi devi devi dasi	Denver	12	1974
Jalasthita devi dasi	London	6	1974
Jalatala devi dasi	Mayapur	3	1976
Jaleyu devi dasi	Melbourne	3	1977
Jalodari devi dasi	Brazil	7	1976
Jamatri devi dasi	Trinidad	4	1976
Jambavati devi dasi	Brazil	9	1977
Jambuvati devi dasi	LA	6	1969
Jambuvati devi dasi	Philadelphia		1969
Jami devi dasi	London		1977
Janaki devi dasi	London	9	1976
Janaki devi dasi	New York	9	1966
Janani devi dasi	New Vrindaban	8	1975
Janani devi dasi	New York	8	1977
Jananigati devi dasi	LA	3	1977
Janardana Prita devi devi dasi	London	12	1974
Janasakti devi devi dasi	Vrndavana	4	1975
Janesvari devi dasi	LA	3	1977
Janesvari devi dasi	Montreal	3	1977
Janjapukandhi-devi devi dasi	San Francisco	11	1974
Janmasunya devi dasi	Atlanta	9	1975
Jara devi dasi	Atlanta	8	1977
Jarati devi dasi	LA		

Name	Location		Year
Jatila devi dasi	Atlanta	4	1976
Jaya devi dasi	London	3	1977
Jayabhadra devi dasi	Vancouver	12	1973
Jayagaurangi devi devi dasi	LA	11	1973
Jayagauri devi dasi	France	8	1976
Jayagopi devi devi dasi	LA	11	1973
Jayalaksmi devi dasi	Paris		1970
Jayalalita devi dasi	New York	7	1976
Jayanti devi dasi	Australia	11	1974
Jayapatni devi dasi	Puerto Rico	10	1977
Jayaprada devi dasi	New Orleans	8	1975
Jayaradhe devi dasi	Detroit	6	1972
Jayaradhe devi dasi	France		1971
Jayarama devi dasi	Venezuela		1976
Jayasri devi dasi	Dallas?		1974
Jayasri devi dasi	Hawaii	5	1969
Jijnasi devi dasi	London	8	1971
Jitamitra devi dasi	New York	1	1973
Jitasakti devi dasi	Australia	3	1977
Jiva devi dasi	Paris	8	1975
Jivana devi dasi	San Francisco		1972
Jivanamukta devi dasi	Paris	9	1977
Jivanausadhi devi dasi	Seattle	5	1975
Jnanamurti devi devi dasi	Melbourne	5	1975
Jotilla devi dasi	LA	1	1969
Jusaniya devi devi dasi	Gainesville	3	1975
Jyestha devi dasi	Paris	6	1974
Jyotiraditya devi dasi	Portland		1973
Jyotirmayi devi dasi	London	1	1970
Kadamba devi dasi	LA	10	1973
Kadambakusuma Priya devi dasi	Tokyo		1973
Kadambaripriya devi dasi	Seattle	7	1973
Kajjali devi devi dasi	Hawaii	1	1974
Kalakantha devi dasi	San Francisco	12	1973
Kalakantha? devi dasi			
Kalalapa devi dasi	Chicago	7	1973
Kalavati devi dasi	LA	5	1972
Kali devi dasi	Philadelphia		
Kalindi devi dasi	Buffalo		1968
Kalindi devi dasi	Vrndavana	4	1976
Kalki devi devi dasi	Sydney	4	1972
Kalpalatika devi devi dasi	San Francisco	11	1974
Kamadhenu devi dasi	France		1972
Kamadhuk devi dasi	Edinburgh	2	1973
Kamadhuki devi dasi	Brazil	9	1977
Kamagayatri devi dasi	Dallas	1	1974
Kamagayatri devi dasi	Sweden	9	1976
Kamagiri devi dasi	Cleveland?		1977
Kamaha devi dasi	Hawaii	5	1974

Kamaksi devi dasi	Hamburg	4	1973
Kamala devi dasi	LA		1972
Kamalakanti devi dasi	London	8	1972
Kamalakara devi dasi	Sydney		1972
Kamalaksi devi dasi	Winnipeg	11	1974
Kamalangi devi devi dasi	London	9	1973
Kamalatika devi dasi	San Francisco	12	1973
Kamalavati devi dasi	Denver	10	1971
Kamalini devi devi dasi	New York	12	1974
Kamanagari devi dasi	Dallas	10	1973
Kamarikanta devi dasi	New Orleans	8	1975
Kamarupa devi dasi	Sydney	2	1973
Kamatavi devi dasi	San Diego	1	1974
Kamesi devi dasi	Dallas	7	1975
Kamesvari devi dasi	New Vrindaban		
Kamini devi devi dasi	Hawaii	3	1975
Kamra devi devi dasi	New York	12	1974
Kamya devi dasi	Buffalo	3	1974
Kancanbala devi dasi	New York	12	1967
Kancani devi dasi	Germany	4	1974
Kandarpa-sundari devi dasi	San Francisco	12	1973
Kanka devi dasi	New York	7	1971
Kansa devi dasi	New York	7	1971
Kanta devi dasi	LA	2	1971
Kanti devi dasi	Paris	2	1974
Kantimati devi dasi	Seattle	7	1973
Kanva devi dasi	Berkeley	6	1976
Kanya Kumari devi dasi	New Orleans		1971
Kapardini devi dasi	London	5	1973
Karanakarana devi devi dasi	Ottawa	1	1975
Karlapati devi dasi	LA	9	1972
Karmasaksi devi dasi	Mexico	6	1976
Karta devi dasi	LA	12	1973
Karuna devi dasi	Berkeley	8	1976
Karunaksi devi dasi	Seattle	2	1977
Karunamayi devi dasi	Berkeley		1970
Karunamayi devi dasi	San Francisco		1967
Karunapurnasakti devi dasi	Atlanta	7	1976
Karyatita devi dasi	New Vrindaban	12	1975
Kasturi devi dasi	Bombay	5	1974
Kasturika devi dasi	New York	4	1970
Katharuci devi dasi	Chicago?	3	1977
Katyayani devi dasi	Pittsburgh	7	1971
Kaulini devi dasi	San Francisco	5	1973
Kaumadi devi dasi	LA	5	1972
Kaumudaki devi dasi	New York	7	1971
Kausalya devi dasi	LA	1	1969
Kelicancala devi dasi	St. Louis	12	1973
Kelilalita devi devi dasi	San Francisco	11	1974

Name	Location		
Kesava-ruci devi dasi	Calcutta	3	1977
Kesavapriya devi dasi	LA		
Kevala Bhakti devi dasi	Denver	9	1977
Khandabasi devi dasi	Berlin		1974
Khandavabha devi dasi	Vancouver	1	1974
Khandita devi devi dasi	Denver	8	1974
Khastha devi devi dasi	New Vrindaban	10	1974
Kilimba devi dasi	Seattle	2	1977
Kirtida Kanyaka devi dasi	LA	3	1973
Kirtika devi dasi	Buffalo	5	1971
Kirtima devi dasi	London	12	1969
Kirtimati devi dasi	Toronto	2	1971
Kisori devi dasi	Amsterdam		1971
Kisori devi dasi	Vrndavana	4	1976
Kisoriballabha devi dasi	Mayapur	3	1976
Klamahara devi devi dasi	Winnipeg	11	1974
Klesagni Bhakti devi dasi	Montreal	1	1977
Kratuphala devi devi dasi	New Vrindaban	2	1975
Kratusrestha devi dasi	Paris	3	1975
Kriyasakti devi devi dasi	Laguna	8	1974
Kriyasakti devi devi dasi	San Diego	11	1974
Krodhasamani devi dasi	Detroit	5	1973
Krpamayi devi dasi	Detroit	12	1971
Krsna devi devi dasi	Dallas	7	1974
Krsna devi devi dasi	San Francisco	2	1967
Krsnabamini devi dasi	New Vrindaban	6	1969
Krsnabhava devi dasi	Buffalo	1	1973
Krsnakamala? devi dasi	London		1972
Krsnakamini devi dasi	Columbus?	8	1969
Krsnakamini devi dasi	New Vrindaban	6	1976
Krsnakamini devi dasi	Paris	7	1972
Krsnakanta devi devi dasi	Geneva	2	1975
Krsnakaruna devi dasi	Toronto	6	1976
Krsnakatha devi dasi	Hyderabad	12	1976
Krsnakirtana devi dasi	France	11	1977
Krsnakrpa devi dasi	Mississippi	4	1977
Krsnakrpa devi dasi	Washington	7	1976
Krsnakumari devi dasi	?		
Krsnakumari devi dasi	New Vrindaban	9	1972
Krsnalaulya devi dasi	Hawaii	9	1976
Krsnalaulya devi dasi	LA	1	1974
Krsnalila devi dasi	Seattle		
Krsnalila devi dasi	Vrndavana	7	1977
Krsnamayi devi dasi	Cleveland		1972
Krsnanandini devi dasi	Brazil	12	1976
Krsnanandini devi dasi	Dallas	9	1972
Krsnanga devi devi dasi	Edinburgh	7	1974
Krsnaparayani devi dasi	London		
Krsnapremanandi devi dasi	London	5	1973

Name	Location		Year
Krsnapremavati devi dasi	Sydney	9	1977
Krsnapremi devi dasi	Sydney	5	1971
Krsnapriya devi dasi	Bombay		1975
Krsnapriya devi dasi	LA		1971
Krsnapriya devi dasi	Mayapur	3	1976
Krsnapriya devi dasi	Seattle	8	1974
Krsnapujya devi devi dasi	New Orleans	6	1975
Krsnarupa devi dasi	Vrndavana	8	1974
Krsnastuta devi dasi	LA	10	1975
Krsnatulasi devi dasi	Bombay	3	1971
Krsnavesa devi dasi	Germany	4	1974
Krsnavilasini devi dasi	LA	2	1970
Ksama devi dasi	Amsterdam	11	1971
Ksamakula devi dasi	New Zealand	1	1976
Ksiracora devi devi dasi	Toronto	1	1975
Kubja Krpamoya devi dasi	New York	7	1977
Kulaja devi dasi	Philadelphia	7	1975
Kulangana devi devi dasi	London	7	1974
Kulapriya devi dasi	LA	10	1975
Kulina devi dasi	Mayapur	3	1976
Kumari devi dasi	Philadelphia	7	1975
Kumkum devi dasi	Dallas	10	1971
Kunjamandana devi dasi	London	8	1971
Kunjari devi dasi	New Vrindaban	1	1974
Kunti devi dasi	Brazil	9	1977
Kunti devi dasi	Hamburg	9	1969
Kunti devi dasi	New Vrindaban	9	1972
Kurmayana devi devi dasi	Detroit	2	1975
Kusa devi dasi	Hawaii		1970
Kusala-devi devi dasi	LA	6	1974
Kusuma-priya devi dasi	LA	5	1972
Kusumapida devi dasi	LA		1972
Kusumika devi dasi	LA	12	1973
Kutila devi dasi	New Vrindaban		1971
Labangalatika devi dasi	San Francisco?	2	1969
Labangamanjari devi dasi	LA	5	1972
Lajjavati devi dasi	New Vrindaban	4	1973
Lakhima devi dasi	Vancouver	6	1972
Laksmana devi devi dasi	Sydney	4	1972
Laksmi devi dasi	Miami		
Laksmi devi dasi	San Francisco	1	1968
Laksmimoni devi dasi	Buffalo	7	1969
Laksmipati devi dasi	LA		1972
Laksmipriya devi dasi	Mexico	6	1972
Lalagopala devi dasi	London	9	1976
Lalana devi dasi	Chicago	3	1974
Lalanamani devi dasi	New York	7	1976
Lalita devi devi dasi	Chicago	7	1975
Lalita devi devi dasi	London	1	1975

Name	Place		Year
Lalita devi devi dasi	Montreal	10	1974
Lalita devi devi dasi	Seattle	5	1975
Lalita-priya devi dasi	Edinburgh		1975
Lalitacara devi dasi	LA	4	1975
Lalitakrsna devi dasi	Houston	4	1977
Lalitakunda devi devi dasi	Frankfurt	6	1974
Lalitasakhi devi dasi	New Vrindaban	9	1972
Lalitasakhi devi dasi	New Vrindaban	6	1976
Lamba devi dasi	Berkeley	6	1976
Lasika devi dasi	Miami	7	1976
Lata-devi devi dasi	Pittsburgh?		1975
Latika devi dasi	Berkeley		
Lekhasravanti devi dasi	Detroit		1974
Lekhasravanti devi devi dasi	Germany	12	1974
Lelihana devi devi dasi	Vrndavana	4	1975
Lila devi dasi	LA	1	1974
Lila devi devi dasi	Denver	12	1976
Lila devi devi dasi	Portland	8	1974
Lilakatha devi dasi	Montreal	3	1977
Lilamanjari devi dasi	New York	7	1971
Lilamanjari devi dasi	Vancouver	7	1974
Lilamohini devi dasi	London	3	1977
Lilamrta devi dasi	Vancouver		1976
Lilarati devi dasi	Trinidad	3	1977
Lilasakhi devi dasi	Miami	3	1977
Lilasakti devi dasi	Detroit	1	1977
Lilasakti devi dasi	LA	4	1971
Lilasakti devi dasi	London	8	1970
Lilasmaranam devi devi dasi	San Francisco	7	1974
Lilasmrti devi dasi	New York	7	1976
Lilasravana devi devi dasi	Hawaii	3	1975
Lilasuka devi dasi	New York	12	1967
Lilasuka devi dasi	Toronto	6	1976
Lilasukha-devi devi dasi	Toronto	7	1975
Lilasukhi devi dasi	Honolulu		1976
Lilasukhi devi dasi	Vancouver	4	1977
Lilavatara devi dasi	Caracas	4	1976
Lingini devi dasi	Seattle	2	1977
Locanapadma devi dasi	Gita Nagari	3	1977
Lohanga devi dasi	?		
Lokadevi devi dasi	New York	3	1977
Lokadrsti devi dasi	Toronto	3	1974
Lokahita devi devi dasi	Dallas	11	1974
Lokalila devi dasi	Denver	2	1974
Lokamangalam devi dasi	France	11	1977
Lokamata devi dasi	Amsterdam	8	1976
Lokesvari devi dasi	Rome	3	1977
Lola devi dasi	Vancouver	1	1974
Madana Mohana devi dasi	Hawaii	8	1977

Name	Location		Year
Madana Mohana devi dasi	New York	7	1977
Madana Mohana Mohini dd	Paris	7	1972
Madanalasa devi dasi	Heidelberg	1	1974
Madanalasa devi dasi	New Vrindaban	1	1974
Madanamohini devi dasi	Atlanta	9	1975
Madanasini devi dasi	San Francisco	5	1973
Madanasundari devi dasi	LA	11	1973
Madhavapriya devi dasi	Vancouver	10	1976
Madhavi devi dasi	Chicago	4	1976
Madhavi devi dasi	LA	6	1972
Madhavi-lata? devi dasi	Montreal?		1968
Madhu devi devi dasi	San Diego	4	1975
Madhumalati devi dasi	LA		1973
Madhumati devi dasi	Detroit		1973
Madhumati devi dasi	Paris		
Madhumati devi devi dasi	Vancouver	12	1974
Madhuprita devi dasi	Mexico	9	1973
Madhupuri devi dasi	New York	7	1971
Madhuri devi devi dasi	Caracas	2	1975
Madhuryalilananda devi dasi	Denver	12	1972
Madhusrava devi devi dasi	Mexico	2	1975
Madhyama devi dasi	Detroit	9	1973
Madira devi dasi	Buffalo	7	1971
Madri devi dasi	Berkeley		1969
Mahabhagavata devi dasi	Portland		1977
Mahabhoga devi dasi	Philadelphia		
Mahadevi devi dasi	Melbourne	5	1975
Mahadevi devi dasi	New Vrindaban	2	1975
Mahadhana devi dasi	Philadelphia		1973
Mahaguna devi dasi	LA	9	1972
Mahakamini? devi dasi	New Vrindaban		1974
Mahalaksmi devi devi dasi	Boston	1	1975
Mahamanjari devi dasi	LA	3	1977
Mahamaya devi dasi	Washington	7	1971
Mahamedha devi dasi	Sweden	10	1974
Mahanandi devi dasi	Santo Domingo	5	1974
Mahanandini devi dasi	Detroit	3	1975
Mahapunya devi devi dasi	Mexico	2	1975
Maharajni devi dasi	Cleveland	3	1974
Maharani devi dasi	Detroit?		1972
Maharha devi dasi	New York	1	1973
Mahasini devi dasi	LA	6	1971
Mahati devi dasi	Austin	1	1972
Mahavegavati devi dasi	LA	10	1974
Mahavegavati devi dasi	Miami	7	1974
Mahavisnupriya devi dasi	Hawaii	11	1975
Mahayogisvari devi devi dasi	Brazil	6	1975
Mahendrani devi dasi	Trinidad	3	1977
Mahesani devi dasi	LA		

Name	Location	Month	Year
Mahesvari devi dasi	Berkeley	11	1976
Mahesvari devi dasi	Toronto		1971
Mahimabhusana devi devi dasi	Paris	3	1975
Mahira-kanya devi dasi	Detroit	6	1976
Mahodhari devi dasi	San Diego	2	1976
Mahojjvala devi devi dasi	Philadelphia	7	1974
Mahojjvala devi devi dasi	Vancouver	7	1974
Maitahili devi dasi	San Francisco	3	1970
Maladhara devi dasi	Auckland		1973
Maladhari devi devi dasi	Portland	2	1975
Malati devi dasi	San Francisco	2	1967
Malini devi dasi	Toronto	12	1973
Mallika devi dasi	New York	7	1976
Mamata devi dasi	New York	7	1971
Mamavi devi dasi	?	11	1976
Manada devi dasi	Germany	4	1974
Manakumari devi dasi	New Vrindaban	9	1972
Manamohini devi dasi	Boston	2	1970
Manasa-ganga devi dasi	LA	9	1977
Manasvini devi dasi	Buffalo	10	1976
Manavi devi dasi	France	11	1976
Mandahasa devi dasi	Paris	3	1974
Mandari devi dasi	Regina	3	1974
Mandodari devi dasi	Guatemala	3	1977
Mangala devi dasi	San Francisco		1971
Mangalada devi dasi	Brazil	7	1976
Mangalya devi dasi	Amsterdam	12	1975
Manimanjari devi dasi	Bombay	5	1974
Manimanjari devi dasi	Germany	1	1974
Manindra devi dasi	LA	12	1973
Manini devi devi dasi	San Francisco	11	1974
Manipuspaka devi dasi	San Francisco	11	1972
Manisa devi dasi	Dallas	3	1974
Manjari devi dasi	Hawaii	6	1971
Manjuali devi dasi	LA	5	1972
Manohara devi dasi	Detroit	8	1972
Manohara devi dasi	San Juan	8	1974
Manohara devi dasi	Vrndavana	4	1976
Manoharini devi dasi	Chicago	3	1977
Mantrini devi dasi	Chicago	7	1973
Manukanya devi dasi	New York	7	1976
Manupatni devi dasi	Rome	3	1977
Marutvati devi dasi	Amsterdam	1	1977
Mathura devi dasi	Mexico	8	1974
Mati devi dasi	Vrndavana	4	1976
Matida devi devi dasi	Sydney	11	1974
Matsya devi dasi	Brazil	12	1976
Mayapriya devi dasi	New Vrindaban	3	1975
Mayapura devi devi dasi	Brazil	9	1977

Name	Location		Year
Mayavati devi dasi	Toronto	2	1971
Mayura devi dasi	LA	10	1976
Medha devi dasi	LA?		1974
Medhya devi devi dasi	Montreal	10	1974
Megha devi devi dasi	Philadelphia	7	1975
Meghamala devi devi dasi	New Vrindaban	7	1974
Mekhala devi dasi	Chicago	3	1974
Mekhala devi dasi	Melbourne	4	1972
Menaka devi dasi	Costa Rica	3	1977
Meru devi dasi	LA		
Meru devi devi dasi	Brazil	8	1977
Meru devi devi dasi	Portland	7	1975
Merumala devi dasi	Paris	6	1974
Merumala devi dasi	Santo Domingo	5	1974
Mina devi dasi	Boston		1972
Mirabai devi dasi	LA	8	1969
Mirabai devi dasi	Paris	7	1972
Misrani devi dasi	Toronto	12	1973
Mitravinda devi dasi	Denver	5	1972
Mitravrtti devi dasi	New York	3	1977
Modani devi dasi	Caracas	1	1974
Mohana devi dasi	New Vrindaban		
Mohanasini devi dasi	LA	9	1973
Mohini devi dasi	Montreal	9	1973
Mohini-sakti devi dasi	Melbourne	6	1974
Moksa Laksmi-devi devi dasi	Vrndavana	4	1975
Moksada devi dasi	Trinidad	3	1977
Moksarupa devi dasi	San Francisco	7	1975
Mondakini devi dasi	London	1	1970
Mondakini Ganga devi dasi	Mexico	4	1977
Mrda devi dasi	Paris	9	1973
Mrdani devi dasi	Heidelberg	6	1973
Mrdapriya devi dasi	San Francisco	5	1973
Mrgaksi devi dasi	Cleveland	6	1973
Mrganetri devi dasi	LA	6	1970
Mrnalini devi dasi	New Vrindaban	7	1972
Mrnmayi devi dasi	Paris	2	1971
Mudakari-devi devi dasi	New Vrindaban	2	1975
Mukhara devi dasi	Dallas		1973
Mukhya-devi devi dasi	Detroit	2	1975
Mukti devi dasi	Caracas	8	1976
Muktihetu devi dasi	Brazil	7	1976
Mukunda-devi devi dasi	Chicago	7	1974
Mulaka devi dasi	Baltimore	8	1977
Mulaprakrti devi dasi	LA	10	1973
Munipatni devi dasi	LA	3	1972
Munipatni devi dasi	LA	10	1976
Murti devi dasi	Brazil	12	1976
Murti-vandya devi devi dasi	New York	6	1975

Name	Location	Month	Year
Murtimurti devi devi dasi	Caracas	2	1975
Nabhalinga devi dasi	Brazil	9	1977
Nabhasvati devi dasi	London	8	1972
Nada devi dasi	Berkeley	8	1976
Nagapatni devi dasi	LA	2	1971
Nagari devi dasi	Gainesville	3	1974
Nairvani devi dasi	Brazil	7	1976
Naiskarmi devi dasi	New Vrindaban	9	1972
Nama Sankirtana devi dasi	Hawaii	8	1977
Nanda devi dasi	Boston	6	1972
Nandadayini-devi devi dasi	Caracas	2	1975
Nandalala devi dasi	LA		1970
Nandapatni devi dasi	Vancouver	7	1976
Nandapriya devi dasi	London	8	1975
Nandarani devi dasi	San Francisco	3	1967
Nandidevi devi dasi	Washington	4	1975
Nandimukhi devi dasi	LA		
Nandini devi dasi	Mayapur	3	1977
Nandirupaka devi dasi	Paris	12	1975
Nandita Gokula devi dasi	Denver	5	1972
Naradevi devi dasi	New York	7	1971
Naradi-devi devi dasi	Atlanta	7	1974
Naravesa devi dasi	Berkeley	6	1976
Narayani devi dasi	Gainesville	7	1971
Nari devi dasi	Pittsburgh	4	1973
Narmada devi dasi	New Vrindaban		
Narmadadevi devi dasi	Costa Rica	3	1977
Nartaka-gopala-devi devi dasi	Miami	1	1975
Nartaki devi dasi	Sydney	5	1971
Nataka Candrika devi dasi	Denver	8	1974
Navalanga-devi devi dasi	Paris	6	1974
Navasi devi dasi	New Vrindaban	9	1972
Navina devi dasi	Laguna	1	1972
Nayika devi dasi	San Diego	4	1976
Nidra-devi devi dasi	Denver	12	1976
Nidra-devi devi dasi	Montreal	3	1974
Nikhilesvari devi dasi	Atlanta	10	1973
Nikunjarasi Vilasi devi dasi	St. Louis	7	1973
Nikunjavasini devi devi dasi	Miami	7	1974
Nikunjavasini-devi devi dasi	Frankfurt	6	1974
Nilacala devi dasi	Costa Rica	5	1976
Nipuna devi dasi	LA	1	1973
Niradhara devi dasi	Mexico	9	1973
Nirakula devi dasi	LA	5	1973
Niranjana devi dasi	New York	6	1975
Nirguna-devi devi dasi	Vrndavana	4	1975
Nirlepa devi dasi	Mexico	9	1973
Nirmala-devi devi dasi	New Vrindaban	7	1974
Nirmala-devi devi dasi	Paris	3	1975

Nirupadi devi dasi	Laguna	10	1973
Nirupama devi dasi	Vancouver	7	1971
Niscintya devi dasi	LA	12	1973
Nitaipatni devi dasi	Montreal	7	1976
Nitigata devi dasi	Sydney		1973
Nitya devi dasi	London	8	1973
Nitya devi dasi	Mexico	9	1973
Nityalila devi dasi	Vrndavana	4	1976
Nityalila-sakhi devi dasi	China	3	1977
Nityamanjari devi dasi	St. Louis	10	1976
Nityarupa devi dasi	Berkeley	4	1976
Nityatrpta devi dasi	LA	6	1976
Nogomala? devi dasi	New Vrindaban?		1974
Nrsimha devi dasi	Minneapolis	11	1976
Nrsimhananda devi devi dasi	Vrndavana	8	1977
Ojasvini devi devi dasi	Mexico	2	1975
Omkara devi dasi	New York	1	1973
Padma devi dasi	Miami	7	1976
Padmahara devi dasi	Buffalo	3	1974
Padmaksi devi dasi	?		
Padmamalini devi devi dasi	Washington	1	1974
Padmamukhi devi devi dasi	Seattle	1	1974
Padmavati devi dasi	Bombay	3	1971
Padyavali devi dasi	Vancouver	7	1974
Palika devi dasi	LA	4	1969
Pampa devi dasi	New York	7	1971
Pancajani devi dasi	Detroit	9	1977
Pancali devi dasi	Baltimore	5	1973
Pandurani devi dasi	Denver	12	1976
Pandurani devi dasi	LA		1972
Papaharinidevi devi dasi	Laguna	6	1974
Papasudana devi dasi	Cleveland	8	1976
Parama devi dasi	Germany		1974
Paramahamsi devi dasi	LA	6	1972
Paramamrta devi devi dasi	Melbourne	5	1975
Paramasakti devi dasi	Brazil	7	1976
Paramprabha devi dasi	San Diego	7	1976
Parasakti devi devi dasi	New York	12	1974
Paratpara devi dasi	Vancouver	1	1976
Parayana devi dasi	Seattle	1	1972
Parijata devi dasi	Paris	7	1972
Parvati devi dasi	LA	5	1972
Parvati devi dasi	Mayapur	3	1974
Pasupati devi dasi	Toronto	8	1972
Patri devi dasi	LA	5	1972
Patrimadhukantha devi dasi	Mexico	6	1972
Pattarajni devi dasi	Philadelphia	6	1974
Paurnamasi devi dasi	LA		1969
Paurnamasi devi dasi	Vancouver	8	1973

Pavani devi dasi	San Francisco	7	1975
Pavitra devi dasi	LA	9	1977
Payahsvini devi dasi	New York	7	1971
Phalini-devi devi dasi	LA	10	1974
Pitambara devi dasi	New Vrindaban	4	1977
Poulastini devi dasi	LA?		1970
Pouravi devi dasi	Philadelphia	7	1971
Prabala-devi devi dasi	San Francisco	7	1975
Prabhavati devi dasi	Bombay		1975
Prabhavati devi dasi	Boulder		1970
Pracetana devi devi dasi	Vancouver	7	1974
Praci devi dasi	Baltimore	7	1971
Pradhana-gopika devi dasi	Denver	9	1975
Praharana devi dasi	Toronto	8	1972
Prajnadevi devi dasi	Toronto	7	1974
Pralambahari devi dasi	Paris	12	1975
Pramada devi dasi	Cleveland	3	1974
Pramada devi dasi	LA	7	1971
Pranada devi dasi	LA	6	1976
Praphullamukhi devi dasi	Victoria	5	1971
Prasuti devi dasi	Melbourne	5	1976
Pratici devi dasi	New York		
Pratima devi dasi	New York		
Pratima devi dasi	Toronto	12	1973
Prayaga devi dasi	New York	7	1971
Premabhakti devi dasi	E. Berlin	8	1977
Premaka devi devi dasi	Buffalo	5	1975
Premamanjari devi dasi	Buffalo	10	1976
Premamayi devi dasi	New Vrindaban	9	1972
Pritha devi dasi	London	9	1969
Prsni devi dasi	Charlotte, NC	2	1977
Prsni devi dasi	LA		1971
Prsnigarbha devi dasi	Seattle		1972
Puja devi dasi	Denver	2	1974
Purnacandra devi dasi	London		1973
Purnamrta devi dasi	Italy		1976
Purnima devi dasi	Hyderabad	12	1976
Purnima devi dasi	New Vrindaban		
Purnima devi dasi	Vrndavana	10	1977
Purvacitti devi devi dasi	Buffalo	12	1973
Puspaka devi dasi	Miami	9	1977
Pusti devi dasi	LA	10	1975
Racitambara devi dasi	LA	6	1974
Radhabhavini devi dasi	New York	7	1971
Radhagokulananda devi dasi	France	10	1973
Radhakunda devi dasi	?		1970
Radhakunda devi dasi	New Vrindaban	9	1972
Radhanarupini devi dasi	Hawaii	2	1976
Radhapriya-devi devi dasi	London	1	1975

Name	Location		Year
Radharani devi dasi	Mexico	6	1972
Radharasabihari devi dasi	Bombay	3	1977
Radhasakhi devi dasi	Hyderabad	8	1976
Radhathakurani devi dasi	Mexico	10	1973
Radhika-devi devi dasi	Boston		1970
Radhika-devi devi dasi	Nairobi		1976
Radhika-devi devi dasi	Vancouver	1	1977
Radhika-devi devi dasi	Vrndavana	9	1975
Radhikaramana devi dasi	New Zealand	11	1976
Raga-bhumi-devi devi dasi	Brazil	6	1975
Ragamathani devi dasi	Seattle	8	1973
Ragatmika devi dasi	Melbourne	10	1973
Ragatmika devi dasi	New York	3	1972
Raghunandini devi dasi	Miami	12	1973
Ragini devi dasi	Paris	3	1974
Rajadhidevi devi dasi	Mexico	9	1977
Rajalaksmi devi dasi	Australia	6	1974
Rajanatha devi dasi	New Orleans	2	1975
Rajani? devi dasi	India?		1975
Rajavidya devi devi dasi	Edinburgh	7	1974
Rama-devi devi dasi	Bombay	3	1977
Rama-devi devi dasi	Edinburgh	11	1972
Rama-devi devi dasi	Melbourne	12	1976
Ramalila devi dasi	Bombay	3	1977
Ramanareti devi dasi	Denver	9	1977
Ramanareti devi dasi	Vrndavana	4	1976
Ramani devi dasi	Miami	1	1973
Ramaniya devi dasi	Amsterdam	8	1976
Ramaniya devi dasi	Melbourne	10	1973
Ramapriya devi dasi	Detroit	1	1977
Ramatulasi devi dasi	Denver	8	1972
Rambhavati devi dasi	New Vrindaban	9	1972
Rambhoru devi dasi	Germany	4	1974
Ramesvari devi dasi	New Vrindaban	9	1972
Ramesvari? devi dasi	Mayapur		1975
Ramya devi dasi	Heidelberg	6	1973
Ramya devi dasi	London		1973
Ranga devi devi dasi	Bombay	4	1974
Rangabhumi devi dasi	Bhubanesvar	1	1977
Rangavati devi dasi	Detroit	1	1974
Ranjani devi dasi	Chicago	7	1973
Rasabihari devi dasi	Brazil	12	1976
Rasajna-devi devi dasi	LA	10	1974
Rasakeli devi dasi	Santo Domingo	8	1974
Rasaliladevi devi dasi	Nairobi	12	1973
Rasaliladevi devi dasi	New Vrindaban	7	1974
Rasalubdha devi dasi	Denver	11	1972
Rasamandala devi dasi	Mayapur	3	1975
Rasamanjari devi dasi	Mayapur	9	1977

Name	Location		Year
Rasamanjari devi dasi	San Diego	6	1972
Rasangi devi dasi	LA	12	1973
Rasaparayani devi dasi	LA	3	1973
Rasapurnada devi dasi	LA	3	1973
Rasarani-devi devi dasi	Sydney	5	1971
Rasasundari devi dasi	Argentina	12	1975
Rasavasini devi dasi	Argentina	12	1975
Rasesvari devi dasi	London	3	1976
Rasottunga? devi dasi	LA		1973
Rastrapalika devi dasi	New York	7	1971
Rathesvasi devi dasi	Berkeley		
Ratimanjari devi dasi	London	8	1972
Ratipriya devi dasi	Heidelberg	6	1973
Ratirupa devi dasi	Vancouver	3	1973
Ratnamala devi dasi	Delhi		1974
Ratnaranjini-devi devi dasi	Edinburgh		1974
Ratnavrnda-devi devi dasi	San Diego	7	1974
Ratnesvari devi dasi	Berkeley	12	1971
Ratri-devi devi dasi	Toronto	4	1975
Rauhina devi dasi	Berkeley	6	1976
Renuka devi dasi	Heidelberg		1972
Renuka? devi dasi	LA?		1977
Revati devi dasi	Germany		
Revati devi dasi	LA	3	1973
Revati devi dasi	New York	4	1976
Rocana devi dasi	Mexico	10	1973
Rocani devi dasi	S. Africa		1974
Rocira devi dasi	Montreal	9	1976
Rohini devi dasi	Frankfurt	1	1975
Rohini-devi devi dasi	Brazil	9	1977
Rohini-devi devi dasi	Miami		1969
Rsabhadevi devi dasi	Sydney	5	1971
Ruci devi dasi	Chicago	3	1974
Rucira devi dasi	London	3	1975
Rudrani-devi devi dasi	Toronto	12	1973
Rudrani-devi devi dasi	Vancouver	4	1975
Rudraramani-devi devi dasi	Detroit	2	1975
Rukmavati devi dasi	LA?		1975
Rukmavati devi dasi	Sydney	2	1973
Rukmini Priya devi dasi	London	7	1973
Rukmini-devi devi dasi	Montreal	8	1968
Rupa Ramesvari devi dasi	Denver	2	1973
Rupacandra devi dasi	LA	12	1973
Rupamanjari-devi devi dasi	LA	5	1972
Rupavati devi dasi	Australia	10	1977
Saci devi devi dasi	LA	1	1970
Sacimata devi dasi	Germany		1975
Sacimata devi dasi	Mayapur	3	1972
Sadabhuja devi devi dasi	Chicago	7	1974

Name	Location		Year
Sadadhyeya devi dasi	San Francisco	7	1975
Sadanandini devi dasi	Buffalo		1969
Sadhvi devi dasi	Montreal	9	1973
Sahadevi devi dasi	LA	1	1970
Sahasraksi devi dasi	France	8	1976
Sailavasini devi dasi	Melbourne	4	1976
Sailendriya devi dasi	London	9	1973
Sailodgata-devi devi dasi	LA	6	1974
Sajjanajivana devi dasi	LA	1	1974
Sakhi devi dasi	Hawaii	2	1976
Saktimati devi devi dasi	Hawaii	6	1971
Saktimati devi devi dasi	London		1973
Sakuntala devi dasi	Boston	7	1971
Sama devi devi dasi	?		
Samapriya devi dasi	San Francisco	7	1975
Sambhavi devi dasi	London	5	1973
Samharina devi dasi	Seattle	8	1973
Samhartri devi dasi	Stockholm	11	1975
Sammita devi dasi	Baltimore	1	1972
Samsaramocana devi dasi	Seattle	1	1972
Samsayaghni devi dasi	Mexico	9	1973
Sanandananda Manjari dd	Atlanta	5	1973
Sanatana-dhama devi dasi	Amsterdam		1977
Sanatani devi dasi	London	10	1977
Sanatani devi devi dasi	Miami	7	1974
Sandamini devi devi dasi	San Diego	5	1975
Sandini devi dasi	Columbus		1970
Sandipani devi dasi	LA	6	1972
Sanga devi devi dasi	Winnipeg	6	1975
Sangita devi dasi	LA	11	1973
Sanjaya devi dasi	New York	7	1976
Sankari devi dasi	LA	10	1973
Sankirtana devi devi dasi	Atlanta	8	1977
Santanandi devi dasi	LA	4	1971
Santanu devi dasi	Paris	8	1970
Santi devi dasi	St. Louis		1971
Santi devi devi dasi	Houston	6	1972
Santimati devi dasi	Hamburg	4	1973
Saptarsi devi dasi	New Vrindaban	9	1972
Sarada devi dasi	Montreal	1	1976
Sarada devi dasi	Seattle	8	1974
Saradi devi devi dasi	Edinburgh	7	1974
Saradiya devi devi dasi	San Francisco	1	1968
Sarala devi devi dasi	LA		1970
Sarana devi devi dasi	Laguna	9	1976
Saranagata devi dasi	LA	3	1973
Saranam devi dasi	San Diego	1	1972
Sararupa devi dasi	San Francisco	7	1975
Sarasani devi dasi	Argentina		1975

Sardhunya devi dasi	London		
Saridvara devi devi dasi	Mexico	2	1975
Sarmistha devi dasi	Boston	7	1971
Sarvadi devi dasi	New Vrindaban	1	1972
Sarvajna devi dasi	Auckland	1	1976
Sarvamangala devi dasi	London		1971
Sarvamayi devi devi dasi	Montreal	5	1973
Sarvani devi dasi	LA	9	1973
Sarvarupa devi dasi	San Francisco	7	1975
Sarvasaktimata devi dasi	Detroit		1973
Sarvesvari devi dasi	Italy	3	1977
Sarvesvari devi dasi	New Vrindaban	4	1973
Sasikala devi devi dasi	San Francisco	12	1973
Sasimukhi devi dasi	Bombay	5	1974
Sasimukhi devi dasi	Caracas	3	1977
Sasimukhi devi dasi	New York	7	1971
Sasthi devi dasi	LA		1971
Sastramayi devi dasi	Mexico	9	1973
Sasvata Pavana devi dasi	Paris	8	1974
Satadari devi dasi	LA	9	1973
Satadruti devi dasi	London	8	1972
Satananda devi devi dasi	San Diego	4	1975
Satarupa devi dasi	Dallas	4	1971
Satarupa devi dasi	Paris	8	1974
Sati devi dasi	Melbourne	4	1976
Satodara devi dasi	Mexico	9	1973
Satya devi dasi	Washington	7	1976
Satya devi devi dasi	LA	6	1972
Satyabhama devi devi dasi	Montreal	7	1968
Satyaki devi dasi	San Diego	4	1972
Satyarupa devi dasi	Melbourne	4	1976
Satyavati devi dasi	Melbourne	4	1972
Satyavati devi dasi	Mexico	9	1977
Satyavati devi dasi	Montreal		1968
Saubhagya-sundari devi dd	Caracas	2	1975
Saucarya devi dasi	Ottawa	10	1971
Saudamani devi dasi	Philadelphia	7	1971
Saumya devi dasi	France	11	1977
Saumyarupa devi dasi	Germany	12	1975
Saursani devi dasi	Mexico		1975
Savitri devi dasi	London	3	1975
Savitri devi dasi	St. Louis	7	1973
Seva devi devi dasi	New York	10	1977
Sevanandi devi dasi	Paris	3	1975
Sevya devi dasi	Costa Rica	4	1976
Siddhesvari devi dasi	London	9	1973
Siddhi devi dasi	Montreal	1	1977
Sikhandi devi devi dasi	LA	6	1972
Sikhandini devi dasi	New York	9	1972

Name	Location		Year
Siladitya devi dasi	Buffalo	3	1974
Silavati devi devi dasi	San Francisco		1968
Silpakarini devi dasi	Germany?	1	1974
Sindhupriya devi dasi	Vrndavana	4	1976
Sindura devi dasi	Montreal	1	1977
Sita devi dasi	Buffalo		1972
Sita devi devi dasi	Hawaii	3	1975
Sita devi devi dasi	New York		
Sitala devi devi dasi	Detroit	12	1970
Sitapati devi devi dasi	Boston	1	1975
Sitarani devi dasi	Detroit	7	1971
Siva devi dasi	Hawaii	10	1975
Sivanidevi devi dasi	Gorakhpur		
Sivanidevi devi dasi	LA	7	1970
Smrti devi dasi	Vrndavana	4	1976
Snata devi devi dasi	Germany	11	1974
Snehalata devi dasi	Boston	2	1970
Snehalata devi devi dasi	Mayapur		1975
Snehalata devi devi dasi	New York	7	1976
Sobhavati devi dasi	New Vrindaban	2	1975
Sonapuri devi dasi	San Diego	6	1974
Sranti devi dasi	Brazil	2	1976
Sranti devi dasi	Gainesville	5	1975
Sravaniya devi dasi	St. Louis	8	1971
Srida devi dasi	Portland	4	1976
Srigopika devi dasi	New York	7	1976
Sriharini devi dasi	Stockholm	4	1974
Sriji devi dasi	Mexico	3	1973
Srikama devi dasi	London	11	1975
Srikari devi dasi	Montreal	9	1973
Srila devi dasi	LA	5	1972
Srilaksmi devi dasi	San Diego		
Srilekha devi dasi	Australia		1975
Srilekha devi dasi	Toronto	7	1970
Srimati devi dasi	Portland		1975
Srimati devi devi dasi	San Francisco	10	1968
Sriprada devi dasi	LA	4	1976
Sriradha devi devi dasi	Boulder	6	1975
Sriradha devi devi dasi	Vrndavana	4	1975
Sriradhika devi dasi	LA	3	1977
Srisa devi dasi	Laguna	4	1976
Srividya devi dasi	Paris	8	1976
Srnkhala devi dasi	Brazil	7	1976
Srutipriya devi dasi	New Zealand	12	1975
Srutirupa devi dasi	Miami	8	1974
Stritama devi dasi	Seattle	2	1977
Striyadisa devi dasi	Sydney	4	1973
Subhada devi dasi	Chicago		1974
Subhadra devi dasi	Chicago	12	1973

Name	Location		Year
Subhadra devi dasi	LA	10	1973
Subhalaksmi devi dasi	Australia	6	1974
Subhanana devi dasi	Buenos Aires	1	1974
Subhangi devi dasi	Germany	8	1975
Subhavrata devi devi dasi	Vancouver		1975
Subhra devi dasi	LA	10	1976
Subuddhi devi dasi	Toronto	6	1976
Suci devi dasi	Edinburgh		1972
Sucikari devi devi dasi	Mayapur	10	1974
Sucitra devi devi dasi	LA		1970
Sudarsana devi dasi	New York		1967
Sudarsani devi dasi	Denver	11	1972
Sudevi devi dasi	Buffalo		1972
Sudhakari devi dasi	New York		1972
Sudharma devi dasi	Berkeley	6	1976
Sujana devi dasi	Toronto	2	1970
Sukhada devi dasi	Boston	7	1971
Sukhada devi dasi	Philadelphia	7	1975
Sukhasagari devi dasi	Detroit	7	1971
Sukhavaha devi dasi	Pittsburgh	5	1975
Sukhi devi dasi	Hawaii		1973
Sukla devi dasi	Melbourne	2	1973
Suksmarupini devi dasi	Atlanta	5	1973
Sukti devi devi dasi	Detroit	2	1975
Sukulina devi dasi	New Vrindaban	11	1975
Sulaksmana devi dasi	Montreal	8	1975
Sulocana devi dasi	Miami	12	1973
Sumana devi dasi	Mayapur	3	1972
Sumati devi dasi	Boston	3	1971
Sumitra devi devi dasi	Calcutta		
Sumukhi devi dasi	Calcutta		1974
Sundari devi dasi	San Francisco	7	1975
Sunita devi dasi	New York	12	1971
Suniti devi dasi	LA	6	1971
Suprabha devi dasi	Chicago	2	1975
Surabhi devi devi dasi	Amsterdam	8	1971
Surangi devi dasi	Seattle	2	1977
Surasa devi dasi	Atlanta	10	1974
Suruci devi devi dasi	LA	7	1970
Susarma devi dasi	Buffalo		
Susarma devi dasi	LA	3	1973
Susri devi dasi	San Francisco	2	1974
Susroni devi dasi	Denver	3	1974
Svaha devi dasi	Atlanta	10	1974
Svahna devi devi dasi	Toronto		1972
Svakiya devi devi dasi	Frankfurt	6	1974
Svarga devi dasi	Denver	2	1974
Svarga? devi dasi	Detroit	7	1971
Svargavasini devi dasi	London	7	1974

Name	Location		
Svarupa devi dasi	Vancouver	12	1973
Svarupasakti devi dasi	Paris		
Svati devi dasi	London	10	1970
Svayamprabha devi dasi	Phoenix	1	1976
Syama devi dasi	New Vrindaban	3	1977
Syama devi dasi	San Francisco		1967
Syamadevi devi dasi	Washington	7	1974
Syamagha devi dasi	LA	9	1973
Syamapriya devi dasi	Gainesville	7	1976
Syamapriya devi dasi	San Diego	9	1977
Syamapriya devi dasi	Seattle	10	1976
Syamasundari devi dasi	Durban	6	1976
Syamasundari devi dasi	London	7	1972
Syamavallabha devi dasi	Montreal	12	1975
Tadita devi dasi	LA	3	1974
Taijasatmika devi dasi	Detroit	5	1973
Taittareya devi dasi	LA	12	1973
Tamra devi dasi	New Vrindaban		1977
Tamra devi dasi	Seattle	2	1977
Tapasvini devi dasi	Philadelphia	7	1975
Tapati devi dasi	LA	3	1977
Tara devi dasi	LA		1974
Tara devi devi dasi	LA	7	1969
Taraka devi dasi	Laguna	3	1973
Tarani devi dasi	LA	4	1973
Tarkikcuramoni devi dasi	Pittsburgh	4	1972
Tarksi devi devi dasi	Melbourne	4	1975
Taruni devi devi dasi	New Vrindaban	6	1969
Taruni devi devi dasi	Vrndavana	4	1975
Tattva-dasini devi dasi	Trinidad	3	1977
Tejovati devi dasi	London	9	1973
Tilaka devi devi dasi	Seattle		1971
Tilakini devi dasi	Buffalo	10	1976
Tilakini devi dasi	Caracas	1	1974
Tirthanidhi devi dasi	Colombia	3	1977
Tirthapada devi dasi	Mexico	6	1976
Titiksa devi dasi	Atlanta	3	1974
Trailokyasundari devi dasi	Vancouver	9	1975
Trayi devi devi dasi	LA		1971
Tribhuvanesvari devi dd	Toronto	1	1975
Tripuramalini devi dasi	Seattle	8	1973
Trisakti devi dasi	Caracas	3	1977
Trisakti devi dasi	Detroit	12	1971
Trpti devi devi dasi	Denver	12	1974
Tryadhisa devi dasi	Boston	1	1975
Tulasi devi dasi	France		
Tulasi devi devi dasi	San Francisco	1	1968
Tulasi-carana devi dasi	LA	10	1976
Tulasi-manjari devi devi dasi	Seattle		1971

Name	Location		Year
Tulasiananda devi dasi	Miami	9	1977
Tungabhadra devi devi dasi	LA		1969
Tungavidya devi dasi	Mexico	6	1972
Tusita devi dasi	LA	10	1976
Tusti devi dasi	LA	5	1973
Ucchalita devi dasi	Germany	4	1974
Ugrasena devi dasi	New York		1972
Ujjvala devi devi dasi	LA	1	1970
Ujjvalaprada devi dasi	Baltimore	10	1975
Ullasanti devi dasi	New York	7	1974
Uma? devi dasi	Philadelphia	7	1976
Urmila devi dasi	Chicago	12	1973
Urvasi devi dasi	New York	7	1971
Usa devi dasi	New York		1972
Usamati devi dasi	Paris	8	1973
Uttama devi dasi	Vancouver	12	1973
Uttara devi dasi	Mexico	9	1977
Vaibhavi devi dasi	Sydney	5	1971
Vaijayanti-devi devi dasi	New York		1973
Vaikunthadevi devi dasi	Brazil	9	1977
Vaikunthadevi devi dasi	Montreal	3	1977
Vaikunthamurti devi dasi	LA		1976
Vaisnava devi dasi	Mombasa	3	1977
Vaisnavapriya-devi devi dasi	Dallas	11	1974
Vajasana devi dasi	New York	1	1973
Vajresvari devi dasi	New Vrindaban	4	1973
Vallidevi devi dasi	New Vrindaban	7	1974
Vamanadevi devi dasi	Dallas	11	1975
Vanamalini devi dasi	Mayapur	3	1974
Vara devi dasi	LA	12	1973
Varaha devi dasi	Berkeley	11	1976
Varahadeva devi dasi	Berkeley	12	1971
Varanasi devi dasi	New York	7	1971
Varuni devi dasi	Toronto	8	1972
Vasudevaya devi dasi	Cleveland?		1972
Vasudha devi dasi	Paris		
Vedagarbha devi dasi	Vancouver	9	1975
Vedajanani devi dasi	New Vrindaban	8	1973
Vedamata devi dasi	New Vrindaban	8	1975
Vedapriya devi dasi	New York	8	1975
Vedasmrti devi dasi	Amsterdam	1	1977
Vedatita devi dasi	Stockholm	11	1975
Vedavati devi dasi	Seattle	4	1976
Vegavati devi dasi	LA	6	1976
Venudhara devi dasi	Australia	5	1977
Venugit devi dasi	Nairobi	4	1973
Venurati devi dasi	Johannesburg	12	1975
Venuvilasa-devi devi dasi	Cleveland	2	1975
Vibhavari-devi devi dasi	New Vrindaban	2	1975

Name	Location		Year
Vicitravasini devi dasi	Italy	11	1975
Vidambha devi dasi	Pittsburgh	11	1973
Vidarbha Kanya devi dasi	Philadelphia	1	1970
Vidarbha-suta-devi devi dasi	New York	7	1971
Vidarbharani devi dasi	Germany		1975
Vidhatri devi dasi	Seattle	8	1973
Viduttama devi dasi	New Vrindaban	8	1975
Vidya devi dasi	LA	6	1976
Vidya devi dasi	New Vrindaban	8	1973
Vidyabhadu devi dasi	London	8	1971
Viharini devi dasi	San Francisco	2	1974
Vijaya-devi devi dasi	Denver		1971
Vijaya-devi devi dasi	Detroit	6	1970
Vijaya-devi devi dasi	Mombasa	3	1977
Vijayamurti devi dasi	Costa Rica	3	1977
Vikramini devi dasi	LA	4	1971
Vikuksi devi dasi	New Vrindaban	7	1977
Vilasi devi dasi	New Vrindaban	9	1972
Vilasini-devi devi dasi	New York	7	1971
Vimala devi dasi	Melbourne	4	1976
Vimalangi devi dasi	New York	8	1975
Vimoha devi dasi	Johannesburg	12	1975
Vinode Vani devi dasi	Houston	6	1972
Viraja-devi devi dasi	Caracas	2	1975
Visakha devi dasi	London	3	1969
Visakha-devi devi dasi	Vrndavana	11	1971
Visalaksmi devi dasi	New Vrindaban	9	1972
Visalini devi dasi	San Francisco		1972
Visesa devi dasi	Paris	8	1974
Visnumurti devi dasi	Berkeley	11	1976
Visnupadi-devi devi dasi	Caracas	2	1975
Visnupriya devi dasi	Portland	6	1972
Visnuvrata devi dasi	Detroit	9	1977
Visodhani-devi devi dasi	Caracas	2	1975
Visoka-devi devi dasi	Germany	11	1974
Visvadevi devi dasi	Heidelberg	6	1972
Visvadharini devi dasi	London	5	1973
Visvadhika devi dasi	New Vrindaban	8	1973
Vrajabhadu devi dasi	Mexico	10	1973
Vrajadevi devi dasi	Portland	6	1972
Vrajalalana devi dasi	Gainesville	7	1976
Vrajaraja-devi devi dasi	Dallas	11	1973
Vrajasakhi devi dasi	LA	6?	1976
Vrajasundari devi dasi	Berkeley	12	1971
Vrajesvari devi dasi	?		1976
Vrajesvari-devi devi dasi	LA		1973
Vrnda-devi devi dasi	Germany		1970
Vrnda-devi devi dasi	LA	8	1972
Vrnda-devi devi dasi	Toronto	7	1974

Name	Location		Year
Vrndavana Viharini devi dasi	London	7	1972
Vrndavana Vilasini devi dasi	LA	8	1972
Vrndavanesvari devi dasi	LA	6	1972
Vrndavani-devi devi dasi	London	7	1974
Vrsabhanusuta devi dasi	Paris	8	1974
Vrsavanu Nandini devi dasi	?		
Vrsnidevi devi dasi	LA		1975
Yadurani devi dasi	New York	10	1966
Yajaniya-devi devi dasi	Mexico	2	1975
Yajnapriya devi dasi	LA	5	1973
Yamini devi dasi	Columbus	6	1970
Yamuna-devi devi dasi	San Francisco	2	1967
Yasasvini devi dasi	London	5	1973
Yasoda devi dasi	Chicago	12	1973
Yasodamayi devi dasi	London		1973
Yasodamayi devi devi dasi	London	7	1972
Yasodamayi-devi devi dasi	Gainesville	4	1976
Yasodanandanapatni devi dasi	Vancouver	9	1975
Yasogami devi dasi	Detroit	8	1975
Yasomati devi dasi	Vancouver	6	1972
Yasomati-stanya-payi devi dasi	London	4	1977
Yayati devi dasi	Sydney	2	1973
Yayati devi dasi	Vrndavana	12	1975
Yogamala devi dasi	Dallas	11	1975
Yogamandakari devi dasi	Rome	11	1975
Yogamaya-devi devi dasi	New York	7	1971
Yogini devi dasi	Brazil	12	1975
Yugapriya devi dasi	Dallas	11	1975
Yuvati devi dasi	LA	10	1975

The Vaishnavi Ministry

The Vaishnavi Ministry is under the auspices of the Governing Body Commission of ISKCON, Founder-Acharya His Divine Grace A. C. Bhakti-vedanta Swami Prabhupada.

Our Mission:

To promote a culture of open-hearted empowerment for Vaishnavis through association, education, representation, support, and service.

Our Purposes:

To:
1. Uphold Srila Prabhupada's legacy in relation to Vaishnavis.
2. Encourage full facility for Vaishnavis to become strengthened by association through various sanga networks.
3. Promote devotional training for Vaishnavis.
4. Facilitate the Vaishnavi voice in diverse aspects of devotional life.
5. Increase opportunities for Vaishnavis to be fully engaged in devotional service according to their God-given talents and inclinations.
6. Develop an enduring network of personal support for Vaishnavis through guidelines, referrals, counseling, and friendship.
7. Inspire women inquisitive about bhakti.

If you were not included in this book but are a direct lady disciple of Srila Prabhupada, please feel free to write a remembrance and submit it to the Vaishnavi Ministry Facebook page.

Profits from this book will go to help support the Vaishnavi Ministry.